A HISTORY OF THE JEWS
IN NORTH AFRICA
VOLUME I

A HISTORY OF THE JEWS IN NORTH AFRICA

BY

H. Z. (J. W.) HIRSCHBERG

SECOND, REVISED EDITION, TRANSLATED FROM THE HEBREW

VOLUME I

FROM ANTIQUITY TO THE SIXTEENTH CENTURY

WITH 4 MAPS

LEIDEN
E. J. BRILL
1974

ISBN 90 04 03820 5

PRINTED IN THE NETHERLANDS

CONTENTS

LIST OF MAPS

PREFACE

This first volume of "A History of the Jews in North Africa" is a revised version in the English language of the corresponding volume of a work in Hebrew published by the Bialik Institute in Jerusalem in 1965. The time interval accounts for changes both in the body of the text and in the notes. I particularly deemed it appropriate to enlarge Chapters Six and Seven and to add two appendices designed to elucidate certain special matters and to describe certain processes at length. I moreover thought it useful to abridge the notes and to transfer them from the end of the volume to the foot of the pages. The revision of the notes took a long time, much longer than I had anticipated.

I am indebted to Mr. M. Kol, Minister in the Israel Government, and Mr. M. Rivlin, now Director-General of the Jewish Agency for Eretz Israel, for initiating the translation and assisting the venture in its early stages. The expenditure involved was later shouldered by the Research Board of Bar-Ilan University, to which, too, I hereby express my gratitude.

I would also like to thank Dr. M. Eichelberg, who did the translation. In consultation with me, he overcame the numerous difficulties that were bound to arise in recasting the material into so different a linguistic mould.

I further thank Mr. A. Attal, research worker at the Ben-Zvi Institute, who rechecked the references and gave every assistance in preparing the indices and bibliography, and Dr. E. Bashan, who greatly helped during the preparation of the revised text and read one proof.

I apologize for inconsistencies in the transliteration of Hebrew and Arabic names of persons and places; where an Anglicized form exists, it is generally given preference, except in the case of names of authors and names appearing in book titles and quotations. I hope that those technical inconsequences will be forgiven.

Jerusalem, March 1974.

ABBREVIATIONS

Abbreviated titles of works not found in this list are contained in the Select Bibliography.

A.	Arab(s), Arabic.
AbZar	Aboda Zara (Talmudic tractate).
ABA	H. de Castries et P. De Cenival, Les sources inédites de l'histoire du Maroc. Archives et bibliothèques d'Angleterre.
ABE	*the same-work*, Archives et bibliothèques d'Espagne.
ABF	*the same-work*, Archives et bibliothèques de France.
ABP	*the same-work*, Archives et bibliothèques de Portugal.
ABPB	*the same-work*, Archives et bibliothèques des Pays-Bas.
Ag	Agada, Agadic.
AI	Archives Israélites.
AIEO	Annales de l'Institut d'Etudes Orientales.
AoF	Altorientalische Forschungen.
AR	Arabica, Revue d'Etudes Arabes.
b.	ben.
B.	Banū (tribe).
Bab.	Babylonia, Babylonian.
BQ	Baba Qamma (Talmudic tratate).
Ber	Berakhot (Talmudic tractate).
BGA	Bibliotheca Geographorum Arabicorum.
BIES	see *BJPS*.
BJPS	Bulletin of the Jewish Palestine Exploration Society, later Bulletin of the Israel Exploration Society.
BO	Bulletin Officiel de l'Empire Chérifien.
BZ	Byzantinische Zeitschrift.
c.	century, centuries.
Chr.	Christian(s), Christianity.
CIG	Corpus Inscriptionum Graecarum.
CIJ	Corpus Inscriptionum Iudaicarum.
CIL	Corpus Inscriptionum Latinarum, vol. VIII, 1-5, Berlin 1881-1942, Inscriptiones Africae Latinae.
CPJ	Corpus Papyrorum Judaicarum.
DArCH	Dictionnaire d'Archéologie Chrétienne.
EI	Encyclopaedia of Islam.
EJ	Encyclopaedia Judaica.
EJ[2]	*the same-work*, Jerusalem 1971 (16 vol. in English).
EJC	Encyclopedia Judaica Castellana.
FO	Folia Orientalia.
g.	geonic.
G.	Gaon.
GAL	C. Brockelmann, Geschichte der arabischen Litteratur, vols I-II, Leiden, 1943-1949.
GALS	*the same-work*, Supplement, Leiden, 1937-1942.
GB	Les Guides Bleus, Algérie-Tunisie. Paris, 1955.
GB Maroc	Les Guides Bleus, Maroc. Paris, 1954.
Git	Gittin (Talmudic tractate).
GK	Ginze Kedem.

GQ	Ginze Kedem.
Gratz CAJS	Gratz College Anual of Jewish Studies.
GSAI	Giornale della Società Asiatica Italiana.
Hal.	Halakha, halakhic.
HCM	Histoire du Commerce de Marseille, publiée par la Chambre de Commerce de Marseille, Paris, 1949-
HESP	Hespéris.
ḤM	Ḥoshen Mishpaṭ (Codex of Personnal Matters).
Ḥul	Ḥullin (Talmudic tractate).
HUCA	Hebrew Union College Annual.
IJMES	International Journal of Middle East Studies.
J	Jew(s), Jewish.
JA	Journal Asiatique.
JAH	Journal of African History.
JBL	Journal of Biblical Literature.
Jeb	Yebamot (Talmudic tractate).
Jer	Yerushalmi (= Palestinian Talmud).
JESHO	Journal of the Economic and Social History of the Orient.
JGJJ	Jahrbuch für die Geschichte der Juden und des Judenthums.
JO	Journal Officiel de la République Française, lois et décrets. Paris.
JPOS	Journal of the Palestine Oriental Society.
JQR	Jewish Quarterly Review.
JRS	Journal of Roman Studies.
Ket	Ketubot (Talmudic tractate).
Kid	Kiddushim (Talmudic tractate).
Kil	Kila'im (Talmudic tractate).
LA	Leo Africanus.
M.	Muslim(s).
Magh.	Maghreb, Maghrebi(s).
Meg	Megilla (Talmudic tractate).
Meg Taʿan	Megillat Taʿanit (Fast Roll).
Mekh	Mekhilta (Hal. Midrash to Ex.).
Men	Menaḥot (Talmudic tractate).
MGWJ	Monatsschrift für Geschichte und Wissenschaft des Judentums.
Mid	Midrash
MJC	A. Neubauer, Mediaeval Jewish Chronicles.
MWJ	Magazin für Wissenschaft des Judenthums.
p.	place.
Pal.	Palestine, Palestinian.
PdRE	Pirqey de Rabbi Eliezer (Ag. Midrash).
PdRK	Pesiqta de Rab Kahana (Ag. Midrash).
PAAJR	Proceedings of the American Academy for Jewish Research.
Pes. R	Pesiqta Rabbati (Ag. Midrash).
PG	Patrologia series Graeca.
PL	Patrologia series Latina.
PRO COP	Public Record Office, Colonial Office Papers.
PRO SP	Public Record Office, State Papers.
PW	Pauly-Wissova, Realencyclopädie.
r.	region (geographical)
R.	Rabbi, Rabbinic, Rabbanite(s).
R	Rabba.
RA I	S. Assaf, Responsa I.
RA II	S. Assaf, Responsa II.

RA III	S. Assaf, Responsa III.
RAf	Revue Africaine.
R Ar	Revue Archéologique.
RaSHBaSH	R. Solomon b. Simon [Dūrān], Responsa.
RC	D. Cassel (ed.), Rechtsgutachten der Geonim.
RCor	N. Coronel (ed.), Gaonäische Gutachten.
REC	Recueil des Notices et Mémoires de la Société Archéologique de Constantine.
REG	Revue des Etudes Grecques.
REI	Revue des Etudes Islamiques.
REJ	Revue des Etudes Juives.
RH	A. Harkavy, Responsa der Geonim.
RHG	Z.W. Wolfensohn and Sh. Z. Schneursohn (ed.), (g. Responsa) Ḥemda Genūza.
RHPhR	Revue d'Historie et de Philosophie Religieuses.
RHR	Revue de l'Histoire des Religions.
RIBaSH	R. Isaac bar Sheshet (Responsa)
RIHP	Studies of The Research Institute for Hebrew Poetry in Jerusalem.
RL	Y. Musafya (ed.), g. Responsa.
RM	J. Müller (ed.), (g.) Responsen.
RMM	Revue du Monde Musulman.
RO	Rocznik Orientalistyczny.
Ro Ha	Rosh Hashana (Talmudic tractate).
RSh	G. Shaʿarey Ẓedeq, Responsa.
RShT	W. Leiter (ed.), Shaʿare Teshubah (g. Responsa).
Sab	Sabbat (Talmudic tractate).
San	Sanhedrin (Talmudic tractate).
Sbornik	Palestinskiy Sbornik.
SEG	Supplementum Epigraphicum Graecum, vol. IX, fasc. 1-2.
Shab	Sabbat (Talmudic tractate).
Sheb	Shebiʿith (Talmudic tractate).
Shek	Shekalim (Talmudic tractate).
SHQ	Sefer ha-Qabbalah.
SOR	Seder Olam Rabba.
SOZ	Seder Olam Zutta, in *MJC* II, pp. 68-88.
SRH	S. W. Baron, A social and religious history of the Jews.[2]
Suk	Sukka (Talmudic tractate).
T.	Tribe or subtribe
tal.	talmudic(al).
Tal.	Talmud
Tan	Tanḥuma (Ag. Midrash).
Targ	Targum (the authorized Aram. translation of the Bible).
TaS	J. Mann, Texts and Studies.
Tosef., Toseph.,	Tosephta (a Tannaic Corpus of Halakhot).
TR	Ch. H. Horowitz (ed.), Toratan shel Rishonim (g. Responsa).
UI	Univers Israélite.
UJE	Universal Jewish Encyclopaedia.
Y.	Yerushalmi (= Pallestinian Talmud).
Yeb	Yebamot (Talmudic tractate).
Yedioth	Bulletin of the Jewish Palestine Exploration Society, later Bulletin of the Israel Exploration Society.
Yer	Yerushalmi (=Palestinian Talmud).
Zeb	Zebaḥim (Talmudic tractate).
ZDMG	Zeitschrift der Deutschen Morgenländischen Gesellschaft.

INTRODUCTION

Background and Outline

The locale of the events we are going to describe in this book has natural boundaries, separating it from the neighbouring areas. An arid zone, the Libyan Desert, extends between North (West) Africa and Egypt and is the reason why the geographical-historical dividing-line between the two blocks, Egypt on the one hand and North (West) Africa on the other, has never been obliterated. In the north, North Africa is bounded by the Mediterranean, in the west by the Atlantic; in the south, it borders on an ocean of sand, the largest on earth, known by its Arabic name, Sahara (*al-Ṣaḥra*), "the white one," whose north-eastern extension is the aforesaid Libyan Desert.

Some generally accepted measurements and figures may give an idea of the spaces and distances in this vast territory. The length of the coast from Egypt's western border to present-day Tunisia is over 1,600 kms., and from here to Agadir another 3,000 kms. The coastal belt and highlands of the interior, which were inhabited at the dawn of history, comprise an area of at least 750,000 sq. kms. Of this, according to the present political dispensation, 100,000 sq. kms. belong to Libya, 100,000 to Tunisia, 200,000 to Algeria and 350,000 to Morocco. All these figures are approximations, since every scholarly work and every guidebook give different assessments. Beyond the highland-and-mountain zone, the interior forms a steppe dotted with permanent settlements. Beyond the steppe is the Saharan Desert, where Berber nomads used to roam, descending from time to time upon the settled land. Adding the steppe and the Sahara to the coastal belt and the highlands, we arrive at a total of about 6,500,000 sq. kms., *i.e.* two thirds of the area of Europe.

The earliest inhabitants of the region, from the end of the prehistoric period, which here lasted longer than in other parts of the world and left comparatively numerous traces, were probably the tribes that the Greeks and Romans called Libyans or Berbers. Scholars who tried to determine the racial affiliation of the Berbers by anthropological criteria did not come to a definite conclusion; they only reached the negative finding that even the dark-skinned people in the southern oases, and called Ḥarthānī, do not belong to the race now known as African. There is no uniformity in either the skull structure or the colour of the skin, eyes or hair of the

Berbers. The prevailing view is that they are members of the Mediterranean race, but form a special group within it. Their language does not belong to any of the established families, although Hamitic affinities may be detected; and since no early literary testimonies of it have reached us, we are unable to trace the development of the various Berber dialects. Only in our days were products of the Berber genius, such as folktales and legal and social usages, recorded in writing, in the Berber language but in Latin script—thanks to the efforts of French scholars, who thus sought to perpetuate the national heritage of the indigenous population.

Nor have the Berbers preserved any historical traditions, any epics, about their mighty kings and doughty warriors, such as Hannibal, Masinissa and Jugurtha. What we know of their past comes from alien sources: Egyptian (from the 4th millennium B.C.E.), Punic-Greek, Roman, Arab, and lately French. Many facts relating to it have undoubtedly been distorted or at any rate presented in a biased manner, thus giving rise to various legends about the early history of the region and the penetration into it of members of different peoples.

Foreign Conquerors

The influx of foreign conquerors into the Mediterranean and Atlantic coastal plains, and thence into the highlands of the interior, lasted from the historical beginnings of North Africa until almost our own time. They operated in various ways. The Tyrians and Sidonites, called Phoenicians by the Greeks and *Poeni* by the Romans, set up a chain of trading colonies along the coast, the most famous of which was Carthage (Qart-Ḥadasht), founded in 814 B.C.E. and called Kartigene in talmudic literature (with slight variations of spelling) from the inflected form of its Latin name Carthago. The establishment of the Tyrians and Sidonites probably began at the end of the 2nd millennium B.C.E. and proceeded peacefully, almost without bloodshed, as befitted sea-faring traders concerned only with economic advantage. Of their voyages (as far as the coast of South Africa?), we know from Hanno's *Periplus*, of the 5th century B.C.E., which was inscribed on a bronze tablet affixed in one of the temples of Carthage.
We only possess a Greek translation of the *Periplus*, prepared two hundred years later.

The Phoenicians presumably did not reach the North African coast in large numbers, and those who settled there gradually merged with the local inhabitants; the result of this merger was the Libyan-Punic population. However, the Tyrians imposed upon the residents of the coastal belt their language, which was related to Hebrew, and the rites of their Canaanite religion. Numerous inscriptions have been discovered in the Punic language (called Neo-Punic in respect of the period following the destruction of Carthage); in all probability, it was still used at the time of the Arab conquests, and even afterwards. This was so despite mounting Greek pressure from the days of Alexander the Great and the fact that the eastern part of the area, Cyrenaica, came under the rule of the Ptolemies in Egypt. The western part was invaded by the Romans, who destroyed the Phoenician metropolis in 146 B.C.E. and, according to tradition, ploughed its site and sprinkled it with salt. The Berber tribes which until then had been subject to the Carthaginians fell under Roman domination. Not all the Berber kings and chieftains upheld their allegiance to Rome; some revolted and tried to achieve independence.

Traces of the events of this period may exist in Talmudic literature and Procopius, in legends of Canaanites settling in North Africa after being forced to leave their country. The tale of the Berber Kāhina, who fought the foreign invaders, may have a similar basis. In fact, a Neo-Punic inscription mentions RB KHNT, *i.e.* the high priestess, and this title may have contributed to the coining of the appellation *kāhina.*

Incidentally, there are those who think that the Neo-Punic script influenced the development of Hebrew cursive writing.

The Roman-Byzantine Period

For the Romans, Africa was not an area of settlement; those residing there permanently were very few. They nevertheless succeeded in holding the entire territory until 429 C.E., that is to say, for over 500 years in the case of some places, such as Carthage, and for no less than about 400 in the case of others, occupied at a later date.

At the time of the conquest, there were still books in the Punic language at the courts of the Berber kings; official documents were still drawn up in Punic, and coins still bore Punic signs. But gradually changes occurred in both the material and spiritual culture of the region. Latin superseded Punic, and Roman law became prevalent. Public libraries were established, and schools where jurists, linguistic scholars and philosophers taught were opened in the great cities. Roads were constructed, and temples, theatres and circuses were built whose ruins still impress the beholder with their size and shape. Even nature changed: lions, elephants and other animals, which had been numerous, disappeared. The population learnt to cultivate fruit trees, cereals and industrial crops until then not known locally. The Romans encouraged the development of olive and grape growing; many centuries later, the remains of oil-presses from Roman times inspired the French to plant olives and revive the oil industry in Tunisia. Josephus Flavius (*Wars* II, 16, 4) reports that the produce of the region was exported to Rome to feed the masses that clamoured for "bread and circus games"; their lust for games was satisfied by the famous Libyan lions, which were captured and sent to Rome until they had become completely extinct in the region.

Changes also occurred during that period in the administration of the areas directly controlled by Rome. They were at first divided into four and later into eight provinces. In time, one district, called Tingitana (District of Tangier), was joined to Spain; this is the area which fell to Spain in 1912.

The region's prosperity lured the Goths, who had overturned Italy and Spain. In 429, the Germanic Vandals crossed the Strait of Gibraltar, and after ten years' fighting, meeting but little opposition from the Romans, they had captured the most fertile and populous parts of the region—those most eagerly coveted by them (Carthage surrendered in 439). After consolidating their grip, they proceeded to attack the mother country by means of their fleet; they landed in Italy and entered Rome in 455. The ensuing sack, the most famous in history, lasted two weeks, but in accordance with a solemn pledge to the Pope by the Vandal king, Gaiseric, no persons were harmed and no buildings or monuments burnt. Fabulous treasures were removed to Carthage, including the Temple vessels brought to Rome by Titus. Three generations later, in 533, the Vandals were in turn defeated by the Byzantines under Belisarius, an outstanding general in the service of the Emperor Justinian, who dreamt of restoring the unity and power of the Roman Empire. From then onwards, discrimination and oppression were practised in North Africa against Jews, pagans and heretics, *i.e.* all those whose views or religion differed from the creed prescribed by the official church in Constantinople.

The Arab Period

Over a century thereafter, North Africa was first attacked in the east by Beduin from the Arabian Peninsula who only a little earlier had embraced

Islam. The complete subjection of the coastal cities, where Byzantine garrisons were stationed, and of the Berber tribes in the mountains, took fifty years. In the meantime, swift-moving Arab cavalry troops repeatedly penetrated to the western end of the region, but always withdrew again to their base at Barce in Cyrenaica. Only when the Arabs had crossed the strait named after Ṭāriq, one of the conquerors of Spain, did the *istiʿrāb, i.e.* the Arabicization and Islamization of the Berbers, begin, a process which owing to the small number of Arabs involved lasted hundred of years.

Not long after the Arab occupation authorities, representing the Umayyad caliphs in Damascus, had established themselves, a process of disintegration and fragmentation of government began in the west, far from the political centre. Arab-Berber dynasties, simultaneously and successively, seized different parts of the region, expanded and shrunk, flourished and waned. A penetrating study of this instability of government led Ibn Khaldūn, an Arab sociologist and historian of the second half of the 14th century, to formulate a rule as to the duration of those dynasties. It is, he says, a hundred or a hundred and twenty years, *i.e.* four generations: (1) the generation of the founder; (2) the generation of the heir immediately succeeding and thus still close to the founder; (3) the generation relying on the tradition of its predecessors; (4) the generation of the destroyer of the dynasty. We may suppose that Ibn Khaldūn is mainly referring to the dynasties founded by nomad Beduin, either Arab or Berber, although he does not expressly say so. Ibn Khaldūn also dealt the first blow to the notion accepted in Muslim society of the superiority of the nomads, pointing to their complete sterility as to permanent cultural values. Moreover, he believed that the Arabs, *i.e.* the sons of the desert, were fundamentally hostile to the settled urban and rural population and its culture. He witnessed the consequences of the invasion of the Banū Hilāl and Banū Sulaym Beduin, who "descended upon Africa and the Maghreb at the beginning of the 5th century (of the Ḥijra, the 11th century C.E.) and attacked and troubled them for three hundred and fifty years, until they had devastated all their flatlands, which previously had been wholly settled, between the Sudan and the Roman (Mediterranean) Sea. This is evidenced by vestiges of culture, monuments, the shapes of buildings and the remains of villages and settlements."

The Muʾminid dynasty, *i.e.* the house of the Almohad leader ʿAbd al-Muʾmin, who subdued North Africa up to the areas bordering on Egypt, ruled for about a century. The region then split up, under three different dynasties, into states roughly coinciding with present-day

Tunisia, Algeria and Morocco; Tripolitania and Cyrenaica were controlled by Tunisia.

The Modern Period

In the 16th century, North Africa came under Turkish rule, except for Morocco, which succeeded in repulsing the Turkish land and sea robbers. The Turkish regime lasted for 300-400 years, but left no mark on the local population, apart from certain religious customs in Algeria and the mixed offspring of the janissaries, who married native women.

The form of government was most oppressive in Algeria: the Council of the rais (captains of pirate ships) and the janissary officers elected one of their number as the dey, the "big brother". The tyranny of the rulers prepared the ground for the French conquest in 1830.

Tunisia achieved a certain stability in the early 17th century. Government was hereditary in two successive dynasties. Dependence on Constantinople was less pronounced, and political developments were much quieter. In 1881, the country became a French protectorate.

A different development took place in the eastern sector of the region, in Tripolitania and Cyrenaica, and the form of Turkish rule was adapted to it. In 1911, the area was conquered by Italy, and after the First World War it became an "inseparable" part of the Italian kingdom.

Morocco, as stated, succeeded in the 16th century in preserving its independence and sovereignty. As a matter of fact, the rule of the Saʿdi dynasty, which then grew powerful, and of its successors, the Filāli (Alouites) (the family of the present king), was confined to a few districts of the interior, known as *bilād al-makhzan* (the countries of the treasury). The important seaports on the Mediterranean and the Atlantic were directly or indirectly controlled by different European powers: Portugal, Spain and Britain. Most of Morocco, and especially the mountain areas, was *bilād al-sibā* (the countries of freedom). These were ruled by powerful sheikhs, the chieftains of Berber tribes, each of whom was associated with one of several *ṭarīqas*, kinds of brotherhoods with special customs and religious beliefs that welded the members into one religious-ideological unit. Through the head of the *ṭarīqa*, the chieftain was able to influence the members of his tribe in any way he chose. The chieftains pursued their own policies, which were determined by European powers and sometimes posed a grave threat to the national ruler, whom the people called *mulay* (master, lord) or *sharīf* (descendant of the Prophet Muḥammad). One recent instance may illustrate this: the overthrow of the Sultan Muḥammad V in 1953. Three opponents of the latter; the Pasha of Marrakesh and leader of powerful Berber tribes in the Atlas Mountains, the head of a *ṭarīqa* who resided in Fez, and a scholar at the famous *madrasa* in that city, combined to depose him, ostensibly for religious reasons, but really at the instigation of France. The verdict of the two theologians provided the French with an excuse for deporting the sultan.

Despite its weakness, the Sherifian regime in Morocco maintained its independent and sovereign status until the early 20th century. Only in 1912, by virtue of an international treaty, did Morocco come under the protectorate of France and Spain, which divided the country between them. France received by far the larger portion, about sixteen seventeenths of the total area, rich in natural resources, while Spain had to be content with one seventeenth, a poor, undeveloped tract in the coastal zone, north of the Rif Mountains.

One hundred and thirty years of French rule in Algeria and seventy-five in Tunisia, the forty years of the French protectorate over Morocco, and the settlement of Frenchmen and other Europeans in those countries, enormously advanced the latters' material culture. The French imparted to the urban population of Algeria and Tunisia a not inconsiderable knowledge of the French language. There can be no doubt, however, that French culture in no way changed the character of the local population, did not bring it nearer to European civilization, and certainly did not affect its religious consciousness or its customs. The influence of the Spanish in their zone was even less, and the territories annexed by Italy lagged in all respects—for objective reasons—behind the French and Spanish areas.

Shifts of the Cultural Scene

From what we have said so far it is clear that North Africa has never been an obscure nook, devoid of influence on the course of events in the Mediterranean and the countries adjacent to it.

In antiquity, it maintained political, commercial and cultural ties with Phoenicia, and afterwards with Hellenistic Egypt and the Rome of the consuls and emperors; the remains of cities and magnificent buildings attest to Rome's position. It was, moreover, the cradle of the Latin Christian Church, whose early great thinkers and writers originated from here.

In the Middle Ages, it was the bridge between the Muslim East, including Egypt, and Muslim Spain. It was the breeding-ground of ideas and values that were subsequently brought to Spain and reached their full development there. From Southern Morocco, the desert borderland, there came, at the beginning of the 2nd millennium C.E., waves of religious awakening, the Almoravid and Almohad movements, which touched off large-scale campaigns of conquest in Africa and Spain. Besides the literary heritage transmitted to us from that period, the region possesses numerous sumptuous mosques and other places of worship in a style identical with that of Spanish Muslim architecture —visible testimonies of a common culture.

From the beginning of the Reconquest, the Maghreb was the first line of defence against Spanish and Portuguese aggression, and later it opposed the commercial and political expansion of European states. The latter coveted the region for its own sake (the Italians also had historical "claims", based on the Maghreb's ties with ancient Rome), but probably even more as a springboard for an advance into Black Africa with its immense resources. The Ottoman Empire, which technically was the suzerain of three of the four Berber countries, played only a secondary role in this struggle, perhaps not even that. With the weakening and ultimate exhaustion of Turkey in the 19th century, the interest and political manœuvring of all the European powers in the Maghreb became still more intense. The fact that the Berber countries had sadly declined, that their population was among the most backward in the Mediterranean area, certainly encouraged the European states to grab many political and economic-social advantages.

The importance of the Maghreb to the European countries is reflected in a wealth of documents and official correspondence preserved in the archives of their governments and public bodies (such as chambers of commerce and admiralty offices) and in innumerable travel books, certainly written not only because of the exotism of the Maghreb or to describe the fate of European captives in pirate hands, but also from a realization of the significance of the region.

French and Italian scholars have carried out numerous excavations to reveal the Maghreb's past; they were joined by British and American archeologists after the Second World War. Teachers at Algiers University and university extensions in Tunis and Rabat made a special study of Maghreb problems and afterwards published the results in the mother country; a substantial historical literature also developed, especially in French, but also in Arabic. Important periodicals devoted exclusively to Maghreb research appeared in the three French-controlled countries;

they dealt extensively with political and social questions, such as were also discussed in general periodicals.

In the two-and-a-half millennia scanned by us, the Maghreb scene shifted a number of times. Seven centuries of Phoenician-Punic hegemony were followed by five centuries of Roman rule and three centuries of Christianization through political pressure and later through Byzantine armed might. The conquerors and rulers may have seemed at the time to make a profound mark upon the Berber population, but all that recalls their presence today is impressive archaeological remains and numerous place-names. Long and splendid historical periods left hardly a trace. In contrast hereto stand the twelve to thirteen centuries of Islam (in the widest sense, comprising many spheres besides religion), which forced upon the conquered population not only its creed, but also its language and literature and even the history of the people to which its founder belonged. These factors combined to produce in that population a consciousness of membership of the Arab nation. Of course, this does not apply to every area to the same extent and in the same way: Muslim religious experience in the Maghreb is very different from the variety evolved in Asia; moreover, the Berber language, despite its cultural backwardness, survives in Tripolitania with 23 per cent of the population, in Algeria with 33 and in Morocco with 40 (only in Tunisia is it down to 1 per cent). But there can be no doubt that Arab consciousness will make further progress in the sovereign states which Libya, Tunisia, Morocco and Algeria have become in the past twenty years.

It should be noted that the areas once subject to Ottoman rule, which lasted three to four centuries, have retained no trace of it except the Ḥanafite *madhhab*, which was the official rite of Islamic theology and law in the Ottoman Empire and is still followed by some *qāḍīs* in Algeria and Tunisia, as well as in the liturgy of some Maghrebi mosques.

An Undervalued Diaspora

Against the background delineated in the foregoing, an attempt will be made to present the history of the Jews of the African Maghreb, a large, well-defined diaspora which in some respects is different from other Jewish groups generally and from those of the Muslim East in particular.

This diaspora has been treated as a backwater of Jewish history. Jewish scholars mostly devoted their efforts to the vibrant centres of political and cultural life and did not give the Jewish periphery the attention to which it is objectively entitled. The author has repeatedly pointed out that they, nearly all of them members of the 19th-century school of historiography, were allured by the relative—and sometimes imaginary—wealth of literary sources available for the study of such diasporas as Babylonia, Spain, France, Germany and Poland. They were dazzled by the prestige of the Geonim and early Decisors; the work of the Tosaphists, for instance, seemed to them—and rightly so—a kind of continuation of the discussions of the Gemara, a living tie with the debates of the Amoraim. On the other hand, halakhic jurisprudence, even in the sphere of civil law, did not attract scholars—and be it only from a theoretical point of view—in the countries where modern Jewish studies developed. Spanish-Jewish literature appealed to the emotions; the philosophic treatises, in part inspired by ideas current in the non-Jewish world, evoked a sympathetic response because of the similarity of their topics to present-day problems. And so, just as there is a contrast in Jewish history between periods apparently all splendour and others apparently all darkness, a contrast accentuated by a lack of interest in periods deficient in source material and therefore difficult to explore, there are countries receiving detailed and penetrating study and others reduced to backwater status.

In the life of these "backwaters" there were times when they played a highly important part in the history of the Jewish people, and in certain cases even in the history of mankind generally. Such a part was played, *e.g.*, by the Jews of the Arabian Peninsula at the time of the rise of Islam; the Jews in the northern border region of the Arab caliphate and of the Byzantine Empire and the Judaizers in the Khazar kingdom; and the Messianic movements which occurred from time to time in the course of centuries precisely among the simple folk, in societies whose physiognomy is hardly known to us, and not at the centres of learning and wisdom in wealthy, well-regulated circles.

A prominent place among these peripheral Jewries is held by the North African diaspora.

The Antiquity of North African Jewry

North African Jewry possibly goes back to the time when Tyrians and Sidonites settled on the African coast. However, no epigraphic or other evidence of settlers from Israel or Judaea at that time has been preserved, which may be due to rapid assimilation of the Jews to the Phoenicians owing to affinity in language and material culture. But even excluding that period, North African Jewry has existed continuously for about 2,300 years, scattered over an enormous area. This continuity is not broken by the wide gap between the late Roman period and the second century of the Arab occupation, when both Jewish and non-Jewish sources are almost completely silent. Here is the first instance of a "dark age" in North African Jewish history, such as is found also in the history of other Jewries.

The position is rather different with regard to the second North African "dark age," viz. the period between the appearance of the Almoravids and especially the Almohads in the second half of the 12th century and the arrival of the first Spanish refugees in 1391. At first sight, it would seem that for this period, too, documents are almost completely lacking. However, painstaking research has produced a number of data which combine into a nearly uninterrupted chain spanning that gulf. This does not mean, of course, that every aspect of social life is fully covered, but we may say with certainty that the reestablishment of Jewish communities in the Mediterranean ports, as well as in Fez and other cities of the Moroccan interior, after the Almohad catastrophe was not a single occurrence following the immigration from Spain and the Balearics, but a slow internal process of rehabilitation, accompanied by an influx of traders and agents from Christian countries and beginning immediately after the cessation of the Almohad persecutions.

But the discovery of those data, which represent only a part of the material preserved in various European archives and still awaiting full study, is not sufficient. We have to reexamine all the problems connected with the survival of remote Jewish communities in times when for geographic-logistic, military, social or other reasons they were unable to maintain regular contact with the centres known to us and were therefore compelled to conduct their spiritual affairs unaided, either according to traditions upheld by them for many generations past or by way of innovations. Our historiography is under the spell of the charismatic leadership of the patriarchs, exilarchs and *geonim* and later of the *negidim* and *nesiʾim*; we almost overlook the fact that in large areas of Europe, Asia and Africa Jewish groups survived which, for reasons this is not the place to discuss, hardly had any ties with those authorities. In all probability, they set up autonomous social regimes of varied forms and representing a mixture of different systems and methods of rule. This is the background against which, on the threshold of the second millennium C.E., the communal agreements (*haskamot*) and ordinances (*takkanot*) mentioned by contemporary rabbis developed. Those *takkanot* and *haskamot* enacted by the community (*qahal*), though somewhat similar, are nevertheless essentially different from the *takkanot* of the sages of old. We know almost nothing about the composition, modes of operation and execution procedures in the period under reference.

At first, the communal *haskamot* and *takkanot* were certainly not constitutional acts, based on clear-cut legislation, but measures dictated by the needs of the hour and place, uncoordinated even between neighbouring communities. They subsequently developed into an extremely interesting, variegated system of social control, far removed from the charismatic rule of the sages and *geonim*, a system which has not yet been studied comprehensively and exhaustively. Its essential function is clear: to ensure the continued normal existence of the community in times when a central spiritual authority was lacking.

What we have said concerning spiritual leadership applies to the administration of justice as well. Persons halakhically qualified to adjudicate cases according to rabbinic law were not to be found everywhere at all times. On the other hand, it was impossible to let a whole community take every dispute to a Gentile court; it was enough that the execution of judgments against an obstreperous party had to be entrusted to the Muslim authorities. So the "courts of the elders" were created which were not only concerned with monetary matters in the narrow sense. There may have been in their case, as in that of the leadership, a revival of ancient forms of tribal organization, such as still existed in the Beduin society in whose midst at least part of the Jewish communities were living. This does not mean that the Jews copied social patterns of their Beduin neighbours, but that certain conditions of life produced similar phenomena.

These conditions of life account also for the theory of the Berber origin of North African Jewry.

The first "dark age", at the end of antiquity, as well as the obscurity of the history of most of the communities of the interior in the first half of the second millennium C.E., provide a certain background for the thesis that the great majority of Maghreb Jews are of Berber stock. This thesis was enunciated in various travel books and adopted in modern historical writings, without anybody giving it a thorough scrutiny. Of course, a visitor to remote corners of the High Atlas, to the South Moroccan valleys descending towards the Sahara, to the small *mellāḥ* that were scattered among Berber villages or to the oases of the French military region in Algeria bordering on the Sahara was likely to believe these stories, especially after reading in serious books about the "Berber *kāhina*", the Jewish queen that fought the Arab conquerors in the second half of the 7th century C.E. No scholar bothered to trace the development of the tale of the Judaizing queen and Judaizing Berbers to its ancient primary version, which later underwent additions and embellishments. The position with regard to sources is different here than in the case of the Ḥimyar Judaizers in South Arabia or the Khazars on the banks of the Volga. We know that the great majority of the former adopted Islam in the days of Muhammad and that only Jews of Jewish stock were left in South Arabia, and it is also well known that the Khazar Judaizers have completely disappeared. Now is it to be supposed that precisely the Berbers in North Africa remained loyal to Judaism, especially as the evidence of their Judaization is extremely flimsy?

To deal exhaustively with the problem of the Berber Judaizers, we must study the character of the Jewish communities and the history of the Berbers in the region during antiquity. We shall then realize that, as stressed by Berberologists and recently by G. H. Bousquet in several places of his book on Maghrebi Islam, almost no trace of Roman or Christian influence on the Berbers is left. Now if these tribes proved rather impervious to both Roman culture and Christian propaganda, if their Islamization took many centuries and they have still not absorbed Arab culture, they were even less likely to adopt Judaism and cling to it in the face of relentless persecution. On the other hand, a study of the history of Maghreb Jewry in the period between Almohad oppression and the recovery in the 15th century may greatly assist in ascertaining the origin of the Jews of the interior.

Relations between African and Spanish Jewry

In geonic times, certain parts of the African Maghreb maintained a much closer connection than other diasporas with the academies of Sura and Pumbeditha and also with Palestine. The past fifty years have seen a steady speeding up of the publication of sources discovered in the Geniza: geonic responsa, halakhic and aggadic writings and fragments of such, letters, commercial documents and court decisions. This material adds to what has long been known of the Maghreb's relations with the East and its major role in halakhic and scholarly matters, but there has not yet been an overall review and evaluation, such as ought to dispose of the preconceived notion of the Maghreb as a backwater and assign to it a paramount position in the history of medieval Jewry in Muslim lands (except Babylonia and Palestine).

A study of the material shows that Maghrebi rabbis were the teachers and mentors of Spanish Jewry. The linguistic scholars and *payṭānīm* held to be the founders of the Spanish school came to Spain from Morocco in the 10th century. Things were similar with regard to *halakha* and rabbinic decisions. Isaac Alfasi, the undisputed doyen of halakhic learning in Spain, came to that country as an old man, after many years' teaching in the Maghreb, where he wrote his great book and his many responsa.

When the plight of Spanish Jewry became increasingly acute, they began to migrate to the Berber countries, whence many of their ancestors had come centuries previously. The first refugees arrived even before the events of 1391, and from then the movement continued through the years of relative quiet that preceded the expulsions of 1492 and 1497 and for a long time thereafter. There were several waves of settlement of Spanish and Portuguese Jews in the Maghreb. The last to arrive were the "Gornim", Spanish expellees who after many wanderings had at first settled in Leghorn and thence proceeded to Africa; they, too, did not all come at the same time. All this immigration greatly benefited Maghreb Jewry both spiritually and materially.

About the time of the settling of the Spanish expellees and emigrants in Africa, certain port cities on the North African coasts of the Mediterranean and the Atlantic were controlled by states of the Iberian Peninsula. Other ports were virtually independent, ruled by the famous Berber pirates who ambushed European merchant vessels; technically, they were subject to the ruler of Morocco. A feature common to all these ports —including those of Algeria, Tunisia and Tripolitania—was that in addition to being pirate anchorages they were centres of international trade and of the redemption of Christian captives from pirate hands. Ships of all seafaring nations called at them under treaties and agreements made in order to ensure the freedom of navigation. Here and in neighbouring towns, Jewish merchants were living, usually of refugee descent, who had an official or practical monopoly on trading with European countries and negotiating the redemption of captives. Trade relations were a key to consular posts for the representatives of the great commercial firms, and on the other hand, the Jews to whom the functions of diplomatic representatives and of agents for peace talks and the redemption of captives had been assigned had to look after the commercial interests of their principals and procure the necessary technical assistance to them in constructing new ports, manufacturing war equipment and the like. In the Maghreb, Jews were thus given tasks the like of which they did not perform in any other Christian or Muslim country in the Mediterranean basin.

Concerning the relevant period, the 16th to 18th centuries, we have a wealth of archival sources unparalleled in any other Mediterranean region: consular and ambassadorial reports, stories of captives' adventures and travel books by emissaries charged with the redemption of captives. Part of this material has been published, part of it is about to be published, and part is still stowed away in the archives of London, Paris, Amsterdam, the Hague, Madrid and Lisbon. From what has so far been published it may be assumed that the unpublished material, too, deals extensively with Jews and the trade with Jews.

The Social Fabric

By responsa collections of refugee rabbis in Algeria and Morocco; the *Sefer Takkanot* of Fez, reproduced in Part Two of *Kerem Ḥemer*; regulations as yet unpublished, preserved in privately-owned manuscripts; and accounts of contemporary travellers, we know of the forms of organization of refugee communities and discern that they were different from those evolved in the Muslim East (in the cities of European and Asian Turkey). Here, too, the difference in organization and way of life between refugees and veteran residents is clear and sometimes striking, but we never find the same division into congregations according to cities of origin, and fragmentation within the congregations themselves, as in the East. It should be noted that the organization of the veteran residents in the Maghreb was stronger and more stable than that of their eastern counterparts: the Musta'ribs in Arabic-speaking countries and the Greek-speaking Romaniots. The indigenous North Africans did not assimilate to the refugees, as did the Romaniots in Rumelia, who after two or three generations almost disappeared as a separate communal entity, and most of the Musta'ribs in places where the refugees founded communities of their own. It seems that throughout the Maghreb, except Fez during certain periods and the Spanish-controlled area, the veteran residents carried greater weight than the refugees in all spheres but one: big business and the representation of the Sherifian state at the courts of European rulers. Another striking feature in the Maghreb was that refugee rabbis served in veteran communities and *vice versa*. Relations between the two groups were generally satisfactory. It is surprising, therefore, that relations between the 'Tuansa', the veteran Jewish population of Tunisia, and the Gornim grew steadily worse, so that in time two separate communities came into being; the Gornim eventually also had a *qāʾid* of their own, who represented them with the authorities. The reasons for this development must be sought in the original social background of the Gornim and in the special circumstances of their settlement in Tunisia.

The form of organization and mode of representation *vis-à-vis* the authorities had a considerable, and sometimes decisive, influence on the appointment of the *nagid* in Morocco, the *muqaddam* in Algeria and the *qāʾid* in Tunisia and Tripolitania—those were the titles of the heads of the communities in these countries. Interference by the authorities was sometimes decisive in apportioning the tax burden among the Jews; once we even find a Moroccan ruler interfering in a matter of personal status by forcing the rabbis to permit refugees to take two wives, contrary to Spanish-Jewish regulations. From the *Sefer Takkanot Fēs* we learn that there was nevertheless a great measure of freedom to make regulations in accordance with current requirements.

The *batey-dīn* were particularly well-ordered and highly esteemed by the public. Refugees and veteran residents had separate *batey-dīn* because of certain differences in the law of personal status, but everything of importance to the Jewish population as a whole was settled by agreement and coordination; an exception was the dispute in Tunisia, which affected the status of the *batey-dīn*, but not the respected position of the *dayyanim* of both communities.

Halakha and Administration of Justice

Throughout the ages (except the period of the Almohad persecutions), the *batey-dīn* in the Maghreb and their full authority to adjucidate all litigations between Jews were not challenged. At a late stage, during the French protectorate over Morocco and Tunisia, they were state institutions maintained by the treasury; only in Algeria did the French authorities, shortly after the occupation, begin to restrict the powers of the *batey-dīn*, until they were mere religious institutions, similar in status to the rabbinate in France.

Clearly, the existence of the *batey-dīn* necessitated a broad basis of religious-legal studies in *batey-midrashot*, which, in addition to teaching the Law for its own sake, trained *dayyanim*, court clerks and the like. Because of the isolation of the Maghreb and its remoteness from other Jewish centres, the communities there preferred to rely on themselves rather than bring *dayyanim* from far away, as did the community heads of Tripoli, which owing to its closer ties with Turkey on the one hand and its rather tenuous link with Tunisia would invite rabbis from Palestine and Turkey to head their *batey-dīn* (a similar situation prevailed in Egypt); however, even in the *batey-dīn* of Tripoli there were *dayyanim* of local origin (or from the island of Jerba), well-versed in the customs regulations and special life conditions of their community.

Just as it created special forms of communal administration, Maghreb Jewry evolved its own methods of rabbinic study and of reaching halakhic decisions. The talmudic foundations and the link with the Spanish heritage are evident, but in the course of time traditions from the geonic era and perhaps from the period preceding it reasserted themselves or gained in strength. It was precisely the teaching of outstanding rabbis from Spain and the Spanish islands, the trainers of generations of disciples in Algeria and Morocco and later in Tunisia, that heightened the veteran residents' sense of independence and made them cling more resolutely to their own halakhic traditions. Moreover, in the course of centuries, a merger of different methods produced special Maghrebi patterns, whose influence can be felt in all spheres of spiritual life, and not only in the Halakha.

Acculturation and Separate Identity

All the epigraphic finds from the antique period attest that North African Jewry adopted the Greek and Latin languages. It seems, moreover, that upon the arrival of the Arabs they were the first among the residents of the region who began to use literary Arabic. Yehuda ibn Quraysh is the first non-Arab in Africa of whom a work in Arabic—in the field of linguistics—has been preserved, and Isaac Israeli was the first non-Muslim student of natural science, medicine and philosophy in the region. Turkish culture had not, to our knowledge, any influence on North African Jewry, any more than it left a trace among Jews or Arabs anywhere in Asia who were ever under Turkish rule. In the French era, many Jews were prominent exponents of French culture; this was so in Algeria and Tunisia and more recently also in Morocco.

The Jewish élite in Fez, Tetuan, Algiers, Tunis and (in the 19th century) Tangier seems to have been intellectually superior to that in other oriental countries. Members of the prominent families were for many generations in the service of the rulers and in contact with Europeans who came to those cities on various business, as stated above. In Morocco, the Jews were the only non-Muslims, and Christian visitors were only permitted to reside in Jewish neighbourhoods and houses; they were not allowed to reside permanently in the royal cities, and as late as the 19th century all the ambassadors and consuls lived in Tangier. As stated, Jews were the only persons who travelled to European countries on political missions, and were agents and vice-consuls of European states. Obviously, this contact with the great world left a profound imprint on the physiognomy of the wealthy stratum that had access to the authorities. At the same time, that stratum did not enjoy a favoured status with the Muslim rulers; they were subject to the same humiliations as their fellow Jews.

The perfect Arabic spoken by the Jews in the Middle Ages gradually dwindled into a Jewish dialect, which has survived until today; it is largely the everyday speech of those who lived far from the centres of French culture, but is understood even by the second and third generations of graduates of French schools. The Arabic of the educated, both written and spoken, has not in recent times been current among the Jews, since they did not attend Arabic schools, whose standard was extremely low, while the schools of the Alliance Israélite Universelle, during French rule, allotted no or almost no room to Arabic in their curriculum. In this respect, the situation of Maghreb Jewry was different from that of Iraqi and even Egyptian.

It is thus not surprising that assimilation to French culture made deep inroads into the Arab sector as well. Algeria, for instance, where some nine million Muslims were living in 1955, had not a single Arabic newspaper, and the only illustrated Arabic weekly in Morocco closed down in that year. A literature or press in any of the Berber languages did not exist at all, except for a few textbooks issued by the French Government for two or three Berber schools founded by it. The propensity of the Jews to linguistic assimilation makes it all the more remarkable that they are the only group in the region that preserved its national-religious identity under all circumstances. The Berbers in the settled areas changed their religion four times: they at first adopted Phoenician-Punic and Greco-Roman forms of worship, then they became Christians and finally all of them became Islamized and most of them Arabicized. We shall have to review the material and spiritual struggle of the Jews with their environment, a struggle frequently varying in form, but always maintaining the characteristic Jewish way of pouring old wine into new vessels.

Needless to say that political developments in the North African countries, as referred to above, largely determined the way of life of the

Jews. This relationship will be dealt with extensively in the body of the book. But we must also mention here the special Maghrebi form of Islam, which manifested itself almost from the beginning of the Arab conquest. Its sectarian movements and puritan trends, the spread of the Malekite *madhhab*, the school most intolerant of non-Muslims (except for the Ḥanbalites, who, however, had no contact with the latter), the establishment of the *ṭarīqas*, mystical fraternities headed by religious fanatics—all these affected the Jews, sometimes favourably, but mostly adversely.

Discriminatory features included the ghetto (*mellāḥ*, *ḥāra*), distinctive clothing (*ghiyār*) and other marks of degradation, which the Jews retained (sometimes voluntarily) until our time. We should not, however, overlook cases in which highly respected *qāḍīs*, in reliance on Islamic law, protected Jews from the designs of sectarian demagogues and the fury of incited mobs.

There is sometimes great similarity between Muslim and Jewish customs. In certain cases, it is impossible to decide whether we have to do with a late influence of the Muslim Berber environment or with ancient traditions adopted from the Egypto-Hellenistic world; this applies, *e.g.*, to the belief in charms and incantations. One feature does not seem to exist anywhere else (apart from the Tombs of the Patriarchs in Hebron), viz. pilgrimages to and prostrations on the graves of "saints" common to Jews and Muslims and revered also by Christians. A number of further parallel or similar customs might be pointed out.

Purpose and Structure of the Book

These are the main characteristics of Maghreb Jewry, which necessitate its study as a separate unit. Since research hitherto conducted in this field is very scanty—especially as far as Jewish scholars are concerned—it is not surprising that writers of Jewish history generally prefer to skip this seemingly unimportant subject, while the authors of the relevant articles in Jewish encyclopaedias repeat "information" such as that discovered by Marcus Fischer in faulty translations of Arabic works and published as facts in his *Toledot Yeshurun* (Prague 1817(!)).

European travellers—Christian scholars, physicians, French army officers, civil servants and education workers—were attracted to the study of Jewish society, especially in Morocco, but also in Algeria and Tunisia, and tried in their own way, to the best of their ability, to fathom its problems. The result is a sizable array of books and articles. These authors, of course, turned to matters they were qualified to handle by their particular training, such as the *mellāḥ* in the great cities, the small communities in the Atlas Mountains and the valleys of the south, and demographic, ethnological and anthropological surveys; we can hardly blame them for not being versed in cultural history or for not knowing the world of Jewry from within. This serious attention given to it by Gentile researchers is one more feature distinguishing Maghreb Jewry from all other Jewish diasporas.

The English edition of the book, which is a revised version of the Hebrew, embodies fundamental changes as to both substance and form. Let us point, for the time being, to the changes made in Volume One. The first six chapters contain additions necessitated by recent researches and publications, and for the same reason certain passages have been omitted. For the convenience of the reader, the notes have been transferred from the end of the book to the foot of the pages. I deemed it desirable to indicate in an annex, in the form of *regesta*, the material available to me on Tunis from the earliest informations to the end of the 15th century. Luckily, a considerable number of documents on Tunis have been preserved from that period, while there is almost no information concerning the period prior to the Almohads and very little for the second half of the 16th and the early 17th century. The reestablishment in Tunis of Jews—descendants of former residents, traders from Europe and refugees from Majorca and other islands—is undoubtedly a typical instance of the reestablishment of Jews in the port cities generally.

The changes in Volume Two will be indicated upon the publication of the latter, which we hope will not be long delayed.

I have refrained from adding notes and references to this Introduction, so as not to swell its pages unduly. A selection of the very extensive literature dealing with problems touched upon here and not dealt with in the body of the book is given in the Selected Bibliography.

CHAPTER ONE

IN THE GRECO-ROMAN ORBIT

The approximately 1,000 years (from 300 B.C.E. to 700 C.E.) that we shall review in this chapter are a very long period even in the history of the "eternal people", especially as they were marked by some of the most fateful events in its existence, bringing about profound changes in its structure, its spiritual and religious development and its relations with other peoples. The Jewish people rose once, twice, three times against the Roman Empire and was vanquished after a great deal of fighting. It eventually lost its freedom, saw its Second Temple destroyed and was ejected from its homeland, which was settled by strangers, while its own sons, as an early Christian writer tauntingly remarks, were forbidden even to visit it. At the same time, this was a period of propagation of the Jewish faith throughout the world on a scale difficult to imagine nowadays. Movements for a closer relationship and even conversion to Judaism sprang up at the ends of what was then the known world: in the Arab Peninsula, in North Africa, in South Russia.

The Position of the North African Diaspora within the Jewish World

North Africa played an important part in those processes. The North African diaspora shared the convulsions of Palestine to a greater extent than other Diaspora countries. The revolt of the "king" Lucuas in the reign of Trajan bears great resemblance to the revolt of Bar-Kokhba, also as regards its political consequences. North Africa saw the birth and development of Latin Christianity, which crystallized in the Roman Catholic Church. Here we find Tertullian, the first anti-Jewish ecclesiastical writer, and Augustine (354-430), the greatest religious thinker in Christendom, the spiritual architect of the Catholic Church, the programme and content of which are outlined in his "City of God". About a hundred years after Augustine's death, North African Jewry came under Byzantine rule, which proved more severe in this region than in Palestine.

The meagreness of Jewish historical sources on the North African dispersion for the period we are dealing with makes it extremely difficult to trace the course of events and draw reliable conclusions. The task is

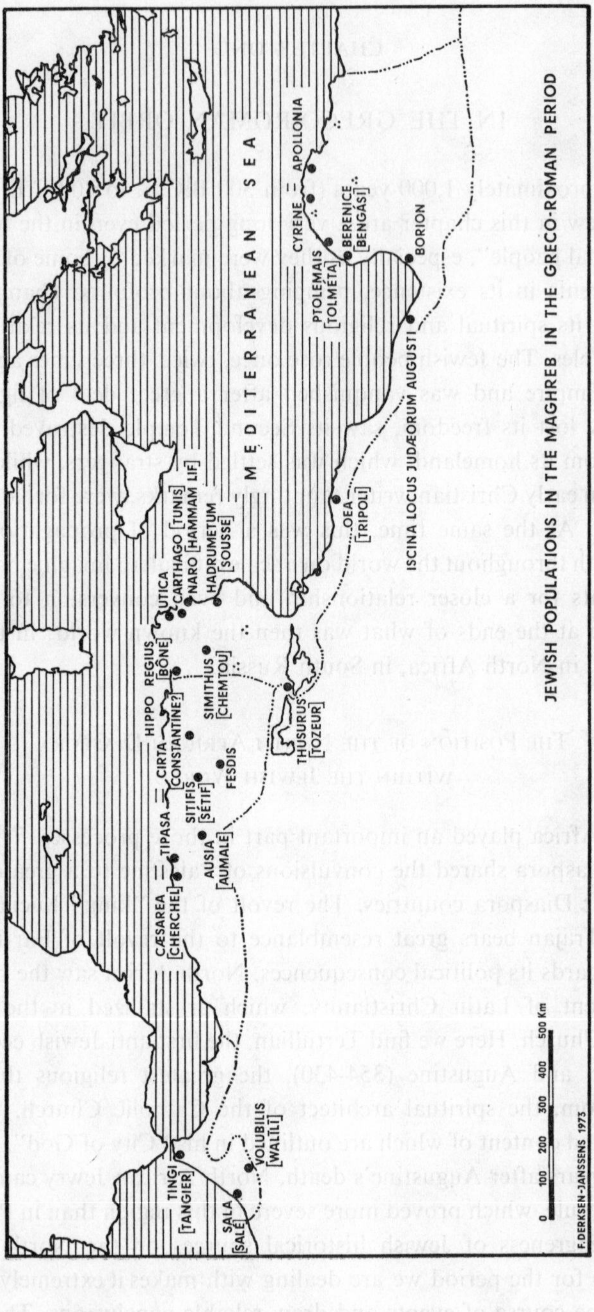
JEWISH POPULATIONS IN THE MAGHREB IN THE GRECO-ROMAN PERIOD
MEDITERRANEAN SEA
SALA [SALE]
TINGI [TANGIER]
VOLUBILIS [WALILI]
CÆSAREA [CHERCHEL]
TIPASA
AUSIA [AUMALE]
SITIFIS [SETIF]
CIRTA [CONSTANTINE?]
FESDIS
HIPPO REGIUS [BÔNE]
SIMITHUS [CHEMTOU]
UTICA
CARTHAGO [TUNIS]
NARO [HAMMAM LIF]
HADRUMETUM [SOUSSE]
THUSURUS [TOZEUR]
OEA [TRIPOLI]
ISCINA LOCUS JUDÆORUM AUGUSTI
PTOLEMAIS [TOLMETA]
BERENICE [BENGASI]
BORION
CYRENE
APOLLONIA
0 100 200 300 400 500 Km
F. DERKSEN-JANSSENS 1973

Map 1

similar to the restoration of a mosaic from which many stones are missing. But while such a mosaic discovered in a Roman villa may be reconstructed by reference to better-preserved specimens, how are we to reconstruct a complete picture of African Jewry, which was unique of its kind and whose epigraphic and archaeological vestiges are few and, moreover, unequal in historical value and scattered over a vast area and a period of a thousand years? Not a single spiritual creation of African Jewry during that period has come down to us to enlighten us on its peculiarities. The information contained in contemporary Palestinian literature is likewise extremely scanty. Any reconstruction, therefore, must rely on secondary sources. In the absence of Jewish documents, we have to fill in essential details from Gentile accounts, which describe events and conditions from their point of view. An important domain like religious and spiritual life—particularly open to the impact of emotions—must be viewed in part in negative pictures, as it were: through polemics and discussions in hostile writings by representatives of a religion that strove to eliminate Judaism.

Jewish history in Africa west of Egypt begins with some wondrous tales: of the promise of the Land of Canaan to the children of Israel; of the withdrawal of the Tyrians and Sidonians, who had controlled the approaches of Egypt, to Africa after being expelled from Canaan in the days of Joshua; of David's victory over the Philistine ("Berber") Goliath; of Joab the son of Zeruiah, who pursued the Philistines to the western and southern ends of Africa;[1] of the ships of Tarshish, *i.e.* Africa;[2] of an ancient synagogue, erected in the days of King Solomon; of a stone from the Temple of Solomon which was inserted in the *Ghrība*, the legend-enwreathed synagogue on the island of Jerba—folk-traditions and stories collected and recorded on ancient times by both Jewish and Gentile (*i.e.* Greek and Arab) scholars or transmitted orally and written down only in recent generations.[3]

These traditions take us back to a remote past, when that unknown continent emerged from the depths of prehistory; whatever happened there at that time appears in the half-light of dawn. There is some resemblance to the Greco-Roman tales of the primeval days of our planet and its inhabitants. Of course the background against which the Jewish legends developed was different, as we shall see below.

---

[1] These legends are mentioned by N. Slouschz, *Heb.*, *passim*; *id.*, *Jud.*, *passim*; Laredo, *Bereberes*, pp. 107-109 and *passim*. Comp. below, pp. 41ff.

[2] Comp. Targum to Jer. 10; 9; Mieses, *REJ* 92 (1932), pp. 114-116.

[3] See, *e.g.*, Hirschberg, *Me-Ereẓ*, p. 43.

From the 4th century B.C.E. onwards, isolated hints begin to accumulate: references in literary sources and archaeological finds, which together permit conjectures as to early Jewish history in those regions.

The Jewish Settlement in Cyrene

The first historical report of the presence of Jews in the area west of Egypt reaches us in the treatise of Josephus Flavius against the Hellenistic Jew-baiter Apion, a native of Libya. Relying on official sources, Josephus notes that King Ptolemy Lagi (r. 323-285) entrusted Jews with the protection of Egyptian fortresses and that, when about the year 300 he intended to conquer Cyrene (the most important of the five Greek cities—Pentapolis—in the region called after it Cyrenaica) and other Libyan cities, he sent Jews to settle there. Josephus relies on the Letter of Aristeas (though he does not expressly mention it), which says that Ptolemy transferred 100,000 Jews from Palestine to Egypt and employed about one third of them to guard fortified places.[1]

Not very informative evidence of a Jewish settlement in Cyrene during that period is provided by a Hebrew seal with the inscription "To Obadiah the son of Y.sh.b".[2] A Cyrenian named Jason described the War of the Maccabees in five volumes, but his book is lost and its contents are known only from a reference in II Maccabees. Jason is believed to have been a companion of Judah the Maccabee.[3]

The relative proximity of Egypt, where many Jews lived in the period of the Second Temple, led to a progressive increase of the Jewish population of Cyrenaica and Libya, which must in all respects be regarded as an extension of the Egyptian diaspora. This is the opinion expressed by the Greek geographer Strabo in connection with a revolt of Cyrenian Jewry. The last Hellenistic king of Cyrene, Ptolemy Apion (d. 96 B.C.E.), had bequeathed his kingdom to Rome, which left the government for a time in the hands of the managements of the Greek cities. After several years (in 87 B.C.E.), the Jews revolted, and Sulla, who was engaged in war against Mithridates, had to delegate one of his subordinates to restore order. The revolt is believed to have resulted from tension over civic

---

[1] Josephus Flavius, *Against Apion* II, § 44; *ibid.*, § 53; *Ant.* XII, 12, 5 § 45. Also *The Letter of Aristeas* (ed. Wendland) § 12.

[2] M. A. Levy, *ZDMG*, (1857), pp. 318f.; *id.*, *JGJJ*, 2 (1861), p. 264; D. Diringer, *Iscrizioni*, p. 193, No. 34.

[3] 2 Maccab. 2, 19-24; also ibid. 15, 38 and 4, 40. Comp. E. Schürer, *Gesch.* III, pp. 482-485, also p. 82; *PW*, 17, col. 778-780.

discrimination which the Greek cities tried to practise against the Jews. Strabo, from whom Josephus derives the information, notes in this context: "In Cyrenaica, there were then four (*scil.* φυλαί "strata"): the first were the citizens; the second were the tillers of the soil; the third were the sojourners (μέτοικοι); the fourth were the Jews. That nation has found its way into every city, and it is not easy to find a place in the inhabited world where that nation has not been admitted and its influence is not felt. This was the case in Cyrenaica, which had the same rulers as the Egyptians and imitated them (the Egyptians) in many things, especially in encouraging the spread of, and assisting, Jewish communities, which adhered to their own religious precepts".[1] A comparison with Herodotus's report of three φυλαί in Cyrene, which were named according to the origin of the settlers, suggests that the Jews were reckoned as a separate stratum because of their origin, which had not yet become obliterated, while the three Greek strata had already merged and were divided according to social status. We may suppose that Cyrenian Jewry enjoyed a national-religious autonomy similar to that of the Jews of Egypt.[2]

Direct Roman Rule

Interference with the rights granted to the Jews did not cease when some years later the country came under direct Roman rule. Although Julius Caesar permitted them to send the half-shekel to the Temple in Jerusalem, local Roman governors, on a complaint by Greek cities that the Jews did not pay municipal rates, tried to prevent the transmission of the contributions. A delegation of Cyrenaican Jews brought the matter before Augustus, who reaffirmed the decisions of his predecessor: that the Jews might observe their ancestral customs, send the half-shekel to Jerusalem and refrain from appearing in court on Sabbaths and Friday afternoons, and that persons stealing sacred books or pious contributions from synagogues or houses of religious study would be considered desecrators and their property forfeited to the treasury. The imperial ordinance was sent to Flavius, the Praetor of Libya, as the province was then called. Indeed, many Jews migrated to that region, and the local community developed and flourished.[3]

[1] Josephus, *Ant.* XIV, 7, 2 §§ 114-116. It should be noted that Plutarch does not connect the Jews with this revolt.

[2] See K. Friedmann, *Atene e Roma*, 10 (1929), pp. 206-207; *id.*, *Giornale Soc. Asiat. Ital.*, N.S. 2 (1934), pp. 323-327. Comp. also Juster, *Juifs* I, p. 417; II, p. 12, n. 2.

[3] Josephus, *ibid.* XVI, 6, 1 § 160; 6, 5 § 169-170. About the development of the area see Kahrstedt, *Kulturgeschichte*, p. 207, also pp. 195-196.

Marcus Titius Sextus, one of the Roman procurators, who implemented the imperial ordinance in letter and spirit, earned a token of esteem in the shape of a stele erected for him by the Jewish community (πολίτευμα) of Berenice (present-day Benghazi), where many Jews lived at that time. The wreath-encircled honorary tablet, which took the place of the wreath-crowned statue usually set up as a memorial, but which the Jews were unable to provide for religious reasons, bears an expression of thanks from the heads of the community to the "fine and good" governor for his benevolence towards the citizens in general and the Jews of Berenice in particular, both in his official capacity and in personal contacts.[1]

That community seems to have been extremely active. Another inscription that has been discovered records a decision to honour the Jew Decimus Valerius Dionysius, a Roman citizen, for having repaired the amphitheatre, apparently the meeting-place of the community.[2] S. Applebaum has published a Jewish inscription recently found in Benghazi of the year 56 C.E., commemorating the renovation of the synagogue and mentioning the donors who had made it possible.[3]

The number of Jews in Cyrenaica increased steadily. Philo reports that in his time Egypt and Libya, from Kabathmos (Sollum) to Ethiopia, had a Jewish population of about a million. Modern scholars do not think this an exaggeration, and the figure is confirmed by papyri and contemporary literary sources. Of course, the great majority of Jews were in Egypt, whose cities—especially Alexandria—and rural districts had densely populated Jewish settlements. But even if we put the number of Jews in Cyrenaica at only one tenth of the figure given by Philo, it is still considerable.[4] Incidentally, Philo makes no mention of the Jews west of Cyrenaica; he probably never heard of them.

After the destruction of the Temple, a new wave of exiles reached Africa. Many settled voluntarily in that vast region, where the cities of the coastal plain and the fertile plateau offered favourable conditions,

---

[1] *CIG* 5361 (vol. III, p. 557-61); Juster, *Juifs* I, p. 438, n. 4; Krauss, *Syn. Alt.*, p. 265. See also below, pp. 61-3 and notes. The exact date of this inscription is difficult to establish. Schürer, *Gesch.* III, p. 80 and n. 21, assigns it to 13 B.C. Another conjecture is 24 C.E.; see S. Applebaum, *Zion*, 19 (1954), p. 47, and recently *id. Jews and Greeks* (Hebrew), p. 138, also pp. 146, 156.

[2] *CIG* 5362. This inscription is discussed by J. and G. Roux, *REG* 62 (1949), pp. 281-296. Comp. Applebaum, *Jews and Greeks*, pp. 137-8.

[3] *BIES* 25 (1961), pp. 167-174; id., *Jews and Greeks*, pp. 140-1.

[4] Philo, *In Flaccum* 43, (trad. Pelletier, Paris 1967, p. 75); comp. Juster, *Juifs* I, p. 209; Baron, *SRH*, I, pp. 168-169. Kahrstedt, *Kulturgeschichte*, pp. 386, 193, also 316, thinks that about half the population of Cyprus and Cyrenaica, and 40 percent of that of Alexandria, was Jewish.

while in Egypt population density and the hostility of the Greeks no doubt acted as a deterrent against further immigration. Others were deported there as prisoners of war sold to Roman masters to work on their African estates. Yosephon reports: "And Vespasian gave his son Titus the country of Africa, and he settled thirty thousand Jews in Carthage, besides those he established in other places."[1] Support for Yosephon's statement may be found in the Tabula Peutingeriana, where a locality south-east of Oea (Tripoli) is marked as "Scina (Iscina), Locus Judaeorum Augusti"; this was probably an estate where slaves of the imperial treasury had been settled. Inscriptions discovered in Rome mention people of Scina, and it is believed that these were inhabitants of that locality concerned with the import of grain to the metropolis.[2]

Africa in Talmud and Midrash

For various reasons, Palestinian scholars took an increasing interest in Africa; it is reflected in the Talmud and Midrash, in sayings of *tannaim* and *amoraim* which reveal their information and conceptions as to people and things African.

Hillel's reply to the man who tried to tease him with questions shows that he knew of the characteristic African marshlands, especially in the Carthage area and the interior of Tunisia. These marshlands produced a reed of which various articles were made, and so the Targum Yerushalmi to Ex. 2:3 describes the "ark of bulrushes" as תיבותא דטונס. The term בַּרְבֻּרִים ("fowl"), I Kings 5:3, is explained folk-etymologically as an appellation of origin: "fowl coming from Barbary". Another geographical reference occurs in a legendary report that the sea flooded the earth "as far as the headlands of Barbary", which probably means the Straits of Gibraltar, known in the Greco-Roman world as the Pillars of Hercules.[3]

Interest in Africa no doubt increased when Glaphyra, the widow of Herod's son Alexander, who was killed on his father's orders, married Juba, the King of Mauretania.[4]

---

[1] Neubauer, *MJC* I, p. 190.

[2] Charles Tissot, *Géographie comparée de la province romaine d'Afrique*, Paris 1884-1888, II, pp. 237-238. *CIJ* I, pp. 12-13, II, pp. 352-53; Baron, *SRH* I, p. 410, n. 17; Reynolds-Ward, *Inscriptions*, pp. 201-202.

[3] Comp. B. Shab. 31a; PdRK 58b; Eccl. R. 7b; also Yer. Shek. VI 2 (50a), PR 81b n.; Gen. R. XXIII 7 (54a). Ex. R. XVIII, 6 (35b) seems to contain a reference to Mauretania Caesariensis.

[4] Comp. Josephus, *Ant.* XVII, 13, 4 §§ 349-353; Schürer, *Geschichte* I, pp. 451-452;

R. Aqiba's visit to Africa has been variously interpreted. Some regard it as a propaganda campaign for the uprising which materialized towards the end of Trajan's reign, while others ascribe no political object to it. It is difficult to reach a conclusion on the basis of very sketchy information and of two linguistic remarks transmitted in R. Aqiba's name: "And R. Aqiba said: When I went to Africa, the *maʿa* (quarter-shekel) was called *qesīṭa*; R. Aqiba says ... *pat* in Africa means 'two'." At the same time, there can be no doubt that the visit was very important in that it strengthened relations between Palestine and the African communities.[1]

Earlier, after the fall of Massada (73 C.E.), Jonathan, one of the leaders of the zealots, who fled to Africa, tried to stir up a revolt against Rome there by fanning the passions of the people, and especially of the exiles. However, the rich Jews informed Catullus, the Governor of Cyrene, who encircled the rebels and destroyed most of them—about 2,000—and captured the remainder. In time, Jonathan was also apprehended, and when he was brought before Catullus, he alleged that the rich had incited him to rebellion against Rome. Catullus, delighted to hear this accusation, put 3,000 rich Jews to death and confiscated their property. When this became known to the Jews of Rome and Alexandria, they were anxious to remedy the situation. Josephus adds that when Jonathan was brought in chains before Vespasian, he tried to convince the latter that it was Josephus who had supplied the rebels with arms and money. The emperor, disregarding his talk, had him tortured and burnt alive.[2]

After this period of unrest, life returned to normal. From those days, we possess coins with Hebrew lettering and specifically Jewish symbols, such as the citron and the *lulab* (festive palmbranch), which attest to the influential position of the Jews in the region.[3]

The Revolt under Trajan

However, the tension that spread after the destruction of the Temple did not abate, and it suddenly erupted into a wayward, mutinous spirit, which caused unrest among the Jews and led them, as Eusebius puts it, to rise against their neighbours. Unlike Jonathan's rebellion, which had

A Schalit, *Herod the King, the Man and His Work*, Jerusalem 1960, pp. 292-294 (Hebrew).

[1] Comp. RoHa 26a; San. 90b; Zeb. 37b; Men. 34b. Also Rapaport, *Bikkure ha-Ittim*, 1823/4, pp. 70-71; Friedmann, *GSAI* 2 (1931), p. 115.

[2] Josephus, *War* VII, II, 1-3, §§ 437-450; *Life* § 424, p. 157.

[3] Friedmann, *Miscellanea Chajes*, pp. 47-48; Applebaum, *Zion* 19 (1954), p. 43, l.c. 15.

been confined to Cyrenaica and been quelled within a short time, the revolt that broke out in the middle of the second decade of the second century was sustained by a powerful impetus. It comprised Egypt, extended to Cyprus and brought about disturbances in Mesopotamia and Palestine.

The revolt started towards the end of the reign of the Emperor Trajan (96-117 C.E.), who until then had been favourable to the Jews. The main source on the events of those days is Eusebius, Bishop of Caesarea, who lived in the early fourth century. In his "History of the Church", he reports that in the eighteenth year of Trajan's reign, which is 115 C.E., the Jews in Alexandria and the rest of Egypt rose in arms against their Greek neighbours. At first the Jews had the upper hand and their adversaries took refuge in Alexandria, but here the Greeks were able to defeat the Jews. According to Talmudic tradition, the Great Synagogue in Alexandria was destroyed on that occasion. However, this setback did not dismay the rebels. The initiative, so Eusebius continues, passed to the Jews of Cyrene. "Under the leadership of Lucuas, after they had not been able to have those (*i.e.* the defeated Alexandrian Jews) join them, they wrought havoc upon the Egyptians and devastated their areas. The Emperor was compelled to send Marcius Turbo against them at the head of infantry units, a war fleet and cavalry. After much fighting, and not within a short time, Turbo had annihilated tens of thousands of Cyrenian and Egyptian Jews who had rallied under their king, Lucuas." This happened in the second and the third year of the revolt; the latter year was the last of Trajan's reign and the first of Hadrian's. At the same time, Lusius Quietus was sent to Mesopotamia, where the Jews had also risen. He was subsequently appointed Procurator of Palestine as reward for subduing and ruthlessly punishing the Jews of Mesopotamia. Thus Eusebius.[1]

In Dio Cassius's "History of Rome", written in the first half of the third century, a special paragraph deals with that war as follows: "For that reason, Trajan departed, and after a short time he became ill. The Jews of Cyrene then destroyed the Romans and the Greeks, making Andreas their chief. They ate their (*i.e.* their enemies') flesh, made belts of their intestines and rubbed themselves with their blood; they dressed themselves in their skins; and they sawed through the skulls of many of them in the middle. Others they threw to wild beasts; others they forced

---

[1] *Historia Ecclesiae*, IV, II, (Kirsopp Lake, *The Ecclesiastical History*, London 1926, pp. 304-7).

to fight each other. As a result, 220,000 persons were killed in all. They did many similar things in Egypt. So they did in Cyprus, where their leader was one Artemion; there, too, they destroyed 240,000 people. This is why no Jew is allowed on that island. If one of them is driven there by the wind, he is killed. Still others (*i.e.* other army leaders) defeated the Jews, including Lusius, who had been sent by Trajan."[1]

The portion of Dio Cassius's work that contains this passage has come to us only in a summary by Xiphilinus, an 11th-century copyist and epitomist, and the exaggerations in the account of those cruelties are ascribed by some to the latter, since Dio himself is regarded as an objective writer, free from Judophobia.[2] It seems to us, however, that he may have found this account in his sources and regarded it as his duty to transmit it, just as he did in the case of stories concerning other peoples. Anti-Jewish propaganda in Alexandria spread reports of Jewish cruelty in Cyrene and Egypt and found willing listeners. In an Egyptian papyrus of the period of the revolt, aged Eudaimonis prays the gods to protect her son from being roasted by the enemies. The methods of that propaganda, as well as Jewish counter-propaganda, will be discussed at some length below.[3]

Short reports have reached us through other writers. Artemidoros Daldianus (2nd c.) devotes a short passage to the fanaticism of the Jews of Cyrene, who fought on even after Lucuas's defeat. Orosius (second half of the 4th c.) notes especially the large-scale destruction caused throughout Libya, which forced Hadrian to bring in new settlers in order to make colonization possible. An important Constantinopolitan historiographer, the monk Synkellos (late 8th and early 9th c.), tells of the defeat of the Jews who had been fighting against their Greek neighbours in Libya, Cyrene and Egypt and of the punishment meted out to them by Hadrian.[4]

Spartianus (late 3rd and early 4th c.) is the only antique writer who —briefly—mentions the revolt of Palestinian Jewry at the beginning of Hadrian's reign. The subject is dealt with at some length by the Syrian Catholicos Ibn al-ʿIbri (so called on account of his Jewish origin) (1226-

[1] Ed. Ph. Boissevain 2, Berlin 1955, vol. III, 32, 1-3, Liber LXVIII, p 220.

[2] Comp. Friedmann, *GSAI* 2 (1931), pp. 110, 117-118, 120, and I. Baer, *Zion* 21 (1956), p. 20 (note). See also I. Heinemann, *PW*, Ergänzungsband V, *s.v.* Antisemitismus, col. 30.

[3] Comp. A. Fuks, *Zion* 22 (1957), p. 6, and below, pp. 40ff.

[4] Artemidoros Daldianus, *Onirocriticon* (ed. R. A. Pacie, (1963), IV, 24 p. 259 (comp. Juster, *Juifs* II, p. 186, n. 10); Orosius, (ed. C. Zangenmeister 1889); Historia VII, 12, §§ 6-8, p. 253.

1286): "And in the last year (of Trajan's reign), the Jews on the island of Cyprus, in Syria and in Ethiopia revolted. The Jews of Egypt gave themselves a king named Luminus (لو مينو س) (!). The latter assembled an army and moved towards Palestine. Roman troops pursued him and killed him and tens of thousands of Jews everywhere".[1]

Many scholars have wondered about the reasons for this outbreak, which was preceded by no provocation on the part of the Roman administration. Each of them has pointed to different factors that might have driven the Jews of Egypt and Cyrene to revolt: national, religious (anti-pagan), social and economic motives. Gentile Judophobia no doubt assumed coarser forms in distant Cyrenaica than in refined Alexandria. Some have credited the rebels with plans for the establishment of a Jewish state in Africa or its renewal in Palestine. The title "king" which Eusebius confers on Lucuas, the leader of the revolt, has been said to attest the Messianic character of the movement. Rabbi Aqiba's journey to Africa has been mentioned in this connection, and a link has been seen between it and the outbreak of the revolt. It is doubtful, however, whether far-reaching conclusions may be drawn from the use of the title "king", especially as Lucuas's identity and role are uncertain and an apparently rival figure, called Andreas by Dio Cassius, looms opposite him. We may indeed reconcile the two sources by assuming that there were two leaders at two different stages of the revolt or that, as held by most scholars, the leader of the revolt had two names, which was common enough with Egyptian and African Jewry. But even if we combine all the possible causes for the spread of the movement, no clear picture of its immediate motives will emerge; they seem to be definitely unascertainable. In any event, the credit for armed revolt against Rome in the Diaspora must go to the Jews of Cyrene.[2]

Talmudic literature contains hints and faint echoes of these events. But before dealing with them, we must discuss the two Roman generals who put down the revolt. One of them was Marcius Turbo, who is not mentioned in Jewish literature at all, apparently because his area of

---

[1] Aelius Spartianus, *Scriptores Historiae Augustae*, (Loeb Classical Library v. I), Vita Hadriani V, p. 16; Ibn al-ʿIbri, *Taʾrikh mukhtaṣar al-duwal*, Beirut 1890, pp. 119-120.

[2] Friedmann, *Miscellanea Chajes*, pp. 39-55, reviews all the sources for Cyrenaica during that period. Applebaum, *Zion* 19 (1954), pp. 51-56, gives the plentiful bibliography of the revolt in an Appendix. Some publications omitted by him, as well as later ones, are indicated in the Hebrew edition of this History (I, pp. 334-335, n. 13), where material on related subjects is also mentioned.

operations was Cyrene and Egypt. After the suppression of the rising, Marcius was given a similar assignment: subduing the Berbers in Mauretania. The other general was Lusius Quietus, the leader of the Mauretanian Berbers, who had risen high in the service of Rome. He commanded the Berber volunteers who took part in the Dacian War. His generalship, daring and ruthlessness won him the confidence of Trajan, who entrusted him with an important task in the Parthian War (114-117) as commander of the Moors and chief of an army corps in Mesopotamia. When the Jewish revolt spread to that area, Trajan ordered Lusius to deport the Jews from there, and if they resisted, to destroy them. Lusius carried out the Emperor's command in his own way. He moved a large body of troops against Mesopotamian Jewry and staged a terrible massacre among the densely-settled Jewish population of the cities, who had no inkling of the danger threatening them. According to Christian writers, tens of thousands of Jews were killed and bodies lay unburied everywhere—in the streets, houses and courtyards.

Lusius Quietus

In recognition of his services in Mesopotamia, Trajan appointed Lusius Quietus consul, put him in charge of Palestine and ordered him to subdue the rebels there. To vest him with the full legal powers of a procurator, Lusius was also appointed imperial envoy (*legatus Augusti*) in Judaea. These positions carried with them a seat in the Senate, and Lusius was the first Mauretanian to belong to that ancient, venerable body. He put down the rebellion in Palestine, apparently without overmuch bloodshed. Besides the permanent garrison, viz. the Tenth Legion (*Fretensis*) and some auxiliary units, a battalion (*vexillatio*) of the Third (Cyrenian) Legion and Quietus's Berber horsemen were stationed in the country.

After Trajan's death (117), Quietus's fortunes changed. He may have imagined that he himself would be proclaimed emperor, and there were rumours that Trajan regarded him as worthy of the office. But it was Hadrian who ascended the imperial throne, and he gave orders to disarm the Berber cavalry. Quietus himself left, apparently to return home. About that time, upon Hadrian's accession, a plot of four high dignitaries against the emperor was discovered in Rome, and the Senate ordered them to be executed without investigation. One of the plotters was Lusius Quietus; the death warrant caught up with him en route, and he was assassinated. On learning this, the Mauretanian tribes revolted and, as stated, Marcius Turbo was charged with crushing the revolt.[1]

Talmudic literature contains four texts which rather cryptically allude to that period. (a) The legend of Trakhinos, whose wife gave birth on the eve of the Ninth of Ab to a child who died at Hanukka (Trajan was childless); (b) the story in the scholion to "Megillat Ta'anit" concerning "the 12th (of Adar), the day of Tiryon", which ends with the sentence: "It is said: He had no sooner departed than a διπλῆ (δίπλωμα) (*i.e.* warrant) of Rome was issued against him, and they injured his brain with slivers and splinters"; (c) the terse data in Seder Olam Rabba: "From the war of Vespasian to the war of Quietus, fifty-two years; and from Quietus's war to Ben Koziba's war, sixteen years; (d) Sota IX, 14 should read, according to some MSS.: "During Quietus's war, bridal wreaths were forbidden etc.".[2]

Echoes of the Revolt against Trajan in the Talmud

There would seem to be many reasons why the Talmud says little about this episode in Jewish history, reasons of external policy and reasons to do with the internal situation. The discoveries made in the winter of 1960/61 in the Judaean Desert indicate that the preparations for the Bar Kokhba Revolt began several years before its outbreak and that leading rabbis were even then preoccupied with the matter—whether or not they were wholeheartedly in favour of it. On the other hand, immediately after the fall of Betar, the rabbis were hardly likely to concern themselves with the revolt against Trajan. It was overshadowed by the Destruction of the Temple in historical respect and the Bar Kokhba Revolt in topical respect. Nevertheless, the figure of the Berber procurator was not forgotten, and a generation later, fairly clear references to the revolt against Trajan and its consequences are made—in the anonymous manner usual in the Midrash and Aggada.

(1) "R. Yudan and R. Ḥonya. R. Yudan in the name of R. Eliezer the son of Rabbi Yosi ha-Gelili, and R. Ḥonya in the name of R. Eliezer ben Jacob, say: The voice of my beloved! behold, he cometh (Cant. 2, 8), this is the King Messiah. When he says to Israel: This month you are re-

[1] Spartianus, *op. cit.*, V, p. 16; Schürer, *Geschichte*, I, p. 647. *PW*, *s.v.* Lusius Quietus (Vol. 26, col. 1874) and *s.v.* Mauretania (Vol. 28, col. 2344).

[2] Yer. Suk. V, 1, 23a; Meg. Ta 'an. XII; H. Lichtenstein, *HUCA*, VIII-IX (1931-1932), p. 346, also p. 272 and *SOR*, XXX; comp. also Schürer, *Geschichte* I, pp. 667-670, Yeivin, *Milḥemet Bar-Kochba*[2], 46-48 and 145.

deemed, they say to him: How can we be redeemed? The Holy One, blessed be He, was sworn to enslave us to seventy nations. And he gives them a two-fold answer, saying: One of them is exiled to Barbary and another to Samatria, so that it is as if you had all been exiled. Moreover, this realm enlists officials from the whole world, from every nation. A Kuthi (Samaritan) or a Berber comes and enslaves you, and it is as if their whole nation enslaved you through them. So that you are, so to speak, enslaved by seventy nations etc."[1]

In the form of an aggadic midrash, two tannaites are here discussing matters of the revolt during the generation following it, *i.e.* after the minds had long quieted down. They mention that Jews were exiled to Barbary, a detail to which we shall have to revert below. This is at the same time a reference to Lusius Quietus, the Berber who came and enslaved Jews. Moreover, I feel almost tempted to read *kushi* (Ethiopian), since Quietus presumably looked like an Ethiopian. In fact, we find the very same phrase in a midrash: "Lest an Ethiopian or Berber come and enslave me".[2]

(2) " 'Consider mine enemies; for they are many; and they hate me with cruel hatred' (Ps. 15:19). If Esau hates Jacob because he took his birthright away from him, then he has a justification for it, but what have I done to the Berbers and Anathians and other peoples?"[3]

This accusation seems somewhat odd. We know that Esau-Edom hates Jacob, but what prompted the Aggada to mention Esau and the Berbers in the same breath? As far as we know, only one Berber did grievous harm to the Jews of Babylonia and Palestine, namely, Lusius Quietus.

The following midrash will now no longer surprise us:

(3) " 'And I will move them to jealousy with those which are not a people' (Deut. 32-21) ... those who come from Barbary, Tunisia and Mauretania, who walk about naked in the market—no one is contemptible and tainted but he who walks about naked in the market."[4]

---

[1] Cant. R. to 2, 8 (16d); comp. also PR 71a; PdRK 47b-48a; Gen. R. 60,2.

[2] Comp. *Pesikta de Rab Kahana* ed. B. Mandelbaum, 1962, I p. 89, so all Mss. I am indebted to Prof. M. Beer, who drew my attention to this Midrash. Comp. also the dialogue of R. Aqiba with an Ethiopian King of the Arabs, Krauss, *ZDMG* 70 (1916), pp. 325f.

[3] Mid. Ps. 25, 14; comp. also *ibid.* 109, 3, where one MS has "Berbers and Kuthim" (perhaps for "Kushim"; see preceding note). Instead of the enigmatic Anathians, Buber (in footnotes to both passages) suggests *gentes* or Goths. But comp. P. Romanelli *Le grandi strade romane nell' Africa Settentrionale*, 1938, map on p. 24: *Getuli*.

[4] Sifre Deut. § 320; Yeb. 63b.

We know that Berbers and Ethiopians in their own countries wore little clothing, and the Mauretanian soldiers who were in Palestine with Lusius Quietus no doubt did—at least off duty—as they were accustomed to do at home.

(4) " 'Her adversaries are the chief' (Lam. 1:5), this is Vespasian; 'her enemies prosper' (*ibid.*), this is Titus. For three-and-a-half years, Vespasian encircled Jerusalem, and there were four chiefs (*dukasin*) with him: an Arabian chief, an African chief, an Alexandrian chief and a Palestinian chief."[1]

The midrash in its extant form is not early. We know indeed that Malkos, king of the Nabataeans, took part in the siege of Jerusalem, but the references to the three other chiefs were added in the course of time and point to other enemies of the Jews. Proof of the late date of the midrash is the title *dukas* (*dux*), which belongs to a later period; also, the name "Palestine" was not used until Hadrian. We may thus presume that the description "African chief" points to Lusius Quietus. He was, in fact, not only the commander of his Berber soldiers, but a high official in the imperial administration of North Africa. Hence his title "African chief", and not "Berber chief". We have seen that not only his Mauretanian cavalry, but part of the Third (Cyrenian) Legion was stationed in Palestine during his procuratorship.[2] The grievous experience of the Jews in the days of Quietus explains how the image of the Berbers as a fierce, ruthless nation found its way into the Aggada.[3]

A few years ago, an attempt was made to prove that Lusius Quietus was a native of Ethiopia, which provoked a rather heated controversy. The sources quoted here undoubtedly decide the issue in favour of the customary assumption of his North African origin.[4]

Epigraphic and Archaeological Testimony

Those literary sources, not very rich in detail, are supplemented by new documents representing an important contribution to the study of

---

[1] Lam. R. 1, 31; comp. Tacitus, *Historia* II, 4, V, 1; Baron, *SRH*, II, pp. 92 and 114.

[2] Comp. Baron, *SRH*, II, pp. 123 and 380. For Quietus's rank comp. Carcopino, *Maroc*, p. 238, n. 7.

[3] Comp. Gen. R. LXXV, 9; XLII, 3. Targ. to Ps. 114, 1; Krauss, *MGWJ* 39 (1895), pp. 2-7.

[4] Comp. V. Den Boer, *Mnemosyne*, Ser. 4, 1 (1948), pp. 327-337; A. G. Roos, *ibid.*, 3 (1950), pp. 158-165. The controversy between them: *ibid.*, pp. 263-267, 336-338 and 339-343. I have not been able to see Carcopino's article in *Istros* 1 (1934), pp. 5ff., or O. Jordanescu's thesis, *Lusius Quietus*, Bucuresti 1941.

the revolt. During the past forty years, epigraphic and archaeological finds in Cyrenaica have yielded first-hand confirmation of the statements of the writers. Moreover, considerable progress has been made in deciphering Egyptian papyri, long illegible owing to their dilapidated condition, which, specifically or incidentally, deal with events of the time of the revolt in Egypt and indirectly shed much light on events in Cyrene as well.

Excavations in the city of Cyrene, in Apollonia and in Teuchira (modern Tócra)— one of the cities of the Pentapolis, between Ptolemais (Arabic Ṭalamuyta (Yāqūt), modern Tolméta) and Berenice (Benghazi)—reveal the extent of the destruction caused during the revolt to major public buildings, such as temples, baths and monuments. Particularly great was the devastation in Cyrene, where the temples of Zeus and Hecate, the Caesareum, the baths etc. were destroyed. Recent examination has shown that the temple of Zeus was not destroyed by an earthquake, but in a revolt, and that organized force and the use of special machinery were required to bring about such destruction. Teuchera in the west was not rebuilt as a city, but became a colony of discharged soldiers. Remains of a temple destroyed in the revolt have been unearthed also in the east of the country, in the part of the coastal zone called Marmarica. The eastern districts were depleted to such an extent that they had to be annexed to Egypt, since impoverished Cyrenaica was unable to undertake their resettlement. In Applebaum's opinion, the Jews adopted a scorched-earth policy, in order to clear the area of Cyrenaica and break through to Palestine.

Commemorative inscriptions and votive tablets proclaim that Hadrian did much to repair the damage and compensate the Hellenistic population. According to one inscription, of approximately 135 C.E., he was still trying towards the end of his life to restore the position of pre-revolt times, but apparently without success.

Here are some of the many inscriptions discovered that tell of the destruction and subsequent rebuilding. This is what we read on a milestone near Apollonia, the port of Cyrene:

Imp[erator] Caes[ar] divi | Traiani Parthici f[ilius] | divi
Nervae nepos, Traianus Hadrianus | Aug[ustus] P[ontifex] M[aximus]
T[ribunicia] P[otestate] ii co[n]s[ul] iii | viam, quae tumultu
Iudaico eversa et | corrupta erat re[stituit pe]r ...
Κδ' στάδ(ια) 'Απολων(ίαν)[1]

---

[1] *SEG* IX, No. 252; Applebaum, *Jews and Greeks*, p. 308. Comp. Kahrstedt,

"The Emperor-Caesar, son of the divine Trajan the Parthian, grandson of the divine Nerva, Trajan Hadrian the August, the Chief Pontiff, during his second tenure as tribune and his third as consul, rebuilt this road, which had been torn up and spoilt in the Jewish revolt . . . 24 miles to Apollonia."

Owing to the importance of the road for all spheres of life, the emperor ordered it to be repaired first (in 118/9). Thereafter, from 119 onwards, the restoration of destroyed buildings was undertaken. Here is the inscription, in two languages, on a tablet commemorating the repair of the temple of Hecate:

Imp Caesar etc. trib pot iii cos. iii templum| restitui iussit Cyr]enensi[um civitati, | quod tumultu Iudaico di]rutum et e[xustum erat Αὐτοκράτω]ρ καῖσ[αρ] | θεοῦ Τραιανοῦ Παρθικ[οῦ κ.τ.λ. τῆι Κ]υρηναίων π[όλει τοῦ | ναοῦ ἐν τῶι ταράχωι Ἰ]ουδαϊκῶι κεκ[αυμένου | καὶ πεπορθημένου τὴ]ν ἀποκατάσ[τασιν προσέταξε][1]

"The Emperor-Caesar etc., during his third tenure as tribune and his third as a consul, ordered the temple which had been destroyed and burnt in the Jewish revolt to be restored for the citizens of Cyrene."

On a marble slab found in Cyrene, we read:

Imp. Caesar etc. trib potest iii cos. iii balineum | cum porticibus et sphaeristeris | ceterisque adiacentibus quae | tumultu Iudaico diruta et exusta | erant civitati Cyrenensium restitui | iussit[2]

"The Emperor-Caesar etc., during his third tenure as tribune and his third as consul, ordered the baths with the porticos and the ball-game fields and the other appurtenances, which had been destroyed and burnt in the Jewish revolt, to be restored for the citizens of Cyrene."

The great effort expended in the revolt and the revenge taken by the Romans after their victory sapped the strength of Cyrenaican Jewry, although the Roman authorities tried to calm the minds in Alexandria and did much to rebuild Cyrene, which had been hit hardest in the revolt. Greek propaganda now found fertile soil for continuing its anti-Jewish incitement. Alexandrian anti-Semites brought charges of xenophobia, atrocities in time of peace and war, robbing the Egyptians, and usurping

---

Kulturgeschichte, pp. 195-196 and 207. On Roman roads in North Africa in general comp. P. Romanelli, *Le grandi strade romane nell'Africa Settentrionale*, 1938; Pierre Salama, *Les voies romaines de l'Afrique du Nord*, 1941.

[1] *SEG*, *ibid*., No. 168.

[2] Friedmann, *Miscellanea Chajes*, p. 42; Applebaum, *Jews*, pp. 308-9.

the country of the Canaanites. The Greeks also used the stage, poetry and narrative literature to influence the masses.[1]

It would be an exaggeration, however, to talk of total extinction. A series of inscriptions with Jewish names have been discovered of which part are apparently later than the Bar Kokhba Revolt.[2] Extremely interesting is a Hebrew inscription found on a site 10 kilometres south of Cyrene:

נתן בר
שלומו תנוח
נפשו ברשת
החיים

"Nathan the son of Solomon. May his soul rest in the net of life."[3]

The letters are similar to those of the Bar Kokhba period. But more significant, in our opinion, is the Mishnaic Hebrew language. We are faced with the same phenomenon of a return to the Hebrew language as in Egypt at the very same period. Here, the last vestiges of Hellenistic Jewish literature vanish completely, and Hebrew papyri and inscriptions appear.[4] A Hebrew epitaph: "To Ezer. May his soul rest in the bundle of life" has been unearthed in Antinoopolis, a city founded by Hadrian.[5]

Cyrenaican Jewry did not disappear, but whereas until then they had been politically active, and Greco-Roman historians and geographers had found it necessary to mention them from time to time, from then onwards, they were no longer a political factor in the country. Part of them turned to spheres where Greek pressure was less heavy, others scattered to all winds.

A curtain of silence fell on Libyan Jewry for several centuries, much as after the persecution by Justinian and the forced conversions by the Almohades. This is apparent from a list prepared by Applebaum of testimonies to Jewish settlement in Cyrenaica in the Greco-Roman period.[1] Only in the early fifth century do we again find references to Jews

[1] Comp. Fraser-Applebaum, *JRS* 40 (1950), pp. 77-90; Kahrstedt, *op. cit.*, p. 231. On efforts to calm the minds comp. Tcherikover, *The Jews in Egypt*, 1945 (Hebrew), pp. 209-213; Fuks, *Zion* 22 (1957), pp. 2-4.

[2] *SEG* IX, 599, 645, 648, 683, 699, 700, 704, 711, 722; comp. also 888 (an amulet) and 245: Sara, Philo. Comp. also Tcherikover, *Hellenistic Civilization and the Jews*, p. 503, n. 76.

[3] Comp. Applebaum, *Zion* 19 (1954), p. 49, No. 43; also p. 26 and n. 24.

[4] *CIJ*, 1536, 1537, 1538; Tcherikover-Fuks, *CPJ*, I, pp. 107-109.

[5] *CIJ*, 1534.

[6] Comp. his *Jews and Greeks*, pp. 170-4.

in contemporary non-Jewish literature. We shall deal below with a letter of Synesios of Cyrene, who travelled home from Egypt in a Jewish ship; it seems that the shipowner was likewise a Cyrenaican.[1] Procopius of Caesarea, who accompanied Belisarius on his expedition to Africa (533) tells of a Jewish community that had existed in Borion since olden times and whose synagogue had been built in the days of Solomon. This story, too, will be dealt with below in connection with contemporary events.[2]

West of Cyrenaica

No local evidence has reached us of Jewish settlement in the western sector of North Africa prior to the middle of the second century C.E. As we have seen, our sources from that time onwards do not mention the Jews of Cyrene, and just as this silence does not prove a discontinuance of Jewish settlement in Cyrene, thus we cannot say with certainty that no Jews lived in the western part of North Africa prior to the second century.

Difficult economic conditions and a poisoned atmosphere tended to make the surviving Jews of Libya and Cyrene—their number was not small—leave for other areas. Many turned westward, to those vast regions which were then experiencing an economic and cultural upswing. Carthage, razed by the Romans 250 years previously, had been rebuilt and was now again a prosperous city, the second largest in the western part of the Empire. Within a comparatively short time, the population of the area doubled and trebled, agricultural production increased, and grain exports to Rome rose from 200,000 modii [3] to 40,000,000 modii, *i.e.* twice the quota of Egypt.

To all appearance, the Jewish population of the western part of the region, *i.e.* from Carthage westward, assumed substantial proportions only after the failure of the revolts subsequent to the destruction of the Temple, when many refugees from Cyrenaica and Egypt arrived. In any event, we may assume that only under the post-Hadrianic emperors did that diaspora actually begin to develop. We may, moreover, suppose that the new immigrants engaged from the start in the same occupations they had pursued in Cyrene and Egypt, *i.e.*, especially, agriculture. Those grain importers in Rome who apparently hailed from Scina, Locus

[1] See below, pp. 65-6.
[2] P. 56.
[3] Greek μόδιος (appr. 8.6-8.7 litres).

Iudaeorum Augusti, east of Oea (Tripoli), where Jewish farmers worked on imperial estates, may be representative of many similar localities.[1]

The socio-economic situation with regard to agricultural lands and imperial estates was very complicated, and the penetration of Jews into this sphere, as into other walks of life, no doubt provoked hostile reactions on the part of the established population, and especially the inhabitants of the cities: the *Poeni*, *i.e.* descendants of the Phoenicians, and the Greeks. The strengthening and increased activity of the Jews afforded a new field of operations for hostile Hellenistic propaganda.[2]

Echoes of Anti-Jewish Propaganda

In the generation following the revolt, Talmudic-Midrashic literature suddenly raises the odd question how inhabitants of the Land of Canaan came to Africa.

1. "R. Simon ben Gamliel says: There is no more gentle people than the Amorites. Also, we have found that they believed in God, for they went into exile in Africa, and God gave them a country as beautiful as theirs, and the Land of Israel was called after them."[3]

Simon ben Gamliel's remarks are most astonishing, for they contradict the appraisal of the Amorites frequently expressed in the Bible (*e.g.*, Gen. 15:16) and in the Talmud ("the ways of the Amorite").[4] A very weighty reason must have compelled the tannaite, who was noted for his nationalist views and who headed the Sanhedrin at Usha after the Bar Kokhba Revolt, to make this favourable statement about the ancient inhabitants of the country. The claim that part of the Canaanites left the country voluntarily occurs several times in midrashim. Judging by the name of the author, however, the passage under reference is early.[5]

(2) A later collection of homilies presents a variety of opinions concerning three peoples whose heirs the Jews are destined to be: "R. Ḥelbo Simon bar Ba said in the name of R. Yohanan: Your fathers inherited a country of seven peoples, and later they will inherit a country of ten peoples. The three others are the Kenite, the Kenizite and the

---

[1] Comp. Kahrstedt, *Kulturgeschichte*, pp. 146, 148-149, 152, 156-157, and above, p. 27, n. 2.

[2] Kahrstedt, *op. cit.*, pp. 231-232.

[3] Toseph. Shab. VIII, 12. Parallel texts: Mekh. Bo 18 (21b-22a); Yer. Sheb. VI, 1 (36c); Lev. R. XVII, 6; Num. R. XIII, 3; Deut. R. V, 14; comp. L. Ginzberg, Legends of the Jews VI, pp. 177-178, n. 34.

[4] Comp. also Book of Jub., 29, 11.

[5] On the political activities of R. Simon ben Gamliel comp. Baron, *SRH* II, p. 141.

Kadmonite. R. Yehuda said: The Arabs, the Salamians,[1] the Nabataeans. R. Simon said: Asa and Spain and Damascus. R. Eliezer ben Jacob says: Asia and Carthage and Turkey. Rabbi says: Edom and Moab and the beginning of the Ammonites."[2]

R. Eliezer ben Jacob's opinion is that the Jews will ultimately inherit Carthage and that they are therefore entitled to settle there. It should be remembered that this *tanna* was a contemporary of R. Simon ben Gamliel, in whose name we are told the homily concerning the exile of the Jews to Barbary and their redemption after having been enslaved by the Berbers.[3] The reference to the Arabs, the Salamians and Nabataeans will be discussed below.

(3) "The Sages said: On the 24th Nisan, the δημοσιῶναι (*publicani*—tax-collectors) were removed from Judaea and from Jerusalem. When the Africans came to litigate with the Jews before Alexander the Macedonian, they said to him: The Land of Canaan is ours, for it is written: the land of Canaan with the coasts thereof (Num. 34:2), and Canaan is the father of this people. Geviha ben Pesisa said to the sages: Give me permission and I shall go to argue with them before Alexander the Macedonian etc." Then comes another story: "The Egyptians once came to litigate with Israel before Alexander the Macedonian etc." A third story follows: "And again, the Ismaelites and the sons of Qetura came to litigate with Israel before Alexander the Macedonian etc." [4]

We must first deal with the "historical" framework of the three discussions. The Aggadist, who placed them together, did not mean to create the impression that they were held in Palestine. The very wording shows strikingly that they do not belong to the same time or the same place. There seem to have been no sages in the places where the claims were brought, so that none were summoned before the king.

It thus appears that the Africans, the Egyptians and the Ismaelites separately complained that Israel was occupying their territory. Each time, Geviha asked permission of the sages to go and answer the pleas of the complainants.[5] It seems that we have to do here with a set of apologetic answers in the form of a debate, then very common in Hellenistic literature.

---

[1] A tribe in the southern neighbourhood of the Nabataeans; comp. *PW s.v.*

[2] Yer. Sheb. VI 1 (36b); Yer. Kid. I, 9 (61d); Gen. R. XLIV, 23 (*ult.*).

[3] See above, pp. 33-4.

[4] San. 91a, also (with variants) Meg. Taʿan. III, 5; H. Lichtenstein, *HUCA* VIII-IX (1931-1932), pp. 328-330, also p. 302; Gen. R. LXI, 7.

[5] As far as the Aggada is concerned, the complaints might have been made in Carthage: according to a famous *aggada*, Alexander visited that city; comp. *PdRK* 74a and many parallel passages; see also Krauss, *MGWJ* 39 (1895), p. 4, n. 4. We know

The numerous papyri reflecting the views of the Jews and their enemies at that time include especially two passages describing complaints and arguments between Jewish and Greek inhabitants of Alexandria, who had their representatives, Greek advocates and Jewish religious scholars, appear before the emperors. One debate was conducted in Rome before Trajan, who, under the influence of his wife, Plotina, adopted a definitely pro-Jewish attitude; the account as now before us is an eminently literary production, but may in part be based on authentic documents. The second debate—whether historical or imaginary—must in all probability be dated to the beginning of the reign of Hadrian. Particularly characteristic is the reference to a Jewish "king of the stage and the mime" who by order of the Roman procurator was paraded through the streets of Alexandria, so that the Greeks might mock him. In this case, too, the emperor (presumably Hadrian) adopted a pro-Jewish or at least neutral attitude, reproving the Greeks with the words: "Such things are done in such tension-fraught situations!" The papyrus is very poorly preserved, and it is impossible to decide whether the reference is to the leader of the Cyrenian revolt, whom Eusebius calls king and who was seized and led through the streets to be jeered at, or whether a farcical show was staged, as was done in Alexandria during the visit of Agrippa I. The significance of the account is summed up by Tcherikover in the words: "We gather from this passage that the appearance of the 'king of the Jews' made a great impression on the Greek population of Alexandria, let alone the Jewish, and sparked a renewal of rioting and hostile acts between Greeks and Jews in that city."[1]

Let us now revert to the debates conducted before Alexander. A. Aptowitzer and J. Lewy, in highly instructive papers, explained the apologetic background of the legends concerning the first masters of the Land of Canaan and the right of the Jews to it. In J. Lewy's opinion, these legends were first told when the Hasmonaeans began to expand the borders of the reborn state and to dislodge the Gentiles who had settled in the country.[2] The Greeks in Alexandria used these events as propaganda

---

that Alexander was never in Jerusalem; comp. B. Niese, *Geschichte der griechischen und makedonischen Staaten* I, p. 83, p. 3.

[1] Comp. *The Oxyrhynchus Papyri*, X (1914), 1242, pp. 112ff.; Tcherikover, *The Jews in Egypt*, p. 211.

[2] Aptowitzer, *REJ* 82 (1926), pp. 275-286; Lewy, *MGWJ* 77 (1933), pp. 84-99, 172-180; comp. also L. Ginzberg, *Die Haggada bei den Kirchenvätern und in der apokryphischen Litteratur*, Berlin 1900, pp. 99-100. Mar Zutra's statement, San. 92a, that the Ten Tribes were exiled to Africa, may have an apologetic purpose: to support a Jewish claim to that continent.

material and began to question the right of the Jews to Palestine *a limine*. The plea of the displacement of the Canaanites from their land was countered with the story of the division of the earth between the sons of Noah in the Book of Jubilees (8:11-10:35), which was written at that time. The sons of Sem were allotted the navel of the earth, *i.e.* Palestine (8:19), and the sons of Ham—Cush, Phut and Canaan—received portions adjacent to one another (9:1). All three sons of Noah solemnly swore not to take away each other's share, appointed by lot (10:14). "And Canaan saw that the land of the Lebanon, down to the valley of Egypt, was very good, and he did not go to the land of his inheritance, west of the sea, but settled in the land of the Lebanon, east and west of the land of the Jordan and on the shore of the sea" (*ibid.*, v. 29); he was therefore cursed by his father Ham and his brothers Cush and Mizraim, and he and his sons were cut off from the world (*ibid.*, vv. 30-35). Thus the Canaanites stole the country, in contravention of the partition and the oath sworn by the sons of Noah.

Another answer is contained in the Book of the Wisdom of Solomon: God hated the early inhabitants of the country because they acted abominably in that they practised witchcraft and held nefarious assemblies: they cruelly killed their children and ate entrails and feasted on human carcasses and blood (12:4, 5). The charge of cannibalism will be further dealt with below.[1]

Whenever the accusations against the Jews by the Greeks and later, with certain variations, by the Romans were renewed, the same old answers—likewise with variations—were given. The statement that the Canaanites stole the country from its rightful owners occurs in slightly varied form in Simon ben Laqish's remarks: There are many biblical passages which should be eagerly absorbed because they are the essential parts of the Tora: and the Avims which dwelt in Ḥazerim, even unto Azzah, [the Caphtorims, which came forth out of Caphtor, destroyed them, and dwelt in their stead] (Deut. 2:23). What do we learn from this? When Abimelech had Abraham swear: that thou wilt not falsely deal with me, nor with my son, nor with my son's son (Gen. 21:23), God told the Caphtorim to dispossess the Avim, *i.e.* Philistines, and Israel to dispossess the Caphtorim.[2] That is to say, it was the Caphtorim who destroyed the Avim-Philistines, whereas the Israelites did not violate the oath Abraham had sworn to Abimelech the Philistine to requite his son's sons for the kindness he had done to him.

[1] See below p. 73 and nn. 2, 3.
[2] Ḥul. 60b.

Not later than the days of the Maccabees, the charge of the spoliation of Egypt was first heard, for it, too, is already answered in the Book of Jubilees (48:8): And they despoiled the Egyptians in return for the slavery to which they had subjected them by force. That complaint was again voiced in the days of R. Aqiba, who indirectly admits its justice: R. Aqiba said: All raised a clamour over the silver and gold which went out with them from Egypt, as it is said: Thy silver is become dross (Is. 1:22); and multiplied their (!) silver and gold, which they prepared for Baal (Hos. 2:10); of their silver and their gold have they made them idols, that they may be cut off (*ibid.*, 8:4).[1]

The third accusation, concerning the wrong done to the Arabs, the sons of Ismael and of Qeṭura, may likewise be of an early date, perhaps of the days of Alexander Yannai, who fought the Arabs, as the author of the First Book of the Maccabees and Josephus rightly call the Nabataeans and the inhabitants of Moab and Gilead.[2]

The three debates supposedly conducted before Alexander the Great were fitted into a single framework, preceded and followed by debate and dialogue of an apologetic character. It seems probable that these discussions were originally reported to have taken place before one of the pro-Jewish emperors, perhaps before Trajan himself, who until the outbreak of the Cyrenian revolt was considered friendly to the Jews owing to the influence of his wife, Plotina. At that time, the reference was certainly not to Africans, but to the Canaanites. Some manuscripts and prints of Megillat Taʿanit in fact have the reading "Canaanites", which is undoubtedly the original one and which alone is consistent with the statement that the episode took place in a sabbatical year, an institution existing only in Palestine. After the revolt, in view of Greek incitement spreading to Africa, the reference to the Africans, *i.e.* the *Poeni*, who regarded themselves as Canaanites, was substituted. It was then, too, that the mention of Alexander the Great was introduced.[3] The conjectured

[1] Gen. R. XXVIII, 7 (R. Aqiba's utterance). According to Israel Lévi, the spoliation of Egypt was a subject of discussion between Jews and Greeks in that country; comp. *D. Kaufmann-Gedenkbuch*, pp. 351-354; *id.*, *REJ* 63 (1912), pp. 211-215.

[2] On the Arab tribes in the vicinity of Palestine comp. Josephus, *Ant.* 13, 13, §§ 374-5; 14, 2, § 382. Hirschberg, *Israel in Arabia*, p. 37 (Hebrew); *PW*, *s.v.* Nabataioi, Salami. Answers to claims ascribed to the latter two are quoted above, in the text to n. 55; for a similar answer to the Moabites comp. Ḥul. 60b (see also above, text to p. 43, n. 2.

[3] Comp. Augustine, *Epistolae ad Romanos* XIII, *PL* XXXV, 2096. According to Augustine (*In Epistolam Johannis* II, 2, *ibid.* XXXV, 1991), the Donatists in Africa were familiar with both Latin and Punic. Comp. also Terrasse, *Histoire* I, pp. 45 and 395.

substitution of Alexander for Trajan is rather unexpectedly supported by a strange textual variant. In the Jerusalem Talmud, the destruction of the famous synagogue in Alexandria is correctly ascribed to the evildoer Trogyonos (*i.e.* Trajan), whereas the Babylonian Talmud speaks of Alexander.[1]

It should be noted that the Talmud makes a clear distinction between the African Carthaginians and the Mauretanian Berbers. The stories referring to Lusius Quietus never use the term "African" (except in the passage mentioning the "African chief", where the title of the Roman general is meant). On the other hand, we never find a mention of Barbary or Mauretania in connection with the alleged migration of the Canaanites to Africa.[2]

Procopius's Story

Seventy years ago, W. Bacher already noted the parallel between Jewish traditions about the ancient inhabitants of Canaan and the story of Procopius of Caesarea about the origin of the Mauretanians.[3]

Here is a summary of Procopius's account:

When the Israelites had left Egypt and were approaching the borders of Palestine, Moses died, and Joshua the son of Nun brought them to the country after winning brilliant victories over the Phoenicians, whose territory extended from Sidon to Egypt. The books of the Hebrews call the Phoenicians Girgashites, Jebusites etc. On seeing that they would not be able to withstand the Israelites, they left the country and went to Egypt. After finding that the latter country was densely populated, they moved on to Libya, where they settled all the way to the Pillars of Hercules. In a city in Numidia, where Tigisis[4] now stands, they built a citadel; near a great spring, two marble pillars can still be seen, engraved with an inscription in the Phoenician language and in Phoenician script:

[1] Comp. Yer. Suk. V, 1 (65a) and B. Suk. 51a. An interesting parallel is the anecdote of a painter changing a portrait of Alexander the Great into one of Augustus to honour the latter; Kahrstedt, *Kulturgeschichte*, p. 302.

[2] The Targum to Ps. 114, 1 therefore translates *meʿam lōʿez* (a people of strange language) by *meʿama barbrāe*; the Greek language was not a strange one. Tarshish (Jer. 10, 9) is called Afrīkē because it was settled by Sidonites (*Phoenicians*). Gen. R. XXXVII, 1 explains Gomer as Africa because Gomer is a descendant of Japhet (Gen. 10, 2).

[3] Comp. *JQR* 3 (1891), pp. 354-357. F. C. Movers, *Die Phönizier*, Berlin 1850, II 2, pp. 427f., was the first to compare Procopius's story with Jewish traditions.

[4] Modern ʿAyn al-Burj.

"We are of those who fled from Joshua the son of Nun, the robber." Procopius subsequently emphasizes that these Canaanites are the ancient inhabitants of Africa. They voluntarily permitted their relatives, who arrived afterwards under their leader, Dido, to settle in Carthage. But the Carthaginians returned evil for good. They fought with their neighbours who were called Moors (= Berbers), defeated them and forced them to settle far from Carthage.[1]

Lewy subjected this account to a thorough literary analysis, pointing out the classical sources drawn upon by Procopius and the parallels in Talmudic literature. He sensed that something was wrong with the structure of the account, but thought that we had to do here with two parallel versions, which Procopius "had welded together superficially and unsuccessfully". Lewy did not perceive the contradiction in Procopius's words, nor did he try to explain how and why the allegation of the ouster of the Phoenicians from Palestine in the days of the Maccabees revived in Africa. Who brought it there, and under what circumstances was it spread about? [2]

Procopius's account combines two stories. One is that of the foreign robber Joshua, who drove the Canaanites from their country, the other that of Dido and her people, also Canaanites, who came to Africa as brothers and enjoyed the hospitality of the old-established settlers, and who afterwards became enemies, so that the Africans were wronged twice. Although the two stories are similar as regards the settlement in Africa, they are opposed to each other in tendency, the second greatly blunting the edge of the first; they therefore do not seem to originate from the same source.

It appears to me that the first story, of "Joshua the robber", is a product of the propaganda of Greeks and Hellenized *Poeni* in Africa, who sought to defame the Jews when these began to arrive there in increasing numbers. It was then that the old story of the ill-usage and ejection of the Canaanites was trotted out, and it was very easy to transfer it to the Africans, who were the descendants of Canaan, or at least of his brother, both of whom the Jews had mistreated. This propaganda is countered by the Jews with the second story, of Dido and the manner of her establishment in Carthage, which was itself a piece of trickery, and of the ingratitude shown by the newcomers to the veteran inhabitants of the country, who were expelled from their patrimony and forced to settle far away. This answer

[1] Procopius, *Opera*, ed. H. B. Dewing (Loeb Library), De bello Vandalico II, x, 286/7.

[2] Comp. H. Lewy, *MGWJ* 77 (1933), pp. 84-99.

is aimed alike at the Phoenicians, Greeks and Romans, who all subjugated and ill-treated the Berbers.

The historian Procopius, who arrived in Africa with the Byzantine army of Belisarius (533) as a military reporter, did not perceive the contradiction between the two episodes, which shows that he already found them combined. It is indeed conceivable that anti-Jewish propaganda resumed under Justinian, when harsh anti-Jewish measures were introced (novella 37).[1] But it seems more likely that Procopius, who was fond of antiquities, just came across the story and put it in without any ulterior design. After all, he tells us of the synagogue that had existed in Borion (Boreium) since Solomon's days and of the age-old autonomous Jewish community on the island of Jotaba at the entrance to the Gulf of Eilat (today Tīrān, *i.e.* Tārān of the mediaeval Arab geographers). Procopius did not quite approve of the oppressive regime introduced in North Africa by Justinian. It therefore seems safe to assume that his account aims at satisfying scholarly curiosity as to the past of the North Africans, without any anti-Jewish intent.[2]

When were those two stories first disseminated? We think it was in the days when the *tannaim* R. Simon ben Gamliel and R. Eliezer ben Jacob and the *tanna* whose words appear in the Barayta in connection with the debate before Alexander the Great set out to explain the conquest of the country. Although this cannot be proved, there are traces of discussions of this kind in the writings of African-born ecclesiastical authors in the 2nd and 3rd centuries C.E.

Before tackling this subject, we should mention that the legend of the Canaanite origin of the Berbers passed into mediaeval Arab and Jewish literature with a significant change: the Berbers do not stem from just a descendant of Ham, but from Goliath and the Philistines.[3] This being so, the tradition of Joshua, who pursued the Canaanites, undergoes a change of names. From now on, it is Joab the son of Zeruiah who pursued the Philistines, and local popular legend knows of monuments in various

[1] According to L. Gernet, De l'origine des Maures selon Procope, *Mélanges de Géographie et d'Orientalisme, offerts à E. F. Gautier*, Tours 1937, pp. 234-244, the tradition of the Canaanites fleeing from Joshua is of different origin. According to him, its author is Justus of Tiberias, an adversary of Josephus Flavius.

[2] Procopius, *De aedificiis* VI, ii (p. 368/9); *id., De bello Persico* I, xix (p. 178/9). A different explanation is given by E. F. Gautier, *Passé* (1927), pp. 115ff. Comp. also R. Basset, *Nédromah*, pp. VIII, XIII-XIV, 74-75 and 194.

[3] For Arab sources comp. Ibn ʿAbd al-Ḥakam, *Futūḥ*, p. 34; Masʿūdī, *Murūj* I, pp. 43-44; Idrīsī, *Description*, p. 88; Ibn Khaldūn, *Taʾrīkh* VII, pp. 3-4; for Jewish sources Assaf, *Teshubot ha-Geonim*, 1942, pp. 83-84; Neubauer, *MJC* I, p. 71; A. Zacuto, *Liber Juchassin*, ed. Filipowski, 215a-b.

places in Morocco, and also on the island of Jerba in Southern Tunisia, which bear the inscription: "Up to here I, Joab the son of Zeruiah, pursued the Philistines" or a similar formula. It is true that these traditions were written down only in recent generations, but as nothing similar exists among Arabs or Berbers, there can be no doubt that they are old and were transmitted from fathers to children for many centuries.[1]

We thus see how the Jews took over a tradition which originally had been directed against them, adapted it to the new reality of their life among Arabs and used it in order to prove their early presence in the country.

The debate between Jews and Africans did not end here, and its sequel in the days of the first ecclesiastical writers in the area will be dealt with below.

Judaizers and Proselytes

The influence of Judaism in the period of Septimius Severus and his son Caracalla (193-217) is apparent from the words of Rab (Abba Arikha): "From Tyre to Carthage, Israel and its Father in Heaven are known."[2] Many Jews were indeed living in Carthage and the whole region at that time, and they spread the tenets of their faith among their neighbours. True, not all the Judaizers were circumcised and properly converted; the ban on circumcision continued in force in respect of Gentiles even after it had been lifted in respect of Jews.[3] But many underwent the proper procedure, and R. Hoshaya, who lived at the time of the Severi, raised the problem of the conversion of the Libyans: "Why should intending proselytes from Libya have to wait three generations?" This rule is based on Deut. 23:9, which limits the acceptance of an Egyptian or Edomite proselyte to the third generation. Libya borders on Egypt and was in part subject to Egyptian rule, so that the *amora* wondered whether the Libyans were to be regarded as Egyptians or as members of other nations, whose immediate acceptance was permitted. A later *amora* (4th c).

[1] Comp. Zacuto, *op. cit.*, 226a; Noah, *Travels*, p. 96. J. Schwarz, *Tebuoth ha-Areẓ*, 1900, p. 248, and Saphir, *Eben Sapir* II, p. 16, assign the abovementioned inscription to Zagora (in the Darʿa Valley of South Morocco). Comp. also Benjamin, *Acht Jahre*, p. 239; Flamand, *Communautés*, pp. 28-29. By a strange coincidence, the name Joab was found in Carthage on a stone of the 7th century B.C.; comp. Berger, *Académie des Inscriptions et Belles-Lettres, Comptes rendus* 1905, t. I, pp. 757-758.

[2] Men. 110a.

[3] Comp. Baron, *SRH* II, p. 107.

decided in favour of the more stringent provision.[1] R. Hoshaya may be identical with the R. Hoshaya in whose company we find R. Ḥinena Qarṭigenaa, who transmits a halakhic rule in his name. R. Ḥinena is called Rab Ḥanan (or Rab Ḥanna) Qarṭigenaa in the Babylonian Talmud.[2]

The next (third) generation of Palestinian *amoraim* likewise included a sage from Africa: R. Abba Qarṭigenaa, who is mentioned in the Jerusalem Talmud in connection with various halakhic matters. One of the halakhot in question is given in the Babylonian Talmud in the name of R. Isaac *demin Qarṭigenin* (from Carthage). It is difficult to decide whether we have to do here with another *amora* or with a textual variant.[3]

We see, at any rate, that Libya and North Africa not only had proselytes, but sent out religious scholars. It should not be supposed, of course, that they came from there fully trained; much of their learning was surely acquired in Palestine. We incidentally glimpse here a movement aimed at settlement in the Holy Land. We have observed the same phenomenon in the generation preceding the destruction of the Temple, and we shall later see that during the Arab occupation Jews from North Africa were among the first to migrate to Palestine.

From the silence about Cyrene we may certainly conclude that the importance of Cyrenian (and Egyptian) Jewry had so much declined that it no longer made any impact. On the other hand, as we have seen, the *tannaim* do speak of Africa. We may suppose that the North West African communities, at least in part, made headway thanks to the eclipse of Cyrene.

It is only from the end of the 2nd century onwards that sources on the life of the Jews in that region are available. They reveal large, well-developed concentrations and isolated points, both along the coastal belt and in the interior. The great majority of sources represent the areas now included in Tunisia and Algeria as a region of dense settlement. Excavations in Tunisia and Algeria during the inter-World-War period uncovered Christian catacombs in which the names of the buried indicate Semitic—perhaps Jewish, but possibly Phoenician—origin. The presence of Jews in Oea (Tripoli) is disclosed incidentally. Clearly, even if full credence is given to Yosephon's testimony as to the banishment of 30,000

---

[1] Y. Kil. VIII, 3 (31c); Y. Shab. V, 1 (7b).

[2] Y. Shab. XV, 2 (15c); Y. Ber. I, 5 (60c); B. Ket. 27b; B.K. 114b.

[3] Comp. Y. Ber. IV, 3 (8a), Y. Dem. V, 2 (24c), Y. Kil. I, 9 (27b), B. Ber. 29a. For the relations between the sages of Palestine and Egypt comp. Tcherikover-Fuks, *CPJ* I, pp. 106-109.

Jews to Carthage under Titus, these were slaves, whose presence at first made no impact in social or administrative respect.[1]

The Geographical Extent of the African Diaspora

To obtain some conception of the geographical extent of the North African diaspora from the time when silence descends upon the eastern region, let us review the sites where unmistakable archaeological-epigraphic remains have been found.[2]

In the 19th century, a Jewish cemetery was unearthed in Gamarth near ancient Carthage, containing several catacombs, each with seventeen or eighteen graves. Moreover, about a dozen tombstones with Latin inscriptions were discovered, some of which show a representation of the seven-branched candelabrum or the word *shalom* in Hebrew or Latin characters (SALOM). Remnants of inscriptions in Hebrew characters were also found, and so were many lamps stamped with the effigy of the candelabrum. Père Delattre, who first published a comprehensive study of this site, originally believed that the candelabrum was also a Christian symbol. He later reversed his opinion, especially in view of the fact that the Christians had a separate cemetery. The Gamarth cemetery dates from the period of the spread of Latin, *i.e.* from the 3rd century C.E. onwards.[3]

More important is the discovery of the remains of a synagogue at Hammam-Lif on the seacoast, 17 kilometres south of Tunis, of the 3rd-4th centuries C.E. In the Roman period, the place was called Naro. In 1881, a mosaic was discovered here with various symbols, including the candelabrum, three inscriptions in Vulgar Latin with faulty spelling (CIL 12457 a, b, c), and fragments of a seven-branched candelabrum.

The inscription on the mosaic floor reads:

"Sancta Sinagoga Naron pro sa | lutem suam ancilla tua Iulia
Na[ronensis] p[uella] de suo proprium teselavit"

---

[1] For archaeological finds in Tripolitania comp. Applebaum, *Zion* 19 (1954), pp. 30-31; Renato Bartoccini, *Africa Italiana* 2 (1928-1929), pp. 187-200. According to Schürer, *Geschichte* III, p. 54, Jews settled in Africa Proconsularis during the Ptolemaean period. For Josephon's report comp. above, p. 24 n. 1.

[2] Comp. Monceaux, *REJ* 42 (1902), pp. 1-28; J. Oehler, *MGWJ* 1909, pp. 525-538; Juster I, pp. 207-209.

[3] Comp. Alfred Louis Delattre, *Gamarth ou la nécropole juive de Carthage*, Lyon 1895 (offprint from "Missions Catholiques"). This pamphlet being very rare, comp. also Monceaux, *op. cit.*, pp. 13-15; *CIL* VIII, Sup. 1, 14097-14106; *PW*, *s.v.* Karthago.

i.e.: Thy servant Julia, the maiden of Naro, for the sake of her salvation, had this mosaic made at her expense in the holy synagogue of Naro.

An inscription on the wall to the right of the mosaic says:

"Asterius filius Rus | tici arcosinagogi | Margarita Riddei filia par | tem portici teselavit"

i.e.: Asterius, the son of Rusticus the synagogue warden, and Margaret, the daughter of Riddeus, inlaid part of the portico with a mosaic.

The third (double) inscription (to the left of the mosaic) reads as follows:

"Istru | menta [1] |	Istru | menta
servi | tui Na	servi | tui a Na |
ritanus	rone

i.e.: The Tora scrolls of thy servant, the inhabitant of Naro.

Upon the resumption of the excavations in 1909, many more earthenware lamps were found with the effigy of the candelabrum, which also appears several times in the mosaic.[2]

Single tombstones, all inscribed in Latin, have been discovered in the central part of North Africa.[3] An inscription from Utica (half-way between Tunis and Bizerta) mentions an archon (Utica 1205). In a lament on a tombstone at Henchir Djouana (Central Tunisia), bereaved (Judaized?) parents mourn the loss of two children.[4] Some more short inscriptions have been preserved: from Sidi Brahim, No. 16,867; Nos. 7150, 7155, 7530, 7710, from Cirta (= Constantine); Henchir Fuara, suppl. 16701; Ksour el-Ghennaia, (in the Aures Mountains) No. 4321; Sitifis (Sétif), 8499, 8640; Khalfoun (7 kilometres west of Sétif) 8423; Auzia (today Aumale), 20759. The tombstone Sitifis 8640 is that of a baptized Jew; it bears the monogram ☧. The supplement to the inscription is No. 20354, but the editor doubts whether the reading *Iudeus* in line 8 there is correct. In other inscriptions (Sidi Brahim, Cirta 7530), we find the letters *D.M.* (= *Dis Manibus*), "dedicated to the (Roman) gods",

[1] For *instrumenta* in the sense of holy books comp. Tertullian, *PL* II 1320, *Index latinitatis, s.v.*

[2] Comp. E. Goodenough, *Jewish Symbols in the Greco-Roman Period*, 1953-1964, II, pp. 89-100 (where a bibliography will be found); Hirschberg, The Fish in the Mosaics of the Synagogue at Naro, *Eretz-Israel* 8 (1967), pp. 305-311.

[3] They are contained in *CIL*, vol. VIII. Some inscriptions were published by E. Diehl, *Inscriptiones Latinae Christianae Veteres*, 3 vol., Berlin 1925-1931. Comp. also René Cagnat et Alfred Merlin avec la collaboration de Louis Châtelain, *Inscriptions latines d'Afrique etc.*, Paris 1923; Alfred Merlin, *Inscriptions latines de la Tunisie*, Paris 1944.

[4] Monceaux discusses this inscription in *R. Ar.*, Troisième série, tome XL, Janvier-Juin 1902, pp. 208-226.

which is the usual pagan dedicative sign. Whatever the meaning of this feature, neither it nor the fact of baptism disproves the ethnic affiliation of the buried.[1]

Inscriptions discovered in the farthest Maghreb are of especial interest both on account of their rarity and their character.

In Volubilis, now Wolili (Oulili), between Meknes and Fez, the following Hebrew epitaph has been found:

מטרונא
בת רבי
יהודה נח

i.e.: Matrona, the daughter of Rabbi Yehuda; may she rest (in peace).[2]

This epitaph is believed to date from the 3rd century C.E. A bronze lamp with the candelabrum stamp has also been discovered among the ruins of that city. A Greek inscription contains the name Σαλέμου, which is believed to correspond to the Hebrew name שלום or שלם (*CIL* 21900, 21901). According to a somewhat vague report, a Greek inscription relating to the local synagogue, as well as a Hebrew inscription, were discovered there a few years ago.[3]

In a cemetery of the Roman period at Chellah near Rabat, H. Basset found a tombstone inscribed in Greek letters:

"M. Aurelios Ptolemaios Ioudaios"

Sherds stamped with the seven-armed candelabrum have been discovered in the area of Tingi (Tanger).[4]

The Rise of Christianity

Under the emperors succeeding Hadrian, the situation of the Jews in general and of North African Jewry in particular improved. The grant of civil rights to the Jews and tolerated status to their religion fitted them into the framework of the Roman Empire, so that nothing but their religion seemed to distinguish them from the rest of the population. In

[1] Some believe it to be due to an error of a pagan mason; comp. Juster I, p. 481, n. 5; II, 234b; Tcherikover, *Jews*, p. 251.

[2] Comp. Ph. Berger, *Bulletin archéologique* 1892, pp. 64-66, pl. XIII.

[3] Comp. Laredo, *Hebreos*, pp. 168-169. For the name Salemos comp. also *SEG* IX, 885-886; Applebaum, *Zion* 19 (1954), p. 41; p. 44, No. 19.

[4] Basset, *La nécropole romaine de Chellah*, 1919, p. 131. J. Carcopino, *Le Maroc Antique*, 1948, p. 287, n. 1, mentions Jewish remains in Volubilis and a Greek inscription in Salé (Chella-Rabat), discussed in articles which I have been unable to trace. For the sherds of Tangier comp. Laredo, *Hebreos*, pp. 147-148.

addition to the Jews, whose number was considerable, there were many σεβόμενοι (God-)fearing persons, who were accessible to Jewish and Christian influence.[1]

At the end of the 2nd and the beginning of the 3rd century C.E., Rome was ruled by the Emperors Septimius Severus and Marcus Aurelius Antoninus (Caracalla), who were known for their favourable attitude towards the Jews. Septimius was born in Leptis Magna (*i.e.* Lebda) in Tripolitania, and all his life betrayed his African origin by his speech. His son Marcus Aurelius Antoninus was brought up together with Jews in Africa. It is reported that at the age of seven he once heard that one of his play-fellows had been severely beaten for being a Jew. Antoninus (his name was then still Julius Bassanius, after his maternal grandfather) long avoided looking his friend's father and his own father in the face because he felt that they were responsible for the suffering of the Jewish boy. Some believe that Antoninus is the friend, frequently mentioned in the Aggada, of R. Yehuda ha-Nasi. The two emperors permitted the Jews to hold positions of honour, and Jerome, in his commentary on Daniel (11:35), says that the Jews interpret the words "and to make them white, even to the time of the end" as referring to Septimius and Antoninus.[2] In the ruins of a synagogue at Qaysūn, north of Safad, a Greek inscription has been found, saying: For the well-being of our sovereign lords, the Emperors Lucius Septimius Severus and his sons Marcus Aurelius Antoninus Caracalla) and Lucius Septimius Geta, because the Jews made a vow. M. Avi-Yona notes that this is the only inscription dedicated to Roman emperors by Palestinian Jews.[3]

True, according to one source, Severus forbade proselytizing for Judaism, but such a decree is mentioned nowhere else. But even if the report is true, conversion to Judaism was probable prohibited incidentally to the prohibition of conversion to Christianity and designed mainly to prevent the latter.[4] Tertullian, a contemporary of the two Severan emperors, complained that many Christians posed as Jews because Judaism was a *religio licita* and its adherents were not liable to the perse-

[1] Comp. *Lexikon für Theologie und Kirche* IV (1960), col. 109-110.

[2] Comp. Spartianus, Antoninus Caracalla 1, 6, and Jerome's comment, *PL* XXV, 570. Comp. also Baron, *SRH*, II, p. 400, n. 19, and Rachmuth, *MGWJ* 50 (1906), p. 37.

[3] Comp. M. Avi-Yona, *In the Days of Rome and Byzantium*, 1946, pp. 26-31 (Hebrew). H. Kohl-C. Watzinger, *Antike Synagogen in Galilaea*, 1916, p. 219, doubt whether the building was a synagogue; but comp. S. Klein, *Jüdisch-palästinisches Corpus Inscriptionum*, 1920, p. 81 and n. 3, where the synagogue in קציון is referred to.

[4] Spartianus, (see p. 31 n. 1) *Septimius Severus* 17; comp. Julien, *Histoire* I, pp. 186-187.

cution to which the Christians were then subject.[1] It is a fact that Judaizing was in many cases a preliminary stage to the conversion of Gentiles to Christianity, and in later days to Islam. The Fathers of the Latin Church, which originated in North Africa, nevertheless regarded the spread of Judaism among the idolaters as a direct threat to Christianity, and fought it in speeches and disputations.[2]

The fight of the Early Fathers against Judaism in the third and the first half of the fourth century was not crowned with success in Africa, where the half- or one-third- or one-quarter-Judaized were numerous. But when Christianity became the ruling religion in the Empire, and the position of the official church consolidated, the emperors and the governmental apparatus were invoked in aid of the representatives of the church in Africa. A number of decrees were launched against Jews, Judaizers and heretics, *i.e.* Christian sects which did not accept the tenets of the official religion. Especial wrath was incurred by the "worshippers of heaven" (*caelicolae*), a Judaizing sect widespread in Africa in the fourth and fifth centuries of whose nature no clear and reliable evidence has come down to us.[3]

Constantine the Great, despite his unfavourable attitude towards the Jews, did not dare to interfere with their legal status. But when Valentianus conquered North Africa in 355, he repealed the law which granted the Jews the *jus testandi* (right to testify in Gentile courts). On the other hand, the Jews were still recognised as Roman citizens in one of the laws (of 392) contained in the Codex Theodosianus, named after Theodosius the Great (379-395), who in 392 declared Christianity the state religion. Not long afterwards, the Emperor Honorius (395-423) issued laws against the Jews and the Donatists, a Christian sect that had spread very rapidly in Africa in the 4th century and posed a serious threat to the official clergy. In those days, West Roman rule in Africa was nearing its end; one procurator even dared to discontinue the grain shipments to feed the metropolitan masses, which had been customary for centuries.[4]

---

[1] Tertullian, *Apolog.* 21, *PL* I, 391-392 (449-450). Opinions as to the legal status of the Jews are divided; comp. Juster, I, pp. 213-226, 246, 422-423, and Baer, *Zion* 21 (1956), 6-7. For Caracalla's *constitutio Antoniniana de civitate* (212 C.E.) comp. Tcherikover, *Jews*, p. 213; Baron, *SRH*, II, p. 109.

[2] See below (pp. 71ff.).

[3] See *Lexikon für Theologie und Kirche* II (1958), col. 881; comp. below, p. 82 of the text and n. 3. Comp. also Jan Burian's contribution to: F. Altheim and R. Stiehl, *Die Araber in der Alten Welt* I, Berlin 1964, pp. 528-32.

[4] Comp. Rachmuth, *MGWJ* 50 (1906), pp. 41-42, and Juster, II, pp. 24-25, also I, pp. 465ff. The Laws of Honorius, *PL* XI, 1218-1220.

According to Jerome (d. 420), a continuous chain of Jewish settlements stretched at that time from Mauretania in the west through the Maghreb, Egypt and Palestine to India in the east.[1]

The Vandals and the Byzantine Conquest

When the Vandals had conquered North Africa (430), a period of quiet ensued for the Jews and the heretical Christian sects. The Vandals themselves belonged to the Arian trend, one of the Christian denominations relentlessly persecuted by the official Catholic Church because of dogmatic differences as to the nature of Christ. The Arians now inflicted upon the Catholics the same measures as the latter had inflicted on them; they vented their wrath upon the Catholic clergy, confiscated their property and expelled them from the region. The Vandals burnt the books of the erstwhile official church and introduced their own rites in its places of worship. The Jews may have viewed this development sympathetically, and perhaps even helped the Vandals. Towards the end of their rule, the Vandals treated their mortal enemies, the Catholics, tolerantly, allowed their priests to return, reinstated the Metropolitan of Carthage and permitted the election of new bishops. However, the orthodox clergy was not satisfied; they harboured suppressed hatred against Arians and Jews. At the same time, the Byzantine Emperor Justin outlawed the Arians.[2]

It was then that Justinian, Justin's nephew and co-regent, and after his death (527) his successor on the imperial throne, began to think of the reconquest of North Africa and the restoration of the Roman Empire to its former greatness. All his political and military advisers, prompted by both political and strategic considerations, urged him not to risk a war with the Vandals, which he was likely to lose. On the other hand, exiles from Africa and clerics prodded him to make war against the heretics. Justinian at first hesitated, but eventually—as Procopius of Caesarea tells us—obeyed an express command from heaven, transmitted to him by a bishop, to fight the Vandals. He ordered Belisarius, one of his most experienced generals, to go to Africa with an army of 16,000 men, carried

[1] Jerome, *Epist.* 129, 4, *PL* XXII, 1104; comp. also W. H. C. Frend, *The Donatist Church*, 1952, pp. 250, 269, 308-309, and Mesnage, *Rev. Afr.*, 1913, pp. 361-700.

[2] Comp. Procopius, *De bello Vandalico* II, IX (278/9). An account of the persecutions is given by Victor, Bishop of Vita, in *Historia Persecutionis Africae*, *PL* LVIII, 179ff.; comp. also F. Ferrère, *De Victoris Vitensis Libro* etc. (thesis), Paris 1898, and Julien, *Histoire* I, pp. 249ff.

by a fleet of 500 transport vessels accompanied by 92 patrol boats. On Belisarius's staff was his friend, Procopius of Caesarea, as a military reporter, commissioned to describe the campaign of conquest. The invasion fleet reached the African coast in September, 533. Belisarius was careful not to attempt to take Carthage, the capital of the Vandals, by a frontal attack. A succession of blunders by the defenders enabled the invaders to win victory after victory, so that Carthage fell within a short time. On that occasion, the vessels from the Temple of Jerusalem, which had been in Carthage since 455, were removed to Constantinople.[1]

When the conquest of North Africa was completed, Justinian immediately set about organizing the administration. The region was now constituted as a separate unit, directly connected with the Byzantine metropolis. According to the Codex Theodosianus, Judaism was still a recognised religion in the Christian state, and it was forbidden to harm its institutions or adherents merely because of their Jewishness. Justinian was the first who, by novella 37 of the year 535, outlawed the Jewish religion. That decree, which according to clause 12 thereof applied only in Africa, contained a severe warning to Arians, Donatists, Jews and others not to make proselytes. Clause 8 of the novella provides that the existence of synagogues shall no longer be permitted and that they shall be converted into Christian churches. Jews, idolaters and other unbelievers were forbidden to maintain "luminaries" (*i.e.* places of prayer and worship).

This decree was the direct result of incitement by the Byzantine-African official clergy against all those who did not accept its creed. As regards the Jews, it was more stringent than Justinian's novella 131 of 545, which forbade the erection of new synagogues, and than his novella 146, issued in 553. The latter merely restricted their activity in the sphere of religious instruction, which was placed under supervision, while novella 37 aimed at eradicating all their religious life.[2]

In 535, the year in which novella 37 was promulgated, the city of Borion, the fifth of the cities of the Pentapolis, at the south-western extremity of Cyrenaica, fell into Byzantine hands. Procopius explains that it was situated near the Berber territory, that it had until then been completely free, never served under tribute and never seen tax-collectors within its gates. Jews had been living here since olden times; they had an

---

[1] Comp. Kornemann, *Weltgeschichte* II, pp. 418-419; Julien, *op. cit.*, pp. 256-261; Rubin, *Iustinian*, pp. 161-162.

[2] For the three *novellae* comp. *PL* LXXII, 1051; *Corpus Iuris Civilis* vol. III, Novellae, Berlin 1899; pp. 245, 663 (XIV, 2), 714-7; Baron, *SRH* III, pp. 9, 12, VII, pp. 94-95; Juster *Juifs* I, pp. 238, 250-251.

ancient, most venerable synagogue, built, according to tradition, in Solomon's days. The Emperor Justinian now forced the Jews to become Christians and converted their synagogue into a church.[1]

These measures brought no benefit to the region. Procopius himself, the court historiographer, criticizes them sharply, noting that Justinian did not concern himself with setting up a stable administration and did not realize that the goodwill of the whole population must be encouraged. He plundered the country, imposed heavy taxes on the inhabitants, took the best land for himself and showed no concern for the welfare of his soldiers. The victims of persecution—Arians, pagans, Donatists and Jews—sought refuge among the free Berber tribes, who treated them sympathetically.[2]

Oppression eased somewhat in the days of the Emperor Mauritius (582-602), who made many changes in the administration and boundaries of the provinces and discontinued the persecution of Jews and Donatists. It was henceforth forbidden to convert Jews forcibly, and they were allowed to use the remaining synagogues. At the same time, the ban on the erection of new synagogues was reaffirmed. Corrupt Byzantine procurators used the relaxations in oppressive legislation as a convenient means to extort payment from the various kinds of "unbelievers" for their implementation.

The condition of the Jews—and of the population at large—deteriorated again under Phocas (602-610). One source reports forced conversions in Carthage in his time, but according to another source they occurred in Jerusalem. A report of the forced conversion of Jews and Samaritans in Carthage in 632 has not been sufficiently clarified, either. In any case, we may suppose that at a time of tension and conflict between the Christian sects the ruling church did not show itself broad-minded towards the Jews.[3]

It is reported that the Jews of Spain, who were ruthlessly persecuted by the Visigoth kings, took advantage of the temporary quiet and the

---

[1] Procopius, De aedificiis, VI, II; comp. *PW* V, 730, *s.v.* Boreion (2). It should be remembered that according to Procopius, De bello Persico 1, 19, Justinian abrogated the autonomous status of the Jews on the island of Yotabe (today Tiran, in the Gulf of Aqaba); comp. Hirschberg, *Elath*, 1963, pp. 182-193.

[2] Comp. Monceaux, *REJ* 54 (1902), p. 27; Julien, *Histoire* I, p. 272; Rubin, *Iustinian*, pp. 173, 182-183, 187-188, 210 and 218. One of the fiercest fighters was the learned priest Ferrandus, who collected the various ordinances against the "heretics"; *PL* MLXXXVIII, 817-828.

[3] Kornemann, *Weltgeschichte*, pp. 456-457; Scharf, *BZ* 48 (1955), p. 109; Avi-Yona, *Rome and Byzantium*, p. 185. See also next page.

weakening of government authority in order to escape to the nearby province of Mauretania Tingitana. It is said that whenever in the 7th century pressure increased in Spain, as in the years 612/613 and 638-642, many Jews fled to Mauretania Tingitana; here, at the periphery of the Byzantine Empire, the authorities were not strong enough to persecute them. It is further reported that King Egica severely punished the Jews in his kingdom for trying to maintain trade relations with the Jewish or non-Jewish population of Africa. In 694, a plot between Spanish and African Jews, aimed at overthrowing Christian rule in Spain, was allegedly discovered, and the Seventeenth Council, met in Toledo, resolved to take drastic steps against the Jews in the Visigoth kingdom. But all these reports originate from Spain, while no other source mentions the Jews of Tingitana of that period. The account of the Jewish-Berber leader *Qawla al-Yahūdī*, who at first took part in the conquest of Spain on the side of the Arabs and subsequently revolted against them, is a late story, of the end of the 18th century, without any basis in the sources.

Meanwhile, the central provinces of North Africa were in steady decline. Corruption, indiscipline and religious fanaticism undermined the administration. In the reign of the Emperor Heraclius, the son of the Exarch (governor-general) Heraclius of Africa, anti-Jewish measures were revived; he was the emperor who waged a campaign of vengeance against Palestinian Jewry for supporting the Persian invasion and seizing power in Jerusalem during the years when the city was in Persian hands (614-628).[1]

According to the sources, Heraclius's conversion decree applied to a large portion of the empire. It was extended to Africa in 632, and it is directly and indirectly referred to in *Doctrina Jacobi nuper baptizati*, the account of a disputation between a Jew converted to Christianity, Jacob, and some of his former co-religionists.[2] Jacob, probably a native of Palestine, lived in the reigns of the emperors Phocas and Heraclius. During the persecution of the Jews in Africa, he was an agent of a Constantinopolitan merchant, who had entrusted him with a consignment of precious clothes for sale in Africa or Gaul. He arrived with the goods in the province of Byzacena and thence proceeded to Carthage. He was a Jew, but posed as a Christian, carrying a document from the owner of the

---

[1] Comp. Juster, *La condition légale des Juifs sous les rois visigoths*, Paris, 1912, pp. 60-61; José Amador de los Ríos, *Historia social, política y religiosa de los Judíos de España y Portugal* (reprint), Madrid 1960, pp. 60-61.

[2] See R. Devreesse, *Revue des Sciences Religieuses* 17 (1937), p. 28; Bonwetch, *Doctrina Jacobi nuper baptizati*, 1910, p. 1.

goods attesting to his Christianity, lest he be apprehended and ill-treated as a suspected Jew. His Jewishness was revealed by chance—as told in detail in the Slavic translation of the *Doctrina*—and he was forced to undergo baptism. Before long, he became an ardent believer in his new religion. He debated with Jews—*inter alia*, with one Justus, a merchant who had also come to Carthage on business—trying to win them over to Christianity; the *Doctrina* refers to another Jew, Nonos, an inhabitant of Carthage, who refused to become a Christian. Jacob left Carthage in 634.[1]

Without going into the question whether the *Doctrina* was written by Jacob himself, who is described in it as an unlearned person, or whether he is an historical figure at all, there can be no doubt that this work truly depicts the Jews, with their various occupations and tribulations, during that period of Byzantine and especially African history.

Heraclius wished to Christianize the Jews forcibly, but in the meantime, an unexpected event took place that radically changed the situation in the Byzantine Empire and left an indelible mark on the history of the three continents then known. Arab tribes sallied forth from the desert with the slogan "There is no God but Allah, and Muḥammad is the Messenger of Allah", which welded them into one people and a militant religious community; they swept Heraclius and his army from most of the areas of the Byzantine Empire in Asia, invaded Egypt and began knocking on the gates of North Africa and Spain.

Even on the threshold of subjection and expulsion, the Byzantines in Africa did not change their ways. The various sects within the Eastern Church continued wrangling about the nature of the Trinity and the formulation of the dogmas—until the day when North Africa succumbed to the Arabs.

Society: Communal Organization

The reports on Jewish military settlements in the Cyrene region under Ptolemy Lagi and Jewish military operations upon the outbreak of the revolt under Trajan highlight the strong ties between Cyrenaican and Egyptian Jewry. It is fair to assume that the form of organization and economic structure of the two Jewries were as similar as the peculiarities of each country and its population permitted. The relative abundance of sources on Egypt is thus a help towards understanding the hints that have reached us concerning Egypt's western neighbour.

[1] Bonwetch, *Doctrina* pp. 89-91; 2. See S. Krauss, *Zion*, Yearbook II (1927), pp. 28-37, esp. 30-31; Y. Dan, *Zion* 36 (1971), pp. 1-26, esp. 17-23.

The Jewish soldier-settlers in Egypt during the Persian period were organized in special units, which were separate entities also in economic and socio-religious respect. On the strength of papyri material, A. Tcherikover reaches the conclusion that Jewish soldiers in the Ptolemaean period were scattered within the Egyptian army without a general national organization of their own.

Because of the importance of the exact wording of his conclusions, some extracts from Tcherikover's remarks may be given here *verbatim*. Talking of the Greek cities in Egypt, he explains that "they had municipal autonomy and their own jurisdiction. As to other ethnic groups, organization in autonomous cities was out of the question since they did not live in cities in their own countries, either; nor could they be allowed to organize in large national associations, which would have comprised all the members of the people throughout the country. On the other hand, it was impossible to ignore their natural propensity to follow their national customs and live in groups somewhat segregated from the rest of the population. This is how the πολιτεύματα (communities) came into being in Egypt, whose names are mentioned in inscriptions, papyri and contemporary literature. The word πολίτευμα, which appears for the first time in the 4th century B.C.E., had a very wide meaning and was used in different senses at different times. In the period we are dealing with, its commonest acceptation was: a community established on an ethnic basis and enjoying certain political rights. We know of a not inconsiderable number of such communities in Egypt: the πολιτεύματα of the Idumaeans (*OGIS* 737), Phrygians (*OGIS* 658), Cretans (P. Tebt. 32), Lycians (*SB* 6025), Cilicians (*SB* 7270) and Boeotians (*SB* 6664). These communities were sometimes—as in the case of the Cretans—bound up with the Ptolemaean army organization and, like every ethnic unit in the Ptolemaean army, likely to lose their ethnic character and become 'pseudo-ethnic' organizations; but there is no reason to suppose that all the πολιτεύματα were bound up with the army, especially as ethnic organizations called by that name existed not only in Egypt, but in other countries as well. Although these communities could not compete with the Greek cities as regards the extent of their rights, their members called themselves citizens (πολῖται), convened to pass certain resolutions, carved their resolutions in stone, elected their own officials, had their own religious worship—in short, presented the picture of a πόλις both externally and internally. We may say that the mode of life within the πολίτευμα was 'pseudo-municipal', that it combined a small amount of the traditional freedom of the Greek πόλις with the vestiges of the national organization of free peoples and tribes. The legal autonomy of such a community was of course rather limited, and we may imagine that while observing national customs, such as traditional festivals and religious rites, the πολιτεύματα conducted all their legal business in accordance with the general Hellenistic law obtaining in the country and resorted to the ordinary government courts."[1]

Here is what Tcherikover says about the Jewish soldiers: "The Jewish πολίτευμα (*i.e.* the Jewish community) was not only a political-national, but also a religious organization, and he who wished to join it had to adopt the Jewish faith. For all the sympathy that Ptolemaeans, such as Philometor, felt for the Jews, they did not intend to convert their subjects to Judaism. We may thus conclude that the term 'Jew' in the Ptolemaean army was not, and could not be, used as a 'pseudo-ethnic' designation, but always meant a genuine Jew. It was so in Elephantine; but whereas in the Persian era the Jews had been organized in special formations with specific assignments (though without supreme powers of command), in the Hellenistic period they were dispersed among and absorbed into the various army units."[2]

Tcherikover's opinion as to the situation in Egypt is made plausible by the fact that there were many Jews in Alexandria and in provincial centres and rural settlements, so that Jewish soldiers could satisfy their religious-communal requirements by attaching themselves to the "civilian" Jewish communities in the places where they were stationed, without having to organize in special groups. Things were different in Cyrenaica, where the military settlers formed separate communities.

Let us refer once again to the inscriptions from Berenice. They were indeed written under Roman rule, but it is well known that the Romans made no changes in the system of the πολιτεύματα; emperors and procurators respected the old-established organizational frameworks.

The stelae CIG 5361 and 5362 contain the term (Jewish) πολίτευμα several times. Outside Cyrenaica, a πολίτευμα is mentioned only once, the reference in that case being to Alexandria. Here is a complete translation of the first inscription:

"In the year 55 on the 25th Faōr. At the time of the Feast of Tabernacles. In the days of the Archons: Kleandros the son of Stratonikos; Euphranōr the son of Aristōn, Sōsigenos the son of Sosippos; Andromachos the son of Andromachos; Marcus Laelius Onasiōn the son of

---

[1] Tcherikover, *Jews*, pp. 130-131; comp. also Juster, *Jews* I, pp. 413ff.

[2] *Ibid.*, p. 45.

Apollonios; Philōnides the son of Agēmōn; Autoklēs the son of Zēnōn; Sonikos the son of Theodotos; Josepos the son of Straton.

It has been found that Marcus Tittius, the son of Sextus and Aemilia, a fine and good man (καλὸς καὶ ἀγαθός), after being called upon to manage public affairs (ἐπὶ δημοσίων πραγμάτων), exercised his leadership kindly and handsomely (φιλανθρώπως καὶ καλῶς) and throughout his tenure of office displayed a friendly attitude; and not only in these matters did he show himself blameless, but also with regard to the private affairs of every citizen; moreover, in exercising his leadership in the manner most favourable to us, the Jewish community (πολίτευμα), all and sundry, he did not refrain from doing what was for our benefit.

We, the Archons and community of the Jews of Berenice, have therefore resolved to mention him honourably at every festival and every new moon and to crown him with a wreath of olive leaves and a ribbon of honour. The Archons shall inscribe this popular resolution on a stela of stone from (the island of) Paros and put it up in the most honourable place in the amphitheatre. Passed unanimously."

The Jewish community of Berenice also deemed it its duty to perpetuate the name of the Jew Decimus Valerius Dionysius, a Roman citizen, who had had the amphitheatre repaired and renovated, as proclaimed by inscription No. 5362. He was granted tax exemption, and the inscription, engraved in his honour on a column of Parian marble, was decorated with an olive wreath at every assembly and new moon. The column was set up in the most conspicuous place in the amphitheatre. In the view of scholars recently studying this inscription, it dates from between 30 to 6 B.C.E. It is older than No. 5361.

A third inscription is later than the preceding ones and, in contrast to their correct style, its wording is faulty and its language more popular. It mentions the members of the community (συναγωγή) who contributed to the reconditioning of the synagogue, likewise called συναγωγή. The amounts donated are not large, and so we may assume that only ordinary maintenance work was carried out. The inscription is not complete; the names preserved are those of fifteen men and three women. The number of archons must have increased, ten being mentioned here. It is noteworthy that this inscription calls the community not πολίτευμα, as do the two preceding inscriptions, but συναγωγή. This permits the inference that the organizational structure of the community had undergone a change, the cause of which is unknown to us.[1]

---

[1] Comp. above, p. 26, n. 1; also Applebaum, *Tarbiz* 28 (1959), p. 423. *Id.*, *Teucheira*,

The importance of these inscriptions cannot be overrated. They tell us of the forms of activity of the Jewish community, the passing of its resolutions, its place of meeting, its relations with the Roman administrator. There are nine or ten *archons, i.e.* wardens, who meet at fixed times, together with the members of the community, and who have to carry out the resolutions. In the region under reference, the *archon* is mentioned also in an inscription from Utica (No. 1205) and in one of Tertullian's homilies. He is further known from the Talmud and from inscriptions in other regions, while the Roman laws are silent about him.

The inscriptions indicate that the Roman administrator had wide powers of supervision over both the community as a whole and its individual members and that much depended on his personal attitude towards the πολίτευμα. It is thought that the very establishment of the community required a permit or approval from the Ptolemaean administrator or Roman procurator. Some wish to differentiate between the terms "the Jewish community" and "every citizen" in inscription No. 5361, which allegedly reflect a clear distinction between the members of the Jewish community and the citizens of the town; this would be additional proof that the Jews in the Greek cities had no citizen rights.

The inscriptions attest to the high level of development of the organization of the Jewish community of Berenice, whose existence is known to us only from these documents. Jewish πολιτεύματα no doubt existed also in Cyrene and other cities in the Pentapolis. The fact of the revolt under Trajan proves the existence of a permanent organization among the Jews, which could be used for various purposes.[1]

The inscription of the mosaic of Naro and the story of a woman saint of Caesarea (Cherchel) mention the *arcosynagogus* (ἀρχισυνάγωγος), whose title corresponds to "synagogue head" in Jewish sources and whose office enjoyed great prestige during the Second Temple and later. The *archisynagogos* was in sole charge of all synagogue affairs, unlike the *archons*, who served collectively. He was usually a person of distinguished family and personal merit. In Juster's opinion, he was also the rabbi and mentor of the synagogue. Unlike the *archon*, the *archisynagogos* is frequently mentioned in the Codex Theodosianus.[2]

Another Jewish notable we may mention is Marcus Avilius Ianuarus

---

p. 48, maintains that this community, too, had its communal organization. *The Letter of Aristeas*, 310, mentions the καὶ τῶν ἀπὸ τοῦ πολιτεύματος.

[1] Comp. Tcherikover, *Civilization*, p. 331. On the archons comp. Krauss, *Syn. Altertümer*, pp. 146-149.

[2] Comp. Juster, *ibid.* I, p. 450; Krauss, *op. cit.*, pp. 114-121.

(or Ianuarius), *pater Sinagogae* in Sitifis, who erected a tombstone for his daughter, Avilia Aster (No. 8499); he is the same who erected a tombstone for his wife, Caelia Thalassa, in Khalfoun (No. 8423). That title seems to have been no designation of office, but a mere honorary style, bestowed both on men and women—for we also find a *mater synagogae*—for activities on behalf of the synagogue. The Codex Theodosianus grants immunity to the *pater synagogae* without specifying the functions of the holder of this title nor why he had received it. In any event, it seems that the Jewish notable, like his Roman counterpart, was expected to concern himself with the common good.[1]

The Economy

References to the occupations and sources of livelihood of North African Jewry are extremely scanty. In Egypt, the Jewish economy of the time was not based exclusively on commerce and finance; Jews also worked on the land, in agriculture and cattle-farming. During the Persian period, they provided a considerable contingent for the Egyptian garrison force, and we know that the Ptolemaeans continued this policy of recruiting non-Egyptians for various military services, mainly for settlement on the frontier. Papyri, both general ones and those dealing with Jews in particular, show us these settlers as tillers of the soil and cattle-breeders, buying, selling and otherwise engaging in workaday pursuits.

If this was so in more highly-developed Egypt, we may certainly assume that the Jews in Cyrenaica, and especially the military settlers among them, engaged in agriculture and stock-farming. It has lately been suggested that Palestinian Jews were sent to the Cyrene region for military settlement already in the days of Herod.[2] What is generally agreed is that surviving Jewish prisoners of the wars of Vespasian and Titus were sold as slaves to work on the estates of Roman aristocrats which covered wide stretches of North Africa. After their release, they settled as tenants on state domains, joining the existing class of Jewish farmers. Others may have taken up the grain trade, some of them moving to Rome, like those people of Scina mentioned in metropolitan inscriptions.[3] S. Applebaum dwells at length on the economic and social position of those

---

[1] Kahrstedt, *Kulturgeschichte*, pp. 63 and 223-226.

[2] Tcherikover, *Jews*, pp. 35ff. It was only in the 4th century C.E. that Jews became debarred from serving in the armed forces.

[3] Comp. Josephus, *War* VI, 9, 2, p. 425, on Jewish prisoners of war sent to Egypt, and above, p. . 26-7

farmers under the Ptolemaeans and Romans, and regards the eviction policy towards them after the destruction of the Temple as one of the causes of the revolt under Trajan. U. Kahrstedt, on the other hand, points to the severe economic crisis that visited the whole Empire under that ruler.[1]

We possess evidence of Jewish farmers in the western region as well. In one of his speeches, Augustine, Bishop of Hippo Regius (present-day Bône), attacks Jewish Sabbath observance, which in his opinion is grossly material and merely a sign of laziness. It would be better, he thinks, for the Jews to do something useful in their fields rather than spend their time in theatres, and for their women to dress wool rather than dance unashamedly on balconies.[2]

The prohibition of the employment of slaves who had become Christians was a severe blow to Jewish landowners and eventually forced them to abandon agriculture. On the other hand, the displacement of the Jews from the cities during the persecution by Justinian caused many of them to move to the interior of the country, to areas where Byzantine rule was not firmly established, and to take up agriculture at least as a subsidiary occupation. Remnants of agricultural activity can be found to this day in Jewish quarters (mellahs) in remote corners of the Maghreb.[3]

Let us now turn to the abovementioned epistle of Synesios, a contemporary of Augustine, in which he describes to a friend, in a lively and charming manner, his voyage in a Jewish ship from Egypt to his home city, Cyrene. The Greek Synesios was still a pagan at the time the letter was sent (appr. 404), and only afterwards turned Christian and became Bishop of Ptolemais.

Synesios sailed from Poseidion in the ship of the Jew Amaranthus. The crew numbered thirteen, including seven Jews (with the captain). At this point, Synesios cannot help cursing the Jews heartily: a plague on them for trying to drown a lot of Greeks! The ship carried about fifty passengers, one third of them women, some young and shapely, as Synesios is careful to point out. But let not his friend envy him: men and women were accommodated separately. Of course—he adds casually—the partition separating them was of decayed, unserviceable canvas, but who would harbour lascivious thoughts on Amaranthus's ramshackle vessel!

[1] Comp. Applebaum, *Zion* 19 (1954), p. 25; and especially id. *Greek and Jews*, pp. 62 passim; Kahrstedt, *op. cit.*, p. 226.

[2] Comp. Augustine, Sermo 9, 3, *PL* XXXVIII, 77.

[3] Comp. Iustinian, Novella 37, 5, p. 245, which reaffirms a decree contained in the *Codex Theodosianus* (Juster, *Jews* II, p. 71).

At first, everything went off pleasantly. The sailors were in a cheerful mood: they jokingly called each other names according to their physical defects—for every one of them had some physical defect. However, all of a sudden, a gale blew up. It was on a Friday, and Amaranthus was at the helm. At sunset, the accursed captain, who was also a student of the Law (νομοδιδάσκαλος), left the helm. The passengers at first thought that he had done so from despair, but they soon understood the true reason. The Sabbath had come and he did not wish to profane it with work, and so, instead of minding the helm, he gazed into a book (βιβλίον) and read to the sailors who were of his faith. The entreaties of the Greek passengers and Arab horsemen that he return to the helm fell on deaf ears. The horsemen even threatened to cut off his head, but this true son of the Maccabees was adamant, declaring calmly and fearlessly: It is Sabbath. Only at midnight, when the storm grew stronger and lives were in peril, whose preservation takes precedence over the Sabbath, did the captain seize the helm again. At last, they were out of danger and reached harbour, together with other vessels which had almost foundered. It then appeared that the ship had only one anchor and not the regulation three. The Jew had sold the second in an hour of need, and the third seemed never to have existed.[1]

We have given an epitome of Synesios's lengthy account because it reveals a variety of interesting facts; the engagement of Jews in shipping; the difficult economic position of the shipowner, who is compelled to sell one of this two anchors; his piety and religious learning when on Friday night he abandons the rudder and sits down to read a book—no doubt the Pentateuch or some homiletic work; the deep-seated hatred of the Greeks for the Jews, which appears several times in the story and which disposes them to believe that the captain intends to drown them, as if he and they were not in the same boat.

The shipowner Amaranthus was probably an inhabitant of Cyrene or the western part of North Africa. We know a good deal about Jews engaged in shipping in those days. Maritime trade flourished in Roman not less than in Phoenician Carthage, and Jews seem to have had a part in it. The participation of Alexandrian Jews in maritime trade is attested by an imperial edict sent to the Procurator of Egypt in 390 C.E., mentioning well-to-do Jews required to carry shiploads of grain to Constantinople (Amaranthus's rickety craft was certainly not suitable for such long

[1] Comp. Synesii Ptolemaidis Episcopi *Epistolae*, Ep. 4, *PG* LXVI, 1327-1336; G. Grützmacher, *Synesios von Kyrene*, Leipzig 1913, pp. 75-79.

voyages). Augustine speaks of the freedom of marine shipping enjoyed by Jews.[1]

Amaranthus was hard up, and the farmers of Cyrenaica were not well off, either. But there was no lack of rich Jews in the area, as shown by the story of the three thousand wealthy men executed by Catullus in the revolt after the destruction of the Temple with a view to confiscating their property. We do not know in what that property consisted: whether in immovables, such as estates and houses, or in goods and cash.

The existence of a well-to-do stratum is hinted at also by the remains of the synagogue at Naro and the inscriptions concerning the archons, the *archisynagogos* and the *pater Sinagogae*. Poor people would not have been able to erect a sumptuous synagogue and decorate it with mosaics or to be archons taking time off their businesses to manage the affairs of the community. We know that North Africa developed and prospered under the Roman emperors, despite the economic crises to which it, too, was subject, and was one of the wealthiest countries of the Empire. Apuleius (middle of the second century C.E.) has left instructive descriptions of the life of the wealthy class, and the testimony of the literary sources is confirmed by the remains of public and private buildings. It is not to be assumed that the Jews had no share in this plenty.[2]

Linguistic Assimilation

The references to Sabbath observance, Tora readings and theatres bring us to the intellectual and religious life of North African Jewry. Judging by the epigraphic material—the only direct source in our possession—linguistic assimilation to the environment seems to have been extremely strong. We have quoted two or three published inscriptions in Hebrew script and language; the others are in Latin or in Latin script or, in some cases, in Greek. But the inscriptions discovered at Tocra (see above, p. 36), part of them of the pre-Christian period and part of the first and second centuries C.E., are all in Greek.

Assimilation is conspicuous in names. The resolution of the πολίτευμα

---

[1] Comp. Augustine, *De altercatione*, *PL* XLII, 1132; Tcherikover-Fuks, *CPJ* I, 105; Krauss, *Talmudische Archäologie* II, pp. 338ff.; Hirschberg, *RO* 9 (1933), p. 124. Pompey charged the Jews with piracy, Josephus, *Ant.* XIV, 3, 2, p. 453. Comp. also S. Katz, *The Jews in the Visigothic and Frankish Kingdoms of Spain and Gaul*, 1937, p. 132; Y. Dan, *Zion* 36 (1971), p. 25, n. 173.

[2] It may be appropriate to mention the Jewish artisans referred to by Cosmas Indicopleustes, *Topographia Christiana*, III, *PG* LXXXVIII, 171-172. Comp. also Pezant, *Voyage*, pp. 307-309.

of Berenice in honour of Decimus Valerius (*CIG* 5362) contains no Hebrew name among those preserved in the inscription. In the inscription listing members of the συναγωγή we find one Hebrew name: Ἰωνάθας, and one Aramaic name: Mario (Μάριο[ν]). But we find several Greek names that were very common among the Jews of that period, such as Dositheos, Jason and Alexandros. It is believed that the female name Ζωσιμήτηρ is a Greek translation of "mother of all living" (Eve). In inscription *CIG* 5361 from Berenice, only the ninth archon—in the order of the inscription—has a biblical name: Joseph (the son of Straton) (the name Joseph was frequent also in Egypt). Seven other archons have purely Greek names and one has a Latin-Greek composite name: Marcus Laelius Onassiōn the son of Apollo. which may indicate that he was a Roman citizen. This external assimilation to the Greek environment is particularly noticeable in the Tocra inscriptions.

It is interesting that an inscription in Greek letters on a tombstone found in the cemetery at Chella, at the other end of North Africa, shows a name of the same type: Marcus Aurelios Ptolemaios the Jew. Most probably, that man obtained Roman citizenship under the law of Antoninus (Caracalla) in 212 and, like many others, added to his Greek name the personal name of that emperor: Marcus Aurelius (Antoninus). His Hellenistic name and the Greek script suggest that he or his forebears came from the eastern region, perhaps from Cyrenaica, or even from Egypt. The name Salimos, found in Volubilis in Greek script, is general Semitic; it was used also by the Arabs, and occurs already among the Jews of Elephantine (שלמציון שלם, שלמיה, שלומם, שלום).[1]

No definite conclusions can be drawn from these two Greek inscriptions from the Maghreb, or from a third found there concerning the synagogue of Volubilis (see p. 52 above), but they may be indicative of a wave of immigrants from the eastern region of North Africa, where Greek was still spoken and written and Latin was not used, whereas in the west, Greek was a second official language.

In inscriptions from the central part of our region, the names are Latin, such as Ampliatus, Arnesus, Asterius, Aster, Victorinus, Tatia, Juliana, Licenia, Lucus, Luciosa, Marcus Avilius Ianuarus (or Januarius), Pompeiana, Rusticus, Sabira. Compare also Irene (*CIL* 1091).

The authors of the inscriptions mostly did not try to conceal the religious and national identity of the buried. In comparatively many cases, we find the ethnic appellation "Jew" or "Jewess", as already seen in the case of

[1] Comp. above, p. 61-2.

Marcus Aurelius Ptolemaeus the Jew. Here are some names followed by it from our region: Avilia Aster Iudea, Iulia Victoria Iudea, Iulius Anianus Iudeus, Satia Rupia Iudaea, Pompeius Restutus Iudeus, Profanius Honoratus Iudaeus, Caelia Thalassa Iudaea. The Tocra inscriptions show the name Ιοδα, Ιουδαις twice.[1]

The Gamarth tombstones show the word *shalom*, in Hebrew and Latin script, which likewise indicates the religion of the buried. Extremely frequent is the representation of the seven-branched menorah (candelabrum), the Jewish emblem at that time, which mostly occurs in Palestinian and Italian cemeteries; it appears at the entrance to catacombs and by the side of inscriptions. In Gamarth, on the other hand, a Christian lamp has been found with a representation of Jesus and the cross and an upturned menorah symbolizing Judaism defeated.

The menorah has been discovered twice in Cyrenaica in conspicuous positions, not in connection with graves. Applebaum here regards it as a political symbol of insurrection. We also find it engraved on a column bearing the inscription [*Deus Abr*]*aham Deus Isac* at Henchir Fuara (*CIL Suppl.* 16701) on the Tunisian-Algerian border, *i.e.* very far from Cyrenaica.[2]

We sometimes find in inscriptions the name *shamayim* (Heaven) in different forms; but this, as we shall see below, is not yet proof of the Jewishness of the persons referred to.

Religious Life

We have mentioned above the synagogue of Naro and the donors who contributed mosaics for its decoration. These donors include a young woman (*puella*) named Iulia. Hence women, too, were instructed in Jewish religion and no doubt also in Greek wisdom. The education of girls was particularly widespread in Africa.

[1] The problem of the names used by Jews is discussed by Tcherikover, *Jews*, 233, 239-240, also 203-4; comp. also Gray, *Inscriptions*, pp. 43-56; Applebaum, *Teucheira*, pp. 49-51.

[2] The symbol of the *menorah* occurs in *CIL* VIII, 12457, p. 1284, along with the *shofar*, the *lulab* and the *ethrog* (for the reading of the second name in this inscription comp. Diehl, *Inscriptiones* II, p. 41; Merlin, *Inscriptions*, p. 171). Comp. also *CIL* 12457, 14102, 14104 (also *lulab* and *ethrog*), 14191, 16701, 22644-243; see also 16701. For the lamp with the upturned *menorah* see Delattre, Gamarth, pp. 40-42. For the *menorah* as a symbol in Cyrenaica comp. Applebaum, *Eretz-Israel*, 6 (1961), pp. 73-76. It should be noted that according to Slouschz, *Travels*, p. 206, Tripolitanian Jews used to swear by the *menorah*.

The inscriptions of the mosaics in that synagogue refer to *instrumenta*, *i.e.* Tora scrolls and perhaps also other sacred writings that were kept there. There were also secular libraries in North Africa, though not such large ones as in other parts of the Empire.

We know that Sitifis had a synagogue (No. 8499, see above p. 64). The stories of the Christian women saints, Marciana and Salsa, reveal incidentally the existence of synagogues at Caesarea and Tipasa. Budarius, who incites the mob against Marciana, is the archisynagogos, and if there was a synagogue head or synagogue elder, there must have been a synagogue. The story of Salsa says that the synagogue at Tipasa had been erected in the place of a pagan sanctuary; afterwards the Christians had converted the synagogue into a church, in spite of strong opposition from the Jews. This permits the conclusion that the synagogue was favourably located and a building worth fighting for. Tertullian complains that the synagogues were the starting-points for the persecution of the Christians. He no doubt means the anti-Christian propaganda conducted there, but also the instruction given to the Jews to enable them to reply to the arguments of their opponents. However, nothing is known to us from Jewish sources as to the nature and forms of that instruction.[1]

It is common knowledge that religious life in the Diaspora was bound up with the Holy Land and with the Temple so long as it existed. The connection of Cyrene, Carthage and the rest of North Africa with Palestine was in fact quite strong.

Jason of Cyrene went to Palestine during the Hasmonaean revolt and wrote a book in five volumes about it. As we have already noted, the Cyrenians complained to the Emperor Augustus of attempts to prevent the sending of the half-shekel to the Temple, won their case and obtained the discontinuance of restrictive practices.

It is certainly accidental that the memory of Libyan Jews making pilgrimages to the Temple is preserved only in the Acts of the Apostles (2:10). They had a synagogue in their name in Jerusalem (*ibid.* 6:9). Some of these pilgrims settled in Jerusalem, such as Simon the Cyrenian, who according to the New Testament, as a chance passerby just arrived from the country, was forced to take part in the Crucifixion.[2] It is not surprising that a tombstone—inscribed in Greek—of one Reuben the

---

[1] Comp. *Salsae passio*, published in *Catalogus Codicum Hagiographicorum qui asservantur in Bibl. Nat. Parisiensi*, t. I, p. 346, 3; also St. Gsell, *De Tipasa, Mauretaniae Caesariensis Urbe*, 1894, p. 13; L. Leschi, *Etudes d'Épigraphie, d'Archéologie et d'Histoire Africaines*, Paris 1957, pp. 412-419. For Tertullian see below pp. 72ff.

[2] Matt. 27, 32; Mark 15, 21; Luke 23, 26.

son of Jacob, of the Pentapolis, should have been discovered in Palestine.[1] The assumption that the settlers in Cyrene may have included Palestinians has already been mentioned. The ties of the Cyrenaicans with Palestine may have been the reason why a good many of them—especially, perhaps, Judaizers—were accessible to Christian propaganda.[2]

Through the Eyes of Christian Ecclesiastical Writers: Tertullian and Minucius

An important supplementary source of information on North African Jewry are the writings of Christian ecclesiastical authors in the area. Their religious views, polemical utterances and replies to various arguments, and even their openly hostile remarks, reflect the image of that Jewry—though mostly in a distorted form, which requires straightening out. The source of inspiration of the Early Fathers were in most cases the anti-Jewish Alexandrian writers.

The first of this series of authors was the earliest Christian writer in the Latin language, Tertullian, a Roman jurist born in Carthage—the son of an army officer—who became a Christian in adulthood. The second was Minucius Felix, a contemporary of Tertullian. He, too, was a native of Africa who settled in Rome, and the characters in his only extant work, *Octavianus*, which is in the form of a disputation on Christianity between a Christian and some idolaters, are Africans.

These two authors wrote in the days of the Severi, Septimius and his son Caracalla, who both took a harsh attitude towards Christianity. Tertullian and Minucius had to fight on several fronts: argue with Jews and Judaizers, struggle against the religion and concepts of the Greco-Roman world, and dissociate themselves from the many heretics within the Christian camp. In fact, Tertullian himself ran afoul of the official views of the Church.

Jewry at that time enjoyed a political lull after the turbulent seventy years from Vespasian to Hadrian. Tertullian's position in his debate with the Jews was uncomfortable in many respects. The Jewish religion was recognized—or at least tolerated—officially, and the Jews were Roman citizens, who must not be incited against or slandered. Moreover, despite their hostility to the Jews, the Christian writers had to defend the Old

---

[1] Comp. Clermont-Ganneau, *Archaeological Researches in Palestine*, II, 143-144. For new finds in the Kidron Valley traced to Cyrenaica comp. Avigad, *IEJ*, 12 (1962), pp. 4-12.

[2] According to Acts 11, 20 and 13, 1, the Cyrenaicans propagated Christianity. But the explanation of a strange inscription in Cyrene as a Christian monogram does not seem very probable; comp. Gray, *Inscriptions*, p. 59.

Testament against various criticism, because an attack against it was an attack against Christianity, and in defending it they used arguments used before by the Jews.

Tertullian boasts that the Christians are numerous in the world, while the Jews are scattered, fugitive and vagabond, and without a leader.[1] This does not prevent him from holding the Jews responsible for all the sufferings of the Christians and claiming that the synagogues are the starting-points of their persecution (*fontes persecutionum*).[2] Tertullian does not here explain the nature of this persecution; he certainly does not mean physical attack.[3]

Echoes of Jewish-Christian Disputations

Particulars of that alleged persecution are given in other places. Both Tertullian and Minucius mention a charge against the Christians which in previous generations had been preferred against the Jews, and which over a thousand years later was again preferred against the Jews in Europe, viz. the blood libel.

In his tract *Ad Nationes*, Tertullian says: "New slanderous reports are being spread about our God. Not long ago, some scoundrel walked the streets of this city with a figure underneath which was written ὀνοκοίτης (he that sleeps with a donkey). He (that scoundrel) is a traitor to his own religion, a Jew only in that he has no foreskin—and this perhaps only owing to the bite of the animals to (fight) which he hires himself, and he trembles every day. The figure has the ears of a beast of burden; it wears a toga and is holding a book; one of its feet is cloven. The mob believed the Jew. What other race could be the source of the malicious reports about us? And now the whole town greets us with the cry: He that sleeps with a donkey!"[4]

A few months later, Tertullian deems it necessary to revert to this subject in his tract *Apologeticus pro Christianis*: "It seems to you, as to others, that our God is a donkey's head"; and he refers to Tacitus, who had tried to explain why the Jews worship a donkey. In the later part of the chapter, he refutes the charge that the Christians worship the sun: "And if we devote the day of the sun (Sunday) to pleasure, we do so for other reasons than sun worship. We are next after those (scil. the Jews) who

[1] *Apologeticus*, 37, 1, *PL* II (ed. 1844, col. 461-464; ed. 1879, col. 524-526).

[2] *Ibid.*, 21, 1, *PL* I (ed. 1844, col. 394; ed. 1879, col. 451).

[3] *Adversus Gnosticos Scorpiace*, 10, *PL* II (ed. 1844, col. 143; ed. 1879, col. 166).

[4] *Ad Nat.*, 1, 14, *PL* I (ed. 1844, col. 579; ed. 1879, col. 650-651). About the donkcy worship in North Africa (Morocco) see E. Doutté, *Magie*, pp. 563-4.

devote the day of Saturn (Saturday) to rest and eating... But lately, a new form (*editio*) of our God was presented in this city when a voluntary hired *bestiarius* displayed a figure with the inscription *Deus Christianorum* ὀνοκοίτης ('the God of the Christians, who sleeps with a donkey'). It had donkey's ears etc. We laughed both at the name and the figure."

A clear reference to the report that the Christians worship a donkey is made by Apuleius, a pagan poet living in Africa in those days who left many descriptions of features of real life. One of his poems tells of a Christian woman who fell in love with a donkey.[1]

In Minucius's work, which is later than Tertullian's *Apologeticus*, the pagan African, in the course of the disputation, utters a series of extremely grave accusations against Christianity. The Christians are steeped in vice: they sleep with their sisters and mothers; and they worship a crucified man. "I understand that on the strength of some foolish belief they revere the head of the donkey, which disgusting animal is sacred to them." "A worthy religion, in keeping with such customs," he concludes with biting irony. He also mentions the manner in which new converts are allegedly initiated into the mysteries of the Christian religion: the neophyte unwittingly stabs to death an infant covered with flour; thereafter all the participants in the ceremony lick the blood and eat the limbs. This ensures the keeping of the covenant, the silence which prevents treason. Similar accusations are mentioned by Tertullian.[2]

It is known that Apion, who was of Libyan extraction, levels similar charges at the Jews, telling stories of a golden donkey's head and of a Greek whom the Jews fatten every year in order to sacrifice him, to taste his entrails and to swear hatred to all Greeks; both features were alleged to have been encountered by Antiochus Epiphanes in the Temple in Jerusalem.[3]

How came it that these two stories were transferred to the Christians in

---

[1] *Apol.*, 16, 1, *PL* I (ed. 1844, col. 364; ed. 1879, col. 420). For Apuleius comp. *D. Ar. Ch.* I, 2044 (*s.v. âne*).

[2] Minucius Felix, *Octavianus*, 9, *PL* III (ed. 1844, col. 261-262; ed. 1879, col. 271-272); *D. Ar. Ch.* XI, 1388-1412, esp. 1396-1397. Comp. also Quispel, *Vigiliae Christianae*, 3 (1949), pp. 120-121; Monceaux, *Hist. Littér. de l'Afrique chrétienne*, 1901, I, p. 39; J. H. van Haeringen, *Mnemosyne*, Ser. III, vol. 3 (1935-1936), pp. 29-32; Tertull., *Ad Nat.*, 1, 7, *PL* I, 569 (639); *Apol.* 7, *PL* 307-311 (358-363); *De Jejuniis*, 17, *PL* II, 977 (1029).

[3] Comp. Josephus, *Against Apion*, 2, 7, 9, p. 325. Bickermann, *MGWJ*, 71 (1927), pp. 171-187, 255-264, reviews the Greek sources of these accusations; comp. also Heinemann, *PW*, Suppl. vol. 5, *s.v. Antisemitismus*, col. 20-21, 28-29; Tcherikover, *Civilization*, p. 365; R. Neher-Bernheim, The Libel of Jewish Ass-Worship, *Zion* 28 (1963), pp. 106-15.

North Africa, and who brought this about? As for the donkey cult, Tertullian says expressly that this "novelty" (*nova*) was the invention of a renegade Jew, whom the common people believed. The absence of the anti-Jewish element in the second version of the story shows that Tertullian did not always deem it necessary to point out the origin of the libel, and he certainly meant incitement and propaganda, and not actual persecution.[1] The date of the first mention of the blood libel, the middle of the 2nd century C.E., may help to understand the atmosphere of mutual accusations and hatred then prevailing in Africa. It was after the two great revolts, when Hellenistic propaganda was busy spreading atrocity stories about the Jews, such as we find in Dio Cassius and in the naive letter of that old woman who prayed the gods that the Jews might not roast her son; as we have seen, there were still other, less dangerous, but no less venomous propaganda stories. The Jews thereupon engaged in counter-propaganda: the Palestinian scholars in their own particular way, by means of *midrashim* and *aggadot*, and the Alexandrian scholars and heads of the Cyrenaican communities, who had left their places of residence and moved to prosperous North Africa, in theirs. The waves of Hellenistic Jewish immigrants swelled in the second half of the century, and as soon as they had established themselves in the country, they began to take action against their enemies. But just as anti-Jewish propaganda was sometimes conducted through people who were not aware of its Alexandrian origin, thus those who brought forward anti-Christian allegations did not always know that they had originally been anti-Jewish.[2]

The Charge of Proselytizing

Tertullian accuses the Jews of making propaganda for the adoption of their religious precepts: the keeping of their festivals and Sabbaths, the lighting of candles on the Sabbath, the eating of ritually pure food, the observance of fasts and the holding of prayer services by some body of water.[3] He is particularly incensed at the Gentiles who adopt Jewish

[1] The Jews accused the Christians of worshipping a human being; *Apol.* 21, 1, *PL* I, 392 (450).

[2] Comp. Bickermann, *MGWJ*, 71 (1927), p. 177. Bickermann does not explain why this propaganda spread to North Africa.

[3] *Ad Nationes*, 1, 13, *PL* I, 579 (650); comp. Josephus, *Apion* II, 39 (282); *Ant.*, III, 9 (217); also Augustine, *De Civitate Dei*, *PL* XLI, 192-193.

customs, who celebrate the Sabbath in the Jewish manner and refrain from various occupations on that day.[1] Elsewhere he explains the nature of the fast practised by Jews wherever resident, and notes that since the destruction of the Temple they have been sending their prayers heavenwards from every shore and every open space.[2] The reference is to prayers at public fasts, which were recited in the streets of the cities (Mishna *Ta'anit* II, 1). Indeed, he remarks that Jews always pray in public and aloud, and what he says about the inner thoughts of the Christians at prayer undoubtedly applies to the Jews as well.[3] Sabbath observance and circumcision are regarded by him as the most characteristic of Jewish religious practices. Tertullian reverts to this subject several times, and Augustine and Synesios likewise regard the Sabbath as the main dividing wall between Jews and Gentiles.[4] Tertullian once has occasion to commend the modesty of Jewish women, who are distinguishable by the veil with which they cover their heads.[5]

In Tertullian's view, many adhered to Judaism because Christianity was forbidden by law and must hide "in the shadow of the permitted religion (... *religionis, certe licitae* ...)".[6] This was not to his liking, and he deemed it necessary to attack Judaism and demonstrate its worthlessness in a polemical tract, *Adversus Judaeos*, in which he enumerates the calamities that befell Israel: the destruction of the Temple and devastation of the country; the dispersion of the people among the Gentiles; the prohibition of Jews from entering Palestine even as visitors.[7] Obviously, Tertullian would not have fought the Jews so bitterly, would not have debated with them in several books, unless they had been a dangerous enemy, led by keen-witted scholars, well equipped to win adherents for their faith. Even proselytes to Judaism were trained in apologetics, and Tertullian gives details—no doubt historical—of a debate between a proselyte and some Christians as to whether the Gentiles had part in the

[1] *De Jejuniis*, 16, *PL* II, 976 (1828). J. Toutain, in his thesis, *De Saturni Dei in Africa Romana Cultu*, Paris 1894, shows that Saturn worship existed in Africa. Tertullian's attacks were probably directed against both Jews and Saturn worshippers. Comp. also above, p. 54.

[2] *Apol.* 19, *PL* I, 381 (473); *ibid.*, 30, I, 442 (504).

[3] *Ibid.*, 16, I, 371-372 (427-428).

[4] *De Oratione*, 23, I, 1191 (1298); *Adv. Jud.* 2, II, 601 (639-640); *ibid.*, 3, II, 603 (641). On Synesios see above, p. 66. Comp. Tcherikover-Fuks, *CPJ* I, pp. 94-95.

[5] *De Corona* 4, II, 80 (100).

[6] *Apolog.* 21, I, 392 (449-450).

[7] *Adv. Judaeos* 13, II, 634-638 (673-678), also 8, 616 (656); *Apolog.* 21, I, 394 (400). Comp. also *Adv. Marcionem* 3, 23, II, 353-355 (382-383).

divine blessings promised to Abraham's posterity (Gen. 22:18). The debate lasted inconclusively until evening.[1]

Tertullian debated with the Jews and combated their influence on their surroundings. But he respected and appreciated the Jewish Bible, whose wisdom was older than that of the Greeks.[2] Moreover, he was influenced by aggadic and halakhic *midrashim*, and his writings contain many biblical interpretations and homiletic expositions borrowed from or directed against the Talmud. In his opinion, the first command issued to Adam, not to eat of the Tree of Knowledge, contained all the commandments afterwards issued to Moses.[3]

We have already mentioned that the spoliation of Egypt was a subject of anti-Jewish polemics in the days of R. Akiba, who deemed it necessary to disavow it, pointing out that the booty eventually became a serious stumbling-block to the Israelites. Tertullian brings up the matter of the spoliation in his debate with the Gnostic Marcion. "They (the Marcionites) reproach the Creator for the artful theft of gold and silver vessels which he enjoined upon the Hebrews to the detriment of the Egyptians ... The Egyptians claim from the Hebrews the return of the gold and silver vessels. The Hebrews make a counterclaim, asserting, by the right of their forefathers and in reliance on the same biblical passage, that wages are owing to them for the work done by those in making bricks and building towns and villages".[4] Tertullian and the Jews here make a common front against the Gnostic attack upon the ethics of the Old Testament; his reply corresponds exactly with the words of the Book of Jubilees and Geviha ben Pesisa's defence in the Talmud (cf. above p. 41).

It is not by accident that the subjects debated by R. Yehuda ha-Nasi and Antoninus, and which the Talmud (*San.* 91b) places immediately after the debates before Alexander, are dealt with also by Tertullian. They were matters at issue between Greco-Roman philosophers on the one hand and Judaism and Christianity on the other. In the debate as to whether the soul is given to man at the time it is decreed what the germ

---

1 *Adv. Judaeos* I, II, 597-598 (635-637).

2 *Apolog.* 18-19, I, 377-378 (433-434), and hence a spiritual kinship between Judaism and Christianity; *ibid.*, 15, I, 357-363; comp. Bergmann, *Apologetik*, p. 92.

3 *Adv. Jud.* 2, II, 599 (637); comp. B. Murmelstein, Biblical Agadot in the Works of Tertullian, *Minḥat Bikkurim*, Vienna 1926, pp. 30-46 (Hebrew). We have to content ourselves with the briefest hints at this subject.

4 *Adv. Marcionem* 2, 20, II, 308-309 (335-336), also *ibid.*, 4, 24, II, 308-309 (335-336), 418 (448). Comp. also F. Ferrère, *La situation religieuse de l'Afrique Romaine depuis la fin du IVe siècle etc.* (thesis), Paris 1897, pp. 274-278.

in the womb is to grow into or at the time it is first wholly covered with flesh, sinews and bones, R. Yehuda agrees with Antoninus that it is given at the former time and adduces a supporting biblical passage (Job 4:12). Tertullian, in his tract *De anima, adversus philosophos,* discusses whether —as assumed by the Stoics and the physician Hegesias of Cyrene—the soul joins the body only at the time of birth or already at the time of conception. He arrives at the same conclusion as Antoninus and R. Yehuda. As to punishment on Judgment Day, R. Yehuda explains to Antoninus that "God brings the soul, throws it into the body and judges them together", and this is also Tertullian's view in his treatise *De resurrectione carnis.*[1]

It is not to be assumed that Jewish and Christian sources on this subject are independent of each other. Nor does it seem likely that the Talmudic sages used Tertullian's arguments. What is probable is that he knew the subjects of certain religious discussions appearing in the Talmud ("Some heretics asked Rabban Gamliel" etc., Sanhedrin 90b-91b), and also the contentions of the parties. His writings show that he was familiar with the Talmudic *aggadot* and sometimes took exception to them.

He challenges the view that the world was created out of something pre-existent and that the angels had a part in this act. In truth, he says, the angels disappeared before the creation of the world.[2] The creation of the world and of Adam is explained by him along the lines of the Aggada.[3] A subject of controversy is the quarrel between Cain and Abel. Cain, the elder brother, whose offering God had rejected, symbolizes Judaism, whereas Abel, the younger, who was murdered by his brother (an allusion to the Crucifixion), symbolizes Christianity. Cain was born in uncleanliness; he was of the seed of Satan.[4] Enoch, on the other hand, was a prophet.[5] The episodes of the sons of the gods and the daughters of man,[6] the serpent of brass and Joshua the High Priest (Zech. 3:3) are

---

[1] *De Anima* etc. 25, II, 690-691 (732-733); comp. *ibid.*, 43, II, 721-724 (765-768), *De Resurrectione* etc. 15, II, 813-814 (859-860), and *ibid.*, 12, II, 810-811 (856-857). For this note and the following ones comp. also Bergmann, *Apologetik, passim.*

[2] *Adv. Hermogenem* 32, II, 227-228 (251-252); *ibid.*, 34, II, 228 (253-254). Comp. Aptowitzer, Festskrift Simonsen, Copenhagen 1923, pp. 112ff. and esp. p. 116.

[3] *Adv. Marc.* 2, 10, II, 297 (323).

[4] *De Patientia* 5, I, 1258 (1369). For the preference of the younger (Christianity) comp. Irenaeus, *Adv. Haer.* 4, 21, 3, *PG* VII, 1045-1046; Augustine, *Contra Faustum*, 12, 9, *PL* XLII, 258-259. Comp. also Aptowitzer, *Kain und Abel in der Agada*, 1922, pp. 23-24, 129-131.

[5] De Idolatria 15, I, 684 (761); *De Cultu Fem.* 1, 3, I, 1307-1308 (1421-1422).

[6] *De Idolatria* 9, I, 671 (747); *De Virginibus* 7, II, 899 (947); comp. L. Ginzberg, *Legends* V, 154-155. Bergmann, *Apologetik*, p. 97, quotes *Adv. Marc.* 2, 27, II, 316-318 (343-345), about the descent of God to man.

symbols of Jesus.[1] Another subject of polemics is the story according to which King Solomon ruled the whole world, this being the prerogative of Jesus.[2]

The influence of the *halakha* is felt in Tertullian's *De Idolatria*, as has been demonstrated extensively by J. Bergmann, F. Y. Baer and E. E. Urbach. Tertullian opposes Christian participation, in public or in private, in anything smacking of idolatry. No pagan festivals or family celebrations may be taken part in if they involve anything like recognition of pagan gods. Tertullian deprecates all handicrafts connected with the manufacture of idols of whatever shape or material, as well as the trading in idols and in any adjunct of idolatry, such as incense. A Christian should not be a teacher because this occupation will compel him to devote his first salary to the goddess of knowledge and wisdom and to use books containing many stories of gods and goddesses.[3]

Unlike the early Christians in the East, who were of Jewish origin, those in North Africa came mainly from pagan circles, where idolatry was widely practised and its influence in everyday life sometimes difficult to recognise. The fight against it therefore seemed imperative. In his sharp polemics against idolatry, Tertullian was able to point to the struggle of the prophets against false gods, and to their vision of a day when carven images and their worship would have vanished from the world.

Two hundred years later, Augustine reverts to this subject in a different historical context. The dispersion of the Jews over all countries and nations, he says, is an act of divine favour towards the Christians. After the statues, altars, groves and sanctuaries of the false gods have been destroyed and their sacrifices prohibited, it can now be shown from the scriptures of the Jews that their prophets predicted this in days of yore; if these prophecies were found in Christian scriptures, they would possibly be regarded as a Christian invention.[4]

Tertullian's tract *De Spectaculis*, directed against visits to theatres, circuses and the like, may also have been influenced by the Talmud. Like the latter, it interprets Psalm 1, 1 as referring to those who do not sit in theatres. The warning: "Neither shall ye walk in their ordinances (Lev. 18, 2)—do not resort to their institutions, the things ordained for

---

[1] *Adv. Jud.* 10, 11, 629 (667-668); *De Idolatria* 5, I, 667 (743); comp. Ginzberg, *Legends* VI, 115.

[2] *Adv. Jud.* 7, II, 611 (650). Comp. Cant. R. 1, 10 (3a); Est. R. 1, 5; Meg. 11b.

[3] *De Idolatria*, I, 662-695 (738-774). Comp. Bergmann, *Apologetik*, pp. 11-24; Baer, *Zion* 21 (1956), pp. 1-13; Urbach, *Eretz-Israel* 5 (1959), pp. 202-204.

[4] *De Civitate Dei* 4, 34, *PL* XLI, 140.

them, such as theatres, circuses and stadia" (*Sifra*, Aḥarey Mot XIII, ed. Weiss 86a)—was timely for Jews as well. We have already mentioned that Augustine reproves them for spending their Sabbaths in theatres. Once, indeed, he holds up as an example to his hearers the Jews of Simitthu, now called Chemtou (a townlet near Hippo, his seat of office), who refrain from visiting such places.[1] Let us note incidentally that in Chemtou, according to testimony of seventy years ago, the ruins of a building of the Byzantine or Roman period (near the famous marble quarries) used to be known as Ṣelā al-Yahūd (the synagogue of the Jews).[2]

As stated, Tertullian was the first of the ecclesiastical writers who were active in the western part of the Maghreb. He acquired his legal training in Carthage. While he himself says that he has been to Rome, we are not aware that he ever visited the seats of learning in the East. It is difficult to assume that his knowledge of the Aggada and Halakha stemmed from the few earlier Christian writers in the East, such as the notable polemists Theophilos of Antioch and Justus of Neapolis, a contemporary of R. Akiba. He probably derived that knowledge from the same circles whose influence on Christians and pagans he combated with all his might. These circles were in close contact with the *tannaim* in Palestine; it was they who spread Jewish learning in Carthage in the days of Rab (R. Abba Arikha), and their sons went to Palestine for study. Tertullian thus gives a picture, though an unsympathetic one, of North African Jewry and some conception of the extent of their religious learning.

Tertullian's contemporary Minucius Felix, who settled in Rome, refrained from attacking the Jews directly and confined himself to incidental strictures. An analysis of his *Octavianus* shows that in refuting the arguments of the pagan opponents of Christianity he used the apologetic weapons prepared by Jews two or three generations earlier (Josephus Flavius). He himself says that he is acquainted with the translation of the Old Testament and with the writings of Josephus and of Antoninus Julianus, an author not otherwise known. *Octavianus* betrays also the influence of apocryphal writings embodying views derived from Jewish sources.[3]

---

[1] *De Spectaculis* I, 627-662 (702-738), esp. chap. 3, 634 (708); Augustine, *Sermo* 9, *PL* XXXVIII, 77; *ibid.*, *Sermo* 17, *PL* XLVI, 880-881. The halakhic sources are quoted by Baer, *op. cit.*, p. 12. According to ecclesiastical writers, Jews would go to the theatre; Bergmann, *op. cit.*, pp. 17-19; Tcherikover-Fuks, *CPJ*, p. 109.

[2] On this locality comp. Cazès, *Essai*, p. 41.

[3] Comp. Quispel, *Vigiliae Christianae* 3 (1949), pp. 113-122; Monceaux, *REJ* 44 (1902), p. 19, n. 7.

The Polemics of Ecclesiastical Writers Subsequent to Tertullian

In the generation following Tertullian, Cyprianus was elected bishop of the Carthaginian eparchy. He, too, was the author of some anti-Jewish writings, but it seems that relations between the two communities had straightened out somewhat; according to Augustine, the Jews bore him no ill-will.[1]

The writings of Augustine, a native of Africa who adopted Christianity in adulthood and became Bishop of Hippo Regius, contains few passages permitting conclusions as to the life of African Jewry. But one general and rather casual remark is worthy of note: "The Jews, although vanquished by the Romans, nevertheless did not disappear. All the peoples subdued by the Romans adopted the Roman laws; this nation was vanquished, but has nevertheless adhered to its own law and observed its ancestral religion and customs in everything relating to divine worship."[2] From this remark, we may infer that the Jews of Africa, too, had preserved their moral energy and loyalty to their ancient heritage. Augustine's *Tractatus adversus Judaeos*, which tried to demonstrate that the Tora should not be observed in the way it was by them, proved ineffective.[3]

In his *Epistle to Jerome*, Augustine criticizes the Greek translation of the Old Testament prepared by the former, charging him with inadequate knowledge of the Hebrew language and insufficient attention to the Septuagint. In this connection, he relates an incident which occurred in the city of Oea (Tripoli). The local bishop read to his congregation the Book of Jonah in Jerome's translation, which had then become accepted. When they came to the verse "And God prepared a gourd (*qiqāyōn*)" (4:6), the rendering of the word *qiqāyōn* caused a stir among the hearers, who knew the Septuagint and regarded the new translation as a distortion of the text.The embarrassed bishop was compelled to call in the Jews as experts because they possessed the Hebrew original, and the Jews rejected Jerome's rendering. The bishop thereupon corrected the translation. We may thus conclude that there were Jewish scholars in the city whose opinion the bishop was prepared to accept.[4] In the letter of Syne-

[1] Comp. *Sermo* 310, 1, *PL* XXXVIII, 1413; Julien, *Histoire* I, 201-207; Baer, *Zion* 21 (1957), p. 13.

[2] *Sermo* 374, *PL* XXXIX, 1667 (Augustine was well acquainted with the Jews who lived in his town); *Sermo* 196, XXXVIII, 1021.

[3] *Tractatus*, *PL* XII, 51-64. Augustine wrote a very indifferent dialogue on the conflict between the Church and the Jewish community; *ibid.*, 1131-1140.

[4] *Epist.* 71, 3, 5, *PL* XXXIII, 242-243. Comp. also Jerome's reply to Augustine, *Epist.* 112, *ibid.*, XXII, 930.

sios, a contemporary of Augustine and Jerome, we have already met the impecunious ship's captain who is at home in Scripture and on Friday night pulls out a biblical book and reads it.

In *De Civitate Dei*, Augustine reports a miracle—one of many—which happened at the shrine of St. Stephen in Uzali near Utica. A certain Petronia, described as *clarissima* (*i.e.* belonging to the senatorial class), of noble birth and a nobleman's wife, who owned an estate near Carthage, was suffering from a protracted weakness which the doctors were unable to cure. A Jew persuaded her to buy a little ring and tie it to her body with a girdle of hair under her clothing. The ring contained a charm, a stone which had been found in the kidney of an ox. But when she came to Uzali, the charm fell off without the girdle having been untied. We thus meet here a Jewish dealer in amulets, no doubt one of many. He probably lived in Carthage—at any rate not, as has been suggested, in Uzali.[1]

Augustine's book contains few aggadic elements. He has heard, for instance, that the Book of the Generations of Adam (Gen. 5:1) contains all wisdom, although he does not know where this is indicated in the Bible,[2] and he also knows the Jewish tradition of Adam's wives.[3] He is particularly interested in the legends of Cain and Abel on account of their importance for a controversy with the Jews, already known to us from Tertullian's writings.[4] Abraham, too, plays an important part in Christian propaganda.[5] It seems that Augustine, who was addressing a Gentile public, utterly unfamiliar with Jewish homiletic literature, deliberately avoided using such material.

Judaizers

Notwithstanding the fight of African Christians against Judaism and the difficult political situation of the latter, Jewish teaching still found willing ears among the pagan inhabitants. There was no large-scale conversion movement, but an infiltration of concepts and beliefs that fell on fertile soil among a population heterogeneous in every respect: ethnic origin, language, ideas and political relationships. In fact, we may

---

[1] *De Civitate Dei* 22, 21, *PL* XLI, 768-769. The custom of setting an amulet in a ring is confirmed by Tosef. Shab. V, 9.

[2] *Questiones in Exodum* 69, XXXIV, 620.

[3] *Contra Adversarium Legis* 2, 5, XLII, 649; comp. Ginzberg, *Haggada*, p. 60, n. 3.

[4] Comp. H. Gutmann, *Semitic Studies in Memory of Immanuel Löw*, Budapest 1947, pp. 272-276; V. Aptowitzer, *Kain und Abel*, pp. 9-10, 120.

[5] Comp. *Epist.* 196, *PL* XXXIII, 891.

conclude from Augustine's utterances that the Byzantine Province (Central Tunisia) numbered many Judaizers in this time precisely among the Christians.[1]

Epigraphic evidence of Judaizers was found by Monceaux on a tombstone from Henchir Djouana, on which bereaved parents express their belief in Judgment Day and the hereafter. The inscription is in Latin and in the metre of an elegy. Monceaux does not think that the authors of the inscription were Jews, but he finds very definite Jewish influences in it.[2]

An inscription: [*fidel*]*is metu*[*endum*] "the faithful one among those who fear" was discovered at Ksour el-Ghenaia in the Aurès Mountains.[3] That title suggests a Judaizer or convert to Judaism, and the use of the Latin language indicates the period.

In Augustine's days, the *Caelicolae* ("heaven-worshippers") gained ground in North Africa, and he invited their leader for a disputation.[4] They seem to have been a Christian heretical sect influenced to some extent by Judaism. Laws enacted at that time against *apostates* dealt extensively with that sect. The factual material in our possession concerning the "heaven-worshippers" is insufficient to decide whether their name indicates any ideological (not historical) affinity between them and the worshippers of *the lord of heaven and earth*, *the merciful one in heaven* or *the master of heaven and earth* in approximately contemporary South Arabian inscriptions. The authors of the latter were undoubtedly Judaizers, and many of them ultimately became Jews, while others embraced Islam upon the appearance of Muhammad. But according to available data, we must deprecate any attempt to draw even partial analogies between the South Arabian situation and African affairs. All we can say is that a sect of *heaven-worshippers* existed who were persecuted by the official church like the Jews and Donatists.[5]

An important source enabling us to trace the Judaizing movement are the poems of Commodianus, a bishop of African origin, whose biographical particulars are obscure. He is assigned by some to the third and fourth centuries, by others to the fifth. Some think that he was at first a Judaizer and then became a Christian and a bishop, whereupon he

---

[1] *Epist.* 196, 1, 4; *PL* XXXIII, 891-892, 897-899; comp. Baron, *SRH* II, pp. 149-150.

[2] *R. Ar.* 1902, pp. 208-226.

[3] *CIL* 4321.

[4] Comp. *Epist.* 44, 6, 13, *PL* XXXIII, 180. See also above, p. 54.

[5] This is too wide a subject to be dealt with here; comp. Honorius's laws of 408 C.E. against the *caelicolae*, *PL* XI, 1218, 1220. Comp. Juster, *Juifs* I, pp. 177, 274-275; Tcherikover, *Jews*, p. 254. For the South Arabian inscriptions comp. Hirschberg, *Israel be-ʿArab*, 1946, pp. 61ff.

began to attack Jews and Judaizers. He spent the latter part of his life in Gaza.

In his "Confessions", Commodianus mocks the Judaizing Gentiles, who cannot find their way: Why do you rush to synagogue, to the Pharisees (*v.l.*: splitting yourself in two)? To win the mercy of him whom you deny in the end? From there, you go to where carven images are, you wish to live between the two; but you will perish! And in another poem: How so? You wish to be half a Jew and half a Gentile? But you will not escape the judgment of Christ after your death.

To hit the Judaizers, Commodianus, in his *Carmen Apologeticum*, lashes out at the Jews, who are unable to see the truth. He mocks at their customs, their propaganda, their belief that they are the chosen people. Was it not they that sawed to pieces the Prophet Isaiah, stoned Jeremiah, beheaded John the Baptist, strangled Zechariah and crucified Jesus? Also, it was they who incited Nero to persecute the Christians. Commodianus's attacks upon Jewry are more stinging and violent than Tertullian's and undoubtedly made an impression.[1]

The story of St. Marciana seems to have likewise been intended to impress Judaizers. Whatever its degree of historicity, the conditions described in it are certainly those of real-life Caesarea (Cherchel). A young woman, Marciana, smashed the statue of Diana which had been erected in a public place. She was arrested and held at the gladiators' school near the amphitheatre. The archi-synagogus Budarius lived close by. This notable and the local Jews incited the populace against Marciana and were punished for it by God. The moment Marciana died a martyr's death, fire fell from heaven and destroyed Budarius's house and all its inhabitants.[2]

Belief in Talismans and Magical "Names"

We have heard the story of the noble Petronia, who bought a supposedly health-giving charm from a Jew. This report by Augustine leads us to a sphere of belief common to the majority of mankind, viz. charms and incantations. The pagan Roman aristocracy, the highest social order in the state, was not alone in believing in the power of such devices. Augustine

---

[1] Comp. Instructiones 1, 24, *PL* V, 219; *ibid.*, 1, 37, *PL* V, 229; Juster, *Juifs* I, 275, n. 3. For Carmen apologeticum, I have to rely on Monceaux, *REJ* 44 (1902), p. 21; Juster, *op. cit.*, p. 294, n. 5.

[2] *Acta Marcianae* IV-VI, in *Acta Sanctorum*, Antverpiae anno 1643, I, pp. 568-570: De S. Marciana, virgine martyre Caesareae in Mauretania, IX Januarii.

himself would not have denounced the amulet-seller had he been a Christian. In fact, his account is designed to show that the dead St. Stephen is more powerful than the living Jew.

For even this sphere, which would seem to be syncretistic and universal, was drawn into the whirlpool of the Jewish-Christian controversy within the pagan world, and a kind of competition sprang up between Jewish and Christian "names experts" as to whose magical "name" was the more efficacious one. Many men and women resorted to supernatural "demonic" forces, both pure and impure, which were mobilized by means of various "names", so as to bring good luck and ward off evil from the applicants or, on the contrary, send evil spirits and hosts of destroying angels against enemies and rivals. The more cryptic and mysterious a "name", the more it was believed capable of helping or harming. And a person who had experienced the superiority of a particular "name" would sympathize and sometimes associate with its devotees. The importance of the plentiful material on this subject for the study of religious and intellectual influences should therefore not be minimized.

Egypt had always been a centre of such beliefs, and Coptic Greeks —both pagan and Christian—as well as Jews had a large share in their dissemination also outside the country. Magic papyri have been discovered which contain prayers, invocations of gods, incantations, spells, occult formulae and the like; and besides various distorted appellations of gods, demons and spirits we find Ἰαω, a shortened form of the tetragrammaton; Ελοίμ; Σαβάωθ; Αδωνάι. Names of angels, such as Raphael, Michael and Gabriel, are frequent, and Moses and Abraham are repeatedly mentioned. The incantations are sprinkled with verse-fragments and phrases from the Bible or ancient Jewish prayers.[1] Incantations of a Jewish character discovered in Egypt have been edited by K. Preisendanz.[2]

The features just mentioned in connection with Greek magic papyri in Egypt appear also in incantations and charms discovered in North Africa. They, too, are all in Greek, though written on different material, according to local conditions. Those inscriptions which make no reference

[1] Comp. Th. Hopfner, *AoF* 3 (1931), pp. 119-155, 327-358, esp. pp. 340-345; *id.*, *ibid.*, 7 (1935), pp. 117-188. *Ibid.*, pp. 355-366, Hopfner published a new Greek-Christian papyrus, in which Ιαω Σαβάωθ Αδονάι the God of Abraham, Isaac and Jacob, is mentioned. For Hebrew, Aramaic, Samaritan, Greek, Latin and Coptic incantations using this formula comp. M. Rist, *JBL* 57 (1938), pp. 289-303.

[2] *Papyri Graecae Magicae,* hggb. von K. Preisendanz, I, 1928, pp. 170; 184; II, 1931, p. 148-149; comp. also Tcherikover-Fuks, *CPJ* I, 110; and *D. Arch.* Ch. I, 127-155, 1784-1860, *s.v.* Abrasax, Amulettes.

to gods or Christianity must be regarded as Jewish, *i.e.* the work of Jewish "experts".[1]

As early as 1848, a report was published of an oval-shaped stone the size of a coin, brought from Cyrenaica and engraved with the names Abraham, Isaac, Jacob and Iao in Greek characters; the other side bears Libyan and perhaps also Greek letters which it was not possible to decipher. This amulet dates from the 4th or 5th century C.E.[2]

Excavations in the late 19th century in the cemeteries and amphitheatre of Carthage revealed lead tablets inscribed with incantations part of which contain Jewish, but no non-Jewish "names". Here is a typical example of such an inscription: "I adjure you (demons) in the name of the God of Heaven, who sits on cherubs, who set a limit to the land and divided off the sea, (in the name of) Iao, Abraio, Arbatiao, Zebaio, Adonai, to harm the horses of the competitors, so that they may not win in the forthcoming contest at the circus."[3] Lead tablets of the same type without any Christian "name" or symbol have been discovered in the cemetery of Hadrumetum, *i.e.* Sousse of the Arab period.[4]

A particularly instructive specimen of the Hadrumetum incantation tablets is a 47-line inscription of the 3rd century, which has come down to us almost intact. The sorcerer adjures the demon (δαιμόνιον πνεῦμα) who haunts that cemetery, in the name of the holy Αωθ Αβαωθ, in the name of the God of Abraham, Isaac and Jacob and in the name of the God of Israel (?), as follows: You, demon, must obey the great, honourable, mighty and dreadful name and hurry to Urbanus the son of Urbana and bring him to Domitiana the daughter of Candida in order that he may ask her, full of desire and lust, to become his wife. This adjuration is repeated three times, each time in stronger terms, combining the "name" with different attributes: eternal and more than eternal, highest of highest, who distinguishes between the just man (and the evildoer), between light and darkness, who set lights to give light upon men, who divided the sea with a rod (!), who made the mule barren, etc., and using terms urging speed, such as "hasten!", "hurry!". The incantation ends with the

---

[1] Comp. *CIL* 16701, 22634; *ibid.* 22658, 34: Ιαω σαβαξ, 'Αβρασαξ, Αβλαβρας

[2] Comp. K. Friedmann, *Miscellanea*, p. 46. A Gnostic talisman from Eastern Cyrenaica is recorded by Applebaum, *Zion* 19 (1954), 26, n. 29.

[3] Comp. *CIL* VIII, *Sup.* I, 12504-12511; the incantation to harm horses is No. 12511, and see Delattre, *Bulletin de correspondance hellénique* 12 (1888), pp. 294-302.

[4] On these tablets comp. *Collections du Musée Alaoui*, Paris 1890, pp. 57ff., 101ff.; Monceaux, *REJ* 44 (1902), p. 6. Copious bibliographical lists will be found in: Schürer, *Geschichte* III, pp. 407-420; Baron, *SRH*, Index to vols. I-VIII, *s.v.* Magic; and Tcherikover-Fuks, *CPJ* I, p. 110.

longest (8-line) reference to the "name" (32-29) and with the demon being addressed—for the fifth time—as follows: Bring Urbanus the son of Urbana and mate him with Domitiana the daughter of Candida, full of love, mad, tormented with love, desire and lust for Domitiana the daughter of Candida, mate them as spouses for all their lives! See that he desires no woman or virgin but her, lives only with Domitiana all his life. Quick, quick! Hurry, hurry!

L. Blau discusses all the particulars of this incantation in a penetrating analysis, proving their dependence on the Bible and ancient Jewish prayer texts. He sums up as follows: The lead tablet of Hadrumetum is an important document of ancient Jewish magic, whether the author was a Hebrew-speaking Jew or Greek-speaking. The characteristic and essential content of this incantation are the divine attributes, taken more or less faithfully from Holy Scripture. In this tablet, the demon is adjured, in the name of God the Almighty, to kindle desire. The demons of disease etc. were undoubtedly invoked in similar fashion.

It is very doubtful whether Domitiana the daughter of Candida, and her beloved Urbanus, were Jews or Judaizers. But there can be no doubt that if Domitiana's incantation was successful, this made a great impression on her and influenced her outlook. This was one of the ways, and not a negligible one, by which the Jewish faith spread. We have already mentioned that Jewish customs, such as the observance of the Sabbath and festivals, and Jewish forms of prayer, exerted considerable attraction in the pagan world.[1]

[1] Comp. L. Blau, *Zauberwesen*, 96-112; for a later bibliography see Schürer, *op. cit.*, p. 412, n. 140. A love incantation was published by Grunwald, *MGWJ* 77 (1933), pp. 248-249. For the use of lead in talismans comp. *ibid.*, pp. 167-168 and 243, n.l.

CHAPTER TWO

IN THE MAGHREB STATES

In the spread of the Jews outside Palestine and Babylonia, their main centres in the first half-millennium of Arab-Muslim rule, the Maghreb (North West Africa), *i.e.* the vast area west of Egypt, played an extremely important part. That area was then described in Hebrew as Afrīqiya,[1] as in the days of the *tannaim* and *amoraim*, or Maʿarab,[2] in imitation of the Arabs, who called it Maghreb.[3] Indeed, Maʿarab in contemporary sources occasionally includes also Egypt and Spain,[4] and on the other hand, Afrīqiya is sometimes a particular town: Kairouan or Mahdiya.[5] Usually, however, the terms Afriqiya and Maʿarab are synonymous (in some cases, they occur side by side). Now and then, the region is called Barbariya, and this name, too, is found already in talmudic times.[6]

Data preserved in the responsa of the Geonim and in letters and other documents discovered in the Geniza of Fustāt (Old Cairo) bear witness to the important role of the Maghreb and the brisk activity of its Jewish inhabitants in all spheres of life. In spite of all the political and social upheavals visiting the population of the area, including the Jews, that activity continued until the collapse of the major Jewish communities during the Almohad persecutions.

Muslim-Arab writers give little direct information about the Jews, and if nothing else had been preserved, we would not know much of the fate of the latter during that period. Most of this chapter is derived from the literature of the Geonim and their contemporaries. However, the responsa of the Geonim and the Arab chronicles tell nothing of what happened in

[1] Comp. *e.g.*, *RHG*, no. 49; *RH*, no. 210; *RA* III, p. 49, 1.21; *MJC* II, p. 78.

[2] Comp. *e.g.*, *RH*, no. 44; *RA* III, pp. 7-8; Lewin, *Iggeret*, p. 104; Mann, *J* II, 26, 1.4, 162, 1.27; and esp. Kairouan of the Maʿarab: *RH* no. 48, and comp. Ibn al-ʿIdhārī, p. 41.

[3] Comp. *e.g.*, ibn Ḥawqal, 60-66; Yāqūt, *s.v.*; Gottheil-Worrell, *Fragments*, pp. 128-129.

[4] Egypt: Mann, *J* II, pp. 81, 352. Spain: *e.g.*, *JQR*, 18 (1906), p. 401. Qābes belongs to the Maʿarab; *RH*, no. 59.

[5] Comp. Brunschvig, *Berbérie* I, p. 178, no. 5, and p. 203. See also below, p. 132.

[6] Comp. *SHQ*, p. 64. *Ibid.*, p. 74, we find the division "Spain, the Maghreb, Ifriqiya, Egypt"; which is subsequently elucidated by the remark: "Sala is at the extreme end of the Maghreb, Tahert at the very beginning of the Maghreb, at the end of Ifriqiya" (p. 92). Barbariya: *RSh* 7b, no. 50.

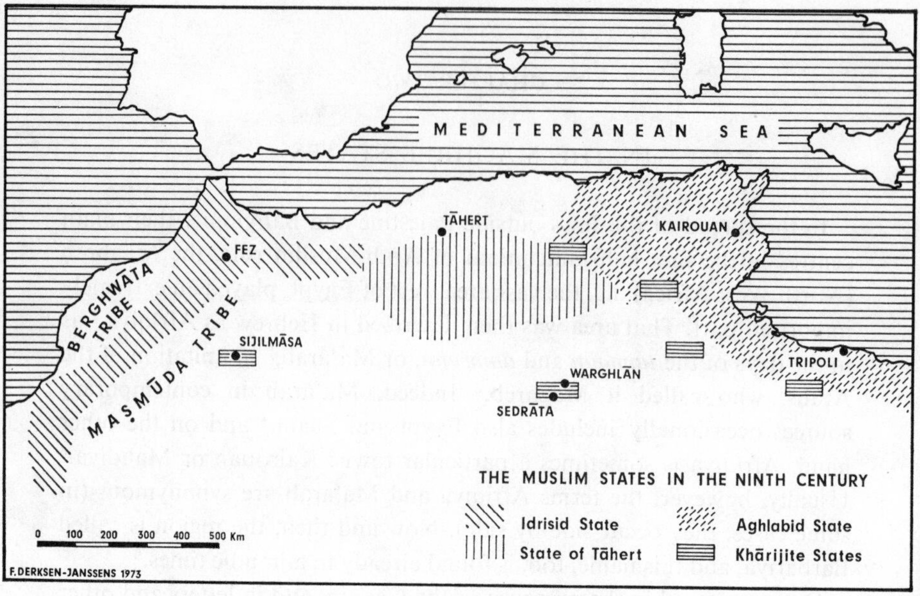

Map 2

the area at the time of the change of regimes, *i.e.* at the end of the Byzantine and the beginning of the Arab era. The conquest of North Africa by the Arabs lasted fifty years, from the middle of the seventh to the beginning of the eighth century C.E. Several able generals succeeded in penetrating deeply into Berber territory, as far as the Atlantic coast, but were afterwards repulsed by the Berbers and forced to withdraw to their base, Barca in Cyrenaica, to wait for reinforcements, whereupon they resumed their offensive again and again. In the last stage of this war, the Berbers were led by a woman of the Jarāwa tribe.

The Kāhina

The figure of that woman, surnamed the Kāhina, prophetess and last queen of the Berbers in the Aurès Mountains in Algeria, holds an important place in the history of the conquest of North Africa by the Arabs. Berber resistance was broken after the ultimate defeat of the Kāhina, thus enabling the invader to occupy the country and attack Spain.

Here is an account of the events, as given (with many variations) in most of the sources and in modern researches.

Kusayla, a Christian Berber leader, made a pact with the Arabs and embraced Islam, but afterwards revolted and, with the help of his Byzantine allies, defeated the famed Arab general ʿUqba, who fell in battle. Kusayla was subdued after a time and killed in action, but the Arab forces nevertheless withdrew to Cyrenaica. Some time later, the Caliph ʿAbd al-Malik (685-705) sent Ḥasān ibn Nuʿmān to Africa; Ḥasān defeated the Byzantines still holding major coastal cities, and captured Carthage.

After these victories, Ḥasān marched against Dahya (or Damya) the Kāhina, queen of the Jarāwa, an important Judaized subtribe of the Zenāta, because it was she who headed the free Berber tribes fighting the Arabs. The Kāhina tackled the enemy and defeated him decisively by the river Balā (or Nīnī or Maskiyāna or Seqtātā) on the slopes of the Aurès Mountains, east of Bajāya (the famous fortress destroyed by the insurgent Berbers) or near Qābes (on the southern part of the Tunisian coast). The date of the event is not certain, either, varying as it does between 68 A.H. (687/8 C.E.) and 79 A.H. (697/8 C.E.).

The Kāhina released all the Arabs taken prisoner, except one youth, Khālid ibn Yazīd, whom she adopted in addition to her own two sons, one a Berber and the other a Greek (*i.e.* of a Byzantine father).

The Arab general retired with the remnants of this troops to Barca, where he waited for fresh instructions from the Caliph. Five years later, ʿAbd al-Malik sent Ḥasān reinforcements, ordering him to move once more against the Kāhina, who had meanwhile devastated the whole of the fertile coastal zone with its cities and agricultural settlements. She believed that the Arabs were coveting the country's riches and that when they found it desolate they would leave the Berbers alone. The situation in the country and the mood of the sedentary population were known to Ḥasān, who would receive information from Khālid, the Kāhina's adopted son.

Ḥasān's campaign against the Kāhina was joined by many Christian town-dwellers. Before fighting flared up, the prophetess foresaw that she would be killed and the Berbers defeated, and she therefore advised Khālid to go over to the Arabs with her two sons. She herself refused to yield to the conquerors and fell in battle at Bīr al-Kāhina in the year 693, 698 or 702 C.E. She died at the age of 125 or 127 years after ruling the Berbers for 35 or 65 years. Their sons embraced Islam and were given command of the Islamized Berber units that became part of the Arab army.

The above picture, a concentrated array of data from Arab authors of the 8th to 14th centuries, contains much divergent and contradictory information as to the occurrence, place and time of events, as well as clearly romantic-fictional elements. It is not surprising that opinions as to the historical value of the Kāhina story are divided. There are those who reject it almost completely, regarding it as a mere legend.[1] Others accept the report of the Jewish Berber queen in every detail.[2] A third group says that a historical nucleus was woven round with many legends.[3] I have attempted elsewhere to subject the sources dealing with the Kāhina to very sober historico-literary criticism with a view to separating fact and fancy. I shall therefore confine myself here to quoting two sources, the earliest and the latest, and summarizing the conclusions arrived at after analysing all the known sources.[4]

The Traditions of the Arab Historians

Al-Wāqidī (d. 822 C.E.), believed to be always weighing his words carefully, says: The Kāhina reigned over all Africa and oppressed her people. She was particularly severe with the Muslims in Kairouan. Furious at the murder of Kusayla, she revolted against the Arabs. After the murder of the Arab commander in the year 67 A.H. (687), ʿAbd al-Malik placed Africa in the charge of Ḥasān ibn al-Nuʿmān, who marched against the Kāhina with a large army. The Muslims were defeated and many of them killed. Ḥasān returned to the Barca region and encamped there until the year 74 A.H. (694), when the Caliph sent him a large army and ordered him to march once more against the Kāhina. This time, Ḥasān defeated the Berbers, killed the Kāhina and her sons and returned to Kairouan.[5]

---

[1] Comp. Basset, *EI*[1], *s.v.* al-Kāhina; Brunschvig, *ibid.*, *s.v.* Tunisia. Comp. also St. Gsell scepticism about legal adoption among the Berbers; *Histoire Ancienne de l'Afrique du Nord*, V, p. 37, n. 4.

[2] Slouschz, *Maroc* II, pp. 11-18; also *ibid.* I, p. 66; *id.*, *Travels*, pp. 309-316; Bourrilly, *Ethnogr.*, pp. 71-73; Gautier, *Passé*, pp. 270-280, also 225, 267; Simon, *RHPhR* 26 (1946), pp. 6, 18, 141-142; Chouraqui, *Juifs*, pp. 46-49; Abbou, *Andalous*, p. 279; Julien, *Histoire* II, pp. 21-22, but comp. pp. 24-26; Laredo, *Hebreos*, p. 180; comp. also the articles "Kahena" in *JE*, *EJ*, *UJE* and *EJC*.

[3] Comp. G. Marçais, *Berbérie*, pp. 34-35; Terrasse, *Histoire* I, p. 83. Mercier, *REC* 12 (1868), pp. 241-254, in describing the Arab invasion, does not indicate the *Kāhina*'s religion. Lévy-Provençal, *Arabica*, I (1954), pp. 17-43, publishes an account of the conquest by ʿUbayd Allah, a contemporary of al-ʿIdhārī, but does not comment on the historicity of the description of the Kāhina's war.

[4] Comp. *Tarbiẓ* 26 (1957), pp. 370-383. For the history of the conquest comp. M. Tshurakov, *Sbornik* 3 (66), 1958, pp. 107-126; L. Kubbel, *ibid.*, 4 (67), 1959, pp. 124-125.

[5] Ibn al-Athīr, *Al-Kamil* IV, p. 33.

Ibn ʿAbd al-Ḥakam (lived in Egypt in the years 803-871) likewise reports that the son of the Kāhina fought the Arabs and that, although he was defeated, the Arabs withdrew to Egypt as they were threatened by a Berber coalition.[1]

We now come to Ibn Khaldūn (d. 1406), the greatest Arab historian, a native of Tunisia. In view of the importance of this author, who is almost the only source for most modern accounts, we give a full translation of all the passages directly connected with the Kāhina story.

(A) After explaining that Christianity was widespread among the Berbers, but not in its Eastern form, and that the foreign Christians were Franks (*i.e.* Latins), and not *Rūmiyūn* (*i.e.* Byzantines), he continues:

"It is possible, moreover, that others among those Berber tribes believed in the Jewish religion, which they had received from the Israelites at the time of the expansion of their kingdom to the neighbourhood of Syria and their rule over it. This was true of the Jarāwa in the Aurès Mountains, the tribe of the Kāhina, who was killed by the Arabs at the beginning of the Conquest. This was true also of the Nafūsa in Africa, Qandalawqa (!), Madyūna, Bahlūla and Ghiyata and the Banū Bāzāz (!) in the outermost Maghreb, until the great Idris (a descendant of Ḥasan ibn Ḥasan), who shone forth in the Maghreb, wiped out all the remnants of religions and communities that were in his area."[2]

(B) "After the death of Zuhayr, Afrīqiya burst into flames (of rivalry). The Berbers split into factions, and authority was divided among many leaders. One of the most respected of them was the Kāhina, Dahya [3] the daughter of Mātyah the son of Tīfān, queen of the Aurès Mountains; her people were of the Jarāwa tribe, kings and leaders of the Butr (a group of Berber tribes). ʿAbd al-Malik instructed Ḥasān ibn al-Nuʿmān al-Ghasānī, his governor in Egypt, to launch a holy war against Afrīqiya and sent reinforcements to him. Ḥasān advanced into Afrīqiya in the year 69, entered Kairouan, fought at Carthage and occupied it by force. The Franks who were still there went to Sicily or Spain. Ḥasān then inquired who was the greatest of the Berber kings, and was told of the Kāhina and

---

[1] *Conquête de l'Afrique du Nord et de l'Espagne*, ed. A. Gateau, Alger 1948², pp. 70-78.

[2] *Kitāb al-ʿIbar* VI, p. 107; de Slane's edition uses variant forms of some names: Fandalaua, Fāzāz (*Histoire* I, p. 132). Traditions of the Judaizant Berbers in the Jebel Nafūsa are mentioned by Mordechay Cohen in his Diary (1906), *Genazim* 3 (1969), pp. 78-9.

[3] De Slane's edition reads Damyā (*ibid.*, p. 135); this may be induced by the name of a Berber tribe, Damyā (comp. Lévy-Provençal, *Documents*, p. 63), but is possibly only a scribe's error.

her people, the Jarāwa. He marched against her and arrived at Wādī Maskiyāna. She, too, marched out and they fought hard. The Muslims were defeated in battle, and a great number of them were killed. Khālid ibn Yazīd al-Qaysī was taken prisoner. The Kāhina and the Berbers did not cease to pursue Ḥasān and the Arabs until they had driven them from the Qābes District, and Ḥasān reached the Ṭarāblus District. Here he received a letter from ʿAbd al-Malik. He remained there and built his encampment, which is known to this day. The Kāhina subsequently returned to her own territory and made a covenant with her prisoner, Khālid, by suckling him with her two sons. She held sway over Africa and the Berbers for five years. Thereafter ʿAbd al-Malik sent reinforcements to Ḥasān, and the latter returned to Africa in the year 74 A.H. (694). The Kāhina had meanwhile devastated all the cities and estates in the area from Tripoli to Tangiers, which had previously been one shady stretch, a continuous chain of settlements. This angered the Berbers, so that they sought, and received, the protection of Ḥasān, who thus succeeded in sowing discord in the ranks of the Kāhina. He marched against her, and she was among the mass of Berbers who were routed. She was killed in a place no longer known in the Aurès Mountains."[1]

(C) "The Zenāta were the most important of the Berber tribes as regards numbers and the multitude of subtribes. The seat of the Jarāwa, who belonged to the Zenāta, was in the Aurès Mountains. The Jarāwa were descendants of the sons of Karau ibn al-Dirat ibn Jānā. They were headed by the Kāhina Dahbā [2] the daughter of . . . the son of Naʿān the son of Bāru the son of Maṣrasrī the son of Afrad the son of Waṣilā the son of Jarau. She had three [3] sons, who had inherited the leadership of the people from their ancestors and who had grown up at her bosom. She treated them and the people despotically, in part because she had magic powers (literally: the qualities of a *kāhina*) and knew the secrets of their condition and the outcome of their affairs; thus she obtained dominance over them. Hānī ibn Bakkūr al-Darīsī says that she reigned over them thirty-five years and lived one hundred and twenty-seven years. It was she who incited the Berbers to murder ʿUqba ibn Nāfiʿ in the plain south-east of the Aurès Mountains, a fact which was known to the Muslims. After the fate of the Berbers was sealed and Kusayla murdered,

---

[1] *Kitāb al-ʿIbar* VI, p. 109. In de Slane's edition (I, p. 214), the place where the Kāhina was killed is called Biʾr al-Kāhina. This is undoubtedly an addition prompted by Ibn ʿAbd al-Ḥakam's account (*Conquête*, ed. Gateau[2], p. 78).

[2] De Slane's edition, I, p. 198: Dihya.

[3] Including the adopted Khālid.

they returned to the Kāhina in her capital in the Aurès Mountains. She was joined by the Banū Yifran and all the Zenāta tribes that were in Africa and the rest of the Banū Butr. The clash with the Muslims occurred in the plain in front of the Aurès Mountains. The Muslims were defeated and she pursued them with their men until she had driven them out of Africa" (sequel as in passage (B)).[1]

Historians posterior to Ibn Khaldūn all follow in his footsteps, without making any material addition.

It is comparatively easy to analyse the material, separating the ancient account from later versions and mere embellishments. The sources are all of a piece, stemming from Muslim historians without any special political or religious-sectarian bias and forming a chain of tradition the historical links of which are fairly clear. We are not faced with a jumble of data from sources representing such divergent and conflicting tendencies that the chronological order is difficult to establish.

Here are our conclusions:

In their last fight against the Arabs, the Berbers were led by a woman. We shall see below that her name was Kahya and that the appellation Kāhina resulted from a faulty reading. She and her sons perished in that fight. One of the causes of her defeat was her method of warfare: the destruction of cities and villages in the coastal region with a view to discouraging the Arabs from conquering areas which had now become waste and useless. Her action led to internal dissension and undermined her position with the population of the region, which included many Christians. We know that the Arabs were aided in their conquest, in each country, by conflicts both within the ruling class and between the ruling class and the population.

The story of the Arab prisoner adopted by the Kāhina is a romantic literary addition. He is described as a noble-minded spy, who passes information to Ḥasān ibn Nuʿmān on the situation in the Berber kingdom, and at the same time saves his adoptive mother's own sons from destruction by guiding them into the haven of Islam. This story was intended as propaganda among the Berbers for whole-hearted conversion to Islam. The data on the prophetic qualities of the leader are to explain the appellation Kāhina, as we shall see below. The report that the Kāhina belonged to a Judaized tribe is important from a general historical and social point of view, but as the narratives give no hint of religious motives

[1] *Kitāb al-ʿIbar* VII, pp. 8-9; de Slane's edition, II, pp. 10-11.

for the war nor—perhaps advisedly—preserve any Jewish feature (unlike the stories of Judaized kings in South Arabia and Khazaristan), this bald statement adds nothing to the image of the Berber leader from the Jewish point of view.

The Kāhina's Name

Ibn Khaldūn gives the Kāhina's name: Dahya or Dahba or Damya, which are variants accounted for by Arabic palaeography. The occurrence of a similar name for the Kāhina with ʿUbayd Allāh, an author preceding Ibn Khaldūn by a hundred years, proves that we have not to do here with an invention by the latter; Ibn Khaldūn certainly obtained the name from an old manuscript or by way of oral tradition similar to that relied upon by ʿUbayd Allah.[1]

Yet another similar name, whose second syllable is identical with the second syllable of Dahya, is preserved in the oral folk-tradition of Algerian and Tunisian Jewry. Cazès, the historian of Tunisian Jewry (second half of the 19th cent.), took down the following interesting lament, in Jewish-Arabic, from a religious scholar in Constantine, *i.e.* in a region very close to the Aurès Mountains:

"Children of Yeshurun, do not forget your persecutors,
The Chaldaeans, the Emperor, Hadrian and Kahya.
This accursed one, she was more cruel than all those (who
preceded her) together.
She delivered our virgins to her soldiers
And bathed her feet in the blood of our infants.
God created her in order that we might expiate our sins.
God hates the tormentors of his people.
Give me back my children, that they may mourn me;
I left them in the hands of Kahya."[2]

Cazès rightly assumes that the Kahya mentioned here is the Kāhina, and he regards this lament as proof that she was not a Jewess. In our opinion, we have to do here with a tradition parallel to a report of the persecution of Christians by the Berber leader, and if such acts of oppression in fact took place, they did not spring from religious motives, but from social antagonisms between the Berbers and the settled population.

---

[1] ʿUbayd Allah (comp. p. 90, n. 3) has: Daḥiya; comp. *Arabica* I (1954), p. 16.
[2] Cazès, *Essai*, p. 46.

It should be noted that according to one of the Church Fathers the Jews collaborated with the Arab invaders.[1]

The variant readings Kahya-Dahya are easily accounted for by Arab palaeography. Oral tradition preserved the correct name Kahya, but in ancient Arabic script the letters *kāf* and *dāl* are not very different, and a blot on the vertical stroke of the *kāf* or even mere negligent writing may lead to *kāf* being read as *dāl*.[2]

After the sudden appearance of the name Dahya (Damya, Dahba) has been explained, there remains the problem of the appellation Kāhina, which is most unusual for a Berber woman. Modern scholars note the Hebrew, Punic or Arabic origin of the word, which means "priestess" in North Semitic and "sorceress" in Arabic.[3] However, we have not found the appellation *kohenet* anywhere in ancient Hebrew literature, but only the terms *nebi'a* and *ba'alat 'ob*. Moreover, though Punic was still spoken in Africa, it was certainly not by the Berbers, and they could not have known Hebrew at all. This means that the Berbers themselves did not call their leader Kāhina. Even assuming that she was a visionary (which is not proved at all by the ancient narrative), their language certainly had a word for it, so that they did not have to fall back on a foreign expression.[4]

The solution may again lie in palaeography. Ancient Arabic script had no diacritic points, and the signs *k h y '* might just as well have been read *kāhina*. It is quite likely, therefore, that al-Wāqidī, who lived in Baghdad and no doubt received his information on Kahya in writing, read that non-Arabic name "Kahina" and derived it from the appellation *kāhina*, well known in Arabic literature. After the reading *Kāhina*, familiar and intelligible to the Arabs, had been received, stories were evolved concerning her particular qualities in order to explain that appellation. It is true that only Ibn Khaldūn states expressly that the Kāhina had a *shayṭān* who furnished her with mystical knowledge.[5]

Clearly, in view of the situation of Berber historiography and the abso-

[1] Comp. Starr, *JPOS* 15 (1935), pp. 287-288.

[2] *Tarbiẓ* 26 (1957), pp. 380-381, reproduces a portion of MS. Ar 155 of the St. Catherine (Sinai) Library, apparently of the 9th century, the time when the Kāhina story began to spread. It shows the similarity of the letters *dāl* (*dhāl*) and *kāf*.

[3] Comp. Slouschz, *Etude sur l'histoire des Juifs*, Paris 1906, II, p. 12; St. Gsell, *Histoire* IV (1929), pp. 396-9.

[4] For divination and female seers in North Africa comp. Gautier, *Passé*, p. 225; Doutté, *Magie*, pp. 32ff.; H. P. J. Renaud, *Hespéris* 30 (1943), pp. 213-221; L. Golvin, *AIEO* 12 (1954), pp. 114-121. T. Lewicki, *Folia Orientalia* 7 (1965), pp. 3-27, esp. p. 6, where the author stresses, that the Berber queen was called Kāhina by the Arab writers.

[5] *Al-'Ibar* VI, p. 110.

lute lack of autochthonous archaeological, epigraphical and literary sources, even for later periods, no confirmation or decision in the matter can be expected, unlike the case, similar in many respects, of the name of Yūsuf Dhū Nuwās (c. 517-525), the Judaized Ḥimyar king, who likewise fell in battle.

Three contemporary inscriptions discovered in the early fifties of the present century give the original South Arabian name of this king: ʾAsʾar Yaṯʾar, and confirm the history of his wars, as told in literary sources.[1]

The Jews as *dhimmī*

The victories of Ḥasān ibn Nuʿmān and Mūsā ibn Nuṣayr in the late 7th and early 8th centuries, through which the whole of the North Africa fell into Arab hands, mark the beginning of a new era for the Jews as well. An inquiry into the particulars of the events of that time meets with numerous difficulties. We possess no Jewish sources for that period, and Arab authors did not trouble to record details important from the point of view of Jewish history. The Jews are mostly described as *dhimmī* (protected persons), an expression which in the Maghreb refers only to them, and not to the Christians.

Here are a few instances of data relating to our region in the period under discussion.

Ibn ʿAbd al-Ḥakam reports that Ḥasān, the conqueror of North Africa, imposed the *kharāj* on the *ʿajam* (the strangers, *i.e.*, Byzantines) and the (native) Berbers who adhered to Christianity. He subsequently says that after a time the Rūm (= Byzantines) reconquered Anṭablus (the Pentapolis) and staged riots against the *dhimmī*.[2]

The reference is undoubtedly to the Jews, not the Christians. The same historian reports the uprising of the Berbers in the Nafzāwa province some fifty years after their subjection by Ḥasān; they seized the *dhimmī*, who were subsequently freed by the Arab commander who put down the rebellion.[3]

---

[1] Comp. G. Ryckmans, *Muséon* 66 (1953), pp. 284-303; W. Caskel, *Entdeckungen in Arabien*, Cologne 1954, pp. 14-26; A. Jamme, *Studi Semitici* 23 (1966), pp. 10, 39-55.

[2] *Futūḥ*, p. 80. Elsewhere (p. 106) he calls a certain woman *naṣraniya*. The expression "Berbers who believed in Christianity" occurs also in *Ibn-ʿIdhārī*, p. 38, and Ibn Khaldūn, *K. al-ʿIbar* VI, p. 110, Ibn Khaldūn, *ibid.*, pp. 116 and 419, mentions the "Franja," who were compelled to pay *jizya* during the conquest. The terms used for the Christians in North Africa are discussed by Hopkins, *Government*, pp. 62ff.

[3] *Futūḥ*, p. 138; comp. Julien, *Histoire* II, p. 31. On Jews and Christians in that area see next page.

Ibn Ḥawqal (middle of 10th century) notes the *jawālī* (poll-tax) imposed on the Jews in Qābes. Immediately afterwards, he relates that the Beduin attacked the *dhimmī, i.e.* Jews, who had entered into a protective covenant by paying the *jawālī*.[1]

A poem describing the rough climate of Tāhert, where winter was jokingly said to last thirteen months, contains the following verse:

"We rejoice at the sun when it shines
as the *dhimmī* rejoice on the Sabbath.[2]

Ibn ʿAbd al-Ḥakam's utterances permit the conclusion that the Jews experienced some relief after the long period of restrictions and humiliations under the Byzantines. Ḥasān certainly did not pass them by when imposing the special tax on Christian landowners, but the Jews had had to pay that tax in the days of the Romans as well, and now they had fellows in adversity, which afforded them some consolation. The difference was felt when the Byzantines succeeded in recapturing Anṭablus (the Pentapolis) for a few weeks and committed outrages against the *dhimmī, i.e.* Jews, apparently because they had collaborated with the Arabs. We also hear that the Jews suffered during the Berber insurrection in Nafzāwa province. Nafzāwa is an extensive region in Central Tunisia, east of the salt marshes of Jarīd and the oases of Nefṭa and Tozeur. It stretches to the approaches of Qābes, al-Ḥāma and Maṭmaṭa and was inhabited by Jews and Christians. R. Abraham, one of the Babylonian geonim, who was active in the early 9th century C.E., was surnamed al-Qābesī, which indicates that he originated from Qābes and proves that Jews lived there in the second half of the 8th century.[3] In any case, that region was inhabited by Jews from the Geonic period down to our time. Christians lived there in the Middle Ages.[4]

Sectarian States

The first hundred years of Arab occupation were not remarkable for peaceful development. Although the Umayyad rulers attached great

[1] *BGA* II², p. 70.

[2] Yāqūt, *s.v.* Tāhert; Ibn ʿIdhārī, p. 25. Gautier found a MS. expressly referring to "the Jew" (*Passé*, p. 324).

[3] Lewin, *Iggeret*, p. IV; and below, p. 341.

[4] Comp. below, p. 141 nn. 5-7. Brunschvig, *Berbérie* I, p. 400; *Tashbeẓ* IV/1, no. 33 (Tozeur), fol. 16, b. Elishaʿ ha-Qashṭilyani, who in 1041 brought a Hebrew MS. from Jerusalem to Warghlān, may have come from Qashṭilya; for the use of that name comp. Brunschvig, *op. cit.*, p. 315. On Christians in that area comp. Lewicki, *RO*, 17 (1951-52), pp. 423 and 463-464.

importance to this conquest, and the governor of North Africa was for a time in charge of Egypt and Spain as well,[1] it was not long after the completion of the military occupation that the Khārijiya, *i.e.* secession, the oldest Islamic sect, began to gain ground in the region. One of the main slogans of that sect was the equality of all races in Islam, a principle suiting the Berbers. The Khārijiya won many supporters among the Nafūsa tribe, which originally settled in Tripolitania. It should be noted that according to tradition that tribe had formerly cherished some Jewish beliefs. In the middle of the 8th century, at the end of Umayyad and the beginning of ʿAbbasid rule, we hear of an armed rebellion of Khārijite Berbers against the Arab governors residing in Kairouan and Western Tripolitania. One centre of the rebellion was the abovementioned Nafzāwa, another was the area of the Berghouata tribes in Western Morocco (Comp. map 2 on p. 88).

The branch of the Khārijites which lived in Tripolitania and Tunisia was called the Ibāḍis. Though the Ibāḍis were defeated, their leader Ibn Rustem succeeded in escaping and setting up a new state in Central Algeria with Tāhert as its capital. About the same time (middle of the 8th century C.E.), another secessionist sect founded a second Khārijite kingdom in Tlemcen. Another Berber tribe in those days established a third Khārijite state in the oasis of Tāfilālet in the Ziz Valley and built its capital, Sijilmāsa. In spite of the theological differences between the various branches of the "secessionists", those states were closely interlinked politically and commercially. It should already be noted that the three new cities mentioned, Tāhert, Tlemcen and Sijilmāsa, will in time be found to contain Jewish populations. As far as we know, the oldest extant evidence of the presence of Jews in those cities is from Tāhert, where R. Yehuda ibn Quraysh (or Qurays), one of the earliest Hebrew philologists, lived in the 9th century. We should further point out that other Ibāḍī centres —*e.g.* Jebel Nafūsa (originally a kind of extension of the Tāhert kingdom), the island of Jerba in the Jarīd region (= Nafzāwa, which extends as far as Qābes) and the oases of Warghlān and Mzāb—always included important Jewish settlements, such as continued to exist in Ibāḍī environments until our days.[2]

The "secessionists" with their various sects were indeed the first, but not the only ones, who tried to establish in North Africa independent

---

[1] Comp. M. Tshurakow, *Sbornik* 3 (66), p. 126.

[2] On sectarian movements in Africa see ʿAbd al-Ḥakam, pp. 134ff.; ibn Ḥawqal, p. 96. Comp. also Goldziher, *ZDMG*, 41 (1887), pp. 31ff.; Marçais, *Berbérie*, pp. 102-103; Terrasse, *Histoire* I, pp. 101-102; Lewicki, *FO*, 3 (1961), pp. 1-134.

states, not subject to the caliphate in Baghdad. In the late 8th century, Idrīs, a descendant of the fourth caliph, ʿAlī, and of Fāṭima, daughter of the Prophet Muḥammad, fled the East to escape ʿAbbāsid persecution and found refuge in the outermost Maghreb. Idrīs was the founder of the Idrīsid dynasty, which set up a kingdom in western Central Morocco, in an area whose chief town had until then been Walīlī, as the Arabs called the Roman-Byzantine city of Volubilis. Near the ruins of that city, on Mount Zarḥūn, is the tomb of Idrīs the First, which is most sacred to the Moroccans and on which the royal family and the masses of the people prostrate themselves in May every year. It is reported that Idrīs, surnamed the Great, found Jews and Christians in that region and wiped out "the remnants of the religions and communities in his area", a report which is certainly not literally true, as we shall see presently.[1]

The Foundation of Fez

In the early 9th century, Idrīs the Second, Idrīs the First's posthumous son, founded the city of Fez, in and near which we find Jews some time afterwards, as known from various sources. One source reports that some Jews, who had to pay an annual poll-tax of 30,000 dinars, came with the Muslim families from Spain who settled in the city a few years after its foundation. According to that figure, we would have to assume that the number of adult males—only they were liable to the tax—was at least 15,000, and hence that the total Jewish population was 45,000 on the most conservative estimate: one woman and one child for every man. But it is impossible that so many Jews should have come from Spain, as against 800 Muslim families, or 6,000 persons, who then came from Spain according to the same sources. We must assume, therefore, that the said amount—if correct—was levied from all the Jews then resident in the Idrīsid kingdom.[2]

The important and influential position of the Jews is evidenced by the story of the Emir Yaḥya al-Idrīsī (in the sixties of the 9th century), whether authentic or not. Yaḥya loved a beautiful Jewish girl and wished

[1] According to *Rauḍ al-Qarṭās* I, pp. 38-39 (Beaumier, p. 34), the Berber tribes in the area of Fez at the time of its foundation partly adhered to Islam and partly to Judaism or Christianity; some were pagans. *Ibid.*, p. 46 (Beaumier, pp. 42-43), we are told that Idrīs II, on founding Fez, met a monk and a Jew on the site.

[2] *Rauḍ al-Qarṭās* I, p. 62 (Beaumier, p. 55); Terrasse, *Histoire* p. 118; Le Tourneau, *Fès*, p. 44; Ashtor, *The Jews in Spain* I, p. 44. Hopkins, *Government*, pp. 4-5, treats with some reserve the sources that mention the arrival of Arabs from Spain about that time.

to marry her. When she remained unresponsive to his wooing, he broke into her house and raped her in her bath. When this wicked deed became known, a crowd of Jews and Muslims gathered under the leadership of a Muslim sheikh, pursued the Emir, who was hiding in one of the city's quarters, and killed him. His widow was compelled to summon her father, the governor of the mountain region, to restore order by force. A present-day French historian notes that this incident shows how integrated the Jews were in the life of the country, how close to their Muslim neighbours, and, moreover, what an honoured position women occupied in a mainly Berber society.[1]

In the late 9th or early 10th century, the abovementioned R. Yehuda ibn Quraysh reproved the Jews of Fez in a famous epistle for neglecting the Aramaic translation of the Bible. He wished to bring home to them how much the use of that translation might promote the knowledge of the Hebrew language.[2]

Kairouan

At the time the Idrsid kingdom was founded, the Emir Ibrāhīm ibn al-Aghlab set up a semi-independent principality, which did not sever its ties with the Baghdad caliphate, in the central part of North Africa. It extended from Mount Nafūsa in the east to the Mzāb region in the west. Its capital, Kairouan, though founded in the early days of the Arab occupation, had suffered much in the fighting between the Khārijite secessionists and the representatives of the Baghdad authorities and its development had thereby been arrested.

It is possible that Jews moved, or were transferred, to Kairouan immediately after its foundation,[3] although there is no confirmation for the belief that the Kairouan community was in contact with R. Yehudai, the Gaon of Sura (middle of the 8th century C.E.), concerning the clarification of halakhic problems.[4] An Arab historian indeed mentions a Jewish physician at the court of an Arab governor then residing in Kairouan.[5]

It was only under the Aghlabid dynasty that Kairouan began to

---

[1] Comp. Bekri, p. 124; Lisān al-Dīn ibn al-Khaṭīb, *Aʿmal al-Aʿlām*, 1964, p. 207; Beaumier, p. 103; Terrasse, *op. cit.*, p. 125.

[2] Comp. below, pp. 308-9.

[3] Comp. below, p. 144.

[4] Comp. below, p. 298.

[5] Ibn ʿIdhārī, p. 41; comp. also Ashtor, *The Jews in Spain* I, p. 31.

develop rapidly, thanks to its central location, into North Africa's largest and most important trading centre. When the Byzantine navy's control of the Western Mediterranean weakened, the Aghlabids seized the opportunity to establish commercial relations with the countries adjacent to its European shore and even undertook—from 827 onwards—campaigns of conquest in Sicily and Southern Italy. These campaigns extended over several decades (the fate of Sicily was decided only in 902) and involved also the Jews resident in those areas. An echo of these events occurs in the *Megillat Aḥimaʿaṣ*, whose author lived in Oria in Southern Italy in the early 11th century. Describing the life of R. Shefatya, a member of his family, Aḥimaʿaṣ relates how the Ismaelites raided the kingdom of the uncircumcised and conquered Calabria and Apulia. The Arab ruler, who resided in Bari, tried to take Oria by a ruse, "to move against it suddenly and to destroy and devastate it". But the lord of Oria, with the assistance of R. Shefatya (d. 886), thwarted the emir's plan and saved the townspeople. R. Shefatya himself seems to have fallen into Arab hands because the capture of the city took place on a Sabbath. It can be assumed that the Jews of North Africa, and especially of Kairouan, made contact at that time with their brethren in Sicily and Southern Italy.[1]

Extremely important is the firm connection established in the early 9th century between the Kairouan community and the geonim of Sura and Pumbeditha, which clearly indicates the respectable intellectual level of the local Jewish population. For, not only the giving of correct responsa, but also the asking of pertinent questions, requires a thorough knowledge of law and tradition.

About the year 880, Eldad ha-Dani visited Kairouan, whereupon "the people of Kairouan asked Rabbenu Semaḥ (ben Ḥayim), the Gaon in Mata Mahsaya, concerning the affair of Eldad ha-Dani, who had come to them from the tribes hidden away in ancient Hawila in the land of Kush" (comp. Gen. 10, 7). We also know of contacts between Egypt and Kairouan in the early 10th century. The Gaon Saadia, while still living in Egypt, carried on a correspondence with a Kairouan resident, R. Isaac ben Solomon the Physician, on problems of worldly learning, as reported by R. Dunash ben Tamim in the introduction to his commentary on the *Sefer Yeṣira*.[2]

---

[1] Comp. Salzman, *Chronicle*, p. 9/74 (Klar, *Aḥimaʿaṣ* p. 24).

[2] A detailed study of the life of the Kairouan community was published by S. Poznanski in *Harkavy Jubilee Volume*, St. Petersburg 1909, pp. 175-220.

In one of his writings, the Gaon Saadia vaguely refers to persecutions of the Jews by Christians: "In these our days, the people of Kairouan composed a work in the Hebrew language on what befell them at the hands of Shnuri (?) the Christian, and that work is divided into sections and marked with accents."[1] Perhaps we may conclude from this that the work was written in the form of a "scroll" (*megilla*) designed for public reading, which would indicate a considerable knowledge of Hebrew. During that period, there were still Christians in North Africa, and one of them may have been an official at the court of a provincial ruler and have stirred up excesses against the Jews. Nor is it impossible that during a change of dynasties a Christian seized the opportunity to worry the Jews.[2]

The Rise of the Fāṭimids

In the early 10th century, a new Arab dynasty, the Fāṭimids, emerged in Africa that was to interfere with, and eventually supplant, the existing kingdoms. Its name purports to indicate that it descended from the family of the Prophet, like the Idrīsid rulers of the outermost Maghreb. Under the leadership of ʿUbayd Allah al-Mahdi (909-934), the African Fāṭimids headed a movement of revolt against the orthodox Sunnite religion. Sunnite tradition, therefore, tried to discredit ʿUbayd Allah in Muslim eyes by alleging that he was the son borne by a bondwoman to her Jewish master. But this vilification did not prevent the Ismaʿilis, one of the extreme Shiʿite sects, from proclaiming ʿUbayd Allah as the Mahdi, *i.e.* the one guided by Allah, the expected Muslim Messiah, who will come at the end of the days to redeem mankind.

In 909, ʿUbayd Allah succeeded in expelling the Aghlabids and establishing himself in Kairouan, but he still had to fight his enemies in the west and east, Sunnites and "secessionists". A few years later, to protect himself against sudden attack, he transferred his seat of government to a new city, founded by him about 915 on a peninsula two days' journey east of Kairouan. It was called al-Mahdiya after its founder. The Mahdi surrounded his city with fortifications, built a citadel in it and used its natural harbour as a base for his navy. The founding of Mahdiya was a

[1] Harkavy, *Zikhron la-Rishonim* V, 1891, pp. 150-151. Harkavy reads שעדי; the Geniza fragment published by Malter, *JQR* 3 (1912-13), p. 489, has שנורי. Comp. also Harkavy, *ibid.*, pp. 162-163 and 180-181, and the Notes *ibid.*, pp. 209-211.

[2] About Christian inhabitants of that region comp. Lewicki, *RO* 17 (1951-52), p. 424; Hopkins, *Government*, pp. 66-67.

significant event. Until then, all the important cities founded by the Arabs: Kairouan, Tāhert, Tlemcen and Fez, had been in the interior, far from the coast, because of the threat of the Byzantine navy. Upon the conquest of Sicily and the partial, temporary seizure of Southern Italy by the Arabs that threat had disappeared, and it was now possible to transfer the seat of government to a port city. The founding of Mahdiya, moreover, indicated the intentions of the Mahdi, his striving for expansion to the east and determination to build up a substantial maritime power. Mahdiya flourished and for centuries played a part similar to that of Alexandria. It is not surprising that it soon became the seat of a large and economically important Jewish community. Commercial documents of the time repeatedly refer to Jewish traders resident or originating from there.

The development of the port of Mahdiya did not prevent the progress of Kairouan, which benefited by the many possibilities opening up to it upon the expansion of Fāṭimid rule over the whole of North Africa, from Fez in the west to Sijilmāsa in the south. Kairouan's position with regard to Mahdiya corresponded to that of Fusṭāṭ-Cairo with regard to Alexandria.

At the same time, the Jewish community in North Africa was increased by exiles and captives from Italy. Shabbethai Donnolo the Physician, in an account of the capture of his native town of Oria by the Arabs in the year 925, says that ten rabbis and many disciples, as well as women and children, were killed on that occasion and the others led into captivity. He himself was redeemed in Taranto with the money of his parents and remained under Christian rule, but his relatives were deported to Palermo and to Africa, *i.e.*, mainly, Kairouan and Mahdiya.[1] In *Megillat Aḥimaʿaṣ*, the author tells of one of his relatives, R. Paltiel, who lived in Oria in the second half of the 10th century. That city was taken by al-Muʿizz, the Fāṭimid caliph (953-975) who was to gain control of Egypt and build his capital, Cairo, there (969). R. Paltiel was taken prisoner with many others, but al-Muʿizz liked him and treated him kindly. Being an astrologer, he foretold al-Muʿizz that he would rule over Sicily, the Maghreb and Egypt. When al-Muʿizz returned to Africa, he took R. Paltiel with him "and he was the king's deputy, and his fame spread in all countries."[2]

---

[1] *Sefer Ḥakmoni* (*Il commento di Sabbato Donnolo*) ed. D. Castelli, Firenze 1880, p. 3; comp. *Ibn ʿIdhārī*, p. 190.

[2] Salzmann, *Chronicle*, transl. pp. 16-17, 89-90 (Klar, *Aḥimaʿaṣ* p. 38). A slightly different version appears in *Sefer Ḥasīdīm*, no. 545, p. 152; comp. A. Marx, *JQR* NS 1 (1910-11), pp. 79-82.

Opinion as to R. Paltiel's functions at the Fāṭimid court is divided. According to R. Aḥimaʿaṣ, he was a viceroy and at the conquest of Egypt (969) went ahead of al-Muʿizz's troops "and set up markets and billets and placed traders therein to prepare and buy bread and water and fish and meat and vegetables and everything needed by soldiers who come from distant lands". R. Paltiel would thus have been in charge of army supplies and billeting.[1] It should be noted, however, that a distinguished orientalist tried at the end of the last century to identify R. Paltiel with Jawhar, the famous general (of Christian origin) who conquered Egypt for the Fāṭimids. Still, the arguments advanced by him for this identification are not satisfactory.[2]

Though there can be no doubt as to the authenticity of the story of the Jewish courtier at the court of the Fāṭimid caliph, historians have pointed out several difficulties in respect of his identity and the date of the events described by Aḥimaʿaṣ. It is hard to accept that the reference should be to the capture of Oria in 925, for al-Muʿizz was not yet living then. On the other hand, there is no indication that al-Muʿizz ever went to Italy. Moreover, Paltiel's name is not mentioned in any Arab source. The question has been reexamined by B. Lewis, who offers a new solution: Paltiel was Mūsā b. Elʿāzār, physician to al-Muʿizz and author of several books on medicine, who accompanied al-Muʿizz from North Africa to Egypt and whose sons and grandsons followed his profession.[3]

One more (renegade) Jew played an important part at the Fāṭimid court, and in his case, too, identification with Jawhar and Paltiel has been attempted. Jacob ben Killis, who according to tradition descended from Samuel ibn ʿĀdiyā, a famous Jewish poet in Arabia in the generation before Muḥammad, came to Africa at that time. In the days of Kāfūr, the Ikhshīdi ruler, Jacob b. Killis was in charge of the revenue of the Divan in Egypt and Syria (residing in Ramle for a time) and embraced Islam to secure promotion. He thus aroused the jealousy of the Vizier Jaʿfar, and after Kāfūr's death (968), Jacob was compelled to flee Egypt and joined al-Muʿizz. Reportedly with the help of Jews at the Fāṭimid court, he entered the service of that ruler, who was then preparing to attack Egypt. According to Arab writers, Jacob rendered great assistance to the Caliph's commander in that campaign. At the Fāṭimid court in Egypt, he

[1] Salzmann, *op. cit.*, pp. 19/93 (Klar, *op. cit.*, p. 43).
[2] Comp. de Goeje, *ZDMG*, 52 (1898), pp. 75-80; D. Neustadt, *Zion*, 4 (1939), pp. 135-141.
[3] B. Lewis, *BSOAS*, 30 (1967), pp. 177-181. See also below, p. 193.

rose steadily and eventually became Vizier, but although he had become a Muslim he maintained friendly relations with the Jews.[1]

Events in the Central and Western Maghreb

In those days, Kairouan, in the words of a legal document dated 978, was "a great city in Africa", although the centre of the caliphate had already shifted to Egypt. Fāṭimid rule extended over vast areas east of Egypt, viz. Palestine and Syria, and west of Egypt as far as Central Morocco. Before long, however, Fāṭimid control in the west weakened. At the first stage, control of Kairouan passed to the Banū Zīrī dynasty, whose founder had been a faithful helper of the Fāṭimids while they still resided in North Africa; his descendants had at first been appointed governors of the Maghreb on behalf of the Fāṭimids. Becoming powerful, the Banū Zīrī eventually severed their political ties with the Fāṭimids in Cairo and recognised the suzerainty of the ʿAbbāsid caliphs in Baghdad.[2]

Zīrī, of the Ṣanhāja Berber tribe, in accordance with the custom of the period, founded and fortified the city of Ashīr as a refuge for his family in an emergency. His son and heir, Bologin-Yūsuf, transferred many of the inhabitants of the vicinity to Ashīr, including the people of Tlemcen, who had revolted against him in the year 971/2. There were Jews among the exiles from Tlemcen, and the event is referred to in a question transmitted to Babylonia: "Reuben had some land in Tlemcen, and they were exiled to Ashīr and the land remained ownerless etc." ...; years later, they all returned to Tlemcen and took possession of their paternal and maternal property. The people of Fez were likewise exiled to Ashīr, probably after Bologin-Yūsuf had captured the city in the year 979.[3]

In the year 987, the people of Fez were still in exile, as we learn from "questions which the displaced community of Fez asked our master, the Academy Head Sherira, and Hay, the Judge of the Porte (דיינא דבבא)" and from the beginning of the only responsum preserved from that fascicle, which doubtless contained responsa to the other questions as well: "To all the rabbis and their disciples and the householders and general public whose residence used to be in Fez and is now in Ashīr

[1] Comp. *Sefer ha-Yishub* II, pp. 56-7; Neustadt, *l.c.*, p. 135. According to *Ibn ʿIdhārī*, p. 298, b. Killis's position was strengthened in 980; Jawhar and other viziers were removed from their posts. Comp. Fischel, *Jews*, pp. 45-68; and Hirschberg, *Nissim*, pp. 12-13, where still other biographical sources are quoted.

[2] Mann, *Texts* I, p. 363.

[3] *RH*, no. 38, and comp. Harkavy, *ibid.*, p. 348. For the history of Ashīr comp. now *EI*², *s.v.*

after being transferred from Fez. The good, excellent, select, enlightened etc." A list of Geonic responsa refers to other answers sent by the Gaon Sherira and his son Rab Hay to the exiles from Fez, who had incidentally mentioned the ritual bathhouses they had had in that city.[1]

An epistle of Samuel bar Ḥofni, Gaon of Sura and contemporary of Sherira and Hay, to the people of Fez mentions a great calamity which befell the Fez community. It reads as follows:

"Samuel ha-Cohen, Head of the Exilic Academy, the son of Ḥofni the Head, Father of the Exilic Academy, the son of Kohen Zedek, Head of the Exilic Academy, the son of Yosef the Nagid, Crown of the Exilic Academy, to the holy congregation, which is like the shining headpiece of the lamp and the greatest candle in the candelabrum, which unhesitatingly fulfils religious commandments, the glorious, superb community, the congregation of God, his jewel, his own people, which dwells in the great ancient city of Fez, the seat of the Law, the threshing-floor of wisdom, the winepress of the testimony, which drives away sleep to study the Law of the Lord, which breathes divine learning even in its sleep . . .

. . . Greetings to our brethren from us and from Israel, the Clerk of the Academy, our son proficient in the Law of the Lord, and from the heads of rows and the heads of colleges and chapters and the heads of closing sessions and heads of study groups, and from the *allufim* (masters scholars), scholars, sons of geonim, judges, repeaters, students and scribes. We shelter in the grace of God, address our supplications to him and utter our complaints in his shadow. We have heard what has happened to you and we are deeply shocked and grieved at the destruction of our sanctuary and the slaughter of the sons of our people and the evil wrought upon the flower of our manhood, and we pray God to slay their slayers, to let evil befall them, to smite with pestilence those who smote them, as it is written: Hath he smitten him, as he smote those that smote him? (Is. 27, 7), and we beg him to comfort us and you, to do good to you and to turn your mourning into joy and make your hearts rejoice from your sorrow, as it is said: Then shall the virgin rejoice in the dance etc. (Jer. 31, 13), and we will praise him and thank him for the evil as well as the good."[2]

The responsa quoted here refer to no specific date or place. Rab Sherira's responsa are clearly not later than the end of the 10th century

[1] *RA* I, no. 9 (p. 39); comp. J. Müller, *Mafteaḥ*, p. 54, note d; Mann, *JQR*, 11 (1920/21), pp. 439-440; Assaf, *Gaonica*, p. 228.

[2] Cowley, *JQR*, o.s., 18 (1906), pp. 403-404.

and were not impossibly sent to Ashīr. Not so R. Samuel bar Ḥofni's letter, of which we have advisedly quoted a large portion. It gives the impression of having been sent to Fez, but offers no clue to the time of the events. It is mere conjecture if we link it with what happened during the struggle between the Umayyads and the Zanāta Berber tribe for power in Fez.[1]

In fact, that period, from the middle of the 10th to the thirties of the 11th century, was a time of trouble and calamities for Fez. Control of Morocco and of Fez as its capital was fiercely contested by the Spanish Umayyads in Cordova, who wished to annex that country, and the Idrīsids, its long-time masters. After the overthrow of the latter there was fighting between the Cordovan rulers on the one hand and the Zīrī dynasty and the Zanāta Berber tribe on the other, and within the Zanāta themselves. This fighting caused suffering to the Jews.

It should be noted that about the same time a Jew was appointed collector of Jewish taxes for the whole of the Caliph's realm, including the areas conquered in Morocco, with Cordova as his seat of office. This happened in the days of the King Hishām II (who occupied the Cordovan throne in the years 976-1009 and 1010-1013) and of his foster-father, the "King" al-Manṣūr Muhammad ibn Abī ʿĀmir. Persons of great consequence at that time were Jacob ibn Jau and his brother Yūsuf, dealers in silk goods and costly garments "and very valuable Arab flags, the like of which were not manufactured in Spain". Al-Manṣūr, who was the actual ruler of the state, put Jacob ibn Jau in charge of all the Jewish communities in the Cordovan empire, as far as Sijilmāsa, which was the end of his dominion, "that he might judge all of them, appoint over them whomsoever he wished and determine every tax and payment due from them." After a year's tenure, however, Ibn Jau was imprisoned by the "King" al-Manṣūr, who had been disappointed of his hope that the *nāsī* would gratefully "bring in substantial contributions to him by levying money, properly or improperly, from all the Jewish communities."[2]

We may suppose that neither the Fāṭimids and their agents nor the Berbers viewed with any sympathy the appointment of the Spanish Jew over the Jews of Morocco, and they certainly suspected the latter of

---

[1] Toledano, *Nēr*, p. 221, thinks that this letter refers to the persecutions of 1033 (see next page). Assaf's reasoning, that R. Samuel b. Ḥofni died in 1033 and that the news of those events could therefore not have reached him (comp. *Ha-Shiloaḥ* 39 (1921), p. 449), is based on a mistaken assumption. R. Samuel died twenty years earlier; it was his son, Israel, who died in 1033. Comp. *MJC* I, p. 189, and Mann, *JQR*, 11 (1920/21), p. 410.

[2] Ibn Daud, *SHQ*, pp. 51/69; *EI*, *s.v.* Fez.

involvement in machinations against the indigenous population. Ibn Jau's elevation may have sparked anti-Jewish excesses in Fez, and perhaps also other localities, of which no information has reached us, although he surely had no authority to meddle in Muslim affairs.

The Jews suffered particularly when in 1032 Fez fell into the hands of the sheikh of a Berber tribe, who devastated the whole city, including the Jewish quarter. It is reported that over 6,000 Jews were killed on that occasion, while others were robbed of their women and their property.[1]

In between calamities there were periods of quiet, when life proceeded normally. This is evidenced by question-and-answer correspondence on halakhic matters between Fez scholars and Babylonian Geonim (Sherira, Hay, Samuel bar Ḥofni), such as the responsa to Mar Abraham and Mar Tanḥum. The Fez people had contacts also with Palestine, and two of them, David the "Workman" (he-Ḥārāsh) and Abudanī, brought from there the Gaon Saadia's commentary on the *Sefer Yeṣīra.*[2] The geographer al-Bekrī (middle of the 11th century) says about Fez: It is the largest city in the Maghreb as far as the number of the Jews is concerned, and from here they would proceed (on their travels) to all the countries of the world. A Maghrebi saying goes: "Fez is a city without people", *i.e.* without Muslims.[3]

Responsa from Babylonia were sent also to Tāhert and Sijilmāsa during that period. R. Samuel ben Abraham al-Tāherti carried on correspondence with Solomon ben Yehuda, the Palestinian gaon (in the second quarter of the 11th century), and with the Babylonian Academy. He undertook a journey from his city to Egypt and stopped over at Qābes.[4]

Muslim Tāhert, once the capital of a Khārijite state, was devastated in the early tenth century, losing its political and cultural significance. However, the local Jewish community continued to exist, no doubt because of the importance of Tāhert as a transit station between the coastal towns and the arid zone. We may perhaps assume that the sectarian relations between the Tāhert Muslims and the Berbers of Jebel Nafūsa were conducive to relations between the Jews of the two areas —for we know that there were Jews in Jebel Nafūsa at that time. Indeed,

---

[1] Lisān al-Dīn, *op. cit.* (see p. 100 n.1), pp. 161, 165; Beaumier, *Roudh*, p. 151; Nāṣirī, *al-Istiqṣā*, I, p. 202.

[2] Assaf, *Ha-Shiloaḥ* 39 (1921), p. 448. It is interesting to note that an al-Dāni appears in Fez at a different time; comp. Cat. Bodl. 2877, No. 31.

[3] *Al-Masālik*, p. 115/226.

[4] Comp Mann, *Jews* I, pp. 117, 119, 182, II, pp. 128, 218, 351, *Texts* I, p. 141.

the figure of the Jew might slip into a description of the climate of the city, noted for its long cold winter, as in the ditty quoted above.[1]

A different fate was that of Sijilmāsa, the great oasis in the southern part of the Ziz Valley. It, too, was founded by Khārijite secessionists, and the whole region was still inhabited by members of that sect during the period under discussion. We have already seen that Jews succeeded best in gaining a foothold in areas populated by Muslim sectarians. Sijilmāsa's importance as a starting-point of caravans bound for the Sahara made it a coveted prize for the political ambitions of the Fāṭimids and their satellites on the one hand, the Spanish Umayyads and their satellites on the other, and the original Berber masters of the country. The area frequently changed hands during the period under review.[2]

But wars and political upsets are one thing and business another. The economic importance of Sijilmāsa forced all the contestants to handle it gently. We see the Jews of Sijilmāsa engage in their classical pursuits—study of the Law and commerce. Halakhic questions are sent to Babylonia, and the Geonim reply by way of the intermediate station, Kairouan. Hay Gaon once replies concerning the permissibility of eating locusts, and we should not consider the matter trivial: in those hot regions, locusts are a staple food in years of drought, famine and disruption of trade routes.[3]

We have noted that the Fāṭimids were assisted in their attacks on the Central and Outermost Maghreb by emirs of the Zīrī family and by local Berber satellites subject to the emirs. Jewish leaders in Kairouan therefore deemed it their duty to see to it that no harm came to the Jews in the conquered areas. This task was undertaken especially by a leading religious scholar, R. Yehuda ben Joseph. A poem probably by a native of Fez and kept at the Geniza mentions the exiles from that city—and especially the women—who had been punished for their waywardness. The unknown poet thanks God for raising up "as a saviour and redeemer, a prince in Judah, Yehuda ben Joseph the divinely favoured one, who bares his arm, gathers in the children of the desolate woman" and uses his wealth to provide for them. Another Geniza fragment reports that R. Yehuda suddenly left for Mahdiya, apparently on public business. Hay Gaon also wrote a poem in praise of R. Yehuda ben Joseph. R. Yehuda died about 1020, and his death was widely noted. We may have to

---

[1] Comp. p. 97.

[2] Comp. Ibn ʿIdhārī, pp. 230-231; Beaumier, *Roudh*, p. 118; Terrasse, *Histoire* I, p. 169; Julien, *Histoire* II, p. 79.

[3] Comp. Ibn Quraysh, *Risāla*, pp. XVI-XVII.

identify him with R. Yehuda Fasi (= of Fez) ben Joseph, mentioned in the list of Hay Gaon's responsa. His origin from Fez might explain why he concerned himself particularly with the Fez victims, instead of leaving this task to the nagid of Africa, to whom it would have seemed to belong. In fact, a letter reporting R. Yehuda's death states that he gave support to those near to him. The question of the identity of the two R. Yehuda ben Joseph is nevertheless undecided.[1]

The Emirate of the Banū Zīrī

In contrast to the noise of battle that resounded again and again in the Outermost Maghreb, quiet reigned in the eastern part of North Africa, in the emirate of the Banū Zīrī. The numerous gaonic responsa of that period, which tell a great deal about the status and importance of the sages of Qābes, a port city on the southern part of the Tunisian coast, make no mention of any tribulations. The leading personalities engaged in halakhic discussions, debating with the Geonim of Pumbeditha problems which seem to have been of merely theoretical significance.

This was during the rule of the Fāṭimid Caliph al-Ḥākim bi-'Amr Allah (996-1021) or, as a Hebrew source calls him, "the one who judges by God's command, who reigns in the land of Egypt and governs in the corners of the earth, in the west, east, north and south." In the early part of his reign, he was sympathetic towards Jews and Christians and even had a Jewish court physician, who was nicknamed al-Ḥaqīr al-Nāfi', *i.e.* the useful wretch. But later he cruelly persecuted Christians and Jews in Egypt and Syria, wrecking and burning their places of worship. He also prescribed special dress for non-Muslims: black garments, and probably also black shoes.[2]

Nothing indicates that this campaign of persecution involved the Maghreb, which, too, was subject to the fierce Caliph—except for a slight hint at black shoes worn by the Jews.

There were two reasons why the Jews and—as far as there were any left—Christians of North Africa were exempt from al-Ḥākim's onslaught.

1. At the time of the persecution, the Banū Zīrī dynasty divided, and one branch tore off a portion of the emirate in the west and established its capital in the fortress Qal'at Banī Ḥammād, founded by it a few years

---

[1] Assaf, *Gaonica*, pp. 220, 224; *idem*, *Tarbiẓ* 20 (1949), p. 184; Schechter, *JQR* OS 11 (1898-99), p. 650. Comp. Hirschberg, *Nissim*, p. 17, n. 29; and ch. V-VI below. Also Abramson, *Tarbiẓ* 31 (1962), pp. 192-5.

[2] Mann, *Jews* II, pp. 35, also 33, 36; also *ibid.*, I, pp. 32-33, 35-36.

previously (1007). Let us note right now that, according to R. Abraham ben Daud, R. Isaac ben Jacob Alfasi (born in the first or second decade of the 10th century) originated from Qalʿat Ḥammād. This means that Jews already came to Qalʿa (Arabic for "citadel") a few years after its foundation. Obviously, at a time of division and internecine strife between the two branches, the Emir of Kairouan, Bādis, whom al-Ḥākim had endowed with the title (and name) Naṣīr al-Dawla, *i.e.* defender of the (Fāṭimid) state, was not anxious to breed conflict within his own country by persecuting Jews and Christians.[1]

2. During the al-Ḥākim persecution, tension increased in Kairouan between two factions in the Muslim population, the Sunnite majority and the Shīʿites, who depended on the Egyptian rulers. After Bādis's death (1016), the emirate fell to his eight-year-old son, al-Muʿizz. The populace, apparently upon a hint from al-Muʿizz's tutors, used this opportunity to riot against the Shīʿites, kill and loot indiscriminately and attack even mosques. Many thousands of Shīʿites were killed in Kairouan in the years 1016-1019. A caravan of Shīʿites who had escaped from the city and intended to cross to Sicily were attacked *en route*, the women raped, and all subsequently killed. After reporting this outrage, the Arab chronicler adds laconically: "In that year (1018/9), there was a great dearth in Afrīqiya and much fighting."[2]

This situation was another reason for the Kairouan rulers, who were already preparing to defect from the Fāṭimids, not to imitate al-Ḥākim's oppression of Jews and Christians.

Nevertheless, in those years of unrest, rebellion, war and famine, the Jews were not exempt from fear and suffered both bodily and material harm, although, as a rule, the rebels and rioters did not aim at them specifically. Two letters then sent to Fusṭāṭ by the brothers Joseph and Nissim, the sons of Berakhya, leading members of the Kairouan community, contain accounts reflecting the state of minds among the Jews and particulars of important events.

One letter says, *inter alia*: "I have already explained to you that, with the help of God the Great and Exalted, quiet has come to our area after the unrest which reigned there and we have calmed down after the fear in which we lived, and I have also told you of the safe return of the Sultan

---

[1] On Alfasi and the judge b. Formash in Qalʿat Ḥammad see Ibn Daud, *SHQ*, pp. 78, 84; comp. Poznanski, *REJ* 58 (1909), p. 297. There were also many Christians living at Qalʿa; Hopkins, *Government*, p. 68.

[2] Ibn ʿIdhārī, pp. 268-269, 277; Ibn Khaldūn VI, 158/II, pp. 18-22; Marçais, *Berbérie*, pp. 166-171.

from the west with large booty and of the return with him of the Sheikh, our Lord Abū Isḥāq the Nagid, and that upon their arrival from the west..."

In the second letter, sent a short time after the nagid's death, Joseph and Nissim describe the dangerous situation created upon the passing of that guardian and mainstay of the community. In precarious times like those, enemies of the Jews raise their heads. The writers note especially the plight of the inhabitants of remote localities when no one intervenes on their behalf and officials are at liberty to harass them. To make matters worse, that other protector and helper of his people, R. Yehuda ben Joseph (whose illness during a stay in Mahdiya is known from an addition on the sheet of the first letter), died in the same year.

Here is a translation of one paragraph of the letter:

"And the affairs of the kingdom, O our brethren, are very perplexed; and our city at this time is tightly closed, no one can go out or come in. The area has become impoverished through famine and drought, and after this year had brought some relief by rains, God passed sentence upon that Lord and took him to himself. And the region has been left unprotected and desolate. I beg God to have his spirit dwell upon us so that we may prosper. The people of Qābes, too, were overtaken by a great calamity through the levy that was imposed upon them in the days of the famine when they were unprotected. Most of them are at this time in our city. And as for the far west, *i.e.* Sijilmāsa and other places, their people have perished by starvation and by the sword, and we are in great fear. May God calm our fear and relieve our anxiety."[1]

As explained below, the nagid was the Emir's physician; this was why he was always in his company.[2]

Neither letter indicates the year. With the help of a datum contained in the second letter, viz. the death of the Nagid Abū Isḥāq, *i.e.* R. Abraham b. ʿAṭā, which probably did not occur before approximately 1020, since at that time the Gaon R. Israel bar Samuel (bar Ḥofni) dedicated his work on prayer rites to him,[3] and with the help of hints at certain events, we shall try, with reference to Arab historians, to determine the years when the two letters were written. We can of course hardly expect to find records of specifically Jewish matters with Arab authors. Nor is it to be

---

[1] Assaf, *Tarbiẓ* 20 (1949), p. 179, 11-4-6. p. 185, 11, 31-38. See also Abramson as quoted above p. 110 n. 1.

[2] Comp. below, pp. 304 f.

[3] Comp. Mann, *JQR* 11 (1920/21), p. 415.

assumed that a chronicler, even a contemporary one, will appreciate and mention details such as frequently appear in letters sent by one person to another in the actual course of events.

The first letter, announcing the quiet prevailing in the area and the return of the emir with the Nagid Abraham b. ʿAṭā, was presumably written in December, 1014. In 1014, the second branch of the dynasty openly revolted against Bādis. Confusion gripped the court of the emir of Kairouan, who evacuated his family and household from the capital to the fortress of Mahdiya, two days' journey from Kairouan, and marched against the rebels. He routed them and took a great deal of booty (in fact, it proved unfortunate for him that his soldiers began to deal with the loot rather than pursue the enemy, who managed to escape).

During the campaign, Bādis learnt that his son and heir, on whom al-Ḥākim had conferred the title *ʿAzīz al-Dawla, i.e.* the one dear to the nation, had died in an epidemic. The chronicler reports that the emir took the blow with courageous resignation. It seems natural that immediately after the victory he should have gone for a few days to see how things were at home and to show the booty he had taken, for the distance between the battlefield and his capital was not great. True, such a short visit is not mentioned in the chronicle, which says only that the emir continued the war and died in camp.

The nagid's stay in the west at that time is easily accounted for. The fate of many communities in the disputed area—such as Ashīr, Mesīla, Tāhert—trembled in the balance, and constant intercession and intervention by the nagid were required to shield them from harm. According to R. Joseph ben Berakhya, the nagid was at first expected to stay longer in the west, but was able to return after two months—probably thanks to Bādis's splendid victory and his return to Kairouan. For, in Kairouan, too, there were things for him to set right. The closing of all (not only Jewish) shops and markets and their transfer to a distant suburb, to which the Ṣanhāja Berbers were also to move, had meanwhile been ordered there, and this measure threatened to ruin Jewish shopkeepers and hawkers.

The second letter probably dates from 1019 or 1020, *i.e.* about five or six years later than the first. The political climate had meanwhile changed radically. Whereas in the first letter Joseph and Nissim tried to reassure their friend in Fusṭāṭ by stressing that all was quiet in their country, a spirit of unrest and the lack of a strong ruling hand were now already making themselves felt. The boy emir—only twelve years old—was dominated by his mentors and guardians, and the governors in the distant provincial towns of the west behaved like independent rulers, since they could always revolt and go over to the Banū Ḥammād, the other branch of the dynasty. Fighting was no doubt rife among the Berber governors and sheikhs as well, which was why the people of Kairouan feared to leave their city. These tribulations were augmented by a severe famine, and it seems natural that it should have been particularly serious in the south, in the Qābes region. Spells of drought were usually accompanied by incursions of nomad tribes with their cattle into farming settlements and cities to escape death from starvation. All this is hinted at in the above-quoted short sentence from Ibn ʿIdhārī. The Sunnite writers tend to glorify the period of al-Muʿizz, when the Shīʿites came in for punishment, and to tone down its negative aspects.

The drought and famine of 1018/9 were—according to the letter-writers—followed by relief at the onset of the rains, but then the nagid died and the joy of the Jews turned into mourning and uneasiness about the future.[1]

The Destruction of Kairouan

This was the situation at the beginning of the reign of al-Muʿizz, which according to Arab historians was altogether a period of peace and prosperity in the emirate until the Fāṭimids began to incite the Beduins against him. It seems that even in those good days the Jews repeatedly endured hardships of which the chronicles make no mention. A letter of the Palestinian Gaon Solomon ben Yehuda to Fusṭāṭ, discovered in the Geniza, mentions incidentally "what happened to the Kairouan community when the hand was extended against them and their enemies would have prevailed but for the mercy of the Merciful . . . the Nagid Rabbenu Jacob was of some help."[2] This letter dates from the thirties of the 11th century, but no particulars of the danger then threatening Kairouan Jewry can be gathered from it, nor is that danger mentioned in the letters of R. Nissim ben Jacob or Rabbenu Ḥananel, distinguished yeshiva heads whose activities in Kairouan at that time will be discussed below.

A few years later, the general situation in the country deteriorated. In the forties, al-Muʿizz openly defected from his Egyptian overlord and swore allegiance to the Baghdad Caliph, whose name again appeared in Friday prayers at mosques. The Fāṭimids sent the Upper Egyptian

[1] The Arab source is *Ibn ʿIdhārī*, pp. 249, 261. *Ibid.*, pp. 256-257, we find an account of the famine of the year 335/1004; comp. Idris, *Berbérie* I, p. 399.

[2] Mann, *Jews* II, p. 163, 11.27-29.

nomad Beduin tribes of the Hilāl and Sulaym against the rebel. These launched recurrent marauding expeditions against Cyrenaican, Tripolitanian and Tunisian cities. The authorities were compelled to withdraw from Kairouan to a suburb and defend Old Kairouan from there. Part of the population also left the city, and the emir sought refuge in the well-fortified and easily defensible citadel of al-Mahdiya. In 1057, the Beduin broke into Kairouan and wrought havoc there. The palaces of the sheikhs of the Ṣanhāja tribe and the houses of the rich were looted; the inhabitants scattered in all directions.[1]

This happened shortly after the death of R. Ḥananel ben Ḥushiel (1056), as we gather from a fragmentary Geniza letter which alludes to those events while noting that the Gaon and Yeshiva Head has appointed Nissim ראש בי רבנן "Head of the Rabbis House" (Academy) and representative of the Yeshiva for the whole of the Maghreb in succession to R. Ḥananel. This information is followed by a brief description of Kairuoan: "God wanted the ruin of this country and the destruction of those in it. We beg God to do good ... and look upon us in his mercy, etc.". And again: "... will write to the community and console them for what happened to them—their subsequent exile from their city and departure from their country. Their quarter and אלמקדש אלגליל (sumptuous synagogue) were the admiration of every passerby ..."[2]

We do not know where this letter was written—whether in Kairouan or in Mahdiya—and are therefore unable to deduce from it whether the Kairouan Jews were vouchsafed to return to their city or were banished from it for ever. The request that comfort be extended to the people of Kairouan permits of no definite conclusion, for the writer may have meant that the Gaon's message should be sent to the place where the community had found refuge. At any rate, if they returned, part of them will surely not have remained there long. The city as a whole was becoming impoverished, for before there had been time to rebuild the ruins of 1057, it was sacked by a nomad Berber tribe in 1060. From then onwards, the actual masters of the country were the Beduin, who extorted and pillaged the population at will.

From a Geniza letter discussed by S. D. Goitein we learn that R. Nissim

---

[1] Arab sources are unanimous about the events, though divergent about dates; comp. Ibn ʿIdhārī, pp. 263-295; Ibn Khaldūn ʿIbar VI, pp. 15-16, p. 158. I, pp. 34-38, II, pp. 20-22. Comp. Julien, *Histoire* II, pp. 74-75.

[2] Mann, *Texts* I, pp. 244 and 246. This synagogue aroused the anger of a Muslim religious scholar, who regarded it as infringing Omar's Ordinance; comp. Idris, *Berbérie*, p. 768.

left his native Kairouan for Mahdiya and died there in June or July, 1062. Another letter, of approximately 1061, mentions the (unnamed) nagid of Kairouan, who was forced to leave the country and moved westward; he was so poor that (Jewish) merchants from Tunisia living in Egypt had to collect money for him.[1]

When al-Muʿizz died in 1063, the state began to disintegrate. Every important city and every region became an "independent" kingdom. Upon the destruction of Kairouan, nodal point of the threads connecting the individual Jewish settlements all over the country, continuous information about them ceases. This must not be taken to mean that these communities ceased to exist, but merely that they are no longer traceable. A handful of Jews seems to have lived in Kairouan for quite a considerable time. It is mentioned in a letter of the middle of the 12th century as a place where Jews can live.[2] According to a late Arab writer, their complete expulsion from the city took place in the second half of the 13th century, when Kairouan was proclaimed one of the holy cities of Islam and Jews and Christians were forbidden to reside in it as well as in Ḥammāmet near Tunis.[3] Although a document of the year 1500 discovered in the Great Mosque of Kairouan mentions one Maimūn the Jew as the lessee of a shop in the Muslim endowment, he was probably a convert to Islam.[4] Joseph ha-Kohen (middle of the 16th century) reports that Jews were forbidden to reside in Kairouan because it was the seat of the "Ismaelite High Priest".[5]

After the destruction of Kairouan, the administrative centre of the state moved westward, at first to Qalʿat Banī Ḥammād. One branch of the Banū Ḥammād succeeded in coming to an agreement with the Beduin who had devastated Tunisia, and by means of an annual tribute protected its country from their incursions. During that period, the importance of the Qalʿa Jewish community obviously increased, and a Jewish historian about a hundred years after the destruction of Kairouan notes that Qalʿa shares Kairouan's spiritual heritage with Mahdiya.[6] The city of Majāna

[1] Goitein, *Zion* 27 (1962), pp. 17-19.

[2] Comp. the letter published by Braslavsky, *Zion* 7 (1942), p. 137, l. 24 and p. 132 below.

[3] Cazès, *Essai*, pp 83-84.

[4] Brunschvig, *Berbérie* I, p. 399.

[5] *Dibrei ha-Yamim*, Amsterdam 1733, f. 114a. ʿAli of Herat (12th-13th cent.; ed. Janine Sourdel-Thomine, Damascus 1953, p. 53) knows that seven of the *tābiʿīn* (second generation of Mohammed's followers) are buried in Kairouan.

[6] Comp. Ibn Daud, *SHQ* p. 58/78. Upon the expulsion of the Muslims from Sicily in 1061, a Jewish immigrant from Spain, Moses b. Joseph ibn Kashkil, left

(north of Qalʿa), with a district rich in natural resources, had also long had a large Jewish population, as evidenced by documents.[1]

In the late 11th century, the Banū Ḥammād transferred their capital to Bajāya (now Bougie) on the Mediterranean, at about the longitude of Qalʿa and Majāna, since it seemed safer to them from Beduin raids. We may assume that Jews moved there together with the Ṣanhāja, although Jewish communities in Bajāya and Algiers are mentioned only in a list of places of Almohad days.[2]

The Almoravids and Almohads; the First Forced Conversions

In the very same period when Beduin marauders descended upon the Banū Zīrī kingdom in the eastern part of the region (Tripolitania, Tunisia) and the Banū Ḥammād consolidated their position in the centre (today Central Algeria), there arose in the west, among the Berbers in the Sūs and Darʿa valleys, the religious-social-military movement of the *murābiṭūn* (Almoravids), *i.e.* people of the *ribāṭ*, the strongholds of bands of defenders of Islam against enemies without and heretical views within. The people called those Berbers "veil-wearers" because they veiled their faces like women. The Almoravids aimed at purifying Berber religious life in the spirit of traditional belief, as represented by the Malikite school, one of the four schools of orthodox Islam.They at first attacked the small Shīʿite principalities at Sijilmāsa and Taroudant. As they became more powerful, under the leadership of Yūsuf ibn Tāshfīn (1061-1106), the founder of Marrakesh (1062), they undertook large-scale conquests in Africa and Spain. After subduing Morocco, they turned eastward, captured Tlemcen, Wahrān (Oran) and Tenes and advanced to east of Algiers, which fell to them (1082) after a siege. They thus reached the border of the Banū Ḥammād state.

We do not know whether the Jews suffered more by that fighting than the rest of the civilian population. This absence of information may indicate that they were not specially affected. Such an assumption may be strengthened by a report that the Jews of the Maghreb paid *jizya* (protec-

---

Sicily for Mahdiya, where in 1079 he wrote a commentary on a biblical story; comp. Mann, *Texts* I, pp. 386-393.

[1] Comp. *RA* II, pp. 2 and 23, no. 69; Mann, *T* I, pp. 143, l. 18, 344, l. 17, and 362, l. 7; Assaf, *Tarbiẓ* 20 (1950), pp. 179, l. 3, and 181, n. 3; Goitein, *ibid.*, pp. 202, n. 38, and 203, n. 46.

[2] Comp. p. 141 nn. 16, 17. A far echo about Kairouan in Eshtori ha-Farhi's, *Caftor wa-pherach* (14th cent.) ed. A. Edelmann, Berlin 1852, p. 26b.

tion tax) under Yūsuf. The story of R. Isaac Alfasi, who fled from Fez to Cordova in 1088, contains no hint of religious persecution. One manuscript indeed has it that in 1071 Yūsuf ibn Tāshfīn imposed upon the Jews a *farīḍa* (compulsory levy), which yielded 100,000 dinars, a very considerable sum; this seems to have been a kind of property confiscation. Anyhow, it stands to reason that many Jews crossed to Spain in those days, which would account for the slackening intellectual activity and general quiescence we now find in Morocco. We know that the army of Alfonso VI of Castile, which fought the Almoravids in their drive into the Pyrenean Peninsula, included Jews, and it is also reported that the Muslim conquerors from Africa were helped by Jews who accompanied them or followed closely behind.[1]

After two generations, Almoravid power began to wane. There arose in that same South Moroccan region the new religious movement of the Almohads, *i.e.* upholders of unity (*muwaḥḥidūn*), who proclaimed the absolute unity of God, maintaining that no physical or moral attributes must be ascribed to him.

This movement, too, whose founder was Muḥammad ibn Tūmart, the Mahdi, *i.e.* the one guided by Allah, did not content itself with preaching, but sought to spread its ideas by the sword. At first, in the twenties of the 12th century, Ibn Tūmart enlisted support among the Berbers of his country. He went to Fez, Meknes and Salé and also to Marrakesh, the capital of the Almoravids. Everywhere he debated with religious scholars, preached purity and staged demonstrations to stir up feelings against moral corruption. Eventually he settled in his home district, the Nefīs and Upper Sūs Valleys. Here, in the wilderness of the High Atlas Mountains, he built the fortress of Tinmalāl, whence he sent emissaries to organize his adherents and carry out purges (*tamyīz*) among those known or suspected to be unreliable. He died—according to most sources—in 1130, and the leadership passed to ʿAbd al-Mu'min, his deputy, as directed in his will. The events and dates of his career are reported with great variations, but the general picture is clear.

ʿAbd al-Mu'min at first operated in the Atlas Mountains and the southern valleys; the Tāfilālet, *i.e.* the Southern Zīz Valley, and its capital, Sijilmāsa, yielded to him in 1140. But only in 1145 did he advance into the northern coastal plain. Here he captured Oran—at the defence of which Tāshfīn ibn ʿAli, who had only recently succeeded to the Almoravid

---

[1] Comp. Beaumier, *Roudh*, pp. 191 and 213; Ibn Daud, *SHQ*, p. 84; Hopkins, *Government*, p. 47.

throne, was killed—and Tlemcen; Sijilmāsa sent a thanksgiving mission to erase the memory of insurrections against Almohad rule which had occurred there during the preceding years. Then the Almohads attacked Fez and Marrakesh (1146/7). In 1147, ʿAbd al-Mu'min sent an army to Spain, where many important cities, including Seville, were conquered; others, such as Cordova, surrendered. The Banū Ḥammād state succumbed to the Almohads in 1152.[1]

The eastern parts of our region, Tripoliṭania and Cyrenaica, did not seem to interest the Almohad leader. Those countries had for a hundred years been a prey to nomad Arabs, the Banū Hilāl and Banū Sulaym, who turned fertile agricultural lands and thriving commercial cities into deserts. This situation had been taken advantage of by King Roger of Sicily, who during the years 1134-1148 captured the important seaports in that area, viz. (in geographical order): Jijilli (Algeria) Sousse, Mahdiya, Sfax, the Qerqina (Kerkenna) Islands, Qābes (1143-1148), the Jerba Peninsula (1134) and the Tripolitanian ports (1146).

In view of the threatening spread of Christian rule, the Muslims asked the Almohads for help, and the latter set out in 1159 from their Moroccan centre to complete what they had begun fifteen years previously. In this campaign, the most difficult part of which was the capture of fortified Mahdiya, ʿAbd al-Mu'min drove the Normans from Africa and shifted the boundary of his state to within the sphere of influence of Egypt, which was still under Fāṭimid rule.[2]

ʿAbd al-Mu'min died in 1163, a few years after completing his work —the union of the whole of North Africa under the Muminids, as the dynasty founded by Ibn Tūmart's deputy is called. But he himself had created the nucleus of the force which ultimately supplanted the Berbers in their own country. To prevent unrest in the newly-conquered territories, and to resettle the Outermost Maghreb, depopulated by the mass extermination of opponents, he had brought Arab Beduin to his homeland. This was the beginning of the end of the sovereignty of the Berber tribes.

---

[1] Comp. Ibn al-Athīr X, pp. 401-402; Goldziher, *ZDMG* 41 (1887), pp. 30-140; Marçais, *Berbérie*, pp. 245 and 253-275. The most important sources for this period are the biographies of Ibn Tūmart and ʿAbd al-Mu'min by their contemporary, Abu Bekr al-Ṣinhājī, surnamed al-Baydhaq; comp. Lévi-Provençal, *Documents*. For the surrender of Sijilmāsa comp. Ibn Khaldūn, *ʿIbar* VI, p. 231 (II, p. 179).

[2] Ibn ʿIdhārī, pp. 313 and 316; Ibn al-Athīr XI, pp. 158-162; Beaumier, *Roudh*, pp. 279-281; Ibn Khaldūn, *ʿIbar* VI, p. 337 (II, pp. 193-194).

Moses Darʿi Predicts the Coming of the Messiah

Arab historians completely ignore the sufferings of Jews and Christians in those days. Ibn al-Athīr reports that upon the capture of Tunis in 1159 ʿAbd al-Mu'min gave them the choice between conversion to Islam and death. Other sources say that the Almohad leader waived the *jizya*, and thus abrogated the protective relationship, and gave those who were not prepared to join him time to leave the country.[1]

These occurrences at the end of Almoravid rule, and particulars of the forced conversions are reflected in several Jewish sources, some of which are near to the events in place and time and may therefore be regarded as faithful first- and second-hand accounts, while others cast the available data into the mould of elegies, without aiming at order, historical correctness or completeness of description.

Two versions of an epistle of Maimonides to Yemen contain a description of an event which deeply perturbed the Jews of Fez in the twenties of that century. After warning against the lure of self-proclaimed Messiahs and telling about a "Messiah" who had appeared in the East, he continues in the shorter version as follows:[2]

"There also arose a man in the west, in the city of Fez, eighteen years ago, saying that he was the harbinger and messenger of the Messiah, who would appear during that year. His prediction did not come true, and the Jews suffered fresh tribulations on his account. The story was told me by a person who was present at all those events."

And here is the longer version:

"And this I am reporting to you as something certain, knowing that it is true because of its nearness in time. For, fifty years ago or thereabouts, a devout, excellent man, a scholar in Israel by the name of Master Moses Darʿi, came from Darʿa to Spain to study the Law under Rabbi Joseph Halevi b. Megāsh, of blessed memory, of whom you have heard. Thereafter he came to the capital of the Maghreb, *i.e.* Fez, and the people of the place flocked to him because he was a devout, excellent and learned man. He said to them: Lo, the Messiah is coming, God has told me so in a dream. He did not, as that mad man had done, boast that he knew he was the Messiah; he only said he had been told that the Messiah had revealed himself. And the people were attracted to him and believed him. My father and teacher, may that righteous man's memory be blessed,

---

[1] Comp. Ibn al-Athīr XI, p. 160; Munk, *Notice*, pp. 40-45.
[2] Halkin, *Maimonides' Ep. T.*, pp. 99 and 101-103.

would dissuade and prohibit the people from following him. But few listened to my father, their rabbi—in fact, all turned after R. Moses, may his soul rest in Paradise. Eventually, he would make predictions, which proved completely correct. If he said: it was revealed to me yesterday that such-and-such a thing would happen, it would be exactly as he had said. One day, he told them that on a certain Friday it would rain heavily, and the liquid that came down would be blood, and that would be the sign of which it is said 'And I will shew wonders in the heaven and in the earth' etc. (Joel 3, 3). It was in the month of Marheshvan, and it rained hard and fast that Friday, and the water that came down was red and slimy, as if it had been mixed with clay. This was the sign by which he proved to all the people that he was undoubtedly a prophet; as I have told you, it is not impossible that prophesy will revive before the coming of the Messiah. And when most of the people believed him, he told them that the Messiah would come on Passover Eve of that year. And he ordered them to sell their property and to borrow money from the Muslims with the promise to pay ten dinars for every one, thus fulfilling the commandment of the Tora with regard to the Passover Festival, because they would never see them again; and they did so. And when Passover came and nothing happened, those people were ruined, for most of them lost all their property and were burdened with debts. The matter became known also among their Gentile neighbours and servants, and if he had been found he would have been killed. He could not remain in the lands of Islam after this, and he went to the Land of Israel and died there, may his memory be blessed.[1] On leaving, as I have been informed by all those who saw him, he foretold everything, great and small, that has happened in the Maghreb, in accordance with what God had announced to him."[2]

This long account, an enlargement of the first-quoted version, is important because of Maimonides' initial statement that he vouches for its truth as he heard the story from reliable persons who had known Moshe Darʿi personally and whom he questioned about details. This emphatic affirmation, which Maimonides saw fit to place at the beginning

[1] For Moses' stay in Palestine comp. *Maimonides' Responsa*, ed. Freimann, 1934, p. 9, l. 7; also *Shebeṭ Yehuda*, ed. Shohet, pp. 77 and 191. For Messianic movements in those days comp. Mann, *Hatekufa* 23 (1925), pp. 243-261; 24 (1928), pp. 335-358; Goitein, *JQR*, 43 (1952-53), pp. 57-76.

[2] Halkin's view (introd., p. XXXII), that the longer version is the original one, is difficult to accept; its extant form, at any rate, is later than the extant form of the shorter version. According to the longer version, Moses Darʿi appeared fifty years previously, and according to the shorter version, forty-five years previously.

of his report, undoubtedly deserves most serious notice. The discrepancy as to the date of the events—fifty years or forty-five years before the date of the letter (allegedly 1122 or 1127)—is not material to our subject; in any case, we do not know the exact date of the Epistle to Yemen in either redaction. The decisive fact is that Moses' Darʿi's prophecies were made after Muḥammad ibn Tūmart had been in Fez. His visit took place before 1120. On that occasion, he debated with the *ṭulabā*, the scholars of Islam, on the principles of religion and went to the market with his disciples to smash musical instruments; according to one source, he was expelled from the city. From Fez, Ibn Tūmart went to Meknes and Marrakesh, and his appearance in these two places no doubt made a great impression and caused unrest not only among the Muslim population.[1]

In this general turmoil, Darʿi's prophecies of the coming of the Messiah on Passover Eve found willing ears, especially as they were accompanied by seemingly corroborating signs. Their non-fulfilment caused acute disappointment. The Muslims, too, must have heard of the episode, and the failure of the prophet surely was a trump-card of the Almohads twenty years later in their attempts to convert the Jews.

In the early thirties of the century, we find at the court of the Almoravid ruler ʿAlī ibn Yūsuf ibn Tāshfīn (1106-1142) the physician Meir ben Qamniel and another Jewish physician Solomon b. al-Muʿallim, who had both been invited from Spain, the latter from Seville.[2] When at that time the local mosque, which had proved too small for the number of worshippers, was to be enlarged, it appeared that many Muslem endowment properties had passed into private hands and that most of the houses to the south were Jewish-owned. In accordance with religious law, the land necessary for the enlargement of the mosque was expropriated from both Muslims and Jews; this happened in the year 529 A.H. (1134/5). But the owners all received fair compensation, which may have been due to the influence of the two Jewish physicians who had access to the king; a sovereign's physicians in ordinary were always persons of consequence.[3]

However, the ban imposed by that ruler on the residence of Jews in the capital, Marrakesh, founded by his father, was a flagrant act of discrimination. Marrakesh was at first only a large encampment of Berber nomads,

---

[1] Comp. Lévi-Provençal, *Documents*, p. 63, and the notes to the translation, pp. 99ff.

[2] Comp. Suesmann Muntner (ed.), *Treatise on Asthma* (by Maimonides), Philadelphia (1963), p. 94 (*Sefer ha-Qaẓeret*, Jerusalem 1940, p. 43); Schirmann, *Tarbiẓ* 9 (1938), p. 52; Halkin, *Marx Jubilee Volume*, 1950, English Section, p. 391.

[3] Al-Jaznāi, *Zahrat al-Ās*, p. 57/125; Beaumier, *Roudh*, p. 75; comp. also *ibid.*, p. 78.

and the city of Aghmāṭ Wāylan, capital of the Banū Maghrāwa, the predecessors of the Almoravids, situated forty kilometres to the south-east in a grandiose landscape at the foot of the High Atlas, continued to be the administrative centre of the country, although it remained unfortified.[1] We may assume that there were Jews at Marrakesh already in its early days, having come there in the course of their business, just as they came to other nomad encampments. In time, solid buildings were erected at Marrakesh, and ʿAlī himself surrounded it with a wall—the hallmark of a royal city—and constructed a mosque which was subsequently destroyed by the Almohads because its *miḥrāb* did not face south but east—in accordance with the Jewish custom of facing east in prayer, as noted by Ibn Tūmart's and ʿAbd al-Mu'min's biographer. In those days began the decline of Aghmāt as the centre of government, and many Jews apparently asked to settle in the new capital. This displeased ʿAlī, who towards the end of his life shut himself up in his palace and harem and listened to religious scholars and his womenfolk. He demonstrated his Muslim zeal by building sumptuous mosques; besides erecting that of Marrakesh, he enlarged the Qarawiyīn (= people of Kairouan) Mosque in Fez and in 1136 constructed the Great Mosque in Tlemcen. He further decreed that any Jews found in Marrakesh at night should be killed and their property confiscated. They were only permitted to be in the capital in the daytime in the pursuit of their business or trade.[2]

The ban on settlement in Marrakesh was only a kind of prelude to the troubles visiting non-Muslims and even many Muslims in Africa and Europe in the fifth and sixth decades of that century, when the Almohads launched their above-described campaign of conquest.

The Almohad Persecutions

Abraham ibn Ezra's famous lament *Ahā yārad* (Oh, there descended) is our main source for that calamity, since it mentions several communities that were destroyed, describing the attendant events. First some in Spain: Seville, Cordova, Jaen (גיאן), Almería. Then some in Africa: Sijilmāsa, "city of the learned and wise"; Marrakesh, "the royal city"; Fez; Tlemcen; Ceuta; Meknes; Darʿa, "where the blood of sons and daughters was spilt on a Sabbath day". According to the poem, the persecution took

[1] For its importance in pre-Almoravid times comp. Ibn Ḥawqal, *BGA* II², p. 91; *Maqdisi*, *BGA* III, p. 227.

[2] Comp. Lévi-Provençal, *Documents*, p. 105/174; Dozy—de Goeje, *Description*, p. 69/79-80 (see below, p. 125 n. 1); also Terrasse, *Histoire* I, p. 290.

place in the year 1070 or, if we follow the Tripoli MS., 1072 after the destruction of the Second Temple, *i.e.* 1138 or 1140 C.E. The events are strung together without chronological or geographical order (those in Spain are placed first), so that we may assume that Ibn Ezra, who was roaming about Europe in those days, did not know their exact sequence. The lament must have been composed not later than the end of the fifties, *i.e.* before the news of the expulsion of the Normans from Africa and the conquests of ʿAbd al-Mu'min in Tunisia and Tripolitania spread in Europe. It was very popular, and several additions and supplements to it have come down to us.[1]

Among the Geniza documents, Schirmann has discovered a fragment of this lament which differs in many points from the previously known version.[2] The main differences between the two versions concern the order in which the events are reported and the story of a disputation held in Darʿa between the Jews and the Muslim conquerors;[3] this story appears only in the Geniza fragment. We shall see below, in Solomon Cohen's letter, that a similar debate in Sijilmāsa lasted seven months. Such debates were fully in accordance with the spirit and methods of ʿAbd al-Mu'min and his predecessor Ibn Tūmart. The Almohads at first tried to win over the population by debate and preaching, and only afterwards resorted to more drastic means of persuasion.

An addition concerning Fez in the Geniza fragment describes that city as an important centre of Jewish religious learning, but does not enrich our knowledge of historical events. The Geniza fragment makes no mention of Marrakesh. The above data as to ʿAlī ibn Yūsuf's ban on Jewish settlement there make it likely that the verse about the "royal city", which appears in only one MS. of the familiar version of the lament, is a late addition by a person who knew that Jews were harmed in that region also, but who knew no particulars. On the other hand, the Geniza fragment mentions Aghmāṭ and Sūs. This detail is important because it proves that the information given here is more exact than that contained in the familiar version.

Aghmāṭ is the name of the ancient settlement near Marrakesh where

---

[1] The lament has been published many times; *e.g.*, D. Kahana, *R. Abraham ibn Ezra* I, pp. 140ff.; I. Davidson, *Thesaurus of Medieval Hebrew Poetry*, vol. I, 1924, pp. 61-62, no. 1301. For the Tripolitanian MS. comp. Cazès, *REJ* 20 (1890), p. 84; I. Loeb, *ibid.*, p. 316.

[2] He published it in *Qobeẓ al-Yad* 3 (13), 1939, pp. 33-35.

[3] Disputations were among the foremost activities of the Almohads; comp. above p. 118, and Munk, *Notice*, pp. 42-44; Tritton, *Materials on Muslim Education in the Middle Ages*, 1957, p. 84.

Jews lived because they had been forbidden to live in Marrakesh itself since the days of ʿAlī ibn Yūsuf. It is not to be supposed that Jews moved to Marrakesh precisely during the three years of war and unrest between ʿAlī's death and the capture of the city by the Almohads.[1]

In referring to the fate of Sūs, the poet meant the region south of Marrakesh and Aghmāṭ, which was the cradle of Almohadism. The Sūs Valley runs south from the Atlas Mountains and then turns towards the Atlantic coast; its mention in the Geniza fragment attests that it had a Jewish population. Hence all three South Moroccan valleys: the Ziz Valley, with Sijilmāsa, the Darʿa Valley and the Sūs Valley, had Jewish populations.

Schirmann has published a fragment of yet another lament, which in his opinion likewise deals with North African events, but which mentions no place-names. It begins with the words *Eykh neḥerāb* (Oh, there was devastated). Schirmann surmises that both fragments stem from Abraham ibn Ezra.[2] If this is correct, we must suppose that "Oh, there was devastated" is a later, amended version of "Oh, there descended", written when the poet had obtained more exact and detailed information, also as regards the chronological order of events.

Jewish historiography has preserved three short notes on the sufferings of African Jewry about the middle of the 12th century. One is by Abraham ben David, who says: "... those were years of distress, oppression and persecution to Israel, and they were exiled from their localities: such as were for death, to death, and such as were for the sword, to the sword, and such as were for the famine, to the famine, and such as were for the captivity, to the captivity (Jer. 15, 2). Jeremiah's prophecy was even added to: and such as were destined to leave the community left because of the sword of Ibn Tūmart, who went forth into the world in the year 4902 (1141/2)[3] and who had decided to eliminate Israel. They said, Come, and let us cut them off from being a nation; that the name of Israel may be no more in remembrance (Ps. 83, 5). And so he left no name of them in the whole of his kingdom nor remnant in the city of Salé, from the end of the world to the city of al-Mahdiya."[4]

---

[1] Idrīsi says of Aghmāṭ: "It is a pleasant prosperous place, inhabited only by Jews."; comp. ed. Dozy - de Goeje (see p. 123 n. 2 above).

[2] Comp. *Qobeẓ* as quoted above.

[3] Cohen, *SHQ*, pp. 66/88 and 141-142, explains the date (4) 873/1112-13 appearing in MS. de Rossi. But the "sword of Ibn Tūmart", *i.e.*, the wars of his followers and their measures against the Jews began only in 536 H./1141. Comp. next page n. 3.

[4] *SHQ* p. 66/88. Cohen reads שלב = Silves (Portugal) rather than = Salé; comp. next page n. 2.

Abraham ben Daud wrote his book after North Africa had been conquered as far as the approaches of Egypt, but for some reason he did not specify all the places that suffered, but mentioned two typical localities, at either end of the region, to circumscribe the area of the disaster: the Atlantic port of Salé and Mahdiya on the Tunisian coast. Elsewhere he writes: "They did not leave a remnant of Israel from Tangiers to al-Mahdiya; turn back thine hand as a grapegatherer into the baskets (Jer. 6, 9)."[1]

For an area to be defined by indicating two port cities at its western and eastern ends, respectively, was quite common. The settlements along the coast were close together and linked by a fixed caravan route in addition to the sea communication. It is reported that there was a signalling service by means of beacons all along the coast.[2] The reason why it is not Tripoli that is mentioned in the east will be given below.

The date of 4902 is absolutely exact, for it was in the year 536 (1141/2) that ʿAbd al-Mu'min set out on his campaign to conquer areas outside his original territory in the Sūs Valley and the High Atlas.[3] From then onwards, tribulations occurred which lasted many years—since there were intervals between one campaign and the next and attempts at persuasion and enticement.

Two other notes originate from R. Solomon ibn Verga.

(a) In connection with the fourth persecution, Ibn Verga reports that in 4872 (!) Ibn Tūmart threatened death to anyone who refused to embrace Islam. The Jews tried to ease their fate by discussion and the offer of their property, but did not succeed in influencing the king. Many communities thereupon foreswore Judaism. A month after the persecutions, however, the king died, and his son appeared to be more moderate, so that numerous converts returned to their former faith, while others, suspecting a trap, did not do so until much later.

(b) Elsewhere Ibn Verga says that a general severe persecution of the Jews for the purpose of conversion occurred in the whole of Barbary and the eastern lands in the year 4906 (1146).[4]

The year 4872 (1112) as the date of the persecution in the first note is clearly erroneous, and since the phrase "the sword of Ben Hūmard (!)

---

[1] *SHQ*, p. 70/96.

[2] This is why צלא (or סלא) = Salé seems more probable than שלב = Silves; against Cohen, *SHQ*, p. 142. Ibn Daud (p. 67/92) confirms that Salé (סלא) had a Jewish community, but we have never heard of one at Silves.

[3] Lévi-Provençal, *Documents*, p. 90/146.

[4] *Shebeṭ Yehuda*, pp. 21-22 and 74. Comp. also Kobak, *Jeschurun* 6 (1868), pp. 1-34, and below, ch. VII, n. 2.

went forth" points to influence of the *Sefer ha-Qabbala*, we should amend it to 4902, as there. The date in note (b), 4906 (1146), is correct, as in that year ʿAbd al-Mu'min in fact began to conquer the important and populous cities.

The story of the debate between the king and the Jews is based on traditions that have some substance, as we have seen above. The dating of ʿAbd al-Mu'min's death "one month after the persecution" is a literary exaggeration, but not far from the truth. He died in 1163 about a year after returning from his last campaign in Spain.

The data so far reviewed show defects which detract from their value as historical material. They are extremely general and indefinite, replete with poetical flourishes and lacking the precision needed to determine facts.

Solomon Cohen's Letter

A detailed account of developments is given in the letter of Solomon Cohen, a resident of Fusṭāṭ, who heard of the events from eye-witnesses, Jewish and Muslim refugees in Egypt, and reported them to his father, then in South Arabia (probably in Aden).[1] The father was eager for news of the Maghreb, since he was a native of Sijilmāsa and still had relatives in Moroccan cities. The letter, written in Judeo-Arabic, is dated of the month of Shebat in the year 1459 of the Seleucid Era, *i.e.* January 1148 C.E.

Here is the story of the persecutions, as told by Solomon Cohen:

ʿAbd al-Mu'min the Sūsī, (*i.e.* the one of the Sūs Valley), leader of the Almohads after the death of Muḥammad ibn Tūmart the Mahdī, marched against the Emir Tāshfīn, who was in Oran, besieged and captured the city, killed Tāshfīn and crucified his body. Thereafter he captured Tlemcen and killed all those who were in it (*i.e.* including the Jews), except those who embraced Islam. At the news of these events, the Berbers in Sijilmāsa rose against the Almoravid governor and expelled him and his garrison force from the city. Some 200 Jews, sensing the impending trouble, fled Sijilmāsa at this juncture. They included two brothers of his fahter Yehuda, as well as Yehuda ben Farḥōn, whom Solomon mentions specially, probably because he was a local notable

[1] It was published by J. M. Toledano, *HUCA*, 4 (1927), pp. 449-458, and a second time, with an introduction and translation into Hebrew, by the present writer, in *Y.F. Baer Jubilee Volume*, 1960, pp. 134-153. We therefore content ourselves with a summary of the historical parts.

and rabbinical scholar or a relative. They escaped to Darʿa, but it was not known what had happened to them afterwards. Following the expulsion of the Almoravid governor from Sijilmāsa, the inhabitants of the latter sent a surrender delegation to ʿAbd al-Mu'min. On entering the city, the Almohads tried to convert the Jews to Islam by debate and persuasion, but after seven months of religious disputations, a new commander arrived in the city, who solved the problem by a more efficient method. One hundred and fifty persons were killed for clinging to their faith; the remainder converted. The first to adopt Islam was the *dayyan* (religious judge) of Sijilmāsa, Joseph ben ʿAmrān.[1] All the cities in the Almoravid state were conquered by the Almohads. One hundred thousand persons were killed in Fez on that occasion, and 120,000 in Marrakesh. Only Darʿa and Meknes had not been captured by the time of reporting. The Jews in all the localities from Bajāya (Bougie) westward groaned under the heavy yoke of the Almohads; many had been killed, many others converted, none were able to appear in public as Jews. The news of the capture of Bajāya reached Fusṭāṭ on the day the letter was written. Large areas between Seville and Tortosa had likewise fallen into Almohad hands.

This account tallies with the sequence of events as given by Arab historians, and in particular by Ibn Baydhaq, the biographer of Ibn Tūmart and ʿAbd al-Mu'min, who was their contemporary and comrade-in-arms. This permits us to date the events as follows: Oran, 1145 or 1146; Tlemcen, Sijilmāsa, 1146; Fez, 1146/7; Marrakesh area, 1147; Bajāya, end of 1147 or beginning of 1148.

It should be noted that with regard to certain details Solomon's account clarifies some obscure passages in the Arab sources. This applies to his remark that Darʿa and Meknes had not yet surrendered to ʿAbd al-Mu'min according to information available in Fusṭāṭ in January, 1148. This statement either disproves Ibn Ezra's lament for the murder of the Jews of Darʿa or postpones the event until at least 1148. The capture of Darʿa is in fact not mentioned in Arab sources as happening during that period. The date of the capture of Meknes is not clear; Ibn Baydhaq and other authors are vague on this point: Solomon Cohen's information was probably correct.

The mention of the capture of Bajāya (Bougie), the capital of the Banū Ḥammād, at the end of 1147 or the beginning of 1148 is surprising. It is

---

[1] He was a friend of Abraham ibn Ezra; comp. N. Ben-Menahem, *H. Albeck Jubilee Volume*, 1963, pp. 81-86. The *dayyān* subsequently reverted to Judaism; comp. below pp. 352ff.

not a slip of the pen, for Solomon had already said that all the communities of the Maghreb, from Bajāya (in the eastern part of this region) onwards, were under Almohad control. Upon examining Ibn Baydhaq and other sources, we find that on this point, too, our letter has preserved an important detail. The biographer of ʿAbd al-Mu'min does not specify when the city was occupied, but notes that its inhabitants surrendered to the Almohads at the same time as the (Andalusian) admiral Ibn Maymūn. This, as he says elsewhere, was at the time of the fighting for Oran and Tlemcen. A year or more may have passed between the revolt of the people of Bajāya against their lawful Banū Ḥammād ruler and the entry of the Almohad garrison force, just as a considerable period elapsed between Ibn Maymūn's surrender and the establishment of control over Spain. It seems that Solomon knew of the coincidence of these dates, for he mentions the surrender of the Andalusians side by side with the conquest of Bajāya.

The private letter of a merchant of Fusṭāṭ, who had no pretensions of writing the history of the beginning of the persecutions that occurred in the Maghreb in the years 1145-1161, is thus revealed as the only source for the sequence and dating of the events.

Tunisia and Tripolitania

We have already noted that several additions to Ibn Ezra's lament "Oh,there descended" have been preserved that refer to the fate of the Eastern Maghrebi communities in the days of the Almohads. But before dealing with the information relating to that area during the period under discussion, we must briefly review the situation in Tripolitania and Cyrenaica in the preceding generations. While much material is found in responsa and the Geniza with regard to Tunisia, little information has reached us concerning other places whose names appear in the additions to Ibn Ezra's lament. However, the few Geniza documents, hints in Arab literature and the literature of the Gaonic period, and some contemporary epitaphs, will suffice—*faute de mieux*—to evoke a continuous chain of Jewish communities in Tripolitania and Tunisia, continuous both in space and time. It is, after all, inconceivable that all the communities mentioned in the laments should have sprung up during the period immediately prior to the Almohads; nor can we assume that only they were then in existence, while others, known from other sources, had completely disappeared—there were no doubt more.[1]

[1] Comp. Cazès, *REJ*, 20 (1890), pp. 78ff.; also Slouschz, *Travels*, pp. 11ff.

The reason why information concerning those Jews is so meagre has in part already been given: those small communities had little religious learning and no rabbinical scholars. Maimonides, in one of his responsa, exposes their ignorance in one sweeping, scathing sentence, which will be discussed in detail in the next chapter.[1] Moreover, the political situation in the area was extremely precarious. Tripolitania was disputed by the rulers of Egypt and those of Tunisia, which latter conquered it in 1022/3; the event is described in one of the Geniza letters. Even when the area was under one suzerainty, there were feuds between the emirs of the local dynasties and the Berber sheikhs. All this, in conjunction with nomad invasions, highway robbery, piracy and general poverty—a land-starved, unproductive agriculture, no natural resources—results in a rather dismal picture of insecurity and economic instability.[2]

Most of the Jewish settlements in Cyrenai,ca Tripolitania and Tunisia were concentrated in the numerous port cities along the seacoast. Outstanding among the latter was Tripoli, an important commercial centre in touch with its counterparts in Egypt, Syria and Sicily. A query addressed to a Palestinian academy reveals that Tripoli had a rabbinical court not subject to the Rabbinical Grand Court of Palestine.[3]

An interesting letter fragment—the names of the writer and addresses are not preserved—reports, in an account of the writer's troubles during a journey to Spain, that a famous Jewish physician, by the name of Tubiya, was living in Tripoli. The "king" of Qābes, we are told, had revolted against the "king" of Mahdiya, and when he contracted the illness of which he was to die, he asked the sheikhs of the Banū Maṭrūḥ, the elders of Tripoli, to send him the Jewish physician from their city. He promised him a generous fee, part of which he paid in advance. But Tubiya did not want to go to Qābes, and he and his four sons went into hiding. Eventually, when the elders had seized all the Jewish notables of the city as hostages, he was compelled to come out of his hiding-place and undertake the arduous journey.[4]

The letter is undated, but the story of the sheikhs of the Banū Maṭrūḥ and the enmity between Qābes and Mahdiya points to the time shortly before Roger's invasion of Africa. The disputes between the rulers of the two cities were one of the causes of that war.

---

[1] Comp. below p. 165.

[2] Comp. Ibn ʿIdhārī, pp. 265-269 and 357; Ibn al-Athīr, IX, pp. 230-231, XI, pp. 79-80; Ibn-Khaldūn, VI, p. 159 (II, p. 22), pp. 166ff. (II, pp. 34ff.); *EI s.v.* Tripoli.

[3] *RA* III, pp

[4] Assaf, *Sources*, pp. 130-134. Comp. also Braslavsky, *BJES* 9 (1942), p. 57.

From the frequency of the surname al-Lebdī, *i.e.* the one of Lebda (the Roman port of Leptis Magna), in the Geniza documents of the late 11th until the middle of the 12th century, and the fact that the bearers of this surname include important traders known beyond their own city, we may infer that Lebda had a sizable Jewish population.[1]

A Jew hailing from another coastal city, Barca, lived in Jerusalem in 1058.[2] On one occasion, Jewish captives were sent to Barca, probably in order that the local Jews should redeem them. Nearby was Ramāda, where, too, Arab pirates brought captives from Byzantium.[3] This area suffered greatly during invasions by nomad Arabs, of the Banū Sulaym and Banū Hilāl, who ruined harbours and fields, *i.e.* both commerce and agriculture.[4]

In the interior, there were several communities in the Nafūsa Highlands in Western Tripolitania. In the past century, Tripolitanian Jews believed that their community originated from that region, then known as Fassato.[5] The earliest news of Jews in Nafūsa occurs in a 10th-century responsum of the Gaon Ḥanināy of Pumbeditha.[6] From it, we learn incidentally that Nafūsa was devastated in a war, but it is not clear whether the reference is to a particular place in the area or to all inhabited localities. In the 11th century and until the middle of the 12th, the people of Nafūsa, Jādū and Mīsīn are mentioned several times, and Arab geographers note that there are many Jews in the region. They seem to have engaged in trade and perhaps also in agriculture; we find a poet among them, as well as a rabbi who somehow got to Naples in the days of Benjamin of Tudela, and a scribe who copied the Tractate Gittin (Divorce) from the Babylonian Talmud.[7] Caravans travelling from the coastal cities to Tunisia passed through the Nafūsa Highlands; this route was very difficult, but apparently less dangerous than the storm- and pirate-infested sea route.[8]

---

[1] Comp. Mann, *Jews* I, p. 23, n. 2; II, pp. 14-15, 78, n. 7; also B. Chapira, *REJ* 56 (1908), pp. 233-234; Goitein, *Society* I, index.

[2] Schechter, *Saadyana*, Cambridge 1903, p. 114, l. 1.

[3] Mann, *Jews* I, pp. 90-91, 123, n.1; II, pp. 87-88; comp. also Assaf, *Sefer ha-Shetaroth le-Rab Hay*, Jerusalem 1930, p. 53; Braslavsky, *Tarbiẓ* 12 (1942), p. 44; Goitein, *Society* I, index.

[4] There was a place named Yahudiyātayn between Surt and Barca; Maqdisī, p. 245.

[5] Cazès, *REJ* 20 (1890), p. 79; Bartarelli, *Guida*, p. 333.

[6] *RSh* 26b, no. 26; comp. Mann, *JQR* 7 (1916/17), p. 484.

[7] Bekri, p. 9; Yāqūt *s.v.* Jādū; comp. Hirschberg, *Zion* 22 (1957), pp. 16-17; Mann, *Texts* I, pp. 412-413; Poznanski, *REJ* 65 (1913), p. 42; N. Epstein, *MGWJ* 60 (1916), pp. 112-113; Strauss, *Zion* 7 (1942), p. 142, l. 25.

[8] Assaf, *Sources*, pp. 130-134 (esp. letters 1, 11, 20 and 29).

At what is today the border between Tripolitania and Tunisia is the large oasis of Ghadāmes. It, too, had a Jewish population at that time, as appears from the surname of R. Moses Ghadāmsi.[1]

Let us now revert to the period of the Almohads and their conquest of Tunisia and Tripolitania. We have already mentioned that this event was preceded by attempts of the Norman King Roger of Sicily to subdue that coastal region. Their echo, as received in Aden in South Arabia, is contained in a letter of the merchant Abraham ben Peraḥya ben Yajū, a former inhabitant of Mahdiya, to his brother Mubashshir, who was still in that city.[2] Abraham has just returned to Aden (in the month of Tishri, 4910 (1149)) from a long trip to India and has heard what has happened to the communities on the African coast: Tripoli, Jerba, Kerkenna, Sfax, Mahdiya and Sousse. To relieve his anxiety, he asks to be told who is dead and who has survived. The reports that have so far reached him are not clear; he intends to marry his daughter, who is with him, to the son of his (other) brother or his sister and considers the possibility of their settling in Mahdiya, Africa(!), Tunis or Kairouan. By "Africa"—mentioned whereas Sousse and Sfax are omitted—Abraham probably means the narrow zone between Sousse and Sfax which had remained in Banū Zīrī hands.[3]

However, nothing is known from other sources of harm befalling Jews during the invasion of Africa by Roger's troops, and we are thus unable to gauge the measure of truth in the rumours current at Aden. We only know that the conquerors imposed the *jizya*, *i.e.* poll-tax, on the inhabitants of the area;[4] but this was nothing new for the Jews, who had formerly paid it to the Muslims.

As stated, ʿAbd al-Mu'min's drive into Africa at the head of the Almohad forces, which ended with the conquest of the territory from Tripolitania to Barca in Cyrenaica, was induced by the victory of the Sicilian troops over the rebels in Mahdiya. During that campaign (1159/60), the Almohads, as already noted, encountered serious resistance only at the maritime fortress of Mahdiya; its siege lasted several months, and ʿAbd al-Mu'min gained possession of it only after granting honourable terms of surrender to the Sicilian garrison. He deterred the rulers of

---

[1] Assaf, *ibid.*, p. 141, l. 8.

[2] Published by Braslavsky, *Zion* 7 (1942). Abraham clearly was not, as assumed by Braslavsky, *l.c.*, p. 136, referring to occurrences during the Almohad conquest. The Almohads did not arrive in the region until 1154-1160.

[3] Comp. Ibn al-Athīr XI, p. 79; Brunschvig, *Berbérie* I, p. 3.

[4] Comp. Ibn Khaldūn VI, p. 162 (II, p. 28); Marçais, *Berbérie*, p. 225.

provincial towns from fighting him by his harsh treatment of the people of Tunis, who had refused to surrender. Half the property of the Muslims of that city was confiscated for the Almohad treasury, and the Jews and Christians were faced with the choice between conversion and death; at the same time, ʿAbd al-Mu'min spared the persons and property of families which had previously sent a peace delegation to him. So the other cities surrendered to ʿAbd al-Mu'min; some of them did not even wait until the Almohad army reached them.[1]

The Communities in the Occupied Area

It was a sacred tradition in Islam from the days of Muhammad and the first Caliphs that populations which surrendered without a fight obtained much more favourable conditions than those worsted in battle, and the victors would honour their agreements with those who had yielded. So would ʿAbd al Mu'min. The rulers who had surrendered voluntarily were confirmed in their positions, although reliable men from ʿAbd al-Mu'min's inner circle were attached to them; this implied no discrimination, since his extreme suspiciousness made him treat his own sons the same way. A sheikh of the Banū Maṭrūḥ tribe, who had revolted against the King of Sicily and hastened with a deputation of notables to occupied Mahdiya, remained in office in Tripolitania. He was readily accepted by ʿAbd al-Mu'min and continued for many years as governor of the country. The prompt surrender of the city governors seems to be the main reason why the conquest of Southern Tunisia and the areas east of Tunisia has not been much noted.

ʿAbd al-Mu'min's rule was severe. He divided the newly-annexed areas, from Barca in Cyrenaica to Tlemcen, into administrative districts, ordered the lands throughout the state to be valued and imposed a tax payable in grain and money, from which only reliable Almohads were exempt, while other Muslims, including Almohads suspected of insincerity, had to pay it.[2]

Additions to Ibn Ezra's lament that have been preserved in the Tripolitanian MS. (formerly in the possession of R. Abraham Khalfon) reflect with striking faithfulness the state of affairs as known from Arab sources.[3] Here is a reference to the communities affected:

---

[1] Comp. Ibn al-Athīr XI, pp. 134-135 and 159-160; Ibn Khaldūn VI, p. 168 (II, p. 37); Brunschvig, *ibid.*, pp. 5-6.

[2] Comp. Beaumier, *Roudh*, p. 281; Hopkins, *Government*, pp. 34-35.

[3] Cazès, *REJ* 20 (1890), p. 85; Kahana, *Abraham ibn Ezra*, p. 250.

"There is not a Jew, not a single one, in Dājayyā or al-Mahdiya,
And for Sabrat and Ṭūrā my eye always weeps."

Dājayyā is corrupt for Bajāya, well known to us from Solomon Cohen's letter. The reading Sabrat for Kasbarā, a little town west of Tripoli which had a harbour already in Roman times, is very plausible.[1] Ṭūrā is difficult to locate; its identification with the Tripolitanian Plateau or the Nafūsa Highlands is mere guesswork. Another addition in the same MS. mentions in correct geographical order Tunis, Sousse, Mahdiya (repeated for the sake of order), Qābes and Tripoli.

There is a third addition.[2] Apostrophizing Ibn Ezra with the question why he had omitted certain places, an unknown poet who knew the particulars of events in that vicinity points out some other communities that suffered in those days: Al-Ḥāma (near Qābes), Qafṣā (in the interior of South Tunisia), the Isle of Jerba, Ṣurmān (a seaport between Sabrat and Tripoli), Mesallāta (a highland in the interior between Tripoli and Ḥomṣ) and Miṣurāta (a seaport east of Tripoli).

The poet especially bemoans the fate of the people of Miṣurāta, who were overburdened with taxes and part of whom had been exiled to Jerba, while others had migrated to Ṣurmān. This means that even in this serious case, particularly dwelt on by the author, persecution was confined to monetary matters and exile. The passage relating to Tunis likewise mentions no forced conversions or killings. It therefore seems that Ibn al-Athīr (see page 133, note 1) mistakenly lumps the Jews together with the Christians, on whom ʿAbd al-Mu'min wished to avenge the murder of Muslims by Roger's men. The Almohads apparently carried out no killings and demanded no conversions in this region. The local rulers, confirmed by them, were compelled to follow their example: worry the Jews, sometimes move them from one place to another, subject them to heavy taxes, all in accordance with ʿAbd al-Mu'min's general policy; but they were not particularly active in this respect.

In Tripolitania and Libya, remains of Jewish tombstones and Hebrew inscriptions have been discovered which may perhaps be assigned to the period following the Almohad conquest, although the evidence is not sufficient.[3] The language of Maimonides' responsum on Reuben, who

[1] Comp. Yaqut *s.vv.* Sabrat, Sabra; Julien, *Histoire* I, 166-167 and 173-175; Bartarelli, *Guida* pp. 312-313. It seems unlikely that the reference is to Ṣabra, a suburb of Kairouan, also called Manṣūriyya; comp. *Yāqūt, s.v.*

[2] Comp. p. 133 n. 3 above.

[3] Comp. Slouschz, *Azkara* IV, pp. 114-117; Gray, *Inscriptions*, pp. 56-57.

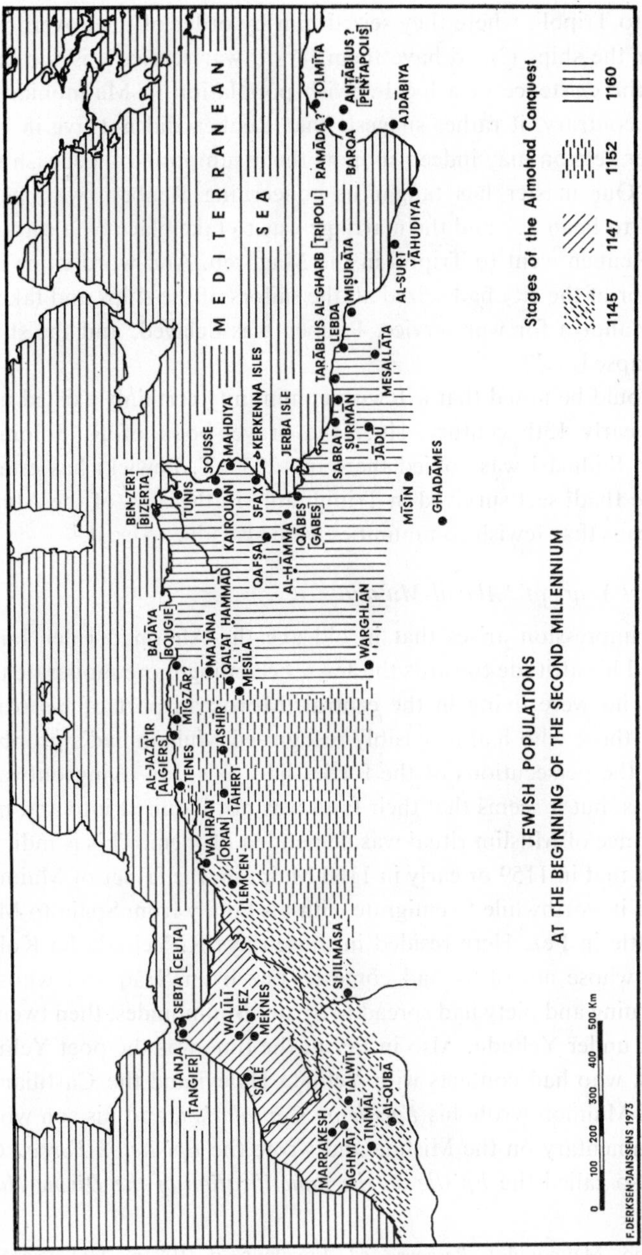
JEWISH POPULATIONS
AT THE BEGINNING OF THE SECOND MILLENNIUM
Stages of the Almohad Conquest
1145
1147
1152
1160
MEDITERRANEAN
SEA
TANJA [TANGIER]
SEBTA [CEUTA]
WALĪLĪ
FEZ
MEKNES
SALĒ
MARRAKESH
AGHMĀT
TINMAL
TALWIT
AL-QUBĀ
SIJILMASA
TLEMCEN
WAHRĀN [ORAN]
TAHERT
AL-JAZĀ'IR [ALGIERS]
TENES
ASHIR
MIGZĀR?
BAJĀYA [BOUGIE]
MAJĀNA
QAL'AT HAMMĀD
MESILA
WARGHLĀN
BEN-ZERT [BIZERTA]
TUNIS
SOUSSE
KAIROUAN
MAHDIYA
QAFSA
SFAX
KERKENNA ISLES
AL-HĀMMA
QĀBES [GABES]
JERBA ISLE
SABRAT
SURMĀN
JĀDU
MĪSĪN
GHADĀMES
TARĀBLUS AL-GHARB [TRIPOLI]
LEBDA
MESALLĀTA
MISURĀTA
AL-SURT
YĀHUDIYA
RAMĀDA?
TOLMĪTA
BARQA
ANTĀBLUS ? [PENTAPOLIS]
AJDĀBIYA
0 100 200 300 400 500 Km
F. DERKSEN-JANSSENS 1973
Map 3

went "to Tripoli, where they seized him by order of the governor of the city for the ships (?), to have them (?) do war service", is too vague to prove the existence of a local Jewish population in Maimonides' time; on the contrary, it rather suggests that Reuben did not live in Tripoli.[1] Another version may indeed support the assumption of a Jewish population: "Our master has taught us concerning Reuben, who betrothed himself to Leah ... and the marriage was to take place by a certain date. Then Reuben went to Tripoli in the Maghreb. And word came that the governor of the city had seized all the sailors of the ships and taken them to al-Mahdiya for war service. Reuben was delayed, and the stipulated time elapsed..."[2]

It should be noted that a Jewish community certainly existed in Barca in the early 13th century, since the prayer-book of R. Solomon bar Nathan Sijilmāsi was copied there in 1203.[3] T. Lewicki has established that the Ibāḍī sect survived in Tripolitania in the days of the Almohads; this means that Jewish communities were also able to exist.[4]

The Last Years of ʿAbd al-Muʾmin

The impression arises that in old age the Almohad ruler somewhat changed his attitude towards the Jews, becoming more moderate towards those who were living in the central, Moroccan part of his realm. Of course, those who had ostensibly recognised Muḥammad's prophethood during the persecutions of the forties had to go on living outwardly as Muslims, but it seems that their faith was not inquired into and no strict observance of Muslim ritual was demanded of them. This is indicated by the fact that in 1159 or early in 1160 Maimon, the father of Maimonides, deemed it worthwhile to emigrate with his family from Spain to Morocco and settle in Fez. Here resided in those days R. Yehuda ha-Kohen ibn Sūsān, whose ancestors had come to Fez from ʿIrāq and whose fame for learning and piety had spread to Spain. Maimonides, then twenty-five, studied under Yehuda. Also in Fez at the time was the poet Yehuda ibn ʿAbbās, who had contacts with Yehuda Halevi and the Castilian poets. In Fez, Maimon wrote his *Epistle on Consolation*, and his son worked at his commentary on the Mishna and wrote the *Epistle on Forced Conversion*, also called the *Epistle on the Sanctification of the Divine Name* (or

[1] Comp. Maimonides, *Responsa*, ed. Freimann, p. 214, n. 225; also Slouschz, *Lub* II, p. 22.
[2] Maimonides, *Responsa*, ed. Blau, I, pp. 138-139, n. 88.
[3] Steinschneider, *Kereṃ Ḥemed* IX, p. 38.
[4] Comp. *RO* 25/2 (1961), pp. 87-120; 26/1 (1962), pp. 97-123.

on Martyrdom). These two letters, as well as Maimonides' utterances after leaving Morocco, do not point to outrages and bloody persecution.[1]

Maimonides' remark to his son Abraham concerning the character of the Jews living in the Berber Mountains, the Isle of Jerba and generally in the area between Tunis and Alexandria, whom he describes as strong in faith but superstitious (see below pp. 165f), permits the assumption that they were not in danger, for he would certainly not have talked about them in this way had their lives been threatened. In a letter to the community of Lunel, Maimonides deplores the decline of religious learning generally and in the Maghreb in particular, "it being known what persecutions that community has suffered". A similar sentiment is expressed by him in a letter to a disciple. The main trouble was the decline of religious learning.[2]

Nevertheless, although no immediate danger threatened the lives of North African Jewry, their residence in the area imperilled their Judaism and that of their children. This appears from the *Epistle on Forced Conversion*. Although, in the opening lines of that *Epistle*, Maimonides most strongly deprecates the condemnation of the forced converts by "the self-styled sage who has never experienced what so many Jewish communities experienced in the way of persecution", his conclusion is that a Jew must leave the country where he is forced to transgress the divine law: "He should not remain in the realm of that king; he should sit in his house until he emigrates, and if he must pursue any occupation he should do so secretly, until he emigrates." And once more, with greater insistence: "He should on no account remain in a place of forced conversion; whoever remains in such a place desecrates the divine name and is nearly as bad as a wilful sinner; as for those who beguile themselves, saying that they will remain until the Messiah comes to the Maghreb and leads them to Jerusalem, I do not know how he is to cleanse them of the stigma of conversion".[3]

R. Maimon and his sons acted in accordance with that advice, and so did Yehuda ibn ʿAbbās and the family of Joseph ben Yehuda ʿAqnīn, all admirers of Maimonides, and certainly many others. Maimonides' departure from the country of the Almohads is commonly assumed to

---

[1] Saadia ibn Danān, *Seder ha-Doroth*, published by Edelmann, *Ḥemda Genūza*, 30b; Toledano, *Ner*, pp. 26 and 225; Ad. Neubauer, *REJ* 4 (1882), pp. 173ff. Comp. also Baron, *PAAJR* 6 (1935), p. 83 and n. 164.

[2] *Iggerot*, Amsterdam 1712, pp. 10b-11a; *Responsa*, Leipzig 1859, Part 2 (Epistles), p. 44a.

[3] Comp. Edelmann, *Ḥemda Genūza*, pp. 6a, 11b and 12a-b.

have taken place in 1165; according to Saadia ibn Danān, it was prompted by the martyrdom of Yehuda ibn Sūsān, who had been called upon to forsake his religion and had preferred death to apostasy. R. Maimon's family tried to establish itself in Palestine, but after he had died in Jerusalem, his sons went to Egypt, where, in Saadia ibn Danān's words, Rabbenu Moshe became very great in wisdom, learning and rank.[1]

The Maghreb was thus depleted of its last remaining scholars and of those who had come to it as refugees from Spain. Still, the Maghrebi communities continued to exist. This is evidenced by what Maimonides says about their sufferings in his abovementioned letters. He also mentions the Fez community in a letter to the leadership of Marseilles Jewry, written after the *Epistle to Yemen* was published. That letter indicates that a missive attributed to him on Messianic matters was circulating in Fez; he explains to the people of Marseilles that this is possibly the *Epistle to Yemen*. On the strength of this, it has lately been suggested that there may be some truth in an apocryphal pamphlet on the life of Maimonides at least in so far as it relates to an *Epistle on the Appearance of the Messiah* circulated among the Jews of Fez.

In 1173, Maimonides appealed to some apparently North African Jewish communities to collect money for the redemption of captives. This suggests that their economic situation was by no means unfavourable. The geographer Yāqūt (1179-1229) reports that most of the merchants in the Darʿa Valley are Jews.[2]

ʿAbd al-Mu'min's reign brought a most serious crisis in the history of Maghrebi Jewry. Its life in the Almohad Empire becomes veiled in obscurity. Even Moroccan-Jewish popular tradition preserves no memory of these events. The author of a 19th-century historical work, who knows R. Yehuda ibn Sūsān from literature, merely adds: "For ʿAbd al-Mu'min exerted heavy pressure on the Jews living in Fez to adopt Islam and resort to Muslim places of worship, and he closed all the synagogues; and R. Maimon and his two sons fled to Alexandria."[3] Little is known of what happened under the descendants and heirs of ʿAbd al-Mu'min. And the little the historians deemed worthy of note is both sad and mortifying: discrimination was practised only against Jews, for only they had remained of the country's non-Muslim inhabitants. The remnants of Christian communities, in so far as still existing at the beginning of the

---

[1] Comp. Saadia ibn Danān, *l.c.* (see p. 137 n. 1 above).

[2] Comp. *Iggerot*, p. 10a; *Responsa* II, p. 26b (for both sources see p. 137 n. 2 above); Halkin, *Ep. Y.*, p. 108f.; Margulies, *MGWJ* 44 (1900), pp. 8-11; Yāqūt *s.v.* Darʿa.

[3] MS. Sassoon 1007, pp. 12b-13a.

Almohad conquest, had been completely wiped out. So the spite of the second Almohad generation was wreaked wholly upon the Jews. The Jews held out even under these circumstances, but the situation left its mark upon them. The particulars of these events, however, belong to a different chapter.

The refugees from the persecutions of those days scattered in all directions. We can trace them in their new places of residence, such as Genoa,[1] Sicily, Egypt and Jerusalem. Part of them may have left the Maghreb before the Almohad period, e.g., the Tripolitanians in Sicily, which was under the rule of the Normans, the temporary conquerors of Tripolitania.[2] But the majority left the Maghreb in response to Maimonides' advice and example.[3] The presence of an "important and good community" of Maghrebis in Jerusalem at the time of Alḥarīzī's visit can only be explained as the result of immigration during the religious persecutions in Africa.[4] Surnames indicating Maghrebi origin were used for centuries.[5]

---

[1] *The Itinerary of Benjamin of Tudela*, ed. Ascher, p. 6. Adler's edition, p. 5, reads: "R. Samuel, the son of the refugee, and his brother. They were dyers and came from Ceuta."

[2] Comp. Roth, *JQR* 47 (1956-57), pp. 322-323; 319, n. 8; and 327, nn. 17 and 24.

[3] Comp. p. 114 (n. 136) above; Goitein, *Jewish Education in Muslim Countries*, Jerusalem 1962, p. 117, tells of a silversmith of Ceuta, who left that city during the persecutions and settled in Egypt, where he lost his eyesight and became a teacher.

[4] *Taḥkemōni*, ed. Kaminka, Warsaw 1899, p. 353; see also *ibid.*, pp. 223-4.

[5] Comp. e.g., A. Milano, *Storia degli Ebrei Italiani nel Levante*, Florence 1949, p. 41: Sabatino Sigilmes.

CHAPTER THREE

JEWISH SOCIETY

Distribution of the Jewish Population

The list of localities and areas in which Jews lived, such as it emerges from the sources,* shows that Jews during that period were scattered over the whole vast area of more than 1,000,000 square kilometres. We give that list in the geographical order of present-day states: from Cyrenaica-Libya in the east to Morocco in the west, along the coast and in the interior. This order enables us to visualize the continuous chain of communities stretching across the Maghreb.

Cyrenaica-Libya

Anṭāblus (Pentapolis) [1]
Ramāda [2]
Ṭolmītā (Ptolemais) [3]
Barqa—Barca [4]

Tripolitania

Al-Surt [5]
Yahūdiya [6]
Miṣurāta [7]
Lebda [8] = Leptis
Mesallātā [9]
Tarāblus al-Gharb—Tripoli [10]
Sabrat [11]
Ṣurmān [12]
Nafūsa [13]

---

* In the notes, on pp. 140-143, we generally refer to the earliest extant source.

[1] Ibn ʿAbd al-Ḥakam, pp. 80-81.

[2] Mann, *Jews* I, p. 90; II, p. 87; comp. Yāqūt, *s.v.*: "A pleasant town between Barqa and Alexandria, near the sea and near Barqa."

[3] The seaport for Barca; comp. Fagnan, *Extraits*, p. 43; Yāqūt, *s.v.*; Applebaum, *Zion* 19 (1954), p. 26.

[4] *RA* II, p. 4; Mann, *Jews* I, p. 91; II, p. 88.

[5] Mann, *Texts* I, p. 465 and n. 23. Ibn ʿAbd al-Ḥakam mentions this locality frequently; comp., *e.g.*, pp. 60-61, 142-143, 144-145 and 155, n. 60.

[6] Maqdisī, *BGA* III, p. 245, has the form Yahūdiyatayn. Bekri, *Masālik*, p. 45, describing the route from al-Mahdiya to Alexandria, says: "Near al-Surt is a place called Yahūdiya, which is not far from Lebda" (see n. 8). Idrīsī, *Description*, pp. 134-135, likewise mentions the fortress of al-Yahūdiya. There still exists a small port in that region by the name of Marsa al-Yahūdiya; comp. Bartarelli, *Guida*, map opposite p. 169, east of 18° long.

[7] Cazès, *REJ* 20 (1890), p. 86.

[8] According to Geniza documents, this place had Jewish inhabitants in the 10th and 11th centuries; comp. Mann, *Jews* I, p. 23, n. 2; II, pp. 14-15; p. 78, n. 7; Goitein, *Society* I, p. 81; p. 380, sec. 49.

[9] Cazès, *l.c.* (above, n. 7).

[10] *RA* II, pp. 125-127.

[11] Comp. above, p. 134.

[12] Cazès, *l.c.* (n. 7).

[13] *RSh*, p. 26b, no. 26; comp. above, p. 131.

Jādū [1]
Mīsīn [2]
Ghadāmes [3]

Tunisia

Jerba [4]
Qābes (Gabes) [5]
al-Ḥāmma [6]
Nafzāwa [7]
Qafṣa [8]
Sfax [9]
Qerqenā-Kerkenna [10]
Mahdiya [11]
Qayruwān-Kairouan [12]
Sousse (Sūsa) [13]
Tunis [14]
Bizerta (Ben-Zert) [15]

Algeria

Bougie (Bajāya) [16]
Algiers (al-Jazāʾir) [17]
Mīgzār [18]
Tenes [19]
Oran (Wahrān) [20]
(in the interior, from east to west)
Warghlān [21]

---

[1] Ibn Ḥawqal, *BGA* II², p. 95; Bekri, *Masālik*, p. 9; Yāqūt, *s.v.* Jādū.
[2] Mann, *Texts* I, p. 412 and n. 3.
[3] Assaf, *Sources*, p. 141, letter IV, l. 8.
[4] Cazès, *l.c.*
[5] *RShT*, no. 74.
[6] Cazès, *l.c.*
[7] Ibn ʿAbd al-Ḥakam, pp. 138/139. Lewin, *Tarbiẓ* I/1 (1929), p. 86, quotes a query concerning the wife of a man from נקטמא(?), which form makes no sense and is probably miswritten for נפזאוה. The reply contains another error: קערות מוכנות "prepared dishes" for העדות מכוונת "the testimony is consistent".
[8] Cazès, *l.c.* (n.l.).
[9] Mann, Texts I, p. 344, l. 17; Braslavsky, *Zion* 7 (1942²), p. 138.
[10] Braslavsky, *l.c.*
[11] Schechter, *JQR*, o.s. 11 (1899/1900), p. 650.
[12] Jewish sources mention it from at least the 9th century onwards; comp. Hirschberg, *Eretz-Israel* 5 (1958), p. 214. Instead of the usual קירואן, which corresponds to Arabic القيروان, T.-S. 13 J 17 (Mann, *Jews* II, p. 109) has כיראואן, which is nearer to Persian كاروان "caravan".
[13] Braslavsky, *l.c.* (n. 9).
[14] R. Nissim b. Jacob of Kairouan mentions one Ibn al-Ṭansāwī in a letter (Mann, *Texts* I, p. 144, l. 18). It is difficult to decide whether this is a man from Tunis (Tunisia) or from Tenes (Algeria); comp. Appendix Tunis.
[15] Comp. Slouschz, *Maroc* II, p. 1.
[16] Comp. above, p. 128.
[17] Mann, *Texts* I, p. 465 (IV, l. 2); comp. also *ibid.*, p. 452, and the next note.
[18] Mann, *Texts* I, p. 466, l. 3, in a document dated Sivan, (4) 898/1138. It seems to be the name of one of the islands on which Algiers stood and which disappeared upon the development of the port. Algiers upon its foundation in the 10th century was called al-Jazāʾir of the Banū Mazghanā or Mazghad; comp. Ibn Ḥawqal, *BGA* II², pp. 76-77; Ibn Khaldūn, VI, p. 154 (II, p. 6); Léon l'Africain, *Description* II, p. 347.
[19] Ibn Ḥawqal, *op. cit.*, pp. 69-70, mentions the *jawālī ʿalā al-Yahūd*, the poll-tax paid by the people of Tenes. In his time, Tenes was an important seaport, frequented by Andalusians; *ibid.*, p. 77.
[20] Comp. above, p. 128.
[21] Mentioned in a letter from Jerusalem dated Shawwāl 432 H. (?)/1040 (*T.S.*

Majāna [1]
Qalʿat Ḥammād [2]
Ashīr [3]
Mesīla [4]
Tiaret (Tāhert) [5]
Tlemcen (Tlemsēn) [6]
Tabāla [7]

Morocco

Sebta-Ceuta [3]
Tanja-Tangier [9]

Salē [10]
Fez [11]
(In the interior)
Walīlī (Volubilis) [12]
Meknes [13]
Sijilmāsa [14]
Darʿa [15]
Marrakesh [16]
Aghmāt [17]
Sūs [18]
Talwīt [19]
al-Qubā [20]

18.J.4[41c], published by Assaf, *Studies in Memory of Gulak and Klein*, Jerusalem 1942, pp. 19-21. Comp. below p. 160-1.

[1] *RA* II, no. 69 (pp. 23-24).

[2] Ibn Daud, *SHQ*, p. 62/84, also p. 58/78.

[3] *RH*, no. 38; *RA* I, no. 9 (p. 39). Harkavy, *RH*, p. 348, quotes Yāqūt as saying that Ashīr, in the Berber Maghreb, is "opposite Bajāna on the mainland". This is a printer's error (also in the Cairo edition) for Bajāya (Bougie). Bajāna (Pechina) is in Spain (comp. Yāqūt, *s.v.*), whereas Bujāya (or Bijāya, comp. Yāqūt, *s.v.*) is indeed opposite Ashīr.

[4] A rabbinical court deed dated [4] 794/1034 mentions the daughter of one al-Jāsūs al-Mesīlī. Hirschfeld, who published this document (*JQR* o.s., 16 (1904), pp. 575ff.), thought the man was from Marseilles, and this was accepted by Caro, *Wirtschaftsgeschichte*, p. 196, Mann, *JQR* 10 (1919/20), p. 323, Neustadt, *Zion* 2 (1937), p. 228, Rabinowitz, *Adventurers*, p. 101, and Lewicki, *Źródła*, p. 307. But Mesīli is a *nisba* of Mesīla, the name of at least two towns in Africa; comp. *Yāqūt, s.v.*, and Eisenbeth, *Juifs*, p. 84.

[5] Ibn Quraysh, *Risāla*, pp. VII-VIII. Comp. Vajda, *Sefarad*, 14 (1954), p. 387. A man from Tāhert is mentioned in a letter published by Starr, *Zion*, I (1936), p. 441, n. 21.

[6] *RH*, nos. 37 and 38; *RR* II, no. 9, p. 31.

[7] Assaf, *Tarbiẓ* 20 (1950), p. 182. But such a place is completely unknown to the Arab geographers.

[8] In the Responsa of R. Joseph b. Megāsh, I. Ta-Shmah, *KS* 46 (1971), pp. 542-3, 551; Abraham ibn Ezra, ed. Kahana I, Warsaw 1894, p. 142.

[9] Ibn Daud, *SHQ*, p. 70/96.

[10] Comp. above, pp. 125-126

[11] Comp. above, pp. 99f.

[12] Beaumier, *Roudh*, pp. 14-16.

[13] Comp. above, p. 128.

[14] Ibn Daud, *SHQ*, p. 51/69; *RH*, nos. 68-81.

[15] Comp. above, pp. 120f.

[16] Comp. above, pp. 123ff.

[17] Schirmann, *Qobeẓ ạl-Yad* 3 (13), 1939, p. 35.

[18] Schirmann; *l.c.*; above, p 124.

[19] *I. F. Baer Jubilee Volume*, p. 151, comm. on l. 19.

[20] *Baer Jubilee Volume, l.c.*

For completeness and precision's sake, let us also mention here some localities or areas in the Sudan and Central Africa in which, according to Arab geographers and historians, Jews or Judaizers were living.

Mallal, in the Lamlam country	Daw in the Lamlam country
Qamnūrī, in the Qamnūriya country	Nighīrā, in the Qamnūriya country
Tātaklātīn, in the Western Sudan [1]	

The information in our possession on Jewish settlements in the Maghreb during the period under review is fragmentary. It is certain, therefore, that the above list, which contains nearly sixty definitely established names of major cities and large geographical areas, is far from being complete, and there are scant prospects of new sources, comparable to the Geniza documents, being discovered that will widen our geographical-historical knowledge of those countries. There can be no doubt, however, that many Jews lived in small unfortified towns and in highland and farming settlements. A certain villager whose village is said to be ten miles from Kairouan was not an isolated phenomenon.[2] Many Jews lived among the Berbers in localities remote from traffic arteries and trade routes, on mountains and heights, in the border regions between the settled country and the desert.

It is hardly necessary to say that not all the abovenamed Jewish communities were established at the same time. Some are attested at a fairly early period, and it may be assumed that a Jewish community existed in or near the places in question continuously (except for possible short breaks during persecutions) for many generations prior to the arrival of the Arabs. For instance, Lebda was Leptis, Qafṣa Capsa, Sfax Taparura, Sousse Hadrumetum and Walīlī Volubilis. Some cities were founded by the Arabs or by Berber dynasties, and we presently hear of Jews living there. Others of the communities listed are mentioned only in late documents or in connection with events occurring in the middle of the 12th century C.E.

The responsa of the first (1391) Spanish expellee rabbis and the following two generations mention places inhabited by Jews along the seacoast and in the interior down to the Saharan border region, such as *e.g.* Mostaganem, Hūnayn, Tozeur, Biskra, Touggourt [Tūqūrt], Mzāb

[1] Comp. Hirschberg, *JAH* 4 (1963), pp. 314-316.

[2] *RH*, no. 5; and comp. Assaf, *Sources*, p. 132, Letter I, l. 18, about a village near Tripolis.

and Tū'āt.[1] It is not to be assumed that all these settlements were established about the time of the arrival of the Spanish rabbis. It stands to reason that at least part of them existed already during the period under review, but that written mention of them was made only from the time that their inhabitants began to apply directly to the rabbinical centre then arising in Algiers. The lack of information on small settlements in the Gaonic period is similarly due in part to the fact that the inhabitants of little towns and villages were not in direct contact with the yeshivot in Babylonia or Palestine, but applied to the major yeshivot and the courts of justice (*batey dīn*) in their own country, in Kairouan, Qābes, Fez and Sijilmāsa, which, in turn, referred to the decision of the Geonim the matters about which they were in doubt; conversely, the Geonim dispatched their missives to prominent persons—*allūfīm*, *negīdīm* and *rāshīm*—who acted as their representatives for the whole of North Africa, and even for Spain.

Only very rarely do we find a hint as to where the Jewish populations of those new or renewed towns had come from—whether they had been residents of the region or the country or voluntary immigrants or whether they were exiles transplanted from other countries and cities. According to a fairly late tradition, the Caliph ʿAbd al-Malik (685-705) ordered his brother, the Governor of Egypt, to transfer 1,000 Copts or Jews from Egypt to Kairouan, which had just been founded. It is reported that the order was carried out immediately, but not whether the new settlers were Jews or Christians.[2] We have told above of Jews exiled from Tlemcen and Fez (in the second half of the 10th century) and resettled—with other deportees—in Ashīr, which had been founded in those days. The physician Shabbetay Donolo says in his book "*Ḥakhmōnī*" that his relatives were deported to Africa during the Arab conquests and that the family of the Nagid Paltiel settled there voluntarily.

We shall nevertheless see that immigration to Africa from other countries was not very large. In the Maghreb we do not, as in Palestine, find synagogues of "Syrians" and "Babylonians", pointing to mass immigration. Let us note, moreover, that while among residents of Egypt and Sicily we find surnames attesting to African origin, we find no surnames indicating Egyptian, Palestinian, Syrian or Babylonian origin in sources relating to the permanent population of North Africa.

---

[1] Some other places will be mentioned below in Chapt. VII, where the sources are also quoted.

[2] Cazès, *Essai*, pp. 44-46. Bekri, *Masālik*, p. 38, reports that the order was to send 10,000 Copts to build a shipyard in Tunis; comp. Hopkins, *Government*, p. 66.

There was certainly constant migration from Africa to neighbouring countries, especially Egypt, Spain and Palestine, and *vice versa*, depending on the political, economic and social-cultural situation. According to documentary evidence, the migrants were chiefly traders and religious scholars, both of whom, by virtue of their occupations were particularly mobile. Most North African Jews, however, were veteran inhabitants.[1]

The Problem of the Judaizers

It is the prevailing view that most of the Jews living in North Africa were of Berber origin. This view is based on hints and fragmentary reports in non-Jewish literary sources and oral traditions recorded in travel literature. There is no trace of it in Jewish literature until the 15th century, and it must especially be noted that there is not the slightest indication of the Judaization or conversion to Judaism of Berbers in sources of the Gaonic period. This fact is by itself calculated to arouse grave doubts as to the correctness of the "Berber theory".[2] It is impossible to assume that the conversion of many Berber tribes to Judaism took place in the Byzantine period, for if so, the church fathers would certainly have decried it and pointed out the danger it spelt to Christianity. On the other hand, we cannot assign it to the period of accelerating Islamization of the Berbers, *i.e.* from the 10th and 11th centuries onwards. The time during which the many Berber tribes mentioned by Ibn Khaldūn might have adopted Judaism narrows down to the two or three hundred years between the defeat of the Byzantines and the consolidation of Islam (8th-10th centuries). This was precisely the time when North African Jewry was in closest contact with the centres in Palestine and Babylonia, and it is hardly conceivable that the conversion of Berber tribes to Judaism should not have come to the knowledge of rabbis, *payṭanim*, writers and authors of late midrashim and that no halakhic questions, necessitating recourse to the Geonim, should have arisen in this connection.

Still, we cannot dismiss all the stories of Berber and other Judaizers and assign them to the realm of legend. In spite of all the adventitious and obscure elements they contain, they add up to a total which should not be slighted, since there is no conceivable reason why the writers, especially the Muslim ones, should have invented them. They reflect no tendency, either pro-Jewish or anti-Jewish. Arab authors cannot be suspected of

[1] It seems that Abū Naṣr Ṣadqa al-Shāmi, who brought a letter from R. Nissim in Kairouan (Mann, *Texts* I, p. 143, l. 13), to Ibn ʿAwkal in Cairo, was only temporarily in Africa.

[2] Comp. above pp. 88ff.

wishing to glorify Judaism, nor can we suppose that hatred of the Jews made them take an exaggerated view of events without real significance.

However, since the elucidation of the problem of the "Berber Jews", as the Jews of North Africa are often called, exceeds the scope of this chapter as to both time and place, we discuss it more fully elsewhere, confining ourselves here to those points that are necessary for the continuity of our account.[1]

As we have seen, Ibn Khaldūn's list begins with the inhabitants of Jebel Nafūsa.[2] We know that Jews lived in Tripolitania in the pre-Arab period. Jewish sources of the 12th century frequently mention Jews from that area. Al-Bekri notes that Jews live in the town of Jādū, in the Nafūsa region. Yāqūt, however, *s.v.* "Nafūsa", says that there are many Christians throughout the area and does not mention Jews; it is only *s.v.* "Jādū" that he mentions many Jewish inhabitants.

The territory of the Jarāwa tribe, ruled by Kahya, the Judaized "*Kāhina*", is difficult to determine. Al-Bekri gives different places for the earliest fighting, and also for the last battle, in which the leader of the revolt was killed. The feature common to all of them is that they were in areas inhabited by both Christians and Jews. This probably accounts for the variety of traditions as to the locale of the events, which may reflect conflicting attempts to claim that illustrious personage. The habitats of the Medyūna, Ghiyāta and Fezāz, *i.e.* the Tlemcen and Fez-Meknes regions, also had Jewish populations both before and after the conquest.

The Judaizing of Berbers indicates that there must have been Jewish communities in those areas both before and after the arrival of the Arabs in Africa. For otherwise, that Judaizing would be almost incomprehensible. As is well known, the Jews do not conduct missionary activities. Judaizing is always the effect of the presence of a local Jewish community, which more or less unintentionally attracts others to its faith. Ibn Abī Zarʿ's and Ibn Khaldūn's reports on the Judaizers thus fill, incidentally, the gap in our knowledge concerning Jewish communities in the interior, but they provide no basis for determining the number of Judaizers and certainly warrant no far-reaching conclusions as to the character of Berber Judaizing or the character of the Jews themselves and their role in the fight of the Berbers against the Arab conquerors. No less important than the fact that there w e r e Judaizers among the Berbers is the question what became of them. Did they merge completely with the Jews of Abraham's stock or did they preserve their racial identity—perhaps so

[1] Comp. *JAH* 4 (1963), pp. 313-39.

[2] Comp. above, p. 91.

well that even now, more than 1,000 years after the last possible date of their Judaization, they are distinguishable as a special racial group within African Jewry?

A reply to these questions can only be given after examining the factual material, and it will be a rather vague one, for the quality of that material makes a definite reply impossible.

The Language of Maghreb Jewry

It is common knowledge that in all their countries of residence Jews tended to adopt the language of the peoples among which they lived and with which they had political, social and economic contacts. This law of adaptation applied even in Palestine, and we have seen that it was operative in Africa during the Roman and Byzantine periods. The period under review, however, is strikingly exceptional in several respects (the relevant material, though not particular plentiful, is generally not inferior, either quantitatively or qualitatively, to that available in regard to other countries).

The most salient fact is that Jewish sources of the Islamic period contain no reference to the use of the Berber language, and it would seem that the Jews did not employ that language at all. One would have expected Judaizing and fully converted Berbers to have exerted some reciprocal influence upon the Jewish inhabitants, enriched their language by some Berber words, proper names etc. But apart from two or three isolated words in Ibn Quraysh's epistle, no use of the Berber language by Jews is attested. Nor have any remnants of an old translation of the Bible into Berber been preserved, no doubt because no such translation existed. The problem of the language and culture of the Berbers, the most veteran inhabitants of the region, is indeed not simple. As is known, we possess no early literary documents in their language, nor any testimony as to their intellectual culture; Arab Muslim literature created in the Berber region contains no residue of Berber creativeness, nor does North African Arabic show any Berber influence either in its literary phraseology or in its various dialects, unlike the position in all the other regions to which Arabic spread. This demonstrates the weakness of the Berbers in the sphere of their original culture, a weakness they never overcame, even at the time of their political expansion over a large part of Africa and Spain in the 11th and 12th centuries.[1] The numerical strength of the Berber

[1] Gautier, *Passé*, pp. 425ff.; G. Marcais, *Berbérie*, pp. 35-42, 194ff.; Terrasse, *Histoire* I, pp. 102ff., 360ff.; Guernier, *Berbérie*, pp. 307ff.

element is evidenced by the fact that the masses cling to their dialects to this day; those speaking or at least understanding them are 40-50 per cent of all Muslims in Morocco and Algeria, one per cent in Tunisia and one third in Tripolitania.

The cultural weakness of the Berbers accounts for the lack of impact of their language and culture upon the Jews. If we accept the reports of the Judaizing or conversion to Judaism of numerous Berber tribes, these events hardly affected intellectual life or social development; at any rate, they left no trace—unlike Judaizing in South Arabia and Khazaria, of whose intensity we have many epigraphic and literary documents. The use of Berber dialects and surnames in recent centuries is a second phenomenon, comparable to the use of Slavonic languages by Yiddish-speaking Jews in Eastern Europe during the same period. Of course, Berber influence is discernible in certain folkways and superstitions, to be discussed below, but this is hardly due to the action of Judaizers.[1]

The foregoing suggests that Berbers were not a numerically, let alone substantively, important element in the Jewish community structure, at any rate in the period of which we possess historical documents. Eventually—already at an early date—part of them merged with the Jews of Abraham's stock; the others were Islamicized, though in some places, according to Arab historians and European travellers, they retained vestiges of Jewish beliefs—their fate was similar to that of the native Christians, whose last remnants disappeared during the Almohad persecutions.

It should be noted that this was not a unique phenomenon in the history of Christianity and Judaism in Muslim countries. A similar development occurred in South Arabia. Here, too, the various Christian communities held strong positions prior to Islam and during the first centuries of the Hijra, and then declined and ultimately vanished; in the same way, according to Arab historians, Judaism fell into oblivion with many South Arabian tribes among which it had spread. A further instance are the Khazars who had converted to Judaism and who in their great majority became Muslims.[2]

We can nevertheless not rule out the possibility that certain groups of

---

[1] A different view of the "Berber problem" presented by D. Corcos appears in many places, e.g., *Jews*, I-II, pp. 273-9; III-IV, pp. 54-5, 61ff., esp. 70; *Folklore Research Center Studies*, 1 (1970), Jerusalem, pp. 1-28; and H. Zafrani in *Une version berbère de la Haggadah de Pesaḥ*, Paris 1970, which is not dealt with here.

[2] Comp. Hirschberg, *Israel in Arabia*, Tel Aviv 1946, pp. 166-168; D. M. Dunlop, *The History of the Jewish Khazars*, Princeton 1954, pp. 261ff.

Judaizing Berbers merged with the Jews at a later date. This is suggested by the story of tent-dwellers whose connection with Judaism was very superficial and who lived with the Arab Banū Mirdās tribe. The manner in which these nomads are referred to indicates that they were a tiny minority.[1]

We may thus say, in fine, that rather than gain by Berber accretions, Jewry lost by the forced conversion drives of Islam, such as occurred in North Africa.

The Arabicization of the Maghreb Communities

The attitude of African Jewry towards the Arabic language was completely different. The pace of their Arabicization was comparatively fast, but at the same time their immunity to Islam did not lessen. These two facts are additional proof that the majority of the Jewish population of the region was not of Berber origin.

One of the oldest literary relics of Maghreb Jewry, in Arabic, is the *risāla, i.e.* missive, epistle, of Yehuda ibn Quraysh of Tāhert to the Fez community concerning the importance of the Aramaic Targum for the understanding of the Bible. It is not really an epistle, but a comprehensive treatise on matters of Hebrew language research. It is estimated to have been written, at the latest, some 200 years after the conquest of North Africa by the Arabs and some 100 years after the founding of Fez, that is to say, during a period when the knowledge of Arabic among the Berbers was extremely limited. Its value for the furtherance of Hebrew language research will be discussed below. Here we shall appraise it as a document of the social-cultural situation of the Jews in the Outer Maghreb at that time.

In this epistle, Yehuda ibn Quraysh reproves the people of Fez for following the advice of the ignorant among them to cease using the Aramaic Targum of the Bible at synagogue because the language of the Bible could be understood without it. The author points out their error, explaining the usefulness of referring to languages related to the language of the Bible, viz. that of the Mishna and that of the Talmud, as well as Aramaic and Arabic, in trying to understand unusual words and expressions and rare grammatical forms in the Bible. In his suggested interpretations, b. Quraysh a few times uses still other languages: Persian and Berber.[2] The use of Berber in only two or three (doubtful) cases is some

[1] Comp. Hirschberg, *JAH* 4 (1963), pp. 326-7.

[2] Comp. Ibn Quraysh, *Risāla*, esp. pp. 64-65, p. 105, l. 9, and notes, pp. 119-120;

indication of the respective prevalence of the two languages. It shows that not only colloquial, but also literary Arabic was quite widespread among the Jews.[1]

More important, in social-historical respect, is the conclusion arising from the claim of simple folk in Fez that they know sufficient Hebrew to understand the Bible and do not understand Aramaic. How did they come to know Hebrew? In earlier years, the Jews had used Greek and Latin in expounding the Bible. I see clear evidence here of a fact noted by Pirqoy ben Baboy about two generations before b. Quraysh, viz. Palestinian influence on liturgical customs and study methods in Africa. One of the results of that influence was undoubtedly the spread of the knowledge of Hebrew, at least to an extent permitting some understanding of the Bible.

The revival of Hebrew in Palestine from the end of the Byzantine period is attested by the *piyyūṭim* of Yosi ben Yosi, Yannai, Eleazar ha-Qalīr, Pinḥas ha-Kohen ha-Payṭān, Samuel (author of *piyyūṭim* on the earthquake in Tiberias in 748), Joshua ha-Kohen and others, in part known by name and in part anonymous, whose works have come to light in the Geniza. Moreover, the *midreshey aggada* known as the *Rabbot* and the *Pesiqta'ot*, whose language is Hebrew and which circulated in Africa, were collected in Palestine during that period. Of particular importance was the Massora, the Tiberian and Palestinian punctuation and pronunciation, which consolidated about that time and spread to Egypt and the Maghreb.

In Chapter One (p. 38), we quoted a Hebrew epitaph discovered in Tripolitania and ascribed to the pre-Arab period. In the area between Barca and Tripoli, some further inscriptions have been discovered whose language is similar to that of the inscription referred to but whose exact date is difficult to determine—even where they seem to contain a date assigning them to the 12th or 13th century. Although they must be treated very cautiously as regards political-historical conclusions, we may suppose that they attest to continuity of the use of Hebrew, at any rate in inscriptions.[2]

Katz, *Iggeret*, pp. 106-107 and 196. A reflex of this problem may be present in *RShT*, no. 64, sec. 2. Comp. also Zucker, *Saadia*, p. 11.

[1] Comp. Steinschneider, *JQR* o.s. 12 (1900), pp. 481ff.; *idem*, *Arabische Literatur*, pp. XIIIff. and XLIV; Hirschberg, *Israel in Arabia*, pp. 242-264.

[2] Comp. Zulai, *RIHP* V, pp. 107ff.; Klar, *Erez Kinnaroth*, Jerusalem 1951, pp. 109-110; above, p. 134.

It has been established that Yehuda b. Quraysh, the philologist of Tāhert, himself wrote *piyyūṭīm*.[1] The language of prayers, *piyyūṭīm* and liturgical songs was Hebrew or Aramaic.[2] Rab Hay forbade cantors to sing in Arabic, even at convivial gatherings. The relevant responsum was sent to Kairouan or at any rate to North Africa.[3]

Kairouan was the home of Dunash ben Tamim, a younger contemporary of Yehuda. It is no accident that two of the earliest Jewish grammarians and philologists, Dunash ben Labraṭ and Yehuda Ḥayyūj, originated from Fez. There must have been some knowledge of, and interest in, the Bible and Hebrew in North Africa prior to their activities. We may perhaps assume that the renewed preoccupation with Biblical Hebrew was furthered, on the one hand, by memories of Punic, which had not completely vanished, and on the other, by Arabic, which already played an important part with Jewry, as attested by Ibn Quraysh's epistle and by other sources, to be discussed below.

The phenomena referred to led to a certain downgrading of Rabbinical Aramaic-Hebrew. Although it was used in the *batey-midrashot* and in most of the questions to the Babylonian academies, as well as in the responsa of the Geonim, it was gradually superseded by Arabic. At first, the questions only were couched in Arabic, so as to state the case in the language of the claimant and the respondent, but later the responsa, too, were framed in that language דפענא הד̇ה אלמסאלה אלי חצ̇רה סידנא גאון בלפט̇ ערבי כמא גרא מן אלכ̇צום מן אגל שגבהם וענתהם [4] that is to say: We have sent this question to His Honour our Lord the Gaon in Arabic, the language in which the parties stated their grievances and misfortunes. The language used by the parties in court (at Qābes) was thus Arabic. Elsewhere we read: "This question has been brought before us, to the Gate of the Yeshiva of the Exile, to two great *batey-dīn* (Sherira and Hay) . . . and we have ordered it to be read before us . . . and we have also ordered the responsum to be written in the language of the Hagareans (*i.e.* Arabs), like the question itself."[5] A query addressed from Kairouan to the Gaon Aaron ha-Kohen (Sarjado) (middle of 10th century) gives the

---

[1] Edited by H. Brody, *Ha-Zofe*, 2 (1912), pp. 63-83.

[2] Comp. e.g., the *Fragments from the Cairo Genizah* published by R. Gottheil and W. H. Worrell, New York 1927, nos. 31, 32, 38, 42, and 46. Some people of Kairouan once asked whether Aramaic might be used for prayer; *RH*, no. 373.

[3] *RShT*, no. 152; comp. also a responsum of Isaac Alfasi (no. 181), and below, pp. 153ff.

[4] *RH*, no. 325 (from Qābes).

[5] *RH*, no. 371, probably also from Qābes.

oath formula in Arabic. There can be no doubt that an oath taken in Arabic was regarded as binding.[1]

In time, we find an increasing number of Gaonic responsa to questions from Kairouan and surroundings accompanied by a note saying that they have been translated from Arabic; some of them state expressly that they emanate from the *beyt-midrash* of Sherira and Hay.[2] But even those preserved in Hebrew and not designated as translations include many originally written in Arabic. Saadia laid down rules for the interpretation of Arabic in legal matters in which the sacred tongue has decisive effect.[3] The apologetic remark that the responsum is given in the language of the question shows that the rabbis were not happy about the use of Arabic by scholars familiar with Rabbinic (Aramaic-) Hebrew. This appears also from the words of R. Naḥum ben Joseph ha-Ḥazzān al-Baradānī, who, in a letter from Mahdiya (or Kayrouan) to the Gaon Samuel bar Ḥofni, explains why he is using Arabic.[4] In a letter from Jerusalem to Fusṭāṭ of the first half of the 11th century, the writer, a rabbinical scholar, deems it necessary to mention to the addressee, also a rabbinical scholar, that he has received a letter in Arabic from him, which therefore does not seem to have been a common occurrence.[5] The scholars of that generation would thus ordinarily use Aramaic-Hebrew in discussions with one another. But the correspondence between Yehuda bar Joseph of Kayrouan and Sherira and Hay is in Arabic,[6] and we also find many responsa in Arabic from Isaac Alfasi.[7] This latter fact is additional evidence that Arabic was widely used in Fez.

We have already seen that parties in court pleaded in Arabic. That language was used also in records of court decisions, business correspondence, promissory notes and contracts.[8] At the same time, specifically Muslim terms were adopted, the rarity of which shows, however, that they were usually avoided. A document fixing the date for a trial at the *Beyt-Dīn Gadol* in Iraq repeatedly uses the term *qaḍiyya* (court case) in

---

[1] *RHG*, no. 37; comp. *ibid.*, no. 40, at the end; and an oath in Arabic or Persian *ibid.*, no. 76.

[2] Comp. *RSh*, p. 31b, no. 18; p. 36a-b, no. 12; p. 94b, no. 6.

[3] Comp. *RM*, no. 90; also Müller, *Mafteaḥ*, p. 52 bottom.

[4] Goldziher, *REJ* 50 (1905), p. 184, l. 18. Nahum was a scholar, comp. Ginzberg, *Geonica* II, p. 69; and so was his father, whose *piyyūṭīm* were published by Davidson, *Ginzey Schechter* III, pp. 51, 92 and 95ff., and Mann, *TaS* I, pp. 151-152.

[5] Comp. Mann, *Jews* II, p. 183, l. 19.

[6] Comp. Ginzberg, *Geonica* II, p. 69; *RH*, nos. 207 and 208; *Harkavy*, *ibid.*, p. X.

[7] Comp. *RH*, nos. 83-177, 443-508.

[8] Comp. Golb, *JSS* 20 (1958), p. 19: three documents in Hebrew, three in Aramaic, twenty-four in Arabic.

varying forms.[1] A man declares before witnesses that in a certain lawsuit documents were forced upon him "in accordance with the laws of the Gentiles or in accordance with the *sharīʿa al-Yahūd*";[2] the suit was heard before a Muslim *qāḍī*, and the "law of the Gentiles" is thus the law applied by him, while the "*sharīʿa*"—the usual term for Islamic law—is the law of the Tora! The date is usually given according to the Seleucid Calendar and sometimes in years of the Creation; the Hijra date is used only exceptionally in legal documents, and then because they were to be submitted to a *bey-doʾar*, a Muslim judicial authority, for confirmation.[3] We sometimes find an isolated Arabic word in a Hebrew responsum, *e.g.*, *biḍāʿa*, goods, *shāriʿ*, street, or an Arabic verb with Hebrew inflection *meṣarfin ōtān 400 zūz*, (that 400 zūz is changed—*ṣarafa*).[4]

As the knowledge of Arabic spread, the homily at synagogue—whether only oral or also in writing—was in that language. It was studded with rabbinical sayings and passages from sacred writings, which were not translated into Arabic nor allowed to be freely rendered in Aramaic by the homilist. The reason for these restrictions is given in a responsum of Sherira and Hay: "But as for him who reads a passage as our teacher Moses said it, in the sacred tongue, and interprets it in accordance with the Targum and the Aggada, saying: *amōn* (Prov. 8:30) pedagogue, *amōn* covered, *amōn* self-effacing" (Gen. r. 1, 1), it is right to mention these different interpretations, for the Aggada and minor commentaries and all *midrashot* are legitimate and should be taken into account"; and on the other hand: "As for him who translates a passage as it is (not using an authorised translation) and he who adds to it (his own explanations), they are both blameworthy."[5]

These usages led to the emergence of a special language, a mixture of Arabic, Hebrew and Aramaic, in the halakhic, aggadic and philosophical writings of the scholars of those generations. Much illustrative material is provided by Rabbenu Nissim ben Jacob, who was a typical representative of Maghrebi scholarship and whose works have reached us in greater numbers than those of others.

In his Talmudistic writings, Nissim uses Hebrew-Aramaic and Arabic alternately, without clear delimitation. Purely accidental causes long

---

[1] Comp. Aptowitzer, *JQR* 4 (1913/14), pp. 25 and 50.

[2] Gottheil-Worrell, *Fragments* 7, p. 34, ll. 16-17.

[3] Comp. *e.g.*, *JQR* 16 (1904), pp. 577-578, ll. 6-7, and *Sepher ha-Yishub* II, Z̠efat, no. 1.

[4] *RCor*, no. 41; *RM*, no. 95; *RH*, no. 210; comp. also *RCor* no. 95, where the value of the *mohar* (*i.e.* the *ketuba*) is given in Arabic.

[5] *RH*, nos. 15 and 248, also no. 208.

created the impression that part of his *Megillat Setarim* (Secret Scroll) was in "Hebrew" (*i.e.* Hebrew-Aramaic) and part in Arabic. But the discovery of large fragments and an index to the book has shown that the author used the two languages indiscriminately, passing from one to the other while dealing with the same subject, just as he did in his *Mafteaḥ le-Manʿulay ha-Talmud* (Key to the Locks of the Talmud).[1] His popular *midrash*, *The Fine Book of Comfort* was deliberately written almost entirely in Arabic, though the author not infrequently changes to Hebrew-Aramaic or quotes rabbinical sayings in their original language. It should be noted that this book contains a greater number of quotations than the works of other thinkers of that generation.

Nissim had complete command of Arabic, and his style has a peculiar charm, noticeable especially in those works to which no parallels have been found in ancient rabbinical literature. At the same time, it should be stressed that his language is not classical literary Arabic; it has a popular flavour, which is possibly intended. Nor is it surprising to find an admixture of Hebrew words and terms, which he took over not only because they were in common use, but because it was difficult to find Arabic equivalents. Although he was not the first to adopt this practice, some expressions were used only by him. Here is an incomplete list of Hebrew words and terms interspersed in the Arabic text of the *Fine Book*: *Al-betūlā* (virgin); *bi-zekhūtāh* (thanks to her); *ketubbathā* (her marriage settlement); *al-pāsūq* (passage, verse); *parnās* (community leader); *al-ṣadaqa* (charity); *al-shushbīnīn* (groomsmen); *al-kippūr* (atonement); *al-mishna*; *al-nebīʾīm* (prophets); *al-pārāsha* (portion of the Law).[2]

Jewish authors as yet saw nothing wrong in the use of the form *kenīsa* for "synagogue", although it denoted also a church (similarly to the plural (*batey*) *kenesiyot*); it was only afterwards that the form *kenīs* was set aside for "synagogue".[3] But it seems rather odd that David ben Abraham al-Fāsī uses the term *al-qurʾān* for the Bible, alternately with *miqrā* or *kitāb*. Does this mean that the Jews did not yet reserve that term for the holy book of Islam? [4]

---

[1] Comp. below, pp. 336-7, and Sh. Abramson, *R. Nissim Gaon*, Jerusalem 1965, esp. pp. 305ff.

[2] Comp. Hirschberg, *R. Nissim*, Introduction, pp. 48-50, also Ginzberg, *Geonica* II, pp. 67 and 69: *al-Kohen, al-Ḥazzān.*

[3] Ibn Quraysh, *Risāla*, p. 1; Obermann, *Studies*, p. 28; Ginzberg, *Geonica* II, p. 69 (vertical line); Mann, *Jews* II, p. 91, l. 14, p. 111, l. 11, and p. 114, l. 20.

[4] Comp. Skoss, *Dictionary* I, p. 3, l. 1; p. 42, l. 19; p. 39, l. 5; p. 3, l. 6; comp. also Introduction, p. LXIII. The Gaon Saadia likewise uses the term *al-qurʾān* for the Bible; comp. *Goldziher*, *Memorial Volume* II (Hebrew part), p. 14, l. 1.

The *Fine Book* contains two clear cases of borrowings from the Koran. In one of them, the Koranic verse is quoted as if it were a Biblical one: "And he also said: The heaven belongs to the Lord, who made it high, and the earth is an edifice" (comp. Sura 13:2; 55:7; 2:2). In the other case, Nissim uses the words of the Koran (Sura 9:119) without realizing that he is drawing upon a non-Jewish source, for he continues: "as (Scripture) says" and then quotes Ex. 20:4. These borrowings are without doubt unconscious and show how much the Jews had been influenced by their environment.[1]

When writing in Arabic, the Jews used Hebrew script, in all the forms then current; only in exceptional cases, as when one of the parties to a contract or bill was a Muslim, or when writing the name of the recipient, did they use Arabic characters.[2] This practice must be regarded as deliberate self-segregation from the Arab-Muslim majority (Syrian Christians likewise used their own alphabet when writing in Arabic). This explanation is supported by the fact that the art of reading and writing was not prevalent in wide circles, not even among merchants,[3] but was the business of professional scribes and sometimes of slaves employed as book-keepers and accountants; these could easily have learnt Arabic script if they had needed it.[4]

The same consistent dualism of assimilation and self-segregation marked another feature of the Jewish scene in Muslim countries, viz. personal names and family names. Some Hebrew names took on Arabic forms: Abraham became Ibrāhīm, Yiṣḥaq Isḥāq, Moshe Mūsā, David Da'ūd, etc. Others were translated into or adapted to Arabic: Elʿazar – Manṣūr, Yehoshūʿa – Faraj, Nathan – ʿAṭiyya or Wahab. In the Maghreb, many Jews bore purely Arabic names with the ending *-ūn*, which was peculiar to that region: Barhūn, Zaidūn, Ḥayyūn, Khalfūn, Maymūn, Faḍlūn, etc., and similarly Ḥasūn, ʿAlūsh. Arabic names were especially frequent among women, some rather bizarre: Sitt al-Bahā (Lady of Splendour), Sitt al-Ahl (Lady of the Family). Maidservants' names had a peculiar flavour: Qamar (Moon), Naʿīm (Lovely One).[5]

---

[1] Comp. Hirschberg, *R. Nissim*, Introduction, pp. 61-62. See also Gottheil-Worrell, *Fragments* 35, p. 160, l. 2, where Sura 1, 1 is quoted; Steinschneider, *Hebr. Bibliographie* 3 (1860), p. 113; Mainz, *Islam* 21 (1933), p. 229.

[2] Comp. Worman, *JQR* o.s., 19 (1907), pp. 728-729, and Gottheil-Worrell, *Fragments* 16, p. 82.

[3] *RH*, no. 238.

[4] Comp. Hirschberg, *R. Nissim*, pp. 94-95.

[5] Klar, *Meḥqārīm we-ʿIyūnīm*, Tel Aviv 1954, p. 66, and Goitein, *Society* I, General Index.

However, among the host of Arabic names, male and female, we find none expressly associated with the founder of Islam, his relatives or the early Caliphs, except ʿAlī, which may be regarded as a Biblical name (with a change of vowel), and Ḥasan, which was considered a translation of Yefet (Japhet). No Jewish man was called Muḥammad, Aḥmad, (Abū) Bekr, ʿOmar,[1] ʿOthmān or Muʿāwiyya and no Jewish woman Khadīja, ʿĀʾisha or Fāṭima.

The Physiognomy of Jewish Society

In default of factual documents, such as taxpayers' lists, court records etc., from which we might have gathered statistical data, we are unable to determine the numerical relations between the different strata of society: the percentage of villagers as against town-dwellers, the number of breadwinners, the standard of living and the level of education. The material in our possession is one-sided and limited, and when trying to ascertain the character of that society, we must beware of unwarranted generalizations. When dealing with the works of thinkers, rabbis, men of letters and scholars, we are apt to regard these as typical of society as a whole, representative of the majority of their generation, though exceptional in degree of achievement. But the sources themselves help us to dispel this illusion. *E.g.*, R. Jacob ben Nissim of Kairouan attests that most of the signatories of bills are ignorant, that they cannot read the bills nor comprehend their own affairs; that is to say, that the art of writing was not widespread even among those who had to do with bills: merchants, property owners and the like.[2] This agrees with the description of the characters in Nissim ben Jacob's stories in the *Fine Book*, which will be extensively dealt with below. Those characters are largely simple folk, laboriously tilling their small plots of land. The fact that Nissim thinks them worthy to be heroes of his stories permits us to infer that they represent the majority of the Jewish population. The underscoring of the virtues of these simple people, who are no less excellent than religious scholars and better than the rich, shows that the author regards them also as the soundest element in the community.

Their standard of religious learning is not high; even the stories of the Bible are not very well known to them. Hay Gaon once explained to R. Nissim that the teachers of Scripture in the cities make many mistakes, "and all the more the teachers in the villages, who are not conversant

[1] For two exceptions see below pp. 235 n. 6, 465 para 6.
[2] Comp. *RH*, nos. 231 and 238.

with the Bible."[1] Still, Hay's strictures indicate that there were teachers in Jewish communities, while the surrounding non-Jewish population was completely illiterate. We know that in the Maghreb—including Spain—there were schools for children.[2] It was the custom, though only in the higher circles, for a Tora scroll, or even a copy of the whole Bible, to be written for an infant, so that he might study it when he grew up.[3]

A perfunctory perusal of hundreds of letters and documents concerning international and intercontinental business activities of Maghreb Jews might give the impression that a very large circle of persons took part in them. But the list of names occurring in documents shows that we have to do here with a small group of members of certain families connected by kinship and intermarriage. Goitein has found that the Geniza documents mention only a few dozen families, including only about ten of special distinction.

We hear almost nothing of disagreements and disputes in the Maghreb concerning religious doctrine or communal government. Of course, absence of information is not proof. Anyhow, we do not find here the division into two communities, as it were, viz. Palestino-Syrians and Babylonians, that occurred in Palestine and Egypt, and this may be due to the paucity of Palestinian and Babylonian emigrants to the Maghreb. But we know that even a single person with a scheming mind is able to create dissension, and the possibility of a split as aforesaid would seem to have existed in the Maghreb as well. It developed in fact at the end of the Middle Ages, upon the arrival of the expellees from Spain. During the period under discussion, there must have been a nucleus of Babylonians in Kairouan, as can be inferred from the term "the Babylonian elders".[4]

The Karaites in the Maghreb

The absence of a tendency to strife and fission is evident also in relations with the Karaite sect, this, too, in contrast to what we find in other countries.

In view of the many and varied ties of the Maghreb with the countries

---

[1] *RC*, no. 78.

[2] Schechter, *Saadyana*, p. 77, l. 1; Ginzberg, *Geonica* II, p. 83, l. 13; Lewin, *Iggeret*, p. XVI.

[3] See below, pp. 177f.

[4] Comp. below, p. 281.

where the centres of Karaism were situated, we are not surprised at the presence of Karaites and Karaite ideas in North Africa. A new sect is usually vital and full of drive, eager to win supporters either by gentle methods or by argument and polemics, according as circumstances suggest. Since the inception of Christianity and even before, North Africa, with its mixed population of Berbers, Carthaginians and Romans, had generally been fertile ground for the development of religious sects. This situation remained unchanged; it persisted especially during the first five centuries of Muslim rule in the Maghreb.

As already hinted in the preceding chapter, the settlement of Muslim sects in the border areas of the Maghreb about fifty years after the Arab conquest encouraged the development of Jewish communities in several remote districts. Karaite propaganda was thus enabled to reach places distant from the usual caravan routes. In fact, it was precisely there that the Karaites established themselves and held their own for a fairly long time. It was also there that conditions for the survival of remnants of Karaism were more favourable than in the large communities, where there were rabbis capable of defending the Jewish heritage.

The question when Karaism first spread to North Africa is a moot one. Two or three generations ago, the prevailing view was that there were Karaites in the African and European Maghreb already at the end of the 9th century C.E. As to Spain, this assumption has almost nothing to rely upon, while there is room for discussion as far as Africa is concerned.[1] The upholders of the antiquity of Karaism in Africa assert that Yehuda b. Quraysh of Tāhert was the first known Karaite to settle in Fez (he is presumed to have flourished at the end of the 9th or the beginning of the 10th century). They quote as evidence his anti-anthropomorphist commentaries and also try to prove that he wrote the *Sefer ha-ʿArayot* or *Sefer ha-Miṣwot*, which is directed against the Talmudists. As has already been shown by some scholars, this view rests on shaky foundations and may be refuted.[2]

Stronger evidence of Karaite leanings may be found with David ben Abraham of Fez, the author of a dictionary of the Hebrew language: he

---

[1] Comp. Pinsker, *Liqqutey Qadmoniyoth*, p. 46 and nn. 3 and 13. There is no evidence that R. Eleazar b. Samuel, the "Alluf of Lucena" saw Anan's "Book of Commandments" in Spain (see *Seder R. ʿAmram*, Warsaw 1965, 38 a-b; also Müller, *Mafteaḥ*, pp. 109-110, no. 101); it seems more probable that he saw it in Iraq. In any case, Ibn Daud's testimony, *SHQ*, p. 69/94-95, that Karaism did not spread in Spain until the late 11th century cannot be disregarded; comp. also Baron, *SRH* V, p. 271 and n. 72.

[2] Comp. Katz, *Risāla*, Introd., pp. 31-38.

designates the Karaites with the epithet *maskīlīm* (wise ones), which was customary with them, and clearly sides with them in matters in dispute between them and the Rabbanites. His note to the verse "And when he had set the brands on fire" etc. (Judges 15:5), viz.: "These words of the text forbid lamplight on the Sabbath, whether it was lit before or on the Sabbath", reflects the view of the early Karaites, who, in reliance on Ex. 35:3, forbade not only the lighting of a fire on the Sabbath, but also the maintenance on the Sabbath of a fire kindled before the Sabbath. Of course, even if we agree that David ben Abraham was a Karaite, we have still not solved the question of the date. We know nothing about his life. He probably lived for a long time in Palestine; at any rate, his book is known only through Palestinian sources. If that is so, it seems likely that he received Karaite influence in Palestine and that while in Fez he was still a Rabbanite.[1]

It is always difficult to determine the sectarian affiliation of a philologist or grammarian on the strength of his "Karaite" views in matters of exegesis. We cannot rule out the possibility that the preoccupation with language induced a freer approach and a disregard for traditional interpretations and methods without any Karaite beliefs being involved. On the other hand, many may have been wavering between the two religious trends. "Mixed" marriages between Rabbanites and Karaites attest that the division, which was to become rigid in the course of time, was not yet complete.

From the middle of the 10th century, Rabbanite literature in the Maghreb propounds ideas which sound like a reply to Karaite propaganda. A question which R. Jacob, on behalf of "the holy congregation of Kairouan", put to the Gaon Sherira in the year 1298 S.E. (987 C.E.), viz. how the Mishna was written, is regarded by some as an echo of the Karaite campaign then conducted in Africa against Rabbanite traditions and the Oral Law.[2]

We know that a dispute arose between the Kairouan rabbis and the Karaites concerning the blowing of the ram's horn on the New Year, when the people of Kairouan were again compelled to seek guidance from Sherira and Hay, his son and successor to the Gaonate, in order to be able to reply to their opponents.[3] Moreover, S. J. Rappaport has

---

[1] Comp. Skoss, *Dictionary* I, p. 253, ll. 131ff., and English Introduction, pp. Lff., also XXXVIff.

[2] Comp. Lewin, *Iggeret*, Introd., pp. XI-XII.

[3] Comp. *Ozar ha-Geonim*, Rosh ha-Shana, no. 117, pp. 60-61.

pointed out a number of passages from R. Ḥananel's Bible commentary, gleaned by him from various books (the commentary itself being lost), which evince anti-Karaite polemical intent.[1]

The above data are supplemented by a letter from Jerusalem to Warghlān of the second half of A.H. 432 (4801 of the Creation, 1041 C.E.). Moses ha-Sefaradi, a resident of Jerusalem originating from Warghlān, is writing to two brothers who used to befriend him and his family. He sends greetings to the elders of the community and mentions that he has despatched to Warghlān, through one Elishaʿ ha-Kastiliani, a very voluminous book with explanations of difficult words in the Bible. He is anxious to know whether the book has reached its destination.

Warghlān or, as it is now called, Ouargla, is a fertile oasis, remarkable for its date-palms, on the eastern edge of the Saharan Atlas. It was very important for the trade between the Mediterranean coast and the interior, being the starting-point for camel caravans that travelled to the Sudan and brought back products of Central Africa. The letter indicates that the Jewish community in Warghlān was well off, and we may suppose that its members took an active part in the caravan trade.

The letter was sent *via* the community of Kairouan, which was an intermediate station for correspondence and responsa between Palestine and Babylonia on the one hand and West Africa and Spain on the other.[2]

We possess two direct references to the Warghlān community of approximately the middle of the 12th century. Abraham ibn Daud, speaking of the "heretics", *i.e.* Karaites, notes that they are to be found "in one city in the west (*i.e.* in the Maghreb), in the Warghlān Desert".[3] Abraham ibn ʿEzra, in his comment on Ex. 12:11, records a custom of the Karaites in that locality: "The heretics in Warghlān do today as follows in memory of the exodus from Egypt: these misguided people all go out of their country on the fifteenth day in memory of the exodus from Egypt."

A letter of the same period from Karaites in Egypt concerning assistance to their leader David ben Ḥasday says that "Warghlāni Gentiles" transmit such letters to the Karaites "in the west".[4] It was no doubt through these Gentiles that the Karaites in Warghlān maintained contact

[1] Comp. *RShT*, no. 92 (kindling of the Sabbath lights); Rappaport, *Bikkurei ha-ʿIttim* 12 (1832), pp. 34-35.

[2] Comp. Assaf, *Studies in Memory of Gulak and Klein*, Jerusalem 1942, pp. 18-22. For the economic importance of Warglān comp. below, p. 251.

[3] *SHQ*, p. 68/93.

[4] Mann, *Texts* II, pp. 155, 138-140.

with Egypt and also with Palestine. Incidentally, the Muslims in Warghlān —as reported by Idrīsī—belonged to the Wahhābī and Ibāḍī sects.[1]

Moses ha-Sefaradi's utterance concerning the large volume, sent by him to Warghlān, of explanations of difficult words in the Bible may indicate the presence of Karaites in that locality already a hundred years before Abraham ibn Daud and Abraham ibn ʿEzra, so that we may regard the despatch of that book as an attempt to spread Karaite ideas.[2] The messenger who transmitted the book, Elishaʿ ha-Kastiliani, was not impossibly a Karaite. Abraham ibn Daud says that many people in Castile were misguided enough to join that sect. During the same period, the Karaites made increased efforts to gain a foothold in Africa.[3]

In the middle of the 12th century, there lived in Egypt the Karaite poet Moses b. Abraham Darʿī (*i.e.* of Darʿa in the Maghreb), about whom a great deal has been written. He was at first dated as early as the time of the Gaon Saadia. His *dīwān*, entitled *Maḥberet Nō-Ammōn u-Miṣrāyim*, contains no data on his life; still, it permits us to infer that he was not born in Darʿa, but in Alexandria. According to Davidson, Moses was not a Karaite from birth, but joined the sect in his youth.[4]

From then onwards, there is a gap in our knowledge of the Karaites in the Maghreb. It may be supposed that the Almohad persecutions did not affect the Karaites in Warghlān, since ʿAbd al-Muʾmin's army did not reach that area at all.

It seems appropriate to deal with the subject all at once, and we therefore pass on to the 14th and 15th centuries. In the first half of the 14th century, there lived in Cairo the Karaite *dayyan*, Israel ha-Maʿarabī, author of several pamphlets dealing, respectively, with religious duties, ritual slaughtering, calendar lore, etc. A reference to a custom which obtained in his country before his arrival in Cairo suggests that he came from the Maghreb. In the 15th century, we find in Cairo the Karaite

---

[1] *Description*, p. 121.

[2] Some halakhic instructions sent to the Maghreb by the geonim appear to be directed against Karaite customs, which were beginning to spread in Africa; comp. the liberal instructions for menstruating women (as against the prohibitions of the Karaites): *RM*, no. 44; *RShT* nos. 5 and 169-171 (comp. also Maimonides' letter below, p. 165). The meal on Sabbath eve is to be eaten by candlelight, *RL*, no. 53; the Decalogue need not be recited every day, *RShT* no. 343 and comp. Mann, *Jews* I, p. 223.

[3] *SHQ*, p. 69/95. Incidentally, a locality named Kastilia existed also in Tunisia at that time, and there seem to have been Jews among its inhabitants; comp. Ibn Ḥawqal, *BGA* II², p. 54, and Maqdisī, *BGA* III, p. 243.

[4] Comp. Pinsker, *Liqqutey Qadmoniyot*, p. 105, and Davidson, *Maddaʿey ha-Yahaduth* II, Jerusalem 1927, pp. 297-308.

physician Samuel b. Moses ha-Maʿarabī, who wrote an important treatise on religious duties, entitled *Al-Murshid*, in Arabic. Maghrebi origin indicated by his surname is the only, though for us important, vestige of the biography of that scholar. The settling of these two men in Cairo illustrates the general tendency of African Jews to move to the East, to Egypt and Syria in search of scholarly contacts.[1]

According to Simon ben Ṣemaḥ Dūrān, Karaism became extinct at that time at least in the major Maghrebi centres: "The Karaites are an insignificant minority; there are only a few of them in Egypt and in some places in the east; and as for one place in the desert, called Warghlān, we have heard that they have all died and that not one of them is left in that locality."[2] Abraham Zaccuto, who wrote his *Sefer Yuḥasin* in Tunis in the year 5264 (1504), comments upon Abraham ibn Daud's remarks concerning Karaites in Warghlān:[3] "But by this time, they have reformed."[4] After an account (also borrowed from Abraham ibn Daud) of the Almohad persecutions, "which left no remnant of Israel from Tangier to Almahdiya,"[5] Abraham Zaccuto goes on to speak of the Rabbanites in Warghlān: "I, Abraham, have now learnt in Tunis that there is a large community there of wealthy people who believe in the receipt of the Oral Law; the place is in the Sahara, three days' journey from the city, and they come to Tunis and Bougie; there is a ruler there from among the rulers of Tunis, and the place is thirty days' journey from Tunis."[6] The reference is undoubtedly to Warghlān, as appears also from the sequel; we have to do here with a second, enlarged, but corrupt version of what the author has said once before. The city whose name is missing seems to be Tūqūrt (Touggourt), then an important centre.[7]

However, remnants of Karaism subsisted at least in two remote regions of the High Atlas in Morocco. Leo Africanus, who describes the

---

[1] Comp. Steinschneider, *Arab. Literatur*, sections 184 and 199. On Israel ha-Maʿarabī comp. also Mann, *Texts* II, pp. 71, 110 and 1416, and Z. Ankori, *Karaites in Byzantium*, Jerusalem 1959, pp. 341-342. The third part of *Al-Murshid* was edited by F. Kauffmann (*Traktat über die Neulichtbeobachtung und den Jahresbeginn bei den Karäern*), the fourth by J. Junowitsch (*Die karaeischen Fest-und Fasttage* etc., Berlin 1904), the eleventh by Julius Cohn (*Abhandlungen über die Pflichten der Priester und Richter*, Berlin 1907 (Inaugural-Dissertation)). Comp. also Baron, *SRH* V, pp. 236, 238, 399, no. 30, 404 n. 45.

[2] *Magen Abot*, ed. Leghorn 1785, Part II, ch. 3, p. 31a.

[3] See above p. 160, n. 3

[4] *Juchassin*, ed. Filipowski, London 1857, p. 215a n. 2.

[5] *SHQ*, p. 70/96.

[6] Juchassin, p. 215b.

[7] Comp. above p. 143.

situation in Morocco in the first quarter of the 16th century, reports that in the Demensera Mountains (south-west of Marrakesh) he found many Jews riding horses, carrying arms and fighting by the side of their masters, the inhabitants of those mountains. The Jews of other regions regarded them almost as heretics; they were called Karaites. In the lofty Hintāta Mountains—named after the Hintāta tribe—south-east of Marrakesh, the like of which he had never seen, he found many Jewish craftsmen, who paid poll-tax to their masters. They were all Karaites and were said to be brave and to carry arms.[1]

The correctness of Leo's account cannot be doubted, nor can we suppose that he is referring to groups of expellees from Spain who had somehow come to the Atlas Mountains. Karaism in Spain never prospered and quickly disappeared from the scene, so there was no infusion of fresh blood in North African Karaite communities, as there was in Rabbanite ones. Leo saw remnants of the Karaite sect who, similarly to their Rabbanite brethren, had escaped Almohad persecution in North Africa and subsisted in remote districts.

The African Kohanim

While discussing the Karaites, we should touch upon the problem of the *kohanim* (priestly class) in the Maghreb, a rather obscure matter, which has some relevance to the dispute between the Rabbanites and the Karaites. The latter asserted that the Rabbanites had deliberately defaced the genealogical documents of the *kohanim*, so that those claiming to be of Aaron's stock could no longer prove their claim. This implied the charge that the Rabbanites had abrogated the Biblical prohibitions regarding the marriage of *kohanim*.[2] The rabbis refrained from directly answering this charge, but were more rigorous from then on as to the conduct of *kohanim* generally and forbidden marriages in particular. Hence the many questions addressed to the geonim concerning a *kohen* who led an immoral life, who had married a divorced woman or who had reneged and subsequently returned to the fold. In these cases, the offender would be publicly censured and disqualified from being "called" first to the Tora at synagogue.[3] The conduct of women of the priestly class

---

[1] Comp. Léon, *Description*, pp. 85-86 and 114 and the map before p. 71. For the Hintata comp. Lévi-Provençal, *Documents*, p. 41-62.

[2] For the Karaite beliefs comp. J. Cohn, *Abhandlung* (see above, p. 162 n. 1), pp. 1/11 and 12/37; Baron, *SRH* V, pp. 236, 239-40.

[3] Comp. *RShT*, nos. 177 (Hay), 180 (Sherira), 207 (Natronāy), 231 (Hay), also *RM*,

was of course also judged by exacting standards.[1] The sources containing the relevant responsa do not indicate their destinations, but the Gaon Hay's *Epistle to the Kohanim* of Africa, "who were utterly lawless", suffices to enlighten us on the situation in that region.[2]

That epistle, which is surprisingly sharp, attacks the following kinds of *kohanim*: 1. those who are over-eager for the gifts due to priests; 2. liars and storytellers; 3. coarse-minded persons; 4. genealogical snoopers, who try to disqualify their fellow *kohanim*; 5. those who sow discord; 6. those who indulge in making presents to women; actors and frivolous persons; 7. the quarrelsome and brazen-faced; 8. smooth-tongued persons and flatterers; 9. those who are greedy of gain; 10. those who know the significance of priesthood and yet do not mount the dais at synagogue; 11. the ill-tempered and over-fastidious; 12. the scoffers and the haughty; 13. those who are proud of their priesthood; 14. those who scramble for wealth; 15. the recalcitrant; 16. those who transgress the precepts concerning *almānōt ʿissōt* (widows whose husbands came of ritually impure families); 17. the sexually licentious; 18. the leprous; 19. the over-punctilious; 20. those who are over-eager to attend banquets; 21. the double-tongued; 22. those who frequently swear oaths and are quick to quarrel.

After twenty-two reprobative expressions, which in the Hebrew original are in alphabetical order, Hay wished to wind up on a positive note. He therefore used the last two letters of the Hebrew alphabet (*shīn, tāw*) once more, this time in descriptions of praiseworthy categories of *kohanim*: 23. those who study (*shōnīm*) two *halakhot* in the morning and two in the evening; 24. those who are perfect (*temīmīm*) in their ways and excellent in their proceedings.

The main content of this epistle is the denunciation of a sad moral decline which had set in among the *kohanim.* It also contains (in the fourth paragraph) a disputation with the Karaites concerning the genealogical documents. B. M. Lewin, who published the epistle, was inclined to think that it was addressed to "a city whose inhabitants are all *kohanim.*" Such a city is in our time the Jewish community on the island of Jerba, where there is a tradition that a Levite who settles there will not

---

nos. 132 and 171. *RC*, no. 4, may contain a polemical reference to the view of some Karaites that a widow is not eligible for marriage to a priest; comp. Cohn, *ibid.*, p. 7/26 and n. 69.

[1] Comp. *RCor*, no. 24.

[2] Published in *Ginzey Kedem*, 4 (1930), pp. 51-54; comp. also Klein's note *ibid.*, p. 111.

outlive the year, but we do not know whether the composition of the community was the same in the days of the Gaon Hay. Maimonides does not mention this detail, which would have seemed to deserve mention. Slouschz found still another *kohanim* settlement in the Maghreb, and he tries to connect this phenomenon with the presence of Judaizers in the region, which led the *kohanim* to protect their genealogical purity. Such a connection cannot be ruled out, especially in view of the existence of two priestly tribes, the "Kāhinān" Naḍīr and Qaraiẓa, in North Arabia in the pre-Islamic period. But the material in our possession is insufficient for any definite conclusion.[1]

Beliefs and Customs

Let us begin with a description by Maimonides, in a letter to his son, of the inhabitants of remote corners of the Eastern Maghreb:

"And you, my son (Abraham), should seek pleasant company only with our beloved brethren, the Sephardim, who are called Andaluzios, for they have sense and perception and a clear brain; you should avoid others than these. You should also beware of certain people who live in the western region called al-Zirbi, *i.e.* localities in the countries of Barbary, for they are dull and coarse. And you should always be extremely cautious of the people who live between Tunis and Alexandria in Egypt and who also live in the mountains of Barbary, for they are more stupid in my opinion than other men, although they are very strong in faith; God is my witness and judge that in my opinion they are like the Karaites, who deny the Oral Law; they have no clear brain at all, neither for dealing with the Bible and the Talmud nor for expounding *aggadot* and *halakhot*. Some of them are *dayyanim*, but their beliefs and actions in matters of ritual uncleanness are like those of the sons of abomination, who are a nation of the nations dwelling in the lands of the Ismaelites. They do not see the ritually unclean woman at all; they do not look at her figure or her clothes, they do not speak to her and forbid walking the ground her foot has trodden and do not eat of the hind quarter of animals, and many more and longer stories may be told of them, their customs and doings."[2]

In connection with this appraisal, we should hear what the well-known Arab geographer al-Idrīsi, a contemporary of Maimonides, has to say concerning the Berber inhabitants of Jerba; they are dusky-skinned, of

---

[1] Comp. Hirschberg, *Zion* 22 (1957), p. 18.

[2] Maimonides, *Iggarot u-Sh'eloth u-Teshuboth*, Amsterdam 1712, p. 3a.

a wicked disposition, and hypocritical; they speak only Berber, are always ready for rebellion and submit to no authority; they belong to the Wahhabites and believe that their clothes are made unclean by contact with strangers; they do not extend their hand to a stranger, do not eat with him and do not eat from dishes not kept specially for them; men and women purify themselves every day, wash themselves before every prayer with water and afterwards with sand; if a strange traveller wishes to draw water from their well, they beat him and dry up the well because it has become unclean; the clothes of unclean persons are not brought into contact with those of ritually pure persons, and *vice versa*; at the same time, they are hospitable—they invite strangers to eat at their houses, treat them well and take care of their belongings.[1]

The similarity of the two descriptions of people of Jerba is not accidental, and it prompts speculation as to mutual influence. Maimonides' principal charge is that the people of the area east of Jerba as far as Alexandria are uncouth and are poor scholars. Sure enough, we hear very little of their scholastic attainments, and neither do we hear much of the culture of the Berbers and Arabs there. The other charge, concerning excessive rigour, like that shown by the Muslims, as regards ritual cleanness, agrees perfectly with what al-Idrīsi says of the Berbers and Muslims. There is no need to look for Karaite influences.

It nevertheless seems that Maimonides, biased in favour of "Andalusian Sephardim", tended to over-generalize. Just as it is difficult to imagine a community consisting entirely of scholarly, godfearing and benign persons, thus we can hardly conceive of a group whose members are all ignorant, crude and coarse. The very continuity of Jewish settlement in the area attests to its vitality.

Let us now see what the Kairouan people had to say about beliefs and customs prevailing among them at that time, both among the rabbis and the common folk.

Hay was once asked concerning an important theological question then exercising the minds. Here is the text of the question and the responsum (with some omissions).

"When Mar Rab Yosef the son of Mar Berakhya and our rabbis and the students of the Bet Midrash of Mar Jacob *Rēsh Kalla* the son of Mar Nissim asked him concerning the (Divine) 'Name' and the belief that there were several magic 'names' and that there were those who did great things with them which a person could do only through a miracle

[1] *Description,* pp. 127 and 123.

—such as making oneself invisible to robbers and shackling them—he replied that all this and the like of it were idle things. He said that even if they were perfectly virtuous persons no such thing would happen to them. It impresses us that several Palestinian and Occidental sages, wise men, *ḥaberim* and trustworthy persons, should say that they have seen someone, in public, take leaves of reed grass and of olives and write on them and throw them at robbers so that they could not pass, and that there is someone who writes it (the Name) on a new potsherd and throws it upon the sea so that it ceases from raging, or throws it at a person so that he dies on the spot; and they tell a great many (other) things. They have reported that in several cases they saw somebody, a certain person, with the miracle workers on the eve of Sabbath in a certain place and that he was seen in another place, several days' journey away, on the same eve of Sabbath, and on the same Sabbath in the first-mentioned place. It seems a certain and well-known fact to the people of Spain,[1] and is a tradition with them from their fathers, that Mar Rab Natronāy came to you by the 'leaping of the way' from Babylonia, gave instruction in the Tora and went back, and that he did not go with a caravan and was not seen on the way. And he left several books with us containing several of the 'Names' and the 'names' of angels and the form of his seal and he said: he who wishes to do so-and-so and he who wishes for such-and-such a thing shall write so-and-so upon so-and-so and shall make himself such-and-such a thing and his wish will come true . . . Does our lord say that all these are idle things? . . . There have also been with us some old and pious men who know about dreams; they fasted several days . . . —Will our lord please explain all this to us." In his responsum, Hay says: ". . . these and the like are idle things . . .".[2]

This belief in the use of the Divine Name to change the order of nature leads us to the innermost core of the faith of the Jew in those days. The question emanated from a circle of rabbis and religious scholars in Kairouan headed by Joseph ben Berakhya, one of the spokesmen of the interim period after the death of R. Jacob, when his son, Nissim, was still young. It surely never occurred to simple folk to doubt established popular notions. The belief in the "leaping of the way" was current among Jews in other countries as well. Ibn Ḥazm, the well-known Spanish-Muslim historian of religion of those days, ridicules his Jewish

[1] This, and not "France", is the correct reading according to Ms. Parma and Yehuda al-Barceloni's *Commentar zum Sepher Jezira*, Berlin 1885.

[2] *Ta'am Zeqēnīm*, ed. E. Ashkenazi, Frankfurt a.M. 1854, pp. 54b-58b. For the "leaping of the way" comp. also *RShT*, no. 18, and *RL*, no. 97. See also above (ch. I).

neighbours for crediting such a concept.[1] It seems to have been connected with Messianic hopes.[2]

According to data in our possession, Daniel al-Qūmasī, a 9th-century Karaite writer who settled in Palestine, was among the first to mention the belief in the "Name". Here is what he says: "Who conjures today in Israel? The Rabbanites do, who pronounce a pure 'name' and an unclean 'name', write amulets, use magic devices and possess books entitled *Sepher ha-Yāshār*, *The Book of Mysteries*, *The Book of Adam*, *The Great Mystery* and several books on witchcraft. If you wish to attract a man to a woman, so that he may love her, if you wish to cause them to feel hatred, if you wish to bring about the 'leaping of the way', [they will use witchcraft to help you]—these and many other abominations, may the Lord keep us from them."[3]

R. Natan ha-Kohen b. Isaac the Babylonian reports of Nissim *Rosh Kalla* Naharwāni that he opened all the locks of Babylonia by means of the Name.[4] *Megillat Aḥimaʿaṣ*, the author of which lived in Italy, mentions the use of the Divine Name for reviving a dead man, for accelerating the progress of a ship, for the "leaping of the way".[5] R. Petaḥya says in reference to Byzantium: "And in the land of Greece, they have a large diaspora and are physically enslaved. And there are (among them) men conversant with 'names'; they conjure up demons, which serve them like slaves."[6] It thus appears that the belief in the power of the Divine Name was prevalent in almost all the countries where Jews lived.

The Gaon Hay scouted the belief in the "leaping of the way" and revival of the dead by using the Name.[7] We also find that R. Ḥananel refuses to believe in "names", saying that those who use them "do not ascend to heaven, but look and see figments of their own minds, like a person who looks into a dim mirror."[8] Hay took a different view of the use of amulets: "But amulets giving health, wisdom, protection and other things

[1] Comp. *Kitāb . . . al-Milal . . . wa'l-Niḥal*, Miṣr 1317/1899 I, p. 156 top, IV, p. 4 top (the better version).

[2] Samau'al al-Maghrebī, *Ifḥām al-Yahūd*, ed. M. Perlmann, New York 1964, p. 92/73; Halkin, *Iggeret*, p. 103. A responsum of R. Hay deals with Redemption and Resurrection; *Ṭaʿam Zeqēnīm*, pp. 59-61. According to Müller, *Mafteaḥ*, p. 258, n. 55, its authorship is suspected.

[3] Mann, *Texts* II, pp. 80-81.

[4] *MJC* II, p. 79.

[5] Ed. Klar, pp. 16-17, 42-43.

[6] *Sibūb*, ed. Grünhut, p. 36 (ed. Carmoly, Paris 1831, p. 109).

[7] *Ṭaʿam Zeqēnīm*, pp. 55b and 56b.

[8] Commentary on Ḥagiga, p. 14b (bottom). He also did not believe in dreams and witchcraft; comp. Rappaport, *Bikkurey ha-ʿIttīm*, 12 (1892), p. 20, n. 14, and p. 24.

exist, and their effectiveness mostly depends on him who writes them; if he is well-practised, the amulet will be useful."[1]

The use of amulets for medical purposes and for protection against evil spirits was indeed very widespread and was not frowned upon by the rabbis.

We find amulets bearing the formula "if you wish", which we have already met in Daniel al-Qumasī and which resembles the phraseology of the question from Kairouan ("he who wishes to do so-and-so and he who wishes for such-and-such a thing shall write so-and-so upon so-and-so"). The Book *The Sword of Moses*, mentioned in Hay's responsum to the people of Kairouan concerning the Name, has also been discovered. Rab Hay knew a *Sepher ha-Yashar*, which is no doubt identical with the one mentioned by Daniel al-Qumasi.[2]

The people of Qābes asked Sherira and Hay to explain the questioning of a deceased person by a "necromancer" or in other ways (Sanhedrin 65b). Their question was certainly not purely theoretical, prompted merely by a desire to understand the sayings of the tannaites.[3]

The problem of prophetic infallibility and immunity to sin is discussed in a responsum of R. Hay sent also to Qābes.[4]

Another belief spreading in those days was that one must not drink water at the four *teqūfōt*, *i.e.* at the change of the seasons. The relevant responsa are ascribed to Hay and may have been addressed to North Africa. This belief may have been connected with the notion that those were times when evil spells were operative.[5] Questions as to customs relating to the blessing of the light at the close of the Sabbath and to the *qiddūsh* (blessing over wine on Sabbath eve) may also have come from North Africa.[6]

A strange custom was observed by Moroccan Jewry at Pentecost. Boys

---

[1] *Ṭaʿam Zeqēnīm*, p. 56b; Sherira and Hay wrote also a Responsum about the nature of mystical writings dealing with Creation and Divine Stature (*Merkaba*); *RL*, no. 29. Comp. Baron, *SRH*, VIII, pp. 11f.

[2] For magical formulae and incantations comp. Mann, *Texts* II, p. 90, also pp. 76, 79 and 81-82. Amulets were published in Gottheil-Worrell, *Fragments*, 15 (pp. 76-81), 24 (pp. 106-107); *ibid.*, p. 22, ll. 8-10, we find a fragment from Cant. for the healing of skin diseases; comp. Baron, *SRH*, VIII, pp. 8ff, 13ff., 233, 281 n. 18, and 282.

[3] *RH*, no. 365. For divination by means of a Tora scroll comp. Mann, *Jews* II, p. 307, l. 14.

[4] *Qohelet Shelomoh*, no. 4, pp. 7-10, esp. 8-9; comp. Zucker, *Tarbiẓ* 35 (1965), pp. 168-170.

[5] Comp. *RShT*, no. 80, sec. 2; *RḤG*, no. 166.

[6] *RL*, nos. 49-54.

equipped with various containers poured water on passers-by, this being generally held to bring luck.[1]

We can hardly accept the assumption of modern scholars that this custom originates in the water festivals called *ʿanṣara,* celebrated by the Berbers about the same time (on June 24 of the Julian calendar).[2] The word *ʿanṣara* is not Berber, but an Arabic form of Hebrew *ʿaṣeret* "assembly"; and *ʿaṣeret* in a pregnant sense means Pentecost. The custom of pouring water during that season occurs also among the Copts, the Christians in Spain, and throughout Iran.[3] A distinct reference to it in the Middle Ages appears in one of the responsa of the Gaon Hay, who is relying on Rabbenu Nissim (of Kairouan): Hay explains the tannaitic saying: "a clear *ʿaṣeret* day is a good omen for the whole year" (Baba Bathra 147a) as referring to Pentecost, since it is said in Tosefta ʿArakhin (Chapter One) that on the day of the Lawgiving, when the Israelites were standing at Mount Sinai, the day was clear, that is to say, the sky was bright, cloudless, and the Israelites were very hot from the fire, and God commanded the "clouds of glory" (cf. Ex. 16, 10) to shower dew and rain upon them. Hay concludes: "For it was a day of rejoicing of the heart of the Almighty. So if the day is clear, it means joy and well-being for the world. This is what Rabbenu Nissim, of blessed memory, wrote."[4]

In one of his works, R. Nissim describes another popular festivity, *meshawarta de-pura* "the stirrup of Purim", the jumping over great bonfires on the eve of Purim in Kairouan, similar to celebrations in Babylonia and Persia.[5] Abraham ibn Ezra reports that the Karaites in Warghlān leave their habitations at Passover so as comply literally with Ex. 12, 11.[6]

It is natural that the customs of the non-Jewish environment should have affected Jewish marriage rites. A question sent from Qābes to

---

[1] Comp. Toledano, *Lumière*, pp. 215-216; Flamand, *Demnate*, pp. 99-100.

[2] Comp. G. Mouette, *Histoire des Conquestes de Mouley Archy*, Paris 1683, pp. 355-366; L. de Chénier, *Recherches historiques sous les Maures*, Paris 1787, III, pp. 224-225; Doutte, *Magie*, pp. 566-567; Westermarck, *Survivances païennes dans la civilisation mahométaine*, Paris 1935, p. 208; comp. also Brunschvig, *Berbérie* II, p. 306.

[3] Comp. Dozy et Engelmann, *Glossaire des mots espanols et portugais dérivés de l'arabe*², Leyden 1869, pp. 136-137; Dozy, *Supplément* II, p. 181b; Aly Mazahéri, *La vie quotidienne des Musulmans au Moyen Age*, Paris 1951, p. 226.

[4] *RShT*, no. 85; comp. Luria's commentary on *PdRE*, ch. 41, n. 78. Hay seems to refer to Nissim's responsum *RL*, no. 107. The extant text appears to be abridged.

[5] Comp. *Hazofeh me-Erez Hagar*, 7 (1922), p. 35; *Tarbiẓ* 11 (1940), p. 253; comp. also San. 64b.

[6] Comp. Ibn Ezra's commentary on Ex. 12:11; comp. Abrahams, *Jewish Life*, pp. 127-128.

Pumbeditha reveals incidentally that one day before the wedding the bride was led with words of "rejoicing and glorification to some other premises, belonging to her relatives or the groo's relatives or some other person (and stays there) until the following day, when she goes in to her husband. The person who recites the seven benedictions does so while standing at the place where she is staying, and then she is led to her husband's house with words of praise and glorification, etc." [1] Addison, a Christian clergyman who was in Morocco in the second half of the 17th century, mentions the Jewish custom that after the ritual immersion of the bride (before the wedding) no man, not even her father or brother, must see the bride until after the marriage ceremony.[2]

The custom of preparing temporary lodgings for the bride before the marriage ceremony is no doubt connected with the belief of the (Berber?) inhabitants of the country that the couple about to be married must be kept from all contact with their closest male relatives: father and brothers. Because of this belief, Muslims rent a special house (called *dār islān*) for the groom, in which he stays until he leads his betrothed into his house, *i.e.* his father's house, which is called *dār al-ʿurs*. Although the bride does not leave her father's house until she goes to her husband's house, it is a sacred custom that her father will not look at her for fifteen or twenty days before she leaves his house.[3]

Another question from Qābes can be reconstructed from the responsum: "It is customary for all Jews at banquets generally, and especially at wedding feasts, to rejoice and sing songs of praise before the Almighty; they remember his miracles and benefactions in ancient times and the hope for the revelation of his kingdom and his good promises and the comforting messages of the prophets. There are many *piyyuṭim* on these and similar subjects which are sung at wedding feasts and other joyful occasions to enhance and dignify them. No Jew in the world refrains from all these. But songs forbidden by Mar ʿUqba, compositions that are not of the kind mentioned, but are songs of human love, songs praising the beautiful for their beauty, the strong for their strength, and the like, such as songs which the Arabs call *ashʿār al-ghazal* (*i.e.* erotic songs), are most certainly forbidden with instrumental accompaniment, but are not allowed even without.[4]

---

[1] *RH*, no. 65.

[2] *Jews*, p. 46.

[3] Le Tourneau, *Fès*, pp. 576-578; Desparmet, *Coutumes* I², pp. 166 and 185; Souhalah, *Société*, p. 172.

[4] *RH*, no. 60 (Müller, *Mafteaḥ*, p. 49, erroneously assigns this responsum to Egypt.)

The "well-beloved (of the Geonim), Neḥemya bar Mar Obadya and Moses bar Samuel bar Jāmiʿ, and the rabbis and students in the city of Kairouan" [1] had certainly asked whether the ban placed by Mar ʿUqba (Giṭṭin 7a) on singing with the accompaniment of instruments, or even without, applied to wedding songs, such as had then spread among Maghreb Jewry under the influence of their environment. Hay permits these, but finally remarks: "What you mention in the question, that women beat drums and dance—if this is done in the presence of men, then there is nothing more objectionable; and if there are no drums and dancing, but only singing, it is still ugly and inadmissible."[2]

In Berber society, women were freer than in Arab society, and this had its impact upon Jewish customs. Even today, Jewish women in the Maghreb mix with men at religious-social gatherings with greater freedom than their sisters elsewhere in similar circles.[3]

We know the Kairouan betrothal customs. The betrothal was effected by means of a ring, as in Palestine, and the ceremony took place in the synagogue: "And such is the custom in our locality when he (the husband-to-be) wishes to betroth the girl to him: if she is of age, she authorizes her father to accept her *qiddushīn* (betrothal token, in this case a ring), and if she is a minor, he (the father) accepts her *qiddushīn* on her behalf, in conformity with rabbinic custom. And the congregation comes to the synagogue where the girl's father worships, and he accepts his daughter's *qiddushīn* at the synagogue. And this Reuben (the father of two girls) was a *talmīd* and elder, and the *talmīdīm* and congregation came to the house of study, and Simon (the groom) rose from his place and gave Reuben *qiddushīn*, and the *talmīdīm*, disciples of Rab Natan, of blessed memory, sat beside them. And Simon said: May your daughter be betrothed unto me by this ring. And they (those present at the ceremony) said to him in the sacred tongue (Hebrew): Specify, specify (which of his two daughters you mean) some four or five times, but he paid no heed to their words because he was flustered standing in front of the *talmīdīm* and congregation."[4]

In connection with the *mishna* "And he shall not read by the light of the candle" (Sabbath 1, 3), doubts arose with the people of Kairouan as to whether they acted properly when "here in Kairouan, in synagogues,

---

[1] Comp. *RH*, no. 59.

[2] Comp. *RH*, no. 60, at the end.

[3] Comp. Goldziher, *ZDMG* 41 (1887), p. 40.

[4] *TSh*, p. 18b, no. 12. This responsum is from the Gaon Saadia. For the meaning of "*talmīdīm*" comp. Ginzberg, *Geonica* II, p. 32, n. 4.

people assemble on the eve of the Day of Atonement and sometimes on the eve of the Sabbath and read psalms by lamplight", and they applied to Hay for a ruling in the matter.[1] Let us note incidentally that at least one synagogue in Kairouan, known as *al-maqdis al-jalīl*, was a magnificent structure.[2] Sumptuous synagogues seem to have been frequent in the Maghreb; Muḥammad ibn Tumart, the founder of the Muslim Almohad sect, knew about their interior layout and the fact that the congregants turned towards Jerusalem during prayers.[3]

Other problems were connected with Sabbath observance. The enormous distances Jewish traders had to cover without being able to spend the Sabbath among Jews were the cause of considerable difficulties. It was necessary to devise special arrangements permitting them to observe the Sabbath *en route*. Sometimes caravans altered their schedules so as to reach their stopping-place before the Sabbath. Resting-places for the Sabbath were planned in advance even when crossing the desert.[4] According to a tradition preserved in an Arab history-book, the Jews in the army of Yūsuf ibn Tāshfīn kept the Sabbath.[5] Under these circumstances, a question might arise concerning a Jew who found himself among Gentiles on the Sabbath with nothing to eat. "He entered the houses of Gentiles and found them consuming fresh bread and milk milked the same day and fruit just picked, and he would eat with them on weekdays; somebody said to him: eat, and he ate, or he ate without their permission. He was asked: And what did you do on the Sabbath? And he said: They did it for themselves, and so it was permitted. Did he argue correctly or not? Is he liable to a legal penalty and a fine or not?" [6]

It is known that the Berbers were not particular strict about Koranic dietary laws, and especially, did nor abstain from wine. Hay was once asked whether one might use Gentile raisin wine with honey, called *nabīdh shamsī* in Egypt. The questioners were thus not in Egypt, and it seems likely that they were Maghrebis. This *nabīdh* was very common among North African Muslims and greatly cherished by the emirs of

---

[1] *RL*, no. 59 (comp. also *ibid.*, no. 87); *RShT*, no. 52.

[2] Mann, *Texts* I, p. 246, bottom. It was destroyed in the Beduin invasion of 1057; comp. above, p. 115.

[3] Ibn Tūmart disliked living in Marrakesh because the mosques there did not face exactly towards Mecca, but to the east, like synagogues. For the same reason, ʿAbd al-Muʾmin, on occupying the city; destroyed all the local mosques, even the Jāmiʿ al-Kabīr; Lévi-Provençal, *Documents*, p. 105/173-174.

[4] Comp. Mann, *Texts* I, p. 137; Yehuda Barceloni, *Sefer ha-ʿIttim*, p. 76 (Sherira's responsum).

[5] Beaumier, *Roudh*, p. 213.

[6] *RCor*, no. 93, and comp. below, p. 259.

Kairouan. Without overlooking the fact that Muslims in other countries, especially the upper classes, included many wine lovers, we may suppose that the Gaonic responsa dealing with the question of wine touched by Muslims [1] were chiefly addressed to the Maghreb, where there were Jews living in villages among Gentiles (as appears from the question concerning a Jew who lived in a village ten miles from Kairouan).[2]

These particulars point to relations between Jews and their environment in the Maghreb, and in Islamic countries generally, that were closer than Jewish-Christian relations in Europe. It therefore seems that Sahl ben Maṣlīaḥ's strictures against rabbis and communal leaders feasting with Gentiles in taverns were not exaggerations, but well-founded in fact.[3]

An opportunity for the establishment of social relations were the popular festivities of Maghrebi Muslims, such as celebrations at the tombs of saints, processions round mosques and annual fairs, which were dominant features of local religious life. The fact that saints' graves common to Jews and Muslims exist in the Maghreb to this day may not justify the assumption of a similar partnership a thousand years ago, but those inquiring whether a Jew might visit such-and-such an annual market of "idolatry" undoubtedly included also Maghrebi Jews; the term "idolatry" does not refer only to pagan or Christian symbols, but also to other cultic features, such as Muslim sacred stones and saints' tombs.[4] Maimonides says that it has been alleged in his time "that the Arabs practise idolatry in Mecca and other places", though he himself does not think so.[5] Against this background, we have to view the decision contained in a responsum that one must not accept alms from a Gentile —no doubt for fear that he may give them for the sake of a false god.[6]

We know that the Jews were integrated in Arab-Berber society in

---

[1] Wine touched by non-Jews is forbidden to Jews. The question of wine touched by a Muslim is often discussed in responsa; comp. *RḤG*, nos. 114-117, *RA* I, pp. 68 (no. 50), 79 (no. 61) and *RC*, no. 46-47.

[2] *RḤG*, no. 164; comp. Marçais, *Berbérie*, p. 78, and Hitti, History, pp. 227-228. For pre-Islamic Arabia see Hirschberg, *RO* 11 (1935), pp. 120-121.

[3] Comp. Pinsker, *Liqqutey Qadmoniyot*, Appendices, pp. 31-32; *Ha-Meliz* 1879, p. 641 (*Sefer ha-Yishub* II, pp. 124-125). Comp. also Daniel al-Qūmisi, Mann, *Texts* II, p. 77.

[4] Ibn Ḥawqal, *BGA* II², pp. 67 and 73, mentions the circumambulations of the Great Mosque of Ajdābiyya and the festival at Monastir (comp. below, p. 258); comp. also *RC*, no. 17, and *RHG*, nos. 19 and 104.

[5] *Iggeret ha-Shemad*, ed. Edelmann, p. 8b; *Iggarot u-She'elot u-Teshubot* (ed. Amsterdam), p. 44. A similar passage in Maimonides' *Mishne Torah*, Hil. ʿAboda Zara IX, was deleted by Christian censorship. The name Mecca is distorted to *makkōth* (plagues); comp. Hirschberg, *Bar-Ilan Annual* 4-5 (1967), p. 454 and n. 6.

[6] *RCor*, no. 26.

Spain, and there is reason to assume that the same was the case in Africa.[1] Precisely under conditions of good neighbourhood, when at joint revelries the wine loosened tongues, it might happen that the Jews jokingly called the *rasūl* or messenger of Allah, *i.e.* Muḥammad, *pasūl* (worthless) or the Korān *qalon* (shame), and the like, and the Muslims might respond by similar raillery.[2] On the other hand, we hardly hear of serious debates between Jews and Muslims, on the lines of the disputations between Jews and Christians (a famous exception is the debate between Ibn Ḥazm and Samuel ibn Nagrela).[3] The Muslims lacked scientific curiosity with regard to Judaism, and the Jews, on their part, avoided teaching them their Law.[4]

Muslim behaviour in matters of prayer and purity—Maimonides already notes that Maghrebi Jews are strict in these matters—prompted questions by Jews as to how they were to act in similar cases. The Gaon Nahshon was asked whether a Jew who had been ill for two months and had recovered was required to say all the prayers he had missed. Doubts had been caused in this matter by a Muslim precept requiring *qaḍāʾ*, making up the deficiency, in such cases. The Gaon gave a lenient decision, absolving the ex-patient of making good the loss, in reliance on the Gemara dictum "When the day for the offering of a person's sacrifice is past, his duty to offer it ceases" (Berakhot 26a).[5]

An anti-Islamic tendency is discernible in the Gaon Yehudai's reply to the question whether a menstruous woman may attend and pray at synagogue; the answer is in the affirmative.[6]

Another question revealing an affinity between Jewish and Muslim law is whether a person wearing clothes through which his flesh is visible may read the Shema; Muslim law, too, forbids praying in transparent dress.[7] Alien influence must have been present in a question to which Sar Shalom,

---

[1] Comp. Hirschberg, *Ha-Tekufa* 34-35 (1950), pp. 693ff.; Skoss, *Dictionary* I, p. LIII.

[2] Comp. Steinschneider, *Polemische und apologetische Literatur*, Leipzig 1877, pp. 302-303 and 316.

[3] Ibn Ḥazm, *Kitāb* ... *al-Milal* ... *wa 'l-Niḥal*, I, p. 152; E. Ashtor (Strauss), *Korot ha-Yehudim bi-Sefarad ha-Muslimit* II, p. 32; S. Baron, *SRH* V, p. 327, n. 4; comp. also E. Strauss (Ashtor), *Sefer ha-Zikaron le-Beyt ha-Midrash*, 1946, pp. 182-191.

[4] Maimonides expressly prohibited teaching the Law to Muslims; Responsa, ed. Freimann, no. 364. Comp. also Baron, *SRH* V, pp. 85-86.

[5] *RḤG*, no. 48. The Muslim precept is discussed on several occasions; comp. *Al-Fiqh ʿala 'l-Madhāhib al-Arbaʿa*, ʿIbādāt, Cairo 1939, pp. 377-383, also 264-265 and 274-276; *EI s.v. Ṣawm.*

[6] *RL*, no. 45 (p. 17a); comp. Wensinck, *Miftāḥ*, Cairo 1934, *s.v. Ḥāʾiḍ*; Juynboll, *Handbuch des islamischen Gesetzes*, pp. 174f.

[7] *RCor*, no. 45; comp. *Al-Fiqh* (n. 5), p. 140; Wensinck, *Miftāḥ*, p. 271b.

a Gaon of Sura in the middle of the 9th century, replies as follows: "As for the wiping of the hands with earth after burying the dead. This is not done here, but there (in the questioner's country); it used to be done to remove death (by striking and rubbing one's hands together)."[1] It seems to me that this responsum relates to a death in the desert, in a caravan, and involves two different matters: the wiping of the hands with earth where there is no water; 2. the duty of those who have handled a dead body to wipe themselves. The duty of wiping with sand (*tayammum*) or with earth (*istijmār*) is well known in Islam; and the duty of those who have handled a dead body to purify themselves exists in Shīʿism.[2]

These questions, which attest to the existence of social ties between Jews and non-Jews, must not cause us to overlook that relations between the Jews and their neighbours in the Maghreb had yet another aspect, reflected in the sources in the statement that the average Gentile is a ruffian.[3]

Moral Attitudes

Let us now consider the tone of that society in fields not directly connected with *halakha*, such as the education of children, the redemption of captives, and the attitude towards women and servants. The physiognomy of Maghreb Jewry, both as it really was and as it appeared in the ideal conception of its outstanding sons, is very clearly reflected in a collection of legends and folktales entitled "*The Fine Book of Comfort*", by R. Nissim ben Jacob, of Kairouan.

This folk-book for the people, clearly datable and the author of which is well known, shows us the little man, the gardener and the butcher, the imprisoned debtor, and all kinds of male and female types not usually much noticed in halakhic literature. This is the *ʿam ha-areṣ* in the primary sense of the term—the common people, whose knowledge of the Oral Law is extremely meagre, and who are not very well versed in the Written Law, either. It is for them that R. Nissim wrote this book, in which he assembled *midreshey aggada* and stories about distinguished rabbis, interspersed with remarks of his own, in order to strengthen their simple

---

[1] *RSh* 21b, no. 19.

[2] Comp. Wensinck, *ibid.*, *s.v. Tayammum*; *EI*, *s.v. Tayammum*, *Ṭahāra.* For Islamic influences on Jewish worship comp. N. Wieder, *Hashpāʿōt Islamiyōt ʿal ha-Pulḥān ha-Yehūdi*, Oxford 1947, pp. 10-20. Solomon b. Natan al-Sijilmāsi, who is quoted *ibid.*, p. 12, lived in the period under reference; his work was copied in Barca in the early 13th century (comp. below p. 354).

[3] Comp. below, p. 198 n. 1.

faith and extol ordinary persons noted for their righteousness. The latter subject is dealt with in seven consecutive chapters, and not finding all the necessary material in ancient Jewish literature, the author was compelled to invent stories or impart a literary form to tales current among the people. This is why some of his interesting narratives have no *vorlage* in earlier sources. R. Nissim's collection is of social-historical significance, especially where supported by contemporary sources.[1]

The Education of Children

Let us begin with the schooling of little children. The custom of commencing their instruction with Leviticus obtained also in Kairouan. In those days, *ghazw* (*i.e.* forays) by desert Beduin against established settlements were frequent, and so were pirate raids against coastal cities and the taking of captives; no one was safe from these attacks. R. Nissim tells how a father prepared a copy of Genesis for his three-year-old only son and had a teacher instruct him at synagogue, so that the memory of Judaism was firmly implanted in the boy's mind and remained alive when he was led into captivity. That copy of Genesis, which the boy was able to read, was the cause of his deliverance: the "king" into whose hands he and his book had fallen was so impressed by his performance that he released him and let him go home.[2]

A similar story is contained in one MS. of R. Aḥāy's *Sh'ēltōth*, and R. Nissim may have used it or a tale current among the people.[3] There was, moreover, factual material which could have been used to lend verisimilitude to the story. R. Elḥanan ben Ḥushiel—a contemporary and fellow townsman of R. Nissim—was once asked concerning a copy of the Bible which a man had left to his minor sons and which had been forcibly taken from them by some Gentile ruffians; nothing daunted, the sons had tried to recover the book from the person who bought it.[4] In recent years, a letter has been discovered that was sent from Mahdiya or Kairouan to Fusṭāṭ in 1062, approximately, when R. Nissim was still alive. The writer,

---

[1] The book was edited by J. Obermann (*The Arabic Original of Ibn Shāhīn's Book of Comfort*, known as the Ḥibbûr Yāphe of R. Nissim b. Ya'aqobh, New Haven, Yale University Press 1933). A new Hebrew translation was published by Hirschberg: *R. Nissim* etc., Jerusalem 1954; comp. the Introduction, pp. 9-82 and below, pp. 331ff.

[2] *Ibid.*, chapters XVI and XVII.

[3] S. Abramson found the story in Ms. Dropsie College 118 and published it in *R. Nissim Gaon*, Jerusalem 1965, pp. 400-403.

[4] The text was published by Mann, *JQR* 9 (1918/19), p. 171.

R. Labraṭ ben Moses of the Banu Sigmār family, who after R. Nissim's death was *rōsh bey rabbanan* (chief rabbi) in his country, congratulates his younger brother on the birth of a son and informs him that the family is presenting him with a Bible that was stolen during the disturbances in Kairouan and subsequently redeemed; part of the manuscript is lost, however, and will have to be replaced before the gift is sent to Egypt.[1]

These few sources permit us to conclude that there was serious concern for the education and religious instruction of children. We may suppose that the situation in Africa was generally the same in this respect to what is known to us of Egypt during that period.[2]

The Redemption of Captives

The duty of redeeming captives played an important part in social life, and there are frequent references to it in Jewish sources of the period, ranging from brief hints in responsa to the story of the "Four Captives". In a letter from Alexandria to R. Ephraim ben Shemarya, we are told of the redemption of two captives, "one a handsome youth with some knowledge of the Law, the other a boy about ten years of age. When we saw them in the hands of the Gentiles, who beat and frightened them in our presence, we took pity on them and ransomed them from their captors ...".[3] The fulfilment of this duty became a heavy burden on Maghreb Jewry, and especially on the people of Kairouan, whose economic position had deteriorated by frequent Beduin raids; the nagid and elders of Kairouan were once compelled to seek assistance from several countries and cities. This is why R. Nissim thought it necessary to stress the reward of those who engaged in this meritorious activity.[4]

Thus he tells us about a butcher who redeemed a captive and in return was granted the same high rank in the next world as a certain *talmīd ḥākhām* of perfect piety and conduct. The butcher saw among a group of captives a little girl, bitterly crying. When she told him that she was Jewish and feared for her religion, he ransomed her for a great sum of money, took her to his house and betrothed her to his only son. He arranged a wedding feast, and among the guests was a youth who had

---

[1] Goitein, *Studies*, p. 326.

[2] Comp. also below, p. 183 and p. 342. For the general trend comp. Goitein, *Sidrey Ḥinūkh*.

[3] Mann, *Jews* II, p. 89, ll. 19-24, and esp. frag. 13 (p. 88) on the captives who were sent to Barqa (l. 14). This subject is very often referred to in the sources.

[4] Comp. Wertheimer, *Ginzey Yerushalayim* II, pp. 17b-18a.

betrothed the girl to himself before she was captured. When the butcher heard this, he annulled the marriage contract that his son had drawn up and married the girl to the youth to whom she had been betrothed.[1]

We dispense with literary parallels to this story and confine ourselves to some actual facts reported in Geniza documents. One of these tells of the redemption of some captives from Arab pirates; among them was "a girl who we begged should not be violated, and all the time we wept for our many sins, and we were taken from place to place."[2] Here is a marriage contract between a man who redeemed a captive and married her, settling upon her 230 *peraḥim* (florins) viz. 50 (her ransom) as the immediately payable part and 180 as the deferred part (of her marriage contract).

Yehuda Mughrabi — The captive, Esther

At a Propitious Hour

On Sunday, the eighth day of the month of Tebet in the year 1823 of the Seleucid Era, an agreement was made between Yehuda the son of Jacob the son of Aharon and the bride, the captive, named Esther, the daughter of R. Moses Siman Tob the son of the Ḥakham known as Kuḥli.

Al-*muqdam*, being her ransom	Al-*me'uḥar*
50	180

It is certainly accidental that the document discovered is late—of the year 1823 S.E., *i.e.* 1512 C.E.; similar cases occurred during the preceding period.[3]

The care of deserted women and girls may have been entrusted to special communal appointees. The Arabic version of the "*Fine Book*" ends with a story (missing in the ancient Hebrew translation) about an orphaned girl whom her uncle and guardian abandoned in a coastal city, ten days' journey from her place of residence, in order to test the truth of Ps. 37, 25. About that time, the *qāḍī* and the *muḥtasib*—the official in charge of markets and the "protected people"—came to the market, and on hearing that the girl was Jewish, they called upon a Jew to take

1 Hirschberg, *R. Nissim*, ch. XV, and Introduction, pp. 77-79; comp. Heller, *HUCA* 7 (1927), p. 383.

2 Mann, *Jews* II, p. 88, ll. 3-5.

3 Gottheil-Worrell, *Fragments* 40, p. 182. It is interesting to note that the captive Esther receives 230 florins as dowry and Dulsa, a girl mentioned previously (on p. 178), only 64 florins. The kind of such marriage contracts will be discussed below (Appendix Tunis).

care of her. Here the manuscript ends, and we do not know what became of the girl. But by reference to a witnesses' memorandum preserved in the Geniza we can easily reconstruct the end of the story. Here is the text of the document:

"Record of evidence given before us, the undersigned witnesses, in the year 1337 S.E. (1026 C.E.) according to the calendar we use here in Fusṭāṭ, Egypt, on the River Nile. This is what Tarīk, daughter of Abraham known as b. Qardūsi, said before us: Let it be known to you, sirs, that I have today ... been living ten years in the house of R. Muḥsin ibn Ḥusayn, the warden of merchants, known as ibn Ukht Shamʿān, of blessed memory, receiving sustenance from his house and by his toil. I had nothing ... [for] my upkeep and he helped me for the sake of Heaven. May the Almighty reward him ..."[1]

On the strength of the above, we may suppose that that Jew, or the local warden of merchants, immediately provided for all that girl's requirements, ascertained her place of origin, took her back there and concerned himself with safeguarding the property left her by her father.

Endowments

In addition to direct charity, given during the giver's lifetime, we find charitable endowments, to begin during the dedicator's lifetime or after his death. An instance of the dedication of the income of property to the poor in general is known to us from a case referred to one of the early geonim (before 4232/872) owing to a jurisdictional dispute between the *batey-dīn* of Kairouan and Majāna in connection with the sale of some estate property.[2] Another responsum mentions that somebody dedicated one quarter of his homestead to the poor of Kairouan.[3] R. Jacob bar Nissim once asks what to make of the will of a person who bequeathed all his property to the poor, leaving nothing to his heirs.[4] Worthy of note is the will of the freedman Bendār, who left one quarter of his property to the local poor and one quarter to the poor of Jerusalem, but only in so far as they were Rabbanites.[5]

Matters of charitable endowments are discussed several times in the literature of the period without an indication of the locality concerned,

---

[1] Mann, *Jews* II, p. 78, n. 7.
[2] *RA* II, pp. 23-24.
[3] *RM*, no. 7.
[4] *RH*, no. 260.
[5] Assaf, *Sources*, p. 141. Comp. also below p. 181, n. 4.

and we may suppose that part of them relate to the Maghreb. There is, *e.g.* the question whether the rent of a shop which was dedicated to the synagogue may be turned over to a destitute *dayyan*. This question reflects conditions in a small, poor African community, unable to pay a salary to its legal functionary.[1]

Slaves

In the social structure and division of labour of the Middle Ages, both at the family level and in the economy generally, an important part is played by the slaves. No description of individual or communal life will be complete without attention being paid to this subject.

According to the Halakha, a Jewish master must Judaize and eventually completely proselytize (*gayyēr*) a Gentile (male or female) slave. The Gaon Amram explains in one of his responsa that one must not keep for any length of time a slave who will not become Judaized (*i.e.* accept part of the principal religious duties, such as observance of the Sabbath and avoidance of idolatry), but one may try for twelve months to achieve complete conversion (circumcision).[2] Some slaves no doubt converted wholeheartedly, accepted the burden of religious duties and became Jews in all respects.[3] We spoke above of the will of the freedman Bendār, who gave one quarter of his estate to the Jews of Jerusalem. The name of a communal leader mentioned in the relevant responsum, al-Ghadāmsī, *i.e.* the one of Ghadames, an important oasis on the Tripolitanian-Tunisian border, and other indications, suggest that Bendār lived in a Tripolitanian city at the beginning of the second millennium C.E.[4] But we easily realize that some Christian slaves refused to embrace Judaism and wished to continue practising their own religion. As they were none the less integrated in domestic and economic life, a variety of religious and social problems arose.

An inquiry addressed to the Gaon Hay illustrates one of the problems connected with female slaves.

In Tlemcen and surroundings, there were Christian slaves, whom Jews were permitted to buy; they were not able to buy any others (*i.e.*

---

[1] *RCor*, no. 82.

[2] *RSh*, p. 25b, no. 18.

[3] Comp. *RSh*, p. 27a, nos. 30 and 32; *RShT*, nos. 254-255; Ginzberg, *Geonica* II, pp. 74, 81, ll. 12-15, 183, ll. 9-11.

[4] The name Bendār would seem to indicate Persian origin. It means "agent" and was common among Muslims and Jews.

Muslim slaves, whom Jews were not allowed to keep) except secretly and at a risk. Some of those Christians converted to Judaism at once, others after a time, but some refused to give up their faith. What was to be done with regard to the latter? The Jews living in those places were in utmost need of Christian slaves because they found no others, and he who had no slave was in great trouble: his children or his wife had to fetch water on their shoulders from the springs, wash clothes and go to the bakehouse with wanton Gentile slaves. The halakhic question related to the resting of Christian slaves on Sabbaths and holydays.[1] In cases where the slave had performed the immersion required for proselytization, but it was not clear whether it had been voluntary or forced, doubts arose as to whether her touch made wine ritually unfit, or whether it was permitted to eat what she had baked or cooked.[2]

It is interesting to note that no Libyan women slaves are mentioned in that area, although they were common elsewhere in Jewish homes. According to the form of a deed of sale of a (male) slave, emanating from the Gaon Hay, Jews kept Indian, Slavonic (*Kenaᶜanīm*), *Rūmī* (*i.e.* Byzantine), Libyan and Zangai (negro) (male) slaves, and there were surely also women slaves of those ethnic groups.[3] In fact, some deeds from Egypt mention Edomite (Byzantine or Italian) and Nubian female slaves. An inventory from Africa possibly mentions (female) dancers, but the reading is not quite clear.[4] Male slaves in North Africa are referred to less frequently, but part of the relevant queries undoubtedly came from the Maghreb.[5]

The slaves included educated persons and craftsmen. R. Nissim, in one of his stories, says that there are those among them who know how to read, write and keep accounts—skills not widespread even among those who could afford to buy slaves. Such slaves were placed in shops and

[1] *RH*, no. 431 (also no. 11); *TSh*, pp. 23b-24a, no. 6; p. 25a-b, no. 15. Most sources have *Miṣriyot*, Egyptian woman slaves; this may be an error for *Noṣriyot*, Christian woman slaves. But the reading *Miṣriyot* may be accepted as referring to Coptish Christians as distinct from Ismaelite Muslims. Woman slaves had to be imported to Egypt from adjacent areas; comp. Hirschberg, *Baer Jubilee Volume*, p. 150. Jews and Christians were not allowed to keep Muslim woman slaves, to prevent marriages between non-Muslim men and Muslim women, prohibited by the Koran (2, 220) and the Sharᶜ. There exists an extensive literature on slaves in Jewish society; comp., *e.g.*, Goitein, *Arabica* 9 (1962), pp. 1-20.

[2] Comp. *e.g.*, *RSh*, p. 25b, no. 16. The question is also discussed in some of the responsa referred to in the preceding notes.

[3] Assaf, *Sefer ha-Sheṭarot le-Rab Hay*, p. 28; *idem*, Zion 4 (1939), p. 100.

[4] Comp. Mann, *JQR*, 11 (1920-21), p. 457; Goitein, *Tarbiẓ*, 20 (1950), pp. 197-199.

[5] Comp. *e.g.*, the slave in Nafūsa (Tripolitania) mentioned in *RSh*, p. 26b, no. 26. A whole chapter in *RSh* (pp. 23a-28b) is devoted to these matters.

entrusted with important business.[1] In one legend, the central figure is the Prophet Elijah, who lets himself be sold into slavery in order that a poor man may enjoy the proceeds, and who subsequently builds a palace in one night.[2] This story, too, contains a feature taken from reality, since North African Jews were no strangers to the building trade;[3] moreover, this story (the subject-matter of a well-known *piyyūṭ*, *Ish ḥāsīd hāyā*, included among the *zemiroth* for the close of the Sabbath) contains a warning to treat slaves honourably because one of them might be the Prophet Elijah.

The Jews were remarkable for their kind treatment of slaves. Many released their slaves and provided for the education of their children. Maimonides, in his code *Mishneh Torah*, says: The essence of piety and wisdom is that a man should be merciful, pursue justice and not oppress or vex his slave.[4]

The Family and the Status of Women

This aspect of the life of North African Jewish society has so far not been explored at all, although the rabbis never shrank from discussing the status of woman and her place in the family or any matrimonial matters and our sources present a wealth of relevant material. The difficulty lies in ascertaining the background on which certain phenomena arose. Reality seems to have been different from the picture emerging from halakhic sources, which reflect only the two extremes: woman and family life within the framework of the Halakha, on the one hand, and instances of breaches of that framework, on the other.

In this matter, too, Jewish society in the Maghreb was influenced by its Muslim environment, which was very different from Muslim society in the East.[5] The Muslim population of the Maghreb consisted of two elements: Arabs and Berbers, with whom the status of woman was not the same. This accounts for a certain confusion, discernible in the *Fine*

[1] *RSh*, p. 73b, no. 10; Hirschberg, *R. Nissim*, ch. XXXI, pp. 94-95.

[2] Hirschberg, *R. Nissim*, ch. XXI, pp. 58-60.

[3] Comp. *RH*, no. 325: skilled workmen in Qābes; and below, p. 200 and n. 28 Hebrew.

[4] Comp. *RSh*, p. 26b, no. 29 (also p. 27b, no. 36); Ginzberg, *Geonica* II, p. 83; Maimonides, *Mishneh Tora*, Hil. *ʿAbadim*, at the end.

[5] Ibn Ḥawqal, (e.g., *BGA* II^2, pp. 93, 95 and 97) remarks that homosexuality, but not prostitution, is common in the Muslim Maghreb; the women are beautiful, and many can be found in the harems of the Caliphs in Baghdad. These remarks seem to refer to the Arab population; comp. Mez, *Renaissance*, p. 275, also Mann, *Texts* II, p. 77, ll. 6-7, and n. 26.

Book and, between the lines, in Gaonic responsa, which lent some curious features to the physiognomy of North African Jewry. There is a great contradiction between the improvements—however modest—in social and legal status which Islam granted or confirmed to woman, such as the right to inherit along with men, capacity to give evidence, the right to divorce her husband if so stipulated in the marriage agreement, and her detention in the harem in the company of legal co-wives and innumerable concubines and female slaves, under the supervision of eunuchs—a custom which the Arabs had adopted from the Persians. The Berber woman, on the other hand, even under Muslim rule, enjoyed a greater measure of freedom than the Arab woman. Her status in her father's and her husband's house was more independent both legally and economically; there was no harem and no veil. All this, of course, affected her general conduct and bearing.[1]

It is universally agreed that the changes occurring under Muslim rule caused the status of the Jewish woman to alter in several respects, for the better and for the worse. It is true that the practice of marrying immature girls continued (it was widespread also among Christians in Christian countries) and that adult girls, too, were married without their wishes being consulted.[2] However, one of the earliest results of the political and social changes was that the Geonim Mar Rab Rabba of Pumbaditha and Mar Rab Huna of Sura, in 660 C.E., enabled the immediate grant of a bill of divorcement to a "obstreperous" wife, "because the sages saw that Jewish women would use the help of Gentiles in order to obtain bills of divorcement by force from their husbands."[3] A further step in favour of women was taken a hundred years later when it was made possible to collect the marriage portion and other debts out of the chattels inherited by the orphans. This regulation was necessary to prevent widows being disadvantaged where the husband had left no immovable property.[4] Muslim influence is clearly apparent in the division of the payment of a marriage contract (see above, p. 179) into two parts: the immediately payable part, due at the time of the betrothal, and the deferred part, paid later, ultimately in the event of widowhood or divorce. Although the place from where the relevant question was sent is not indicated, we may

---

[1] Comp. Guernier, *Berbérie* I, pp. 362-365; Terrasse, *Histoire* I, p. 129; Marçais, *Berbérie*, p. 245; *Initiation à l'Algérie*, 1957, pp. 272-273.

[2] Comp. *RH*, no. 194; E. Power, *Medieval People*, pp. 130-131.

[3] We content ourselves with the following references: Lewin, *Iggeret*, p. 101; Tykocinski, *Die gaonäischen Verordnungen*, ch. I, p. 4ff.; Baron, *SRH*, VI, pp. 132-133.

[4] Lewin, *Iggeret*, p. 105; Tykocinski, *ibid.*, pp. 37ff.; Baron, *ibid.*, p. 132.

suppose that it came from North Africa. It did not necessarily come from Egypt, though S. Assaf states that the practice of dividing the *ketūba* was adopted only there.[1]

An interesting story of a "civil" marriage has been discovered in the Geniza documents. Marriages contracted in accordance with Islamic law were usual in North Africa in the Almohad period and thereafter until the times of R. Isaac bar Sheshet.[2]

The improvement of the status of women in Africa is evidenced by certain customs which took root in the region. In Kairouan, women were permitted to collect their marriage settlement without taking an oath.[3] Furthermore, in the whole of North Africa, the additional part of the marriage settlement was a fixed amount, neither more in the case of a rich woman nor less in the case of a poor one: the main part was 25 zūz and the additional part 375 zūz, and these amounts were combined into 16 large gold dīnārs, which at the time of payment were converted into current coin (Arab dīnārs).[4] It is true that this equality of the marriage settlement was not always maintained; various ways were found of circumventing it:[5] according to some, it was customary in Africa to over-evaluate the clothes of the bride by fifty per cent and to debit the resultant amount to the groom by means of a promissory note; the presents made by the groom were declared to be dowry and their value debited to him in the same way. But this concern for her financial rights is another indication of the esteem in which woman was held.[6]

When certain Maghrebi rabbis ruled that the marriage settlement of a woman who had forsworn the faith was inherited by her father, a gaon queried on the subject rejected this view vehemently, declaring that the father had no such right whatsoever.[7]

In countries where most of the inhabitants practised—and practise—polygamy, it is important to note every feature tending to restrict that practice. The people of Kairouan asked how the duty of procreation

---

[1] *RH*, no. 370; comp. also the Ketuba of the year 4767/1007 published by Golb, *JSS*, 20 (1958), pp. 39-40 and 30, which provides for such instalments, and above, p. 179, n. 3. Assaf, *Sefer ha-Sheṭarot le-Rab Hay*, Jerusalem 1930, p. 62, and *Geonica*, pp. 92 and 97, overlooked the responsum *RH*, no. 370.

[2] Goitein, *Fourth World Congress of Jewish Studies*, Vol. II, p. 179; Isaac Bar Sheshet, *Responsa*, no. 174; comp. also p. 179, n. 3 (above).

[3] *RH*, no. 1 (p. 2); comp. also *ibid.*, no. 370.

[4] *Ibid.*, no. 210.

[5] Comp. *TSh*, p. 56a-b, no. 16.

[6] *Geonica* II, pp. 77-78. This responsum was addressed to North Africa; comp. Assaf, *KS* 3 (1926/27), p. 98.

[7] *RSh*, p. 63b, no. 40; and comp. below, p. 192, n. 3.

should be fulfilled by a man who had lived with his wife without issue for ten years and had not enough money either to divorce her and pay her marriage settlement or to support two wives. The gaon's reply was short and peremptory: that man is exempt from that duty.[1] Another responsum states explicitly that a man may not take a second wife without the consent of the first; if he nevertheless does so, the first wife may collect her marriage settlement and he may be compelled to grant her a bill of divorcement.[2]

A question from Qābes confronts us with another problem. A man had sworn before witnesses that his wife was to be his wife no longer, and therefore had had to divorce her. After a time, he changed his mind and wished to return to her, alleging that he was unable to pay her marriage settlement. The rabbis disagreed as to whether to have him swear that he could not pay or to chastise him and let him return to his wife. Hay, in his responsum, gives a lenient decision, imposing neither oath nor chastisement. He concludes: "Moreover, he has several possible ways of retracting, and if a rabbi consents to question him so as to give him an opening, and he says: if I had known, I should not have sworn, how good this will be; for the Holy One, blessed be He, has said that His name, which is inscribed in sanctity, shall be blotted out upon the waters in order to make peace between a man and his wife (cf. Num. 5:23)" Hay's remarks constitute a warning to respect the marital bond, and perhaps a veiled criticism of Islam, which makes it very easy to repudiate one's wife.[3] We do not know the destination of the Gaon Ḥananya's responsum concerning amends to be made by a man who pulled out some of his wife's hair during a quarrel, but we have evidence here of the concern of the rabbis for woman's dignity.[4]

Thus far the information provided by halakhic literature. R. Nissim's stories that are not drawn from ancient sources likewise reflect a monogamous environment and relations of mutual respect and affection between the spouses. A whole series of characters: Yosef the Gardener; the husband of the wicked woman; the poor man visited by the Prophet and Builder Elijah; Yehuda, the host of R. Meir; the husband of Hannah the Virtuous; the poor man who found a treasure in his house, each have

[1] *RH*, no. 211.

[2] *RSh*, pp. 67b-68a, no. 6, and comp. Yeb. 65a (the opinion of R. Ammi); a responsum to the contrary, *RCor*, no. 66, is in accord with Raba (רבא) Yeb., *ibid.*

[3] *RḤ*, no. 319; comp. *ibid.*, no. 345 (a similar question from Kairouan). Comp. also *RḤG*, no. 37.

[4] *RSh*, p. 30b, no. 13.

only one wife. All these are not rich or even moderately well off, but it is they who are typical of the main section of the people, and not the wealthy Nathan de-Ṣūṣītā, who covets the virtuous Hannah.

It is even more important to note that the picture which emerges from most of those stories is one of marital happiness, of mutual affection and devotion. Joseph the Gardener's wife suggests that her husband sell her into slavery and apply the proceeds to charitable purposes in order that he may receive a whole robe in Paradise. And how tender and delicate is the conversation between the poor man whom Elijah has visited and his wife! Their condition is desperate, they and their children are starving, and yet they do not indulge in bickering and mutual recriminations, but try to cheer each other up. The first wife of Yehuda, the host of R. Meir, was gentle and modest, so that her husband need not fear she might cast an eye upon the illustrious guest; he therefore harbours no suspicion against the woman he married after the first wife's death. Hannah's husband urges her to obtain the means of redeeming him from debtor's prison by giving herself to Nathan de-Ṣūṣītā, but she remains faithful to the poor wretch, managing at the same time to liberate him and to reform the profligate Nathan. When another poor man's wife advises her husband to devote part of a treasure God has given them to charitable purposes, he agrees with the words: I have not disobeyed you in the past, and I shall not disobey you in the future.

The merit of the *Fine Book* lies in the fact that it does not describe an ideal, Messianic world. The characters are almost all simple folk, living by their toil, but the author is aware that there are men and women ready to do wrong for the sake of gain and social advancement. Such is the woman in the story of Solomon and the members of the Sanhedrin, who would have murdered her husband unless she had cunningly been provided with a tin sword. Yehuda's second wife is prepared to take advantage of her husband's and his guest's drunkenness to commit adultery. In another story, a husband feels tempted to kill his wife in order to be able to marry the king's daughter; he desists when he sees his beautiful wife asleep with their children at her bosom.[1]

We would emphasize again that, at least as far we have been able to ascertain, these stories are essentially R. Nissim's own creations. Though part of the subject-matter and accessory elements is drawn from the stock of folk-tales then current, the special colouring and form reflect the status of women and married life in his time. We see the wife as the faithful

[1] Comp. R. Nissim, *op. cit.*, chapters XI, XII, XXI, XXV, XXVII and XXXI.

helpmate, sharer of all her husband's joys and worries. The unfaithful wife is not a harlot, but a weak creature who gives way to her impulses. The most noteworthy fact is that woman was dealt with in fiction by R. Nissim, a veteran Talmudic scholar, head of the Academy of Kairouan, official representative of the Babylonian Academies in Africa, whom early generations honoured with the title of Gaon, and who was a gifted narrator. R. Nissim originated the social short story in Jewish literature.[1]

A book for the people had no room for descriptions of the life of the rich, their wives, concubines and slaves. Such descriptions would hardly have strengthened the faith or improved the conduct of the ordinary man. The figure of Nathan de-Ṣūṣītā was introduced only as a foil for Hannah's virtue and in order to show that a rich man's repentance and reform are also accepted.[2] Another figure of this kind appears in the story of the woman who suggests that her husband sell her into slavery to secure for himself a shining white robe in Paradise (by the charity he will perform with the proceeds of the sale). The husband fears that her master may rape her, but she swears that she will allow herself to be killed rather than let a sin be committed upon her person; and when the master wishes to hand her the keys to his treasure-house, *i.e.* make her a member of his harem, she refuses. The master sends her to a shepherd as the latter's assistant, and the shepherd, too, vainly tries to corrupt her, until her husband redeems her and takes her home. This story, too, presents a woman whose virtue passes the severest tests.[3]

The control of sexual desire was a much-discussed subject in those days. According to R. Nissim, his father delivered many homilies on it, apparently to the Kairouan congregation.[4] One of a collection of responsa addressed to R. Jacob ben Nissim is devoted to the interpretation of the passage: "Desire, a child and a woman should be pushed away with the left hand and drawn close with the right" (Sota 47a); in it, the geonim explain how the urge can be overcome: "time after time, little by little, until one gets used to it." But of course, as the sources do not conceal, man does not always succeed in conquering his appetites.[5]

Many difficulties were caused by the presence of slaves in the house.

---

[1] We shall revert to this subject below in ch. VI.
[2] R. Nissim, *op. cit.*, ch. XXVII, and comp. Beer, *Tarbiẓ* 33 (1964), pp. 354-355.
[2] R. Nissim, *op. cit.*, ch. XI.
[4] R. Nissim, *op. cit.*, ch. XXVII, p. 76 and esp. p. 81 (Obermann, *l.c.*, nn. 31 and 32).
[5] *RH*, no. 246.

The Geonim protected the honour of bondwomen, threatening heavy punishment to the transgressor, but theirs was a hard struggle in the countries of Islam, which intends every female slave to be her master's concubine (Koran, Sūra 70:30).[1]

Several responsa deal with the question of the law applicable to fornication with a bondwoman. Here are a few excerpts: "She is taken away from him and sold and the proceeds are distributed among the Jewish poor, and he is beaten, has his hair shaved off, and is excommunicated for thirty days; this is the *halakha*."[2] But the Jewish authorities were not always able to enforce these rules, and the Muslim authorities could be hoodwinked, especially if the woman was in collusion with her master, who was kind to her and treated the children she bore him as his legitimate offspring. Such concubines were to be found in many households.

Free women were also sometimes guilty or suspected of misbehaviour. Cases in point are known from Europe, but seem to have been more frequent in the East.[3] This was in part due to husbands being away on business, sometimes overseas, for very long periods. Such circumstances gave rise in North Africa to the story of the child which lingered in the womb for over a year.[4] R. Nissim does not overlook those transgressions; in fact, he talks long and warningly about wicked women, just as he does not spare words of praise for the good and chaste ones.[5]

In a review of the Geniza material concerning the position of women, Goitein stresses that it was far more favourable than might be gathered from halakhic treatises. Jewish society was almost entirely monogamous. The hundreds of documents studied by him refer to only one case of bigamy. It seems that in this case the first wife was insane or ill, because it was stipulated that the second wife should take care of her husband's daughter by the first wife. Normally, a marriage contract provides that the husband shall not take an additional wife or a concubine. But flesh is weak and, as the responsa indicate, violations of the contract may sometimes have occurred.

In the Geniza papers, women often dispose freely of their property and a husband sometimes grants his wife the right to dispose of his property.

---

[1] *RSh*, p. 2b, no. 17; p. 25a, no. 15; p. 27b, no. 38; p. 28b, no. 42.

[2] *RSh*, p. 25a, no. 13.

[3] *RCor*, no. 24; *RSh*, pp. 1b-2a, no. 8; pp. 10b-11a, no. 9; *RShT*, no. 179; *RA* III, p. 111.

[4] Gottheil-Worrell, *Fragments* 9, pp. 52-54.

[5] *Op. cit.*, ch. XII; for a similar opinion concerning Islamic peoples see Mez, *Renaissance*, pp. 276-277 and 341.

Women appear in court and make contracts of sale or partnership in which their counterparts are also sometimes women.[1]

The material from responsa addressed to North Africa and from R. Nissim's *Fine Book* indicates that the position of woman in the Maghreb was not unlike her position in Egypt.

Proselytes

We have mentioned slaves converting to Judaism. In Muslim countries, these were always Christians or heathen. Although Jews sometimes took the risk of buying ostensibly Muslim slaves, they certainly did not try to convert them, for Islamic law threatens apostasy with death.[2]

We may suppose that free persons who converted to Judaism in the Maghreb in those days had also previously been Christians; we know of a similar phenomenon in Egypt and Europe.[3] The frequency of such cases is attested by queries concerning proselytes in Gaonic literature.[4] Most of these adopted Judaism for its own sake, and R. Nissim, therefore, warns against slighting them.[5] We must, however, take into consideration the special conditions then prevailing in North Africa. The Christian community was dwindling, though not as a result of persecution or coercion, but owing to a variety of political-economic factors; at the beginning of the second millennium C.E., only an insignificant remnant was left.[6] The Christians who abandoned their faith embraced the ruling religion, but those loyal to Christianity may have preferred to pose as Jews rather than become Muslims. The reason for this was simple: if they voluntarily adopted Islam, they were liable to the death penalty if they reverted to their former religion, but they were in no such danger if they became Jews and it was discovered that they secretly adhered to Christianity. This is the social background of the story of the disavowal of a deposit (according to R. Nissim's version) by a Christian couple posing as Jews.[7]

---

[1] Comp. Goitein, *Studies*, pp. 292-293; *idem*, *Fourth World Congress of Jewish Studies*, Papers II, Jerusalem 1968, pp. 177-179.

[2] Comp. Mez, *Renaissance*, p. 29; *EI*, *s.v. murtadd.*

[3] Comp. Ashtor, *Zion* 30 (1965), pp. 69-70; Golb, *Sefunot* 8 (1964), pp. 85-104; Mann, *Texts* I, pp. 31 and 33.

[4] *RSh*, p. 5a, no. 34; p. 22b, no. 12; p. 27b, no. 36; *RCor*, no. 23.

[5] R. Nissim, *ibid.*, ch. XIII, pp. 40-41.

[6] Comp. Julien, *Histoire* I, p. 279; Brunschvig, *Berbérie* I, p. 430, 451-452; also T. Arnold, *Preaching of Islam*, Lahore 1958, pp. 121ff.

[7] R. Nissim, ch. XIII, p. 40; ch. XXII, pp. 60-61. According to accepted custom, a Jew in Muslim lands could become a Christian, and *vice versa*; comp. Mez, *Renaissance*, p. 30; Strauss (Ashtor), *Egypt* II, p. 236.

Renegades and Marranos

The Maghreb in the wider sense, *i.e.* North Africa and Spain, was in the Islamic period a haven for political refugees and a convenient field for the activities of leaders of religious sects and religious-social movements which rebelled against the secular and religious authorities of the states controlling the area. This is well accounted for by the ethnic and geographical condition of that vast region and its remoteness from the political centres. The political and police authorities in Baghdad, Cairo and Kairouan were unable to supervise and control everything that went on in it. The same applies to the Jewish authorities, whose power was wholly spiritual, dependent on the internal discipline of a voluntary organization. The wide spaces of North Africa thus offered favourable conditions for Jewish renegades, who could easily hide here from their brethren, and for Jews who had voluntarily or involuntarily defected in other countries and wished to live again openly as Jews. Persons of both categories fled to the far-off Maghreb when they were unable to remain in their countries of residence because of their defection or their return to the fold.

Here is an extract from a responsum of which we do not know positively that it was addressed to the Maghreb, but which is definitely relevant to an appreciation of political and social conditions in that region: "A Jew who defected and has subsequently returned to the fold . . . shall go to a place where he is not known and shall observe all the commandments; he shall be received like a proper Jew and shall not be required to return to the place where he is known, because everybody knows that if he returns there he will be killed."[1]

The above shows why, as the evidence of the responsa, the number of converts to Islam was greater in the Maghreb than elsewhere. Moreover, in drawing conclusions as to their number, we should bear in mind two important points; 1. Though most of the relevant questions emanate from that region, the absence of questions from other countries is no absolute proof that there were no defections there; 2. while we have seen above (in the section on proselytes) that almost the entire Christian population of the African Maghreb became Islamized, we should now add that the percentage of Christians adopting the dominant religion was very high in Muslim Spain as well.[2]

---

[1] *RSh*, p. 26, no. 28; also *ibid.*, p. 24b, nos. 8 and 11, and *RḤG*, no. 54.

[2] Among the Christian population in the East, including the high clergy, conversions to Islam seem to have been frequent, while the proportion of Jews who

Here are a few factual accounts from the responsa. There were two brothers, one a Jew, the other a renegade. The Jew betrothed himself to a girl and subsequently died. The renegade lived in Barbary; he had two sons; he had settled among the Gentiles, in a remote locality, where there were no caravans. The betrothed girl thus became tied to the levir [like] an *ʿagūna*, a woman tied to a missing, presumably dead husband (because she could not perform the *ḥalīṣa*, cf. Deut. 25:5-11).[1] One question from Africa concerns the circumcision of a boy born on the Sabbath to a renegade Jew and his Jewish wife.[2] Many questions deal with the succession of renegades. It was said in the Maghreb that the marriage settlement of a renegade Jewess was inherited by her father, that is to say, that her change of religion did not affect her father's right to her property.[3] Similarly, the Gaon Hai said that her immovable property and the clothing and jewelry that were part of her dowry should go to her heirs.[4] In the same way, a male renegade was to be succeeded by his offspring, whether Jews or renegades. At the same time, the Maghreb accepted the Gaon Natronāy's view that a renegade could not inherit from his father; this view was supported by a reference to the Muslim law of succession, which does not permit members of different religions to inherit from one another.[5] The Maghrebi practice is mentioned by Maimonides: "A Jew who has changed his religion inherits from his relatives just as he would otherwise have done, but if the *beyt-dīn* sees fit to disinherit him, in order not to encourage defection, it may do so. If he has children who are Jews, their father's heritage shall be given them. Such is the established custom in the Maghreb."[6]

So far we have reviewed questions asked in respect of individual men

---

accepted Islam seems to have been small. Comp. Steinschneider, *Arabische Literatur* p. XXI; Hitti, *History*, pp. 510-511, 512-513 and 517, also p. 544; Hirschberg, *Israel in Arabia*, pp. 110-111.

[1] *RSh*, p. 7b, no. 50; comp. *ibid.*, p. 4b, no. 29, and *RM*, no. 182. Comp. also *RSh*, pp. 4b, no. 28; 8a, no. 53; *RCor*, no. 96.

[2] *RḤ*, no. 21; *RSh*, p. 22b, no. 8 (from R. Sherira). For other legal problems concerning renegades comp. *RSh*, p. 8a, no. 54; p. 15a, no. 29; *RCor*, no. 16.

[3] *RSh*, p. 63b, no. 40 (comp. also p. 54b, no. 5). According to Lewin, *Ha-Tor* 1926, no. 32, p. 7, this responsum was addressed to the Maghreb. Comp. above, p. 185. n. 7.

[4] *RM*, no. 87. R. Palṭoi makes a distinction between the dowry and the immovable property of a renegade Jewess: *RSh*, p. 63b, no. 41; *RḤG*, no. 53 (R. Natronāy).

[5] *RH*, no. 541; *RA* I, p. 50, no. 19. For R. Natronāy's view see *RH*, no. 332; *RSh*, p. 48b, no. 25; *RḤG*, no. 52; *RL*, no. 23; *RM*, no. 11 (reference to Muslim law); comp. Lewin, *Oẓar ha-Geonim* IX, pp. 30-36. See also Bergsträsser, *Grundzüge*, p. 45; Baron, *SRH* III, pp. 143-144.

[6] *Mishne Tora*, Hil. Naḥaloth VI, p. 12; comp. also Lewin, *Oẓar ha-Geonim* IX, p. 34, no. 87.

and women who in varying circumstances changed their religion. In the days of the Almohad persecution, the problem of the renegades became a general one and brought a considerable part of the Jewish people to a state of crisis. The North African and Spanish communities were faced with the alternative of adoption of Islam or death. Many, perhaps most, Maghrebi Jews saved their lives by submission. The period of persecution was followed by relative calm, when no mortal danger threatened those who had survived by outwardly professing Islam or by benefiting from the doubt since nobody asked their religion. After a time, the ordeal resumed, at any rate in Fez, the temporary abode of Maimonides, and later severe discrimination was practised against the second and third generations of those who were ostensibly Muslims, but secretly adhered to the religion of their fathers and transmitted it to their children.

It seems that during that period acute pangs of conscience began to assail the remnant of North African Jewry: had they or their fathers acted rightly, and had they still a part in the God of Israel? We find an echo of these qualms in the words of three sages: R. Maimon ha-Dayyan, his son, R. Moses (Maimonides), and R. Joseph ben Jehuda ben ʿAqnīn. All three were eyewitnesses of the events and were themselves affected by them; their utterances, therefore, are of extreme importance [1] especially as they seem to be the only extant testimony of this kind.[2]

At the beginning of his *Epistle of Consolation*, R. Maimon ha-Dayyān says that he is writing in Fez in the year 1471 S.E. (1160 C.E.). He does not mention the Almohad persecution expressly, but his allusions to it are plain enough. He tries to comfort the despondent, who think that God "is angry with us because we disobeyed him (p. 10)". We are God's children, whether we believe in him or desert him (p. 13), and he will keep his promises to us (p. 14). Man must occupy himself with the Law both secretly and openly (p. 15) and fulfil the commandments mentally and physically (p. 15). The strongest link between man and his Creator is the *ʿamīda* prayer recited three times a day, but if a man has omitted it once and its time is past, he need not make up for it (p. 23), and if it is

---

[1] B. Klar published a new Hebrew translation of the *Epistle of Consolation* (Jerusalem 1945). Excerpts from the *Epistle* were published in Hebrew in Edelmann, *Ḥemda Genūza*, Königsberg 1856, pp. LXXIV-LXXXII; the same publication (pp. 6-12) contains Maimonides' *Epistle on Forced Conversion*, as it is called by R. Isaac b. Sheshet, Responsum no. 11 (R. Simon b. Zemaḥ Duran, *Responsa* I, no. 63 (p. 31d), calls it Tract on Martyrdom). Ibn ʿAqnīn devotes a chapter to this problem in his book *Ṭibb al-Nufūs*, extracts from which were published by A. Halkin in *Starr Memorial Volume*, New York 1953, pp. 103-110.

[2] Comp. Saadia ibn Danān's remarks in the "Responsum on the Forced Converts", *Ḥemda Genūza*, ed. Edelmann, p. 16a.

not possible to recite it fully (because of the danger involved), he shall recite a short, even a very short, prayer, which may even be in the Arabic language, so long as its contents are in accordance with rabbinic regulations. Such a prayer is sufficient for a person who knows no more and does not wish to forgo communion with God (pp. 18-26). The second tenet is belief in Moses: he who believes in him believes in God (p. 26), and he who denies him will go to hell (p. 33). A considerable part of the Letter (pp. 26-36) is devoted to a description of the qualities of Moses, for the obvious purpose of exalting him above all other prophets. There is a veiled thrust at the descriptions of the outstanding virtues of Muḥammad, which occupy an important place in the collections of Muslim traditions —although his name is not mentioned in the Letter. Daniel is incidentally referred to as the last of the prophets (p. 12) a concealed attack upon the Koran (33:10), according to which Muḥammad was the last prophet.[1]

For all its restrained tone, the *Epistle* is very revealing of the despair that gripped the renegades when they were almost completely debarred from openly observing the precepts of Judaism, when they could not always say even a short prayer without endangering themselves. One anonymous rabbi tries to deprive them even of the hope of communing with God by some sort of prayer. In his opinion, a converso who is forced to enter a Muslim place of worship, though he may not say anything there, and who afterwards goes home and recites a Jewish prayer, loses the reward of a meritorious action because he is in a state of sin. The same applies to a converso forced to acknowledge Muḥammad's prophethood; he is an evildoer and disqualified by the Tora from giving evidence. Maimonides, in the *Epistle on Forced Conversion*, which refutes these and similar views, does not reveal the name of that zealous rabbi; he merely stresses that he lived in a country unaffected by Almohad persecution.[2] Only a few years separated the composition of the *Epistle of Consolation* and the *Epistle on Forced Conversion*. The contents of the latter suggest that a change for the worse had meanwhile occurred in the situation of the Maghrebi conversos, who were again compelled to

[1] This evaluation of Moses (comp. also *Epistle of Consolation*, p. 58) occurs in the *Fine Book* of R. Nissim (comp. Index). According to Maimonides, Moses is greater than the Messiah; comp. Halkin, *Epistle to Yemen*, pp. 86-87; also Introduction, p. XXVIII; Baron, *SRH* V, p. 138.

[2] *Epistle on Forced Conversion*, pp. 6a-b and 8b. Toledano's view (*Lumière*, p. 33) that he was R. Yehuda ibn Sūsān, the *dayyan* of Fez (and, according to Ibn Danān, Maimonides's teacher), is untenable, though not for the reason given by Halkin, *Starr Volume*, p. 102, n. 15; unlike Ibn Sūsān, who lived in Fez and died there as a martyr, the unnamed rabbi did not live in the Maghreb.

attend at mosque, to acknowledge the mission of Muḥammad and to acquiesce in the assimilation of their sons and daughters to the Gentiles. In view of the deterioriation of the situation and the harsh words of that rabbi, it was necessary to adopt a clear stand, so as to encourage and guide the conversos. Maimonides declares in trenchant language that a Jew must not accuse a fellow Jew: even Moses was punished for suspecting guiltless persons. Secondly, Islam must not be regarded as idolatry, and especially, "the religious coercion which we are experiencing does not lead us to worship strange gods, but merely to profess belief in what the Muslims tell us; and they have already realized that we do not believe it at all, but that we mislead the king: they did flatter him with their mouth, and they lied unto him with their mouths (Ps. 78:36)." Thirdly, a Jew who, having been compelled to apostatize, fulfils a religious duty in secret will be rewarded for it. And notwithstanding the sublime quality of martyrdom, not everyone is competent to decide what is martyrdom, and he who wantonly endangers his life is committing a sin and is himself to blame for his predicament, as it is written: he shall live in them (Lev. 18:5), on which the Talmud (Yoma 85b) comments: and not die in them.

Maimonides concludes by advising those who are asked to adopt Islam by merely verbal profession to do so and thus to save their lives, but he urges everyone to leave areas of religious coercion for places where one is able to observe Jewish law. Those who say that they will stay where they are until the Messiah comes to lead them from the Maghreb to Jerusalem are sinning and causing others to sin. But those whose departure is delayed for various reasons shall try to follow whatever precept they can and shall not think that since they have already transgressed important commandments they might as well spurn minor ones. Those who have succeeded in escaping from areas of forced conversion shall be accepted and encouraged to keep the Law; they shall not be turned away.

As a result of persecution and the urgings of Maimonides' *Epistle*, the Maghreb was left by rabbis and religious scholars, and their exit entailed a lowering of standards. Maimonides briefly and tellingly describes the situation in a letter to his disciples: "In the Maghreb, all joy is darkened, every seeker of the Lord has vanished, the light of Israel has died, the House of Israel is on fire." It is not to be assumed that all educated persons left the area; Saadia ibn Danān notes that some grandsons of R. Judah ibn Sūsūn are in Fez in his time (late 15th century).[1] But

[1] Comp. *Ḥemda Genūza* p. 30; and below pp. 368f.

Maghreb Jewish society now entered upon a period of decadence and degradation, the initial stage of which is described by R. Joseph ben Yehuda ibn ʿAqnīn.

R. Joseph ibn ʿAqnīn came of a family of Spanish origin. He himself was born in the Maghreb, and when the Maimon family arrived in Fez, he was attracted to Maimonides and became one of his admirers. He admits that he had ostensibly been brought up in the Islamic faith, which had been forced upon his family, and the thought that he had eventually become a voluntary renegade, because he might have escaped to another country, preyed upon his mind. Moreover, the temporal affairs of the converts were not in good shape, either, for, unlike other cases of forced mass conversion, they were not treated gently by the Muslim authorities. "The more it appears that we obey them as to everything they tell us, and incline after their Law, the more they oppress and enslave us." Even the grandchildren of the first converts (of the forties of the 12th century), who had been brought up as Muslims, were discriminated against, which is why many of them fully reverted to Judaism. Those who were caught were treated as Muslims changing their religion, *i.e.* they suffered the death penalty unless they recanted. Ibn ʿAqnīn mentions a series of further measures inflicted upon those Jews, which will be dealt with presently in the section on discrimination.[1]

Restrictions and Discrimination

He who is familiar with the literature of the period will not be surprised that it contains almost no information on personal relations between Jews and the non-Jewish society within which they lived. Similarly, Arab-Muslim authors almost completely ignore the existence of non-Muslim communities, mentioning them only rarely and incidentally. This attitude is a true mirror of reality. Such was the way of life in Eastern countries in the Middle Ages. The ties of blood, origin and religious-communal affiliation came first, and only what happened within one's group was of real interest. Even important historical events were disregarded if they did not affect the members of the group.

We find no actual complaints of excesses, coercion or malice on the part of the authorities. Only incidentally, in connection with a commander's undertaking not to harm the women on entering a city, do we learn

[1] Maimonides, *Iggarot*, ed. Amsterdam 1712, pp. 10b-11a; comp. Halkin, *Starr Volume*, pp. 103ff.

how troops sometimes behaved. Elsewhere we hear that a certain person "suffers harassment at the hands of the authorities: they harass him, and sometimes his wife is victimized in his stead." The imprisonment of women was apparently not unusual since R. Nissim begins his *Fine Book* with an instance of it.[1]

If occurrences of this kind were not spotlighted, then usual practices, familiar for many generations, were certainly not thought worthy of attention and recording. To people in those days, measures which to us seem utterly degrading did not appear humiliating at all. Both those who enacted them and those to whom they were applied regarded them as the logical outcome of a factual situation evolved over a long period. It was of course advisable to evade some of these measures, to try to have them forgotten, to pay bribes to secure impunity for transgressors, but there was no reason or need to denounce them as novel inflictions. Several of them—such as the special poll-tax and restrictions on public worship, legal competence and civic rights—originated in the distant past prior to the Arab conquest. In this connection, we should note that Arab historians regarded the Christian Romans living in Africa as aliens (*ʿajam*), while describing the Jews as *ahl al-dhimma*—protected persons.[2]

There can be no doubt that in the major cities, such as Kairouan, Fez and Sijilmāsa, the Jews lived in separate quarters. This is to be inferred from an account of the disaster of the Kairouan community which says that the *ḥāra*, *i.e.* the Jewish quarter, and *al-maqdis al-jalīl*, the magnificent synagogue, were laid waste.[3] But segregation in special quarters was certainly not imposed, or arranged for, by the authorities in the early days of Islam. It was a voluntary concentration for reasons of convenience. We know, *e.g.*, that Jewish tribes in pre-Islamic Yathrib each lived in an area of its own.[4] When the Arab conquerors arrived in regions until then under Persian rule, they found *maḥallāt al-Yahūd*, Jewish quarters, there.[5] The delimitation of a Jewish quarter did not prevent the settling of non-Jews in it nor the settling of Jews in other quarters. We find Muslims living among Jews and Jews renting dwellings among Muslims. In a responsum to R. Shabīb bar Jacob in Kairouan (middle of the 9th

---

[1] Comp. *RM*, no. 47; *RH*, no. 346; Hirschberg, *R. Nissim*, ch. I (p. 2).

[2] See above, pp. 96-7.

[3] Mann, *Texts* I, p. 246.

[4] Comp. Hirschberg, *Israel in Arabia*, pp. 119-121 and *passim*.

[5] Hamadāni, Buldān, p. 129; Balādhurī, *Futūḥ al-Buldān*, ed. de Goeje, p. 332. About the *ḥārat al-Yahūd* in Jerusalem in the 11th century: Gottheil-Worrell, *Fragments*, p. 120, l. 30. A Jew living among Muslims in Jerusalem: *ibid.*, p. 126, l. 12.

century), an anonymous gaon prohibits the letting of premises to Gentiles: "Shall a Jew who owns some premises let them to a Gentile to live there? There is no question with regard to a strong and wicked Gentile, to whom one must not let in order that he may not trouble a Jew; but one must not let even to a Gentile who is not (manifestly) a ruffian, because every Gentile is presumed to be a ruffian."[1] If a Jew proposes to sell any premises or share in premises to a Gentile, the *beyt-din* may stop him and warn him. If he does not heed the warning, he is to be excommunicated and compelled to make good the damage caused to the inhabitants of the premises by the Gentile if the latter destroys and spoils the property of the Jews.[2] But we shall see that this rigorous attitude relates only to residence on the premises of Jews, while the rabbis were more lenient, permitting partnerships with Jews, with regard to business premises.

In the eastern part of the Arab Caliphate, the rules of the *ghiyār*, *i.e.* the difference in dress, applied, which were binding on Jews, Christians and Samaritans already at a fairly early period. An Arab historian of the middle of the 11th century reports that in the days of the Aghlābids (9th century) a *qāḍī* ordered Jews and Christians to wear on their shoulders a patch of cloth, with the design of a donkey in the case of the Jews and a pig in the case of the Christians, and to affix a tablet depicting a donkey (or pig) to the doors of their houses. But a hundred years before, an Arab author speaks of friendly relations between Muslims and Jews.[3]

Our sources contain no more than a hint at distinctive footwear. R. Nissim adds a gloss to the story (Taʿanit 25a) of R. Berōqā and the prison guard who wears black shoes to conceal the fact that he is a Jew; we gather from his words that it was not "the custom" for Jews in those (R. Berōqā's) days to wear black shoes. R. Nissim uses the word *sunna* (the Muslim term for customs ascribed to Muḥammad) to denote oppressive measures which the Fatimid Caliph al-Ḥākim bi-Amr Allah adapted in those days in Cairo against Jews and Christians. The order prescribing black clothing and black shoes may have applied to Kaiιouan as well, since Fāṭimid rule theoretically comprised also the eastern areas of the African Maghreb. But the placid remark of R. Nissim shows that the severity of that measure was not felt in his part of the world.[4] On the other hand, an Arab source reports that when the Nagid Abraham ben ʿAṭā once came to the mufti on a mission on behalf of the Emir al-Muʿizz,

---

1 *RA* II, p. 35; *RSh*, pp. 33a-b, no. 22; also *ibid.*, nos. 19, 95 and 158.
2 *RSh*, p. 33a, no. 21.
3 Hopkins, *Government*, pp. 60 and 66.
4 Comp. Hirschberg, *R. Nissim*, ch. I (p. 2) and Introduction, p. 75.

the former sent him away angrily because he was not wearing the *ghiyār*.[1]

The special poll-tax from the protected persons, Jews and Christians, is not expressly mentioned in Maghrebi Jewish sources of the period under reference. But there can be no doubt that it was levied, and we may suppose that it is referred to in R. Abraham ben Daud's story of Jacob ben Jau, whom the King al-Manṣūr set over all the Jewish communities from Sijilmāsa to the Duero River, which was the border of his realm, to judge them all and to appoint for them whomever he wished and to apportion every tax and payment due from them. The poll-tax was nothing new for the Jews, since they had paid it also to the Byzantines and Persians.[2]

That tax is generally called *jizya* in Arabic, but in Africa the term *jāliya* (plur.: *jawālī*), *i.e.* exile (tax), was used, which was obviously coined in relation to, or by, Jews. This latter term occurs frequently in Arab sources,[3] but we find it in later Jewish sources as well.[4] No data on the rate of the *jāliya* in the Maghreb subsist, nor do we know particulars concerning its collection. We may suppose that it was collected by the Jewish authorities, together with other taxes and charges to which the members of the community were liable, the amounts due to the government being set apart from the general collection. This assumption is based on the collection procedure obtaining in Babylonia during the same period and on Abraham ben David's above-cited remarks concerning Jacob ben Jau. Religious scholars do not seem to have been exempt from taxes in Egypt, but it is difficult to decide whether we may assume a similar state of things in the Maghreb.[5]

---

[1] Comp. Idris, *AIEO*, 13 (1955), pp. 55-56; *idem*, *Berbérie*, pp. 178, 767-768.

[2] G. D. Cohen, *SHQ*, p. 51 and 69; comp. *MJC* II, p. 63, about the *jizya* paid to the Exilarch instead of the Persians. Text B, *ibid.*, p. 76, uses the word "tax".

[3] According to Yaʿqūbī, *BGA* VII, pp. 343-344, the annual income from the *jawālī* of Barqa was 15,000 dinars. Ibn Ḥawqal, *BGA* II², mentions the "*jawālī ʿala al-Yahūd*" from Qābes (pp. 69-70) and the poll-tax from Tenes (p. 77). He also gives the amounts of income from the *jawālī* and other taxes, *ibid.*, pp. 96-97. Comp. Hopkins, *Government*, pp. 24-26 and 42. For the use of the term *jalwa* "(period of) exile" by Ibn Khaldūn comp. Fischel, *Goldziher Memorial Volume* II, 1958, p. 155.

[4] Moses ibn Ezra uses *jāliya* in its original meaning; comp. Munk, Notice sur Abou 'l-Walid Merwan ibn Djanaḥ, *JA*, July 1850, pp. 49-50. Maimonides uses this term in his autobiographical letter; comp. Assaf, *Sources*, p. 165, l. 6. In Egypt there was a, *Dīwān al-Jawālī* (register of poll-tax payers); comp. Neustadt, *Zion* 2 (1937), p. 222 n. 8. We also find there a "*jābi al-jāliya*", *i.e.* collector of contributions to the poll-tax of the poor (Ashtor (Strauss), *Zion* 30 (1965), p. 132; comp. also Goitein, *Studies*, pp. 289-290).

[5] A list of taxpayers published by Strauss in *Zion*, 7 (1941), p. 143, includes 143 rabbinical scholars.

The provision of Muslim law that *tarīka*, *i.e.* heirless property, devolves on the treasury applied to the population in general and was not aimed specifically at non-Muslims, but in practice it affected Jews more than others. The other population groups, viz. Muslims, Christians and members of various sects, had been living on their land or in their quarter for many generations, and it hardly ever happened that one of them died without an heir. Not so the Jews, who for economic and religious reasons and as a result of persecution had become a wandering people. When a Jewish pilgrim or trader died abroad, especially at sea, it was usually difficult to prove that he had heirs and where they were. Much depended, moreover, on the attitude of the local authorities, who sometimes, exceeding their power, took a share in the estate even where there were heirs, especially if they were all daughters.[1] This is why the Jews regarded the regulation concerning heirless estates as discriminatory. But we know of cases where Jews circumvented that regulation either by concealing the property or by their leaders bribing the authorities so that most of the estate went to the coffers of the community.[2]

Segregation and social barriers did not prevent business connections and reciprocal relations between members of the two religions. Jews joined Muslim caravans passing through their places of residence and went on long business trips with them. The only caravans including no Jews were those returning from Mecca—no doubt because of the fanaticism of the pilgrims, who did not want their holiness impaired by contact with infidels. Jews also used Muslim merchant vessels when travelling overseas. Such voluntary companionship on extended journeys perforce resulted in closer relations and joint business ventures. Even *qāḍīs* are found taking part in the latter. One of the geonim prohibited activities of this kind because of the complications likely to result.[3] Questions to Geonim show that Jews leased land, inns and baking-houses to Muslims and took shops and fields in partnership with them. Particularly frequent were partnerships in which the Gentile partner worked on the Sabbath.[4]

---

[1] Assaf, *Sources*, p. 141, l. 11; *RA* III, pp. 125-127; Strauss, *Zion* 4 (1939), pp. 222, 226-227; Mez. *Renaissance*, pp. 107-108. For the later period comp. Basola, *Masʿot Eretz-Israel*, published by I. Ben-Zvi, 1938, p. 62; Pollak, *Toledoth ha-Yaḥasim ha-Qarqaʿiyim*, Jerusalem 1940, p. 47; Strauss (Ashtor), *Egypt* II, pp. 233-234.

[2] Mann, *JQR*, 9 (1918-19), p. 163; Assaf, *Sources*, pp. 138-140; *Yaʿarī*, *Iggerot Eretz-Israel*, 1943, pp. 128-129.

[3] *RM*, no. 102.

[4] Comp. *ibid.*, nos. 53-56; *RC*, no. 51; *RL*, nos. 64-65, 67-68; *TR* II, pp. 57-58, no. 5, Ginzberg, *Geonica* II, pp. 186, 194-196. But comp. Goitein, *Studies*, pp. 348-350.

This, too, indicates that the Jewish quarter was still open to non-Jews, although the lease of dwellings to non-Jews in Jewish neighbourhoods was not considered permissible. Nor had Jews misgivings about entering the Muslim quarter.

The Almohad Regulations

A marked change for the worse in the situation of the Jews occurred in the days of ʿAbd al-Muʾmin's grandson, Abū Yūsuf Yaʿqūb al-Manṣūr (1184-1199). The Arab historian ʿAbd al-Wāḥid al-Marrākeshi, a younger contemporary and countryman of al-Manṣūr, reports that this ruler, towards the end of his life, ordered Muslims of Jewish origin to wear a dark blue robe with sleeves reaching to the feet, so as to distinguish them from the rest of the population. He also forbade them to wear a turban after the fashion of those days, and commanded them to don the *qalansawa*, a cap of strange and ugly shape which reached down to the ears. This dress was peculiar to Maghreb Jewry until the end of Abū Yūsuf Yaʿqūb's reign and during the early part of the rule of his son, Abū ʿAbdallah (1199-1214). Upon the entreaties of the Jews, supported by self-interested recommendations from veteran Muslims, that ruler consented to modify the regulations, permitting Jews to dress after the current fashion, but insisting that their robe and headgear must be yellow. Al-Marrākeshi adds that this has remained the Jewish garb until his own time (621/1224). According to him, the reason why Abū Yūsuf Yaʿqūb compelled the new Muslims to wear distinctive clothing was a sneaking doubt as to the sincerity of their belief. "If I were sure," said Abū Yūsuf, "that these Jews have wholeheartedly embraced Islam, I should permit them to mix with the Muslims by marriage and in every other way. And if I were certain that they are infidels, I should put the men to death, sell their children into slavery and confiscate their property in favour of the believers. But I am perplexed about the matter.[1]

Al-Marrākeshī's account indicates clearly that those converts were not permitted to marry the daughters of veteran Muslims because al-Manṣūr was not sure whether to regard them as Jews or as true believers. On the other hand, R. Joseph ben Jehuda ibn ʿAqnīn, a contemporary of Abū

---

[1] R. Dozy, *The History of the Almohades by ... al-Marrákoshi*[2], Leyden 1881, p. 223; al-Zarkashī, *Taʾrīkh Dawlatayn*, p. 11; comp. E. Fagnan, *RAf*, 36, pp. 264-265; idem, *REJ* 28 (1894), pp. 294-8; Marçais, *Berbérie*, pp. 269-270; Hopkins, *Government*, pp. 61-62; for the *ghiyar* regulations in Iraq in the 12th century comp. *KS* 30 (1955), pp. 95-96. Comp. also *Shebeṭ Yehuda*, p. 78.

Yūsuf, reproves those of his generation who contract marriage by means of the *ṣadāq*, *i.e.* the Muslim marriage contract dealing with the marriage settlement, rather than—at least in secret—by means of *ḥuppah* and *qiddushīn* according to Jewish custom; he regards this as a grave offence. Those people apparently wished to convince the government of their adherence to Muslim law.[1]

Besides the *ghiyār* regulations, Ibn ʿAqnīn mentions several other discriminatory measures inflicted upon the pseudo-Muslim Jews.

Until the time of the Almohads, Maghreb Jewry had ramified business connections and played a significant part in intercontinental trade and in trade with the countries bordering on the Indian Ocean; no less important was its share in local trade and in peddling. But now the authorities ousted the Jews from these occupations and stripped them of their property. Moreover, they—*i.e.* the pseudo-Muslims—were forbidden to keep slaves. This disability, in addition to the social stigma it involved according to the concepts of the period, was a serious economic handicap.

Ibn ʿAqnīn further mentions the limitation of the capacity of those forced Muslims to be trustees and guardians. The Almohads deprived them of the right to bring up their children and ordered them to hand them over to trustworthy Muslims to be given a truly Muslim education. They were moreover disqualified for testamentary guardianship, although our author notes that the Muslim guardians were not very strict in the matter and left the minors to be cared for by their own families.

All these regulations were a logical consequence of the approach to Muslims of Jewish origin. According to Islamic law, a non-Muslim cannot be the natural or testamentary guardian of Muslim children. We have already seen, in connection with the question of marriage to Muslim women, that Abū Yūsuf did not regard the forced converts as full Muslims; he consequently denied them the guardianship of their children, who were considered Muslims from birth.[2]

After the Jews were permitted to revert openly to their religion, these regulations lapsed automatically. But the regulations concerning special clothing did not become void; they continued in full force, even though details as to colour and cut were changed. In contrast to the pre-Almohad period, the *ghiyār* is now mentioned in Tunisia (1199) and Spain (end of the Middle Ages); at the instigation of Maghrebi fanatics, it was

---

[1] Comp. Halkin, *Starr Memorial Volume*, p. 104 and n. 35; and comp. *RSh*, p. 8a, no. 54.

[2] Comp. *K. al-Fiqh*, III, p. 486; IV, p. 26; Bergsträsser, *Grundzüge*, p. 45.

reintroduced in Egypt, where it had fallen into oblivion.[1] We possess a text on the duties of the *muḥtasib*, the official—with judicial powers—in charge of markets, morals and protected persons (*ahl al-dhimma*), by an author of African origin who lived in Spain at the end of the Middle Ages; here is what he says of the duties of the *muḥtasib* with regard to protected persons:

He must prevent protected persons from looking down upon Muslims in their houses (*i.e.* from living in houses higher than those of Muslims); from wielding authority (over Muslims); from displaying wine and pork in Muslim markets; from riding saddled and decorated horses in Muslim streets, and other acts of ostentation. He must prescribe signs for them that enable them to be distinguished from Muslims, such as the *shikla* [2] for men and bells for women. He must prevent Muslims being asked to do anything degrading and offensive to them, such as removing refuse, transporting wine containers and tending pigs, or anything expressive of unbelief or superiority over Islam.[3]

The continuity of the clothing regulations is attested by European travellers, who visited Berber countries with increasing frequency from the 16th century onwards. They all noted the special Jewish dress and other humiliating and discriminatory features and did not fail to record them. The restrictive measures subsisted almost until our time—though not with equal strictness in all countries—and there are still some areas where both Muslims and Jews adhere to them.[4]

The Jews eventually prevailed in this heavy struggle. The disabilities imposed upon them caused many descendants of forced converts to return wholeheartedly to Judaism. This process is particularly significant in view of developments in the case of the Christians, who vanished completely from North Africa although their social and political condition was more favourable than that of the Jews. Most of the Maghreb rulers had Christian garrison troops whom they permitted to practise their religion and who had priests and churches and even church bells. If crypto-Christians had wished to return to their religion, they could have

---

[1] Comp. Zarkashī, *Ta'rikh*, pp. 11, 25 (and Appendix Tunis); Pelissier et Remusat, *Histoire*, p. 224; Hopkins, *Government*, p. 62. For the *ghiyār* regulations in Egypt comp. L. A. Mayer, *Mamluke Costume*, p. 65.

[2] The exact form of the *shikla* or *shakla* is not known. It seems to have been different in each Maghreb country.

[3] Comp. Lévi-Provençal, *Traités*, p. 122.

[4] Comp. Beaumier, *Roudh*, pp. 357-358, 372; Brunschvig, *Berbérie* I, pp. 499, 453 and 469; Hopkins, *Government*, pp. 69-70.

taken advantage of these facts. But, like the Christians in South Arabia, they assimilated to the Muslims.[1]

However, North African Jews paid a high price for their resistance and perseverance. Despised and vilified by the local Muslims—Arabs and Berbers—they lived under the most trying economic, social and cultural conditions, segregated and cooped up in special quarters known as *mellāḥ* or *ḥāra*. Even the expellees from Spain, the Mediterranean islands and Portugal, who began to pour into the area, scorned the "residents", so different from them as to customs, manners and livelihood. The merging of the two strata took centuries and is still not complete.

[1] Comp. *e.g.*, Budgett Meakin, *Empire*, pp. 239-250, 307-334; Le Tourneau, *Fez-Merinids* p. 73; Corcos, *Jews*, I-II, pp. 284-5.

CHAPTER FOUR

COMMUNAL ORGANIZATION

The forms of Jewish communal organization in the Maghreb were different from those known to us from other countries. This was due to the special character of the region, which was both a transit area and a self-contained unit, and to political changes occurring in it.

The Negidim of Kairouan

We surmise that when the Fāṭimids set out to conquer Egypt (in 969) R. Paltiel the Italian (or Mūsā b. Eleazar) was the leader of Jewry in that part of North Africa which was already under Fāṭimid rule. He became the first holder of the office of nagid in Egypt, followed in the course of centuries by a succession of others.[1] About the same time, Manṣūr, the guardian of the Umayyad Caliph in Cordova (977-1002) placed Jacob b. Jau in charge of the Jews of Spain and the Outermost Maghreb, which latter was also under Umayyad rule. He "issued to him a document placing him in a charge of all the Jewish communities from Sijilmasa to the Duero (this is the correct reading), which was the border of his realm ... Then all the members of the community of Cordova, young and old, assembled and signed an agreement [certifying] his position as *nasi* (prince), which stated: 'Rule thou over us, both thou and thy son and thy son's son also.'."[2] It is a well-established fact that negidim appointed by the authorities served in those days also in that part of Africa which extended from Egypt westward to the Umayyad territory in Morocco. But our sources give no indication as to when and how the office of nagid was created here. Judging by the situation in Egypt and Spain, it was the caliph or emir who appointed a man acceptable to him to be the agent and representative of the Jews, responsible to him for the fulfilment of their obligations towards the government (payment of taxes etc.). This man was empowered to collect taxes from the members of his community and

[1] The identity of Paltiel, an enigmatic figure appearing in two medieval Jewish sources, has not been definitely established, but B. Lewis (*BSOAS*, 30 (1967), pp. 177-181, where the sources and a full bibliography are given) seems to be on firm ground when he says that he is Mūsā b. Eleazar, physician to al-Muʿizz, who accompanied that ruler from North Africa to Egypt. For the title *nāgid* see next page.

[2] Cohen, *SHQ*, 51/69.

to appoint persons to various offices (perhaps also *dayyānim*).[1] Usually, the nagid owed his position to a decision and official acts of the ruler of the country, and not to election by his Jewish brethren or to the consent or approval of Jewish authorites abroad, such as the Exilarchs and Geonim in Babylonia or the Academy Heads in Palestine.

The nagid generally held an important post at the ruler's court. He was the *kātib*, *i.e.* secretary at the caliph's chancellery, in one case perhaps even a vizier, or the physician in ordinary or banker and treasurer to the sovereign. His devoted services earned him the confidence of his lord, thus facilitating his task as spokesman and intercessor.[2]

Rabbi Paltiel

The description in the Chronicle of Rabbi Paltiel's office as that of deputy to the king—*i.e.* vizier—at al-Muʿizz's court has been suspected of exaggeration, especially in view of a description in the same source of his functions during the conquest of Egypt. According to the latter, Paltiel enabled the long trek from the centre of government Tunisia, to Egypt, through "a wilderness, a land of trouble and anguish, there being no water or food or tent or hostelry all the way, and Rabbi Paltiel went before... and set up camps and provided ... everything necessary for the soldiers coming from the provinces etc.";[3] that is to say that Paltiel's task was that of quartermaster-general of the army. This description indicates that the author of the Chronicle was familiar with the geographical and logistic conditions of North Africa and perhaps also with Fāṭimid administrative practice. As for the title "deputy to the king", a loftily-styled family chronicle cannot be expected to use exact official terminology. Some suppose that there were no viziers at all at the beginning of Fāṭimid rule and that only al-ʿAzīz, the second Fāṭimid in Egypt, appointed a vizier, namely a Jew converted to Islam, Yaʿqūb ibn

[1] On the responsibility of the *nāsī* or *nāgid* for the collection of taxes comp. also R. Petahya, *Sibūb*, pp. 5-6; Gottheil, *Gaster Jubilee Volume*, 1936, p. 174 Respons. 1, l. 5.

[2] For the rank of Samuel ha-Nagid at Bādīs's court in Granada comp. Munk, *JA*, July 1850, pp. 211-212 and 217. For the whole problem comp. Ashtor, *Spain* II, pp. 26ff.; Baron *SRH* V, pp. 38-46, 310 n. 49, 311 n. 54. There is no hint in our sources that, as Goitein assumes, the title *nagid* was conferred the first time by a foreign Jewish authority; Comp. *Zion*, 27 (1962), pp. 11-23, 156-165 and 165 n.; also below, p. 212 n. 1. In an epistle published by Cowley *JQR* o.s., 18 (1906) pp. 403-4 (see above p. 106) calls the Gaon Samuel b. Hofni his great grandfather: Joseph ha-Nagid.

[3] See above p. 104.

Killis. It should further be noted that there was in Fāṭimid Egypt an official known as *wāsiṭa*, a government secretary ranking below a vizier and believed to have been concerned with army administration. Aḥimaʿaṣ may have had such an official in mind when describing Paltiel's functions during the Egyptian campaign.[1]

Paltiel had control over all the Jews in the Fāṭimid state; in the words of Aḥimaʿaṣ: he was "the *menaggēd* (*i.e.* nagid) of the communities of the people of the glorious God in Egypt, Palestine, Palermo, Africa and the whole of the Ismaelite realm."[2] The nagid may perhaps be described as a kind of exilarch on a smaller scale and with lesser powers; in fact, he is sometimes called *negīd ha-gōlā*.[3] There was no room for such an office so long as the principle of the unity of the Arab caliphate and of loyalty to the Abbasid dynasty—expressed by the mention of the name of the reigning caliph at Friday prayers—was preserved at least in appearance. Upon the disintegration of the Abbasid empire and the severance of relations between the local dynasties and the Abbadids, which expressed itself in the replacement of the name of the ruler in the Friday *khuṭba* (sermon), a desire was felt to emphasize this change also with regard to the Jews by giving them a leader appointed by the local emir or caliph. Practical exigencies, too, made it advisable that the ruler should have beside him a Jew who might be held responsible for everything in his community. His functions were nowhere expressly defined, as if they had been self-evident. *E.g.*, the collection of the *jizya*, the poll-tax imposed on protected persons, is mentioned only rarely and incidentally. But there can be no doubt that the nagid was responsible for the levying and punctual payment of that by no means negligible tax. It need hardly be added that the Jews were interested in the presence at court of a man with official status and personal influence, who might obviate or mitigate action directed against them by the autorities or even by foreign enemies.

This clarification of the general background solves two problems arising in connection with the office of nagid in Kairouan. We know that in the early tenth century the Exilarch Mar ʿUqba was compelled to leave

---

[1] Comp. Ibn al-Ṣayrafī, *Al-Ishāra ilā Man Nāla al-Wizāra*, Cairo 1924, pp. 78 l. 12; 79, ll. 2, 7, 9, 13; 80, ll. 7, 10; Al-Maqrīzi, *Al-Mawāith waʾl-Iʿtibār*, Būlāq 1270, I, p. 356 l. 2; Al-Qalqashandi, *Subḥ al-Aʿshā* III, p. 489; de Sacy, *Exposé de la Religion des Druzes* I, Introduction, 1838 p. 282. Originally the meaning of the word is mediator, go-between, e.g., the prophet Isaiah held such a post; al-Thaʿlabi, *Qiṣaṣ al-Anbiyāʾ*, Cairo 1937, p. 277.

[2] Comp. Mann, *Jews*, I, p. 252 n. 1; Baron, *SRH* V, p. 310 n. 48.

[3] Comp. Mann, *Jews*, II, p. 156, l. 14.

Baghdad. He went to the Maghreb and settled in Kairouan, where he was received with all the honours due to his rank: "It was customary in Kairouan for the chief, Mar ʿUqba, to have a seat of honour reserved for him in the synagogue next to the ark, and after a priest and a Levi had read their portion of the Tora, the Tora scroll would be handed down to him.[1] Nevertheless, neither Mar ʿUqba nor his descendants were appointed negidim of African Jewry. Those were the last days of the rule of the Aghlabids, who bore formal allegiance to Baghdad and were reluctant to do anything contrary to the wishes of the caliph who had banished the exilarch. After the Aghlabids were ousted (in 909), power was assumed by the Fāṭimids, who did not at once concern themselves with Jewish affairs and, when they did so, were not interested in the descendants of the Baghdadi Exilarch, but found a reliable supporter of their dynasty in Paltiel.[2]

The other problem is the silence of our sources on the establishment of the nagidship in Kairouan, already referred to above. Precisely from the late tenth century, these sources are comparatively rich, increasing our knowledge of other fields of Jewish social life in the region. If the appointment of the nagid of Kairouan had been a public political act, similar to the elevation of Paltiel or the appointment of Jacob b. Jau it would undoubtedly have left its mark in the sources. Here, too, the explanation is provided by the political background. When the Fāṭimids moved to Egypt, they left the actual rule of North Africa to emirs of the House of Zīrī, who at first were their faithful vassals.[3] So long as this tie was not severed, Paltiel, the nagid in Fusṭāṭ, and his successors were theoretically negidim for the whole of the Fāṭimid-controlled area. Under these circumstances, the appointment of a nagid in Kairouan by the Banū Zīrī and his acceptance by the Jews would have been interpreted as an unfriendly act both at the Caliph's court in Egypt and in the Egyptian nagid's circle; the Egyptian nagid would certainly have refrained from helping the North Africans in times of need—not out of vengefulness, but because they would themselves have said that he had no call to do so as they had a nagid of their own.

---

[1] Abraham b. Nathan of Lunel, *Sefer ha-Manhig*, Hilkhot Shabbat, fol. 26a no. 58; also *MJC* II, pp. 78-79. About the background: Mann, *Tarbiẓ*, 5 (1936), p. 148.

[2] Joseph Sambari's story (*MJC* I, pp. 115-116) of a Baghdadi princess suggesting the establishment in Egypt of a scion of the exilarchic dynasty is therefore unacceptable; comp. Baron, *SRH* V, p. 309 n. 45.

[3] For this chapter in the history of Tunisia comp. Marçais, *Berbérie*, pp. 156-162; Gautier, *Passé*, pp. 374-375.

The Date of the Establishment of the Nagidship

It has been suggested that a contemporary of Paltiel, viz. Joseph, the father of R. Yehuda (surnamed *Allūf* and *Rēsh Sidrā*, and a well-known personality already in the late tenth century) was the first nagid in Kairouan.[1] This was inferred from a few words in a rhetorically styled laudatory epistle from the Gaon Hay to Yehuda, "our beloved, who is *allūf* and rēsh *sidrā*". In that letter, we read:

> And your father, the lord and chief (*sālār*) of his people—May our God grant him long life and quickly fulfil all his hopes.

Sālār in Persian means elder, prince, chief, "general" leader, judge or any person in high office. Hay may have used this expression for the sake of the verse, but is seems more likely that the choice of a foreign word, uncommon in the Maghreb, was intended to impress the reader. In any case, it is noteworthy and revealing that Hay does not here mention the title nagid, although we find it in a poem he composed in honour of the Nagid Abraham.[2]

Here is the closing passage of a fascicle of responsa sent by Sherira and Hay to R. Yehuda ben Joseph; it, too, makes no mention of the nagidship of either Joseph or Yehuda, in spite of all the praise it lavishes on the latter: "And you, my lord Yehuda *Rōsh Kalla*, (college head), son of my master and rabbi Joseph, who have asked these questions. May the Merciful illuminate your eyes with the light of the Tora. And may he gird you with strength and power to interpret its difficulties. And may he support your studious efforts to hew out steps to wisdom, and may he disclose and elucidate treasures of darkness, hidden riches, to you in your learning. And may he raise the banner of the Tora through you. And may he lend you valour in the battle of the Tora. May he go before you and make the crooked places straight. May you break in pieces the gates of brass and cut in sunder the bars of iron. And may thy fountains be dispersed abroad, and rivers of water in the street. May you inherit substance, and may he fill your treasures. And may your stem blossom

---

[1] Comp. Mann, *Texts* I, p. 116; but Baron, *op. cit.*, p. 309, no. 46, does not accept this suggestion.

[2] Comp. Ginzberg, *Geonica* II, p. 278 l. 3; Mann, *Texts* I, p. 129; Brody, *RIHP* 3 (1937), p. 38 l. 57. It should be noted that R. Solomon b. Yehuda, along with the title *sālār*, uses another Persian title: *dustūr*, nobleman; comp. Mann, *Jews*, II, pp. 140 ll. 28, 30; 155 l. 10; Also *ibid.*, p. 376, and Assaf, *Studies in Memory . . . Gulak and Klein*, Jerusalem 1942, p. 26. Gardizī who wrote in Persian (c. 1050), so describes the commander of the Khazars; comp. D. M. Dunlop, *The History of the Jewish Khazars*, 1954, p. 107.

and bud and the face of world be full of fruit. And these questions were noted down and written out in the month of Kislev of the year 1308 of the Seleucid era" (997 C.E.).[1]

Since the office of nagid was hereditary, the assumption of Joseph's nagidship would entitle us to suppose that his son Yehuda was also a nagid, especially as we find a verse similar to the above in a poem by an unknown author, who was probably referring to Yehuda *Rēsh Sidrā*:

> And God, the God of Israel, raised up, to save us, a redeemer like a prince in Judah,
> Yehuda ben Joseph, the God-appointed chief, who bares his arm and gathers in the children of the desolate woman.[2]

To disprove the assumption that Joseph and his son Yehuda were negidim, it is not sufficient to declare that the words of R. Hay and the unknown poet are rhetorical flourishes. After all, everything we know about Paltiel himself derives from a family chronicle by one of his kinsmen, which, too, is full of rhetoric and anecdotes. But reference may be made to the political situation, as described above, which did not permit the appointment of an independent nagid. Yet, there is even more evidence that those two were not negidim appointed by the Muslim government.

R. Ḥushiel, in his letter from Kairouan to R. Shemaryahu ben Elḥanan in Fusṭāṭ, reports that Rabbana Yehuda (ben Joseph) had suddenly had to go to the political centre of the Banū Zīrī, Mahdiya (thus the correct reading) apparently on urgent public business. The letter mentions also Rabbana Joseph ben Berakhya and Rabbana Abraham the son of Rabbana Nathan, each of whom played a very important part in the life of the Jews in the Banū Zīrī state. But R. Ḥushiel describes none of them by the title nagid.[3]

Two of the letters of Joseph ben Berakhya, the representative of Pumbeditha in Kairouan, to Joseph ben 'Awkal in Fusṭāṭ, an official of Babylonian Academy in Egypt, mention the nagid and Yehuda ben Joseph.[4] The first letter speaks of the activities of the *negīd ha-gōlā* Abū

---

[1] *RH* no. 442, at the end; comp. *ibid.*, no. 434, at the beginning, and nos. 207 and 208.

[2] Schirmann, *MGWJ*, 32 (1932), p. 348; Assaf, *Gaonica*, p. 220; Mann, *Tarbiẓ*, 5 (1934), pp. 301-304. Isaac ibn Khalfūn likewise composed a poem in praise of Yehuda ben Joseph; comp. Mirski, *Ibn Khalfūn*, pp. 71-73. Yehuda exchanged letters with the Gaon Solomon b. Yehuda; comp. Goldziher *REJ* 50 (1905), p. 184 l. 15.

[3] Comp. Schechter, *JQR*, o.s. 11 (1899/1900), pp. 647ff., esp. 649 and 650.

[4] Published by Assaf, *Tarbiẓ*, 20 (1950), pp. 177-187. Comp. esp. letter i, ll. 5, 12,

Isḥāq, *i.e.* R. Abraham ben ʿAṭā (= Nathan in Hebrew), who went to the Maghreb and returned from there safely two months later on successfully completing his mission. Now that he has returned, so the letter goes on, it will be possible to conclude several matters, which have been pending for two years, in connection with the raising of contributions for the Academies in Babylonia and Palestine. In the margin of the letter, Joseph adds that Yehuda b. Joseph is ill in Mahdiya. In the second letter, Joseph feelingly bemoans the death of "the excellent lord, our nagid and *negīd ha-gōla*", and mentions incidentally that Yehuda ben Joseph, who was the support and shield of those near to him, died in the same year. On comparing what is said of these two, we conclude without a shadow of doubt that Yehuda ben Joseph never held the official position of nagid. He was a rabbinical scholar and man of action, and undoubtedly engaged in many activities for the good of his brethren, near and far. But he was not appointed nagid in the official sense of the term.

Abraham b. ʿAṭā

To all appearance, Abraham ben Nathan—ʿAṭā was the first nagid officially appointed by an emir of the Banū Zīrī dynasty. It seems that he came of a distinguished family. In a letter he calls his father "Head of the Communities", which suggests that he was the representative of the Babylonian Academies.[1] Abraham's appointment seems to have taken place unobtrusively between the date of R. Ḥushiel's above-discussed letter (early eleventh century) and that of Joseph ben Berakhya's first letter. The time may perhaps be narrowed down even further. The ruler of the eastern Maghreb (Tunisia and Algeria) was then the Emir Bādīs (996-1016). During the early part of his reign he was still loyal to the Fāṭimid Caliph al-Ḥākim bi-Amr Allāh (996-1021), ill-famed for his oppression—which bore all the marks of madness—of Jews and Christians during the second half of his rule; al-Ḥākim bi-Amr Allāh lived in a world of fantasies. The Jews in the Fāṭimid caliphate were seized with fear. Moreover, the Banū Zīrī dynasty split at that time into two branches. The seceding branch tore off part of the emirate and established its centre of government in Qalʿat Ḥammād, whither Jews

17 and 18, and the scholion l. 1: letter ii, ll. 5-18, 22 and 23. For the historical background comp. above, ch. II, pp. 78ff. (Hebrew).

[1] Comp. Goitein, *Tarbiẓ*, 34 (1965), pp. 164-169. In the letter, Abraham mentions his grandfather's burial in Jerusalem; he describes himself as "*negīd ha-gōlā*, Abraham b. Nathan (and not, as more usual, ʾAṭā), Head of the Communities."

at once began to stream. These circumstances may have provided Bādīs with a suitable opportunity to appoint a nagid for the Jews without having to worry about the caliph's possible reaction, and thereby to win the sympathies of the Jews within and outside his country. If this reasoning is correct, Abraham was appointed in the years 1010-1011 approximately, for in a letter of the end of 1014 we read about his efforts on behalf of the academies two years earlier and see him at the height of his activity by the side of the Emir Bādīs upon the latter's marching against the Banū Ḥammād, the secessionist members of his family.[1] We know that Abraham was physician-in-ordinary to Bādīs and as such accompanied him on his expeditions. It is easy to imagine that one of his tasks was to win the Jews for the Emir of Kairouan. Abraham was physician also to Muʿizz ibn Bādīs, who had surely been attended by him while still crown prince.[2]

Hay addressed a letter in verse to Abraham also, concluding with the words: "Nagid of peoples, head of their sanhedrins and rabbi and chief (*sālār*) of the elders of the Jews."[3]

Joseph b. Berakhya, in his first above-mentioned letter to Joseph ben ʿUkkāl in Fusṭāṭ, speaks of Hay's admiration for Abraham, as revealed in his letters to the Kairouan community and to Abraham himself. The title by which Hay describes the nagid, "chief of the elders of the Jews", is no figure of speech, as we shall see below.[4]

The nagid of Kairouan was highly esteemed also by the gaon of Sura. At the nagid's request, R. Israel ben Samuel ben Ḥofni, who acceded to the gaonate in 1017, wrote a book entitled *Kitāb fī Wujūb al-Ṣalāt*, the dedication of which reads as follows: "A *Book on the Duty of Prayer*, composed by Israel ha-Kohen Gaon, the son of our master Samuel ha-Kohen Gaon ben Gaon, for the illustrious elder, the oriflamme of religion and crown of the nation, Mar R. Abraham *negīd ha-gōlā*, the son of Mar R. Nathan, the head of the communities, may the just man's memory be blessed; he composed it for him because he had commanded it and his command had seemed important to him."[5]

In view of these words of praise from the heads of the two Babylonian academies, it is not surprising that Isaac b. Khalfūn, a roving minstrel

[1] Goitein, *Zion*, 27 (1962), p. 162, surmises that Abraham b. ʿAṭā was appointed nagid by Hay in 1012; comp. also *ibid.*, pp. 22 and 23.

[2] Comp. Idris, *AIEO*, 13 (1955), pp. 55 and 56.

[3] Comp. Brody, *RIHP* III (1937), p. 31.

[4] Assaf, *Tarbiẓ* 20 (1950), p. 179 ll. 11-13.

[5] Mann, *JQR*, 11 (1920/21), pp. 415, 431 and 432; Davidson, *JQR* (1910/11), pp. 239-242.

whose art was his livelihood, should have made the nagid the subject of a glowing panegyric. B. Khalfūn visited Kairouan, saw the nagid in his splendour, enjoyed his liberality and, as a mark of appreciation and gratitude, wrote the poem "When my heart remembers its experiences". The poem concludes with a self-appraisal of the author, who knew the power of his pen, and a gentle admonition to the nagid not to be chary of his gifts—he does not always seem to have responded to Khalfūn's solicitations—because man does not live forever.[1]

This is a specimen of a literary genre highly developed in Arabic literature since olden times (*madḥ*, *i.e.* praise) and the purpose (*qaṣd*) of which was to stimulate the generosity of the person praised. This genre began to develop then in Jewish literature, too, with Khalfūn as its first avowed representative.

The Nagid Jacob b. ʿAmram

We suppose that the nagid Abraham died about the year 1020. We do not know whether Jacob b. ʿAmram, the second of the Kairouan leaders bearing the title nagid, assumed office immediately after Abraham's death or somewhat later, say, in the middle of the twenties, when the Emir al-Muʿizz reached majority. Extant documents permit of no conclusion as to commencement of his tenure.

The Nagid Jacob b. ʿAmram's fame spread beyond the boundaries of the Banū Zīrī state. A rabbinical court in Sicily applied in a certain matter to R. Elhanan ben Ḥushiel (surnamed *beyt dīn*), Jacob ha-Nagid and all the worthy elders in Mahdiya, regarding them as rescuers, whom God had raised up "to close their gaps and mend their cracks".[2]

The beginning of another letter to that nagid has been preserved: "From Yeḥezkiyahu, Head of the Exiles of All Israel, the son of David the son of Yeḥezkiyahu, Head of the Exiles of All Israel. To our mighty and noble Nagid, Master and Rabbi Jacob, leader of the hosts of Israel, who was raised up for them in their exile and given to them as a shelter from the enemy who oppresses them, an eternal light to flee to, an iron pillar to lean upon and a brazen wall to shield them, to close gaps and strengthen the fence, and to endear the Tora to its students by the honour he accords them, his bountiful gifts, the tables he lays for those of them who are near, his bread which is laid on the tables of those of them who are far and the sumptuous garments in which he clothes them: fine linen,

[1] Mirski, *Ibn Khalfūn*, pp. 63-66.
[2] Comp. Mann, *JQR*, 9 (1918/19), pp. 175 and 176.

silk, and embroidered work. Their sucklings suck his milk, their babes grow up on his dainties, mention of him is like wine in the mouths of their young men, their middle-aged men are glad and proud of his love, their old men pray for his life. May the Almighty prolong it; may he add days to his days, and may his years span many generations; may he give the upper hand of his enemies, and may all his adversaries be cut off; may he rule over many nations (*goyim*), and may they not rule over him; and may he lend him grace before the king and his counsellors and commanders and mighty men. He is great in the king's house like Bilshan (a prodigious polygot according to the Talmud);[1] he is famous in all countries; for he is (the son of) the master and rabbi ʿAmram, may he be remembered for blessing, resurrection and everlasting peace."[2]

The letter is undated. Yeḥezkiyahu acceded to the Babylonian exilarchate before 1021, and after Hay's death questions were addressed to him as they had previously been to the head of the academy.

The exilarch's words to the nagid were not empty phrases. The latter's efforts on behalf of Kairouan Jewry in an emergency are attested by a letter of the year 1037, approximately, from R. Solomon ben Yehuda, Gaon of the Palestinian Academy, to R. Ephraim ben Shemaryahu in Fusṭāṭ: "As for the Kairouan community, a hand was outstretched against them. Their enemies would have overpowered them but for the mercy of the All-Merciful .... helped somewhat; it was the Nagid Rabbenu Jacob, may (God) set him up on high, may the star of Jacob shine in his days."[3]

The nagid is referred to without mention of his name in a letter from Kairouan of the middle of Ab, 1346 S.E. (1035 C.E.), likewise addressed to R. Ephraim b. Shemaryahu. The writer wishes to excuse the nagid for not having replied to a letter from Ephraim: the messenger may not have carried out his mission, so that the letter never reached its destination. The fact that this point was not cleared up at once shows that the writer and the nagid were not in the same place. The writer subsequently refers to a consignment of money from Mahdiya for the academy in Palestine and which the Gaon Solomon ben Yehuda had seized: "I have been told that a letter has arrived from the nagid in Mahdiya saying that he sent a man with money—some 60 pieces of gold—in order that all the members of the *ḥabūra* (*i.e.* the Academy) might benefit from it, but that the head of the Academy took it for himself, so that all were left empty-handed and

[1] Comp. Men, 65b, Meg. 13b: PdRE, chap. 50.
[2] Comp. Mann, *Texts* I, pp. 183, 184 and 179.
[3] Comp. Mann, *Jews* II, p. 163.

came away from him disappointed. If God decrees that I meet with the nagid after his arrival from Mahdiya, he will tell me the truth of the matter."[1] We have already seen, in connection with the activities of Abraham b. Nathan, that it was one of the functions of the nagid to determine the apportionment of the amounts collected for the academies.

The nagid's sphere of operations was quite extensive. In addition to his official duties towards his community and the authorities, which obliged him to pay frequent and lengthy visits to Mahdiya, where political life was concentrated, he, like his predecessor, concerned himself with the requirements of the academies both in Palestine and Babylonia.

Just as the date of commencement of Jacob b. ʿAmram's tenure as nagid is not ascertainable, our sources provide no indication of its length. The latest known document mentioning the Nagid Jacob by name is of 1041;[2] but later information concerning him may yet come to light. The publication of Geniza fragments may still yield surprises in this respect.

We have seen that in a particular matter the rabbinical court of Sicily linked the Nagid Jacob with R. Ḥananel, who headed the court of Kairouan at that time; Ḥananel may already have been the official representative of the Academy of Pumbaditha, a respected position which he held in his old age. The nagid was moreover assisted by elders, who played a specific part in the management of communal affairs. It was not without definite intent that Hay described Joseph, Yehuda's father, as *sālār*, *i.e.* chief, leader, and the Nagid Abraham as "*sālār* of the elders of the Jews"; and the Sicilian court addressed itself to R. Elḥanan- Ḥananel, the nagid and "the worthy elders" in Mahdiya. It should be noted that Mahdiya had only a small Jewish community at the time since most of the Jews were still living in Kairouan. But Mahdiya must nevertheless have been the place of assembly and official seat of the elders.

We possess a letter from a nagid of Kairouan extending greetings "from us, the *Negid ha-Gola*, the Light of Israel... and the Elders and the rest of our community, the members of the community of Kairouan." It is significant that just as the Geonim of Babylonia and Palestine, in their greetings, mentioned the names of those next to them in authority immediately after their own names, thus the nagid conveys the greetings of the elders immediately after his own.[3]

---

[1] *Ibid.*, I, pp. 123 n. 1 and 124.

[2] Comp. Goitein, *Zion* 27 (1962), pp. 13-15.

[3] Catalogue of Hebrew Manuscripts in the Collection of E. N. Adler, no. 4009, facsimile 5; comp. Mann, *Texts* I, p. 47.

Contacts between the negidim of Kairouan and the academies were not confined to matters of donations. Among the responsa of the Geonim, we find some relating to questions addressed to them from Kairouan in the name of the nagid. Neither the questions nor the answers indicate which nagid is meant, and it has been suggested that the reference is to Samuel ha-Nagid in Spain. The author of the *Sefer ha-Qabbala* indeed tells us that Samuel ha-Nagid drew upon the wisdom of Hay along with that of Rabbenu Nissim of Kairouan. But we have seen that the negidim of Kairouan were held in high esteem at the Babylonian academies and frequently received responsa and epistles from there, and it is therefore possible that questions asked from Kairouan or by Kairouan people were asked in the name of the Kairouan negidim. The point remains in doubt.[1]

The Decline of the Nagidhood

The destruction of Kairouan in the middle of the 11th century compelled its merchants to move to Mahdiya, which since its establishment, and especially in the days of the Banū Zīrī, had been a second capital and stronghold of the country's rulers. During the period under discussion, that city had a rabbinical court, and its Jewish merchants and agents participated in the developing trade with India.[2] A Geniza document of slightly prior to 1062 reports that Tunisian merchants in Egypt collected donations for the nagid, who at that time was somewhere west of Mahdiya. His name is not mentioned, and we do not know whether the reference is to Jacob b. ʿAmram, who may or may not have yet been alive. More likely his successor is meant.[3] A request by the nagid and community elders of Kairouan for help in redeeming captives probably dates from the time of the decline of Kairouan and the impoverishment of its population, when the latter was no longer able to fulfil that religious duty unaided.[4] From the late 11th century onwards, documents no longer mention the Kairouan negidim. The political position of the Banū Zīrī was tottering at that time; their power dwindled, until at last they controlled only a small section of the region. Under these circumstances, there was no room for the appointment of a nagid for the Jews, and be it only as the

---

[1] Comp. *RH*, no. 227 and Harkavy's remarks *ibid.*, p. 362; *Qohelet Shelomo*, p. 71, and Mann's amendment *Tarbiẓ* 6 (1935), p. 240; *SHQ*, p. 57/77.

[2] Comp. below, p. 225.

[3] Comp. Goitein, *Zion* 27 (1962), p. 19.

[4] Comp. Wertheimer, *Ginzey Yerushalayim*, 1901, II, pp. 17b-18a.

holder of a title devoid of practical significance. Just as the office of *negid ha-gola* in Kairouan had arisen out of certain political conditions, it disappeared again when these conditions ceased.

The Organization of the Rabbinical Courts

We know the organization of rabbinical courts and the modes of appointment of *dayyānīm* (rabbinical judges) in Egypt and Babylonia in the Gaonic period. The heads of the Palestinian Acedemy appointed *dayyānīm* in Palestine and in communities of Palestinians resident in Egypt and subject to their jurisdiction.[1] In Babylonia, appointments seem at first to have been a prerogative of the exilarch, but in the course of time a change occurred; Nathan ha-Kohen's account of the Babylonian Academies contains an instructive description of how the exilarch and the heads of the academies appointed *dayyānīm* and for what reasons they removed them from office.[2] A later source reports that the "grand court" in Babylonia, that is to say, the gaon, appointed the *dayyānīm*. Both Academies had grand courts, before which any matter could be brought directly, without recourse to a lower court.[3] The position was no doubt similar in the area of the exilarch.

We have no direct information (descriptions of court procedure, official missives, letters of appointment) as to the mode of appointment of *dayyānīm* in North Africa. The remoteness of the Maghreb from the centres in Palestine and Babylonia and its political independence of the Muslim governments in Cairo and Baghdad make it impossible to assume a parallel situation. Although a most lively correspondence was conducted between the Maghreb and those centres on matters of Tora, *halakha* and commerce, there is no hint in it that Jewish (or non-Jewish) authorities at those centres had any legal power or standing in determining the organization of North African Jewish communities. Fortunately, certain —though indirect—references to this subject are contained in questions sent from the region to the Babylonian Geonim and in the latter's responsa, as well as in the Geniza material. The same sources also include

---

[1] Comp. the letter of the Nasi and Gaon Daniel b. ʿAzarya, Mann, Jews II, p. 216 ll. 9-12; also *ibid.*, p. 217 ll. 13-15. For appointments in Egypt comp. Schechter, *Saadyana*, p. 113 ll. 47 and 48; Mann, Jews I, pp. 126 and 127; also *ibid.*, II, p. 345. Comp. also *Sefer ha-Yishub* II, Introd., pp. 32 and 33.

[2] Comp. *RShT*, no. 217; *MJC* II, pp. 85 and 86.

[3] *RH*, no. 180 and Harkavy's annot. *ibid.*, pp. 355 and 356; see also below, pp. 221 and n. 1. *RHG* no. 20 mentions a total of four courts in the two academies; comp. Aptowitzer, *JQR*, 4 (1913/14), pp. 31ff., esp. pp. 35ff.

numerous court decisions, witnesses' depositions etc. enabling us to discern the organization of Maghreb rabbinical courts. From them, we can gather information not only as to Africa, but also as to the organization of courts in other countries—such as Spain, Italy, Byzantium and the Arab Peninsula—which were not under the direct jurisdiction of exilarchs and academy heads.

In this connection, we should note that a different situation prevailed in Egypt, which maintained very close relations with both Palestine and Babylonia. Just as the local communities of Palestinians obeyed the Palestinian Geonim, thus the Babylonians accepted the authority of the Babylonian Academies; the Babylonian synagogue in Fusṭāṭ was named after the academy of the Gaon Hay.[1] Egypt only emerged from this inferior position in the 12th century, when it established independent academies. The appointment of *dayyānīm* began at the same time.[2]

Rabbinical Courts in Different Localities

On the basis of court decisions, we are able to say that rabbinical courts existed at that time in the following communities west of Egypt (in geographical order, from west to east): 1. Tripoli; 2. Kairouan; 3. Qābes; 4. Majāna; 5. Mīgzar; 6. Qal'a(t Ḥammād); 7. Sijilmāsa; 8. Mahdiya (when after the destruction of Kairouan it had become also a commercial centre). We may suppose that important communities such as Tāhert, Tlemcen and Fez also had rabbinical courts, with an organization similar to that in those first-mentioned localities. A question addressed to Hay Gaon indicates the existence of a rabbinical court in an unnamed city.[3]

1. Tripoli

A question was addressed from Egypt to a *nāsī* and Gaon in Palestine (probably Daniel b. Azarya) concerning the goods of two partners which had been on a ship travelling from Alexandria to Sicily. The partner who had been accompanying the goods had fallen ill and died, and been burried at sea. When the ship reached Tripoli, the local rabbinical court (*beyt-dīn al-balad wa-l-shuyūkh*) had seized all the goods in order to secure the share of the heirs of the deceased. In the further part of the document, it appears that the Gaon, the "rabbinical grand court", could order the court in Egypt to administer an oath to the living partner, but that the

[1] Mann, *Texts* I, p. 139.
[2] Comp. Baron, *SRH* V, p. 42.
[3] Comp. *RH*, no. 180.

court in Tripoli was not subject to the authority of the Palestinian Gaon.[1]

We are thus confronted with two important facts: a. The attachment of the goods was effected by the local rabbinical court and elders: b. the rabbinical grand court in Palestine was not competent to interfere with the decisions of the court in Tripoli. What applied to Tripoli must have applied even more to Kairouan and places west of it.

2. Kairouan

The earliest indication of the existence of rabbinical courts in Kairouan and Majāna dates from the third quarter of the 9th century C.E. A Babylonian gaon was asked to give an opinion as to the validity of a decision of a court in Kairouan. The case is interesting, and it is worthwhile to present it here, as it enlightens us on various matters. A man had died in Kairouan, and the court of that city had appointed an administrator for his property in Majāna and informed the court there accordingly. The administrator went to Majāna, where, after a proclamation by the court, issued as a matter of benevolence, not in strict adherence to the law, he sold the property to an *ashfashandi* (Persian for cook). A deed of sale was made out in the court of Majāna. However, the cook wished to make payment in the court of Kairouan. When his representative arrived in Kairouan with the administrator, a man appeared before the court claiming that he had acquired the property situated in Majāna. The Kairouan court vested the property in him on the grounds that the sale effected in Majāna was invalid since the cook had wished to pay in Kairouan. The gaon was asked whether the Kairouan court had been entitled to sell the property after a deed of sale had been made out in the court of Majāna, although payment had not yet been effected. The gaon (R. Naḥshon or R. Zemaḥ) replied that the Kairouan court had not been entitled to issue a deed of sale to that other man—"they are wrong and the deed should be torn up"; and if that man was a dangerous bully and the annulment of the deed was not practicable, the Kairouan court should compensate the cook for his loss; the rule that a qualified court (*beyt-dīn mūmḥe*) was not liable to pay compensation did not apply in this case because only a court authorized by the *nāsī* or the academy head was qualified.

The gaon's reply shows clearly that the Kairouan court had not in those days the status of a qualified court and that its *dayyānīm* had not been

[1] Comp. *RA* III, pp. 125-127. One of the Tripoli *dayyānīm* is known by name; Assaf, *Sources*, pp. 132 l. 18; 134 l. 59.

authorized by any competent authority. On the other hand, we see that the Geonim had no authority to enforce their decisions upon the court and that the gaon was only asked for a legal opinion.[1]

In the year 4638 (977/8), the court in Kairouan, "a great city in Africa", took evidence in the matter of the sending of some goods from Egypt to Kairouan, which had taken place according to instructions. The record was to be transmitted to Egypt to serve as proof to the sender, who was resident there, in case he was asked to account for the goods, which had been entrusted to him before a court.[2]

Questions addressed to the Babylonian Geonim by Kairouan rabbinical scholars in the late 10th and early 11th century show that the latter were not familiar with court procedure obtaining in Babylonia.

R. Jacob he-Ḥaber [3] ben Mari we-Rabbana Nissim did not know the meaning of the term *beyt-dīn ḥāshūb* (competent court) and had to have it explained to him by the Gaon Sherira: "A court which includes a scholar noted in his locality and its surroundings for his learning. When it is said: 'so-and-so is a *dayyān* in such-and-such a court and many listen to his words in silence', and when, in enumerating the scholars and courts of Israel, he is included, then that court is a *beyt dīn ḥāshūb*."[4]

The scholars of the school of R. Jacob *Rosh Kalla* in Kairouan, in a question to R. Hay in the year 1322 S.E./1011 C.E. (*i.e.* a few years after the death of their master), were wondering how to deal with a man who refused to litigate before an established court which the townspeople had agreed to invoke for the settlement of their disputes. That man claimed the right to select his own *beyt-dīn*. Hay explained that "it is the custom in Babylonia for the grand court to appoint *dayyānīm* in each province, and the *dayyan* receives a letter of authorization called *pitkā dedayyānūtā* in Aramaic . . . And if somebody swears that he will not litigate before a *dayyān* so appointed, he is to be made to appear before him and whipped for his oath, because he (the *dayyān*) is like a grand court. Nevertheless, if the lender demands recourse to a grand court, the borrower is to go with him. . . This (that a party is to be compelled) applies only where the

[1] *RA* II, n. 69 (pp. 23 and 24), also p. 1.

[2] Comp. Mann, *Texts* I, pp. 361-363. For other deeds from Kairouan comp., *e.g.*, Hirschfeld, *JQR*, 16 (1903/04), p. 378; Assaf, *Tarbiẓ*, 9 (1938), p. 215; *idem*, *Sources*, p. 138 ll. 3 and 12. See also Goitein, *Studies in Islamic History and Institutions*, 1966, p. 314; *idem*, *KS*, 41 (1966), pp. 263-76.

[3] Fellow, title of a scholar below *rab*.

[4] *RH*, no. 240. From the fascicle's headline (*ibid.*, no. 230), in which R. Jacob is given no honorific title, we may infer that he was still young at the time. This is also suggested by the stern tone of the reply.

court in that town has been authorized by a court. Courts in distant towns, which have not been appointed by a grand court, are to be considered like *ʿarkhāōt* (offices of gentiles) in Syria, and if somebody declares as the man did you ask about, he cannot be compelled to break his oath, especially if it preceded action by the other side against him . . . But if the man who swears that he will not appear, and who thus infringes communal discipline is an important person, then although he cannot be compelled to break his oath, because of the sacrilege involved, he is to be excommunicated and chastised, so that others may not do like him."[1]

There has also been discovered among the Geniza Fragments a responsum concerning a man who had sworn that he would only litigate before the 'Holy Academy' (of Rab Hay). As correctly surmised by Ginzberg, that responsum, too, was sent to Kairouan, to the same rabbis and at the same time. Both were in the same fascicle of responsa, and the fact that they were copied in different collections is accidental. A. Buechler has already pointed out that it was precisely in Kairouan that the Academy of Pumbeditha was called *Metībtā Qadīshtā*, "the Holy Academy".

Here is the text of the question, followed by the responsum: (p. 62) "We asked you how to deal with persons who had sworn not to submit to Jewish jurisdiction and with persons who had sworn not to litigate before the *dayyān* of that town, who had been set over them. And you replied, stating how each category was to be dealt with. Now here is a person who has sworn to litigate only before the 'Holy Academy' and has said to his opponent: Let us write down my contentions and yours and have them witnessed, and send them to the gaon, and let us pledge ourselves not to deviate from what you will ordain in your responsum; if I go back on my pledge, I shall have to pay you twice the amount of your claim and to pay so much to the poor and so much to the Academy. And his opponent has said: You demand referral to the Academy merely in order to put off the determination of my claim, and I will not let you do so. Are we (p. 63) to help the claimant by deciding in his favour and compelling the other man to accept the jurisdiction of his town or are we to help the other man by compelling the claimant to apply jointly with him to the grand court, the gaon. What if the defendant says: I shall provide a guarantor for the amount of the claim pending application to the gaon, and I shall pay what the latter orders me to pay. And what if the plaintiff

[1] *RH*, no. 180; comp. above, p. 217 and n. 3.

says: Let my case be decided by the people of my town, and I shall provide a guarantor for the refund of any balance in favour of the defendant that may be created by an overriding decision of the gaon? Whose request shall we fulfil? Please instruct us."

And here is the responsum:

"This is how we have found this matter decided in the Talmud etc. ... (p. 64). Those people did not wish to resort to the grand court, but to put off the matter until the question reached the grand court. The same is the case in the present instance. Of course, if the grand court is nearby, then, if (p. 65) a question appears necessary, the proceedings may be stayed and a question despatched. And moreover, even in a distant locality, if the local court is in doubt, a question may be addressed to a rabbi who is near.[1] But anyhow, although the debtor in this case is willing to provide a guarantor for the amount to be adjudicated by the grand court, the creditor cannot be compelled to agree to a postponement. One should say to the debtor: Your guarantor is himself in need of a guarantor. Who guarantees the creditor that he will live until the reply arrives from the Academy? He is therefore not obliged to agree to a postponement." [2]

This responsum is both illuminating and practical. It shows clearly that the gaon does not support the party who demands referral of the case to his grand court, as usual in Babylonia. If the legal position is clear to the local court, the demand for referral must be regarded as procrastination; and if a doubt has arisen as to a legal point, there is always a nearby grand court or a rabbi who may be consulted. That is to say, the claim is not to be referred to that grand court or rabbi, but—as R. Hay stresses repeatedly—it or he is to be asked for a legal opinion, which is to guide the local court in its decision. The identity of the nearby grand court or rabbi referred to by R. Hay can only be conjectured. He probably meant the court of R. Shemaryahu ben Elḥanan in Egypt, while the rabbi seems to be R. Ḥushiel in Kairouan, of whom Hay had written in 1006: "We have heard that there is in your locality a man of great wisdom, a mountain of rabbinic learning, at home in the inner compartments of the *halākhā*, Mar Rab Ḥushiel the son of Mar Rab Elḥanan." [3]

[1] The sentence is not clear in the source. I suspect two or three scribe's errors, induced by the preceding mention of the grand court. The emendations are explained in the Hebrew edition, vol. I, p. 364 n. 30.

[2] *Ginzey Schechter* II, pp. 62-65; comp. Ginzberg's Introduction *ibid.*, pp. 47 and 48, and Büchler, *REJ*, 50 (1905), p. 168.

[3] Mann, *Texts* I, p. 120. R. Ḥushiel died in the twenties of the 11th century; *SHQ*,

In another responsum, R. Hay explains to the rabbis of Kairouan, with reference to his book *Mishpetey ha-Shebuōt* (Law of Oaths), under what circumstances a debtor who pleads insolvency is sworn, how he is excommunicated, when a ban for contempts of court is pronounced and how those presumed poor are declared so. We have to do here with a whole set of provisions relating to civil procedure, legal aid and the legal relevance of social conditions.[1]

R. Yehuda *Rōsh Kalla* the son of *Mārī Rabbānā* Joseph, being uncertain as to the rules governing corporal punishment asked R. Hay to explain them to him. It may be supposed that he had a practical interest in the reply, perhaps because he was a *dayyān* in Kairouan.[2]

Several documents indicate that Rabbanu Ḥananel the son of Ḥushiel was the head of a *beyt-dīn* in Kairouan. His name is mentioned in a court decision given before him in the year 4792 (1032). Once, when presented with a question concerning a Tora scroll that had been stolen, he is addressed as "Great Rabbi, Head of the Court and School Head". Another time, in a letter from Sicily, he is given the title *beyt-dīn*.

R. Ḥananel was undoubtedly a qualified *dayyan*, and we may suppose that he was ordained *ḥaber* by his father, R. Ḥushiel. But we have no explicit information as to the manner of his appointment as *dayyān*.[3]

3. Qābes

We possess no documents of or concerning the rabbinical court of that city. But we rely on R. Samuel b. Jacob ibn Jāmiʿs statement that he was *dayyān* in Qābes and his father head of the court.[4]

4. Majāna

This was an important city, four days' journey west of Kairouan, with which it maintained close commercial relations. A decision of its rabbinical court is referred to in a question sent to Babylonia in the 9th century.[5]

---

p. 57/77; Eppenstein, *Beiträge zur Geschichte und Literatur*, 1913, p. 105; Aptowitzer, *R. Chuschiel*, p. 26.

[1] *RH*, no. 182; comp. *RSh*, p. 77a no. 32.

[2] *RH*, no. 440; *TR* II, p. 41; comp. also *RShT*, no. 16. On R. Yehuda see above, pp. 209f.

[3] Comp. Hirschfeld, *JQR*, o.s., 16 (1904), p. 578; Mann, *ibid.*, 9 (1918/19), pp. 161, 171 and 175. The letter from Sicily is referred to above, p. 213 n. 2. In all these documents he is called Elḥanan the son of R. Ḥushiel; comp. below, p. 320.

[4] Comp. below, pp. 343-4.

[5] Comp. above, pp. 219f.

5. Mīgzār

On the 10th Sivan, 4798 (1038), according to authenticated testimony, a Jew called Jazā'irī appeared before the elders of the coastal town of Mīgzār, equipped with a power of attorney from a man called Ben al-Sirti (*i.e.* a person from the city of Sirte on the western part of the Gulf of Tripolitania), and demanded a certain amount of money from a resident of Mīgzār, probably as the dowry of the daughter of the man from Sirte. The document was found in the Geniza, and there is reason to believe that both Jazā'irī and Ben al-Sirti lived in Fusṭāṭ at the time. Jazā'irī, travelling to his native city, had been asked by al-Sirti to sue a certain person in Mīgzār (which seems to have been near Algiers (al-Jazā'ir)) and been given a power of attorney for that purpose. The local Jewish community seems to have yet been small, so that it had no *beyt-din* and claims were brought before the elders.[1]

6. Qalʿa(t Banī Ḥammād).

A letter from one Abraham the Ḥaber, the son of ʿAmram, to a man in Ramle says, *inter alia*: "I have written two letters to the Maghreb, to Qalʿa, one to the *dayyān*, may God preserve him, the other to the sons of al-Garāwī, may God protect them, R. Maimon and his brother, ʿAmram the Ḥazzan."[2]

Abraham the Haber seems to have lived in Fusṭāṭ, for, in addition to Qalʿa, he mentions correspondence with Alexandria, Mahdiya and Kairouan. The term Qalʿa *tout court* (i.e. citadel) here undoubtedly means Qalʿat Banī Ḥammād, the capital of the Banū Ḥammād, that branch of the emirs of the house of Zīrī in Kairouan who had split the emirate and set up an independent emirate in the western part of the country. Other Geniza letters, of the second half of the 11th century, mention one Abraham al-Qalʿī, who may be assumed to be our Abraham the Ḥaber.[3] These data permit us to conclude that a rabbinical court existed in Qalʿa by that time at the latest. But it is possible that such a court—perhaps for the whole Banū Ḥammād state—was established there shortly after the founding of the city (1007), when Jews began to flock to the new capital. The community, moreover, had a *ḥazzān*. The *dayyānīm* of Qalʿa gained no distinction whatsoever, and we know

---

[1] Mann, *Texts* I, pp. 465-6, 451 and 452; comp. also above, p. 141 n. 18.
[2] Neubauer-Cowley, *Cat. Bodl.* no. 2878, 12.
[3] Gottheil-Worrell, *Fragments*, letter 33, p. 152 ll. 27 and 28; letter 34, p. 156 l. 7.

nothing about them except the name of Solomon the Dayyan, the son of Formash.[1]

7. Sijilmāsa

We possess a set of questions from R. Joseph ben ʿAmram, "head of the court of the city of Sijilmāsa in the Maghreb, and the rabbis and students there". Joseph ben ʿAmram was a *dayyān* during the persecutions, and a member of the Farḥōn family served in that capacity several years afterwards.[2]

8. Mahdiya

Al-Mahdiya was strategically and politically important from its inception, but only in the second half of the 11th century did it become the centre of Tunisia's economic life, so that its Jewish community felt the need to establish a permanent *beyt-dīn*. At the time this was done, the office of *dayyān* seems to have been a prerogative of the Banū Sigmār family. We know of two, possibly three, members of that family who were *dayyānim* in Mahdiya: R. Labrāṭ the School Head, who lived in the second half of the 11th century, his son Moses the Dayyān and his grandson Labrāṭ the Dayyān. The last-mentioned held office in the late forties of the 12th century, shortly before the occupation of the city by the Almohads, and we may suppose that the line of *dayyānīm* of the Banū Sigmār family in al-Mahdiya ended with him or his successor.[3]

Summary of the Discussion of the Rabbinical Courts

Let us now summarize the data and definite hints supplied by the sources.

Rabbinical courts existed in cities of major political, commercial and social importance, such as the great seaports Tripoli, Mahdiya and Algiers, the centres of intercontinental trade: Kairouan and Sijilmāsa; the emirate capital of Qalʿat Banū Ḥammād; and the mining town of Majāna. Courts of qualified *dayyānīm* or of elders probably existed also in some other no less important places, which, however, maintained no

Letters 3, 12, 22 and 33-35 form one group. Letter 3 is from Abraham the Reader of the Tora to his brother Abū ʿImrān the Reader of the Tora (p. 22, margin). This seems to indicate the identity of Abraham the Ḥaber and Abraham al-Qalʿī.

[1] *SHQ*, p. 58/78.

[2] *RH*, headline before no. 68.

[3] Comp. Hirschberg, *Zion*, 22 (1957), pp. 239-241. Comp. also S. D. Goitein, A letter by Labrat ben Moses ben Sighmar, Dayyan of Al-Mahdiyya, *Tarbiẓ*, 36 (1967), pp. 59-72; also *Sefer ha-Yishub*, II, p. 52 no. 6 about Isaac b. David Sigmar in Fusṭāṭ.

regular ties with Fusṭāṭ, so that no documents relating to their courts have been preserved in the Geniza.

The North African *dayyanīm* were not appointed by authorities outside the region. The beginnings of the courts were modest; even the court of Kairouan in the late 9th century was not regarded as "qualified" by the gaon. We have already referred to questions asked by Kairouan rabbis a hundred years later, which show that they were still not conversant with matters of procedure and competence.[1]

The situation improved in some localities (Kairouan, Sijilmāsa, Tripoli) in the early 11th century, when the courts there were headed by rabbis bearing the title of *beyt-dīn*.[2] Though this title was undoubtedly at first an abbreviation of *ab beyt-dīn*, it acquired in the course of time a special factual significance. The term *rosh* (head) or *ab* (father, president) implies that there were still other members, while *beyt-dīn* or *beyt-dīn gādōl* as the title of a person means that he represented the whole of the court, whether he was a qualified *dayyān* sitting alone or whether there were two or even six assessors. So the title *beyt-dīn* meant a *dayyān* whose powers were actually wider than those of an *ab beyt-dīn*, whose colleagues were rabbinical scholars like him. In Iraq and Palestine *beyt-dīn gādōl* meant the gaon.[3] This cannot be an abbreviation of *ab beyt-dīn ha gādōl* (the title *rōsh beyt-dīn ha-gādōl* was not in use at all) because the *ab* was always second after the gaon and usually his successor. The transfer of the name of an institution (*beyt-dīn* court; *beyt-dīn ha-gādōl*—grand court) to a person has a parallel in the title *sultān*, which originally meant authority, government, and then came to mean ruler, sultan. The elders who sat with a *beyt-dīn* in monetary cases or gave decisions without a qualified *dayyān* were not *ḥabērīm*, i.e. accredited rabbinical scholars, fit to be qualified *dayyānīm*, or *talmīdīm*, i.e. *talmideyḥakhāmīm* (rabbinical students), fit to be accredited, but notables whose

[1] Comp. also *RH*, nos. 178, 233 and 180; *RSh*, p. 84b no. 4 (according to Müller, *Mafteaḥ*, pp. 18 and 191 (n. 114), this responsum is by Sherira). For the authority of the Gaon in Babylonia-Iraq comp. Ginzberg, *Geonica* I, pp. 6ff.

[2] In addition to instances quoted by Goitein, *JQR*, 43 (1952), p. 61 n. 1; *idem*, *Kaplan Jubilee Volume* (Hebrew Section), 1953, p. 58 n. 39; and Hirschberg, *Eretz Israel*, 5 (1958), p. 217 n. 44, *beyt-dīn* as the title of a person is attested in material quoted by Schechter, *Berliner Jubilee Volume*, 1903, p. 108 (twice); Mann, *JQR*, 9 (1918/19), p. 175 (*Elḥanan beyt-dīn*); and idem, *Texts* I, p. 466 (*Zakkai ha-dayyān ha-muflā, beyt-dīn hāgūn*; Zakkai's son and grandson are only described as *dayyānīm*).

[3] *RH*, no. 180 (comp. above, p. 217, n. 3 and p. 221, n. 1); also "I the *bayit ha-gādōl*", *JQR*, 9 (1918/, pp. 151 and 152. In later times, R. Naharāy, in Egypt, assumed the title *beyt-dīn ha-gādōl*; Goldziher, *REJ*, 55 (1908), pp. 54-56.

practical experience of monetary affairs might be greater than the *dayyān*'s, but who lacked the theoretical knowledge of civil law based on rabbinical jurisprudence.[1] When elders sat alone, without rabbinical scholars, their decision was not sufficiently reliable—"because they are not learned and may therefore be mistaken" [2]—to warrant resort to a non-Jewish court, which was a grave step. On the other hand, the Gaon Sherira, in a responsum apparently addressed to North Africa, writes that resort to a Gentile court is permitted and even required in the event of non-compliance with a judgment given, in the words of the question, "in a locality where there is no permanent *dayyān* and where a Jew claims a loan or a deposit or an inheritance from another man and has sued him before the elders, the *talmīdīm* and the notables (*ṭobey hā-ʿīr*) and they have ordered the defendant to pay what is due from him by rights, and he refuses to do so"; this permission is given "even if the person robbed is a Gentile and the robber a Jew". In this case, the presence of *talmīdīm* was the deciding factor.[3]

The elders mentioned in connection with a "*beyt-dīn*",[4] *i.e.* a *dayyān*, sat with him, as in Babylonia, where the *dayyān*, on arriving at his place of sitting, "selects two of the inhabitants of the place to cooperate with him in all the judgments which he is to give."[5] At the same time, it should not be forgotten that according to Babylonian practice (attested to by Hay), the *dayyān* appointed by the *beyt-dīn gādōl i.e.* by the gaon, is the main factor, "equivalent to the *beyt-dīn*" by whose authority he is acting.[6]

The procedure of the appointment of *dayyānīm* is unknown. They may have been appointed by the nagid while there was such a dignitary in North Africa or by the academy head of Kairouan during the golden age of that city. We know from Abraham ben Daud's report that an Umayyad caliph set Jacob ibn Jau over all the Jews in Spain and in Morocco as far as Sijilmāsa, "that he might judge all of them and be permitted to appoint for them whomsoever he wished", and this surely included also the appointment of *dayyānīm* in the different localities.[7] We moreover hear incidentally that R. Joseph ibn Megās granted letters

---

[1] For "people" who served as judges where there was no appointed court see *RSh*, p. 90a no. 29; also above, p. 224n. 1.

[2] Comp. *RH*, no. 233.

[3] *RSh*, p. 84b no. 4 (comp. above, p. 226, n. 1).

[4] Comp. above, p. 219 and n. 1.

[5] *RH*, no. 178.

[6] Comp. *MJC* II, p. 85; *RH*, no. 180.

[7] *SHQ*, p. 51/69.

of appointment to his students.[1] It seems plausible that in the Maghreb the local elders—who will be discussed separately—assumed the functions of a permanent *beyt-dīn* or selected a *beyt-dīn* of laymen. R. Hay was once asked what to do with a *dayyān* who wronged the poor. He replied most forcefully: "As to your question concerning *dayyānīm* who put in pawn the beds of the poor and articles not legally pawnable, you must not enforce their decisions. May the breath of life depart from these *dayyānīm*; they are *dayyānīm* of Sodom, robbers and extortioners, of whom it is written: ye have eaten up the vineyard; the spoil of the poor is in your houses (Is 3:14). Word should therefore be passed concerning them to all your neighbours and places near to you, so as to bring them into disrepute and stop them from being your judges, for they heed not the Tora and the words of our Rabbis, of blessed memory. Since you know the law of the Tora and the precepts of the Rabbis, you should hold thorough consultations and select from amongst you godfearing men, solicitous of the honour of the Tora, and set them over you. You should have no hesitation about this."[2]

Incidentally, we cannot, in view of this evidence, entirely dismiss the charge levelled against the rabbis by the Karaite Sahl ha-Kohen ben Maslīaḥ (lived in Palestine in the middle of the loth century) "that they treat them (their coreligionists) arrogantly and domineeringly by means of excommunication, ban and appeal to the Gentile authorities, that they punish the poor, compel them to borrow at interest, and take what is theirs and give it to the rulers, who in turn protect them." The Karaites, who in their beginnings were a fanatical sect, were probably more successful in maintaining internal discipline than the Rabbanite majority. This seems to have been what prompted Sahl ben Maslīaḥ's attack.[3]

Hay's responsum was obviously addressed to a country where the appointment and dismissal of *dayyānīm* were not handled as in Babylonia or Palestine. We may thus suppose that it was addressed to the Maghreb. A similar situation to that described in the question is referred to in a story contained in the *Fine Book of Comfort* of a dead man who testifies about himself: "I was a rich man and a *dayyān*, I was one of the leaders of the people, and I favoured the rich and killed the poor."[4]

Not all *dayyānīm* were rich, however. In one question, we find that a

[1] Comp. Hirschberg, *J. F. Baer Jubilee Volume*, 1960, pp. 143 l. 19, 151 and 152 ll. 19 and 20.

[2] *RShT*, no. 86.

[3] Comp. Pinsker, *Likkutey Qadmoniyot*, *Nispāḥīm*, pp. 31 and 32; Assaf, *Batey ha-Din we-Sidreyhem*, p. 41 n. 1.

[4] Comp. Hirschberg, *R. Nissim*, p. 140.

community was in doubt whether the income of an endowment destined for synagogue purposes might be used for paying "him who looks after their judicial matters, who had no source of livelihood."[1] The wording of the question suggests that the reference is to a small community, which had no permanent *dayyān*, but only somebody who "looks after their judicial matters", and we can draw no conclusions here as to the situation in the major cities. We know, for instance, that Rabbenu Ḥananel, who was a *beyt-dīn* in his city, was rich and certainly needed no salary from the community.[2]

The *dayyānīm* were generally invoked in civil matters and matters of personal status. But once an interesting problem arose concerning the testimony of two men who had been in their respective houses at night after returning drunk from a party, and who thought they had heard the voices of two persons passing behind their houses, one of whom was making a "heretical remark". After an exhaustive analysis, the gaon explains in his responsum that this is not evidence, so that the suspect must be acquitted. Another responsum lays down that no person be put on his oath, as to whether or not he has committed an offence—even if he has a bad reputation, and only specific testimony is lacking—because "a person is close to himself."[3]

Religious Functionaries

Extant literary sources contain no information about holders of religious offices in the Maghreb, such as *ḥazzānīm* and *sheliḥey ṣibbūr*. Only incidentally do we come across some persons from that region whose names have the title *ḥazzān* attached to them, denoting the office they held. In Egypt and Babylonia during that period, the *ḥazzān* had important functions, especially in small communities. He "looked after judicial matters" and at the same time was a preacher, prayer-leader (*shelīaḥ ṣibbūr*) and schoolteacher. He surely had the same functions in the Maghreb.[4] A 15th-century Arab writer in Egypt assigns the *ḥazzān* to the

[1] *RCor*, no. 82.

[2] *SQH*, p. 58/77.

[3] *RCor*, no. 83; *RShT*, no. 7.

[4] The *ḥazzān* of Barqa: Assaf, *Sefer ha-Sheṭarōt*, p. 55; of Mahdiya: Braslavsky, *Zion*, 7 (1941), p. 138 l. 36; of Qalʿa: above, 224; the *ḥazzān* Isaac al-Fāsī: Mann, *Jews* II, p. 113 (no. 30); a *ḥazzān* who uses Arabic (in Kairouan?): *RShT*, no. 152. The "*muqaddam* (leader) of all *ḥazzānīm* in Babylonia" is mentioned in a letter of Hay to Kairouan, Mann, *Texts* I, p. 122 l. 34; comp. also pp. 113 and 151-153. The *ḥazzānīm* in Egypt: Mann, *Jews* I, pp. 268 and 269; Baneth, *Marx Jubilee Volume* 1950, Hebrew section, pp. 75-93; Golb, *JSS*, 20 (1958), pp. 33ff.

second place (after the *ra'īs*, *i.e.* nagid, whom he equates with the *baṭrak*, *i.e.* the Christian patriach) remarking that his functions are like those of the Muslim *khaṭīb* (preacher), who mounts the *minbar* (pulpit) and admonishes the people. The third in rank is, according to him, the *sheliaḥ ṣibbūr*, who leads in prayer like the Muslim *imām*.[1]

Two responsa of the Gaon Hay, to an unspecified destination, deal with *sheliḥey ṣibbūr* who had made themselves a bad name. Here, too, the reference is to small communities, where replacements for the offenders were difficult to find, so that the gaon was inclined to be lenient with them if they repented.[2]

Elders and Ḥashūbīm

We have repeatedly mentioned the elders and local notables (*ḥashūbīm*), and shall meet them again below in rather important functions. Still, we know less about them than about other office-holders. The terms "elder" and *ḥāshūb* are clearly not mere honorific titles, without practical significance. This is borne out by expressions such as "Rabbi So-and So the son of So-and-So the Elder", "Sheikh So-and-So the Elder", "the *beyt-dīn* and the elders consent", "we, the elders and leaders (*sārīm*)", "the scholars (*talmīdīm*) and the elders".[3]

No source indicates how the body described as "the elders" was formed or what its powers were. It is not to be supposed that it was elected. The most likely assumption is that the elders were the heads of the most important and influential families. Support for this view is found in a passage of a letter of an anonymous gaon which mentions a donation made to the academy by the Babylonian elders in Kairouan. These were the heads of the Babylonian families settled in Kairouan.[4]

The elders were a kind of communal management recognised by the authorities, and their task was to provide for the needs of the local community and to fulfil some more general functions, such as the apportionment of the tax burden imposed by the authorities, participation in the sittings of the communal court and assistance in the enforcement of its decisions.[5]

[1] Al-Qalqashandi, *Ṣubḥ al-Aʿshā*, V, p. 474.

[2] *RSh*, nos. 50 and 51.

[3] Assaf, *Sources*, pp. 139/l. 15; 158a l. 1; 160b l. 1; *idem*, *Tarbiẓ*, 9 (1938), p. 196; below, p. 302, in the responsum of R. Zemaḥ, head of the *dayyānīm* at the Exilarchs' court.

[4] Mann, *Texts* I, p. 189.

[5] A donor was not satisfied with a receipt from the Gaon Solomon b. Yehuda, so another had to be given by the elders; Mann, *Jews* II, p. 147 l. 9.

One of their functions, to be discussed below (p. 237), was to appear before a *bey-dō'ār* (non-Jewish court) in order to testify concerning a person who was unwilling to obey a Jewish court. The elders were accredited with the Gentile authorities and testified before the *bey-dō'ār* by public mandate; they were thus not, in this case, what was described by the common term *ḥashūbā b'almā* (mere notable). For how could they have known the particulars of the action, or the pleadings and the judgment, unless they had somehow taken part in the proceedings? It is true that the Geonim Sherira and Hai forbade the elders to testify on the particulars of proceedings conducted before a Jewish court, because they had not been witnesses before it, but they allowed them to testify on the judgment.

Nor is the *ādām ḥāshūb* mentioned in Hay's fundamental directions to the rabbis of Kairouan a mere notable, such as was sometimes included in the bench in civil cases. Unlike the latter, who is not granted full recognition, the *ḥāshūb* is protected by the rules of the Jewish community, and the gaon decides that a defendant who swears that he will not submit to his jurisdiction shall be excommunicated and chastised.

We may draw a parallel between the elders and *ḥashūbīm* and similar functionaries in Muslim society. Let us point here to the institution of the *'udūl*, the trustworthy (witnesses), who will be discussed more fully below, to the *ḥisba*, a municipal body, and to the *muḥtasib*, who is an inspector of markets, weights and measures, as well as of morals, and in charge of non-Muslim affairs.[1] We also once find a Jewish elder being called "the eye of the community", which is a clear loan-translation from Arabic.[2] There is, however, no need at all to assume loans and imitations of non-Jewish organizational forms. Jewish society developed according to its own nature and custom and its age-old traditions.[3]

Bey-Dō'ār (Non-Jewish Courts)

In the Gaonic responsa it occurs sometimes that we are faced with the problem of the attitude towards the *bey-dō'ār*. In view of the fundamental importance of the attitude to Muslim courts, it will be useful to present the available material on this subject even if it concerns areas outside the Maghreb.

---

[1] See above p. 203.

[2] *TR* II, p. 31; Mann, *Jews* II, p. 218.

[3] *He ādām ḥāshūb* is mentioned many times in talmudic literature, *e.g.* Ber. 19a (and parallels); *Tan.*, Shemini sec. 9.

The term *bey-dō'ār* (variant forms: *dawwār*, *dawwar*) occurs in the Babylonian Talmud with a twofold meaning: a) post office;[1] b) [Persian] government courts with judicial and administrative functions.[2] A similar double meaning of the term exists in the Gaonic period: a) Muslim religious court (in some sources perhaps government secular court), which exactly corresponds to *'arkhāōt*, a term likewise used occasionally; this sense is the usual one in the sources of the period; b) post office which meaning I have found only once.[3]

The attitude towards the *bey-dō'ār* as a judicial institution of the Muslim authorities was generally not a sympathetic one, and may even be defined as hostile. This had many reasons. A Gentile court impaired the sovereignty of rabbinical law and the competence of rabbinical courts. The Jews had courts of their own, and "he who informs against his fellow with an alien court is an out-and-out informer; if he is called an informer in civil matters, then all the more in penal matters."[4] Nor were the justice and honesty of Gentiles relied upon. The Gaonic responsa repeatedly state the rule: "The average Gentile is a violent, lawless person, as it is written: Whose mouth speaketh vanity etc. (Ps. 144, 8)" (B.B. 45a). Gentile judges and witnesses were consequently not trusted.[5]

A similar position was taken by the Karaites. Benjamin al-Nahawendi, one of their earliest scholars, who lived in Media in the middle of the 9th century and was a *dayyān* at his place of residence, applied many provisions of law more leniently than his predecessors, while particularly strict in other matters. Like 'Anan, he was very strict about the sovereignty of Jewish law and Jewish judges: "You must not subject a Jew to the courts of the idolaters, neither to their documents nor to their judgments, even if they apply Jewish law; you shall subject a Jew to a Jewish court only."[6]

The Karaites accepted and observed this direction, and attacked the Rabbinites for having violators of communal discipline among them. R. Solomon ben Jehuda, a Palestinian gaon (second quarter of the 11th century), refers to the contentions of the Karaites of his time in one of his epistles: "And they (the Karaites) say that we (the Rabbanites) desecrate

---

[1] Shab. 19a

[2] Ab. Zar. 26b; also Git. 58b; *B.K.* 114a; comp. *Arukh s.v. dawwar*.

[3] *Qohelet Shelomo* no. 56, p. 60: "... *bey dōār* is the man who has been appointed to deliver letters from town to town for a remuneration; he is called *katabī*(!) and in the language of the Sages *dawwār*."

[4] Parma MS of Gaonic Responsa; comp. Müller, *Mafteaḥ*, p. 54 n. 3, at the end.

[5] Comp. *RH*, no. 278; *RA* III, p. 23.

[6] *Mas'at Binyamin*, p. 6b; Mann, *Jews* II, p. 156 n. 3.

(the Jewish festivals); they denounce everyone who applies to a Gentile court and takes an inheritance on the strength of its decision, and say that many will appeal to a Gentile court from the judgment of a Jewish court."[1]

The Christian Church, too, viewed with disfavour resort by its members to the Muslim courts. Its leaders issued regulations to prevent it and imposed fines on offenders. This was of no avail, however, and many sought justice with the *qādī*.[2]

It should be noted that the Muslim state did not compel the "protected people", Jews and Christians, to litigate their internal disputes before its religious or secular judicial institutions. But if they did so, the latter would decide according to Islamic law.[3]

On the strength of the material before us, we may divide the cases in which resort to a non-Jewish court was had into two classes: a) one of the parties ignored the existence of a Jewish court from the outset; b) the parties had accepted Jewish communal jurisdiction, but the loser refused to comply with the judgment. Needless to say that in both classes the circumstances of each individual case were different, so that several sub-classes may be distinguished.

The branding of a man suing his fellow Jew before an alien court as an informer was not always sufficient to stop the practice. This is why in one place the whole community was made to take a solemn pledge that whoever applied to a Gentile court in preference to a Jewish court would be fined one silver dinar. However, our source adds, "the whole community now sins by going to a Gentile court, even on the Sabbath". The wording of the report indicates that the reference is to suing in a Gentile court from the outset. To prevent such occurrences, a nagid in Egypt prohibited taking a case to a Gentile court before it had been tried by a Jewish court. This prohibition must be regarded as a compromise with reality.[4]

---

[1] Mann, *ibid.*, p. 156 ll. 6-8; comp. Baron, *SRH* V, pp. 220, 223, 224 and n. 18. In 1500, the Damascus Karaite community threatened all those resorting to Muslim courts with dishonourable burial; Neubauer, *Aus der Petersburger Bibliothek,* pp. 28 and 118.

[2] Comp. Mez. *Renaissance*, pp. 40 and 41.

[3] Tyan, *Histoire de l'organisation judiciaire en pays d'Islam* II, Larissa, 1943, p. 155 n. 2, mentions a case where the Caliph Maʾmūn refused to hear a Christian plaintiff.

[4] Comp. Marmorstein, *MGWJ*, 50 (1906), p. 599; Mann, *JQR*, 10 (1919/20), p. 140. The *dayyān* of Hebron asks that litigants be dissuaded from recourse to a Gentile court: Assaf, *Studies in Memory of Gulak and Klein*, p. 16 l. 48.

Resort to Muslim courts was indeed frequent. In a letter of the year 1148 from Fusṭāṭ, we read that a man called upon to litigate before a Jewish court, refused to do so, saying: "We shall litigate only before the *Qāḍī al-Quḍā* (the chief *qāḍī* in the land); if I owe him anything, let him swear and take it."[1] In that case, an out-of-court settlement was reached by the intervention of third persons.

In a statement made before witnesses in the year 1151 (presumably also in Fusṭāṭ), a man declared that his partner—both were apparently from North Africa—had compelled him to litigate before the *qāḍī* of Alexandria. He now annulled all the documents he had been compelled to sign: "(10) He (the partner) said that he had bought some goods and that (11) their value had decreased by a certain amount. And he (the declarant) alleged that he had been a dealer (*mitʿassēq*) and not a partner, and he (the partner) said: we shall not (12) litigate save before a Gentile court. And the *qāḍī* al-Athīr, the pride of *qādīs*, required of me (13) and imposed on me proofs as to the goods and the oath according to Gentile and Jewish law (14) and as to what accrued to me from what had been bought and the goods he (the partner) had delivered to me and what (15) he had brought me (?). I declare to you that I was under duress as to everything (16) that was made over to Abū al-ʿAlā by any document I wrote out against me in the court (17) of the Gentile or according to Jewish law (*sharīʿa*!). As to everything that was made over to him, I, Samuel (18) bar Yehuda, was under duress. And we, the witnesses, know that the plea of duress is true (19) and we confirm it. Every document that he (the partner) dictated to him and that is not certified by the *ḥākhām*, (20) the just man, the scribe of the rabbinical court, R. Nathan the son of the late R. Samuel, is (21) void."[2]

The declarant had agreed to litigate before the *qāḍī*, hoping to recover his investment. He was disappointed, however: it seems that he not only did not get his share back, but had to sign certain undertakings in favour of his partner, which he now disowns.

Appearance before a Muslim court in answer to the suit of a fellow Jew was not voluntary. A document of the year 1016 reveals that a Sicilian Jew had R. Ephraim ben Shemaryahu, who afterwards won fame as the leader of the Palestinian community in Egypt, put into "the prison of the Gentile oppressors" for refusing to litigate an action brought against him

[1] Hirschberg, *J. F. Baer Jubilee Volume*, p. 141 ll. 30 and 31.

[2] Gottheil-Worrell, *Fragments*, p. 34 l. 20. The scribe Nathan b. Samuel was a person of note; comp. Mann, *Jews* I, pp. 224-226, II, pp. 277-279 and 286; *idem*, *TaS* I, pp. 250 n. 7, 257 and 259.

before a Gentile court, "And they hunted him and eventually brought him to the *bey-do'ar* which in the language of the Ismaelites is called *shurṭa*."[1]

R. Ephraim tried to excuse himself for not obeying the summons with the plea: "We are Jews", that is to say, we have a court of our own.[2] The prison was in the governor's house, and in the morning R. Ephraim was brought before the Muslim court. The writer explains that *bey-do'ar* means *shurṭa, i.e.* place of custody, police; the prison was in the house of the governor because the latter was at the same time the chief of police.[3]

According to a document of the month of Tebet, 1393 S.E. (1081 C.E.), a Jew was taken to the *shurṭa* following a slanderous complaint by a convert to Judaism (*gēr*), Abū al-Khayr. An accidentally preserved list of tax-payers (undated, but in view of the mention of Abū al-Khayr *al-gēr* to be assigned to the same period) [4] includes one Abū ʿAmrān (Amram) "who is with the police" (*ʿand al-shurṭa*), which indicates that Jews were employed by the Muslim police.[5] But it is not impossible that there was also a Jewish police, just as we find a communal lock-up in which offenders were detained to prevent them from absconding.[6] However, a Jewish prison is mentioned only a few times in our sources, and not always in connection with a judgment.[7] When the Gaon Hay was once asked what to do with obstreperous people who disobeyed the court and did not accept its judgments, he replied that they should be excommunicated and after repentance whipped.[8] Had imprisonment been usual to enforce obedience to the court, Hay and other geonim would certainly have

---

[1] Poznanski, *REJ*, 48 (1904), pp. 171 and 172.

[2] Comp. Mann, *Jews* I, p. 36 n. 2. Assaf, *Batey Din we-Sidreyhem*, 1924, p. 18 n. 22, discusses the case of a Jew invoking the help of Gentiles against his family.

[3] Comp. Tyan, *Histoire de l'organisation judiciaire* etc. II, pp. 428ff. and p. 484; R. Levy, *Structure*, pp. 332 and 333.

[4] The *kunya* Abū al-Khayr was indeed common at that time (comp. Mann, *Jews* I, p. 233, II, p. 225 no. 26, p. 292; Assaf, *Tarbiẓ* 20 (1950), pp. 179 and 180, letter 1 ll. 15, 24 and 25), but the addition *al-gēr* hardly leaves room for doubt.

[5] Golb, *JSS*, 20 (1958), p. 44 ll. 22-24; Gottheil-Worrell, *Fragments*, p. 68 ll. 30 and 35.

[6] Comp. *RM*, no. 146; *RShT*, no. 182. Sherira's responsum may be addressed to a community in Spain, where we find Jewish prisons in the 12th century; comp. *Responsa* of Joseph ibn Megās no. 122; comp. also Toledano, *Sarid u-Paliṭ* I, p. 11 (a reference to the time of R. Asher ('Rosh')). The title *ṣāḥib al-shurṭa*, chief of police, conferred on some prominent Jews in Spain (such as Moses b. Ezra, Abraham b. Ḥiyya ("Savasorda"), but also on an otherwise unknown Abū Omar), seems to be an honorific without actual meaning; comp. Gottheil-Worrell, *Fragments*, p. 94 ll. 8 and 9, and Goitein, *Tarbiẓ* 24 (1955), p. 243.

[7] Comp. Petaḥya, *Sibūb* p. 6.

[8] *RM*, no. 42; comp. also *RH*, nos. 233 and 440.

recommended this measure, similarly to the Gaon Sherira in his reply to a relevant question,[1] and would not have referred to ban and excommunication.

Even excommunication did not always prove an effective deterrent. It could not be applied to everybody, and not everybody took it equally seriously. A person who intended to abscond or emigrate was not likely to heed the threat.

The main difficulty facing the Jewish courts were the limited means of enforcement; they had no police to compel the attendance of the defendant or to carry the judgment into effect. True, the *qāḍī* had no direct powers of execution, either, but he was assisted by the *shurṭa*, whose duty it was to enforce the judgments of the Muslim religious courts at the behest of its commander, who in turn took orders from the governor.[2]

Under these circumstances, the Gaon Paltōy decided that if the defendant refused to litigate before the *beyt-dīn* it was permitted to have recourse to the Gentile authorities in order to obtain redress.[3] In a letter to Aleppo from an unknown locality, Eliya ha-Kohen, *beyt-dīn*, *i.e.* *dayyān* appointed by the *Sha'ar ha-Nesi'ūt* (Patriarchal Porte), the highest Jewish authority, complains that "from most of our people it is difficult to recover ill-gotten gains except by resort to the state authorities. May the Holy One, blessed be he, enlighten us by his Tora and grant us success, for this is the nation whom the prophets were unable to bring under control. But for the state authorities, we would never be able to recover ill-gotten gains from those who hold them."[4] In view of the Gaon Paltōy's decision, we are not surprised at the open avowal of this "*beyt-dīn*" that he applies to state agencies for help in enforcing his judgments.

This problem was discussed and elucidated in a number of gaonic responsa. The Gaon Sherira was asked whether, in a place where there was no permanent *dayyān* and where the elders, *talmīdīm* and *tōbey-hā'īr* had ordered a defendant to repay a loan or surrender a deposit or an inheritance, but found themselves unable to enforce the order, one might apply to an incorruptible, impartial Gentile court which accepted the testimony of a Jew concerning another Jew. The inquirers pointed out the

[1] Comp. above, p. 235, n. 6.

[2] Gibb and Bowen, *Society* vol. I, part 2, p. 116; R. Levy, *Structure*, pp. 332-338; Hopkins, *Government*, pp. 146-147.

[3] Comp. R. Asher (ROSH) to BQ (92b) VIII, no. 17; Beyt Joseph to *Ṭur* HM, no. 26; also Aptowitzer, *JQR*, 4 (1913/14), pp. 27 and 45; Mann, *ibid.*, 11 (1920/21), pp. 460 and 461.

[4] Comp. Schechter, *Berliner Jubilee Volume*, 1903, pp. 108, 112 ll. 67-70, 111 ll. 34-36. Comp. also *RM*, no. 153.

danger of swindlers and extortioners multiplying in the community unless the debtor was compelled to pay up. The gaon's reply indicates that the elders, *talmīdīm* and witnesses in question may, and even must, apply to the Gentile authorities; "even if the injured party is a Gentile and the wrongdoer a Jew, they may testify against the latter before an honest Gentile judge."[1]

Let us now go on to questions expressly designated as coming from North Africa:

An instructive responsum is that given by the Geonim Sherira and Hay in a matter similar to the last-mentioned one. The question, asked by the *Ḥaber Mar Rab* Jacob the son of *Mari Rabbana* Nissim of the city of Kairouan, reveals that instances of non-compliance with the decisions even of qualified courts had recently become more numerous. However great the aversion to suing before Muslim courts, it was impossible to refrain from doing so if collection of the debt was to be ensured. This is apparent from the way the question is framed. The Kairouan rabbi asks, not concerning the fundamental matter of litigating before a Gentile authority, but concerning a procedural problem which arose during such a litigation. On such occasions the witnesses who had attested the claim before the Jewish court were usually not heard, and two notables of the community had to come forward in order that the evidence of the former might be accepted. R. Jacob asks whether these notables may testify as to the substance of the case.

In their responsum, (comp. above, p. 231), the two geonim explain that the notables must not testify as to the substance of the case, since they did not do so before the Jewish court, and that their testimony would be deemed false; but they may declare that they have judicial knowledge of A's indebtedness to B. The geonim subsequently point out that an action may be brought before a Gentile court only if the debtor has been under excommunication by the Jewish court for thirty days and it is known to the Jewish court that he is able to pay and is merely trying to evade compliance with the judgment. If the debtor's ability to pay is not certain, no testimony against him may be given before a Gentile court. However, recourse to a Gentile court may be had if there is any apprehension that the debtor may abscond before an attempt is made to reduce him to obedience by excommunication. If the judgment was not given by

---

[1] *RSh*, p. 84b no. 4; comp. Müller, *Mafteaḥ*, pp. 18, 191 (114). In a place where no Jewish authority existed, it was evidently permitted to a Jew to complain to the governor; comp. Goitein, *Tarbiẓ* 21 (1950), p. 186.

a qualified *beyt-dīn* or by *talmīdey-ḥakhāmīm*, then, even though the case had been heard before elders and notables, no statement by notables should be made before a Gentile court, for elders and notables "are not legal experts and may therefore have erred"; in this case, the persons who gave evidence before the Jewish body and attested the claim may give evidence before the Gentile court, but the notables may not testify on the sentence of the elders.[1]

One important fact emerging from the question is that a Gentile court would, as a rule, accept a statement from Jewish notables, but not hear the evidence of ordinary members of the community. This point will be further discussed in the following.

Two outstanding personalities of the period, Sherira and Hay, we conversant with the procedure of Muslim courts. In reply to a question (also from Kairouan), they rule that there is no need to be as punctilious about deeds made out for presentation before a Gentile authority, and signed by Gentiles, as about deeds made out for presentation before a Jewish court, because they (the Muslims) themselves do not rely at all on those deeds: "They present and accept nothing in their courts save the testimony of witnesses acceptable to their judges and who testify orally, declaring: This man, whom we know personally and by name and by his family connections, (has called us. etc)" It was unreasonable to expect that Jewish courts should value such deeds higher than the Muslims themselves did.[2]

The matter of witnesses acceptable to Muslim judges is brought out clearly in a responsum from an anonymous gaon which, in view of its importance, we quote here in full:

"In the city in which we now are, viz. Baghdad, Gentile courts accept only mentally sound, adult and well-to-do witnesses, who have not been known to have stolen or lied or broken their word, who are noted for a religious way of life, and who are called *muʿaddilīn* (!) (witnesses declared to be trustworthy). If such have given evidence concerning a deed of sale or a

---

[1] *RH*, no. 233. A *sharīʿa* court would only accept testimony from a Jew against a Jew, not against a Muslim (comp. *RSh*, p. 84b no. 4: "and accepts testimony from a Jew against a fellow Jew"), but secular courts accepted evidence from non-Muslims against Muslims; Levy, *Structure*, p. 333. The responsa *RH*, nos. 230-264, were addressed to Kairouan.

[2] *RH*, no. 239; comp. also *ibid.*, no. 82; also *RM*, no. 199. According to the *sharīʿa*, a written document (*ṣakk*, title-deed) has merely secondary evidential value, and only witness evidence carries full weight. This is contrary to the Koran (Sura 2, 282); comp. Bergsträsser, *Grundzüge*, p. 113; see also below, pp. 239-40 n. 1.

loan, and the evidence has been formalized in their (*i.e.* a Muslim) court and accepted by their judge, then we, too, treat that deed as valid. This is now our daily practice. Among the other great cities of Babylonia, there are those in which the Gentile witnesses thus designated are (really) noted for a religious way of life and are very careful about not breaking their word, let alone lying. Of course, we do not know what is in their hearts. We should not regard every Gentile as a sinner, but they remain suspect to us, since they are hypocrites.[1] Our masters said: Although their signatories are Gentiles, they (*i.e.* the deeds) are valid (Mishna Gittin I, 4), and so we, too, recognise them as valid. But there are towns and villages and regions where things are different, where lying and deceit are rampant and witnesses are corrupt. We do not recognise deeds emanating from those places, as you have found in the responsum mentioned by you. We of course apprehend forgery everywhere, and those Gentiles, too, apprehend forgery and do not accept a deed on the strenght of its written attestation by witnesses. Even if they come and say: this is our handwriting, their testimony is not accepted until they say: we remember the evidence we gave for So-and-so the son of So-and-so, whom we know personally and by name, in his dispute with So-and-so the son of So-and-so. We, too, do not rely on their (the Gentiles') deeds unless they are recognised by their courts; and this being so, there is no room for forgery."[2]

A similar position is taken in another responsum. To the question whether an Ismaelite court which is strict about theft and does not decide against a Jew except on the testimony of unimpeachable witnesses should be regarded as extortionist, the gaon replies: Although we hold that Gentiles in general are untrustworthy, some (courts) are strict about the precepts of Islam concerning theft and do not decide against a Jew except on the testimony of reliable witnesses. However, the gaon cautions, a *bey-dō'ār* which prevents a Jew from being robbed does not exist in every town, and not every Muslim obeys the *bey-dō'ār*, and *muʿaddilīn*(!), trustworthy witnesses, are not to be found everywhere; where there is no *bey dō'ār*, all Gentiles must be regarded as extortioners and thieves.[3]

The *muʿaddilūn*, *i.e.* persons recognised as reliable witnesses, are a

---

[1] The translation of this sentence is based on our conjectures; see Hebrew text, vol. I, p. 368 n. 65. This responsum was undoubtedly translated from Arabic into Mishnaic Hebrew.

[2] *RH*, no. 278; comp. also *RCor*, nos. 51 and 13.

[3] *RA* III, p. 23; comp. also Idris, *Berbérie*, p. 768.

special institution of the Muslim legal system. On the basis of the Koran's remarks concerning the two honest (*dhū ʿadl*) witnesses present at a person's death (5:105) or at the repudiation of a wife (65:2), there developed in the course of time the custom of preparing lists of witnesses whose reliability, character and morals had been ascertained by examination. Although according to Islamic law the *qāḍī* is a single judge, two or four such witnesses would sit with the *qāḍī*, investigate the matter at the preliminary inquiry and give evidence at the trial itself. The lists of witnesses were subject to constant review; witnesses whose reliability had become doubtful were struck off and others added. Some believe that non-Muslims were also eligible for inclusion in those lists. The witnesses were headed by the *muqaddam al-shuhūd i.e.* chief witness. This institution of official witnesses, called *ʿudūl* or *shuhūd* in Muslim lawbooks and documents, functioned in all the Muslim countries, eastern and western alike.[1]

The gaonic responsa adduced by us reflect a positive, even respectful attitude towards Muslim courts relying on these witnesses, who were regarded as trustworthy. In the gaonic view, the Gentile court most laudable in this connection was the Muslim court of Baghdad, which was noted for its rectitude and justice. Petaḥya of Regensburg likewise commends the integrity of Muslims in that city.[2] Muslim courts in other major cities were also regarded as honest, although the geonim emphasize that not all countries and localities were the same in this respect. At the same time they note that a serious situation—legal anarchy—prevails in places where there is no *bey-dōʾār* at all.

A favourable opinion of the *bey-dōʾār* is apparent also from a question addressed to R. Elḥanan b. Ḥushiel, the great rabbi, court president and academy head, concerning the theft of a Tora scroll by Gentile rowdies. "And there is no *bey-dōʾār* (marginal note: *ḥākim, i.e.* judge) in that place and no authority to save the robbed from the robber etc."[3] The questioners are thus certain that if there were a *bey-dōʾār* or secular authority in that place it would come to their aid.

Similarly, we once read in a responsum that booty taken in one city and sold in another may be recovered with the help of the authori-

---

[1] References to literature in European languages may be sufficient: Bergsträsser, *ZDMG*, 68 (1914), pp. 409 and 410; Mez, *Renaissance*, pp. 218-220, also p. 214; Tyan, *Histoire* I, pp. 353-372, esp. 371; Levy, *Structure*, pp. 344-346 (comp. also a R. Isaac b. Sheshet, Responsa no. 467: *ha-muqaddamīn weha-muʿaddilīn*).

[2] *Sibūb*, p. 23.

[3] Mann, *JQR*, 9 (1918/19), p. 171.

ties (the *sarey hā'īr*).[1] Still more revealing is a question addressed to Sherira concerning a lost or stolen article which had come into the hands of a Gentile and been bought from the latter by a Jew at less than its value. The owner wishes to redeem it from the purchaser at the price the latter paid for it, but the offer is rejected. The owner declares: "I do not despair of him, for I have witnesses of whom I always inquire into whose hands any goods have fallen and where the thieves or robbers have gone. I can bring them before the king or their (*i.e.* the Gentile) judge and compel them to surrender my property. Failing this, I bribe their (the Gentile) elders and notables, and they can help me to recover my property."[2] It thus does not occur to the questioner that he might bribe the "king" or the judge, but only the "elders and notables".

The question acquaints us with the three judicial authorities that existed in the Muslim state: (a) the "king", *i.e.* the ruler of the state, who represented especially the criminal jurisdiction; (b) the judge, *i.e.* the *qāḍī*, who was principally concerned with civil matters and personal status; (c) the "elders and notables", *i.e.* the city elders (*ḥisba*), whose task it was to watch over morals and prevent wrongful practices, such as the sale of prohibited (*e.g.* stolen) goods. The official empowered to perform the last-named functions was called *muḥtasib*. He was also in charge of the affairs of protected persons, which explains why the Jewish complainant mentions the "elders and notables" who help him recover his property and why it might become necessary to bribe them. Their functions were not well-defined and based on law, like those of the *qāḍī*, or based on physical power, like those of the ruler; therefore it was necessary to "earn" their goodwill.[3]

No far-reaching conclusions should be drawn from those responsa with regard to the period as a whole, for here is a responsum that flagrantly contradicts them by exposing a different face of the authorities: "R. Shesh(i)na. When a king or ruler or toll-gatherer, in the interest of his requirements and desires, orders that information be demanded under threat of interdict, and it is possible to disobey the order because of duress, then such an interdict (*ḥerem*)[4] is ineffective and need not be feared, whereas an oath administered by order of a king or ruler or toll-gatherer must be taken seriously. When a Jew has deposited some money

---

[1] *RC*, no. 93.

[2] *RSh*, p. 32a no. 20.

[3] For criminal and *ḥisba* jurisdiction comp. Tyan, *Histoire* ii (1960), pp. 141ff.; Levy, *Structure*, pp. 222, 334-337; *EI s.v.* Ḥisba; Hopkins, *Government*, pp. 134ff.

[4] According to *RShT*; see next note.

with another Jew and somebody has informed against him, and the king orders the depositary to be examined under threat of interdict, and the depositary refrains from declaring the deposit because he wishes to preserve it for the depositor's heirs, then the depositary shall be blessed. He has nothing to fear from that interdict. He deserves thanks and shall be blessed, for he has acted faithfully and shown consideration for heirs, as it is written: "Mine eyes shall be upon the faithful of the land" (Ps. 101:6)."[1]

Rab Sheshna, one of the earliest geonim, lived in the initial period of Muslim rule.[2] The reference here seems to be to booty taken by the conquering Arab armies on entering new territories. The distinction between the interdict imposed by others and the oath taken by the person in question himself seems logical and fair also in ethical respect.

The Oath in the Bey-dō'ār

The oath was a serious matter for both Jews and Muslims. The Gaon Sar Shalom went so far as to forbid a Jew to enter into partnership with a Gentile because that Gentile might have to swear an oath to him and he might thus find himself administering an oath by strange gods. If, however, such a partnership had nevertheless been formed, it was permitted to have the Gentile swear before a court of his own community because in this case it was that court that administered the oath, and secondly, because it was in the interest of good order to ensure that Gentiles did not deny the receipt of Jewish money in the knowledge that they would not have to take an oath.[3] Indeed, we have found a responsum where a Gentile borrower was prepared to reduce the amount of the loan because of the oath that had been imposed upon him.[4]

As mentioned in a statement (above p. 234), Muslim judges would administer oaths to Jews as well. We know the formula of such an oath which has been preserved in a work of the Mamluke period, but was in use already in the days of the Abbasids.[5] Hay was once asked whether an

---

[1] *TR* I, p. 49 no. 13; but the reading in *RShT*, no. 195 (see preceding note) is preferable.

[2] Comp. Müller, *Mafteaḥ*, pp. 63 and 64.

[3] *RM*, no. 102.

[4] *Ibid.*, no. 204. *Ibid.*, in no. 47, we find an interesting oath formula: A Muslim commander who had captured some Jewish (including priestly) and Gentile women declared that his wives should be regarded as divorced and his concubines as freed if he had touched the captives.

[5] Comp. Qalqashandī, *Subḥ al-ʾAʿshā* XIII, p. 266. For similar formulae comp. Mann, *JQR*, 11 (1920/21), pp. 460 and 461; *RHG*, no. 37.

oath which a Gentile administered to a Jew in the Gentile manner, "by Allah the One and Only", because he did not wish to administer it the Jewish way was as binding as a Jewish oath and should therefore be taken seriously, or whether it might be treated as of no consequence. He replied: "It is a binding oath and is not to be trifled with."[1]

It should be noted that even Muslim scholars and writers were critical of the *qāḍī*'s office and methods; while lavish in the praise of honest judges, they did not shrink from publicly exposing bribe-takers and perverters of justice.[2] Though similar complaints were voiced against Jewish *dayyānīm*, we may suppose that they were not frequent. Hay clearly places greater confidence in the honesty of a Jewish court than in that of a Gentile one. He therefore advises, under certain circumstances, taking action to prevent a suit before a Muslim court, even though it may be objectively justified and the *bey-dō'ār* be competent to hear it because it customarily deals with cases between Jews and Gentiles.

The people of Qābes once consulted Hay concerning the widow and minor orphans of a man against whom a Gentile had a monetary claim. The responsum indicates that the Gentile wished to proceed against the property of the orphans by means of a *bey-dō'ār*, and the rabbis of Qābes wondered whether they might forestall him by selling that property. Hay's reply is most characteristic: "Generally speaking, the paramount consideration in a case like this is the interest of the orphans... for our Sages permit the sale of the property of orphans to provide for immediate requirements. And so long as we can prevent that Gentile from taking anything, it is meritorious to do so. But if we are satisfied that the *bey-dō'ār* will seize and sell with or without justification, then it is like an extortioner ... and if it appears to be in the interest of the orphans that we should sell and pay rather than the *bey-dō'ār*, then we should do so —not because of the religion of the Gentiles, but because of the advantage accruing to the orphans."[3]

The gaon's opinion is clear. There is no intention to deprive the Gentile of what is due to him—the debt must be paid. And the Gentile court is not disqualified because of the difference of religion. But the interest of the orphans must be the foremost concern, and there can be no

---

[1] Comp. *RL*, no. 40; also *RHG*, no. 76.

[2] Comp. Mez, *Renaissance*, pp. 205ff.; Levy, *Structure*, pp. 340 and 341; Hopkins, *Government*, pp. 112ff.

[3] *RH*, no. 324; comp. also *RM*, nos. 201 and 204; Mann, *JQR*, 11 (1920/21), p. 458.

doubt that it will be best served if the sale of the property is conducted by Jews.

As is known, Islam grants women a certain advantage in the distribution of inheritances in that it allots them half of the share of a man of the same degree of relationship to the deceased. Nevertheless, we hardly possess any documents showing that Jewish women applied to Gentile courts with claims in this respect, in order to benefit from the more favourable Muslim dispensation. There is only one fragment concerning a woman who claimed from her brother a share in her father's estate: "... and she went to the chief judge, and the foot-soldiers seized and humiliated him (her brother) and he was compelled to flee from her, and she persistently and brazenly demands her father's inheritance from her brother in the Gentile court, and she has some five men who assist her and who do not fear God."[1] This seems to have been a woman married to a Karaite or inclining to Karaism and therefore demanding her share according to Karaite law, which recognises the right of daughters to a share in the parental heritage.

Differences between Rabbanite and Karaite law as to the status and rights of women were the reason why in cases where the husband was a Jew and the wife a Karaite the spouses undertook in the marriage contract "that they will not resort to Gentile courts instead of Tora jurisdiction."[2] The need to insert such a clause in the marriage contract shows how difficult it was to find a common legal basis in the event of a dispute between partners to such "mixed marriages", which were frequent in the 11th and 12th centuries. It may be supposed that the aggrieved party—usually the Karaite wife—was inclined to apply to a Gentile court, and it was this possibility that the clause in the marriage contract was designed to prevent. The absence of complaints in this respect in our sources warrants the conclusion that the parties indeed adhered to it.[3] We should also note an improvement as to communal discipline on the part of Jewish women, the lack of which in the early Islamic period forced the geonim to devise a divorce procedure that was of a novel character since it bore great resemblance to a *get me'usse* (enforced writ of divorce).[4]

---

[1] Mann, *Jews* II, p. 173; comp. also p. 377. The foot-soldiers mentioned here —*raqqāṣīn* in Arabic—are policemen; comp. Golb, *JSS*, 20 (1958), p. 40 l. 22.

[2] Comp. Mann, *Texts* II, p. 180; Lunz, *Yerushalayim* 6 (1903), p. 238 bottom.

[3] Comp. Mann, *ibid.*, pp. 159-161; Baron, *SRH* V, pp. 221 and 222, 241 and 242, 265-267.

[4] Comp. *RSh*, p. 56a no. 15; Levin, Iggeret, p. 101; *RC*, no. 91; *RHG*, no. 140; Baron, *SRH* VI, p. 133.

Let us conclude with a remark by Maimonides: "Anyone resorting to Gentile judges and courts, even though their laws may be like the laws of Israel, is an evildoer. He, as it were, insults and attacks the Tora of our teacher Moses, as it is written: Now these are the judgments which thou shalt set before them—before them and not before Gentiles, before them and not before unqualified persons. Where the Gentiles are powerful and the opposite party is obstreperous, and the injured party cannot obtain redress through a Jewish court, the matter shall nevertheless be first brought a Jewish court. But if the opposite party refuses to appear, the injured party may, after obtaining permission from the *beyt-dīn*, seek redress in a Gentile court."[1]

Our survey of responsa shows that the attitude of the geonim was more reserved both in reproof and approval. They did not scorn all Gentile courts, and on the other hand, they did not go so far as to permit recovery through any Gentile court, even an ill-reputed one. They were mainly concerned with preventing irregularities in matrimonial law or anything connected with it, and would not allow disputes in that sphere to be brought before Gentile courts. Judging by the material in our possession, they were essentially successful in their endeavour: they preserved the authority of rabbinical law, although they were not always able to preserve the jurisdiction of Jewish courts.

The sources reviewed by us—gaonic responsa, court decisions and private correspondence—reflect changing political and cultural situations over a period of three or four centuries. Obviously, conditions were not the same at all times, in all countries and under every ruler. The circumstances under which Muslim courts functioned and the factors influencing them are not always clear to us, though reasons for their satisfactory or unsatisfactory operation can sometimes be found.[2]

In sum, we may say that the record of non-Jewish courts in the Gaonic period is not, on the whole, unfavourable. Eminent rabbis regarded them as useful and directed that they be resorted to and assisted in their work "lest immoral persons learn to extort and robbers and extortionists multiply", as Sherira says in one of his responsa.[3] A similar view is expressed by Maimonides in a responsum,[4] while he is more intransigent in *Mishne Tora*—a change of attitude possibly dictated by changed circumstances. Rabbis and *dayyānīm* had to weigh the damage likely to

---

[1] *Hilkhot Sanhedrin* XXVI, at the end.

[2] I am unable to check the Muslim sources mentioned by Idris, *Berbérie*, p. 768.

[3] *RSh*, p. 84b no. 4.

[4] *Responsa*, ed. Freimann, no. 298.

be caused to the community and individual in their time by the intervention of the authorities in internal Jewish affairs. R. Isaac Alfasi ruled that even a person who merely raised his voice against a fellow Jew in Gentile market-places and thereby endangered his property must be treated as an informer and was disqualified as a witness, and that of course even greater caution was required where relations with Gentile courts were involved.[1]

---

[1] *RSh*, p. 30b no. 11; *RH*, no. 57; comp. also *RSh*, p. 30a no. 9.

CHAPTER FIVE

ECONOMIC LIFE

Under Roman rule, North Africa was one of the most fertile and affluent regions in the Mediterranean Basin.

Throughout that period, new commerical cities sprang up in this area, and large and small harbours were built or expanded along the coast, including some that had existed already in Phoenician-Carthaginian days and were now awaking to a new life. In the cities, amphitheatres, temples, baths and markets were built, the remains of which have been uncovered in recent centuries.

Forests and orchards covered the countryside. A continuous chain of agricultural settlements stretched along the seaboard and across the fruitful highland. In many places, vestiges of ramified canals have been discovered that conveyed water for drinking and irrigation from the mountains and helped overcome successive years of drought, which were of frequent occurrence. Other features, such as remnants of terraces indicative of intensive cultivation, add to and corroborate the testimony of written records. Though after the Vandal conquest a depression ensued, a new upswing occurred under Byzantine rule, when North Africa was again the granary for the masses of the Western and Eastern Empires, the supplier of choice olive-oil for the tables of the citizens of Rome and Constantinople.

The Geopolitical Position of the Region

Arab historians, in their accounts of the Arab-Muslim conquest, note that the Berber *kāhina* adopted the method of defence now known as scorched-earth policy in order to deter the Arab invaders. According to them, the action of the Berber leader, following sixty years of fierce fighting between Byzantines, Visigoths, Berbers and Arabs for control of North Africa, caused the region's economic ruin.[1] However, this version is gainsaid by Arab geographers. True, the many changes of government in North African countries, the numerous shifts of dynasties and the upheavals of regimes wrought by religio-social movements were not

[1] Comp. above, pp. 93f.

conducive to the rehabilitation of the region and its restoration to a normal life, but these adverse factors were neutralized by other powerful forces, whose effects were more far-reaching and which influenced the development of the North African peoples in a favourable sense.

The first century of Arab rule in North Africa and Spain was a period of incessant tension between the Arab-Muslim Caliphate and the Byzantine-Christian Empire.

The Byzantine fleet blockaded Muslim shipping in the Mediterranean and generally obstructed maritime communications of the Muslim state, which had as yet no warships of its own. The 8th century C.E. saw a conquering Islam at the summit of its power. It directly controlled vast areas in three continents: Asia, Africa and Europe, bordering on spaces which, by the standards of those days, were almost infinite. The Arabs knew about that huge hinterland, its many countries and peoples, its remarkable natural and cultural wealth. True, they did not actually rule over it, but they dominated it in economic respect. Moreover, they looked towards European countries not under Byzantine control or whose ties with Byzantium had weakened. Here, too, treasures beckoned to them such as their own countries did not possess. Under these circumstances, it was impossible that the fertile, opulent area of North Africa, from which immense booty had been taken in the campaigns of conquest, should not again have prospered; it played an important part as a connecting link within the framework of the Muslim state.

So long as the Byzantine fleet controlled the Mediterranean, and the coastal cities faced the danger of landings, traffic proceeded by land. The rulers, therefore—whether governors on behalf of the Caliphs in Damascus and later Baghdad or vassals recognising or repudiating the authority of the caliph—took care to establish administrative-commercial centres in the interior of the country, some distance from the coast, and transit stations at the junctions of caravan routes in the border areas between the inhabited zone and the Saharan Desert.

Centres then coming into being were Kairouan, Tāhert, Tlemcen, Sijilmāsa and Fez.

In the 9th century, a change occurred in the function of the ports in the Muslim zone of the Mediterranean, especially in the western part of the basin. The war fleet of the Arabs grew stronger and enabled their armies to attack Byzantine positions in Cyprus, Crete, Sicily and Southern Italy. The principal beneficiary of this change was North Africa. The Mediterranean became an Arab sea, and the Byzantine fleet ceased to play an effective role in Mediterranean trade. North Africa now became an important link in maritime trade between east and west, south and north. Muslim merchant ships began to ply from Tripoli, from Mahdiya (in the 10th century), and subsequently also from Bajāya (Bougie), Ceuta and Salé. They went in all three directions—eastward to Egypt and Syria, northward to Sicily and Southern Italy, and westward to Spain—to load and unload goods brought from far away. The southern route via the Red Sea towards the Indian Ocean was not yet open to shipping, and goods had to be brought from Alexandria to the Red Sea ports, and vice versa, by a combination of different means of transport.

Hence the decisive importance of Fusṭāṭ, the capital of Egypt.[1]

Prosperity

North Africa had another period of prosperity. This was due in no small measure to political stability during the 9th century: the Maghreb, in the wide sense of the term, was firmly ruled by the Aghlabids in the east (Tunisia and Algeria), the Idrīsids in the west (Morocco) and the Umayyads in Spain.

Reliable witnesses who toured the area for years, such as Ibn Ḥawqal and Maqdisi in the 10th and Bekri in the 11th century, extol its fertility.[2] Large tracts in Southern Tunisia (now covered with sand) yielded different kinds of fruit, several varieties of citrus and figs, as well as olives and vines.

Extensive oases produced delicious dates, and the northern part of the country brought forth wheat and other cereals. The Carthage, Kairouan and Majāna regions produced saffron, that wonder plant from which so many things were obtained—a drug, a perfume, a pigment and a seasoning—and which was a main export article (especial mention is made of *ʿuṣfūr* "flowering saffron",[3] flax, hemp, caraway and cumin; cotton came from Mesīla and Ngaous, sugarcane from Qābes and Jarīd. Industrial crops, sheep's wool and silkworms in the Qābes region supplied material for textile fabrics, tapestry and carpets. Qābes silk was famous for its beauty and delicacy. All the geographers mention the iron, lead and

---

[1] Comp. Pirenne, *Social History*, pp. 3ff.; Lewis, *Power*, pp. 111ff.; Mez, *Renaissance*, p. 475.

[2] Ibn Ḥawqal says that he has travelled in this region; comp. pp. 71, 83, 90 and 99. Maqdisī, p. 246 stresses that the route between Kairouan and Sijilmāsa passes through settled areas. Comp. also Marçais, *Berbérie*, p. 23; Mez, *Renaissance*, pp. 265, 266 and 417.

[3] Cf. Dozy, who notes only the adjective *ʿuṣfūrī* or *muʿaṣfar*, "saffron coloured".

silver mines of the Majāna area; and where iron and lead ore was mined, there must have been a metal industry as well.[1]

In describing the coastal cities from Tunis to the Atlantic seabord, inclusive, Ibn Ḥawqal invariably stresses the fertility of the district. Of course, the almost identical wording may give the impression of stereotyped repetition without actual meaning, but his mention of unfavourable aspects of the local economy contradicts this impression: grain and fruit had to be brought to Marsā al-Kharaz (bead anchorage) west of Tabarka, so called on account of the corals found there—the principal coral centre in the region, superior to Tenes and Ceuta both quantitatively and qualitatively; and barley had to be brought to Nefta in Southern Tunisia.[2]

The country of the Outermost Maghreb, Morocco, was likewise noted for its fertility: its cornfields, orchards and grazing grounds for large and small cattle.

The Atlas Mountains were still covered with primeval forests; luxuriant vegetation filled the Darʿa, Sūs and Ziz valleys in the south. Especially famous was the Meknes region—to this day the most fertile district of Morocco—for its apples, pears, peaches, almonds, nuts, citrus, figs, dates, grapes, olives, sugarcane and cereals. Many new cities were established in Morocco.

Unlike their counterparts in Tunisia and Algeria, they were built in places which had not been inhabited during the earlier period. Fez, Marrakesh, Meknes and Rabat are of wholly Muslim origin, and their medieval buildings show a unique mixture of Spanish art and Berber tradition.

Morocco's position gave it paramount importance as regards relations with the nomad Berbers of the Sahara (the Western Sudan), who were the wealthiest and most powerful of all Berber tribes. Trade with the desert concentrated at Sijilmāsa, the great oasis in the Ziz Valley, which developed into a desert "port" of the first order. Traders from Baghdad, Kufa and Basra came here to exchange goods they had brought by a combined sea and land route, or by land only, for Sudanese gold and for agricultural produce. If they found it worth while to come thus far, it seems all the more understandable that, as Ibn Ḥawqal tells us, traders from Andalusia, Fez and Aghmāt (Marrakesh and Meknes did not yet

[1] Comp. Ibn Ḥawqal, pp. 70, 74 and 84, also p. 88, where he mentions the iron mine and saffron crops between Mesīla and Kairouan. Comp. also Yāqūt *s.v.* Majāna; *REI*, 1935, p. 303.

[2] Ibn Ḥawqal, pp. 75 and 94; Maqdisi, p. 239; Idris, *Berbérie*, pp. 622ff.

exist in his time) were attracted by the profits beckoning at this centre. The merchants of Sijilmāsa itself were rich; Ibn Ḥawqal mentions several times that he once saw a promissory note (*ṣakk*) for forty-two thousand dinars which a man in Awdhaghāst (Sudan) owed to a Sijilmāsan; when he told this in Iraq and Persia—where extremely wealthy people were living—he caused utter astonishment. But not only business magnates were to be found here. The same geographer notes the gentle manners of the townspeople.

They included many religious scholars, as well as persons who had improved their minds on extensive travels throughout the world.[1] According to Leo Africanus, Sijilmāsa's trade declined, and its splendour waned, after the Almoravids conquered Awdhaghāst and devastated Ghana. Darʿa then emerged as a rival centre.[2]

A by no means negligible role was played by the outposts of other avenues of commerce with the Central Sahara: Warghlān, Jarīd, Qafṣa and Ghadāmes, but it was confined to regional trading and never reached international proportions.

The importance of the Algerian oases seems to have increased upon the spread of the Beduin in the eastern part of the area. Trade then sought other points of egress, less exposed to the attacks of the latter. We observe the rise of Warghlān, not previously mentioned, and places such as Touggourt (Tūqūrt), Mzāb and Tū'āt.[3]

Of course, the principal economic centre in North Africa was Kairouan, and no other major commerical town was able to develop in its immediate sphere of influence.

Kairouan and the Port Cities

Kairouan was the metropolis of North Africa, athrob with economic activities: the marketing of agricultural produce and its exchange for industrial products, the import of spices from India and distant islands and the export of precious metals.

Here, about halfway between Alexandria on the one hand and the Western Moroccan ports and Spain on the other, near to the fortified harbour of Mahdiya, but far enough from the coast to be safe from

[1] Ibn Ḥawqal, pp. 61, 91 and 99f.; Terrasse, *Histoire* I, pp. 204-206. For *ṣakk* comp. Fischel, *Jews*, p. 20.

[2] Comp. Léon, *Description*, pp. 426, 458, 461, 468; Yāqūt *s.v.* Darʿa; also Maqdisi, p. 219.

[3] Comp. below, p. 369 and Hirschberg. *JAH* 4 (1963) pp. 323ff..

sudden landings, the great merchants or their agents would meet and all important business be transacted. Everybody in that city, including Aghlabid princesses, engaged in trade. Accordingly, Ibn Ḥawqal follows up a description of Kairouan with an account of North Africa trade: Exports from the Maghreb to the East were women of mixed Byzantine-Berber-Muslim origin and beautiful slave girls, such as would become great ladies and legitimate wives at the caliphal courts, Byzantine boys and slave girls, amber, silk, clothing, wool, hides, iron, lead, mercury, Slavonic slaves, black slaves from the Sudan coming by way of the Nile, horses, mules, camels and large and small cattle.

Food prices were low, and choice meat, oil and fruit plentiful. Maqdisi mentions as goods exported from Afrīqiya olive oil, saffron and various leather goods: provision bags, garments (*anṭāʿa*) and bottles, as well as various fruits.[1]

For 250 years, from the early ninth to the middle of the eleventh century, a great deal of property accumulated in Kairouan: immovables such as sumptuous mosques, palaces and suburban villas, and movables such as gold, silver and other valuables. Ibn ʿIdhāri al-Marrākeshi gives a detailed description of the splendour which Muʿizz (at the end of whose reign Kairouan was destroyed) displayed on various occasions, such as his sister's wedding and his mother's funeral. Referring to the ruler's own wedding, he contents himself with one short sentence: no Muslim ruler ever had the like.[2]

In the east of the region was a string of seaports, the most important of which were Barca and Tripoli. Barca was the first intermediate station between Egypt and Kairouan. According to Ibn Ḥawqal, here was the first *minbar*, *i.e.* large public mosque, on the route from Egypt to Afrīqiya, visited by traders from east and west.

The goods to be found in its markets were tar (*qiṭrān*), raw materials from the interior, such as hides for the Egyptian tanneries, dates, wool, wax, oil, as well as finished products, such as clothes and woollen fabrics. All these were intended for export, and so was the cattle sent from Egypt. The main imports were linen from Sicily, pepper and certainly other spices as well.

According to Maqdisi, the production in Sicily of white ammonia (*nushādhir*), which had in the past been exported to the Maghreb and used

[1] Ibn Ḥawqal, pp. 73f. and 96-99; Maqdisi, pp. 225f. and 239; Nuwairi (in de Slane, *Histoire des Berbères*, Algiers 1847-1851, I, p. 435); comp. Idris, *Berbérie*, pp. 411ff.

[2] *Histoire* I, pp. 270 and 272; comp. also Lewis, *Power*, pp. 209f.

there as a medicament, had stopped. We read of a cargo of pepper in a vessel sold by one Jewish trader to another in Kairouan.

Ibn Ḥawqal dwells at particular length on Tripoli, which then belonged to Afrīqiya. It had numerous markets, some outside the city wall, and an abundance of fine, tasty fruit, such as could hardly be found elsewhere in the Maghreb, and of woollen fabrics and magnificent multicoloured tapestries. Ships called here by day and night, and commerce with Christian countries and with other parts of the Maghreb was thriving. The local inhabitants were of pleasing appearance and of agreeable disposition and character.

Entry to the harbour was made difficult by wind and waves, but the townspeople would lend a hand with the mooring of ships. Ibn Ḥawqal describes also the ports between Tripoli and Tunis: Qābes, Sfax, Mahdiya and Sousse.[1]

Decline and Stagnation

In the eastern half of North Africa, *i.e.* Tripolitania, Tunisia and part of Algeria, the period of prosperity ended upon the invasion by Arab nomads, the Banū Hilāl, which reached alarming proportions in the middle of the 11th century. Arab Berber historians unanimously confirm that the havoc wrought by those Beduin was unparalleled.

The population scattered and towns were devastated; flourishing settlements turned into ruins and heaps of rubble. The people of Kairouan also left their city. Commerical activity continued only the ports of Mahdiya, Sousse, Monastir and Sfax, but here, too, it shrunk when the hinterland had been lopped off.

The impoverished population ceased to play a part in the region's economy. As usual, one calamity was followed by others. After the Beduin incursions came landings by the Pisans and Genoese at Mahdiya which upset the established order. In the 12th century, there were repeated Norman attacks from Sicily.[2] The situation in the Central Maghreb (Western Algeria) and Outermost Maghreb was better. Of course, economic dislocation was caused by the Almoravids rise to power, and especially Sijilmāsa was hard hit. But the religious-social revolution then occurring had no immediate adverse effect.

The decline of Sijilmāsa was offset by the rise of Darʿa and Marrakesh.

[1] Ibn Ḥawqal, pp. 66-73; Maqdisi, p. 239; Wertheimer, *Qohelet Shelomo*, p. 71a; comp. also Pezant, *Voyage*, pp. 307-309.

[2] Ibn ʿIdhārī, *Histoire* I, p. 301; Marçais, *Berbérie*, pp. 210f.; Pirenne, *Social History*, p. 29.

Traffic Routes by Land and Sea

The picture of economic life will not be clear and complete unless we discuss means of communication and transport and everything pertaining thereto, *i.e.* a main prerequisite for the development of human culture.

Without proper land and sea transport, no orderly commercial exchange of raw materials and manufactured articles between one region and another is possible; and but for the regular, constant communication between them, the Jewish communities scattered over the vast areas of the Maghreb—several months' journey apart—would not have been able to withstand the pressure of circumstances; they would have wilted and ultimately vanished.

The study of these matters at the beginning of this chapter provides a key for the understanding of the organization of Jewish society in both material and spiritual respect.

For the Jews as well, North Africa—especially Kairouan—was a bridge between Babylonia, Palestine and Egypt on the one hand and Spain, Sicily and Italy on the other. Let us content ourselves with two examples. A Babylonian rabbi who stopped over in Kairouan and Mahdiya on his way to Spain relates his experiences in a letter to the Gaon R. Samuel b. Hofni.

Another letter, from some Sevillian merchants and presumably addressed to the Palestinian Gaon Solomon ben Judah, came into the hands missed the Palestinian Gaon Solomon ben Judah, came into the hands of one Samuel ben Sahl "from the land of Kairouan". The fragment in our possession does not permit us to determine Samuel ben Sahl's occupation or how the letter reached him, but the maintenance of communication by way of Kairouan is an indisputable fact.[1]

On the basis of the Geniza documents, S. D. Goitein gives an extensive picture of the land and sea communications of the Southern Mediterranean Basin.

This picture naturally assigns a very important place to the Maghreb, especially to the area now known as Tunisia. Although Kairouan had already declined at the time to which most of those documents belong, people of Kairouani origin still held foremost places in activities involving land and sea travel.[2] The Muslim authorities were anxious also for political and financial reasons to ensure free traffic on the land routes.

---

[1] Comp. Goldziher, *REJ*, 50 (1905), pp. 182 and 184; Mann, *Jews* I, p. 102, II, p. 109.

[2] Goitein, *Society*, pp. 273-352.

They set up stations for the protection of caravans, the relay of animals in the postal service and the supply of commodities and services to caravans and to the treasury officials who collected customs at those places.

Most of the contemporary geographers devote their treatises—or at least the major part of them—to a description of those routes and stations, and even indicate this in the titles: *The Book of Roads, The Book of Travels* and the like.

The principal route from Baghdad to Afrīqiya (= Tunisia) was by Aleppo, Damascus, Ramle, Cairo, Barca (Cyrenaica), Lebda, Tripoli, Sabra; thence, via the Nafūsa Mountains or along the coast, to the oasis of Ghadāmes (on the Tripolitanian-Tunesian border) and Qābes. From there, it went on to Sousse and Mahdiya; from these two ports, branch routes led to Kairouan. From Mahdiya, the principal route continued westward to Ceuta, Tangier and Salé. All along that route, a beacon service was maintained by which news could be conveyed from Ceuta to Cairo at surprising speed. This was the coastal route, which, though long, could be traversed in a comparatively short time, since it led through inhabited, fertile territory.

From Qābes and Kairouan, a ramified system of caravan routes extended in a general westerly direction, connecting the two places with the cities of the interior—including capital cities—and with the border towns between the settled country and the desert: Majāna, Mesīla, Ashīr, Tāhert, Tlemcen, Fez and Sijilmāsa. Ibn Ḥawqal and Maqdisi give the exact alignment of the routes, indicating the distances between one locality and another, intermediate stations, provisioning facilities, commercial features (export of quinces and saffron, outlet for iron), customs collection etc. There were, *e.g.*, three routes connecting Mesīla with Kairouan: one via Majāna, the other via the south (Nefta, Qastiliya, Qafṣa). Mesīla itself was the junction of the routes to Fez and Sijilmāsa.[1]

The journey from Sijilmāsa to Kairouan by the coastal route or by Qastiliya lasted from fifty days to two months, while the journey by way of the desert lasted only thirty days. However, according to the Gaon Sherira, this shorter route was in fact longer: "The route by which the caravans of the Maghrebis come (to Egypt) is very long, and most of the Sabbaths are spent in the desert. Some of the travellers know the way and

---

[1] Comp. Ibn Ḥawqal, as quoted above, p. 249 n. 2; also *idem*, pp. 83-90, esp., pp. 85 and 87; he stresses that he has travelled along these routes himself. Comp. also Maqdisi, pp. 244-248; Sauvaget, *Poste*, pp. 39-41.

fix the stopping-place for each Sabbath at the start, but some of them do not know the way."[1]

Sijilmāsa, in turn, was the starting-point for the journey across the Sahara to the Western Sudan, to Awdhaghāst, Ghana and Koga. The journey to Awdhaghāst lasted two months. There had once been a direct route from the Eastern Sudan to the Western, but the wind had covered the track with sand and enemies had dislocated traffic, and trade had thereupon moved to Sijilmāsa.[2]

Customs-collectors were stationed along the routes: in Barca, Ajdābiya, Surt, Lebda, Tripoli, Ṣabra, Qābes, Kairouan, Tenes, Ceuta and Sijilmāsa, between Sijilmāsa and Awdhaghāst, between Sūs and Fez and in Aghmāt. A glance at the map reveals the principle according to which customs offices were located: in ports cities and at terminal stations of the Sudanese trade. Our sources mention the collection of customs only incidentally, and there is no hint of discrimination between Jews and Muslims. The rate of customs duty seems to have been ten per cent of the value of the goods, to which illegal levies by the local ruler and bribes to officials usually had to be added.[3]

The land routes were used also by the *barīd*, the postal service, which in Muslim countries was organized by the method inherited from Persia and Byzantium. The post was first of all at the disposal of the authorities for official business, while individuals were permitted, for a suitable payment, to use it for their commercial or personal requirements. However, the latter generally abstained from using the post for the transmission of secret information, for the postal employees carried out also the functions of police agents and formed a spy network.

There was of course no inter-state postal union, and for their correspondence with the Babylonian Academies, the Maghreb people availed themselves of the commercial caravans or of private couriers, both Jews and Muslims. This, indeed, did not always prevent consignments being damaged.[4] To secure the authenticity of letters, the senders would seal

[1] Yehuda al-Barjeloni, *Sefer ha-ʿIttim*, p. 76.

[2] Ibn Ḥawqal, pp. 60f. and 93; Maqdisi, p. 246.

[3] Ibn Ḥawqal, pp. 66-70, 77, 79 and 102; Mann, *JQR*, 10 (1920/21), p. 323. Muslim pirates bringing in their loot also had to pay tax at the rate of 10 p.ct.; Marçais, *Berbérie*, p. 143. For a comparison with Europe see Pirenne, *Social History*, pp. 86f. and 92f.

[4] Comp. a complaint in Gottheil-Worrell, *Fragments*, pp. 228f. ll. 4f.: "I do not know whether the letters reach my lord, for it is said that they are taken away from the couriers (*fuyūj*)." The *fuyūj* (sing. *fayj*) are mentioned in R. Nissim b. Jacob's complaint to Joseph b. Jacob in Fusṭāṭ; Mann, *Texts* I, pp. 143-4. For the *barīd* comp. *EI*[2] *s.v.*; also Goitein, *Studies*, pp. 303f.

them with their signet-rings. Copies of gaonic responsa sometimes bear the remark: I copied it from the ring-sealed letter.[1]

The transmission of letters by Muslims accounts for the fact that we often find the name of the addressee in both Hebrew and Arabic script, or even only in Arabic script, which was hardly ever used by Jews. Recourse to Muslims was especially necessary for the despatch of letters to distant places with which no regular communication existed, such as Warghlān in the Algerian Sahara.[2]

A letter from Karaites in Egypt, of the middle of the 12th century, concerning assistance to their leader David ben Ḥasday says that "Warghlāni Gentiles" deliver such letters to the Karaites in the Maghreb. These Gentiles no doubt enabled the Karaites of Warghlān to maintain contact with Egypt and Palestine. At the same time, we find contact between Palestine and that oasis maintained by Jews via Kairouan.

R. Nissim of Kairouan, in a letter to R. Joseph ibn ʿAwkal of Fustāt, complains that couriers have brought responsa from Hay to questions asked by others, while he himself has not yet received a reply to a question he asked him in a most important matter and which he sent to Ibn ʿAwkal through a Syrian Jew. He asks that his letter be quickly transmitted to Hay by courier, in order that Hay, in turn, may use a courier for his answer.[3]

The rabbis of Qābes asked Hay whether instructions issued by letter were legally valid. The parties in the case lived in places widely apart and had been dealing with each other by way of such instructions, but they had eventually fallen out, and an account-book in the possession of the defendant was now invoked as evidence. The question dates from the year 1015 C.E.[4]

Land and sea convoys would be planned in accordance with some *mawsam*, which, like its Hebrew equivalent *mōʿēd*, means both a fixed time and a fixed place. This was in order to assemble the greatest possible number of travellers and also to meet the requirements of religious celebrations and pilgrimages that were held in specific localities.[5] Ibn

---

[1] Comp. *RA* II, pp. 128 and 139.

[2] Comp. Worman, *JQR*, o.s., 19 (1907), pp. 728f. That form of address is also usual in letters published subsequently. For correspondence with Warghlān comp. above, p. 141 n. 21.

[3] Comp. Mann, *Texts* I, p. 143 ll. 10, 14f., 21, 25f. and 28; also Assaf, *Sources*, p. 134 l. 53; Goitein, *Tarbiẓ*, 24 (1955), p. 45 l. 3.

[4] Comp. *RH*, no. 59; Ginzberg, *Geonica* II, pp. 284 and 280. Many account-books from Tunisia have been found in the Geniza; Goitein, *Studies*, pp. 314f. Comp. also below, pp. 292-3 and n. 1.

[5] Comp. Assaf, *Tarbiẓ*, 20 (1950), pp. 179 l. 2, 180 l. 23, 185 marg. l. 5, and 188 marg. l. 7; Goitein, *op. cit.*, pp. 303 and 320.

Ḥawqal mentions incidentally the annual *mawsam* for all North Africa in Monastir, and tells about Berbers holding a *tawāf* (processional circuit round a sacred place) at the mosque of Ajdābiya between Barca and Surt.[1] But the main *mawsam* was of course the one connected with the pilgrimage to Mecca. It is common knowledge that pilgrim's caravans were a suitable opportunity for commercial transactions. Hay was once asked "concerning a caravan of celebrants who come on the intermediate days of a festival and to whom things can be sold with a profit, while not selling to them spells a loss."[2]

One letter is explicitly stated to have been sent with the *ḥajj* (the annual pilgrimage to Mecca). One merchant writes that he will send his goods "*fī ʿīd al-gōyīm*", on the festival of the Gentiles, as if whishing to avoid the terms *mawsam* and *ḥajj*, which might be taken to refer to secular caravan seasons.[3] As is known, the modes of delivery of a writ of divorce were insisted upon with particular strictness. In a query to the Gaon Samuel b. Ḥofni we read: "The Ismaelite celebrants come to Egypt only once a year, and on their return to their country no Jews go with them. If a man wishes to send with them a letter of divorcement to his wife, wrapped in a garment, etc."[4] In this case, there can be no doubt that the reference is to pilgrim caravans returning from Mecca, and the country of origin of the celebrants was probably North Africa.

In a letter written in Kairouan ((1)310 Sel./999) by an anonymous merchant to his Master Samuel b. Ḥofni the *ḥajj* is mentioned twice.[5]

The North African caravans were subject to strict control, the authorities insisting on their passing through Kairouan in order to pay the prescribed imposts; it may be assumed that they passed through Kairouan on their way back, too.[6]

It is easy to imagine that the Jews were not eager to join caravans of fanatics still in the mood of the *ḥajj*. Generally, however, for reasons of safety and convenience, the caravans were mixed, consisting of Arabs, Jews and Christians.

---

[1] Comp. Ibn Ḥawqal, pp. 73 and 67 (for Ajdābiya also Maqdisī, p. 216); Yāqūt *s.v.*

[2] Comp. R. Isaac b. Sheshet, *Responsa* no. 320; R. Joseph Karo's Commentary, Beyt Yosef to *Ṭur*, Oraḥ Ḥayyim para. 539. A similar responsum of the Gaon Paltōy (*RM*, no. 149), concerning merchants from Ashkenaz (France? Germany?), was probably addressed to Spain; but it is not impossible that merchants from Europe came also to Kairouan. Comp. also Assaf, *Tarbiẓ*, 12 (1941), pp. 40f.; Abramson, *R. Nissim Gaon*, Jerusalem 1965, p. 258.

[3] Comp. Strauss (Ashtor), *Zion*, 7 (1941), p. 153 (col. b, l. 3.).

[4] *RH*, no. 312; *RHG*, no. 29.

[5] Goldziher, *REJ*, 57 (1905), pp. 184-5 (ll. 8, 20).

[6] Comp. Ibn ʿIdhāri, p. 265.

Moses ben Samuel ben Jāmiʿ of Qābes writes to Joseph ben ʿAwkal in Fusṭāṭ that the well-known Samuel b. Abraham al-Tāherti passed through Qābes a few days previously with a caravan "and we sent with him twenty-five dinars for our Master Hay (the Gaon), and we hurriedly wrote some questions (to Hay) and sent them with one of the Gentiles in the caravan in order that they might reach R. Samuel, for he had gone ahead of the caravan on account of the Sabbath." Samuel had left earlier in order to spend the Sabbath in a place which the caravan would reach after the Sabbath. Incidentally, this letter shows that the route from Tāhert to Fusṭāṭ was via Qābes, in accordance with the itinerary given by Ibn Ḥawqal.[1]

Apart from the prohibition of travelling on the Sabbath, which greatly impeded the movements of Jewish traders, other problems arose in connection with Sabbath observance. The Jewish traveller would find himself in a non-Jewish place: "He who was among Gentiles on the Sabbath and had nothing to eat entered the dwellings of Gentiles and found them consuming bread and milk which had been milked the same day and fruits torn from the ground, and he would eat with them in the sand." The picture is that of an oasis or Beduin encampment, and the problem is not the ritual fitness of the food *per se* but its preparation on the Sabbath.[2]

A voyage on the Nile with Muslims and Christians is referred to in the discussion of the case of an *ʿagūnā* whose husband "went to the towns of Egypt with merchandise and whose pack was heavy. He came to one city and deposited some of his goods with a Jew, intending to return in three days, but he did not return even after three months. His wife and parents believe that he intended to return in the month of Tishri and spend the whole of the festival month at home. We think that something may have happened to him, and the man with whom he deposited the goods is also worried. His parents went to search for him, and some Muslims and Christians told them: We knew how to swim and got out, but he was drowned because he did not know how to swim..." In the further part of the account, the outstanding fact is that the inhabitants of the locality near which the accident occurred knew where the body of the drowned man was, but claimed that they were "afraid to recover it from the river for burial because of the high-handedness of the authorities."[3]

This story comes from Egypt, but accidents of this kind happened in

---

[1] Comp. Mann, *Texts* I, p. 141; see also Gottheil-Worrell, *Fragments*, p. 228, l. 9.
[2] *RCor*, no. 93.
[3] *RH*, no. 27.

North Africa as well, both on land and at sea. Incidentally, we do not in the sources of the period meet with problems of *ʿagūnōt*, which are very frequent in a later period.

This silence points to a certain order and government control, which ensured the safety of travellers—a matter to be dealt with presently—and to proper functioning of the *batey dīn*, which were able to take evidence of the murder or accident, establish the death of the husband and declare the woman to be a widow. In our case, the fault lay largely with "high-handedness of the authorities". Did that "high-handedness" mean that the authorities were likely to confiscate all or part of the deceased's property? Perhaps the Jewish trader and his fellow travellers had infringed the severe Egyptian passport regulations, which required all those leaving their own district to obtain visas, and the offence would have come to light by taking up the case of the death man.[1]

We have already seen that Jews were wary of joining caravans returning from the *ḥajj*. On the other hand, we find that Jews did not refrain from going to places "where markets for the purpose of idolatry are held once a year and where no other traders come from anywhere; they do business there, and as they leave, a duty is levied from them for the purpose of idolatry; such a market is described as an idolatry market."[2] A ban on attendance at such markets was imposed because of the duty collected for the purpose of an alien faith.

We would very much like to know to what countries the questions concerning "idolatry markets" refer; they may have been Christian or heathen markets, or even Muslim ones, which took place on the occasions of pilgrimages to the graves of saints and the like. The most likely assumption seems to be that we have to do here with fairs in honour of Christian saints, usual in Europe already in the Middle Ages, and in which Jews would also participate. But the questions do not seem to have come from Europe, and it is not impossible, therefore, that the questioners were merchants who went, *e.g.*, to Monastir or Ajdābiya or Rādhānites who visited heathen countries, or traders who toured Berber regions, where the observance of Islamic religious law was extremely lax.[3]

Security on the roads was at first fairly satisfactory. It was effectively attended to by the Umayyad governors, and the emirs who succeeded them likewise took strong measures against highway robbery.[4] Towards

---

[1] Comp. Lewis, *Power*, pp. 90f. and 171; also *RH*, no. 299.
[2] *RC*, no. 17; *RHG*, no. 104.
[3] Comp. Pirenne, *Mohammed*, pp. 253f. For the Rādhānites see below pp. 275-7.
[4] Comp. Ibn Ḥawqal, p. 104; Terrasse, *Histoire* I, p. 199; but see Hopkins, *Govern-*

the end of the period, however, the situation deteriorated in the areas in which the Beduin grew powerful. Thus we find some people of Tlemcen asking about the liability of a partner who had gone to a distant place with some merchandise and who, because of the presence of robbers in the area, had not done business as stipulated.[1] A Maghrebi Jew who had been taking some goods to Egypt tells his partner that upon arrival at Ajdābiya he sent all his baggage and gold by a Gentile for fear of the dangers of the journey.

But this did not save him from the robbers, who seized the whole caravan, stripped the Jew of what he had on his person and threatened to kill him.[2] A similar situation prevailed in Tripolitania. A merchant who came to Tripoli and wished to go on to Mahdiya was advised to go by sea to Seville—by one of the ships that went there to buy wheat—and from there to Mahdiya. The same advice was given him in case he wished to go on to Egypt because the land route was infested by marauders who plundered travellers and led them into captivity. But the sea route was by no means safe, either.

That portion of the sea was stormy, and ships often foundered. Our traveller eventually decided to go by land, as he had joined a physician who had been summoned by the ruler of Qābes and the caravan had been given a strong escort. He afterwards learnt that the ship by which he had intended to travel had sunk and that only a few persons had been saved in a small boat.[3] But the main danger came from pirates. Piracy in those days was a perfectly legitimate trade, and all the warships and merchantmen of major nations carried on the hunting of foreign vessels as a sideline. The capture of Jews was particulary aimed at because it was known that Jewish communities spared no effort or expense to redeem their brethren.

This latter subject has already been dealt with in the chapter on Jewish society.[4]

The Geo-Economic Distribution of the Jews

We have already observed that Jews lived in all the administrative centres and emiral capitals of the many dynasties then arising. The same applies to commercial cities, caravan stations and ports, both old and

ment, pp. 43f. In Europe, no measures were taken against highwaymen until the 11th century; comp. Pirenne, *Cities*, p. 90. Under Mongol rule, the long route across Central Asia was perfectly safe for traders; E. Power, *Medieval People*, p. 69.

[1] *RH*, no. 426.

[2] Ginzberg, *Geonica* II, pp. 150f.

[3] Assaf, *Sources*, pp. 130-134.

[4] Comp. above, pp. 178ff.

new. This drive towards the major centres is by no means surprising; it resulted from a very natural stimulus: the Jews who lived nearby took an active part in the economic development of the new settlements, and this attracted others, who had learnt of the opportunities offering there.

The scarcity of the material does not allow us to answer the question from where the Jews streaming to the new cities originated, from near or far, from the same region or from neighbouring countries. Nor are there any data to show where part of the Jews were hiding during the Almohad persecutions. For not all of them embraced Islam, and not all the rabbis emigrated. It seems that many resorted to isolated villages in the mountains or the steppe, where the authorities did not notice them and the local population was not interested in handing them over since they fulfilled an important function in the village economy as craftsmen and pedlars.

Agriculture

In this sphere, too, the Gaonic responsa and the Geniza fragments —court decisions and letters—make larger or smaller contributions to a reconstruction of the facts. Let us begin with the smallest: information evidencing or hinting that Jews engaged in soil cultivation or cattle raising. Some of the questions addressed to the Gaon Hay by the rabbis of Qābes refer to a field irrigated by means of a watercourse which passes through the field of another owner, a situation that led to disputes between the owners over the right to the water and the crops growing beside it.[1] Other questions relate to land—*i.e.* probably agricultural land—of orphans, its division between the heirs or the need to sell it in order to repay a loan to a Gentile. Nor does a question from Qābes concerning the sowing of a bed (Mishna Shabbat 9, 2) seem purely theoretical.[2]

Once a Jew who lived in a village ten miles from Kairouan sent some cheese to the city by a Gentile, each cake imprinted with the word *berakha* (blessing) in Hebrew lettering. The townspeople, not sure whether that cheese was permitted food, asked the Gaon Hay about it. This suggests that that Jew manufactured cheese on a commercial scale and that many did the same. For otherwise, if this was an isolated occurrence, what could have induced the people of Kairouan to bother the gaon of Pumbaditha with their question and wait months for a reply? This must have been an individual instance from which conclusions

---

[1] Comp. *RH*, nos. 318, 322 and 342.

[2] *RH*, nos. 324, 343 and 425.

were to be drawn for many similar cases. In fact, not long ago, a boxwood seal of the Fāṭimid period, engraved with the word *berakha*, was found in Egypt.[1]

We do not know whether the raising of small cattle for milk, wool and meat was the main livelihood of part of the inhabitants of villages and suburbs, but it is clear that the situation depicted here was different from that in Egypt, where—as appears from a responsum of Maimonides—small cattle was entrusted to non-Jews to be raised for meat only.[2]

Some of Nissim ben Jacob's stories in his *Fine Book of Comfort* indicate that Jews in his time and country raised bovines. He also tells of a man of good family who became impoverished and was presented with a pregnant cow by each of his father's friends. *Nota bene*: neither money nor goods, but a cow which would calve after a time and would give milk.

Among the wondrous tales of Elijah reported by Nissim (cp. Koran, Sura 18: 66-80), there is one according to which Elijah killed a cow in the house of an extremely poor man. Thus even the poorest of the poor had a cow.[3]

That Jews cultivated the soil can be inferred from a question from Kairouan, presumably addressed to Hay's Academy. It concerns the practice prevalent in Kairouan of lending money on security of land, the fruits of which were enjoyed by the lender until payment of the debt, so that a kind of interest was charged. The townspeople avoided that practice after they had been warned against it by the Academy. In effect, however, they continued it under the cloak of a sale transaction, *i.e.* the field was ostensibly sold to the borrower, who undertook to return it if he received his money back after a certain time. This was a subterfuge to enable the "buyer" to obtain possession and usufruct without the taint of interest. The "sellers" would give up their fields at less than their value because they were certain to get them back if they returned the "price" at the due date.[4]

The above-mentioned fruits of the land are not proceeds of commercial

---

[1] *RH*, no. 5; comp. Narkiss, *BIES*, 12 (1945/46), pp. 72-74; comp. also *RC*, no. 127. Documents in the Geniza also deal with the making of cheese, ritually fit for Jews, in villages of Egypt; Ashtor, *Zion*, 30 (1965), p. 67. For later periods comp. Zimmels, *R. David ibn Abi Simra* (1933), p. 40; Rosanes, *Histoire des Israélites de Turquie* V, 1937/8, pp. 331-2.

[2] Moses ben Maimon, *Responsa*, ed. Freimann, no. 139.

[3] Comp. Hirschberg, *R. Nissim*, pp. 68f. I assume that *RC*, no. 92, about breeding cattle, was addressed to Kairouan like the preceding responsum. Agriculture as an occupation of Jews in the Maghreb: Baron, *SHR* IV, p. 160; Goitein, *Society* I, pp. 116-126.

[4] *RSh*, pp. 36a-39a no. 12; Müller, *Mafteaḥ*, p. 14 n.

transactions in urban land entered into by the "buyer", but, as proved by the subsequent mention of the field, fruits in the proper sense. In fact, we know that the Muslim inhabitants of Kairouan had cornfields, pasture-land and orchards, cultivated by tenants or slaves, in the border areas and suburbs of the city. The situation was similar in many cities and towns in the Maghreb, especially in Morocco, where open cities, surrounded by gardens, fields and pastures owned by the local inhabitants, were particularly frequent. A combination of date-growing, handicraft, hawking and trading was perfectly natural, and even necessary, in the oases of the south.[1] The land in Tlemcen of certain brothers who had been exiled to Ashīr may likewise not have been house property and building plots, but agricultural land. Another question from Tlemcen deals with vine-growing.[2]

A rural or semi-rural scene is the background to some of Nissim ben Jacob's stories in the *Fine Book of Comfort*, stories for which no midrashic or talmudic source can be found although they describe events which supposedly took place in Palestine. Nissim clearly used Palestinian ingredients for artistic purposes only. There is Joseph the gardener, a simple soul and industrious tiller of the soil, whose father is one of the local notables. When the father dies, almost all his wealth evaporates, and when his fellow citizens hear this, they chase him out of town. He retires to the only piece of land that is left to him and makes a living by cultivating it.

The strange sequel of the story, concerning the sale of Joseph's wife, shows that this is not a Palestinian story. Elsewhere Nissim tells of an orphan girl whose father left her the premises on which she lives and some gardens and fields which give a good crop: he also left her a hundred gold dinars.[3] Soil cultivation naturally raised halakhic questions. Hay was consulted in the following matter: "We have gardens and orchards in which there are areas planted with corn and areas planted with trees. Some of them can be watered at any time and some, by virtue of an inviolable law in force since olden times, only on the Sabbath. We have Gentile tenants, who take one fifth of the fruits; they do whatever they please, and the Jewish owner knows nothing about it."

---

[1] Comp. Marçais, *Berbérie*, p. 18; *idem*, *Histoire* I, p. 206. I observed this combination in the mellahs in the fifties of the present century; see Hirschberg, *Inside Maghreb*, pp. 99ff.

[2] *RH*, nos. 38 and 430; *RM*, nos. 133-136, also no. 153.

[3] Comp. Hirschberg, *R. Nissim*, pp. 26-29 and 102f. In that period, the Jews had a predilection for ornamental gardens; comp. Mez, *Renaissance*, p. 364.

Another problem was as follows: "Some people in our locality raise silkworms, which have since olden times been fed on festival days, though not on the Sabbath."[1]

We do not know from where the two questions come. But as some questions concerning irrigation come from Qābes, and we know that silk was cultivated in Qābes and its surroundings, we may assign them to that area.

Sabbath observance and its attendant difficulties may have been one of the reasons for the abandonment of agriculture. Nor should it be overlooked that actual farm work, the personal physical exertion of the landowner—as distinct from the ownership of large estates tilled by others—was not in Muslim countries one of the most esteemed occupations. Needless to say that a labourer on an estate ranked very low in the society of those days. We are inclined to forget that the vast majority of peasants in Christian countries in the Middle Ages, and in some areas until the nineteenth or twentieth century, were semi-slaves, bound to the soil and sold together with it like chattels. In both cases, a feudal class used slaves, serfs and tenants to cultivate its lands. We have already seen that large Jewish landowners followed the same method.[2]

Artisans

It is hardly surprising that the gaonic responsa have not much to say about handicrafts and handicraftsmen. These occupations usually raised no special halakhic or legal problems, which would have necessitated instruction and guidance from the Babylonian Academies. We should therefore not be entitled to draw conclusions from this silence even if we were not able to fall back in this matter on important material provided by other kinds of literature. It would indeed be inconceivable that the Jews should have refrained in the Maghreb from callings they had followed since time immemorial, such as spinning, weaving, dyeing and, especially, the fashioning of precious metals.[3]

Muslims in Islamic countries were virtually forbidden to engage in gold and silver work. Islamic law regards the taking of payment for work in precious metals as usury and lays down that for articles of precious

---

[1] *TR* II, p. 57, nos. 3 and 4.

[2] Comp. Hirschberg, *R. Nissim*, pp. 93f. The situation in 9th-century Europe is depicted by Power, *People*, pp. 11-33.

[3] The main occupations of Jews in the border countries in pre-Islamic times are mentioned, *e.g.*, by Cosmas Indicopleustes (6th century) in Topographia Christiana, *PG*, p. 88 col. 172.

metal a Muslim may receive their material value only (by weight if payment is made in the same metal), that is to say, without recompense for the work and without compensation for wastage. The resulting abstention of Muslims from all dealing with gold or silver that might involve interest accounts for the fact that in Muslim countries—especially during the initial stages of economic development—the trades connected with the manufacture of precious metals were a monopoly of non-Muslims. Also Muslim magic prejudices are given as reason against occupations with those handicrafts by Muslims.[1] These trades included not only the gold-and-silversmith, but also the examiner of precious metals; the moneychanger (who was originally also the lender and banker); and the toll and tax gatherer, who had to be familiar with the different currencies and be able to calculate their value according to their precious metal content, denominations and weight and, moreover, to keep proper books—an art not at first be found among Beduin. All these trades were originally related or even identical, and also in more developed stages of the economy some of them were called by the same name, so that it is sometimes difficult to decide which of them is meant. *E.g.*, the Persian word *jahbadh*, the primary sense of which is "one who understands, discerns", came to denote a moneychanger, a tax-collector, a lender-and-banker, etc.

From the discussion of a will, we learn that the deceased had "a millstone for the grinding of gold and silver ore". Questions from Kairouan and Fez bring up matters of currency and precious metals in connection with marriage ceremonies involving money (what is the value of a *perūta*, an Italian *īsar* etc.) or interest (loans in deficient *zūzīm*, the purchase of crushed gold). Until the middle of the 10th century, the situation in our region was less complicated because the only currency there—and even as far as Damascus—was the *dīnār* (lighter than the *mithqāl*, which circulated in Iraq and east of it). It was therefore sufficient to count the coins.

From then onwards, however, the Maghrebi rulers flooded the market with coins minted by themselves: *ʿAzīzī*, Almoravid and *Marrākeshī* dinars and various silver coins. Moreover, the reprehensible practice of clipping spread. It was now also necessary to weigh the coins and not to

---

[1] Comp. *EI*, *s.v.* Ribā; *K. al-Fiqh*, Qism al-Muʿāmalāt II, pp. 270-272; Léon l'Africain, *Description*, p. 234. Le Tourneau, *Fez ... Merinids*, pp. 94, 105, also 75. The Muslim attitude in this matter seems to have changed. H. I. Cohen, in a Ph.D. thesis on the occupations of Muslim religious scholars, notes fifty-five gold- and silversmiths and other workers in gold and silver; comp. Goitein, *Society* I, p. 416 n. 10.

rely on merely counting them, and a knowledge of the methods of casting and the proper weight was required.[1] The fact that Muslims shunned gold and silver work led to minting in Muslim countries being done by Christians and later also by Jews. Though precise information about the earlier period is lacking, we know, *e.g.*, that mints in the Aghlabi kingdom were operated by Christians. At a later period, the mint in Egypt was managed by Jews, and Jews also minted the coin of Yemen and North Africa.[2]

Lists of Occupations and Livelihoods

As stated, direct information as to the occupations of North African Jewry, except the wholesale trade, is scarce. One Geniza document mentions three goldsmiths travelling from Aden to Ceylon, one of them of Maghrebi origin. Another time we hear of two Maghrebi goldsmiths sailing for India. A letter probably from Kairouan refers to a man named Ibn al-Ṣabbagh, *i.e.* the son of the dyer, and to *lawwānīn*, *i.e.* dyers. Once a basketmaker in Jerba is mentioned.[3] An Arab geographer reports that the masonry trade in Sijilmāsa is entirely in Jewish hands. Questioners in Qābes want to know whether a technical problem may be taken up with Gentile masons where no Jewish experts are available. This means that skilled Jewish masons were usually to be found.[4]

Geniza lists of payers of taxes (*kharāj, jizya*) and charges and recipients of alms in Egypt should be consulted. Many of those mentioned are shown by their surnames to be of North African origin, while those not mentioned by appellations of origin, but by other appellations and designations, may also be assumed to have included Maghrebis; and all these may be supposed not to have learnt their trades in Egypt, but to have been following the callings traditional in their families.

Moreover, we may take it that the trades and livelihoods then practised by Egyptian Jewry were also frequent in Kairouan and other major

---

[1] Comp. *RH*, nos. 370 (from Qābes), 386 and 552; *RSh*, pp. 34a nos. 3f. and 96b no. 12; *RCor*, no. 52. Comp. also Fischel, *Jews*, pp. 2-5 and *passim*; Goitein, *Society*, pp. 248-250, 368-392 and *passim*.

[2] Comp. Marçais, *Berbérie*, p. 82; Pollak, *Zion*, 1 (1936), pp. 24-36; Neustadt, *ibid.*, 2 (1937), pp. 232 and 234; Assaf, *ibid.*, 6 (1941), pp. 256f.; Romanelli, *Masā be-ʿArab*, ed. Schirmann, Jerusalem 1968, pp. 70f.; Chénier, *State* I, p. 157; de Paradis, *Alger*, pp. 163f.; Brauer, *Ethnologie*, p. 242; Eisenbeth, *Algérie-Tunisie*, pp. 345 and 375; Mayer, *BIES*, 18 (1953/54), pp. 230-232; Goitein, *Society*, Index *s.v.* mint.

[3] Goitein, *Society* I, ch. 2, contains information particularly relevant to this section (comp. *e.g.*, p. 100 no. 6).

[4] Bekri, pp. 148f./284; *RH*, no. 325.

urban settlements, since the social structure was similar and economic relations were extremely close, as will be shown below.[1]

In going over the lists, we shall give the occupations in the order in which they appear, without grouping them under headings such as: craftsmen, pedlars, merchants etc., so as not to have to revert several times to the same list and because in many cases it is not clear whether the reference is to the maker, processer, wholesaler or retailer of a certain commodity. In doing so, we shall also realize at once that Maqdisi's statement concerning the occupations of Jews and Christians in Syria: "Most of the *jahbadh*, dyers, moneychangers and tanners are Jews, most of the physicians and clerks are Christians" is applicable neither to Egypt nor to the Maghreb.[2] Moreover, we get rid of the notion that the Jews were mainly members of lowly, despised trades: moneychangers, tanners, shoemakers, dyers, weavers and street-cleaners. We find among them dealers in cloth and silk, spices, pearls and corals, *i.e.* representatives of highly respected branches of commerce.

A. *The Gottheil-Worrell List* [3]

Al-sukkarī – one who deals (as manufacturer or trader) with sugar or sweets; *al-dūsturī* – registrar; *al-kātib* – clerk, scribe; *al-ṭabīb* – physician; *al-sharrābī* – one who deals with beverages (especially wine and brandy); *al-meqōnēn* – threnodist; *al-ṣayrafī* – moneychanger; *ʿind al-shurṭa* – one who is with the police; *al-qaṭāʾif* – one who deals with dainties; *al-khayyāṭ* – tailor; *al-zajjāj* – glazier; *al-dhahabī* – one who deals with gold; *al-ʿassāl* – one who deals with honey; *al-fiḍḍī* – one who deals with silver; *al-zayyāt* – one who deals with oil; *al-jahbadh* – moneychanger.

B. *The Braslawsky List* [4]

Al-khādima, *al-khādim* – female servant, male servant; *al-sharrābī* (twice) – seller (manufacturer) of beverages; *al-sukarī* – sugar manufacturer; *al-dahqan* – merchant, village headman, expert; *al-munqī* – cook's assistant; *al-ʿashī* – cook; *al-mīrāthī* – mirror-maker; *al-ḥazzām* – packer; *al-munajjim* (three times) – astronomer, astrologer; *baqqāl* – grocer; *khayyāṭ* – tailor; *warrāq* – copyist or bookseller; *al-meshorer* – poet;

[1] Comp. the surnames in the Gottheil-Worrell List (below, n. 3): al-Qābisī, al-Majānī etc., and in the Strauss List (below, p. 269, n. 1): al-Nafūsī etc. An indication of North African origin is the elision common in the Maghreb of the aleph in Abū-Bū, Ibn-Ben.

[2] Maqdisi, p. 183; Levy, *Structure*, pp. 53-73.

[3] *Fragments*, pp. 66-71.

[4] *Tarbiẓ*, 13 (1942), pp. 48-51.

al-parnās (twice) – community leader; *al-bayyāʿ* – dealer in goods; *al-ḥazzān* – synagogue official; *baʿal ḥālōm* – interpreter of dreams; *ṣāʾigh* – goldsmith; *khabbāza* – baker; *ben dayyān Barqa* – son of communal judge in Barca; *aṣḥāb al-ibghāl* – owners of mules.

C. *The Strauss List* [1]

Al-kaḥḥāl – one who deals with kohl, "eye doctor"; *al-nākhoda* – shipowner; *al-nushādrī* – one who deals with *nushādir* (ammoniac); *al-khaṣābī* – one who deals with dyes (henna); *tājir al-ṭal* – one who peddles milk; *al-ṣayrafī* (four times) – moneychanger; Habba *darb al-baqqālīn* – Hibah (proper name) of the street of the grocers; *ṣabbāgh* (twelve times) – dyer; *kātib* – clerk, scribe; *bazzāz* (three times) – one who deals with cloth; *al-ghazūlī* – one who deals with textile fabrics; *al-ṭabīb* (twice) – physician; *al-sōfēr* – writer of Tora scrolls etc.; *al-ʿanbarī* – one who deals with amber; *ḥarīrī* (twice) – one who deals with silk; *al-rabbāṭ* – packer; *al-ḥazzān* – synagogue official; *khuḍrī* – greengrocer; *mustaʿmal* – employee, servant; *naqqād* (three times) – tester of coins and precious metals; *al-zajjāj* – glazier; *al-dayyān* (twice) – communal judge; *al-rāṣūy* – apparently a title: the esteemed one (of the academy);[2] (*awlād*) *al-ṣanīʿa leviyyīm* – the Levites (sons of) the quick one (at her work); *al-talmīd* (*ben al-ʿAjamī*) – the student (at the academy) (the son of the Persian); *sharrābī* – one who deals with beverages; *ben ḥadīd*: perhaps misspelt for *ḥaddād* – black smith;[3] *sukkarī* – one who deals with sugar.

These three chance records contain only a small part of the vocations followed by Jews. There were others, referred to in other sources; *e.g.*: clerk of the merchants; *al-ʿaṭṭār* – perfume dealer; *al-zayyāt* – oil merchant; *al-qazzāz* – silk merchant; *al-ṭaḥḥān* – miller; *al-dallāl* – public crier; *al-ṣaydalānī* – pharmacist; *samsār bi-al-ʿaṭṭārīn* – middleman for perfumes. Goitein, on the basis of the Geniza documents, noted 265 vocations, adding: "the actual number of manual occupations represented in the Geniza papers was a multiple of the 265 listed so far."[4]

Statistically, the great number of dyers attracts attention. The importance of the dyeing trade is apparent also from the list of a merchant who had given a large quantity of silk to be dyed in several colours. Revealing in various respects are detailed instructions to dyers which have been

---

[1] *Zion*, 7 (1942), pp. 142-144.

[2] Comp. Mann, *Jews* II, p. 337, I, p. 279 n. 5; also I, pp. 259f. and 272.

[3] For Jewish blacksmiths in the Maghreb comp. p. 270, n. 2; also Goitein, *Society*, pp. 83 and 92.

[4] Comp. Goitein, *Society*, p. 100; Neustadt, *Zion*, 3/4 (1937), pp. 237f.; Golb, *JSS*, 20 (1958), pp. 22f.

found in the Geniza: *A Description of the Finishing of Silk and Its Dyeing in Differing Colourṣ*. A list of goods sent to Kairouan and available in its and other markets, such as *baqam* (brazilwood), which yields a red dye, and other dyestuffs, but especially raw materials to be dyed, such as wool, flax, cotton and silk, shows that weaving and dyeing were among the principal crafts in the region. The absence of weavers in the lists suggests that this craft was mainly practised by Muslim and Christian women.[1]

Some conception of Moroccan-Jewish livelihoods, about which we have hardly any information relating to the period under review, may be obtained from an account by Leo Africanus, a 16-th century Maghrebi Muslim who turned Christian and lived in Italy; we may assume that what he says concerning Jewish occupations reflects a situation which existed also hundreds of years earlier: In the Shishawā Mountains (west of Marrakesh), the Jews are smiths who make axes, scythes and horseshoes, and masons performing the most simple tasks. In Safi (on the Atlantic coast), they are craftsmen (no details), while for the Tadla region Leo mentions merchants as well as artisans.

In Fez, the rulers gave the Jews a licence to practise gold- and silversmithery.

In the encampments in the Dar'a region, on the route from Fez to Timbuctoo, there were Jewish craftsmen, especially goldsmiths, and in the Sijilmāsa district Leo saw Jewish merchants.[2]

The "Professions"

We must now discuss those who might be said to correspond to present-day "professional people": astrologers and interpreters of dreams; clerks with commercial firms and in communal and governmental offices; the *kaḥḥāls*, of which it is not quite clear whether we ought to describe them as vendors of kohl or as a kind of oculists; and physicians, who are frequently mentioned; on the other hand, there were threnodists; scribes of sacred texts; poets who made a living by composing panegyrics in the holy tongue; synagogue officials (*ḥazzānīm*); and communal judges. The second group of "professions" is here dealt with only in so far as [3]

[1] Comp. Gottheil-Worrell, *Fragments*, pp. 72-75; Neustadt, *op. cit.*, p. 236 and n. 11.

[2] Léon l'Africain, *Description*, pp. 112, 117, 142, 149, 234, 423 and 428.

[3] For writers of charms etc. comp. Gottheil-Worrell, *Fragments*, pp. 22 and 76; Braslavsky, *Tarbiẓ*, 13 (1942), p. 48 ll. 44, 46 and 50; Neustadt, *Zion*, 2 (1937), p. 238; Bookkeeping: Ginzberg, *Geonica* II, p. 284; *RSh*, p. 96a no. 11.

they were livelihoods; the role of not a few of their members as religious scholars, as men of learning and research, has been evaluated elsewhere.[1]

The number of those resorting to interpreters of dreams to have their future told, and of those seeking charms against disease or the evil eye, appears to have been considerable. We should not delude ourselves into thinking that the physicians mentioned in the lists were even remotely comparable to Isaac Israeli, court physician of the Aghlabids and Fāṭimids in Kairouan, or to Tobiah the Physician in Tripoli, whom the ruler of Qābes summoned when stricken with disease, promising him a very high fee.[2] The scribes of Kairouan were famous for their neat writing and their exact copies, which circulated in Jerusalem and Europe.[3] In the middle of the 11th century, a merchant from Kairouan in Jerusalem, for want of another livelihood, copied books which had been ordered from Egypt.[4]

In Fusṭāṭ, a man critically ill, in giving an inventory of his estate, mentions, *inter alia*, consignments of books from the Maghreb.[5] The form of the script in secular documents, such as letters and accounts, likewise arouses our admiration.[6]

This art, however, seems to have been confined to a single district. In Tlemcen, people did not know how to make hides into parchment.[7] We are told of a benefactor who sent a Tora scroll from Fusṭāṭ to Fez as a gift.[8] This might of course have had some special reason, but in view of the great distance between the two cities we may suppose that had there been expert scribes in Fez the task of writing the scroll would have been entrusted to them.

We are not sure what the duties of the *ḥazzān* were in large communities. In small communities, he seems to have been the headman—no doubt salaried—and to have acted at the same time as teacher, slaughterer and *dayyān* (the same combination of functions is found with rabbis of small communities today). R. Isaac the *ḥazzān*, of Fez, is reported to have made the Passover pilgrimage to Jerusalem.[9] Surely not all talmudic

---

[1] See above pp. 229-30, below next pages.
[2] See below, pp. 304ff; Assaf, *Sources*, p. 133.
[3] Comp. Mann, *JQR*, 9 (1918/19), p. 152.
[4] Comp. Starr, *Zion*, 1 (1936), p. 443.
[5] Comp. Golb, *JSS*, 20 (1958), p. 41 l. 15.
[6] Comp. Goitein, *Studies*, pp. 314f.
[7] *RH*, no. 432.
[8] Comp. Hirschberg, *Baer Jubilee Volume*, pp. 135, 143 ll. 22-25, and 152 ll. 22-25.
[9] Comp. Mann, *Jews* I, p. 104; II, pp. 113-115 and 246f.

scholars, religious judges (*dayyānīm*) and heads of academies made a living in commerce or medicine, like Rabbenu Ḥananel and Maimonides, and not all heads of academies received tuition fees from students, like R. Nissim ben Jacob.

We find that in one (unspecified) locality the people used the rent of some endowment property, earmarked for the requirements of the synagogue, to pay the man in charge of communal jurisdiction, who had no other source of livelihood.[1]

At this point, we should discuss the share of Jews in seafaring, which was both a craft or profession and a commercial activity. There can be no doubt that Jews engaged in it in earlier times. We have already met the Jewish owner and crew of the vessel in which Synesios travelled to Cyrene. In a later period Nostamnus the Jew owned a ship in Palermo. An Arab poet of the pre-Islamic period mentions brave Jewish sailors manning ships on the Tigris.[2]

The list published by Strauss refers to the son of a *nākhodā*. Elsewhere we are told that certain gifts were sent to India in the ship of the Sheikh Maḍmūn, through the *nākhodā*.[3] *Nākhodā* is a Persian word denoting the shipowner or the "manager" in charge of the passengers and goods.[4] In "the son of the *nākhodā*" the reference is certainly to a Jew, while this is not certain in the other case. During the period under review, there may still have been Jewish sailors on the Nile and in coastwise shipping, but the masters and crews of large seagoing vessels seem to have included no Jews. Nor do any of the names of shipowners occurring in two Geniza fragments sound Jewish; they were Muslim names, and some ships are expressly said to belong to *qādīs*.[5] However, we do find some Jewish shipowners in the Mediterranean, both in waters under Christian control and in Muslim areas.[6] So far, we know of two Indiamen owned by Jews, one of them being that commanded by Sheikh Maḍmūn, which, according to testimony given before the *beyt-dīn* of Aden in the matter of a Jew who went down with that ship, belonged to Ḥalfon, the nagid of Fusṭāṭ. Indiamen were privately-owned, while the ships plying the Mediterranean

---

[1] *RCor*, no. 82; Baneth, Marx Jubilee Volume (Hebrew Section), pp. 77-79.

[2] Comp. above, pp. 65ff; Katz, *JQR*, 24 (1933), p. 126; Hirschberg, *RO*, 11 (1936), p. 124.

[3] *Zion*, 7 (1941), pp. 142 l. 2 and 149 ll. 19f.

[4] Comp. Goitein, *Studies*, p. 350 n. 1.

[5] Comp. Gottheil-Worrell, Fragments, p. 50 l. 25; Starr, *Zion*, 1 (1936), pp. 439f.; Assaf, *Tarbiz*, 20 (1950), p. 187 l. 10; Strauss, *Zion*, 7 (1941), pp. 152-154.

[6] Comp. Golb, *JSS*, 20 (1958), p. 41 ll. 7f.

included also government-owned ones, which were sometimes used by Jews.[1]

Before passing to the next section, we should note a strange incident involving a coral dealer concerned with alchemy. It was the subject of a court case heard by the Chief Rabbi of Egypt, R. Shemariah and his son, R. Elḥanan (first quarter of the 11th century). Two brothers, Abraham and Ḍabyān, were living in Kairouan. When Ḍabyān once went to Egypt on business, Abraham gave him a parcel of *marjan*, *i.e.* corals, worth 500 (dinars?), to sell there. He also paid him the "wage", *i.e.* probably the travelling expenses, and all the customs duties payable at the different stations. Abraham's son, Ṭibb, accompanied Ḍabyān in order to bring back the goods which the latter would buy in Egypt. On arrival in Egypt, Ḍabyān "began to concern himself with a matter which is a royal prerogative and meddling in which is tantamount to suicide, to wit, alchemy." Privy to this entreprise was a man connected with the authorities. "And my brother Ḍabyān—so Abraham reports—met with him to learn from him that art, wishing to profit by something that in reality involves danger and brings no benefit." That man, perceiving that he was liable to be arrested, made good his escape. Now Ḍabyān was falsely accused of "having smuggled him to the Maghreb in order that he might practise that art for him there and they might both profit." Ḍabyān did not wait until they arrested him, but went into hiding. However, the boy Ṭibb and another of their relatives were apprehended, and the authorities demanded that Ḍabyān's hiding-place be revealed to them. When they were unable to find him, they beat the two of them to death and confiscated the corals. Ḍabyān managed to escape punishment and even to recover and sell the corals, while Abraham got nothing of the proceeds. The whole story was well known to all the Maghrebis and to other strangers, and Abraham relied on their testimony when he came to Egypt to plead his case before the *beyt-dīn* and claim his money.[2]

I have found no other instance in the sources of Jews in our region concerned with alchemy.

Pedlars and Merchants

According to our sources, the main Jewish livelihood was commerce in all its forms. In Eastern countries, the merchant class had been highly

---

[1] Comp. Strauss, *Zion*, 4 (1939), p. 219; id., *ibid.*, 7 (1941), p. 150 l. 19: for the organization of shipping see Goitein, *Society* I, pp. 309-313.

[2] *RA* III, p. 115 no. 110.

respected since olden times. It continued to be so in Islamic days. Although the Caliph Omar had voiced an adverse opinion of commerce, this branch of the economy was not in Muslim lands regarded with any of the hostility developed towards it by the Roman Catholic Church in the West. Most retailers were either merchants who kept a shop or pedlars who toured villages and nomad encampments. The methods of the latter are described in a question sent to Babylonia—probably from North Africa, since it mentions wax, a main export article of the region: "The question comes from traders who visit towns and villages, selling metalware, flax, wool and spices and obtaining wheat, barley, wax and other things; they have previously received money from householders for the acquisition of the wax, wheat and barley, stipulating with them for so many *qefizim* [1] per dinar; with this money, they have bought the merchandise they sell, and they ultimately make a profit from that cycle of transactions."[2]

Those itinerant traders were poor people who bought their wares—petty metal articles, spices, perfumes and spinning materials—with money borrowed from persons of means, on the understanding that they delivered to them, at a prearranged price, the goods they brought from the villages in return for their merchandise. The halakhic problem prompting the question was whether the pedlars were obligated to supply the wax, wheat and barley at the prearranged price even if the price of the product had gone up in the meantime; if so, the lenders would be making an excessive profit, which would be a kind of interest. There can hardly be a doubt that the trade carried on by pedlars in small towns, villages and nomad encampments was barter, for whence should either sellers or buyers have obtained money? The few dinars needed to buy the pedlar's stock-in-trade had to be taken on loan and repaid in goods, or else it was bought on credit.

One responsum mentions shops in Majāna, a locality frequently referred to in the sources. As there were silver mines in the area, as well as cultures of saffron, which was a major export article, we may suppose that the local shopkeepers did not content themselves with the ordinary business of small-town merchants, but were agents for the shipping of the mining output and saffron and the supply of various goods required by labourers. They must also have engaged in the refining and testing of silver and allied occupations.[3] There was close contact between Majāna on the one hand and Kairouan and Fusṭāṭ on the other both as regards

---

[1] Name of a small measure; *cf.* קפיזא in the relevant dictionaries.

[2] Ginzberg, *Geonica* II, p. 80.

[3] Comp. above, pp. 249 and 250, n. 1.

halakhic debate and commerce. A question sent from Kairouan to Babylonia—probably before 872—refers to some immovable property owned by an inhabitant of that city in Majāna which after his death became the subject of a deed of sale issued by the Majāna *beyt-dīn* on the authorization of its Kairouan counterpart.[1]

People from Majāna are mentioned in a decision of the Kairouan *beyt-dīn* of the seventies of the 10th century and in letters of R. Nissim of Kairouan and other rabbis to Joseph ben ʿAwkal in Fusṭāṭ. It can be inferred from this material that Majāna was a kind of affiliate of Kairouan. The distance between the two cities was relatively small—four or five days' journey—and there were Majāna people in Kairouan.[2]

On the whole, we may suppose that all those moneychangers, spice and perfume dealers, wine and oil sellers and keepers of grocery "shops" were far from being well-to-do; their operating capital was a few dinars. Similarly, the wholesale and export-import transactions of the period involved goods worth some tens of dinars.[3]

He who has seen the great majority of "shops" in the Jewish quarters of North African cities in our days can easily visualize the petty traders and pedlars of a thousand years ago, their goods and volume of business.

The Rādhānites

The economic activity of North African Jews was not confined to the retail trade: they were concerned in business encompassing almost the whole of what was then the inhabited world. The earliest information to this effect is preserved in the famous Ibn Khordadhbeh text (middle of the 9th century), which tells of the travels of Jewish traders, the Rādhānites (or Rahdānites), in Europe, Africa and Asia. They spoke all the languages then current in the world: Arabic, Persian, Greek, French, Spanish and Slavonic. They dealt with a wide range of commodities. They brought eunuchs, female servants, young boys, brocade (*dibāj*), furs, hides and swords from Europe to the East. In the East, they bought musk (*misk*), incense, spices and perfumes, which were much in demand in Europe. It should be noted that in tracing the movements of the

---

1 *RA* II, no. 69 (p. 23); comp. also *ibid.*, pp. 1f., and above, pp. 219f.

2 Comp. Mann, *Texts* I, pp. 143 l. 16, 344 l. 16 and 362 l. 6; Assaf, *Tarbiẓ*, 20 (1950), pp. 179 l. 3 and 181 n. 3; Goitein, *ibid.*, pp. 202 n. 38 and 203 n. 46.

3 Comp. *e.g.*, the letter of Israel b. Nathan to R. Nehorāy, *Zion*, 1 (1936), p. 441, the letter of Abraham b. Peraḥya, *ibid.*, 7 (1941), p. 137, and the letter of Solomon Kohen, Hirschberg, *Y. Baer Jubilee Volume*, pp. 149-151.

Rādhānites, Ibn Khordadhbeh incidentally mentions the port of Ubulla at the outlet of the Euphrates into the Persian Gulf, near Basra, whence ships sailed to Oman and on to India and China.[1]

The question of the origin of the name Rādhānites, and the itineraries, extent and significance of the Rādhānite trade as far as it concerns countries outside our region, do not come within the purview of this book.[2] But we should pay particular attention to one sentence of Ibn Khordadhbeh's remarks concerning the African trade. The text before us, after indicating the route followed by Russian traders, goes on to say: "There are those among them who, starting out from Spain or the country of the Franks, go to Outer Sūs (Sūs al-aqṣā), thence to Tangier and afterwards to Africa, Egypt and Ramle." As confirmed by an abridged version of the author's words, preserved in a work by another geographer, the reference here is to Rādhānites, and not to Russian traders.[3] Ibn Khordadhbeh does not say by which route—land or sea—the traders reached Outer Sous, nor do we know which part of Outer Sous he means. If he at least told us what goods were exported from there, we would have an indication of the area visited by the Rādhānites. In the writings of the ancient Arab geographers, Sūs al-aqṣā, *i.e.* Outer Sūs, is that part of Southern Morocco which extends at approximately the latitude of Marrakesh from the Ziz Valley in the east to the Atlantic in the west; it is bounded in the south by the Sahara. We have already seen that this was an area of the utmost economic importance both on account of its agricultural produce and its relations with the Western Sudan.[4] Arab historians maintain that it was already occupied by the earliest Arab conquerors in the second half of the 7th century and only the waters of the ocean prevented ʿUqba from proceeding further west.[5] Yaʿqūbi, a contemporary of Ibn Khordadhbeh, reports that ships built at Ubulla for the carriage of grain would come to Māssa on the Atlantic coast (in Outer Sūs) and thence proceed to China.[6] The agreement between this story of relations between Ubulla and Outer Sous and Ibn Khordadhbeh's above-

---

[1] *BGA* VI, pp. 153f.; comp. also al-Ḥamadhānī, *BGA* V, pp. 270f.

[2] There is an extensive literature on the Rādhānites; comp. Fischel, *Jews*, p. 31; Lewicki, *Źródła*, pp. 43ff.; Baron *SRH* IV, pp. 180f. Cl. Cahen, *REJ*, vol. 123, 1964, pp. 499-505, is very sceptical of their historicity.

[3] Comp. al-Ḥamadhāni, *BGA* V, p. 271.

[4] Comp. Ibn Ḥawqal, pp. 91f.; Maqdisi, p. 221. Comp. also *EI s.v.* Sous; the French edition, which gives the article in the language of the author (Lévy-Provençal), has "Sous al akca," the English edition, wrongly, "Sous al adna."

[5] Comp. Ibn al-Athīr, IV, p. 90; Ibn ʾIdhāri I, pp. 26f. (also 51); Ibn Khaldūn, VI, p. 108.

[6] *BGA* VII, p. 360.

mentioned statement concerning Rādhānites sailing from Ubulla to China is remarkable.

We cannot decide whether the Rādhānites reached Outer Sūs by land or by sea. But one conclusion may be drawn from Ibn Khordadhbeh's words: the presence of the Jewish traders in Sūs is somehow connected with permanent Jewish settlements there, be it that the Rādhānites were assisted by local agents and merchants already in residence or that, on the contrary, reports of that region's natural wealth reached Jewish communities through the Rādhānites and prompted emigration thither. The progress of the Rādhānites from Tangier eastward is easier to determine. The most usual and most convenient overland caravan route led across the coastal plain via a chain of stations, which enabled both rest and trading. At some stations, the Rādhānites would find Jews and they were able so to time their journey that they spent Sabbaths and holydays among them. The terminus of the western part of the trip was Kairouan, where they put up near a gate called Bāb al-Rahdāna (Gate of the Rahdānites or Rādhānites), near the Moneychangers' Gate. Thence they proceeded eastward, stopping at Fusṭāṭ, Ramle, Damascus etc.[1]

INTERNATIONAL AND INTERCONTINENTAL TRADE

The activity of the Rādhānites declined and stopped at the beginning of the 10th century, their place in Africa being taken by the traders of Kairouan and Fusṭāṭ.

From the second half of that century, our sources—and especially the Geniza documents—supply a wealth of material on North Africa's international and intercontinental wholesale trade. Let us first study some questions connected with that trade which were sent to Babylonia. As these are rather vague, we will presently turn to some court decisions and correspondence, which prove extremely revealing.

A question "asked by our brethren, the rabbinical scholars in the city of Tlemcen in the land of the sunrise" concerns a father and two sons; "when the younger son went overseas on business, his brother gave him some of his money etc."[2] Another question from Kairouan turns upon some money that is overseas and how it may be recovered.[3] R. Jacob the son of R. Nissim asks the Gaon Sherira and his son Hay as to the mainte-

---

[1] Comp. Maqdisi, p. 255 l. 15, also p. 30 l. 16; see also above, p. 255, n. 1; Lewicki, *Źródła*, pp. 307f.; Marçais, *Berbérie*, p. 214.

[2] Comp. *TR* II, p. 31; also *RH*, no. 37 and *ibid.*, note on p. 347.

[3] *RH*, nos. 199f.

nance claim of a woman whose husband has gone overseas. In one case, the heir of a deceased person was in Spain.[1]

It is not surprising that relations between Kairouan and Egypt, *i.e.* Fusṭāṭ and Alexandria, were extremely close so long as the Fāṭimids controlled both Egypt and North Africa and the Banū Zīrī recognised Fāṭimid suzerainty. Notwithstanding the importance of Kairouan as the capital of North Africa, Fusṭāṭ was the natural meeting-place of merchants from the Maghreb and Sicily and those who brought goods from the East—the countries on the Indian Ocean and as far as China. This is why, in addition to Babylonians and Palestinians, we find there a great number of emigrants from the Maghreb, who had settled in the city or were staying there for long periods on business.

This forms the background for various questions: Reuben, who lives in Egypt, owns some premises in the Maghreb, etc.[2] In a statement to a *beyt-dīn* in Fusṭāṭ in 967, the Maghrebi merchant Isaac acknowledges the receipt of a loan in fine silver and undertakes to repay it whenever he might be called upon to do so in Kairouan, his place of permanent residence.[3] The brisk commercial traffic between Alexandria and al-Mahdiya is dealt with in a report by Ephraim b. Jacob al-Mahdāwi (*i.e.* the one of Mahdiya), the Alexandrian agent of Joseph b. Jacob ʿAwkal, an important Fusṭāṭ merchant and official of the Babylonian and Palestinian academies in the first third of the 11th century. The report says that twenty-five bales of goods have been received; twenty of them have been loaded onto one ship, three onto another, and the ships have left for Mahdiya (two sacks have been sent to Sicily by a Spanish ship): when the other bales arrive, they, too, will be sent to Mahdiya and Sicily: Ephraim will send still other goods to Mahdiya, which will be sold at the time of the *mawsam* through an uncle who lives there. Ephraim is in regular correspondence with his uncle, who keeps him informed of prices quoted at the Mahdiya (or Kairouan) "exchange" for flax; *baqam* (later known as brazil), a dyewood; Kermān indigo; another dyestuff, known as yellow *lilaj*; ammonia; olive oil; and substances or products called *qemāṭ* and *mellāl*, which we have not been able to identify. The report mentions a letter from Mahdiya, addressed to the servant or clerk (*naʿar*)—probably in Alexandria—of a merchant, which confirms that *qemāṭ* is in great demand, while *mellāl* is not.[4]

---

[1] *RH*, no. 230; *RM*, no. 19.

[2] *RA* III, no. 5, pp. 7f.

[3] Mann, *Texts* I, pp. 360f.; comp. also the following document there.

[4] Assaf, *Tarbiẓ*, 20 (1950), pp. 187-190. *Qemāṭ* and *mellāl* seem to be kinds of

A kind of supplement to Ephraim's report is a letter to Ibn ʿAwkal from Samḥōn ben Da'ūd al-Siqīli, who presumably lived in Kairouan or Mahdiya. This is a detailed business communication, a refutation of charges levelled by Ibn ʿAwkal against Samḥōn both orally and in writing. The business activities in question were extremely extensive. A large quantity of brazilwood had been despatched to Spain, but part of it had been held up by one Faraḥ of Fez, because the price had meanwhile dropped from 265 dinars, for which it had been bought in Kairouan, to 125 dinars; both the despatch and the detention of the goods were apparently not to Ibn ʿAwkal's liking. Four qantars and twenty rotls of silk had been sold by Samḥōn in Kairouan, where the conditions of sale were more favourable than in Egypt. Ibn ʿAwkal was not pleased with this transaction, either, in which Samḥōn's brother Moses, Slāma al-Mahdāwi, ibn al-Ṣabbāgh (*i.e.* the son of the dyer) and the *lawwānīn* (*i.e.*, the dyers) were involved. Samḥōn sends one hundred less one quarter *ʿAzīzī* dinars (minted in the days of the Fāṭimid Caliph al-ʿAzīz, 975-976), which he himself has weighed, by the caravan of the Sijilmāsans. As against Ibn ʿAwkal's complaints, Samḥōn contends that b. ʿAwkal had not let him in on a large pearl transaction in which he, Ibn ʿAwkal, made a 100 p. ct. profit. In view of the tension between them, both sides are withholding payments due to third parties on their joint accounts. B. ʿAwkal has issued a circular to many persons to the effect that it is Samḥōn who withholds the payments, while in reality it is Ibn ʿAwkal who has failed to transmit certain sums to Samḥōn's creditors.

A report spread by "our friends in the Maghreb" in the name of a certain person (apparently an associate of Ibn ʿAwkal), that Samḥōn has attempted to encroach on the domain of Ibn ʿAwkal's agent, Ibn al-Majāni, is described as untrue. The writer stresses repeatedly that he is trading with Ibn ʿAwkal, mainly, because of the latter's high standing in the community and well-known piety. Actually, he says, the Maghrebis have no need of the Egyptians, for "what is little in the Maghreb is much with you". The letter concludes on a friendly note, with greetings to Ibn ʿAwkal's two sons, Hillel and Benjamin.[1] Other letters to Ibn ʿAwkal, interesting from a general economic and not merely a commercial point of view, will be discussed below.[2]

---

textiles. *Qemāṭ* is miswritten for *qemāsh,* comp. *RH*, no. 182: *qemāsha*; *mellāl* is named after a locality in Morocco where this fabric was made; compare *sūsiya*, textiles manufactured in Sousse (Tunisia); Goitein, *Studies*, p. 266.

[1] Goitein, *Tarbiẓ*, 20 (1950), pp. 202f.

[2] Comp. Goitein, *Tarbiẓ*, 34 (1965), pp. 162-182. Additional material from the

A document of 1034 of the *beyt-dīn* in Kairouan deals with the estate of a merchant of Qābes, consisting of garments (*aksiya*) and brocade (*dibāj*). The case was very complicated. The man had left a widow originating from Mesīla (not Marseilles, as the editor of the document thought, whose view, uncritically adopted by many, led them to assume relations between North Africa and Marseilles at that early epoch).[1] There were also two sons, one of whom, a resident of Tripoli, was in Egypt at the time, while the other spent some time in Sicily (on business?). The proceedings for the release of the estate, after the widow had received her settlement, lasted at least two years.

R. Elḥanan b. Shemarya, the famous head of the Fusṭāṭ Academy (beginning of the 11th century), informs his addressee in Damascus, *inter alia*, in a letter, of the sad news he has received. His son-in-law has been drowned while travelling on business. All his wealth and "he had much of it with him, from what was despatched and received by him" has been lost. He left a pregnant widow and their daughter in Kairouan, a strange land.[2]

Trade relations between Kairouan, Mahdiya, Sfax, Tripoli, Barca and Sicily, involving also a man from Andalusia and one from Majāna, are reflected in a document drawn up in 1040 in Egypt at the *beyt-dīn gādōl* of Nathan, head of the Palestinian Academy, a rival of the Gaon Solomon ben Yehuda. The goods in dispute included a few bales of indigo and sixty skins of olive oil acquired in exchange for the indigo.[3]

We should not be surprised at the small quantity of indigo for which the matter was brought before the *beyt-dīn gādōl*. Indigo was a valuable and much sought-after commodity.

Already in the year 977/8, we find the *beyt-dīn* of Kairouan, "a great city in Africa," receiving an admission concerning two skins of *astis*, *i.e.* Syrian indigo, weighing one qantar and twenty pounds, which after the death of their owner had arrived in Kairouan and been taken in charge by the estate administrators, one of whom hailed from Majāna.[4]

A letter fragment, in which the names of the writer and the addressee are missing, mentions relations with Pisa and Genoa, which both had contacts with the Maghreb from the second half of the eleventh century.

---

latter's archives has been published by Goitein, *ibid.*, 38 (1969), pp. 18-42, and in vol. II of his *Mediterranean Society*, 1971, see Index *s.v.* Ibn ʿAwkal.

[1] Comp. above, p. 142 n. 4.

[2] Mann, *Jews* I, p. 38, II p. 40 ll. 19-21.

[3] Comp. Mann, *Texts* I, pp. 343-345.

[4] Comp. *ibid.*, pp. 361-363.

The tenor of the letter indeed indicates that it belongs to that period and that the writer was in Tripoli at the time, but the dilapidated condition of this document makes it difficult to say any more.[1]

An anonymous writer, in a letter (dated 999 C.E.) to the Gaon R. Samuel B. Ḥofni, mentions countries and places visited by him: Andalusia, Kairouan, Mahdiya.[2]

From a letter written in the thirties of the 12th century, by a merchant in Spain, whose name has not been preserved, we learn incidentally, that he has sent merchandise to Fez and is now waiting to receive the proceeds.[3]

The Firm of Nahrāy b. Nissim

Most instructive from the point of view of commercial relations is the correspondence of R. Nahrāy ben Nissim, comprising hundreds of letters that were discovered in the Geniza and apparently belonged to the archives of his firm, which was leading in Jewish trade in Africa and Asia for at least half a century.[4]

Nahrāy ben Nissim was born in Kairouan or came there at a tender age with his family (his cousins also lived there). The family originated from Iraq. In fact, various documents from the 10th century onwards indicate that in those days Babylonians settled or stayed for lengthy periods in Kairouan and Mahdiya.

An anonymous gaon says in a letter: "The contribution donated by the Babylonian elders in the city of Kairouan has reached us through R. Shemaryah the Elder, our emissary, and they are prepared to send the remainder."[5] After moving to Fusṭāṭ, Nahrāy headed the Babylonian community there; he and his son are mentioned in the list of the community leaders: "Nahōrāy (*sic!*), the great rabbi and great *yeshiva* scholar, and his beloved son R. Nissim, the wise and understanding." The view that Nahrāy's father was born in Jerusalem is difficult to accept; it seems

---

[1] Comp. Assaf, *Sources*, pp. 130f.

[2] See Goldziher, *REJ*, 57 (1905), pp. 184-5 and comp. above p. 258.

[3] Published by Goitein, *Tarbiẓ*, 35 (1966), pp. 275-7, from the Geniza materials preserved in Leningrad (MS. Antonin 1105). Comp. also the letter published by Goldziher quoted in the preceding note.

[4] Goldziher seems to have been the first to publish material concerning the Nahrāy family; comp. *REJ*, 55 (1908), pp. 54f.; *ibid.*, 56 (1908), p. 239. The known Nahrāy papers now number over 250 items. Part of them are included in a Hebrew University Ph.D. thesis by M. Michael; comp. Goitein, *Society* I, index and esp. pp. 153-155.

[5] Comp. Mann, *Texts* I, p. 189.

more likely that he was surnamed al-Maqdisi because he had lived for a time in Jerusalem and perhaps died there.[1]

J. Starr has published four letters of Nahrāy's cousin, Israel b. Nathan b. Nahrāy. The first is from Alexandria, where the writer was staying as Nahrāy's agent and partner. It reports various commercial transactions: the purchase, for their joint account, of one third of two loads of indigo of choice quality and half a consignment of packets of pearls; the purchase of ten bottles of musk and of some cinnamon and pepper; some furs bought earlier are still in Fusṭāṭ and will be dealt with when the writer gets there in a few weeks' time. As to the garments (*kiṣāwīn*) mentioned in Nahrāy's letter to him, he saw only one that was attractive, *viz.* the one in which Nahrāy's goods were wrapped during transport on camelback. A certain Andalusian alleges that nothing is due from him. In exchange foı a parcel of hides received from a certain person, Israel has acquired furs for him, which are being sent by ship. For another person he has bought horseshoes, which he is sending by a man from Qābes. Moreover, he is sending Nahrāy three packets of pearls by two different ships. The account for a bead necklace has not yet been prepared; this will perhaps be done simultaneously with the sale of the furs in Fusṭāṭ. Israel has also bought grain, which has been loaded onto al-ʿArūs's ship. The letter was written in haste and without proper order. There are greetings to Nahrāy's mother and sister and to Aaron and Samuel (probably Nahrāy's brothers). Finally, Israel remembers that according to a rumour reaching Alexandria the *Rūmīs*—which usually means the Byzantines, but here undoubtedly refers to Christians from Sicily or Southern Italy—have bought many strings of (coral?) beads from Nahrāy; he hopes that a good profit has been made and asks not to be kept in the dark about it. The letter is undated. However, since we know that in 1050 Nahrāy was already living in Fusṭāṭ, because he signed a marriage contract there in that year, we may place the date of the letter to Kairouan in the fifth decade of the century. At that time, Nahrāy was not yet married (as we shall see, he married only when resident in Fusṭāṭ) and was orphaned of his father, for Israel sends greetings to his mother, sister and brothers. But even then, he was head of the firm, whence we may conclude that he was the eldest brother. Perhaps we may narrow down the time of the letter to Kairouan to 1046/7, considering that in the early days of his residence in Fusṭāṭ he was still fairly young, though already an accomplished rabbinical

---

[1] Comp. Mann, *Jews* II, p. 101 ll. 6f.; also Gottheil-Worrell, *Fragments*, p. 158 ll. 1 and 2 of the address.

scholar. Nahrāy died between 1083 and 1098. A more precise date is so far not known.[1]

We may suppose that Nahrāy moved to Fusṭāṭ in the years 1047/8, approximately, probably because of the severance of North Africa from Fāṭimid Egypt by al-Muʿizz, the Zīrī ruler in Kairouan. The young merchant settled in Egypt because he foresaw developments in North African trade. After a time—perhaps in 1049/50—Israel left Egypt for Byzantine territory; it may not have been necessary for both partners to reside in Egypt. After some wanderings in Christian countries, including Constantinople, Israel settled in Jerusalem, where he engaged in copying books (he mentions the Mishnaic orders *Nashim* and *Nezikin*).

This and other information is contained in three letters he sent from Jerusalem to his wealthy cousin in Fusṭāṭ. The third letter, probably not later than 1053, which alludes to dissensions in the Palestinian Academy, congratulates Nahrāy on his marriage to a daughter of one of the most respected Fusṭāṭ families. At the same time, Israel intimates that he has received a sum of money through Abū Yaʿqūb Yūsuf ha-Kohen b. ʿAlī of Fez, who lives in Ramle and Tyre and is in contact with Nahrāy.[2]

The fourth letter expresses anxiety over the situation in the Maghreb, where Israel's brother is. The writer still has business interests there and wishes to appoint an agent to look after them because he has again been assessed to *kharāj* in Egypt although he left that country ten years ago. These data and the writer's concern about the Maghreb lead us to suppose that the letter was written in the late fifties, when Kairouan had been plundered and the situation in North Africa was extremely disturbed. Israel knew that Nahrāy still maintained close business relations with the Maghreb and had reliable information.

The letter from Nahrāy to the abovementioned Yūsuf ha-Kohen of Fez contains details of business in the Maghreb: the Maghrebis buy indigo, arsenic, Syrian and Eastern metalware, silver (probably in bars) and perforated pearls; from the Maghreb, Nahrāy receives soap, though he has not yet sold any of it. Nahrāy mentions a person surnamed Sūsi, but we cannot tell whether he is from Sousse (Tunisia) or from the Sūs Valley in Morocco.[3]

These trade relations are also referred to in a letter to Nahrāy from

---

[1] Comp. *Zion*, 1 (1936), pp. 436-452; Worman, *JQR*, o.s., 19 (1907), pp. 736f.; Mann, *Jews* I, p. 205, II, pp. 245-247.

[2] *Zion*, 1 (1936), pp. 438 and 446-448. The R. Joseph who aspired to be head of the academy was the son of the Gaon R. Solomon; comp. Mann, *Jews* II, p. 66. He died in 1053. On Abū Yaʿqūb comp. Strauss, *Zion*, 7 (1941), pp. 151-155.

[3] Comp. Strauss, *l.c.* (preceding note).

Ṣadqa al-Maghrebī, a resident of Jerusalem, who asks for news of the Maghreb.[1] A Jew who emigrated from Kairouan to Jerusalem asks Abū Yaʿqūb Yūsuf b. ʿAlī ha-Kohen—mentioned twice before—to buy for his orphaned (female) cousin Ṣebiya some green veils for twenty dinars and some blue ones for three dinars and to buy a cover for a Tora scroll; all these are to be handed to someone who is going to Kairouan for transmission to the addressees. It seems reasonable to assume that the errand is to be carried out through the firm of Nahrāy.[2]

Maghrebis in the Indian Trade

In the first half of the 12th century, Jewish trade between Egypt and India by a land-sea route via South Arabia grew considerably. The general picture is fairly clear from preliminary surveys of the Geniza material, although only a small percentage of the latter has so far been published in full. These sources disclose the large share of Maghrebi Jews in this important economic activity. The reason for their participation is obvious. In addition to general factors, especially the Crusades, they were actuated by a decisive local factor: the decline of Kairouan and of Tunisia in general compelled Tunisian merchants to seek new sources of livelihood.

As far as known hitherto, the earliest documents of Indian trade carried on by Maghrebis via South Arabia are of the late 11th century. Joseph ha-Labdi (*i.e.* of Lebda on the Tripolitanian coast) or ha-Trabulsi (he seems to have stayed for a time in Tripoli) settled in Egypt and thence conducted his far-flung business activities. In the last decade of the 11th century, he left Egypt with goods of his own and of others, including the *pāqīd* (warden) of merchants in Fusṭāṭ. Some time before his departure, the *dayyān* of Mahdiya, Moses ben Labraṭ, entrusted to him a consignment of corals for sale in Alexandria. Joseph got into business difficulties on the way to India, and on the way back his ship foundered and part of the cargo was lost.

However, he arrived safely in Marbāṭ in South Arabia. The dispute with which that journey ended will be discussed below. Joseph's son, Berakhot, also went to India; he returned from there in 1135 after a successful trip.[3]

[1] Gottheil-Worrell, *Fragments*, Letter XXVII; see especially p. 126 l. 7.

[2] Comp. B. Chapira, *REJ*, 56 (1908), pp. 237f.

[3] Comp. Goitein, *Speculum* 29 (1954), pp. 191-195; Hirschberg, *Zion*, 22 (1957), p. 240. The poet Isaac b. Khalfon dedicated a poem to an earlier Samuel ibn al-Lebdi; see A. Mirski, *Ibn Khalfūn*, pp. 80-82; also Mann, *Jews* I, p. 23 n. 2.

In the early 12th century, frequent mention is made of ʿArūs ben Joseph of Mahdiya, a resident of Fusṭāṭ, whose business activities extended to the Maghreb and Yemen. According to a decision of the *beyt-dīn* of Fusṭāṭ of the year 1428 S.E. (1116 C.E.), he seems to have gone to Yemen with R. Yefet (possibly the father of Maḍmūn, the *pāqīd* (warden) of merchants); upon his return, he had a dispute with a creditor, which was terminated by a compromise settlement.[1]

In the thirties and forties of that century, two other Maghrebi merchants were prominent, viz. Yehuda ben Joseph Sijilmāsi and Abraham ben Peraḥya ben Yajū of Mahdiya, who have already been mentioned because of references to contemporary events contained in their letters. Yehuda *nīn (descendant of) geonim* b. Joseph probably not only originated from Sijilmāsa, but grew up there or at least visited the city and knew its rabbis. He sent a Tora scroll as a gift to a synagogue in Sijilmāsa or Fez. In the late forties, his brother and other members of his family were still in the Maghreb, and he was greatly concerned about their fate. Yehuda Sijilmāsī was *pāqīd* of merchants in Fusṭāṭ and engaged in Indian trade in partnership with Ḥalfon ben Netanel, a highly respected businessman, whose ramified activities in three continents, Africa, Asia and Europe, are much spoken of in documents in our possession. Yehuda sailed several times to India and was once taken prisoner there. This is reported by his wife's brother, Maḥrūz b. Jacob, who also traded with India and whose permanent place of residence was Aden. Maḥrūz was in India at the time Yehuda was taken prisoner; he worked for his brother-in-law's redemption, probably together with the abovementioned Abraham ben Peraḥya ben Yajū, who lived in India for many years. It seems that Yehuda became impoverished at that time; his family, which lived in Fusṭāṭ, was in "mediocre circumstances," as his son Solomon wrote in Shebat, 1459 S.E./January-February, 1148 C.E., to his father, who lingered in South Arabia. Yehuda had a sister in Aden, who was married to Maḍmūn ben Yefet, the local *pāqīd* of merchants.[2]

Of the archives of Abraham ibn Yajū, 30-odd letters are left, only two of which have so far been published. In a letter sent from Aden in Tishri, 1461 S.E./1149 C.E., to Mahdiya or wherever else in Africa his relatives might be, Abraham informs his brothers Mebasser and Joseph that he has recently returned from India, where he was on business, and that he and his children are now in Aden; he has amassed great wealth, which

---

[1] Comp. Gottheil-Worrell, *Fragments*, pp. 2-11; 164-169; Goitein, *Studies*, p. 337.
[2] Hirschberg, *I. F. Baer Jubilee Volume*, pp. 134ff., and above pp. 147ff.

will suffice for the livelihood of all of them. He is angry with Mebasser, who, while in Egypt, did not go on to Aden to meet with him. Abraham has sent forty dinars' worth of perfumes to Egypt in a consignment destined for the master and sheikh Maḍmūn, and Maḍmūn's brother-in-law, Yehuda Sijilmāsī, has told him that the consignment has arrived safely; as Mebasser was not available at the time, the goods were taken to Sicily by a reliable Sicilian; Abraham hopes that they will reach Mebasser. He entreats Mebasser to come to Aden, promising to defray all his expenses. Mebasser will then take with him Abraham's son and daughter, as well as all his property, so that it may not fall into the hands of the people of Jerba. Abraham will give his daughter in marriage to the son of his brother Joseph or the son of his sister Berakha. The young couple will live in Aden or in Egypt or in one of the North African cities. The letter ends with greetings to relatives and friends, and especially to the *dayyān* b. Labraṭ, and with a question concerning the truth of reports about events in North Africa. A second letter—also, in all probability, from Abraham—speaks of the despatch of goods to Persia through the Sheikh Maḍmūn.[1]

The other published letter was sent to Abraham ibn Yajū from Aden by a Jew named Khalaf in 1148, *i.e.* while Abraham was still in India, one year before his return to Aden. The writer was probably the agent of Abraham, who had once himself been in India for a long time, although he had promised every year to return to Aden (l. 24). He informs Abraham that he has not been able to ascertain whether his brother Mebasser has been in Syria. At any rate, Mebasser is well, and if he comes to Aden, Khalaf will look after him even without being asked to do so, out of regard for Abraham. Khalaf has received the present Abraham has sent him, and he reciprocates by sending some bowls of sugar, almonds and raisins, which will be taken to Mangalor (on the Malabar Coast, an important trading centre in those days) in a ship of Sheikh Maḍmūn, under the care of the captain (ll. 19-20). Khalaf sends greetings to Abraham's son (but not to his daughter, who was still little and whom one would not expect to be mentioned) and to "the brother"—no doubt Abraham's Indian associate or partner.[2]

The list of Maghrebis proceeding to India is not, of course, confined to these three oı four names. Many more appear in the letters (some mentioned frequently, others only once or twice), the North African

---

[1] Braslavsky, *Zion*, 7 (1941), pp. 148-151. Commercial partnerships: Goitein, *Society* I, pp. 169-179.

[2] Strauss, *Zion*, 7 (1941), pp. 148-51.

origin being indicated by the surnames. Here are a few of them: a man from Barca, Abu al-Khayr al-Barqī; the people of the islands of Jerba; ʿArūs ben Joseph of Mahdiya; Isaac al-Nafūsi; Samuel ben Abraham al-Majāni; Jacob al-Qalʿi; Isaac al-Tlemsāni; Isaac Sijilmāsi. They were certainly not all important merchants; and there must, in addition, have been agents, brokers, clerks, assistants and servants whose names are not mentioned.

We have incidentally noted a few particulars concerning sheikh Maḍmūn ben Yefet, a person of consequence in his day, a *pāqīd* of Jewish merchants in Aden. His official position brought him into close contact with merchants from the Maghreb and Egypt. Abraham ben Yajū addresses him reverently as "my lord the Sheikh"; and Maḍmūn, on the other hand, sends various gifts to him in India by ʿAbd al-Masīḥ *al-Shammās*, *i.e.* the deacon. A document of the *beyt-dīn* in Fusṭāṭ calls him "Our lord and great man, our master and rabbi; Maḍmūn the great lord in Israel", and a Maghrebi poet composed a panegyric on him, no doubt during a stay in Aden.

By virtue of his office, Maḍmūn dealt with the estate of two merchants from the Maghreb who had drowned in the sea, one of them a "Nafūsi" resident in Tripoli. The document in question mentions a man from Tripoli as one of those empowered to receive the estate. In another letter, Maḍmūn recommends that the nagid and the *pāqīd* of merchants in Egypt should protect two Jews from Tripoli, Ben Ḥaddāda and al-Baṭīṭi, who had been robbed in Sicily.[1]

We find Jewish merchants not only in South Arabia at that time. They also appear at the port of ʿAydhāb on the African coast of the Red Sea, Egypt's southern customs station. According to reports of the middle of the 11th century, ʿAydhāb was then a port of entry for goods from North West Africa and the Arab Peninsula and a port of departure for Egyptians on their pilgrimage to Mecca. Soon after, ʿAydhāb was a major centre of international trade. This change was certainly in part due to the dislocation of land communications by disturbed security conditions in Palestine and the Hejaz and by the Crusades. Until a few years ago, nothing was known of Jewish merchants in that place. It now appears that they are mentioned in at least thirty Geniza documents, of which only one has so far been published in full and another in summarized form. The published document confirms—not surprisingly—that the Jews visiting ʿAydhāb included also Maghrebi merchants.[2]

[1] About him see now Goitein, *Society* I, pp. 336 and 347-350.
[2] Comp. Goitein, *Tarbiẓ*, 21 (1951), pp. 185-191; also oral information by the same.

Taxes and Tolls

The silence of Jewish sources as to everything connected with property taxes and customs duties on goods in the Maghreb compels us to rely on Arab authors, especially on Ibn Ḥawqal, who was himself a merchant and recorded figures of the revenue of the treasury and administration from the various imposts. Moreover, we can draw conclusions from the situation in Egypt, since North Africa belonged for a long time to the same administrative unit as that country. Of course, we know little enough of the taxes paid by Egyptian Jewry. They had to pay the *kharāj*, a tax on immovable property, not to be confused with the poll-tax, the *jizya* or, as it was called in the Maghreb, the *jawālī*. This appears from a list of taxpayers which has come down to us. The fact that a Jew who had left Egypt complains that he has been assessed to that tax shows that it must by rights have been a tax on real property, and not a personal obligation.

The *kharāj* was not based on Islamic law but on government regulations, which is why many changes occurred in its nature and mode of collection. Ibn Ḥawqal says that local governors would levy sums in excess of these prescribed by regulations. The ordinary revenue of North Africa totalled 800,000 dinars in one year, and as much again was exacted by the governors on their own authority.

We may assume that North African Jews, too, had to pay the *kharāj* in so far as they owned immovable property. Moreover, they surely had to bear their share of extra-legal imposts.[1]

Organization of Trade and Methods of Payment

The dimensions of international trade called for new methods so as to overcome technical and legal difficulties in its organization. Individuals, albeit members of one family, could not carry on business in different parts of the world, buy and sell, barter, make trips to distant lands, lasting months and sometimes years, without availing themselves of agents, representatives and partners acting under special agreements. For the sake of completeness, the situation according to the Muslim law has to be compared. It seems that some business practices go back to Byzantine pre-Islamic times.[2] The hazards of travel led to the develop-

---

[1] Gottheil-Worrell, *Fragments*, pp. 66-70. For *jawālī* and *kharāj* see above, pp. 96 and 199; comp. now Idris, *Berbérie*, pp. 609-616.

[2] See *e.g.* A. Sayous, *Commerce* pp. 29-31, 139-40, and bibliography. Comp. the stipulations of a business agreement between a Gentile merchant in Constantinople and his (Jewish) agent, discussed by Dan, Two Jewish merchants in the Seventh Century, *Zion,* 36 (1971), pp. 14-18.

ment of new methods of transmitting moneys. Merchants were organized in partnerships on a family basis, with functions divided between the partners. They did not all of them travel all the time; they did not rely on chance for the delivery of goods and their preparation for sale.

Our sources provide a wealth of information on the organization of Mediterranean and Indian trade in the 11th and 12th centuries. Upon the entry of Jews into the overseas trade, the problem arose of the form of the authorization to collect money overseas. According to the halakha, the principal has to convey to the agent four cubits of land, by the acquisition of which the agent becomes duly empowered to collect the money (a similar provision exists with regard to monetary gifts). But it would happen that the principal had no real property to convey, in which case the people of Kairouan originally fell back on the four cubits of land which each Jew is deemed to own in Palestine, as they found in the responsa of the first geonim to a question addressed by their ancestors to the Gaon Mar Hilāy. However, in the days of Hay, they had doubts concerning this solution and therefore consulted him on the matter.[1] Jacob b. Nissim of Kairouan further asked Hay how to effect the authorization if the agent was a Gentile who was to collect the money in a distant country where Jews did not go. The reply was that for the purposes of the acquisition (of land by the agent), there was no difference between Jew and Gentile and that the authorization of both (to collect money) should be effected in the same way.[2]

In Kairouan, where visiting merchants were numerous, a problem was likely to arise in respect of well-to-do and even rich people who had no immovable property. The hazards of transferring money in cash and the difficulties of collecting it over great distances led to the development of means of payment which considerably facilitated trade and were proof against robbery and loss. Thus, the *suftaja*, a money order by means of which moneys could be transferred to distant places without risk, was introduced in Muslim countries. Its use was opposed by Muslim religious scholars, who regarded it as involving a kind of interest owing to the advantage accruing to a person by the protection of his money against loss. Doubts arose also with the rabbis because the *suftaja* was contrary to the

[1] *RH*, nos. 199-200. It is doubtful which R. Hilāy is meant, the first (792-801) or the second (825-829); comp. Mann, *JQR*, 10 (1919/20), p. 315. (The acquisition of four cubits of land in Palestine is still mentioned in *Mishkenot ha-Roʿim* "A" (2) (fol. 1b). The author lived in the 18th century.

[2] *RH*, no. 237; comp. Müller, *Mafteaḥ*, p. 43; Assaf, *Sefer ha-Sheṭarot*, 1930, p. 32 n. 9.

opinion of the Gemara (Baba Kama 104b) that money must not be sent in the form of a symbolic substitute. Eventually, however, they agreed to permit it, giving the following explanation: After seeing that people use it, we have begun to deal with it (*i.e.* to treat it as a commercial document), in order that trade might not be paralysed; we have decided to deal with it in accordance with the way it is dealt with by merchants, without adding or taking away anything; this is now the law, which should not be deviated from.[1] The *suftaja* was in use in Iraq, North Africa and Palestine. By such an order, R. Nissim transferred an amount of money to Hay's Academy in Baghdad, as stated in his letter to Joseph b. ʿAwkal.[2]

From the collection and transmission of moneys let us now pass to the conduct of business through another. There has come down to us an agent's power of attorney: in 1115 an Egyptian Jew, before the permanent *beyt-dīn* of Fusṭāṭ, issues to a man described as *ṣāḥib shamʿah* (candle-maker?) an authorization to act as his agent in the Maghreb and Sicily.[3]

Partnerships, differing in form and conditions, were very common. This was due to the prohibition of interest, which led to a search for methods of linking the capitalist with the merchant who actually conducted the business, and who was in need of working capital, in a way which was worthwhile for both and free of the taint of interest. Accordingly, it was necessary to even up the risks and profits of the two parties. So long as precedents and procedure had not been established, disputes were submitted for decision to the geonim and later to Maimonides.

Some questions contain information as to the forms of transactions and the trade routes. A capitalist in Tāhert, upon the advice of a fellow townsman, invested his gold in the business of a man in Kairouan in return for a quarter of the profits. "Simon came to Africa and went into partnership with Benjamin. Each of them contributed 100 dinars. Simon went overseas with the goods. He travelled from place to place, from country to country, but sold nothing etc."[4]

Changes in the practice with regard to sharing between partners are

---

[1] *RH*, no. 423; comp. also *ibid.*, nos. 548 and 552; Mann, *Jews* II, pp. 125 l. 18, 195 l. 12 and 349 ll. 9f. (on symbolic substitutes for money); comp. Fischel, *Jews*, pp. 18-20; Goitein, *Society* I, pp. 242-246. Against Goitein's assertion that "between the Muslim West and Egypt, no *suftajas* are mentioned at all," comp. next note.

[2] Comp. Mann, *Texts* I, pp. 143 l. 17 and 144 l. 23.

[3] Hirschfeld, *JQR*, 16 (1925/26), pp. 280f.

[4] *RA* II, no. 68 (p. 23). The matter was complicated by the fact that the two Tāhertis bought goods for the gold and sent them to Kairouan as the property of the Tāherti who gave the advice, and not of the real provider of the capital. As to the stipulation for a quarter of the profits see Maimonides, *Mishne Torah*, Hil. Sheluḥin we-Shutafin VII, 5.

dealt with in a question addressed by the Chief Rabbi Jacob (the father of R. Nissim) to Hay. Some years earlier, Jacob had addressed the same question to Sherira, who had replied that if the capital-giving partner paid the working partner a remuneration, however small, for his work, he must share profits and losses with him equally. Hay's answer is different; according to it, the working partner is liable for half the losses only if he receives two thirds of the profits. Hay says: "We do not remember what we wrote nor what the Gaon our father wrote", and after discussing the views expressed in the Gemara, he sums up: If a capital-giver who has given a person a business to conduct has decided to pay a wage to him in order that he may have no share in either profits or losses (*i.e.* that he may really be an employee and not a partner), he must fix a wage for him of an amount equal to that of a worker in the trade which he has given up in order to conduct that business; he cannot fob him off with a trifle. As to the sharing of profits and losses where the working partner receives no fixed wage, the rule is: If the capital-giver receives half of the profits, he is liable for two thirds of the losses; and if he assumes liability for half of the losses, he takes one third of the profits. In other words: If the working partner receives half of the profits, he is liable for one third of the losses, and if he assumes liability for half of the losses, he takes two thirds of the profits. In this way, the working partner is, as it were, assured of his wage, and the capital-giver does not benefit from the business in the same measure as the working partner, which would amount to taking interest.[1]

Different conditions are mentioned in another question asked by R. Jacob. Simon received from Reuben 150 dinars' worth of goods as their joint stock-in-trade and made out to him a loan deed for half the amount and a partnership deed for the whole amount. Reuben gave him a wage and his upkeep in order that he might sell the goods in other places, and both profits and losses were to be shared equally between them. These terms must be understood in the light of Hay's view according to which, since the working partner received a wage and his upkeep from the capital-giver, there was no kind of interest involved.[2] About two generations later, a Maghrebi Jew living in Jerusalem mentions incidentally

[1] As to the partners contributing equally, see *RHG*, no. 49. For Hay's responsum see *RSh*, 94b-95a no. 6. The wording is different from B.M. 68b-69a; see Rashi and Tosaphot *ad hoc*, as well as Maimonides, *ibid.*, VI, 3; comp. further Maimonides' *Responsa*, ed. Freimann, no. 268, as well as Ginzberg, *Geonica* II, pp. 186ff. On the subject as a whole comp. A. A. Hildesheimer, *Das jüdische Gesellschaftsrecht*, Leipzig 1930, pp. 120-150; Bergsträsser, *Grundzüge*, pp. 45 and 71.

[2] *RH*, no. 235; Maimonides, Hil. Sheluḥin we-Shutafin VI, 2.

that a certain man travelled to Damascus with a merchant who had asked him to accompany him, promising him one third of the profits. Clearly, his whole upkeep was on the merchant, who was therefore permitted to allow him only one third of the profits.[1]

Among "India traders", it seems to have been customary to give the working partner one third of the profits without his being liable for the losses. Maimonides confirms that in his day the terms of the deed were in accordance with "Gentile business practice", *i.e.* one third of the profits for the working partner, two thirds for the capital-giver, and no liability of the working partner for losses. These terms reflect the personal risk the working partner was taking on long journeys to distant lands, when he and the goods in his charge were exposed to all sorts of dangers and adversities.[2]

In view of the variety of conditions, revealed by the responsa literature, which then governed business partnerships—the questions were of course practical, not academic—we can realize the tangle in which a certain merchant from Lebda was caught. It led to a series of pleas and counter-pleas which were heard in the years 1097 and 1098 before the *batey-dīn* of Egypt, Aden and Mahdiya. The deeds under which the man acted have not been preserved, but it seems that the terms were in accordance with "common (non-Jewish) practice", so that he was not liable for losses. However, as he had not acted in conformity with the wishes of his principals, having sold their goods and bought others contrary to instructions, he was sued for defaulting on his commission. The proceedings ended with a compromise settlement, no doubt because the *beyt-dīn* was unable to decide in accordance with rabbinic law, the transaction having been effected in accordance with "common" practice.[3] As we have seen, the geonim sanctioned the *suftaja*, although they had initially been reluctant to do so. Maimonides, too, in one of his responsa, rules that the capital-giver cannot be compelled to give up what he has taken unlawfully if he took it in accordance with established practice.

A typical question was probably addressed to the Gaon Saadia: "Reuben died, leaving heirs. His books and accounts were produced to some merchants, faithful Jews, and appeared to be in order. They included accounts of business dealings between Reuben and Simon, according to

---

[1] Gottheil-Worrell, *Fragments*, p. 124 verso ll. 1 and 2.

[2] Some documents in Goitein's as yet unpublished *India Book*; Maimonides, *Responsa*, ed. Freimann, nos. 267f. In one case (*India Book* no. 115), the partners provided 60 per cent and 40 per cent, respectively, but shared the profits equally.

[3] Comp. above, p. 284.

which Simon owed Reuben some money. The heirs claimed from Simon accordingly. To ascertain the true position, they, as usual in dealings between merchants and petty traders, asked him to produce *his* books. Simon found nothing and said, 'I have no books and I know no book-keeping, but I owe you nothing', etc." The question came from an Arabic-speaking country. A fragment of a question from Qābes likewise refers to an account-book that was to serve as evidence in the hearing of mutual claims.[1]

Another question concerns the return of the capital to a partner in a case where the king had meanwhile changed the currency. The reply is: "Let it be returned according to what petty traders say; they will know how much that money was worth at that time."[2]

We have to do here with absolutely modern methods of discussion, taking into account usages which have developed between merchants and petty traders and for which the gaon is trying to find support in the Bible. The *peqīdīm* (wardens) of merchants in Fusṭāṭ, Ramle and Aden may have been competent to deal with problems of this kind. It is worth noting that the consolidation of the *jus mercatorum* in Europe began during the same period.[3]

Summary

The statements of 10th-century Arab geographers on the fertility, natural wealth and ramified, variegated trade of the region are supplemented by the responsa of the Geonim and stories of R. Nissim, which relate to the period from the late 10th to the middle of the 11th century. The commercial records and court files of the Geniza supply information concerning the situation until the middle of the 12th century, including a period for which no other sources exist. The combined yield of these sources, which show surprising agreement, enables us to determine the place of the Jews in the economy of the region. We find Jews at all levels

[1] *RSh*, p. 74b, no. 13; Ginzberg, *Geon.* II, p. 284; comp. also above, p. 182-3, and p. 257 n. 4. See also R. Nissim's story about an illiterate man who bought himself a literate slave to keep his account of sums spent for charity; Hirschberg, *R. Nissim*, pp. 94-5.

[2] *RCor*, no. 43.

[3] Merchants' usages and customs in Ramle: Mann, *Jews* II, pp. 29 and 112. For the duties of a "*paqīd* (warden) of merchants" according to a Geniza fragment of 1203 see Strauss, *Jews in Egypt* II, p. 224. See also *idem*, *Zion*, 30 (1965), p. 64; in n. 22 a *wakīl* in Tenes (?) is mentioned. The simultaneous development of usages in Europe is discussed by Pirenne, *Cities*, pp. 90f.; *idem*, *Social History*, p. 51.

of the occupational structure of medieval society, except high government bureaucracy and state leadership.

The isolated cases of Paltiel the Italian, who attained high office under the Fāṭimid al-Muʿizz, and of the Babylonian-Syrian Jacob al-Killis, who converted to Islam, underscore the fact that Maghreb-born Jews were not to be found among functionaries at these levels. On the other hand, we at first find Christians in the North African tax administration.[1]

Jews engaged in agriculture, which was not socially esteemed, and in humble occupations such as bricklaying and street-cleaning in Sijilmāsa. They also practised goldsmithing, an art shunned by Muslims for religious reasons, and ironwork in remote areas of Morocco. It should be remembered that goldsmithing and ironwork were Jewish callings in the Arabian Peninsula in pre-Islamic times. We may suppose that there were also Jewish dyers and weavers. Many Jews were pedlars or small shopkeepers. But Jews were no less active in what was the most respected category of commerce in Muslim society, the trade in perfumes and spices, corals and pearls, chemicals and dye-yielding plants. As dealers in these products, Maghrebi Jews achieved an important position in international trade. Since this trade was largely barter, import and export were combined in the hands of firms operating in different countries and continents.

All this activity, as reflected in the sources, presents a bright, impressive picture. The Maghreb possessed an abundance of grains, fruits of every kind, olive oil, industrial crops (cotton, flax, hemp, saffron (the later also as a condiment), large and small cattle, hides, wool, silk (from Qābes), wax, corals, iron, silver and probably also gold ore and smelted gold, which were brought from the interior of the African continent,[2] and home-industrial products, such as various textiles. All these commodities were put on the market. On the other hand, Jewish pedlars toured the countryside trading wheat, barley and wax in for petty metalware, women's jewelry and perfumes of local or foreign—mainly Indian—manufacture which they had obtained on credit from wholesalers in the large cities against the promise of goods in return. They also carried on barter between one area and another: wool produced by shepherds and nomads for cotton and flax which grew in certain parts of the region or were imported. The *kisā* (covering), which was the poor man's garment by day and blanket by night, and other kinds of wearing apparel, for which there was a demand even in India, must have been important items

[1] Comp. Hopkins, *Government*, p. 53.

[2] Idrīsi, p. 121, says that gold would be brought from the Western Sudan (Ghana) to Warglān and smelted and coined there.

of merchandise at the pedlar level, for wholesalers' branch establishments bought them freely. The trade in textile fabrics and clothing became a "Jewish" occupation already at that period. The same goes for the trade in hides, from which *anṭāʿa* (table-covers-*cum*-tables-*cum*-bedding) and other leather articles, such as travelling-bags, cases, pouches, satchels and bottles were made. Those pedlar-agents brought to the wholesalers' warehouses corals from the south-western Mediterranean coast and saffron from the Maghreb. All these were in demand in the East. Maghrebi soap is once mentioned among imports to Egypt, where it competed with the renowned Palestinian soap.[1]

Branches of large trading establishments existed at caravan stations and road junctions, in commercial cities and small port towns. They were staffed by relatives and friends of the proprietor of the firm. They received goods from pedlars, giving them other goods in return, and strove to maintain proper contact with their headquarters. The headquarters of the large firms—offices and warehouses—were in the major commercial cities, Kairouan and Fusṭāṭ, and in the main seaports, Mahdiya and Alexandria.

Large-scale business was concentrated in the hands of a few families connected with one another by ties of kinship and intermarriage. The transmission of commercial information between headquarters and branches was regular and frequent. Prices on the commodity market, and even slight fluctuations of supply and demand, are reflected in incoming and outgoing reports and letters.

Thanks to that material, we know exactly what the Maghreb exported to Egypt. Some items not yet referred to are cotton, precious metals in bars, gold and silver coins, silver beads and biblical manuscripts. Egypt supplied the Maghreb with crystal vases, ammonia and *kuḥl* antimony, (*collyrium*, for painting the eyelids).

Exports to India, via Fusṭāṭ and Alexandria, included textile fabrics and garments of Russian flax, which were much in demand, iron, silverware, copperware, drugs and spices from plants growing in the Mediterranean area, and freshly minted gold coins. Imports from India were pepper, indigo, lacquer, and musk.

As examples, let us note some items mentioned in a letter of Solomon Kohen of Fusṭāṭ to his father, Yehuda, who was in South Arabia at the time.[2] Solomon acknowledges receipt of consignments including sandal-

---

[1] Comp. Strauss, *Zion*, 7 (1941), p. 153.
[2] Comp. Hirschberg, *Y. F. Baer Jubilee Volume*, pp. 143-149.

wood, a coat and a mantle, and a medicinal herb (*māmīrān*). He asks his father to bring a maidservant and some special material (*'arḍi*) for a prayer shawl. He himself has sent a box with various drugs, such as white lead, opal, (which was used for medical purposes), medicinal flowers and plants and their roots, and hyssop powder with ammonia (a red dye); he still has to send some fans with handles.[1]

We should not be surprised at the small quantities of the various drugs. These were very valuable, and even small quantities yielded handsome profits, so that dealers could, with luck, become wealthy within a short time.[2]

Just as we have pointed out the occupations mentioned in the sources, we must note the absence or scarcity of references to three branches of the economy in which Jews engaged during that period in other countries: the production of and trade in salt; the production of wine and liquors; and the trade in slaves.

Ibn Ḥawqal says that Muslim countries export 200-300 dinars' worth of salt to the Sudan (*i.e.*, probably, *per annum*). Abraham ben Jacob, a 10-th century Jewish traveller from Spain, indicates that Jews own salt mines in Europe.[3]

We have seen that many Jews were engaged in the production and sale of wine and liquors in Egypt. We know of Jews carrying on this trade in the Maghreb at a later period. In fact, there are frequent references to the making of wine in Muslim countries. But this was a local industry, the product of which was not an article of export.[4]

The economic system of the Middle Ages was based on the use of slaves. We therefore find occasional references to the purchase of slaves for various services and to their sale when they were no longer needed.[5] But the hundreds of published fragments of letters and court decisions from the Geniza contain only a few passages concerning slave trade during our period generally, and in the Maghreb in particular. Now, the

---

[1] Source references for all these activities, as far as not already given here, are now easily available in vol. I of Goitein's *A Mediterranean Society*, 1967.

[2] The same thing happened in Europe; comp. Pirenne, *Social History*, pp. 46f.; *Cities*, pp. 82-84.

[3] Ibn Ḥawqal, p. 101; comp. T. Kowalski, *Relatio Ibrāhīm ibn Ja'ḳūb*, Cracow 1946, pp. 146 also 49, 87 and 88.

[4] *RC*, nos. 46f.; *RHG*, nos. 114-117 and 164; *RA* I, no. 61 (p. 79).

[5] Trading in slaves, male and female, and eunuchs: *RA* II, pp. 39 and 76-78; *RSh*, pp. 23b no. 6 and 26b no. 27; *RH*, no. 431. Castration was forbidden to Jews (Lev. 22, 22), but Gentiles were permitted to perform it: *RCor*, no. 78; comp. also *RSh*, pp. 27b no. 34. For this practice in Muslim lands comp. *Maqarrī* I, p. 92; Mez, *Renaissance*, p. 333; Mazehéri, *Vie*, p. 63.

material under reference was not intended for publication, so that the writers had no need to be apprehensive about what they said. But even supposing Jews were nevertheless reluctant to allude to matters such as slave trade or castration, Arab authors certainly had no reason to keep silent on them, any more than Ibn Khordadhabeh and Ibn al-Faqīh suppressed them with regard to the Rādhānites. We may therefore conclude that Maghrebi Jews did not engage in this kind of trade.[1]

Kairouan's decline directed Jewish trade into new channels. The Almohad advance to the gates of Egypt, religious coercion and the resulting emigration, changed the whole pattern of economic life and completely paralysed it in certain occupations. The refugees continued in their former vocations in their new places of residence. We read that one of them, who arrived in Alexandria almost empty-handed, began to deal in textiles.[2] A refugee from Ceuta, the physician and philosopher R. Joseph ben Yehuda, a disciple of Maimonides, went into business after settling in Aleppo and undertook journeys to Iraq and India. After becoming wealthy, he stopped travelling, without retiring from trade, while at the same time lecturing on philosophy and practising medicine. In doing so, he followed in the footsteps of his master, who, on arrival in Cairo, went into the India business with his brother and, when they were unsuccessful (his brother drowned on the way to India), turned to medicine for a living.[3]

The curtain fell on the life of Maghrebi Jewry. Of course, the continuing discovery of Geniza documents should warn us that there may yet be surprises in this field. We should note, however, that the Crusades brought about a revolution in all spheres of Mediterranean trade. They led to the rise of Italian commercial cities and Marseilles, thus changing the direction and nature of that economic activity. This change, of necessity, affected the economic effort of Maghrebi Jewry.[4]

---

[1] A vast bibliography of this subject will be found in the notes to Baron, *SRH* IV, pp. 187ff. and 332ff.; see also Goitein, *Society* I, Index *s.v.* slaves, slave girls.

[2] Hirschberg, *J. F. Baer Jubilee Volume*, p. 143b l. 26.

[3] Mose ben Maimon, *Epistulae*, ed. D. Baneth, 1946, pp. 1 and 2.

[4] It is well known, however, that war as a rule did not interfere with trade between nations in the medieval East; comp. *e.g.*, S. Runciman, *A History of the Crusades* I, p. 78.

CHAPTER SIX

SPIRITUAL LIFE

Ancient Ties with Palestinian and Babylonian Talmudic Academies

In spiritual-cultural as well as in economic life, our region played an important role, viz. that of a transition zone between the East and South-Western Europe, Sicily, Italy, Spain and the Balearic Islands. Although the Maghreb was a part of the "Islamic East", it must, in cultural respect, be regarded as a separate unit, together with the Muslim sector of South-Western Europe. Socio-religious trends, life-patterns and customs, originating from the Maghreb shaped, directly and indirectly, the way of life of the inhabitants of the north-western Mediterranean area. Close social and cultural relations existed between the populations of both sides of the western Mediterranean, not excepting the Jews. There was fairly keen competition, therefore, between the Babylonian Academies, and between them and the Palestinian Academies, for the strengthening of their respective positions in that important area.

North African Jewry's relations with Palestine were based on a tradition dating from the period of the Second Temple and of Roman and Byzantine rule. However, the expansionist aspirations of the Babylonian Academies, which tried to impose their usages on both Palestine and North Africa, already made themselves felt a short time after the final annexation of North Africa to the Arab Caliphate.

Some of the earliest information contained in our extant source-material concerns the influence of the Palestinian *halakha* on customs prevailing in the Maghreb. Although the words of the Gaon Yehudāy, head of the Academy of Sura about the middle of the 8th century, as quoted in a letter of Pirqōy ben Bābōy, are addressed to Palestine, it is clear from a new fragment of that letter that Pirqōy himself, the disciple of a disciple of Yehudāy, is addressing himself to North Africa.[1]

Here are a few extracts from Pirqōy's epistle to North African Jewry: "... and we have heard that the (Almighty) has favoured you and has

[1] Comp. Ginzberg, *Ginzey Schechter* II, pp. 557f. Mann, *JQR*, 7 (1916/17), p. 482, and Assaf, *Ha-Shiloaḥ* 39 (1921), p. 445, maintain that Yehudāy's utterance is addressed to Africa. For the ties with North African sages comp. Ginzberg, *Geonica* I, p. 204, and Baron, *SRH* VI, pp. 28, 49, 53 and 64f.

established houses of study in all the cities of Afriqiya and in all the localities in Spain and that the Holy One, blessed be He, has granted you to meditate upon the Law and occupy yourselves with it day and night... We have heard that there have come to you students from an academy, including some who were formerly in Palestine and learnt apostatic customs practised by the Palestinians; five hundred years ago, the latter were coerced into apostasy, forbidden to study the Law, and they practised apostatic customs and have not abandoned (apostatic) customs to this day... Some of them interpret mishnaic texts and certain talmudic texts concerning women, and each of these sages interprets those texts according to his own lights, as his fancy takes him, because they have not been taught *halakha* by the ancient sages and are untrained in rabbinic debate... Furthermore, Mar Yehudāy, of blessed memory, said that the Jews had been coerced into apostasy, forbidden to say the *Shemaʿ* (Hear, O Israel) Deut. 64-9 and to pray; but they had been suffered to assemble on the morning of the Sabbath to recite and sing *maʿamādōt* (miscellaneous texts forming daily portions), and so they had said a *maʿamād*, a *qādōṣh* (sanctus) and a *Shemaʿ* by stealth; they had acted in this way under duress. Now that the Holy One, blessed be He, had destroyed the Kingdom of Edom, and its decrees had become void, and the Ismaelites had come and permitted studying the Law and reciting the *Shemaʿ* and praying, it was forbidden to say anything save as prescribed by our Sages, etc."[1]

Pirqōy notes expressly that the establishment of study houses in Africa and the arrival of men who had studied in Palestine occurred in the recent past, which means that although Africa, too, had in pre-Islamic days been under Roman and Byzantine rule, Pirqōy considered that the "apostatic customs" of African Jews were not attributable to measures taken against them by the Byzantines two hundred years before. Pirqōy's statement as to the reestablishment of academies and perhaps also that concerning the arrival of students from Palestine should be accepted as historical evidence, whereas the "apostatic customs" attacked by him were partly rooted in the Jerusalem Talmud and in Palestinian traditions.[2]

At any rate, it is clear that the Maghreb communities were subject to

---

[1] The leaf containing the passages quoted was published by Lewin, *Tarbiẓ*, 2 (1931), pp. 396f.; comp. also pp. 398 and 383f. See moreover Aptowitzer, *HUCA*, 8/9 (1931/32), pp. 415-417.

[2] Comp. *Ginzey Schechter* II, pp. 504ff.; Epstein, *Tarbiẓ*, 2 (1931), pp. 312f.; Margalioth, *Ha-Ḥilluqim*, 1938, pp. 15-23.

the influence of both centres: Palestine and Babylonia. In sacral matters, such as religious ritual, they largely followed Palestinian usage, while questions of civil law, partnerships and land law, and the elucidation and interpretation of difficult passages of the *halakha*, were referred to the Babylonian Academies.

In the days of Hay, Maghrebis still used the formula "it which is designated for you by the Tora" in the *kethūba* (marriage contract), in accordance with the Palestinian *halakha*; the use of a ring in affiancing the bride was another instance of Palestinian practice in the Maghreb. Particularly strict rules concerning the ritual impurity of menstruating women may likewise be of Palestinian origin. There was some disagreement as to prayers: some Maghrebis preferred the Palestinian liturgy, others the Babylonian. Palestinian influence was present even in the use of *raqq*, a kind of parchment, while Pirqōy calls this an "apostatic custom."[1]

Pirqōy's appeal proved effective, at least as regards the rule about cattle suffering from *sirkha*, (see below) whose meat Rab Yehudāy declared absolutely forbidden, without examination in each individual case. The Palestinians rejected Yehudāy's (written) admonition in this matter, on the plea that "custom supersedes *halakha*," whereupon he eventually allowed them to continue as they were wont, in order "that they might not become *apikorsim*," wilful offenders against religious law. On the other hand, Yehudāy's ban was endorsed—probably under the influence of Pirqōy's strictures—by all Maghrebi communities except Fez and some Spanish towns, where the *sirkha* (adhesion of the lobs of the lung) was examined in reliance on permission granted by the Gaon Jacob of Sura, a contemporary of Pirqōy (thus even in this more moderate attitude the authority invoked was a gaon of Sura).[2]

From then onwards, *i.e.* from the early ninth century until the eclipse of the Babylonian Academies, contact between the Maghreb and Babylonia in matters of *halakha* did not cease. The North Africans, first and foremost the people of Kairouan, were in constant correspondence with the Babylonian geonim, whose most important responsa—including Sherira's

[1] Comp. Hirschberg, *Eretz-Israel*, 5 (1958), p. 214 and notes 6-9; Margalioth, *Ha-Ḥilluqim*, pp. 114 and 139. For the manufacture of *raqq* see the question from Tlemcen *RH*, no. 432; Ginzey Schechter II, pp. 560-562, also pp. 140-144; and below, p. 346. The Kairouanis once asked how to write the *kethūba* of a widow: like the Jerusalemites or like the people of Judea; *RH*, no. 389.

[2] *Ginzey Schechter* II, p. 559; *RHG*, no. 15; Ginzberg, *Geonica* II, p. 30; comp. Müller, *Mafteaḥ*, pp. 73f., also p. 100, note 3. The readings אפס and פרס (in *RHG* and *Geonica*) are copyists' errors for פאס.

letter on the "redaction of the Mishna"—were addressed to Africa.[1] The Maghreb takes pride of place also as regards the quantity of gaonic responsa, which, to judge by the responsa collection published by A. E. Harkavy, where the names of the writers and communities are given more plentifully than in other collections, were mostly sent to North African cities and through them to Europe. Rabbi Meir ben Barukh of Rothenburg (13th century) mentions that he once possessed "a large book consisting of responsa of African sages, who had queried Babylonian geonim and received responsa from them."[2]

The Maghrebis also maintained direct relations with the Exilarchs. The Geniza Fragments include a remnant of an epistle which according to S. Abramson was sent by the Exilarch Yehuda ben David [Ben Yehuda] to the Kairouan community. This fragment is greatly blurred on one side, the writer's name is missing, and only the word *rōsh* is left of his title, but the legible parts indicate that this is a reply to supplications addressed to the *rōsh* by the Kairouan community for intervention on their behalf at the caliph's court, since "harsh decrees" and "calamities" had come upon them. On the other hand, the writer complains that the Academy of Sura has taken the lion's share of the gifts sent by the people of Kairouan, although "the Academy of Pumbeditha has seven *allūfim*" (the epistle names only four) and other eminent sages, while the Academy of Sura has not a single *allūf*. The date of the epistle is not preserved, but we may suppose that it belongs to the middle of the 9th century.[3]

It is reported that two exilarchs took up residence in the Maghreb after being forced to leave Babylonya. In the first quarter of the 8th century, the heads of the two Babylonian Academies deposed the Exilarch Natronāy bar Ḥabibāy (or Ḥakhīnāy), who had assumed office without their consent, and the deposed exilarch went to "the Maghreb". It is not clear whether the reference is to Africa or to Spain; another source says expressly that Natronāy reached Spain and that "it was he who wrote the Talmud for the people of Spain from memory, not from a written text." But this does not rule out the possibility that he stopped in Africa *en route*. The Exilarch ʿUqba (on the threshold of the 10th century) is said

---

[1] Poznanski, *Harkavy-Festschrift* (Hebrew part), pp. 179-183, gives a list of geonim who sent responsa to Africa. Mann, *JQR*, 7 (1916/17), and Assaf, *Ha-Shiloaḥ*, 39 (1921), pp. 445 n. 3, and *RA* II, p. 2, add some names to that list.

[2] R. Meir Rothenburg, *Shaʿarey Teshubot*, ed. Bloch, 1892, no. 99 (p. 193); comp. also *RC*, no. 91: "R. Sherira sent this responsum to the sages of Kairouan; I copied it from a book brought from there by R. Itiel". According to Aptowitzer, *R. Ḥushiel*, p. 20, the book was brought to Germany.

[3] Abramson, *Ba-Merkazim*, pp. 9-20.

to have come to Africa after efforts to make peace between him and his opponents in Babylonia had failed. The people of Kairouan honoured him greatly, as befitted a prince in Israel: "It was customary in Kairouan for the chief, Mar ʿUqba, to have a seat of honour reserved for him in the synagogue, next to the ark, and after a priest and a Levite had read their portions of the Tora, the Tora scroll would be handed down to him." These two brief reports do not disclose the nature of the activities of the banished exilarchs in Africa in either spiritual or organizational respect.[1]

A question addressed to Hay shows that already in the days of the Gaon Hilāy (early 8th century) the people of Kairaouan had asked how they were to frame an authorization to collect a debt when the principal had no land. In such a case, the present questioners would have recourse to the four cubits of land which everyone had in Palestine, "as they had found in the responsa that their ancestors had obtained from the first geonim to a question addressed to the gaon Mar Hilāy."[2]

Some fifty years after Hilāy, there lived in Kairouan Mar Nathan ben R. Ḥananyah, one of the earliest Kairouan rabbis whose names are known to us. Mar Nathan corresponded with the gaonim of Sura and Pumbeditha and with the *beyt-dīn* of the exilarch. The opening of a responsum of the head of the *beyt-dīn* shows that Mar Nathan was highly respected. It reads as follows: "This is the text of a responsum which R. Ṣemaḥ, head of the *dayyānim* of the court of the Exilarch Mar Ḥasdāy, the son of the Exilarch Mar Natronāy, sends to Rabbi Nathan, the son of Rabbi Ḥananyah, and to all the students, scholars, elders and other brethren who live in Kairouan in the country of Africa. Beloved and cherished ones, take greetings from me and from the *allūfīm* and from the high-ranking senior rabbis, who stand in the place of the Great Sanhedrin, and from the rabbis who stand ... and from all the students and scholars in Babylonia, who always wish you well and pray for you."[3]

Rabbi Nathan was in contact with several Babylonian scholars, but would not address the same question to more than one of them, to avoid giving offence. This earned him a commendation from Naḥshon bar Ṣadoq, a gaon of Sura (died about 882), who deplored the recent practice

---

[1] Lewin, *Iggeret*, p. 104; *SOZ*, pp. 78f.; Yehuda al-Barjeloni, *Sefer Ha-ʿIttim*, p. 267; comp. Ginzberg, *Geonica* I, pp. 16-18 and 55-58.

[2] *RH*, nos. 199f. Comp. above, p. 289.

[3] Dukes, *Ben Chananja*, 4 (1861), pp. 141f. Comp. *Or Zaruaʿ* no. 640 (I, p. 176); *Graetz-Jubelschrift* (Hebrew part), p. 17; *RSh*, p. 84a no. 3; Ginzberg, *Geonica* I, pp. 31-33, also p. 7 n. 1.

of approaching both Academies with the same question: "R. Nathan ben Ḥananyah, whose soul rests in Paradise, and your earliest rabbis, whose minds were directed to Heaven, never did so. They wrote questions for thirty-seven years, either all to us (*i.e.* to Sura) or all to Pumbeditha, or part to us and part to Pumbeditha, but they never addressed the same question to both Academies; to do so is offensive to Heaven, as was the action of King Ptolemy" (who had seventy scholars translate the Tora for him).[1] The gaon explains that the distance between the two Academies is twenty-eight leagues and that there is no coordination between them: Pumbeditha does not know what Sura replies, and vice versa; matters of discretion are, after all, liable to be decided in different ways, and divergent responsa will mean a desecration of the Divine Name. Naḥshon's exhortations seem to have borne fruit: the Maghrebis sometimes ask to be told the viewpoints of both Academies, so as not to become involved in dissensions, "lest the congregations of Israel go apart in throngs and the Law become as two Laws."[2]

Nathan is not the only rabbi of that generation who is known to us by name. R. Meir of Rothenburg mentions a set of responsa which Natronāy bar Ḥilāy, a gaon of Sura, sent to Rabbi Yehuda ben Rabbi Saul in Kairouan.[3] In the year 1183 S.E./872 C.E., the Gaon Naḥshon b. Ṣadoq sent some responsa to R. Shebib bar Jacob and all the other rabbis of Kairouan, who had corresponded with Amram b. Sheshna, Naḥshon's predecessor as gaon of Sura, and apparently corresponded also with Nahshon's son, Hay, who was appointed gaon in the year 1198 S.E./887 C.E. This means that Shebib was in touch with the Babylonian geonim for at least twenty years.[4]

Moreover, a large group of responsa has been discovered that is addressed to R. Ḥonāy (or Honāy) of Kairouan, not known to us from any other source, but who seems to have been a contemporary of Shebib.[5]

About the year 880, Eldad ha-Dani visited Kairouan, and it was then that "the people of Kairouan asked Ṣemaḥ (ben Ḥayim), the gaon of Meta Maḥsaya (*i.e.* Sura), concerning the affair of Eldad ha-Dani, who had come to them from the tribes hidden away in ancient Ḥavila in the

---

1 Mann, *Texts*, p. 654f.

2 *RH*, no. 347 (the question is from R. Jacob b. Nissim); *RHG*, no. 15; Ginzberg, *Geonica* II, p. 30.

3 Comp. above, p. 301, n. 2.

4 Mann, *JQR*, 11 (1920/21), pp. 455-457 and 458; *RA* II, pp. 2f. and 27. A Shebib b. Jacob lived in Barca about a hundred years later; he may have been a descendant of our Shebib; comp. *RA* II, p. 4.

5 *RA* II, pp. 4-27.

land of Kush."[1] A question addressed to Ṣemaḥ in the matter of an inheritance was probably also sent from Kairouan.[2]

R. Saadia was asked concerning an incident that had occurred in Kairouan, where a man betrothed himself to a little girl, whose father accepted the betrothal in the synagogue in accordance with local custom. This had happened in the presence of some students, the sons of R. Nathan, who was probably R. Nathan ben Ḥananya. Not impossibly Saadia gave his reply while still resident in Egypt. As we shall see presently, he had close contact with Kairouan even then in various matters. His prayer-book was known there, and it is believed that he influenced the methods of North African exegesis.[3]

On the other hand, a commentary attributed to one of Saadia's disciples mentions several times the people of Kairouan, who were "students of Bible and Mishna, great scholars".[4]

Kairouan's relations with the Babylonian Academies and Egypt permit the conclusion that intensive study of the Tora was usual in the city at an early date and that its rabbinic scholars were known beyond the boundaries of the region.

Physicians, Researchers and Men of Learning

A similar statement may be made with regard to other fields of knowledge. Kairouan was the home of noted physicians, including two of particular distinction, known in the world at large as the founders of a medical school. The Muslim Isḥāq ibn ʿImrān, physician to the Aghlabid Emir Ziyādat Allah the Second (middle of the 9th century), had a Jewish pupil, Isaac b. Solomon (Abū Yaʿqūb al-Isrāʾīlī), physician to the last Aghlabid ruler and the first Fāṭimid caliphs.[5]

[1] Comp. A. Epstein, *Eldad ha-Dani*, Pressburg 1891, pp. 1, 4 and 9; D. H. Müller, *Die Recensionen und Versionen des Eldad Had-Dânî*, pp. 16 and 19; M. Schloessinger, *The Ritual of Eldad ha-Dani*, Leipzig—New York 1908, pp. 98ff.; Baron, *SRH* VI, pp. 220f. E. Kupfer and St. Strelcyn published a new fragment of Eldad; *RO*, 19 (1954), pp. 125-41.

[2] *RM* no. 19.

[3] *RSh*, p. 18b no. 12; *RH*, no. 208; comp. Ginzberg, *Geonica* I, p. 32; Baron, *SRH* VI, p. 28. R. Jacob b. Nissim knew R. Saadia's *Sefer ha-Sheṭarot*; *RH*, no. 231.

[4] *Commentar zur Chronik*, ed. Kirchheim, Frankfurt 1874. pp. 16, 18, 22 and 27.

[5] Comp. Neubauer, *MJC* II, pp. 233f.; Gedalya ibn Yahya, *Shalshelet ha-Qabbala*, Amsterdam 1697, p. 30a; Steinschneider, *Hebräische Übersetzungen*, pp. 388-402 and 755-761; idem, *Arabische Literatur*, § 28, pp. 38-45; Hirschfeld, *JQR*, 15 (1902/3), p. 689; idem, *Steinschneider-Festschrift*, 1896, pp. 233f.; Poznanski, *Harkavy-Festschrift*, pp. 207-209. According to *EI s.v.* Ḳairouan, Ibn ʿImrān was a Jew; but Ibn Abī Uṣaybiʿa, *ʿUyūn al-Anbāʾ* II, p. 35, says that he was a Muslim.

According to the prevailing view, Isaac, a native of Egypt who settled in Kairouan, died in 955 at the age of a hundred. M. Plessner has tried to prove that this dating is wrong and to reestablish the former assumption (based on Ibn Abīʾ Uṣaybiʿa) that Isaac died in the mid-thirties, probably after the death of the Fātimid Mahdi, ʿUbayd Allah (A.H. 332/934 C.E.), who is said to have used a drug Isaac had warned against. However, a similar story is told also of the Caliph al-Manṣūr, who is said to have died (at the end of January 953) because he had disregarded the advice of his physician, Isaac b. Solomon, who had warned him against catching a cold; the question can thus not be decided by an anecdote of this kind. Anyhow, it is apparent that Isaac was known as a skilled physician.[1] His many medical books, which circulated in the East, made a name for him in the profession. They were translated into Latin in the 11th century and thereby found access also to Europe, where they served for several centuries as textbooks and manuals. Part of them were printed in Latin in 1515, *i.e.* shortly after the invention of printing. Among the most famous are *The Book of Drugs*, *The Book of Fever* and *The Book of Urine*.[2] Something between a medical manual and moral treatise is the *Guide for Physicians*, containing advice to physicians on how to treat their patients.[3] Philosophic thought is expressed in *The Book of Elements*, which deals mainly with natural sciences. Fragments of the original, and translations into Hebrew and Latin, have reached us of an epistemological work, *The Book of Limits and Delineations* (*Kitāb al-Ḥudūd wa-l-Rusūm*).[4]

From the preface to Abraham ibn Ezra's Bible commentary, we learn that Isaac ben Solomon wrote an extensive commentary on the first chapter of Genesis, which did not commend itself to Ibn Ezra, as he openly declares: "... Isaac ... wrote two books. From 'In the beginning' to 'Thus the heavens and the earth were finished'. And he had so many things to say that he never finished. And at the verse 'let there be

---

[1] Comp. Slane, *Histoire des Berbères* II, Paris 1927, p. 541; Steinschneider, *Arab. Literatur*, pp. 38-45. But see now Plessner, *RSO*, 31 (1956), pp. 239f., and Altmann-Stern, *Israeli*, pp. XVII-XXII, who re-examine the bibliographical data and are inclined to accept the later date of Isrāʾīli's death.

[2] For an appraisal of Isrāʾīli's medical work see S. Muntner, *Revue d'histoire de la Médecine hébraïque* N. 17, 1953, pp. 85-90; comp. also Baron, *SRH* VIII, p. 394 n. 29.

[3] Comp. D. Kaufmann, *MWJ*, 11 (1884), pp. 93-112; *Ozar Tob* 1884, pp. 11-16.

[4] The discussion of Isrāʾīli's philosophic doctrine was reopened upon the discovery of new fragments of his works; comp. Stern, *JSS*, 6 (1955), pp. 135-145, 7 (1956), pp. 13-29; Altmann, *ibid.*, pp. 31-57; Wolfson, *JQR*, 50 (1959), pp. 1-12; and esp. Altmann-Stern, *op. cit.*, note 21.

light' he mentioned the belief in the forces of light and the forces of darkness. And he walked in darkness and did not discern. And in interpreting 'Let the earth bring forth' he brought forth things from his imagination ..." From another source we know that Isaac was acquainted with the Tiberian way of reading and tried "to introduce into his speech" the sounds *ẓ* (ظ) and *ḍ* (ض), which, according to him, existed in the Tiberian pronunciation of certain biblical words.[1] According to Dunash ben Tamim's testimony, which we shall presently quote *verbatim*, Isaac corresponded on questions of the "external (secular) sciences" with Saadia when the latter was still resident in Egypt. We have already referred to contacts between Saadia and the students (*talmīdīm*, probably rabbis not yet ordained) in Kairouan. We have also seen that Saadia was interested in the fate of African Jewry; he mentions a Hebrew work by some Kairouanis, in the form of a scroll, divided into verses and provided with biblical cantillation signs. Their interest in "external sciences" led them to concern themselves also with historical matters.[2]

Two of Isaac's disciples acquired great fame: a Muslim who wrote some medical treatises and the Jew Dunash ben Tamim, also a physician, but whose reputation is based on his occupation with philosophy, Hebrew linguistics, astronomy and mathematics.

Some biographical data concerning Dunash are known from the introduction to his commentary on the *Sefer Yeṣira*:

"... there arrived with us from Palestine Abūdāni and David he-Ḥārāsh (the 'Artificer'), both of the city of Fez, and brought with them this book, interpreted and expounded by R. Saadia the Fayyumi. And I studied his commentary and considered what he says therein, in order to know and understand his great achievements in the external science, that is the science of philosophy, and to what level he had attained therein; for letters had frequently come from him to our renowned city of Kairouan, to our elder R. Isaac ben Solomon, of blessed memory, on questions of the external sciences while he was still in the Fayyum, before he went to Babylonia. And R. Isaac used to show them to me, who was then twenty years of age, and I would point out to him passages where the writer had erred, and he would be pleased at this because of my youth. And when Saadia's commentary on this book (scil. *Sefer Yeṣira*) came to

---

[1] Only small fragments of this commentary are preserved; comp. Zaks, *Hateḥiya*, 1850, pp. 39-41; Dunash b. Tamim, *Commentary on Sefer Yezira*, ed. M. Grossberg, p. 22.

[2] Comp. above, p. 102; also Margoliouth, *JQR*, 8 (1896), pp. 274-288, and Neubauer, *ibid.*, p. 541.

us, I discerned the passages which he had successfully interpreted and those where he had erred, deviating from the right course, understanding nothing of the mysteries of the Kabbalists, while believing that he understood and knew them. Regarding many things, he felt that he did not understand them, so he left them alone and abstained from interpreting them. And he introduced many things irrelevant to the intention of the compiler of the original work. I therefore saw fit to give up all my current preoccupations in favour of that book, to engage in interpreting it, to reveal what its original compiler hid in it and to clarify the matters in which R. Saadia erred, in order that I might be remembered by my people and rewarded by my Creator."[1]

Saadia left Egypt in 915, and since Dunash was then at least twenty years of age, we may assume that he was born in the early nineties of the 9th century. His family may have been of Babylonian origin, for Abraham Ibn Ezra calls him "the Babylonian" or "the Easterner", but he himself was born in Kairouan.[2] Saadia ibn Danān (15th century) mentions that Dunash is alleged by Arabs to have converted to Islam, but this is not reported by any other source.[3] His commentary on the *Sefer Yeṣira* has been known for a long time, and additional fragments have been discovered among the Geniza fragments in recent years. According to Moses ibn Ezra, Dunash wrote a treatise on the relationship between the Hebrew and Arabic languages; no trace seems to be left of this work.[4]

During the following generations, the interest of Kairouan Jewry in the "external sciences" did not slacken. There were in its midst thinkers and physicians, such as Abraham ben ʿAṭā, Ziyād ben Khalfon and Abraham ben ʿAlī.[5] Some of the responsa addressed to Kairouan concerned pathology, geography and geodesy.[6] There is a remarkable description of a water clock consisting of a copper bowl with a perforated bottom, which is placed in water and indicates the time by the rise thereof. The description is given in connection with the interpretation of the word *shenatot* (notches) (Mishna Menaḥot IX, 2).[7] The people of Tāhert

[1] Mann, *Texts* I, p. 74 n. 25. Fragments of this book were published by Vajda, *REJ*, 105 (1939), pp. 132-140; 107 (1946/47), pp. 97-156; 110 (1949/50), pp. 67-92; 112 (1953), pp. 5-33; 113 (1954), pp. 37-61. Comp. Poznanski, *Harkavy-Festschrift*, pp. 190f.

[2] Abraham ibn Ezra, Introduction to *Moznaim*; commentary on Qohelet 12:5.

[3] Edelmann, *Ḥemda Genūza*, p. 16a.

[4] Moses ibn Ezra, *Shirat Israel* (transl. by B. Z. Halper), p. 54.

[5] Comp. Idris, *AIEO*, 13 (1955), pp. 55-56; Mann, *ibid.*, pp. 342 and 329; Poznanski, *Harkavy-Festschrift*, pp. 185 and 192.

[6] Comp. *RH*, nos. 264, 401, 374, also 12.

[7] *RH*, no. 385.

requested a description of a tube that had been in the possession of Rabban Gamliel ('Erubin 43b) and in this connection were given a description of the astrolabe.[1]

Yehuda ibn Quraysh

Interest in scholarly and scientific subjects was not confined to Kairouan. In Isaac Israeli's generation, there lived in Tāhert Yehuda ibn Quraysh, who, as far as we know, was the first comparative linguist: he studied the relationship between Hebrew and its sister languages, Aramaic and Arabic.

We know almost nothing about Yehuda's life; even the time when he lived is in dispute. Some put it as early as the 9th century, but it seems that those who assign him to the beginning of the 10th century are right. His treatise does not indicate whether it was written in Tāhert or in Fez. Even the opening of the book tells us nothing definite: "Epistle of Yehuda ibn Quraysh to the Jewish community of Fez concerning the revival of the study of the Targum and the love for it and the enjoyment of its benefits and the blameworthiness of its rejection."[2]

Ibn Quraysh is believed to have been a physician by profession. The assumption that he was a Karaite seems unlikely. His linguistic treatise frequently mentions the Mishna and both Talmuds, and his *piyūṭīm* show influence of rabbinical writings; the Karaites are known to have shunned these sources.[3] The autor did not give his epistle a special title; it is known as *Risāla* (epistle) or as *Abī wa-ummī* (my father and mother) from the opening words of the third chapter. In the introduction, he explains that he wrote the treatise to demonstrate the importance of the Aramaic Targum, which the people of Fez had ceased to use in reading the Tora at synagogue. The first part is devoted to a comparison of Aramaic words with Hebrew ones; the comparison is arranged in alphabetical order, like the book as a whole. The second part deals with the relationship between the language of the Bible and that of the Mishna and the two Talmuds and seeks to prove that Aramaic enriches and deepens the knowledge and understanding of the Bible. The third part, "On What Arabic and Hebrew Have in Common", compares the vocabulary of the two languages. The remainder of the work discusses the relationship between

---

1 *RH*, nos. 28 and 314; comp. also below, p. 345.

2 R. Jehuda Ben Koreisch, *Epistola*, ed. J. J. L. Bargès and D. B. Goldberg, Paris 1857, p. 1; Vajda, *Sefarad*, 14 (1954), pp. 385-387.

3 Comp. Mann, *Tarbiẓ*, 6 (1934), pp. 66-68.

the three languages as regards conjugation (the metathesis of letters in the reflexive form of the verb), as well as the rules determining the various sound-changes between them: Hebrew *shīn* – Arabic *sīn* (*shalom* – *salām*); Hebrew *shīn* – Arabic *ṯ* (*sheleg* – *ṯalj*, *mashal* – *miṯl*); Hebrew *sīn* – Arabic *shīn* (*bissar*, Jer. 20:15 – *bashshara*, *sereṭ*, Lev. 19:28 – *tashrīṭ*); Hebrew *ḥ* – Arabic *kh* (*taḥbōṭ*, Deut. 24:20 – *takhbūṭ*); Hebrew *z* – Arabic *dh* (*ze'eb* – *dhīb*); Hebrew *ṣ* – Arabic *ḍ* or *ẕ* (*ereṣ* – *arḍ*, *ṣēl* – *ẕill*).

Ibn Quraysh's *Risāla* attests not only to his great proficiency in languages, but also to his originality and his sure instinct, which led him in the right direction although Hebrew language research was then in its infancy and linguists were still grappling with the structure of the Hebrew verb two generations after Ibn Quraysh. We have indeed seen that Dunash was aware of the relationship between Hebrew and Arabic, but he lived about a generation after the author of the *Risāla*. Ibn Quraysh had considerable influence on later grammarians and commentators and is mentioned by them with respect.[1] We do not know whether questions concerning the use of Aramaic and the Aramaic Targum at synagogue, answered by the Gaon Natronāy with a denunciation of those wishing to abolish the Targum, are an echo of the controversy that arose in consequence of Ibn Quraysh's epistle. Nor can we tell whether the epistle indeed caused the people of Fez to give up their negative attitude towards the Targum.[2]

Ibn Quraysh has been credited with other linguistic works (a grammar, a dictionary) and with a commentary on Deuteronomy and a book on religious precepts, but this is pure surmise so long as no remnants of these writings are found. On the other hand, there can be no doubt that he was a liturgical poet, for *piyyūṭīm* by him for the holydays have been discovered in the Geniza.[3]

Linguistic Scholars in Fez

We have seen that the question whether Ibn Quraysh al-Tāherti moved to Fez or sent his epistle to the people of Fez from Tāhert cannot be decided. At any rate, in the generation after him, we find three lin-

---

[1] Comp. Bacher, *Anfänge der hebräischen Grammatik*, pp. 63-70; Eppenstein, *MGWJ*, 44 (1900), pp. 486-507; Skoss, *Dictionary* I, p. XXXV.

[2] *RH*, no. 373, also 248; *RShT*, no. 84 para. b. comp. Hirschberg, *Bar-Ilan Annual* I (1963), pp. 16-23.

[3] Comp. Brody, *Ha-Zofe*, 2 (1912), pp. 63ff. Ibn Quraysh is quoted in an anonymous commentary (see above p. 304 n. 4) on I. Chr. 3.

guistic scholars, noted for their research in Hebrew, who where connected with Fez: Dunash ben Labrāṭ ha-Levi, Judah Ḥayyūj and the Karaite David ben Abraham al-Fāsī. Though they flourished outside the region we are dealing with (which is why we confine ourselves to a brief reference to their work), they acquired their learning in Fez. The *Risāla* must have had its effect on them, directly or indirectly, kindling their interest in the study of the Hebrew language. The fact that four linguistic scholars appeared in North Africa about the same time was probably no coincidence, though we are at a loss to account for it.

Dunash ben Labrāṭ originated from Baghdad, but was educated in Fez, whence he went to Spain and became a rival of Menaḥem ben Sarūq. He was the first Hebrew poet to use the Arabic metre.[1]

Judah Ḥayyūj or, as Moses ibn Ezra calls him, Abu Zekharya Yaḥyā ben David al-Fāsī, was Ben Labrāṭ's contemporary, fellow townsman and antagonist. According to Ibn Ezra, he composed the first complete Hebrew grammar, and the author of the *Sefer ha-Qabbala* says that he "completed the exploration of the sacred tongue"; both mean that he was the first to perceive the existence of weak consonants in the Hebrew verb.[2]

David ben Abraham al-Fāsī left a thesaurus of the Hebrew language with the title *Kitāb Jāmiʿ al-Alfāẓ*, written, to all appearance, in Palestine; it was probably here that he joined the Karaite sect. He knew Ibn Quraysh's book and used it extensively, although, in keeping with the practice of those days, he never mentions him.

Why these three left Fez is not clear. One reason may have been the precarious political situation in Fez since the early 10th century, another the attractive power of Spain, where Ḥasday ibn Shapruṭ and Samuel ha-Nagid were living. Upon their departure, all linguistic scholarship in North Africa ceased, and the people of Kairouan were henceforth compelled to turn the Babylonian Academies not only for guidance in practical halakhic matters, but also for the interpretation of biblical and talmudical words and expressions which had no immediate practical significance. They could have sought such information from local scholars without religious qualifications—if there had been any.[3]

---

[1] Comp. Munk, *JA*, July 1850, p. 27; Ibn Ezra, *Shīrat Israel* (transl. Halper), p. 64. His poems were edited by N. Aloni (Jerusalem 1947). More about him E. Ashtor (Strauss), *Qōrōt ha-Yehūdīm bi-Sefarad* I, 1960, pp. 271-2.

[2] Ibn Ezra, *Shīrat Israel*, p. 64; *SHQ*, p. 73/101f.

[3] But comp. Skoss, *Dictionary*, Introduction, pp. XXVIIff. and XLIf. Linguistic matters are discussed, *e.g.*, in *RH*, nos. 229, 364, 378, 379 and 398-418.

In the context of the migration of scholars from Africa to Spain during that period, we should also name Isaac b. Khalfūn, a contemporary of those referred to. The details of his life are not yet sufficiently known; his poems—he was a pioneer of courtly forms of poetry in Hebrew—are not very helpful in this respect.[1]

Isaac's already mentioned particular attachment to Kairouani personalities, such as Abraham b. ʿAṭā, Yehuda ben Joseph and R. Nissim (and perhaps Samuel al-Lebdi also lived in Kairouan), suggests that he not only originated from North Africa, but that his childhood, and perhaps youth, spent in that region left him with memories that in turn led to his close connection with Kairouan, where he is believed to have resided for some time, and to his writing poetry in honour of its notables. Ben Khalfon was the first Hebrew poet who wrote panegyrics professionally, for monetary reward, but although his poems contain clear references to the generosity of Abraham ben ʿAṭā and Yehuda ben Joseph, they also strike a note of sincere friendship.[2]

It should be observed that just as linguistic scholars were lacking in Kairouan in its golden age, in the 11th century, we find no poets there during that period. Though, according to Samuel ha-Nagid, Nissim ben Jacob was a poet, no poem has been preserved that can be ascribed to him with certainty. During the following centuries, we find a few *payṭānīm* in North Africa, but their work is of a mediocre, routine quality.[3]

Academies and Heads of Academies

In the middle of the 10th century, ties between Africa and Babylonia loosened for a generation. This seems to have been due to several causes: a) the power struggle and political upheavals in Africa, as a result of which the Fāṭimids conquered Egypt; we may suppose that the Fāṭimids did not look favourably upon relations with Baghdad, the capital of the Abbasids, so long as their rule in the newly-conquered territories was not firmly established; b) conflicts in and between the Babylonian Academies, which weakened their influence upon the Diaspora; c) we cannot completely rule out the possibility of increased Karaite influence in Africa,

[1] For a selected bibliography of Isaac see Schirmann, *Tarbiẓ*, 7 (1936), pp. 291-318; *ibid.*, 28 (1959), pp. 330-342; Mirsky, *Itzhak Ibn Khalfun*, Jerusalem 1961, pp. 14-19; Stern, *KS*, 38 (1963), pp. 25-28.

[2] For the lament over Ibn ʿAwqal comp. Schirmann, *Tarbiẓ*, 28 (1959), p. 336. For the poem in honour of R. Nissim comp. Mirsky, *op. cit.*, pp. 89f.

[3] Comp. below, p. 346 n. 6 and p. 354 n. 3.

which was certainly likely to affect the closeness of relations with Babylonia. Thus, of that period, we only have four responsa of the Gaon Aharon ha-Kohen bar Mar Joseph Sargado, who headed the Academy of Pumbeditha in the years 943-54; according to Müller,[1] they were all sent to Kairouan.

It is believed that in those days there was staying in Kairouan R. Nathan ben Isaac ha-Babli, who was asked about the procedures and history of the Babylonian Academies, and fragments of whose account have been preserved in *Seder ʿOlām Zūṭā*; we have already seen (above p. 102) that a propensity existed in Kairouan to inquire into and record historical events. Those interested in the subject—whether because it helped to study the development of the halakha or from scientific curiosity—were apparently not fully satisfied with Nathan's account, for about a generation later a question concerning the same subject was addressed to Iraq.[2]

It is difficult to determine the time and the name of the author of an epistle in which the request is expressed, that the sums collected for the Academies in Baghdad be sent to R. Saul b. Joseph in Kairouan. He will dispatch the money to Rabbana Merwān b. Rabbana Abraham ha-*Maʿrabi*, who is a faithful treasurer of the fixed [donations] destined for the Academies in Baghdad.[3]

Upon the recovery of the Babylonian Academies after the period of decline, relations between them and Africa were resumed. Those were the days of the headship of the Geonim Sherira and Hay in Pumbeditha and Samuel b. Ḥofni, Dosa b. Saadia and Israel b. Samuel (b. Ḥofni) in Sura.[4] The initiative may have come from Babylonia, but it undoubtedly answered the needs of the Maghrebi communities. The responsa were sent to Kairouan, Qābes, Tāhert, Tlemcen, Sijilmāsa, Darʿa and Fez, which latter played a leading role in the Outer Maghreb. They indicate the presence of students (*talmīdīm*) and sages (*hakhāmīm*) eager for guidance by the Eastern academies.

The nature and authority of the students and sages mentioned in the responsa is not always clear. The term *talmīd* is not strictly defined in relation to the academic hierarchy. Sometimes it means an older man

---

[1] Comp. *RHG*, nos. 37-40; Müller, *Mafteaḥ*, p. 177.

[2] *MJC* II, pp. 77-88. A fragment in Arabic was published by Friedlaender, *JQR*, 17 (1905), pp. 747-761; comp. also Ginzberg, *Geonica* I, pp. 30, 33f. and 61; Baron, *SRH* VI, pp. 213f.

[3] Mann, *HUC Jubilee Volume*, 1925, 249-52.

[4] The date of Dosa's responsum, *Qohelet Shelomo* 71a-b, is difficult to determine; comp. Ginzberg, *op. cit.*, p. 7 n. 1; Mann, *Texts* I, p. 117.

still studying under a master, sometimes a rabbi deciding religious questions, but not formally accredited, and sometimes it is short for *talmīd-ḥākhām*, *i.e.* a person fully qualified to give decisions and judgments.[1]

Most of the responsa were sent to Kairouan, which in one judgment is called מחוזא רבא שבאפריקא "the great market city in Africa". As to content and volume, the responsa to Kairouan balance those sent to all the other localities in Africa together; it is widely assumed that even where merely "the Maghreb" or "Africa" is mentioned the reference is mainly to Kairouan. At first, no rabbi in that city seems to have been especially prominent, the responsa being sent simply "to the people of Kairouan"; only later are R. Jacob b. Nissim and others mentioned as heads of the "houses of study". This anonymity indicates that although there was a considerable number of *ḥakhāmīm* and *talmīdīm*, they had not yet achieved that crystallization of internal procedures which is characteristic of a particular stage in the organization of academies, nor evolved a definite pattern in their relations with Babylonia. A permanent staff had not yet been formed, and suitable persons to head those "houses of study" had not yet emerged. We are thus unable to identify the querying "people of Kairouan".[2]

The responsa were sent in fascicles. One of them, the famous *Epistle* written by the Gaon Sherira and his son Hay, then *ab beyt-dīn*, is dated 1298 S.E./987 C.E. They are in part extremely simple explanations and interpretations, in reply to questions from students. Some do not bear the name of the author, but seem to have likewise emanated from the academy of Sherira and Hay.[3] One fascicle contains a remarkable question referring to a responsum given in the same matter more than a hundred years previously.[4] It indicates the respected position of women in North Africa, which is further confirmed by another question mentioning the *talmīdīm* of Kairouan.[5] Once the rabbis of Kairouan applied to Sherira in the matter of a woman who refused to contract a leviratic

---

[1] For the term *talmīd* see, *e.g.*, *RH*, nos. 1 (p. 2), 319 and 345. According to Ginzberg, *Geonica* I, p. 32 n. 4, the *talmīdīm* mentioned in *RSh*, p. 18b no. 12, are distinguished scholars. Comp. also Goitein, *Education s.v. talmīd, talmīd ḥakhāmīm.* An interesting hypothesis as to the meaning of *talmīdīm* in some of Sherira's and Hay's responsa is put forward by Aptowitzer, *HUCA*, 8/9 (1931/32), pp. 421-441.

[2] Mann, *Texts*, I, p. 363; comp. also *RH*, nos. 44-47; *RA* III, pp. 7f.; *RHG*, no. 49.

[3] *RH*, nos. 372-418 are dated 992. No. 381 says that the same question was asked from Kairouan three years before.

[4] *RH*, nos. 209-219 (esp. 210).

[5] *RH*, no. 1 (p. 2).

marriage.[1] Some responsa were sent by Hay to Kairouan in reply to a question put in the name of the nagid—the reference seems to be to Abraham bar ʿAta, the nagid of Kairouan, and not to Samuel ha-Nagid of Granada.[2]

The Ibn Shāhūn (Shāhīn) Family

In the late 10th century, our attention is attracted in Kairouan by the Shāhūn family, which for two—or possibly three—generations played an important part in Maghrebi life. The name Shāhūn (or Shāhīn), which is the appellation of the family, points to Persian-Babylonian origin, although still other explanations exist.[3] As far as we know, the Banū Shāhīn settled in Kairouan already in the days of Nissim, the father of Jacob ibn Shāhūn. Sherira and Hay addressed the first Nissim by the title *mārī we-rabbānā*, which indicates that he was a rabbi (*ḥākhām*).[4]

The material of that period enables us to trace Jacob's development. In 1298 S.E./987 C.E., he applied to Sherira, in the name of the Kairouan community, with the question "how the Mishna was written" and received the famous responsum entitled *Sherira's Epistle*, which Sherira composed jointly with his son, Hay, then head of the *beyt-din* at the Academy of Pumbeditha.[5] Some think that Jacob asked that question in order to know how to reply to the Karaites, who had established themselves in Kairouan and were harassing their Rabbanite brethren by challenging the tradition of the Oral Law. He made a few supplementary inquiries concerning particulars of matters discussed in the *Epistle*.[6]

In Shebat, 1302 S.E./991 C.E., the two geonim replied to the questions of Mar Rab Jacob bar Mar Nissim.[7] The absence of any honorary title indicating his position and the existence of responsa to "the people of Kairouan" of 1303 S.E./992 C.E. seem to indicate that Jacob was not yet the only official address for gaonic responsa to Kairouan.[8] But we

---

[1] *RC*, no. 91, and comp. above, p. 301, n. 2.

[2] *RH*, nos. 227-229; *Qohelet Shelomo*, p. 71a; see also Mann, *Tarbiẓ*, 6 (1935), p. 240.

[3] For the form Shāhūn see Mann, *Texts* I, p. 124 l. 11; Abraham ibn Daud, Sepher Ha-Qabbalah, p. 57/77. For the meaning comp. Poznanski, *Harkavy-Festschrift*, p. 204; Steinschneider, *JQR*, o.s., 11 (1898/99), p. 614. See also *MJC* II, p. 80.

[4] Mann, *ibid.*, p. 107; *RH*, no. 230.

[5] Lewin, *Iggeret*, pp. 2 and 123-131; comp. also *RH*, nos. 218f. and 364, also 349 and Harkavy's note p. 370. *RM*, no. 131 is a similar responsum from Hay; comp. also *TR* II, pp. 39f.

[6] For the anti-Karaite trend in the *Iggeret* see Lewin, *op. cit.*, pp. V-VII.

[7] *RH*, nos. 345-350.

[8] *RH*, nos. 372-418.

may suppose that Jacob's connection with the geonim was already well-established, for, a responsum to the people of Qābes which to all appearance dates from 1302 or 1303 S.E. contains the following: "We have already been asked this year from Kairouan concerning that rumour and have ordered a reply to be written to Mar Jacob ben Mar Rab Nissim."[1]

We possess a list of thirty-two questions sent by R. Jacob to Pumbeditha. Some of them appear in Harkavy's edition of Responsa.[2]

One of Hay's epistles may attest to the appreciation enjoyed by R. Jacob in Pumbeditha:

"We have written responsa to the wonderful, precious questions written by Mar Rab Jacob the *ḥābēr*, may the Merciful protect him. Moreover, we, Hay, head of the *beyt-dīn*, have composed a writing in Arabic, divided into several chapters, intended to smooth the paths and point out the rules of the Talmud; it contains several examples from all the chapters of traditional subject-matter; it straightens out tangles and solves riddles. We shall send it to the *ḥābēr*, may the Merciful protect him, after having composed it in his name and made it for him: it is almost finished and will soon go to him. Although he is an eminent personality and illustrious rabbi, it should be of use to him."[3]

We do not know whether the expression "wonderful, precious questions" refers to Jacob's question concerning the writing of the Mishna. At any rate, the exchange of letters and information between him and the heads of the Academy of Pumbeditha had become most friendly. It may be that the treatise "to smooth the paths of the Talmud" had also been inspired by Jacob and that this was why it was dedicated to the Kairouan rabbi whom the author praises so highly.[4] Here is what Sherira wrote to Jacob: "To the desire of our eyes and that whereupon we set our mind, our coveted treasure, our confidant and ally, our heart's delight, Master and Rabbi Jacob, colleague, the most honoured fellow of our Academy, the most eminent associate of our Sanhedrin, our most cherished vessel . . ."[5]

R. Jacob was the head of the Kairouan Academy and became the official representative of the Academy of Pumbeditha for the whole of

---

[1] *RH*, nos. 351-371, to Qābes, come between two fascicles to Kairuan of the years 991 and 992. The quotation is from no. 364 and refers to no. 244.

[2] Comp. Ginzberg, *Geonica* II, pp. 67f. Some other relevant responsa were published in *RA* II, pp. 127f. and 139.

[3] Lewin, *Iggeret*, Appendix, pp. XXXIf.

[4] Comp. also *RH*, nos. 230-364 (the heading of the fascicle and the benediction at the end).

[5] Mann, *Texts* I, p. 107; comp. also *RH*, no. 257 (the complimentary close).

North Africa (and also for Spain?); questions to Pumbeditha and the answers to them were transmitted through him.[1] He received several honorary titles which the Babylonian Academy awarded to its distinguished correspondents and friends, such as *rēsh kallā* (academy head), *allūf* (master) and *ha-rab ha-rōsh* (chief rabbi), which seems to be short for *rōsh bey rabbānān* (school head).[2] The title *rōsh bey rabbānān* was conferred on some other renowned rabbis in that generation, viz. Ḥushiel, and afterwards Ḥananel; after the latter's death, it was bestowed on R. Nissim.[3]

From a book-list found in the Geniza we know that R. Jacob wrote at least one book: a commentary on part of Genesis; moreover, a remark of R. Nissim b. Jacob concerning homilies by his father on texts dealing with reward and punishment may refer to a written composition. However, no work by him has come down to us.[4] R. Jacob died in the winter of 4867/1006-7 C.E. The Gaon Hay eulogized him publicly and grieved deeply at his passing; when mentioning his name, he added the epithet *qādōsh* (holy). We do not know how old Jacob was at his death. Calculations based on a corrupt text in one of the manuscripts of Dunash ben Tamim's commentary on the *Sefer ha-Yeṣira*, according to which he reached the age of 110 years, are unacceptable.[5]

R. Jacob's academy was not the only centre of rabbinical learning in Kairouan. A very important letter from Hay to Kairouan, of Elul 1317 S.E./1006 C.E., mentions several rabbis who had great influence on developments in the Maghreb. The beginning of the latter is missing, and it is doubtful whether it is addressed to R. Jacob b. Nissim or to the Alluf Yehuda b. Joseph.[6] It reads as follows:

"...and to our dear and worthy Rab Bahlūl, may the Merciful protect and preserve him, the son of Rab Joseph, of blessed memory, will the

---

[1] *RH*, no. 178 and Poznanski, *Harkavy-Festschrift*, p. 207. Comp. also Sherira's letter requesting R. Jacob to forward the responsa attached to it to Sijilmāsa; it was first published by Abramson, *Ba-Merkazim*, pp. 42-57.

[2] Comp. Mann, *REJ*, 72 (1921), p. 164; *idem*, *Texts* I, pp. 124 and 159; Assaf, *Tarbiẓ*, 12 (1941), p. 42; Lewin, *Ozar ha-Geonim* III/II, p. 112 no. 303. Hay, *RSh*, 94b, no. 6, calls Jacob *ha-rāb ha-rōsh*; comp. also Assaf, *Mi-Sifrut ha-Geonim*, p. 121, and Hirschberg, *R. Nissim*, p. 25 n. 12. For *rōsh bey rabbānān* see next note.

[3] R. Nissim, *Ha-Mafteaḥ*, ed. Goldenthal, Wien 1847, p. 13a; Mann, *Texts* I, p. 333; pp. 204-5, 246.

[4] Mann, *REJ*, 72 (1921), p. 164; Hirschberg, *R. Nissim*, p. 81 and Introduction p. 26 n. 19.

[5] Comp. Mann, *Texts* I, pp. 124, 112 and 114; Hirschberg, *R. Nissim*, Introduction p. 26.

[6] See Abrahamson's analysis of the letter, *Ba-Merkazim*, pp. 77-99.

Allūf,[1] long may he live, make known that I am yearning for a letter from him—for his pleasant words and wonderful scholarship. We received two fascicles of questions from him after an interval of several years, and we wrote the answers to both of them and sent them to Rab Shemarya (in Fusṭāṭ), may the Merciful protect him, because the questions had been sent through him. He wrote that one of the fascicles had reached him, but after we had sent the other there were no more letters from him because he had joined the 'Company of the Holy Land,'[2] and we do not know what has become of him. May he inform us whether the other fascicle has reached him, so that our mind may be at rest or, if it has not reached him, that we may send him the text of the answers once again. We are also astonished that Rab Bahlūl, may the Merciful protect him, has ceased to write to us his doubts and queries, because it is a very meritorious thing for him to do and he and all his relatives and his whole community—the holy community [3] will be rewarded for it from Heaven.

We have heard that there is in your locality a man of great wisdom, a mountain of learning, at home in the chambers of the Halakha; his name is Mar Rab Ḥushiel the son of Mar Rab Elḥanan, may his Creator preserve him. We are astonished that he has not sent his scholarly observations to the gate of the Academy, in order to participate in its debates, as the first ones did . . . (lacuna) so that our wits might be sharpened by his marvellous questions and that the students might understand them and knowledge be increased. May our beloved, the Allūf, whom the Merciful may protect, give him thousands of greetings and myriads of blessings from us and may he inform him (lacuna) . . . and if he . . . (?) may the Allūf explain to him that he is our precious one, our peculiar treasure. And may the Allūf obtain a letter from him and transmit it to us; this will be for us a delightful gift, a welcome present. May he do so, and may God fulfil his every wish. Amen.

We ask the Allūf, may the Merciful protect him, to urge Mar Rab Ḥanokh (in Spain) to reply to the letters that were written to him by the great Gaon, our father, long may he live; he should not leave him alone until he does so.

We rejoice at the words of our dear and beloved one, Mar Joseph the son of Mar Rab Berakhya, may the Merciful protect him, at the pure and pleasant saysings he utters, which increase learning. We apply to him the passage: The wise in heart shall be called prudent and the sweetness of

---

[1] A title conferred by the Babylonian Academies.

[2] *Ḥabūrat Ereẓ ha-Ẓebi*. So the Palestinian Academy was sometimes called.

[3] *Ha-sīʿa ha-qedōsha*, i.e. the Palestinian Academy.

the lips increaseth understanding (Prov. 16:21). Who would make friendship with the Allūf—may the Merciful protect him—but such a one, and who would be his companions but the chosen of the world?

With this letter, we are sending two open letters to the whole Maghreb. Do as we request of you—send their text to several places. And inform us as to the arrival of the responsa to the questions of our brethren, the people of Fez—may the Lord, the living God, bless them—and of two open letters to them."[1]

The heads of Pumbeditha were thus keenly alive to everything happening in the Maghreb. This was in part due to anxiety lest they lose their hegemony, lest any rabbis having connections with Babylonia join the "Company of the Holy Land."

The rabbis mentioned in Hay's letter are well known to us. Rab Bahlūl ben Joseph (and two others) were the addressees of a fascicle of responsa of Sherira and Hay. We also possess a fascicle of questions of Rab Ṣalaḥ the son of Mar Bahlūl, "the great Sanhedrin and Rabbi of the city of Kairouan in the Maghreb", which means that the son of the "rebel", who had joined the "Company of the Holy Land," again addressed his questions to Pumbeditha.[2]

We should note the esteem for Rab Ḥushiel ben Elḥanan reflected in the words of Hay, as against his negative attitude towards Ḥanokh of Cordova, the leader of Spanish Jewry at that time. Moses and his son Ḥanokh had severed their relations with Babylonia, and Hay did not delude himself that it might be possible to heal the rift.[3] The case of Ḥushiel seemed different to him. We shall see that Hay's appraisal of the situation proved correct, though only after a time: relations with Ḥushiel's son, Ḥananel, were indeed better.

Hay's fears had a most real basis also as far as North Africa was concerned, in spite of the loyalty of R. Jacob ben R. Nissim and his son, Rabbenu Nissim, to the Babylonian Academy. In Hay's day, ties between the Maghreb and Palestine and its academy became closer. The assumption that the Gaon Solomon ben Yehuda was born in the Maghreb is well founded. He originated from Fez, and his rival, Nathan ben Abraham, studied at Ḥushiel's Kairouan academy after his father's death in that

[1] Mann, *Texts* I, p. 119-121.

[2] *RH*, nos. 16-36; 48-58.

[3] Comp. Mann, *op. cit.*, pp. 111f. The reason given by Mann for the severance of relations between Ḥanokh and Hay is not convincing. A similar political rift at that time between Fāṭimid North Africa and Abbasid Iraq had no repercussions on relations between the Jewries of the two countries.

city.[1] In the next generation, the Gaon and Nasi R. Daniel ben ʿAzarya sought support from the Maghreb on the plea that he was of Davidic descent: "And may they remember and proclaim the word of the Creator Afterward shall the children of Israel return, and seek the Lord their God, and David their king etc." (Hos. 3:5).[2] Economic relations between the Maghreb and Palestine have been discussed above (ch. V). In Fusṭāṭ, Maghrebis joined the synagogue of the Palestinians, which seems to be the reason why the archives of that synagogue contained such a wealth of material on Tunisian and Kairouani affairs.

Rabbenu Ḥushiel

Having mentioned Ḥushiel and Ḥanokh the son of R. Moses b. Ḥanokh of Cordova, this is where we should discuss Abraham ben Daud's story of four sages who set out from Babylonia to collect donations for the "fitting out of the bride", *i.e.* the maintenance of the Academy (a play on the words *kalla* "bride" and *kallā* "academy"), a story having a direct bearing on Kairouan. According to it, those sages fell into the hands of the *shālīsh*, the commander of the Cordovan fleet, who sold them singly into slavery in African and Spanish cities. One of them, R. Ḥushiel, was taken to Kairouan, where he was redeemed by the local community. Ḥushiel founded the academy which made Kairouan a renowned centre of rabbinic learning. His son Ḥananel, one of the early commentators of the Talmud, was born in the city.[3]

The story purports to relate an incident which occurred in the year 4634/974. Its credibility, however, was shaken when a letter from Ḥushiel to R. Shemaryahu b. Elḥanan (one of the four sages, redeemed in Fusṭāṭ) and to his son Ḥananel was discovered. In view of its importance for the history of the whole community, the closing passage of the letter may be quoted here *verbatim*:

"As I have already stated in my letters three or four times, our migration from our birthland to the land of Ismael was motivated by the wish to see the rabbi for whom I had yearned long since and whom I had not till then been able to meet. And as for all those years that we stayed in

---

[1] Comp. Mann, *Jews* I, pp. 132 and 150; II, pp. 128 l. 35, 162 l. 27, 172 l. 8; *idem Texts* I, pp. 118 and 338.

[2] Mann, *Jews* II, p. 216.

[3] *MJC* I, pp. 67f., and now the critical edition of *Sefer Ha-Qabbalah* by G. D. Cohen, pp. 46-48/63-66, and idem, *PAAJR*, 29 (1960/61), pp. 55-131 (The story of the Four Captives).

Kairouan, we have already told you in our letters why we did so. We were waiting for the arrival of our son, R. Elḥanan. When he came last year, we said: Nothing remains (to be done) this year so we may go. And we prepared everything we needed; nothing remained (to be done) but to provide food for the journey. When the people of the Kairouan community—may their memory be blessed—saw that we were determined to go, they began to speak to us in view of our having stayed for all those years: could we not stay on now? And they appealed to us with urgent entreaty. . . .* wished us well and regarded us as their own brother. . .* And he let us find favour in the land of our sojourn both with them and with the government. But although we knew that it was for the love of us that they wished to detain us, we were utterly disinclined to listen to them. While we were debating, *rabbāna* Yehuda, *rēsh kallā*, and *rabbāna* Joseph b. Berakhya unexpectedly left for Mahdiya. . .* And when R. Abraham b. R. Nathan heard the name of this city, he solemly swore that from among us and all the notables. . .* we wished it in deference to their wish. . . . . . .* the sons of R. Joseph and R. Nissim—may God protect and preserve them and let them grow up. . .* came to us yesterday, and now we cannot separate him from us. . ."[1]

Although the writing is blurred and obliterated in some places, several things are quite clear:

The letter shows unequivocally that the writer came to Kairouan of his own free will from a Christian country, possibly from Italy. He spent several years in Kairouan. After the arrival of his son Elḥanan—not Ḥananel—for whom he had been waiting, and who was already grown up (since he travelled alone), he stayed on in Kairouan for another year, until he decided to go to Fusṭāṭ.

Obviously, this testimony from the protagonist himself undermined the credibility of Abraham ben Daud's story and gave rise to scholarly debate. Some tried to save that story by assuming that there were two Rabbis Ḥushiel in Kairouan at that time: one the captive who arrived in 974 from Iraq and to whom a son, Ḥananel, was born in Kairouan; the other arriving voluntarily from Italy at the end of the century, followed by his son Elḥanan. Others rejected entirely the version of the author of *Sefer Ha-Qabbala*; in their opinion, there was but one R. Ḥushiel, who had come from Italy about the year 1000 C.E. and who had one son, Elḥanan, *alias* Ḥananel; we in fact find that Moses ibn Ezra sent an

* Some unintelligible letters.
[1] Schechter, *JQR*, 11 (1901), pp. 649f.

epistle to one Rab Ḥananel who is called Elḥanan in the opening passage.[1] According to another view, R. Ḥushiel had two sons, Elḥanan, born in Italy, and Ḥananel, born in Kairouan. The holder of this view thinks that a person could not possibly have been called by two almost identical names, which might easily have been confused: Elḥanan and Ḥananel. But how can we assume that two sons were given almost identical names? We thus see that this point, at least, will remain undecided so long as no new material is discovered.[2]

But uncertainty as to these important details cannot obscure the undisputed fact that at the end of the 10th and the beginning of the 11th century there were two academies in Kairouan, one of which was headed by R. Ḥushiel. R. Ḥushiel—thus we may summarize the course of events—arrived in Kairouan about the year 1000 C.E., intending to go on to Fusṭāṭ. He was waiting for his son, and when the latter had come, he stayed on in the city for about a year. Eventually, ceding to the entreaties of the people of Kairouan, he decided to settle among them. It is difficult to say what prompted them to make that request. Here, too, there may have been those who wished to end dependence on the Babylonian Academies, and not impossibly, personal interests may also have been involved.[3]

Fate has been most unkind to the writings of many outstanding rabbis in Eastern countries. They were gradually forgotten and were only rediscovered—wholly or in part—during the past three generations or in our very days. This was the case with the writings of the rabbis of Kairouan. Just as almost nothing is left of the teachings of R. Jacob, so only one responsum of R. Ḥushiel has come down to us.[4] His method of studying the Oral Law can only be inferred from the works of his two outstanding pupils, viz. his son, R. Ḥananel, and R. Nissim ben Jacob, both of whom will be dealt with extensively below.

Another of R. Ḥushiel's pupils was R. Nathan ben Abraham, a scion of a family some members of which held important positions at the Palestinian Academy. Nathan came to Kairouan about the year 1011 on

---

[1] Comp. Reifman, *Ozar Tob*, 1881/82, pp. 46-48 and 57 n. 7.

[2] Of the very large bibliography of this problem we will mention only Mann, *JQR*, 9 (1918/19), pp. 160-171; *idem*, *Tarbiẓ*, 5 (1934), pp. 286ff.; Aptowitzer, *HUCA*, 8/9 (1931/32), p. 437, and *R. Chuschiel*, pp. 4ff. Comp. also the summaries: Baron, *SRH* V, p. 312 n. 56; VI, p. 342 n. 50; also V, p. 386 n. 70.

[3] Comp. *e.g.*, Mann, *Texts* I, p. 338; below, n. 23; Aptowitzer, *R. Chuschiel*, p. 13; Eppenstein, *Beiträge*, pp. 189f.

[4] *RA* III, p. 54.

business connected with the estate of his father, who had died in Africa.[1] He stayed there several years, studying under R. Ḥushiel. After the death of his maternal uncle, Nathan claimed the post of *ab* (Relieving Head) of the Palestinian Academy, which the deceased had held. Moreover, he tried to supplant R. Solomon ben Yehuda, the gaon of the Academy. His term of study at R. Ḥushiel's academy seems to have stood him in good stead when he needed the support of influential rabbis. R. Solomon himself at first favoured the new *ab*, which was undoubtedly due to the reputation of Ḥushiel.[2]

Ḥushiel's fame also spread to Spain. Samuel ha-Nagid wrote a poem in his honour, and after his death sent a long letter of condolence to Ḥananel.[3]

It is most significant that apart from that single question in a letter from R. Hay no trace of R. Ḥushiel is to be found in the extensive correspondence on halakha and material aid between the Babylonian Academies and their officials and associates in Kairouan and Fusṭāṭ that has been preserved from the early decades of the 11th century. This seems to indicate that his attitude towards those Academies did not change.[4]

R. Ḥananel

Abraham ibn Daud continues: After R. Ḥushiel's death, his son and disciple, R. Ḥananel, of blessed memory, and R. Nissim b. R. Jacob ben Shāhūn, who had both received traditions from R. Ḥushiel, were ordained in the city of Kairouan.[5] Ibn Daud does not say when R. Ḥushiel died; it was probably in the late twenties of the 11th century. R. Ḥananel was older than R. Nissim, and according to R. David of Estella (who greatly appreciated him) he was R. Nissim's teacher. Here is what R. David of Estella says: After Hay "there arose R. Ḥananel and wrote commentaries in the manner he had adopted from the Geonim; we have had some tractates in our possession. And in his days there was R. Nissim, who

[1] Mann, *ibid.*, I, p. 338, ll. 7-17; comp. Abramson, *Ba-Merkazim*, pp. 32f.

[2] Mann, *l.c.* and *ibid.*, pp. 323-345.

[3] *Diwan of Shemuel Hannaghid*, published by D. S. Sassoon, Oxford 1934, p. 1; D. Kaufmann, *Ozar Tob*, 1878, pp. 64-68; *MWJ*, 5 (1878), pp. 68-75; comp. also *Diwan*, p. XIX.

[4] This silence may of course be accidental. For R. Ḥananel's attitude see below, p. 323 (also p. 328, n. 4.).

[5] *Sefer Ha-Qabbalah*, p. 57/77; according to Eppenstein, *Beiträge*, p. 195, he died in 1027/28.

had received instruction from him."[1] R. Nissim himself mentions R. Ḥushiel most reverently: "I learnt this from my master, our lord, the holy rabbi, R. Ḥushiel, the school head, may his memory be blessed and may he be granted resurrection."[2] It seems, however, that R. Ḥananel, the son, was greater than his father. We may conclude this from the titles assigned to them respectively by R. Nissim: R. Ḥushiel is "the great, distinguished rabbi," but "his darling (his son) is the distinguished rabbi, the exemplar of the generation, from whom instruction goes forth to all Israel."[3]

What is left of Rabbenu Ḥananel's writings is commentaries—some complete, some fragmentary—on most of the tractates of the Babylonian Talmud, as well as a certain number of responsa. He also wrote commentaries on the Pentateuch and the Book of Ezekiel and on the *halakhot* concerning forbidden food.[4] A liturgy and a "Book of Subjects" (*sefer miqṣōʿōt*) have been wrongly attributed to him. He wrote in Hebrew, but he knew also Arabic and, as befits a scholar originating from Italy, Greek.[5]

R. Ḥananel's Talmud commentary enables us to ascertain his method of study and rule-making. Several features of that method occur also with R. Nissim, whence we may conclude that both were influenced by R. Ḥushiel in these matters. This commentary embodies a great deal of material from the Palestinian Talmud, which is mentioned hundreds of times. It is certain that the Palestinian Talmud was known in Africa before R. Ḥushiel's arrival, but we must nevertheless ask ourselves why he introduced its study at the academy. Was he actuated by a predilection for the Palestinian Academy, which admittedly was not able to make a significant theoretical contribution to the study of the halakha? The Geonim and R. Isaac Alfasi likewise rely on the Palestinian Talmud, but only where it does not conflict with the Babylonian. R. Ḥananel, however, apparently following R. Ḥushiel in this respect, uses the Palestinian

[1] *MJC* II, p. 230; comp. also Saadya ibn Danan, *Ḥemda Genuza*, ed. Edelman, Königsberg 1856, p. 29b.

[2] *Mafteaḥ* to Berakhot, p. 13a.

[3] Assaf, *Mi-Sifrut ha-Geonim* I, p. 122 top.

[4] Most of the commentaries were first published in the Romm edition of the *B. Talmud*, Vilna 1859-1867. Comp. the descriptions of the Mss. used, *ibid.*, vol. I, final remarks, p. 5. A fragment of the commentaries on Berakhot was published in *Ginzey Qedem* II, pp. 11-13. In *Oẓar ha-Geonim* I, Appendix, pp. 1-72, B. Lewin presents commentaries on Berakhot by Ḥananel found in early sources. Other fragments were published by L. Ginzberg, *Ginzey Schechter* II, pp. 351-356, also Assaf, *Gaonica*, pp. 185-191, and *RA* III, pp. 206-225; comp. Baron, *SRH* VI, p. 342 n. 51. Two responsa of Ḥananel appear in *RA* III, pp. 53 and 58; a list of his responsa is given by Poznanski, *Harkavy-Festschrift*, p. 195. Comp. also Aptowitzer, *Chuschiel*, p. 18.

[5] Comp. Rappaport, *Bikkurey ha-ʿIttim* 12 (1831), pp. 11-15; Poznanski, *op. cit.*, pp. 194-198; Aptowitzer, *op. cit.*, pp. 16ff.; Ginzberg, *Geonica* I, 178.

Talmud and the *midreshey halakhā* to deepen his study and to lay down rules even in contradiction to the Babylonian Talmud.[1]

Ḥananel is apt to be critical of the Babylonian sages; he does not balk at dissociating himself from their utterances where they seem unacceptable to him, unlike other scholars, for whom the views of the Geonim were sacrosanct: "We have seen a different interpretation by the Geonim, but this is the tradition accepted by us." This tradition came to him from his teachers, *i.e.* his father and the Italian sages ("so we have been taught by our masters"), he once says in his commentary (Shabbat 145a).[2]

R. Ḥananel's utterances evince a striking tendency away from anthropomorphism. However, he inveighs against "the wicked heretics (*i.e.* the Karaites) who invent things that are not, thus bringing themselves into disrepute"; the Karaites taunted the Rabbanites with interpreting biblical anthropomorphisms literally. Ḥananel opposes the use of the Divine Name (again, in contrast to most of his contemporaries), explaining, in his commentary on Ḥagiga 14b: "Ben ʿAzzai peeped inquisitively that is to say, continued to mention (magic) 'names' in order to look into the radiant mirror, and he died."[3]

R. Ḥananel's teachings spread rapidly in Africa and Europe. The first to mention his utterances include R. Isaac Alfasi, R. Nathan ben Yeḥiel (the author of the *ʿArūkh*), who refers to Ḥananel's commentaries 142 times, Rashi and R. Yehuda al-Barceloni. He died in the mid-fifties of the 11th century, shortly after the destruction of Kairouan in 1057.[4]

R. Jacob b. Nissim's Academy

Let us now return to R. Jacob b. Nissim's academy, which continued to exist by the side of that of R. Ḥushiel and R. Ḥananel even after R. Jacob's death. The latter's son, Nissim, was too young at first to succeed to his father's post, and the affairs of the establishment were managed for a long time by R. Joseph ben Berakhya. We have seen above 317) that R. Hay praises Joseph in a letter to R. Jacob, while he does

[1] Comp. *e.g.*, *RH*, no. 434; Weiss, *Dōr, dōr we-dorshāv* IV, p. 270; Aptowitzer, *HUCA* VIII/IX (1931/32), pp. 428, 435 and 440f. For R. Nissim's attitude comp. below, p. 338 (Engl.), for that of Isaac Alfasi, *RH*, Introd., p. X.

[2] See his commentary on Erubin 26a, 83b; *Ọzar ha-Geonim* I, Appendix, p. 20 no. 66.

[3] *Ginzey Qedem* I, pp. 26-29; *RL*, nos. 115-117; comp. also Rappaport, *Bikkūrey ha-ʿIttīm* 12 (1831), p. 20 no. 14 and pp. 24 and 34f.; *RH*, *Introd.*, pp. XVIf.

[4] *RH*, nos. 510, 513 (p. 256), 520; A. Kohut, *Introduction to Arukh*, pp. XIIf.; Rashi to Yoma 29b; *RA* I, nos. 96 (pp. 97f.), 123 (p. 111), 124 (pp. 113, 117 and 119).

not mention Nissim at all; and R. Ḥushiel refers to Joseph by the title *rabbānā*. Joseph must thus have been a person of consequence in those days.[1]

R. Joseph was the representative of the Babylonian Academies in the Maghreb, under a general agreement concluded by the Geonim R. Samuel b. Ḥofni and his son-in-law Hay with a view to preventing rivalry between the two Academies. Here is what R. Samuel b. Ḥofni says concerning the appointment: "We have delegated the administration, trusteeship and treasurership to our wise, learned and distinguished Mar Yosef, the *ḥābēr*, the deputy head of the academy and representative thereat of the Babylonian Academies, may the Merciful preserve him, the son of Mar Berakhya, may he rest in Paradise. We have appointed him one of the wise men and charity wardens." Elsewhere, Samuel b. Ḥofni says that R. Joseph has taken the place of R. Jacob, the academy head, who has been gathered to his people.[2]

A more detailed conception of the relations between the "representative of the Academies" in Kairouan and the centres in Iraq and Palestine is conveyed by two letters addressed in those days to Joseph ben ʿAwkal in Fusṭāṭ. Their author was Joseph ben Berakhya, but he added the name of his younger brother in order to introduce him as a newly-installed public functionary. We have already noted that these letters were written in the years 1014-1020, approximately. Joseph, the "representative of the Academies" was the liaison man between the African communities and the Academies of Iraq and Palestine. Letters and donations were transmitted through Mar Joseph ben ʿAwkal, the "representative of the Academies" in Egypt. The Nagid, R. Abraham ben ʿAṭā, and R. Joseph ben Berakhya determined how much each academy was to receive. Of an amount of 200 gold dinars, only ten were allotted to Palestine and the remainder to Iraq—probably for apportionment between the two Academies according to instructions from the donors (Letter No. 1, ll. 22/23, 28). This too, was based on the general agreement between R. Samuel b. Ḥofni and R. Hay.[3]

Joseph ben Berakhya was praised by R. Hay for his "pleasant sayings",

---

[1] Aptowitzer, *Chuschiel*, pp. 4 and 10.

[2] Lewin, *Ginzey Qedem* II, pp. 20f.; Mann *Texts* I, p. 112 n. 9 and p. 159.

[3] Assaf published both letters in *Tarbiẓ*, 20 (1950), pp. 177ff.; comp. above, pp. 211-214. A donation destined wholly for the Palestinian Academy is mentioned in a letter from Egypt; comp. Goitein, *Ḥinnūkh*, p. 177. *RL*, no. 46 is a question to Hay from Naḥshon b. Berakhya, who according to Poznanski, *Harkavy-Festschrift*, p. 204, was a brother of our Joseph; comp. also *Tarbiẓ*, *l.c.*, p. 181 scholion l. 6. The source for the agreement is indicated in the preceding note.

but not awarded one of the Babylonian honorary titles, such as *allūf* or *rēsh kallā*. At the beginning of a fascicle of responsa of the year 1322 S.E./1011 C.E., we read: "These questions were sent by *māri we-rabbānā* Joseph ben *māri we-rabbānā* Berakhya and some rabbis of the *beyt-midrash* of Mar Jacob *rōsh-kalla* b. Nissim etc." Nor is he given any title in a responsum addressed to him and the rabbis and *talmīdīm* by Hay in the matter of the Divine Name. The fact that he is mentioned together with the other rabbis of the *beyt-midrash* suggests that he was, in the words of R. Samuel b. Ḥofni, the "deputy head of the academy and representative thereat (of the Babylonian Academies)", but not its head. R. Joseph once asked Pumbeditha what to do in the case of a defendant who had sworn not to litigate before the regular local *beyt-dīn* and wished to choose his own *dayyān*. It seems that after R. Jacob's death the authority of the Kairouan *beyt-dīn* waned and people refused to bow to its decisions. A technical question from R. Joseph concerning the validation of deeds indicates that there was no qualified *dayyān*, familiar with the law of deeds, in Kairaoun at the time. In his second letter to Joseph ben ʿAwkal (lines 10/11), R. Joseph himself complains that there is no shepherd to tend the flock in Kairouan, that the elders—the reference is no doubt to the Nagid Abraham ben ʿAṭā and R. Yehuda ben Joseph—have passed away.[1]

The *allūf*, R. Yehuda b. Joseph, *rōsh kallā* and *rōsh ha-sēder*, has long been known to us from the responsa literature of the time of Sherira and Hay. Hay composed a poem in his honour, praising him greatly. Isaac b. Khalfon calls him *sar* and extols his munificence and wisdom, and even allowing for the fact that he does so in a panegyric ("To whom shall I bind a diadem with my song?"), there emerges the picture of a worthy, generous man, which is confirmed by other sources. The material in our possession is insufficient to determine his place in the system of public offices of Kairouan. As far as we know, he did not head the academy, although he is called *allūf ba-yeshība shel gola*. But he may have been president of the city's *beyt-dīn* in the second decade of the century. At any rate, the available information suggests that he was active in communal life and the holder of official status: R. Ḥushiel relates (see above p. 320) how Yehuda, *rēsh kallā*, and Joseph b. Berakhya once left suddenly for Mahdiya and met with the Nagid Abraham b. Nathan (= ʿAṭā)

[1] Comp. *RH*, no. 178, and *Taʿam Zeqenim*, ed. Ashkenazi, p. 54b. *RH*, nos. 180 and 181 are likewise contained in the fascicle of the year 1011. No. 180 is discussed above, pp. 164-5.

there, and this is confirmed by a letter of Joseph ben Berakhya to Joseph ben ʿAwkal in Fusṭāṭ. R. Yehuda died in the late twenties of the 11th century.[1]

Rabbenu Nissim

After R. Joseph ben Berakhya, R. Nissim ben Jacob dealt with the affairs of the Academy of Kairouan and the Babylonian and Palestinian Academies. A letter from him to Joseph b. ʿAwkal has been discovered concerning questions and money—cash and drafts—sent by him through various persons for transmission from Fusṭāṭ to Hay. The letter indicates that it was written at a time when R. Nissim had begun to work for the Academy of Pumbeditha, but was not yet properly appreciated by it; for otherwise it is difficult to understand his bitter complaint that others have already received replies to their questions whereas his question, despite its urgency, has not yet been answered. This suggests that he was by this time a locally recognised religious authority, whom many people would consult, and that his earnest request to expedite the answer to his query was prompted by this fact. Nissim may have been called upon to head his father's Academy already in R. Ḥananel's lifetime. One of Hay's responsa indicates that it "was sent to the *beyt midrash* of R. Nissim in the Arabic language."[2] The *beyt midrash* was thus named after Nissim in 1038 (the year of Hay's death) at the latest, but possibly earlier. Nissim was in regular contact with Hay, as evidenced by the many responsa received by him from the latter. It has been asserted in this connection that Nissim went to study under Hay. We have proof, however, that he did not. Although he learnt a great deal from Hay, he did so through his responsa, and not by way of oral instruction. This and no more is what Hameiri means when he calls Nissim a disciple of Hay.[3]

Of Nissim's private life, more is known to us than of that of other

[1] *RH*, nos. 207f. and 434-442 (*RA* III, p. 102). In a responsum published in Warnheim, *Qebūẓat Ḥakhāmīm*, (Vienna 1861), p. 106, and Mann, *Jews* I, p. 40 n.1, Judah is called *allūf*. A list of questions asked by him appears in Ginzberg, *Geonica* II, p. 69; comp. also *RA* III, p. 101. For his activities see above, p. 113, also p. 109. For the poem in his honour see now Mirski, *Ibn Khalfūn*, pp. 71-73.

[2] Mann, *Texts* I, pp. 142-145; idem, *JQR*, 11 (1920/21), p. 453; *RH*, p. 361; Abraham ibn Daud, *Sefer ha-Qabbalah*, p. 57/77; comp. also Mann, *op. cit.*, I, p. 654 l. 81, for a list of Hay's responsa copied for Nissim. The responsum in Arabic appears in Mann, *JQR*, *l.c.*, p. 499.

[3] An account of Nissim's stay in Iraq is first given in Ibn Danan's *Seder Ha-Dorot*, published in Edelmann, *Ḥemda Genūza*, p. 29b; see also Hameiri, *Beyt-Abōt*, Salonica 1821, pp. 32b and 34a.

members of that generation. In discussing relations maintained between Hay and Samuel ha-Nagid through the intermediary of Nissim, Abraham ibn Daud mentions that Samuel ha-Nagid "accorded great material benefits to R. Nissim, who was not wealthy". Nissim married his daughter to Joseph, the son of Samuel ha-Nagid, but the marriage does not seem to have been a success: the husband did not like his wife, who, though devout and well-taught in the Law, was of "dwarflike" stature.[1] Nissim also had a son, who died young. Samuel ha-Nagid sent Nissim a consolatory poem on the death of his son, whose name is said in it to have been Jacob, like that of Nissim's father. Solomon ibn Gabirol may also be referring to him in one of his poems.[2]

The title-page of the Hebrew editions of the *Fine Book of Comfort* indicates that the latter was written for "his son-in-law (*ḥatānō*) Dunash in order to talk to his heart and console him." Since only one daughter of Nissim is known to us, who was married to Joseph, the son of Samuel ha-Nagid, the reference must be to Nissim's father-in-law (*ḥotnō*)—if, indeed, this apocryphal datum has any basis at all. Dunash does not seem to have been a talmudic scholar, although Hay, in one of his letters to Nissim, sends greetings to "*rabbānā* Dūnash". However, in addition to the doubt as to whether the reference is to Nissim's father-in-law, the reading of the word is altogether uncertain.[3]

After Ḥananel's death (about 1157), R. Nissim was given the title of *rōsh bey rabbānān* (school head) and entrusted with the representation of the Academy in the Maghreb.[4] He was not vouchsafed to hold this position long, however. After the invasion and destruction of Kairouan by the Beduin he probably moved to Mahdiya. He died in 1062.[5] His only daughter, following the murder of her husband, Joseph ha-Nagid, in 1066, depended on the charity of the community of Lucena, since neither her father nor her husband had left her any property. Abraham ibn Daud's account suggests that Nissim was not rich, although Ibn Khalfūn, in a panegyric to a Nissim who according to H. Schirmann is our Nissim, praises the addressee's liberality towards him.[6]

---

[1] *Sefer Ha-Qabbalah, l.c.*

[2] *Diwan of Shemuel Hannaghid*, published by D. S. Sassoon, London 1934, no. 6 (pp. 3f.); comp. also no. 7. For Ibn Gabirol comp. below, next page.

[3] Comp. Hirschberg, *Nissim*, p. 33; Abramson, *Nissim*, p. 22.

[4] *Texts* I, p. 246. It is a moot question whether the title was bestowed on him by a Babylonian or a Palestinian Gaon; see Mann, *ibid.*, p. 206, and Aptowitzer, *Chuschiel*, pp. 28f.

[5] This date was established by Goitein, *Zion*, 27 (1962), pp. 17-19.

[6] *Ibn Khalfūn*, published by Mirski, pp. 89f.; Schirmann, *Tarbiẓ*, 7 (1936), pp. 297f.

We possess some information concerning Nissim's disciples. One of the earliest noted rabbis who drew upon his teachings was Isaac Alfasi, but a report that he was his disciple has nothing to rely upon. Alfasi does not mention him as his teacher even where he makes use of his pronouncements; on the other hand, he takes issue with Nissim without naming him.[1] According to a report preserved by Saadia ibn Danān, Nissim visited Granada on the occasion of his daughter's marriage to Joseph ha-Nagid "and taught pupils there, one of whom was Solomon ben Yehuda ibn Gabirol, the poet." Ibn Gabirol, in his poems, describes himself as Nissim's disciple and expresses regret at their parting. He does not make it clear, however, whether he studied under him in Kairouan or in Spain.[2] R. Nissim himself mentions some disciples of his, especially one who is a Spaniard. We possess a responsum addressed by Nissim to a *talmīd-ḥābēr* resident in Palestine, containing an interpretation of the first *halakha* of the Tractate Rosh ha-Shana. S. Assaf published extracts from a work, already mentioned by Maimonides, of Nissim's disciple Ibn al-Gasūs (or al-Gasūm) on liturgical matters. The Geniza Fragments include a responsum of a Kairouan rabbi who was Nissim's disciple.[3] Another document refers to an anonymous rabbi, a disciple of Nissim, who settled in Fusṭāṭ and, by his method of study, raised the level of rabbinical learning in that city.[4]

A Babylonian rabbi, Meborakh ben David, came to Nissim's Academy and asked him a question at a *shabethā de-riglā*. We thus learn of a *shabethā de-riglā* (sabbath meeting) in Kairouan, while we knew of such an event only from Babylonia, where a *shabethā de-riglā* took place annually in honour of the Exilarch. It seems likely that the Kairouan *shabethā* was held in honour of the Nagid. If this assumption is correct, that custom indicates not only that the nagid was equated with the exilarch, but that the head of the academy where the event took place ranked equal with a gaon.[5]

Nissim's academy, as well as that of Ḥushiel and Ḥananel, was very

[1] Comp. David of Estella, *MJC* II, p. 230; Rappaport, *Bikkūrey ha-ʿIttīm*, 12 (1831), p. 68 n. 18; Poznanski, *Hazofe*, 6 (1922), p. 350; B. M. Lewin, *Festschrift J. Freimann*, Hebrew section, p. 75; Assaf, *Tarbiẓ*, 11 (1940), pp. 232f.

[2] Ibn Danān in Edelmann's *Ḥemda Genuza*, p. 29; Bialik-Ravnitzki, *Shirey Shelomo ibn Gabirol* I, p. 81; according to the Schocken Ms., as Professor Schirmann has been kind enough to inform me, Ibn Gabirol dedicated some more poems to Nissim. Comp. also Ashtor, *Korot Ha-Yehudim bi-Sefarad*, II (1966), p. 216 and n. 148.

[3] Comp. Hirschberg, *Nissim*, p. 32.

[4] Goitein, *Zion*, 27 (1962), pp. 20-22.

[5] Comp. Sh. Albeck, *Sefer ha-Eschkol*, Berlin 1910, p. 73 and n. 4; Mann, *Texts* I, pp. 69f. n. 16 and p. 329.

careful in editing talmudic texts; the version given in books from Kairouan would be relied upon by rabbis in Europe.[1]

A commentary (in Arabic) mentions some MSS. of Talmudic tractates in Andalusia. A high price was fetched for them "because their version was correct and they were in the handwriting of R. Nissim." It is noteworthy that according to Maimonides the books in the Maghreb were written on parchment.[2] It has been assumed that one version of the Geonic *Halākhōth Gedōlōt* was edited in Kairouan.[3]

Nissim was widely renowned already during his lifetime. The Gaon Hay honoured him greatly, calling him *ḥabrā, ḥakīmā* and *nehīrā*,[4] perhaps because, like his father, he maintained liaison between the Academy of Pumbeditha and the Maghreb and Spain, as attested by Abraham ibn Daud's remark: "And Samuel ha-Levi ha-Nagid (of Granada), through the intermediary of Nissim, would drink the waters of R. Hay."[5] R. Nissim's high standing with the heads of the Babylonian Academies was known in Spain. We possess a letter to him from Joseph ha-Nagid, the son of Samuel ha-Nagid, which says, *inter alia*: "If the Babylonian Academy heads and geonim, may they rest in Paradise, recognised his great wisdom, ascertained his virtue, were aware of his rectitude and commended his greatness and learning, what are we, the young ones of Spain, compared with the saints that are in the earth, and the excellent in whom is all my delight? And what is our honour, that of the Spanish 'locusts,' compared with that of the giants?" [6] The Babylonian geonim expressed their appreciation by awarding Nissim the titles *rōsh ha-seder* and *allūf ha-yeshība*, reserved for those they particularly esteemed and cherished.[7]

Nissim's books and method of study had considerable influence on the following generations. The first generations of post-gaonic rabbis made frequent mention of him, referring to him by the title "gaon." It is fitting, therefore, that we should deal at length with his writings.[8]

---

[1] Poznanski, *Harkavy-Festschrift*, pp. 177, 216f. and 193.

[2] *GQ*, 5 (1934), p. 144; comp. Lewin's note be *ad loc.*; Maimonides, *Responsa* ed. Freimann, p. 257 (Addenda to no. 26, p. 23).

[3] A. Epstein, *Ha-Goren*, 3 (1903), pp. 46-84. That assumption is now refuted by A. Hildesheimer, *Sefer Halākhōt Gedōlōt*, Jerusalem 1971, pp. 21-2 (Introduction), p. 360 (explanation to l. 85).

[4] Comp. *RH*, no. 22.

[5] *SHQ*, p. 57/77.

[6] Reifman, *Ozar Tob*, 1881/82, pp. 45f.; comp. now Abramson, *Nissim*, Introduction, pp. 22f.

[7] Comp. Mann, *Texts* I, p. 467. For the meaning of *rōsh ha-seder* comp. Poznanski, *Harkavy-Festschrift*, p. 204, and Ginzberg, *Geonica* II, p. 54.

[8] The number of medieval rabbinical authorities who mention R. Nissim and draw

Nissim's Writings

Owing to the passage of time and the tribulations that befell Eastern Jewry, none of R. Nissim's writings has been preserved in its entirety, except one, which was published in Hebrew translation in the early 16th century, viz. *A Fine Book of Comfort*; it at first appeared anonymously under the title *Tales of the Talmud*. About sixty years ago, the Arabic original of the *Book of Comfort* was discovered and subsequently published. Its especial value for the study of Jewish society has already been noted above. It has been preserved almost completely and is therefore more calculated than Nissim's other books to show his qualities as a writer and teacher and his vast learning.

A Fine Book of Comfort [1]

The *Book of Comfort* is a work aimed at offering in popular, attractive and universally intelligible form a reply to problems exercising the people of Kairouan. Nissim was actually queried about these matters, as shown by *The Secret Scroll* and *The Key to the Secret Scroll*, both of which will be discussed below.

Let us first consider the structure of the book.[2] The first part (chapters

upon his writings is about seventy. Comp. Rappaport, *Bikkūrey ha-ʿIttīm*, 12 (1831), p. 56 and n. 49; Poznanski, *op. cit.*, pp. 211; Goldenthal, *Ha-Mafteah*, Introduction, p. 5a (see below p. 336 n. 1); Sh. Albeck, *Sefer ha-Eschkol*, p. 73 n. 3; Lewin, *Iggeret*, p. 4; Assaf, *Tarbiẓ*, 11 (1940), pp. 231 n. 14, 252 n. 7, 258f. Especially noteworthy is a collection by Poznanski, published in *Hazofe*, 5-7 (1921-23), of quotations from Nissim's *Megillat Setarim* in early rabbinical writings. See also Agus, *Horeb*, 12 (1957), p. 207. S. Abramson, in his monumental *R. Nissim Gaon*, Jerusalem 1965, presents all available fragments of Nissim's writings from the Geniza and mentions the later authors referring to him.

[1] The full Arabic title of this book is *Kitab al-faraj baʿda al-shidda wa al-saʿ baʿda al-ḍayqa* (The Book of Comfort after Distress and Relief after Anguish); comp. Schechter, *Saadyana*, p. 79 ll. 11f., and Abramson, *Nissim*, p. 364. In the first print of the Hebrew translation (Constantinople 1519), it is called "Tales of the Talmud," in the Ferrara edition (1557), "*Ḥibbūr Yāfe me-ha-Yeshūʿah*" "A Fine Book of Comfort." Comp. Hirschberg, *Nissim*, pp. 39-43. Abramson, *KS*, 41 (1966), pp. 529-532, shows how this latter title originated. J. Obermann edited *The Arabic Original of Ibn Shāhīn's Book of Comfort known as the Ḥibbūr Yaphê of R. Nissim b. Yaʿaqobh*, New Haven 1933. He gives a complete heliotype copy of the Ms., which is written in Hebrew characters, and a printed transliteration into Arabic script.

[2] Quotations in the following are according to the abovementioned Obermann edition and Hirschberg, *Rabbēnu Nissim b. Jakob, Ḥibbūr Yāfe me-ha-Yeshūʿah*, Jerusalem 1954 (Introduction, pp. 9-82, and Hebrew Translation (from Obermann's text), pp. 1-107). Abramson, *Nissim*, pp. 361-502, gives many new fragments from the Geniza and collates the text of the Qāfaḥ Ms. with the Obermann text.

I-X) is designed to prove that God judges justly and acts righteously, even if it seems that virtuous persons are punished and evildoers rewarded. The presentation and solution of the problem show influence of the fifth chapter of Saadia's *Beliefs and Opinions*. Nissim adduces a series of stories from the *gemara* and the *midrashim*, but also narratives we have not found in rabbinical literature, to prove that man's behaviour is justly assessed and requited.

Nissim gives a first summing-up at the end of chapter VII (p. 32/19): The ways of the Almighty must not be questioned, "whether you see a virtuous person faring well and an evildoer faring ill, or an evildoer faring well and a virtuous person faring ill." To explain the seeming inconsistency of some virtuous persons faring well and others ill, chapters VIII-X relate incidents in which a person is rewarded for fulfilling a minor commandment or fulfilling a commandment with particular punctiliousness, that is to say, for matters not regarded as of great consequence. The subject of the virtuous person faring ill in this world is taken up again in stories about Ḥanina ben Dosa, for whose sake the whole world is nourished, while he himself lives in dire distress. This part concludes with a homily on the verse "Though thy beginning was small, yet thy latter end should greatly increase" (Job 8:7).

That verse is the theme of the second part (from chapter XI to the beginning of chapter XIII), which is devoted to stories about good and bad women. The heroine of the first story is a wife thanks to whom her husband, a gardener, is granted a shining white robe in the next world. This is followed by several other stories about the character of women. It is interesting to note that especially this part contains stories which have no parallels in ancient literature (the shining robe, Solomon and the wicked woman) or are only alluded to (Yoḥani bat Reṭībi).

The story of Kalba Sabua''s daughter, who married R. ʿAqiba, forms a pleasant transition to the part dealing with the duty of studying the Law and with the qualities required in rabbinical students (chapters XIII and XIV). After a digression on the titles of rabbis, the main subject of this part is taken up again.

Besides tales from rabbinical literature, we find a number of stories about simple people and children who achieved exalted status by the fulfilment of only one precept (chapters XV-XXI). The evident purpose is to strengthen the faith of simple people by stories concerning persons of their own class who were richly rewarded in the next world. The material is mostly taken from sources unknown to us.

There follows a group of stories concerning hypocrites (chapters XXII and XXIII). After a digression, the author reverts, at the end of chapter XXIII, to the subject of the deposit, which served as the starting-point for this part, but unlike the first time, he now adduces the example of an honest man, who returns many times more than what was entrusted to him. Chapter XXIV explains that a charitable deed is a deposit which yields a profit.

The theme of chapters XXV-XXVII is the evil urge and its conquest. At first, we are told of R. Meir and others who were suspected of, or had, illicit sexual relations; this is followed by a dissertation on repentance.

The author felt that he had strayed far afield, so, in the following part (chapters XXVIII-XXXI), he reverted to his subject, dealing with the duty of charity as incumbent even on the poorest people. After mentioning the homily on the letters *gimmel* and *dalet* ("a person who renders (*gōmēl*) benefactions will run after poor people (*dallīm*)"), he again digresses, but subsequently resumes the main theme by telling of a poor man who becomes rich and then poor again and is ultimately repaid by God all he has expended on the poor.

Thus far, the plan is clear and easily intelligible. From here onwards, however, problems arise for which it is difficult to suggest a solution on the basis of the material in our possession. The book evidently did not end with chapter XXXI. Nissim, who took great pains with the literary form of his work, surely wrote a conclusion to it. On the other hand, it is doubtful whether the three chapters that appear only in the Arabic manuscript are authentic. Chapter XXXII, dealing with King Solomon's three pieces of advice, is apparently fragmentary, the main thing: how the youngest brother used the three pieces of advice, being missing. There is no certainty that the sequel, as appearing in *Beyt ha-Midrash* IV (pp. 148-50), is authentic, since it was not before the copyist of the Arabic manuscript. If the whole chapter is in fact authentic, it belongs, in a way, to the stories about women to be guarded against.

A perusal of the story of the sixty philosophers (Chapter XXXIII) leaves the impression that it was not written by the author. Its opening: "A question by the people of Sarandib. They are the sixty philosophers..." is different from the other openings in the book, each of which begins with an apostrophe to the reader or links up with what goes before (in the present case, of course, as stated, we do not know how the preceding chapter ended). Moreover, the disjointed, jerky mode of presentation lacks the qualities of Nissim's epic style.

On the other hand, it seems that the story of the forsaken little girl (Chapter XXXIV) links up readily with chapter XXXI. Both narratives are intended to prove the truth of Ps. 37:25, quoted at the beginning of the story of the forsaken little girl: "I have not seen the righteous forsaken"—this is the poor man grown rich who lavished charity and was therefore not forsaken when in distress; "nor his seed begging bread"—this is the forsaken little girl. Although the end of the story is missing, we may suppose that it was most satisfactory, with the girl finding friends and helpers among the Jewish community of the strange town in which her father's brother had abandoned her. In any event, it was not the end of the book, but we can say nothing concerning that end, except that it no doubt existed and is lost.

Nissim obviously had a definite plan for his book, witness the fact that whenever he digresses—usually for didactic reasons, in accordance with his secondary purpose—he is aware of it and upon reverting to the main theme notes this expressly. Compare: the dissertation on the titles of rabbis (pp. 75-8/44-6) is followed by the words: "I return to the subject" (the story of the three rich men). After the remarks on repentance (pp. 151-3/85-6), the main topic—citrons for medical purposes—is resumed. The story about Abbaye's generous charity in chapter XXX (pp. 157-8/88) is followed by a letter *midrash* (homiletic interpretation of letters of the alphabet) on the same subject, leading to further letter *midrashim*. But afterwards, in chapter XXXI, the theme of the book is taken up again. The story of Kīdor (pp. 110-13/63-64) is followed by the story of Rabbi Yehuda ha-Nasi and Antoninus and another story about Yehuda ha-Nasi (pp. 113-7/64-66); however, the author reverts to the subject of the deposit (pp. 117-8/67), though not noting this specially this time. The collection of sayings of R. Yosi and what is told in this connection separate the stories about R. Meir and that disciple of his (pp. 120-5/68-70) from the story of Natan de Ṣuṣīta and his conquest of the evil urge (pp. 129-40/73-76).

The three stories appearing at the end of the book in the ancient Hebrew editions (Appendix, pp. 104-107, in Hirschberg's edition) do not fit in well with the general pattern of the book and have no inner connection among themselves. This suggests that they may be later additions, perhaps only to the Hebrew version. Although L. Ginzberg thinks that the Arabic version of the book is the source of the story of R. Meir and the dead man, as figuring in Jewish literature, the arguments for this view are not conclusive. Nor can the fact that the story of King Solomon and the thief is included in the Midrash *'Aseret ha-Debārīm*, some of whose stories indeed appear in the *Fine Book*, serve in itself to decide the question either way.

As to the sources which supplied the material and background for Nissim's stories, we may say, summarily, that the latter were culled in all fields of Jewish literature, from the Bible to the writings of Nissim's contemporaries, the geonim, including books and midrashim which apparently were lost in their original form and have in part been preserved in later works. A careful comparison between the *Fine Book* and Arab sources reveals great similarities as regards certain stories which appear in both. Nissim was undoubtedly familiar with Arab literature. Twice the *Fine Book* obviously borrows verses from the Koran. In one case, there is the passage: "The heaven belongs to the Lord, who made it high, and the earth is an edifice" (34 1.11-35 1.1/21); cp. Sura 13:2-3, 55:9 and 2:27. In the other (172 1.11/95), the language of Sura 9:121 is used. Still more instances of Koranic language might be pointed out. As regards folk-tales and legends, it is sometimes difficult to decide wether the original is Jewish or Arab. A third possibility is that the Jewish and Arab versions go back to a common, no longer extant source.[1] At the same time, there are themes for which as yet no literary parallels have been found, and it is perfectly possible that Nissim, who reveals himself in this book as a true artist, took them from real life. The themes in question are: the thief (p. 17/10), the shining white robe (pp. 44-48/26-9), Solomon, the Sages of the Sanhedrin and the wicked woman (pp. 51-54/30-3), hidden saints (pp. 81-87/48-51), a man must not despair (pp. 97-100/56-7), Solomon's three pieces of advice (pp. 173-4/96-7), the forsaken little girl (pp. 181-3/102-3).[2]

The Book of the Key to the Locks of the Talmud

We possess large portions of the original of a halakhic work by Nissim entitled *The Book of the Key to the Locks of the Talmud*. The plan and purpose of that work are explained by the author himself in the introduction. Here are a few extracts from the latter: "The Talmud... which is now in the hands of our people... was written down by persons who knew it by heart, the names of the copyists were known, and the different parts were connected with one another. To permit the adduction of evidence in

[1] For a detailed discussion of the subject see Hirschberg, *Nissim*, pp. 61-71.

[2] Our conjectures in this matter are presented in our discussion of the *Fine Book* as a social document (*Nissim*, pp. 74-82). Parallel legends on heavenly garments in Jewish esoteric literature, the Zohar and late Zoroastrian writings are discussed by G. Scholem, *Tarbiẓ*, 24 (1955), pp. 290-306. D. Z. Baneth, *ibid.*, 25 (1956), pp. 331-336, unlike Scholem, thinks that the ultimate source of the legend is not Zoroastrian but Muslim.

a particular matter from two or three places, short references were given to the relevant earlier passages; it was deemed sufficient to mention the author of the utterance in question. Sometimes the utterance referred to is in the same chapter, sometimes it is in the same tractate, but not in the same chapter, and sometimes it is in the same *seder* (order of the Talmud), but not in the same tractate..." That is to say: Nissim had found that the Talmud contented itself with a short reference when the same matter had been treated in detail elsewhere. Since he had noticed "that many students in our time are not familiar with this method and therefore labour in vain to trace a certain argument and thus do not arrive at a definite conclusion, I have seen fit to collect and coordinate the material in a book, which is to serve as a key to those obscure references, so that the student, when he needs any of the passages referred to, will find them quickly and easily."[1]

The introduction enumerates fifty matters mentioned in the Talmud in obscure language or hintingly in one place, while their principal mention occurs in another place, where they are set out clearly and extensively.

Besides the *Key* to the tractates Berakhot, Shabbat and ʿErubin, published as we have seen long ago by J. Goldenthal, important—though fragmentary—material from the *Key* to other tractates is supplied by the Geniza and by a fascicle of selected passages brought from Yemen. This material shows that the *Key* was written alternately in Rabbinical Hebrew and in Arabic. The text published by Goldenthal indicates that parts of the *Key* were translated into Hebrew at an early period; selections, too, were already prepared then.[2]

Megillat Setārim—The Secret Scroll

Great difficulties are presented by the *Secret Scroll*, which Nissim seems to have written after the *Fine Book*, because the latter does not mention it at all although there are many parallels between them. It is frequently mentioned in the writings of rabbis in North Africa, Egypt, Italy, Spain, France, Germany and the Slavic countries. The *Scroll* thus enjoyed a wide circulation; this is also attested by the fact that it is mentioned in the booklists of the Geniza and in an early philosophic treatise. However, it has been lost for centuries. Solomon Lurya and the

---

[1] J. Goldenthal (editor), *Sefer ha-Maftēaḥ shel Manʿūley ha-Talmūd* etc., Wien 1847, p. 3b.

[2] For material on the *Key* see now Abramson's *Nissim*, pp. 3-90.

publisher of the *Yuḥāsīn*, Samuel Sholem, seem to have been among the last to see the original.

S. Poznanski published almost all the extracts from the *Scroll* contained in ancient writings, arranging them by subjects: (a) faith and research; (b) commentaries on biblical texts; (c) halakhic commentaries; (d) commentaries on aggadot and midrashim; (e) prayer, the phylacteries, the doxology and the reading of the Tora; (f) the Sabbath, *qiddūsh* and *habdālā*; (g) Purim, Passover and holydays; (h) fasting and the Ninth of Ab; (i) the nations of the world and ritual baths. Fragments from the *Scroll* discovered among the Geniza documents were published by J. N. Epstein, B. M. Levin and S. Assaf. But the structure and purpose of the book were still not clear to us, although we knew from the Geniza fragments that it was written alternately in Rabbinical Hebrew and in Arabic, like the *Key*. The title *Secret Scroll* seemed to point to a collection of halakhot and apocryphal traditions.[1]

Then S. Assaf, among the large collection of Geniza fragments in Cambridge, discovered a key to the *Scroll*, prepared by a rabbi who was close to Nissim in point of time and probably also place and who tells us that the *Scroll* contains 230 responsa of Nissim, "without order, no doubt in the sequence of the arrival of the questions". For the convenience of the user of the book, that anonymous rabbi composed the key "in order that he may find it (a halakha) quickly and easily."[2]

Talmud Commentaries and Other Writings

Nissim also wrote more detailed commentaries on Talmudic tractates. He himself mentions his commentary on Chapter 1 of Yebamot. His commentary on the tractate ʿErubin was seen by the author of the key to the *Scroll* and by Nathan, the author of the *ʿArūkh*; Maimonides; Abraham ben David (of Posquières) and Meiri. B. M. Levin discovered the first three pages of the commentary on ʿErubin among the manuscripts of the Adler Collection and published them with the addition of passages from the *ʿArūkh*. He also published a fragment, intercalated between the words of an anonymous author, of Nissim's commentary on Ḥullin. David de Estella and others saw Nissim's commentaries on various

[1] Comp. Poznański, *Hazofe*, 5 (1921), pp. 177-193, 294-301, 6 (1922), pp. 329-350, 7 (1923), pp. 17-46. Abramson, *op. cit.*, pp. 283-360c, adds new finds to the fragments published earlier.

[2] *Tarbiẓ*, 11 (1940), pp. 230f.: see also Abramson, *op. cit.*, pp. 246-283.

tractates, such as Berakhot, ʿErubin, Rosh ha-Shana and Sanhedrin. In the *Fine Book*, Nissim mentions a book of *halakhot* he had written concerning the festive palm branch and which seems to be lost. He remarks that he is planning some more work, viz. a pamphlet on word-plays and allusive language in the Talmud. Elsewhere he says that he will write a book entitled *The Sequence of the Recipients of the Tora* and Meiri mentions a *Sequence of Reception* by Nissim, which seems to be the aforesaid.

Nissim once mentions *Halakhot on Faith* that he wrote. Poznański thinks that these *halakhot* were contained in Nissim's *Book of Commandments* and that this book dealt with matters of both faith and research; Nissim in fact states in the *Fine Book* that he will mention matters of reward and punishment, repentance etc. in another work. Two of his responsa have so far been published; others have been found among the papers of B. M. Levin. Nissim is also said to have written a commentary on the Pentateuch and a liturgical work, but, as has been observed, this assumption is doubtful so long as no sufficient material to support it is found.[1]

Nissim was also a poet, and Samuel ha-Nagid replied to a poem he had sent him as follows: "Balanced by Arab rythm / And prepared with Greek wisdom, / Containing words like music / And rich in content like pearls, / How can I repay your poem with (prosaic) orations (*sīḥīm*), / Which are like scarlet on white bushes (*sīḥīm*)?"[2]

In spite of this testimony, we possess no poem that can with certainty be ascribed to Nissim. Davidson's *Thesaurus of Poems and Piyyutim* contains a *piyyuṭ*, "We have sinned before you from the beginning", for which a R. Nissim is given as the author; this name also appears acrostically in the last verses of the piyyuṭ, which, judging by its style, may well stem from Nissim ben Jacob.[3]

Nissim was a disciple of Ḥushiel and Ḥananel, and their teaching is reflected in his extensive use of the Palestinian Talmud, which he calls *Talmud Ereṣ-Yisraʾel, Gemārā di-Beney Maʿarābā* or simply *Beney Maʿarābā*. At the same time, the influence of the Babylonian geonim —Saadia, Sherira, Samuel bar Ḥofni and Hay—was nevertheless decisive. In view of Nissim's extensive correspondence with Hay, it is permitted to regard the latter as his teacher in the Law and guide in giving decisions.

---

[1] Comp. Hirschberg, *Nissim*, pp. 37f.; Abramson, *op. cit.*, pp. 93-153 and 360 d-g.
[2] D. S. Sassoon, *Diwan of Shemuel Hannaghid*, p. 35 ll. 18-20.
[3] I. Davidson, *Thesaurus*, vol. II, letter ח p. 232, no. 202 (חטאנו לפניך בראש).

Thus, the Babylonian Talmud is "our Talmud" to him, and the method evolved in Babylonia was followed by the African rabbis in the subsequent generations.[1]

Mahdiya

Abraham ibn Daud writes: "... with the demise of these two (R. Ḥananel and R. Nissim), talmudic learning came to an end in Ifriqiya, except for a meagre representation in al-Mahdiya through the leadership of the Banu Sogmar [Zōgmār] and in Qalʿat Ḥammād through the leadership of Mar Solomon the Judge b. Formash. However, these men did not attain rabbinic posts, nor did they gain general recognition."[2] Kairouan was devastated and stripped of its political, economic and cultural importance: its Jewish community scattered in all directions and is hardly mentioned any more in literary documents. Mahdiya now became the permanent capital of the Banū Zīrī. As a result, the size and importance of its Jewish population increased, and it was felt necessary to continue here the tradition of Kairouan as a centre of learning and seat of a *beyt-dīn*.

Mahdiya became the home of R. Moses ben Joseph ibn Kashkīl, a native of Spain well versed in science, philosophy and the Hebrew language, who migrated to Sicily and there served Ṣamṣām al-Daula, the last Muslim emir of that country before its conquest by the Normans (after 1061). During the wars between the Arabs and the Normans, many Jews probably left the island for Mahdiya, where we find Moses ben Kashkīl in 1079 according to the colophon of a pamphlet in which he takes issue with the Geonim Samuel ben Ḥofni and Saadia concerning the witch of Endor (I Sam. 38:7): "Here ends the discussion, by the grace of the God of Israel, may He be exalted upon his heights; it was concluded on Monday, the 12th of Nisan of the year 4839 of the Creation (1079), in al-Mahdiya."[3]

From Mahdiya, Moses went to Acre, where he died before the arrival of the Crusaders; by sheer accident, his work was discovered by a rabbi who came to Acre after his death.

It was in Mahdiya that the B. Sogmār (Sigmār) mentioned by Abraham ibn Daud first entered the scene; they are a family well known to us from

[1] For source references see Hirschberg, *Nissim*, pp. 29f.

[2] According to *SHQ*, p. 58/78, the Banu Sogmar and the B. Formash "were not ordained for the rabbinate." We shall deal in vol. ii with the meaning of the term סמיכה, ordination, in those days.

[3] Mann, *Texts* I, pp. 386-393; the colophon: *ibid*., p. 390.

the Geniza archives. They were principally merchants and men of action, but the record of a session of the *beyt-dīn* in Fusṭāṭ of Thursday, the 5th Kislev, 1409 S.E. (November, 1097), in the matter of the *dayyān* Moses ben Labrāṭ against Joseph Lebdi, names the father of that *dayyān* with the addition of the title *rēsh bey rabbānān* (school head). We have not here a private letter, such as usually abounded in high-sounding titles, but a weighty official document. Nor was the title *rēsh bey rabbānān* awarded for a generous donation or fund-raising activities for the Academies. The geonim awarded it only to the greatest rabbinical scholar in the country in question, who headed the most important local academy and directed the whole organisation of religious life. That title, which thus also points to a practical function, had been borne by the leading rabbis of Kairouan. Upon the rise of al-Mahdiya, Rabbi Labrāṭ was appointed *rēsh bey rabbānān, i.e.* chief rabbi of the whole country.

The *dayyān* Moses, the son of the *rēsh bey rabbānān* Labrāṭ, is addressed by rhetorical epithets used only for outstanding rabbis: "to the chief, the mighty and noble potentate, the powerful hammer, the distinguished son of a distinguished father." The fact that he engaged in commerce does not by itself detract from his rabbinical standing. In those days, rabbis received no salaries and had to make a living in other ways. Abraham ibn Daud says that R. Ḥananel "was a very rich man, with whom many Kairouan merchants deposited stocks of goods, who had nine daughters and left ten thousand dinars." It seems that the Kairouan merchants made him a partner in their business.

Abraham ben Yajū, in a letter from Aden of 1149 to his brother in Mahdiya, sends greetings to "*Rabbenū* Labrāṭ, the *dayyān*, the son of the honourable *marenū*(!)*we-rabbenū* Moses, the *dayyān*." This is the third of the B. Sogmār *dayyanīm* known to us. He is probably referred to in a letter telling of Yehuda Halevi's stay in Mahdiya when, following a denunciation by a Jew converted to Islam, he had to appear before the secret police and did so in the company of the *dayyān* and one of his friends. It should be noted in this connection that the *dīwān* of Yehuda Halevi's poems includes a poem and a letter he sent to a rabbi in Mahdiya by the name of Ḥabib. Yehuda Halevi was well known in Mahdiya and his arrival made a great impression.

The first Labrāṭ was certainly an ordained rabbi, and in view of prevailing local custom, it seems likely that his son, Moses, and his grandson, the second Labrāṭ, both *dayyānim* of Mahdiya, were also ordained and widely known. The second Labrāṭ may have been the last *dayyān* of Mahdiya, for, about ten years after the date of the abovementioned letter (1149) the city was conquered by the Almohads, who forced the local non-Muslims to choose between expulsion and conversion. The Geniza documents confirm and add to the statements of Abraham ben Daud.[1]

Let us now review some other localities that were for a time under the direct influence of Kairouan.

Qābes

Our information concerning the rabbis of Qābes, a South Tunisian city with an important Jewish community, begins with a somewhat strange item. Hay was once asked for an explanation of the Gemara passage (Sukka 28a) concerning the conversation of the date-palms. In his responsum, he refers to Abraham Qābesi, a gaon who lived in the year 1140 S.E./829 C.E., who "understood the conversation of the date-palms and reported very wonderful things, by which he perceived the truth about human beings."[2] The mention of a gaon originating from Qābes who lived some 200 years before Hay is puzzling. A passage in the *Halākhōt* of R. Isaac Alfasi: "And R. Hay Gaon sent messages to Mar Abraham Qābesi" [3] gave rise to the suggestion that the "gaon" R. Abraham might have to be identified with a contemporary of Hay.[4] A rabbi named Abraham indeed lived in Kairouan in Hay's time and addressed questions to the gaon of Pumbeditha.[5] But on the other hand, a letter of Sherira mentions a gaon named Abraham bar Mar Rab Sherira who lived in the early 9th century C.E. Although his origin is not indicated, it seems reasonable to assume that he is the gaon referred to by Hay in connection with the date-palms. Reliable information as to the origin of that gaon might lend substance to various conjectures concerning relations between Qābes and Babylonia. However, in view of the many doubts in the matter, no conclusions as to the antiquity of the Qābes *talmūd-tōrā* can be drawn, and the identity of the rabbi known to us by that name, who must be credited with the introduction of rabbinical learning in the region, remains obscure.

Definite information on Qābes scholars is available only of the period

---

[1] Comp. Hirschberg, *Zion*, 22 (1957), pp. 239-241; Goitein, *Tarbiẓ*, 24 (1954), pp. 21-47.

[2] *RShT*, no. 74; *RL*, no. 33 (Lewin, *Iggeret*, Appendices, p. IV); Rashi to Sukka 28a.

[3] Alfasi, Ket. 45b.

[4] Lewin, *Iggeret*, p. 110; and comp. Musafia's note to *RL*, no. 33, S. Buber's remarks, *ibid.*, p. 10, and Harkavy, *RH*, p. 369 note to p. 167.

[5] *RH*, nos. 336, 344 (see also below p. 343).

of Sherira and Hay. There was then in the city a group of *talmīdīm*, *i.e.* scholars who had not yet been ordained as rabbis or *ḥaberim*, who addressed questions to the Academy of Pumbeditha either directly or through Jacob b. Nissim. We sometimes find the same question asked from Kairouan and from Qābes. Some of the questions do not mention the names of the inquirers, but simply "the people of Qābes," similarly to those addressed "to the people of Kairouan". Some of the responsa can definitely be described as early, because they are given in the name of Sherira or through Jacob b. Nissim, who both died at the beginning of the second millennium C.E. In others, Hay refers to his correspondence with Qābes, which was rather lively, but we are unable to determine whether he is speaking of matters decided by him in his father's lifetime or when he was already the sole head of the Academy.[1]

Gradually the veil of anonimity lifts from the people of Qābes, and several rabbis of the Ibn Jāmiʿ family come into the limelight. From the headings of several responsa, and especially from the blessing at the end, we gather that Hay esteemed the B. Jāmiʿ. The study of four or five generations of that family acquaints us with one of the characteristics of African congregations: heredity of office within certain families. The surname of the Ibn Jāmiʿ rabbis of Qābes is most interesting, since it is the name of the Muslim rulers of the city during that period.

A distinguished member of the group of *talmīdīm* who received responsa from Sherira and Hay seems to have been Moses bar Samuel (ibn Jāmiʿ), since he is mentioned first in the closing formula of the fascicle: "And the *talmīdīm* who framed the questions, R. Moses ben R. Samuel, R. Solomon ben R. Joseph Levi, R. Isaac ben R. Jonah, R. Reuben ben R. Samuel and R. Solomon ben R. Judah, may be jointly instructed by God and be ... (?) vouchsafed (?) the crown of the Tora. Great salvation."[2]

The naming of five rabbis suggests that by the early 11th century Qābes had a large, important *beyt-midrash*. A consignment of responsa of Hay to Qābes, of Tebet, 1327 S.E./1016 C.E., which postdates the preceding fascicle by some fifteen years at least, designates R. Moses b. Samuel by the title *ḥabērēnū*, but mentions before him a scholar named Nehemiah bar Obadiah, which means that R. Moses b. Samuel was not

---

[1] *RH*, nos. 339, 351 and 425; Worman, *JQR*, 19 (1907), p. 734 no. 40; Assaf, *Mi-Sifrut ha-Geonim*, p. 228; *RH*, no. 371 (at the end). The same question from Kairouan and Qābes: *RH*, no. 364. Hay here appears as *ab*, so the reply is not later than the beginning of the 11th century; comp. also *RH*, nos. 319 and 345.

[2] *RH*, no. 369.

the leader of the rabbis and *talmīdīm* to whom the responsa are addressed.[1]

Another responsum of Hay, concerning some Talmudical problems, answers questions asked by "our dear Moses b. Samuel b. Jāmiᶜ and other *talmīdīm*". A letter has also been published of our R. Moses to Joseph ben ᶜAwkal, the representative of the Babylonian Academy in Kairo, indicating that the former would send questions and gifts of money through Joseph to the Academy. In the case dealt with by that letter, they were sent through R. Samuel b. Abraham Tāherti, a rabbi whom we shall yet meet.[2]

We have followed the rise of Qābes as a Jewish centre in the days of R. Moses. The *talmīdīm* became rabbis, and new *talmīdīm* were added. At the time of his correspondence with Joseph ben ᶜAwkal, which is also the time of the correspondence of Joseph ben Berakhya of Kairouan with the same Academy representative, Moses was the head of his community: the latter was autonomous, independent of the African metropolis. This appears to have been the situation at the end of the second and the beginning of the third decade of the century, when that metropolis had no spiritual leader recognised by the Babylonian Academy.

Moses ibn Jāmiᶜ concludes his letter to Joseph ben ᶜAwkal with greetings from his two sons, Jacob and Abraham. Both were rabbinical scholars who sent letters of their own to Pumbeditha during their father's lifetime, when he was old. From the order in which they are mentioned, it seems that Jacob was the elder, but the closing formulas of the responsa fascicles may justify the conclusion that Abraham was the more learned. A letter full of praise to Jacob from an anonymous gaon has also been preserved.[3]

One Moses ben Abraham ibn Jāmiᶜ is mentioned in an exchange of letters between Naharāy b. Nissim and his cousin Israel. Naharāy has asked that efforts be made to locate Moses in Palestine, and Israel replies that he has achieved no results in the matter.[4]

The line of rabbis of the house of Jāmiᶜ extends to the middle of the 12th century, *i.e.* until the arrival of the Almohads in the region. Samuel ben Jacob ibn Jāmiᶜ wrote additions to the *ᶜArūkh* under the title *Agur* (in

---

[1] *RH*, nos. 59-67. Some of the responsa are difficult to date; see a reference in *RC*, no. 85 (in the fascicle nos. 70-90 to R. Nissim), as well as *RL*, no. 1 (p. 5a) and *Qohelet Shelomo* 2b.

[2] The responsum published in *RA* III, p. 93, and the letter to Ibn ᶜAwkal, Mann, *Texts* I, pp. 140f., seem to be the last item of this correspondence.

[3] *RH*, nos. 315-328 and 336-344; Lewin, *GQ* II, pp. 20f.; Mann, *Texts* I, pp. 190-193, also p. 185 (see also above p. 341 n. 5).

[4] Starr, *Zion*, 1 (1936), p. 446 ll. 27f.

allusion to his surname: Jāmiʿ from Arabic *jamaʿa* "to collect," Hebrew *ʾāgōr*) and *Halakhot* concerning ritual slaughter. From quotations in the latter tractate appears that Samuel was acquainted with an early Gaonic compendium called *Hilkhōt Reʾū*, *e.g.* "I have seen in *Hilkhōt Reʾū*, *i.e.* the *halakhot* ascribed to our Master Mar Rab Yehudāy Gaon...". It is assumed that he saw also the *Halākhōt Gedōlōt*. The introduction to the additions indicates that Samuel was *dayyan* in Qābes and his father head of the local *beyt-dīn*, but it is unlikely that the latter was Jacob the son of Moses mentioned above. Samuel exchanged letters with Yehuda al-Barjelōni, and Abraham ibn Ezra composed panegyrics on him, which indicate that Abraham had stayed at the Jāmiʿs' house in Qābes.[1]

Qalʿat Ḥammād

The flowering of this capital was too brief to leave its mark upon the life of the Jews. We happen to know that Isaac Alfasi and possibly also his disciple Ephraim hailed from there. But the former achieved distinction in Fez and the latter in Lucena. Of the *ḥaber* Abraham al-Qalʿi and the *dayyān* Solomon Formash we know nothing but their names, which have already been mentioned in connection with the local *beyt-dīn*. Those data on the Qalʿa congregation which, as hinted by Abraham ibn Daud, were preserved for some time, seem to have been lost upon the city's eclipse.[2]

Tāhert

At the beginning of this chapter, we met Yehuda ibn Quraysh of Tāhert. It is impossible to assume that this scholar grew up and developed in an uneducated, ignorant environment. He probably had teachers, associates and colleagues, and perhaps disciples; but all this will remain

[1] *RH*, p. 351; S. Buber, *Graetz-Festschrift*, 1888, p. 2ff. (Hebrew part). The ritual slaughter rules: Steinschneider, *Geigers Jüdische Zeitschrift für Wissenschaft und Leben* 1 (1862), pp. 232-43, 304-318; 2 (1863), pp. 76-80 (esp.), 297-310; 3 (1864/5), pp. 305-6; 4 (1866), pp. 155-60; A. Hildesheimer, *Sefer Halākhōt Gedōlōt*, Jerusalem 1971, Introduction pp. 28-9; N. Ben-Menahem, *Sefer ha-Yobēl le R. Hanokh Albeck*, Jerusalem 1963, pp. 81-3; cf. also B. Dinur, *Tōledōt Yisrāēl*, II/3, Jerusalem 1968, p. 77.

[2] Comp. below, pp. 347 and above, p. 224. Toledano, *Ner*, pp. 26f., suggests that Solomon b. Farḥon, who completed his treatise on Hebrew roots in Salerno in 1161, was a native of Qalʿat Ḥammād.

conjectural so long as no documentary evidence is found. The city of Tāhert had suffered by political upheavals and its importance had declined in every respect, but in the 11th century it still had a Jewish community; we possess information on the activities of its members and their relations with Palestine and Babylonia.

We have seen above that Moses ben Samuel ibn Jāmiʿ sent money destined for the Babylonian Academy through Samuel b. Abraham ibn al-Tāherti. Samuel was a Talmudical scholar; we possess a fascicle of responsa adressed to him, to R. Bahlūl b. Joseph (also known to us) and to a third rabbi. Samuel al-Tāherti frequently visited Fusṭāṭ, and he is mentioned in connection with an exchange of letters with the Gaon Hay. The Palestinian Gaon, Solomon b. Yehuda, likewise sent him a letter —through Ephraim ben Shemarya in Fusṭāṭ. He seems to have moved to Fusṭāṭ and been a local notable in the days of the Nāsī and Gaon, Daniel ben Azarya.[1]

Before taking leave of Tāhert, we might note that once some Jews in that city wished to know what was the *shefoferet* (tube) referred to in the Talmud (ʿErubin 43b). The responsum describes an optical instrument used in surveying, mentioning in this connection the astrolabe used by *ḥobrīm* (astronomers).[2]

Tlemcen

The Jews of Tlemcen experienced many adversities, culminating in their expulsion. They came back, however, life returned to normal, and we then find scholars among them who sent to Pumbeditha "those questions which have been asked by our brethren, the scholars in the city of Tlemcen in the land of the setting sun."[3] The questions relate to topical matters, arising out of the distress in which Tlemcen Jewry found themselves after their temporary exile. Another set of questions from Tlemcen likewise reflects local problems. Tlemcen is nearer to Spain

---

[1] *RH*, nos. 16-36. Müller, *Mafteaḥ*, pp. 36-38, thinks that these responsa are by Sherira or by Sherira and Hay, but Samuel's ties with Solomon b. Yehuda and Daniel b. ʿAzarya suggest that they are later and by Hay alone; comp. Mann, *Jews* I, p. 182; II, p. 128 l. 35, pp. 218 and 351. For the Tāherti's family comp. also Assaf, *Sources*, p. 137, and Goitein, *Studies*, p. 317.

[2] *RH*, nos. 28 and 314; comp. Baron, *SRH* VIII, p. 359 note 30, and L. A. Mayer, *Islamic Astrolabists and their Work*, 1956, esp. p. 84.

[3] *RH*, nos. 37-43; comp. also *RM*, nos. 133-136, *TR* II, p. 31 no. 9, and Ginzberg, *Geonica* II, pp. 134-142.

than any other city of the region, so that the question of Christian maidservants arose here with particular acuteness.[1] Another question, how to manage in a place where nobody knows how to prepare *gwilin* or *raqq*, a not fully processed parchment, is understandable in a city remote from the major centres of both the East and the West (Fez). We should note that, according to the testimony of Pirqōy ben Bābōy, Palestine faced the same problem after the period of Byzantine persecution.[2]

From the Eastern and Central Maghreb, we now pass to the cities of the Outer Maghreb, *i.e.* present-day Morocco.

Fez

Fez was the most important community in this region. Yehuda ibn Quraysh's letter indicates that the knowledge of Arabic and Hebrew was quite widespread among Fez Jewry. During the tribulations visiting them in the late 10th and early 11th century, they were in touch with Sherira, Hay and Samuel b. Ḥofni. The responsa mention two brothers, Abraham and Tanḥum the sons of Jacob, who had sent questions to Babylonia. The date of one of the responsa is 1315 S.E./1004C.E.; it was sent to Fusṭāṭ for transmission to Fez. We possess a number of other responsa sent to Fez or mentioning responsa sent there.[3] The questions from Fez disclose, *inter alia*, an interest in mysticism. Two residents of Fez, Abū Dānī and David he-Ḥārāsh (the Artificer), on returning from Palestine, brought with them Saadia's commentary on *Sefer-Yeṣira*.[4]

The rabbis of Fez had a more than local reputation already in early days. One of them, Samuel ha-Kohen ben Yoshiya, became head of the community in Pechina, then an important Spanish city. Another, Yehuda Fāsi ben Joseph, who corresponded with Hay, resided in Kairouan.[5] The suggestion that the Gaon Solomon ben Yehuda came from Fez has already been mentioned. We know, moreover, several poets hailing from that city.[6]

---

[1] *RH*, nos. 426-433; the question of the maidservants: no. 431 (comp. also above, pp. 181-2.

[2] *RH*, no. 432; *Ginzey Schechter* II, p. 560; above, p. 000, n. 0.

[3] *RA* I, pp. 81f. no. 63; Mann, *JQR*, 11 (1920/21), pp. 439-442; Assaf, *GQ* V, pp. 108-123; *RH*, nos. 47 (p. 24) and 386 (p. 200); *Qebūẓat Ḥakhāmīm*, pp. 108f.; Mann, *Texts* I, pp. 114f.

[4] Comp. Mann, *ibid.*, p. 74 no. 25.

[5] *SHQ*, p. 49/67; Mann, *Tarbiẓ*, 5 (1934), p. 283; Assaf, *Mi-Sifrut*, p. 224.

[6] Comp. Aloni, *Sinai*, 21 (1958), pp. 392f.

ISAAC ALFASI

The fame of Fez was permanently established in the Jewish world by Rabbi Isaac b. Jacob ha-Kohen Alfasi, known acrostically as "RIF" and sometimes simply called *Ha-Alfas*, although he was born in Qalʿat banī Ḥammād in present-day Algeria and died in Lucena in Spain.

The date of his birth is uncertain. According to Abraham ibn Daud, he died in the year 4863 at the age of ninety, which would assign his birth to approximately 4773 (1013 C.E.). Those were the early days of Qalʿat Ḥammād, which had been founded only a few years previously, and it is inconceivable that the local Jewish community should already have been able to establish a *beyt-midrash* where a student of the calibre of Isaac Alfasi might have been educated. We do not know who taught him. His *Halākhōt* show the influence of two Kairouan scholars, Ḥananel and Nissim, and Abraham ibn Daud in fact says in *Sefer ha-Qabbala*: "He was a disciple of R. Nissim ben R. Jacob and of R. Ḥananel." Many accepted Ibn Daud's statement at its face value, but they were mistaken. Alfasi's own words indicate that he was not a disciple, in the narrow sense of the term, of those rabbis. He seems to have studied in Fez, where he taught for many years.

Isaac was forced to leave Fez at the age of seventy-five after being denounced to the authorities by al-Aʿjab b. al-Khalifa and his son, Ḥayyim. He went to Spain, stayed for a time in Cordova and eventually settled in Lucena. Here, too, he knew no peace at first owing to writers' squabbles and rivalry between him and Isaac al-Bāliya and Isaac ibn Ghiyyāt. Only towards the end of his days, upon the death of ibn Ghiyyāt, did he accede to the rabbinate of that great and famous congregation.[1] It is not to be supposed that he wrote his *magnum opus*, the *Halakhōt*, after attaining the age of seventy-five. As we know, he revised that book many times, making corrections, deletions and additions. This revision many in part have been prompted by criticism from other scholars when the book was already in circulation, and must have extended over many years. Nor is it conceivable that his many reponsa were all written during the last years of his life. Moreover, the lengthy explanations deemed necessary by him for several halakhot of the tractate Ketubot are in Arabic, and so are many of his extant responsa. They were evidently written in an Arabic-speaking country for Arabic-speaking readers, *i.e.* in Morocco.[2]

---

[1] *SHQ*, pp. 62/84 and 64/86; Simon b. Zemaḥ Dūrān, *Responsa* I, no. 72.

[2] Comp. the Hebrew translation of these explanations in the Romm edition at the bottom of Alfasi, Ket. 36b-37b; 51a-55a; Shebuot 31a-33a. Epstein, *Tarbiẓ*, 1/4 (1930), p. 44, also supposes that he wrote his *Halākhōt* in Africa.

Thus, Alfasi is rightly so named and is to be regarded as a Maghrebi and not a Spanish rabbi. Of course, as a result of circumstances, his fame is mainly due to his Spanish admirers and disciples and to the influence of his teachings in that country. Yehuda Halevi lamented his death, and his epitaph was written by Moses ibn Ezra.[1] Abraham ben Daud regarded him as the greatest of the five Isaacs who arose in Spain in that generation; he concludes the account of his life with the words: "He passed away in Nisan, 4863, at about the age of ninety, after having raised many disciples and having gained world-wide recognition. He composed a code (*Halākhōt*) in the form of an abridged Talmud. Ever since the days of R. Hay there has been no one who could match him in scholarship."[2]

The plan of the *Halākhōt* betrays the influence of Nissim's *Key*. Alfasi perceived that the dispersal of the discussion of one subject over several tractates made it difficult to follow the debate and to arrive at a conclusion. He therefore concentrated the material in the place which seemed to him most appropriate, set out the problem briefly and summed up the discussion. He thus made it easier for the student to find his way about and to discern the resultant rule. Being mainly interested in practical precepts, he omitted debates within tractates, and even whole tractates, which had no practical significance in his days, while gathering elsewhere those parts of them that were nevertheless of interest to him. At the same time, he followed the order in which the tractates are arranged in the Talmud. In drawing the halakhic conclusion, he made use of the Palestinian Talmud, but only where it did not conflict with the Babylonian. He also drew upon the Geonim and Ḥananel, referring to them expressly. However, he did not always agree with them, but used his own judgment, relying of the Gemara as he understood it.[3]

Alfasi's *Halākhōt*, which were once regarded as a kind of "Little Talmud", had a decisive influence upon his contemporaries. Leading

---

[1] The lament: *Diwan*, ed. Brody, II, p. 100. The epitaph: *Kerem Ḥemed*, IV (1839)' p. 93; comp. also Halper, *Shirat Yisrael*, p. 73.

[2] *Sefer Ha-Qabbalah*, p. 62/84. Much attention was paid to Alfasi's teachings by later rabbinic scholars; see Tchernowitz, *Toldot ha-Poseqim* I, pp. 131-192; Benedikt, *KS*, 25 (1948/49), pp. 164ff.; Baron, *SRH* VI, pp. 84-87.

[3] For his use of the Jerusalem Talmud comp. *e.g.*, Alfasi Sab. 21a and 47a. In Erub. 35b (at the end), he explains why the decision of the Jerusalem Talmud cannot always be accepted; comp. Rappaport, *Bikkurey ha-Ittim*, 12 (1831), p. 26 n. 20. He expressly mentions Ḥananel, *e.g.*, in Sab. 60b, but in many other places he refers to Ḥananel's teachings without mentioning him; this seems to prove that he was not Ḥananel's pupil; comp. also Benedikt, *KS*, 25 (1949), p. 170. Guided by his own judgment, he accepts the comments and decisions of earlier sages, *e.g.*, Jeb. 21b-22a and Kid. 19a, or rejects them: Sab. 12b.

Spanish and Provençal rabbis wrote commentaries on them, and Maimonides found only a few passages that required correction because the author had erred.

Alfasi's chief disciple was Joseph ha-Levi ibn Megāsh, who was brought up at his house and succeeded him after his death in spite of his youth and although Alfasi's son, Jacob, was also a Talmudical scholar.[1] We know only the disciples who belong to the Spanish period, of whom, for the purposes of our subject, we must single out Ephraim, surnamed al-Qalʿī, *i.e.* the one of Qalʿa, which is probably Qalʿat Ḥammād, Alfasi's birthplace. The community in Qalʿat Ḥammād had developed in the course of time and become a centre of rabbinical learning and the seat of a *beyt-din*, as we may conclude from Abraham ben Daud's above-quoted words concerning the *dayyān* Solomon ben Formash, who held office there in his days. Ephraim felt impelled to study the Law under his great fellow townsman, and wrote the first book intended to supplement Alfasi's *Halākhōt*. He was an excellent scholar and is frequently quoted by early authors.[2]

Sources are lacking as to conditions in Fez after Alfasi's departure, but the experience of recent years raises the hope that documents relating to that period will yet be discovered. Indirect information suggests that the attraction of the Lucena school increased, and that students flocked to Joseph ibn Megāsh from Morocco, particularly from its southern cities, such as Sijilmāsa and Darʿa.[3] He received questions from there, as we may conclude from responsa dealing with events that had occurred in the congregations of Ceuta and Fez, Darʿa and the *Hār* (Hebrew: mountain), by which without doubt a community in the Atlas region is meant, most probably Aghmāṭ, south of Marrākesh. Aghmāṭ has then been settled mostly by Jews. From that place did come Zachariah al-Aghmāṭi, a scholar who deserves a study and appraisal on his own merits, maybe a student of Ibn Megāsh. Unfortunately we lack any information about his biography.[4]

Incidentally a responsum of Ibn Megāsh seems to contain the first mention in our sources of Ceuta, whose Jewish community, as reported by Abraham ibn Ezra, suffered in the days of the Almohads. Abraham ben

---

[1] *SHQ*, p. 63/85.

[2] Comp. Benedikt, *KS*, 25 (1948-49), pp. 164, 170 and 229f., and 26 (1950), pp. 332 and 338, esp. p. 331 n. 39; and now Schepansky, *Tarbiẓ*, 41 (1972), pp. 188ff.

[3] Comp. below pp. 352, 354.

[4] Ibn Megāsh, *Responsa*, Warsaw 1870, nos. 137, 101; 93 (Dāʿa is an error), 152 (*Har*). Comp. I. Ta-Shmah, *KS*, 46 (1971), pp. 136-46, 541-53, esp. 551; *ibid.*, 47 (1972), pp. 318-22. More about Zechariah al-Aghmāti in Appendix I.

Daud mentions it, as well as Tangier and Salé, solely in connection with these sufferings.[1] Anyhow, the reference to those three places on the northern and western coasts of Morocco suggests that Jews had begun to move northward, seeking the proximity of Spain. It is clear that spiritually, too, this can hardly have had a favourable effect on the status of Fez, the largest city in the centre of the country relatively close to those three ports, and which had ceased to be the capital. The Spanish communities increased in importance, and Morocco, especially Fez, marked time, or even receded.

The decline in scholarly zeal was at first slow, the major communities still preserving their tradition and the fund of energies accumulated in more auspicious times. The *batey-dīn* still functioned, and the houses of study were well frequented. Although the *Lament on the Destruction of the Maghreb*, which pays tribute to the Maghreb scholars, is, in both its versions, not free from rhetoric, it would be wrong to regard it as mere poetry and deny its historical significance, especially in view of the close relations then existing between the Spanish poets and their Maghrebi brethren. Maimonides' account of the appearance of Moses Darʿi, the harbinger of the Messiah in Fez, and of the crowds gathering round him (which were not to the liking of his father, R. Maimon, who forbade joining Darʿi), suggests that there was no qualified rabbi and scholar in the city at that time.[2] But when in 1159 or 1160 Maimon decided to move to Fez with his family, he no doubt did so because he regarded that city as most suitable for the further education of his sons. Both studied under R. Yehuda ha-Kohen ibn Sūsān, who was martyred in 1165. As we know, Maimon and his sons left Fez soon afterwards. Though the residence of Maimonides' family in Fez was not of long duration, it left a deep impression both on him and the people of the Maghreb. Strong mutual ties were established, which both sides continued to foster when Maimonides had settled in Cairo.[3]

Among those who left Fez during the second wave of persecutions was the scholar and poet Yehuda ben ʿAbbās or, as the Arabs call him, Abū al-Baqā Yaḥyā ibn ʿAbbās. He was a friend of Yehuda Halevi, but al-Ḥarizi's opinion of him as a poet was divided: "He went from the lands of the west to the east, but his poetry fell by the wayside. Some of his poems are lovely and pleasant, but others are worth nothing, neither

---

[1] *SHQ*, 66/88 (we do not accept the identification with Silves suggested by Cohen, p. 88 to l. 463), 67/92 and 70/96.

[2] Comp. Halkin, *Iggeret*, pp. 99f., and above, pp. 120ff.

[3] Comp. above, pp. 137f., also 194ff. (Hebrew).

pleasant nor good. He begot a son that is a rogue, and he behaved very wickedly."[1] Yehuda ben ʿAbbās settled in Aleppo. His son, Samuel —alluded to by al-Ḥarizi—had previously converted to Islam in Mosul; he gained notoriety as the author of a diatribe against Judaism, entitled *Ifḥām al-Yahūd, i.e.* denigration of the Jews.[2]

Marrakesh

As will be remembered, Jews were forbidden to settle in Marrakesh; they were only permitted to stay there briefly on business. This did not prevent the ruler of Morocco, ʿAlī b. Yūsuf ibn Tāshfīn, from inviting over from Seville the Jewish physician Abū al-Ḥasan Meir ibn Qamniel, a friend of Yehuda Halevi, who dedicated some poems to him. Ibn Qamniel arrived in Marrakesh with another Jewish physician, Abū Ayyūb Solomon Abū al-Muʿallim. Abū al-Muʿallim was extolled, in resounding panegyrics, by Moses ibn Ezra and Yehuda Halevi and, while resident in Marrakesh, by Abraham ibn Ezra.[3] The two physicians bore the title "vizier", which in those days designated a holder of high office generally, and not necessarily a minister of state. Court physicians, as we know, had a certain political status; they were not only familiars, but also advisers of the ruler. According to Ibn ʿAqnin, Ibn al-Muʿallim interpreted the Song of Solomon to ʿAli in the literal sense, thereby arousing the anger of Ibn Qamniel.[4] The invitation of two Jewish physicians from Spain to the court of the Almoravid ruler of Morocco, who was not remarkable for friendship towards the Jews, requires explanation, since highly-skilled Muslim physicians were not lacking in the Maghreb; in fact, Maimonides had studied medicine in Fez. ʿAlī may have wanted to establish a medical school or first-rate hospital in Marrakesh, so as to be able to compete with Fez, and this may have prompted him to bring over experts from Spain.

Ibn Qamniel's and Ibn Muʿallim's presence in Marrakesh is also significant from a Jewish point of view. We may suppose that in addition

---

[1] *Taḥkemoni*, ed. Kaminka, p. 42; comp. also p. 89.

[2] Comp. Munk, *Notice*, pp. 7f. no. 2; Schreiner, *MGWJ*, 42 (1898), pp. 123ff.; *ibid.*, 43 (1899), p. 521; Ginzberg, *Ginzey Schechter* II, p. 524; Baron, *SRH* VIII, pp. 141 and 249; M. Perlmann, *Ifḥām al-Yahūd*, New York 1964. For refugees from Fez comp. Hirschberg, *J. Baer Jubilee Volume*, p. 143, ll. 22-26.

[3] Comp. Schirmann, *Tarbiẓ*, 9 (1938), p. 52; *idem*, *RIHP*, 4 (1938), pp. 249f.; *idem*, *Ha-Shira* I, pp. 541-543.

[4] Halkin, *Marx Jubilee Volume*, 1950, English Section, p. 391; *idem*, (ed.), Ibn ʿAqnīn *Divulgatio* etc., pp. 490-500.

to them, and with their active assistance, other Jews, with their families, settled in the "royal city" permanently or semi-permanently, that, in fact, the nucleus of a Jewish community was created there. This may account for the mention of Marrakesh in one of the manuscripts of the *Lament on the Destruction of the Maghreb*. In the 14th and 15th cent. Marrakesh is only casually mentioned.[1]

Sijilmāsa

A Jewish community undoubtedly existed in Sijilmāsa at least as early as the 10th century.[2] The first indications of relations between Sijilmāsa and Iraqi Jewry are of the 11th century, when questions were addressed from the city to Hay, including one concerning the eating of locusts.[3] In the 12th century, students from Sijilmāsa seem to have begun flocking to the Spanish Academies. One letter mentions incidentally that a man named Joseph ben Mellāl studied in Lucena under Joseph ibn Megāsh and received a letter of appointment from him (*i.e.* was ordained to the rabbinate). As Joseph died in 4901/1141, this must have been before the Almohad campaign. When the Almohads came to the city, the local Jewish scholars debated with them on religious matters, until the commander imposed *ha-pish'ūt*, *i.e.* conversion to Islam, on them. Some 150 persons were martyred on that occasion, as Solomon, a merchant in Fusṭāṭ, informs his father in a letter of the beginning of 1148; he goes on to say: "Where the word of a king is, there is power" (Eccl. 8:4)—the others reneged. The first of the renegades was Joseph ben 'Amrān, the *dayyan* of Sijilmāsa.[4] It has lately been suggested that this *dayyan* was Abraham ibn Ezra's benefactor, who generously assisted the poet during his stay in the Maghreb and was thanked by him with panegyrics in his honour.[5]

In the *Lament on the Destruction of the Maghreb*, the poet (who, according to Schirmann, is Abraham ibn Ezra) describes Sijilmāsa as a city of geonim (scholars)—as it is also called in another, long-known

---

[1] Comp. above pp. 123ff; R. Asher, (ROSH) *Responsa*, chap. 51 no. 4; RaSHBaSH, *Responsa* no. 512. Comp. Corcos, *Zion*, 37 (1967), pp. 158-59.

[2] According to *SHQ*, p. 51/69, Ibn Jau (10th century) was in charge, *inter alia*, of the Jewish community of Sijilmāsa. For the economic role of Sijilmāsa comp. above, p. 250; also Dufourcq, *Espagne*, pp. 136-138.

[3] Ibn Quraysh, *Risāla*, p. XVII; *RH*, nos. 68-81; comp. Mann, *Texts* I, p. 634 n. 6. As one of the questions shows Nissim's name, it seems that they were transmitted through him; Ginzberg, *Geonica* II, p. 67 (a reference to the subject of *RH*, no. 74).

[4] Comp. Hirschberg, *I. Baer Jubilee Volume*, p. 143 ll. 18-25, p. 142 ll. 44-49.

[5] Comp. Ben-Menahem, *Albeck Jubilee Volume*, pp. 84-86.

lament—and mourns its martyrs, but makes no reference whatever to the conversions which took place there.[1] On the other hand, we have found an interesting parallel between the *Lament* and Solomon's letter. Solomon calls his father, who hails from Sijilmāsa, *nīn ge'onim* "descendant of geonim", a title which in those days was no mere figure of speech; the designation "city of geonim" may point in the same direction.[2]

Solomon goes on to tell his father—who maintained close contact with Morocco, and especially with his native city, Sijilmāsa, and with Fez, who had sent a Tora scroll there as a gift and was interested in every detail relating to that country—that before the arrival of the Almohads part of the population of Sijilmāsa, including Mar Yehuda, the son of Mar Farḥōn, had managed to escape to Darʿa.[3] Now, in a letter to his disciple Joseph ben Yehuda, of the end of 1191, Maimonides mentions discussions he had with scholars in the Maghreb when he was of Joseph's age, *i.e.* about thirty years old—which means that he himself lived in Fez at the time; and in view of the conclusions to be drawn from this passage, we will give it *verbatim*:

"... You have undoubtedly heard what befell between me and R. Yehuda ha-Kohen, the son of Mar Farḥōn, of blessed memory, concerning two questions as to forbidden food, and between me and the *dayyān* of Sijilmāsa (his son) concerning a bill of divorcement, and between me and Abū Yūsuf, the son of Mar Joseph, may he rest in Paradise, concerning a captive woman, and with regard to many similar (issues)..."[4]

Baneth has already suggested that the two Yehuda ben Farḥōn are identical, and it seems safe to assume that Yehuda returned to Sijilmāsa during the lull following the tribulations of the forties. There was in that city, moreover, a *dayyān* with whom Maimonides debated. According to one version, he was a son of R. Yehuda Farḥōn; however, the acceptance of that version will not add to, nor its rejection detract, from the fact referred to by Maimonides. Abū Yūsuf, the son of Mar Joseph, seems to be the son of the *dayyān* R. Joseph ben ʿAmrān, who reneged under duress. If this assumption is correct, we can draw two conclusions from it: a) Joseph ben ʿAmrān returned to Judaism—otherwise Maimonides would not have added the words "may he rest in Paradise", though he did

---

[1] Comp. above, pp. 124-5.

[2] Comp. Hirschberg, *op. cit.*, (p. 352, n. 4), p. 144 (the salutation). Solomon b. Yehuda, the writer of the letter, may have been a distant relative (on the mother's side) of R. Solomon b. Yehuda, the gaon of the Palestinian Academy from 1025 to 1050.

[3] Comp. the passages referred to in p. 352, n. 4 and the lines following them.

[4] Baneth, *Iggerot ha-Rambam*, Jerusalem 1946, p. 90.

not, in view of what had happened, call him rabbi or mention his position; b) this *dayyān*'s son was a distinguished scholar, who debated with Maimonides.

The sources mentioned indicate that in the 12th century, both before and after the first Almohad persecution, Sijilmāsa was a centre of rabbinical learning, with scholars important enough for Maimonides to call them his opponents in debate after a lapse of fifty years. This is confirmed by further information concerning Sijilmāsans. One, Solomon b. Nathan, compiled a liturgy which was copied in Barca in 1203.[1] Another attended the academy of Samuel ben ʿAli, a Babylonian gaon at the end of the 12th century, and was given a letter of recommendation to Egypt.[2] As late as the 14th century, we find in North Africa Yehuda ben Joseph Sijilmāsi, a gifted sensitive *payṭan*, whose works were received into the liturgy of Maghrebi synagogues.[3]

Darʿa

The sources on the Jews of Darʿa are few. One Dunash of that city addressed questions to Isaac Alfasi, who replied in Arabic.[4] Joseph ibn Megāsh, Alfasi's distinguished disciple, mentions in one of his responsa a scholar named Dunash, who may be identical with the aforesaid.[5] A famous man was Moses Darʿi, of whom Maimonides says that he was a disciple of Joseph ibn Megāsh (another disciple of Ibn Megāsh, Joseph ben Mellāl, has already been referred to (above p. 352)); although Moses' prediction of the coming of the Messiah proved wrong, Maimonides pays high tribute to him in his "Epistle to Yemen".[6] Darʿa was one of the places hit by disaster after 1147, though in the *Lament on the Devastation of the Maghreb* the debate conducted there with the Almohads is mentioned before the events of Sijilmāsa and Fez. Maimonides met some rabbis from Darʿa in Egypt, who may have migrated there at the time of the Almohad persecution.[7]

---

[1] Steinschneider, *Kerem Ḥemed*, 9 (1856), pp. 37ff.; Mann, *Jews* II, p. 295 n. 1.

[2] Comp. Goitein, *Ḥinnūkh*, p. 182.

[3] Comp. Bernstein, *Ḥoreb*, 12 (1957), pp. 217-233, and Mirski, *KS*, 34 (1959), p. 363. For Jews of Sijilmāsan origin in Sicily see Roth, *JQR*, 47 (1956/57), pp. 322f.

[4] *RH*, nos. 443-453.

[5] Ibn Megāsh, *Responsa* no. 49; *RH*, p. 392 (to no. 443).

[6] Halkin, *Iggeret*, p. 101; Maimonides, *Responsa*, ed. Freimann, no. 7, p. 9; comp. above, p. 121. In the quoted Responsum (p. 8) a scholar, Jacob Qalʿi is mentioned; as there have been many Qalʿas it is difficult to identify that one.

[7] Comp. above pp. 124 ff; Gottheil, Gaster Anniversary Volume, p. 174, and Assaf, *Sources*, pp. 165 f.

In fact, we find people from Darʿa in Egypt two generations before Maimonides. One of them, Abraham ben Jacob Darʿi, is the first signatory of a decision of the *beyt-dīn* of Fusṭāṭ of the late 11th century (as well as of a deposition of the end of 1103), and may therefore have been president of the *beyt-dīn*.[1]

Also of Darʿi origin was the Karaite poet Moses ben Abraham. The dating of his life was the subject of controversy until it was proved that he used a *piyyut* by Yehuda Halevi and could thus not have been earlier than he. He is believed to have been born in Alexandria and to have joined the Karaites in his youth.[2]

The village of Tinzulin in the Darʿa Valley is mentioned in a short note.[3]

Ceuta

Two Geniza fragments containing responsa wear the title: "Questions asked by students [in Ceuta and Almeria] to Alfasi, Hay Gaon, R. Joseph ha-Levi b. Meir [ibn Megāsh] and their answers." As the names of the questioners and of the responding scholars are not given, not much can be concluded from the title. In any case the presence of Jews in this port city, the nearest to Spain, is not attested before the late 11th century. It can hardly be doubted that the emergence of the local community is connected with the development of trade with Italian cities, the migration of Jews to the Iberian Peninsula, and generally with the movement between the two regions (the African and the European) of the Almoravid state, and especially of the Almohad state at the time of the persecutions.[4]

This explains why Ceuta, as far as we know, appears first in our literature in the responsa of Joseph ibn Megāsh and why a copy, ordered by a merchant in Fusṭāṭ, of Nathan ben Yeḥiel's *ʿArūkh* was supplied from here. It seems that even artisans in Ceuta were Talmudical scholars and knew pure Arabic; witness the case of a silversmith who became a teacher. This man had fled from Ceuta to Egypt via Sicily during the first Almohad persecutions. Weak eyesight, due to old age, made it impossible for him to practise his trade and he therefore took up teaching children. His fee was too small for the upkeep of his family, however, and

---

1 Goitein, *KS*, 41 (1966), p. 264; A. Yellin, *KS*, 2 (1925/26), p. 293.

2 Comp. Davidson, *Maddaʿay ha-Yahadūt*, II (1927), pp. 297-308.

3 D. Sassoon, *Ohel David*, p. 896 (8). For it see Hirschberg, *Me-Ereẓ*, p. 102.

4 Lewin, *GQ*, 4 (1930), pp. 38-49; I. Ta-Shmah, *KS*, 46 (1971), pp. 542-3, 551; comp. also above p. 142 n. 8; p. 349.

so he made a petition for assistance. This petition, written by himself in Hebrew and Arabic, is remarkable for calligraphic script and polished language.[1]

The two Joseph ben Yehuda: Ibn ʿAqnīn and Ibn Shimʿon

It seems that in Ceuta as in other cities the Jews did not all leave during the first persecutions. It was here that in the early sixties Maimonides' favourite disciple—for whom he wrote the *Guide of the Perplexed*—was born and brought up;[2] and another scholar, who fled from Spain at that time, may have stayed for a time in Ceuta before proceeding to Fez and becoming there a disciple and associate of Maimonides. The fact that both their first names were Joseph and both their fathers' names Yehuda (and perhaps also that both lived in Ceuta) caused a confusion of their biographies, particulars being transferred from one to the other or even both regarded as one. Baneth, by a comprehensive and penetrating analysis, has proved once again that we have to do here with two persons, distinguishable by their surnames and their writings.[3]

The greater writer of the two is Joseph ben Yehuda ben Joseph ben Jacob ha-Sefaradi (or ben Jacob ha-Dayyān ha-Barjeloni), surnamed Ibn ʿAqnīn. We know almost nothing of the particulars of his life. As stated, he left Spain and met with Maimonides during the latter's residence in Fez. Upon Maimonides' departure, he wrote a farewell poem.[4] Ibn ʿAqnīn was probably of the same age as Maimonides. In his writings, he repeatedly mentions Maimonides with great respect, but does not fail to dissociate himself from him where he cannot accept his views. We may suppose that, like most scholars in those days, he was a physician, or had at least studied medicine. On the strength of hints in the sixth part of his philosophic treatise *The Cure of Souls* and a passage at the end of his commentary on the Song of Solomon ("that he may help me to be cleansed of the impurity of apostasy"[5]), A. S. Halkin decides that Ibn ʿAqnīn was

---

[1] Goitein, *Ḥinnukh*, pp. 159, 117. Refugees from Ceuta are mentioned in Genoa by Benjamin of Tudela, *Itinerary* ed. Adler, p. 4/5.

[2] I deduce his age from Maimonides' remark in a letter to him of 1191 that at the time of his disputations in Morocco (in the early sixties) he had been as old as Joseph was now; Baneth, *Iggerot*, p. 90.

[3] The first to suggest that they were different persons was Munk, *Notice*, pp. 8-10. From then on the debate never ceased until Baneth, *Ozar Yehudey Sefarad* 7 (1964), finally proved that Munk was right; comp. also *idem, Iggerot*, p. 1, and *Tarbiẓ*, 27 (1958), pp. 234-238, and Baron, *SRH* V, p. 296, n. 8.

[4] Halkin (ed.), Ibn ʿAqnīn, *Divulgatio*, pp. 430f.

[5] *Ibid.*, pp. 500f.

forced to embrace Islam. He witnessed the mental distress and social degradation of the forced converts and described their extremely critical position during the second stage of the persecutions, at the time of ʿAbd al-Muʾmin's grandsons; Halkin therefore surmises that he died in the late 12th or early 13th century. At the same time, he continued to study the Law, as he himself attests: "I have given you a hint concerning the generations of forced conversion, when we keep the commandments of the Law while a sword is lying on our necks, and especially (concerning) our present forced conversion (may the Almighty cancel it), when, despite it, as is known, we engage in the study of the Law; conclusive proof of our words is the appearance of the great scholar, Rabbenu Moses, the son of the honourable R. Maimon, in Fez, who is peerless in rabbinical learning and whose knowledge is attested by his writings: *A Commentary on the Mishna*, *Mishne Tora*, *The Book of Commandments*, *The Guide of the Perplexed* etc."[1] The mention of those writings is further proof that Ibn ʿAqnīn was still alive at the end of the century. He does not seem to have left his place of residence for another country, and there is no indication that he corresponded with Maimonides after the latter's departure from the Maghreb.[2]

Ibn ʿAqnīn wrote most of his works in Arabic and only a minority in Hebrew; some have been preserved:

(a) a commentary (in Hebrew) on the Sayings of the Fathers entitled *Sefer ha-Mūsār* (the Book of Instruction), published by W. Bacher;

(b) *Introduction to the Talmud*, published by Graetz;

(c) *Fī Maʿrifat Kammiyat al-Maqādir al-Madhkūra fi Tōrā she-bi-Khetab we-Tora shĕ-beʿal-Peh* (Treatise on Weights and Measures mentioned in the Bible and Talmud) published in Hebrew translation by Sh. Z. Ch. Halberstamm;

(d) an allegorical commentary on the Song of Songs, *Inkishāf al-Asrār wa-Ẓuhūr al-Anwār* (*Divulgatio* etc.; Revelation of the Secrets and Appearance of the Lights), published, with a Hebrew translation, by A. S. Halkin;

(e) *Ṭibb al-Nufūs* (Cure of the Souls); in the author's own Hebrew:

---

[1] *Ibid.*, pp. 398f. In a previous passage (*ibid.*, p. 336/7) he mentions a "great and perfect scholar," R. Yoseph b. Isaac *Shāmi* ("the Syrian"), whose commentaries on the Book of the Judges he read. For two Yoseph b. Isaac in Egypt at that time see Mann, *Jews* II, index.

[2] His biography—as far as it is known—is usually discussed together with that of Maimonides' disciple Joseph b. Yehuda; comp. Lewis, *Meṣūda*, London 1945, pp. 178f., Baneth, *Iggerot*, p. 1, and *idem*, *Ozar Yehudey Sefarad* 7 (1964), pp. 11-20.

Refu'at ha-Nefashot, a philosophic treatise on ethics, the cure of tainted souls, forced conversions and their causes, and the way back; only the 27th chapter has so far been published by Güdemann, with a German translation (it has also been translated into Hebrew); a survey of the sixth part was published by Halkin. Other works by Ibn ʿAqnīn are lost and are known to us only by references to them: a) *The Book of Laws and Judgments*, on precepts obtaining after the Destruction of the Temple; b) *Risālat al-Ibāna fī Uṣūl al-Diyāna*, an epistle on the reasons of the precepts (as Baneth surmises) and principles of religion.[1]

Those works are trustworthy evidence that the light of the Law did not die in the countries of forced conversion—that a rabbi forced to pose as a Muslim continued to disseminate it even after Maimonides had left the Maghreb. In this context, we may see some practical significance in the 27th chapter of the *Cure of Souls*, which deals with *ādāb al-muʿallim wa-al-mutaʿallim*, the qualities of the teacher and the pupil, and which bears some resemblance to the rules for the study of the Law set out in Maimonides' Code (*Mishne Tora*). Ibn ʿAqnīn enumerates seven qualities that the teacher must have in order to guide his pupils and exert a favourable influence on them. The seventh quality is the ability to arrange the material in the order of progressive difficulty, in accordance with the pupils' power of comprehension, so as to lead them to eventual perfection. The recommended sequence is as follows: reading and writing; Bible, Masora, grammar and Mishna; poetry (*shiʿr*), *i.e.* religious poetry (*al-zuhdiyāt*, *Selīḥōt*), avoiding poems likely to have an adverse moral effect (extolling misconduct, love poems); Talmud; apologetics; philosophy and logic; mathematics and logic; selected chapters of physics and astronomy. The author also enumerates the sciences to be imparted to the pupil, and it goes without saying that medicine ranks high in the list. He concludes by mentioning nine qualities required in the pupil, *viz.* cleanliness, which leads to moral purity; readiness to ask questions, for "the shamefast man cannot learn"; devotion to study without expecting material gain; etc. In short, we are given an exposition of the method of education of the perfect Jew. We may suppose that this method was indeed applied in the case of outstanding individuals. Ibn ʿAqnīn's exposition greatly impressed

---

[1] Comp. Güdemann, *Das Jüdische Unterrichtswesen während der spanisch-arabischen Periode*, Vienna 1873, pp. 7-15; Halkin, *Marx Jubilee Volume*, English Section, pp. 389-420; *idem*, *Starr Memorial Volume*, pp. 101-110; *idem*, Ibn ʿAqnīn, *Divulgatio*, pp. 11-14.

succeeding generations and was recommended as a guide in determining the sequence of religious studies.[1]

Better known in the history of literature than Ibn ʿAqnīn is Joseph b. Yehuda ibn Shimʿōn (surnamed ha-Maʿarabi—the Westerner) because of his great teacher, with whom he corresponded, and especially because of two letters accompanying the *Guide of the Perplexed* in which Maimonides dedicates the book to him. He also had the good fortune, when in Aleppo, of becoming friendly with the Muslim writer Ibn al-Qifṭi, a physician like himself, who incorporated ibn Shimʿon's biography in his *Lives of Scholars*. Thanks to al-Qifṭi, we know ibn Shimʿon's birthplace, the course of his education as a forced convert in Ceuta, and the fact that he reached Egypt by means of a ruse. Other particulars can be gathered from his correspondence with Maimonides and from al-Ḥarizi's *Taḥkemōnī*. While still in Ceuta, and not older than about twenty-five, he managed to study the Law and Hebrew and acquire considerable knowledge of philosophy, medicine and astronomy. He reached Alexandria via Spain; the passage from Ceuta to Andalusia was not difficult, and transport facilities from there were better and safer than from the port of his native city.

Of the literary works of Ibn Shimʿōn (this is probably the family name, and not Shimʿōn the grandfather's name), only a few epistles and a metaphysical treatise have been preserved, the latter in a bad Hebrew translation under the title *Maʾamar bi-Meḥuyab ha-Meṣiʾūt* (Treatise on the Necessarily Existent), full of errors and confused in the presentation of the subject-matter.[2]

Twilight over the Maghreb

In the foregoing, we have outlined the dispersal of Maghrebi scholars over the Eastern countries and Spain. At first, it was due to socio-economic causes and fairly slow, in the end it was precipitate, to escape death or forced conversion. Al-Ḥarizi saw some of the emigrants in Syria and Palestine. Others went to Egypt or Southern Italy. Let us point out one of them: Nahum ha-Maghrebi, poet and translator from Arabic into Hebrew. The dating of his life is a subject of controversy. Some put his

[1] Comp. Güdemann, *Unterrichtswesen*, Appendix I; German translation *ibid.*, pp. 43-138. S. Eppenstein gave an abridged Hebrew translation in *Sefer ha-Yobel le-Sokolow*, 1904, pp. 371-88.

[2] Comp. above p. 357 n. 2; Al-Ḥarizi, *Taḥkemoni*, ed. Kaminka, pp. 361f. and 364, also pp. 185 and 405.

residence in Fez as early as the days of Maimonides, some assign him to the middle of the 13th century. Of his translations, we possess Saadia's *Book of Inheritances*, *Commentary on the Thirteen Rules of Interpretation*, Maimonides' *Epistle to Yemen* and Israeli's *Commentary on Sefer Yeṣīra*.[1]

The Maghreb fell silent. Maimonides indeed notes that his *magnum opus*, the *Code* (*Mishneh Torah*), the *Book of Commandments* and some other writings reached it and found attention. He mentions halakhic decisions of the rabbinical courts in the Maghreb, their customs and questions sent to him from there. But at the same time he says, in a letter to Joseph b. Yehuda and the rabbis of Lunel, that the state of rabbinic studies there is utterly unsatisfactory. Objectively speaking, Maimonides' appraisal is undoubtedly correct, but we should nevertheless ask ourselves whether he is not ignoring the claim of Zekharya ben Berakh'el—one of the faithful assistants of the Gaon Samuel b. ʿAli, who married the latter's daughter and became president of his *beyt-dīn*—that contacts between the Maghreb rabbis and the Academy in Baghdad had not ceased. Maimonides reports this claim in the letter to Joseph b. Yehuda, and if he had known it to be unfounded, he would certainly not have failed to deny it. The continuance of contacts is further confirmed by the fact—accidentally known to us—that a student from Sijilmāsa attended Samuel ben ʿAli's Academy. However, Maimonides had no high opinion of the head of the Baghdad Academy or of Eastern scholars generally.[2] On the other hand, if he had been confronted with the testimony of Ibn ʿAqnīn and Ibn Shimʿōn that even while forced to conceal their Judaism they were able to pursue rabbinic studies in the Maghreb, he would no doubt have said that special cases cannot serve as proof.[3]

Eventually even those scholars who had remained in the Maghreb followed Maimonides' earnest advice to leave the countries of forced conversion. It is pointless now to wonder what difference it would have made to the masses if their rabbis and spiritual leaders had stayed with them in their distress.

---

[1] For the different suggestions concerning Naḥum see Toledano, *Ner*, p. 38 n. 19; Halkin, *Ep.J.*, p. XXXIII n. 377; Baron, *SRH* VI, p. 334 n. 34.

[2] See Marx, *HUCA*, 3 (1926), p. 349; Ibn ʿAqnīn's testimony above p. 357; Maimonides, *Iggerot* ed. Amsterdam 1712, pp. 10a-12a; id. *Responsa* ed. Leipzig 1859, II p. 44a; *Responsa* ed. Freimann, no. 72 (p. 72); *Responsa* ed. Blau nos. 143 (I pp. 274/5), 156 (II p. 301), 271 (II p. 519), 365 (*ibid.*, p. 640). For his opinion of the heads of the Eastern Academies see especially *Responsa*, ed. Freimann, no. 57 = ed. Blau, no. 300 (II, pp. 558f.); comp. also Mann, *Texts*, p. 202 and 207 no. 10. For the student from Sijilmāsa, see above p. 354, n. 2.

[3] See above, pp. 356f., 359.

The decline of the Maghreb must be viewed in the context of a similar process in all the Middle Eastern countries, even those not ruled by the Almohads. An increase of ignorance, an appalling drop in the standards of rabbinical studies, can at that time be observed in Iraq and Egypt as well. Maimonides and Abraham ibn Daud refer disdainfully to the people of the West (Maghreb) and East, not concealing a feeling of Spanish superiority towards those brethren of theirs. We have already mentioned the letter in which Maimonides advises his son to eschew the Maghrebis living in Berber countries and consort only "with our beloved Spanish brethren, called Andalusians".[1] There is a wide gap between this unqualified disesteem—even if Maimonides may not have meant all Maghrebis—and the commendation of African scholars in Joseph ben Samuel ha-Nagid's letter to Nissim or the praise of Alfasi in Moses ibn Ezra's *Shirat Yisrael.*[2] Abraham ben Daud expresses his opinion of Eastern learning in a caustic remark on that well-known Isaac ben Moses (know as Ibn Sukkari), whose claim to the title *ḥaber* was doubtful, but who went "to the land of the east and was ordained gaon there and seated on the chair of R. Hay, of blessed memory."[3] A person not otherwise known, in a letter to the Nagid Samuel ben Ḥananya in Egypt (middle of the 12th century), refers to the sorry state of Egyptian Jewry, which he is trying to excuse: "Since no Talmudic scholars have settled among them to show them the path they should follow, the Almighty treats them as unintentional transgressors."[4]

We may well say the same of Maghrebi Jewry. In their hour of stress, many of them were unintentional transgressors, sinning from ignorance. After a time, when conditions improved, and open return to Judaism became possible, they were eager to resume contact with the Law and its exponents. And when the fugitives from Christian Spain arrived, they found many congregations that had survived the trials of the dark era.

[1] Comp. above, pp. 165ff.
[2] Comp. above, pp. 330 n. 6, 348 n. 1.
[3] *SHQ*, p. 61/82f.
[4] See Elijah b. Kaleb's letter, Mann, *Jews* II, p. 288.

CHAPTER SEVEN

THE PERIOD OF RECOVERY

ABSORPTION OF REFUGEES FROM SPAIN AND PORTUGAL (1200-1550)

We have already mentioned Ibn Khaldūn's remarks about a special sociological law applying to the Beduin dynasties, both Arab and Berber. Observation had taught him that they were limited to four generations, *i.e.* approximately 100 to 150 years, in which the cycle of rise to power, apogee of power, standstill, decay and disintegration was completed. He reached this conclusion, especially, by studying the history of the Mu'minids, the family of Abd al-Mu'min, the actual founder of the mighty Almohad state, the ideological foundations of which were laid by the *Mahdi*, Muḍammad ibn Tūmart, the great reformer of Maghrebi Islam.

We are particularly interested in political developments in the Maghreb after the disaster which overtook African and Spanish Jewry as a result of hostile measures by the early Almohads. Those developments were of decisive significance for Maghreb Jewry, affecting it until our time.

Almohad rule brought an improvement of the security situation, cultural prosperity and an enhancement of the state; all made themselves felt throughout the country. However, already in the days of Abd al-Mu'min's grandson, Abū Yūsuf Yaʿqūb al-Manṣūr (1184-1199), the results of internal friction in the Almohad camp became clearly discernible. The brilliant victories of that ruler over the Christians in Spain, which earned him the honorific title al-Manṣūr (the Victor), cannot alter the fact that all his days he had to fight the dangerous aspirations of prominent Almohad sheikhs of the families of Ibn Tūmart's companions and to make war against rebel Beduin led by the Berber Banū Ghāniya. These allied themselves from time to time with the Muslim enemies of the Almohads, especially the remnants of the Almoravids on the eastern border and the fringes of the state, in order to attack al-Manṣūr from sea and land bases. Their onslaughts from the steppes of Southern Tunisia repeatedly carried them as far as Constantine, Bougie and Algiers on the Mediterranean coast and Sijilmāsa at the south-western extremity of the Central Maghreb. Al-Manṣūr, the great general in the war against the infidels, was at home locked in bitter combat with independent, rebellious

Muslim rulers, who threatened the unity of his realm. This struggle against internal enemies may have been the cause of his intolerance, which expressed itself in severe discriminatory measures—already referred to above (see end of Chap. III)—against Jewish forced converts in his country, as well as in the banishment of the philosopher Ibn Rushd from his court and the burning of his books.[1]

The reign of his son, Muḥammad al-Nāṣir (1199-1213), ended with a crushing defeat in a battle with the Christian Spanish kings, outweighing his victories over the Beduin in the east of his realm. That battle, at a place called Ḥiṣn al-ʿUqāb (Citadel of the Eagles) by the Arabs and Las Navas de Tolosa by the Spaniards, marks the beginning of the decline of the Muʾminids.

The Heirs of the Muʾminids

However, the destroyers of the great Almohad state came from the ranks of the Almohads themselves. The grandsons of comrades-in-arms of ʿAbd al-Muʾmin's small circle, on the one hand, and the offspring of those who—due to tribal interests—had long been hostile rivals, on the other, regarded the defeat of 1212 as an opportunity for tearing the kingdom to pieces, establishing practically independent regimes in the areas under their charge and soon turning the latter into sovereign states. The Almohad realm disintegrated into three successor states, whose areas very roughly foreshadow the countries now known as Morocco, Algeria and Tunisia, (Libya was ruled also in the subsequent period by semi-independent tribal sheikhs, sometimes loosely controlled by the Ḥafṣids). The process of division and severance lasted forty years. The Banū Ḥafṣ, supporters and vicegerents of the Muʾminids in the Afrīqiya region, were the first who, in 1228, broke off relations with the rulers of Marrakesh and set up an independent state in Tunisia. This was in the days of the Sheikh Abū Zakariyā Yaḥyā, a descendant of Abū Ḥafṣ Omar of the Berber Maṣmūda tribe, one of the closest and most loyal associates of the Mahdi Ibn Tūmart and his heir, ʿAbd al-Muʾmin. Yaghmorasīn ibn Ziyān of the ʿAbd al-Wād tribe (a branch of the Zenāta), the Muʾminid ruler's vicegerent in the central region, went in the footsteps of his Tuni-

[1] On the lights and shadows of Muʾminid rule see Brunschvig, *Berbérie* I, pp. 5-15; Terrasse, *Histoire* I, pp. 344-346; II, pp. 17-19 and 97f. The statement of Ibn abī Zarʾ (14th century; comp. *GALS* II, p. 340) concerning safety on the roads during the reign of Abū Yūsuf Yaʿqūb (comp. Beaumier, *Roudh*, p. 306) does not seem to be exaggerated. For the attitude towards Jews see Corcos, *Zion*, 32 (1967), 137-60.

Map 4

sian opposite number, proclaiming his independence in 1235; it was he who made Tlemcen the capital of the "Algerian" state of the Banū Ziyān. The sheikhs of the Banū Merīn (another branch of the Zenāta), the earliest and principal rivals of the Mu'minids, were the last to attain their political objective, mainly because of the nearness of the areas held by them to the centre of government in Marrakesh. They gradually expanded their boundaries and, in 1250, established themselves in Fez. Eventually, Abū Yūsuf Yaʿqūb al-Merīnī (1258-1289) conquered Marrakesh, the Mu'minid capital (1269).

Three generations after Abd al-Mu'min, whose realm extended from the Atlantic to the approaches of Egypt in Africa and over a considerable portion of the Iberian Peninsula, his dynasty exits from the stage of history. The last of his descendants, who had escaped to the fortress of Tinmāl, their ancestral home in the High Atlas, were murdered there with the remnant of their followers in 1276.

The end of the Almohads is adduced as evidence in a polemical epistle to the Christians written in those days; J. Mann thinks that it was addressed by R. Jacob de Lattes of Carcassonne to the renegade Pablo Christiani, who debated with Nahmanides. Here is the relevant passage: "And now I will remind you of something that you know, that you have heard: how our God brought retribution upon their heads for having devoured his people. They said: We are free from guilt. It is known who was the king of Marrakesh whose excellency mounted up to the heavens and whose head reached unto the clouds (cp. Job 20:6)—how he gave no rest to the people of the Lord (cp. Is. 51:4); he devoured us, troubled us, turned us into an empty vessel, and swallowed us like a whale; he destroyed our prayer-houses in his fury and burnt our books; he caused all our gladness to cease—our feasts, our new moons and our Sabbaths, and all our holydays. But for all that, the people of the Lord did not forget the Covenant of the Lord, the God of their fathers, and did not forsake their Tora. Each dug a cave in his house, withdrew into the rock, hid in the earth (cp. Is. 2:10); and there they disobeyed the command of the wicked one, kept the trust of the Lord, worshipped him and cleaved unto him. And the children of Israel sighed by reason of the bondage, and they cried, and their cry came up unto God, and he heard their cry (cp. Ex. 2:23-4). And our God did not delay wreaking vengeance upon those evildoers, and smote them, and discomfited them utterly (cp. Deut. 1:44): He poured out his wrath upon him and his lords, so that whosoever heard it, both his ears tingled (cp. I Sam. 3:11), and the vast and great kingdom sank in miry clay, in the deep, and it became the basest of the kingdoms (cp. Ezek. 29:15). And the harassing taskmasters were no more, and all the kings of that seed of evildoers came to an end, were cut off, for their blood was spilt like water. They have no son and no son's son among their people."[1]

The political failures of the Mu'minids, accompanied by manifestations of weakness and decay in every field of public life, diverted their attention from the forcibly converted Jews, so that the latter began to reassert themselves, not only in distant border provinces and in areas which may never have been under effective Almohad control, but even in the Outer Maghreb, *i.e.* at the centre of the Mu'minid administration. In the following, we shall review the existing direct and indirect information on the presence of Jews in the region during the period under reference. It is of particular importance that in addition to European records Jewish literary sources, which are again available from the late 13th century, abound in data concerning Jewish communities in the ports, the coastal plain and the interior—the highlands and the southern steppe—almost as far as the Saharan Desert. This material permits the conclusion that these communities had already been in existence for at least a few generations. It stands to reason that many Jews escaped during the perse-

[1] Published by Kobak, *Jeschurun*, 6 (1878), pp. 1-34; our passage: p. 23. See Mann, *REJ*, 82 (1926), pp. 363-377; also Baer, *Spain*, p. 91.

cutions and joined the old-established Jewish population of the southern border region, which in part had not been conquered at all in ʿAbd al-Mu'min's campaigns and in part was disputed territory actually controlled by nomad tribes. Here they were able to live under the protection of the sheikhs of the Ghāniya tribe, who, like all Beduin, were far removed from religious fanaticism and mainly concerned with their material interests: the collection of protection taxes and the development of trade. We are witnesses here to a seemingly paradoxical phenomenon: the worse the economic decline of the population centres of the northern plain following the Beduin invasions in the 11th and 12th centuries, the greater the development of trade with the Saharan and Central African areas under Beduin protection.[1]

Various factors combined to bring Jews back to the great capital cities and cause Jews to settle in the port cities of Tunis and Bougie, which had already begun to flourish in Almohad days. The main factor was the consolidation of the three successor states, the histories of which interlock. Relations between the near neighbours, the Merinids and the Ziyanids, were usually strained, though both descended from the great Zanāta tribe, and there was likewise enmity between the Ziyanids and the Ḥafṣids. Politically the weakest was therefore the kingdom of the Ziyanids, whose eastern and western neighbours repeatedly, and not unsuccessfully, tried to subdue it.

The Merinids held that good and fertile portion of the Almohad state which was not impaired by Arab Beduin invasions. Their constant struggle with the Almohads during their rise to power kept them from the excessive fanaticism of the latter. They also regarded themselves as the heirs of the Almohads in Spain. To be sure, in spite of the Sultan Abū Yūsuf Yaʿqūb's brilliant victory over a strong Castilian force (1275) and his subsequent achievements, the Muslims in Spain were faced with the steadily increasing pressure of the Christian Reconquista: the recapture of territory from the Muslims, the liquidation of their principalities, the restriction of their religious and economic rights, and the like. Most characteristic is a condition of the peace treaty signed in 1285, a short time before Abū Yūsuf's death between him and King Sancho of Castile, that the latter should return the Arabic manuscripts that had fallen into Christian hands during the fighting. This literary hoard of thirteen muleloads is magnificent evidence of Ibn Yaʿqūb's appreciation of religious and cultural values, but as the only practical result of many

[1] Terrasse, *Histoire* I, p. 347f.; Brunschvig, *Berbérie* II, pp. 162f.

battles it was a bitter disappointment for the Muslims. The process of the Reconquista served warning of the aggressiveness of the Christian states to all the African rulers, who saw the refugees from Andalusia settling in their cities.[1]

On the other hand, the Merinids were successful in their undertakings in Africa. Abū al-Ḥasan ʿAli (1331-1351), one of the outstanding sultans of that dynasty, gained control of the territories of the Ziyanids and Ḥafṣids. He captured Tlemcen and took the Governor of Tunis under his protectorate. The entourage of the Merinid included important scholars; their arrival in Tunis proved a blessing for the young Ibn Khaldūn, who studied under them. The campaign against Tlemcen and Tunis was resumed under Abū al-Ḥasan's son, Abū ʿInān. Those were the golden days of the dynasty. In the late 14th century, a steady decline set in. The Merinids came under the tutelage of their relatives, the Banū Waṭṭās, who from then on performed important functions in the state.[2]

The fortunes of the Ḥafṣids now rose again, so that they were able to gain control of the Tlemcen kingdom of the Ziyanids. But even the weaker Ziyanids were sometimes lucky: by alliances with the enemies of their opponents, they occasionally succeeded in freeing themselves of the latters' pressure and expanding their small territory. From the early 15th century, however, their country was in constant vassalage, sometimes to the rulers of Fez and sometimes to those of Tunis. In the 16th century, it was subject to Spain. In 1551, the kingdom of the Ziyanids was overthrown by the onslaught of the Ottoman Turks.

Jewish and Arab Sources on Jews in North Africa in the 13th and 14th Centuries

In the foregoing, we have seen that bits of information may be gleaned concerning Maghreb Jewry in the second half of the 12th century, *i.e.* in the fifty years that followed the rise of the Almohads to power.[3] On the other hand, no explicit data on the political situation in the 13th century are to be found in Jewish sources. Testimony as to the first half of the 14th century is likewise confined to general hints.

More information is left as to relations between Spain and Morocco in religious matters.

[1] Terrasse, *op. cit.*, II, 4-6 and 38; Julien, *Histoire* II, pp. 165-167 and 170-173; Marçais, *Berbérie*, pp. 303f; Corcos, *Jews* I-II, pp. 280-2, III-IV p. 53.

[2] See Fr. Rosenthal, *Ibn Khaldun, The Muqaddimah* I, pp. XXXIXf.

[3] Comp. above, pp. 356ff., also 201ff.

R. Solomon ibn Adret ("RaSHBA"), a leading talmudic scholar and rabbi in Barcelona (d. 5070/1310), refers to two contemporary rabbis in Morocco who asked him questions on halakhic and aggadic subjects. Some of the responsa are addressed to R. David b. Zikhri in Fez.[1] One responsum mentions a R. David who asked questions during a stay in Barcelona, and it has been surmised that this is the said David b. Zikhri.[2] In his *Commentary on the Aggadot*, Ibn Adret quotes a responsum sent by him to R. David b. Zabdi in Fez in which an aggadic motif is explained in a critical-philosophical way.[3] R. Joseph b. Galil says that he visited R. David in Fez in 1307, when the latter was stricken with the illness of which he subsequently died. Together with him he mentions R. Yehuda b. Ghiyān of Marrakesh and R. Isaac b. ʿAmmār of Ceuta. All had been consulted on a halakhic problem, which R. Joseph finally submits to Ibn Adret for an authoritative opinion. The responsum arrived from Barcelona through the good offices of R. Vidal Shulam, and was in accordance with R. Joseph's decision.[4] It seems very likely that R. Joseph b. Galil came from Spain and belonged to the family of the Abengelel, diplomatic agents of the kings of Aragon and Castile. (see later p. 376 and note 1). A responsum of Ibn Adret is addressed to a R. Moses b. Zibdi (or Zabdi) in Fez. But it is likely that the first name is a scribe's error for David, and Zibdi a variant of Zikhri.[5]

Several responsa of Ibn Adret to R. Isaac b. Māymōn (sic) b. Elhanan in Tāza indicate that ignorance had spread at the seat of b. Māymōn's activities. There can be no doubt that the reference is to the well-known North Moroccan city.[6]

We have no authentic information on the life of R. Judah b. Nissim ibn Malka, a philosopher and cabalist originating from Morocco (Fez?), who lived in the middle of the 14th century. Nor is there more than a passing reference to R. Joseph ha-Kohen ha-Dayyan, a descendant of Maimonides' teacher in Fez, R. Judah ha-Kohen ibn Sūsān. R. Joseph was the teacher of R. Judah Khorosani(?) (middle of the 14th century), an astrol-

---

[1] *Responsa* vol. I, no. 1185; comp. *ibid.*, II, no. 230 at the end, where responsa to David are mentioned.

[2] *Ibid.*, II, no. 250; comp. H. Michael, *Or ha-Ḥayyim*, Jerusalem 1965, no. 717.

[3] The full text was published by L. A. Feldman in *Bar-Ilan Annual* VII/VIII (1970), pp. 153-161.

[4] H. J. D. Azulai, *Shem Gedolim*, letter J, no. 120; Benbenishti, *Keneset ha-Gedola*; Eben ha-Ezer, *Hashmatot*, fol. 218.

[5] *Responsa* III, no. 228.

[6] *Responsa* III, nos. 244-248. On Tāza see below, pp. 390, 405.

oger and the author of a book that was still in manuscript at the end of the 19th century.[1]

Between 1315 and 1320, the Merinids extended their territory southeastward to the oases of Ghurāra and Tū'āt (both today belonging to Algeria). It is difficult to decide whether the tombstone of a woman, Nasfa(?) bat ʿAmram, of the year 5089/1329, which was discovered in the Tū'āt region, is connected with that campaign of conquest. On the face of it, it is early evidence of Jewish inhabitants of that region, of whom we shall have much to say below.[2]

The Communities in the Border Region

We have already hinted in the foregoing that responsa of rabbis of Algiers—expellees of 1391 and their descendants—mention Jews, both individuals and communities—resident in the Sahara border region. We find Jews in Biskra, Tūqqūrt (Touggourt) and Warghlān, *i.e.* along the eastern route from Bougie southward on the border between the settled country and the salt steppes; we find them also in the Mzāb region, west of Tūqqūrt and Warghlān. Reports on the community in Tū'āt, a chain of oases in the Western Algerian Sahara, are very important in several respects. The responsa of R. Isaac bar Sheshet to the Tū'āt community were sent *via* Hūnayn; Hūnayn was then the port of Tlemcen, the capital of the Ziyanids.[3] The sources do not indicate how the indigenous Jews managed to survive the period of tribulations.

We are accustomed to the historical accounts of Arab writers, who almost completely ignore the existence of Jews and Christians, mentioning them and their affairs only incidentally. Still, oddly enough, in describing certain events, they treat the presence of Jewish communities in the Almohad realm and its successor states as a matter of course. They apparently regarded it as quite natural that Yaʿqūb al-Manṣūr's harsh measures against forcibly Islamized Jews and their children, already born and brought up as Muslims, should have lapsed in course of time.[4] The

[1] On Ibn Malka and his writings see for the time being G. Vajda, *Juda B. Nissim ibn Malka*, Paris 1954. The Hebrew summary of his *Uns al-Gharīb*, edited by G. Vajda, is to be published shortly. On Joseph ha-Kohen ha-Dayyān see H. Edelman, *Ḥemda Genūza*, Königsberg 1856, p. 30, and Toledano, *Ner*, pp. 41-42.

[2] The inscription on the stone is difficult to read and explain stylistically; comp. Schwab, *REJ*, 48 (1904), pp. 137f.; comp. also below, p. 402. On the conquest see Terrasse, *Histoire* II, p. 48; Julien, *Histoire* II, p. 177.

[3] RIBaSH, *Responsa*, nos. 16-19; comp. also Hirschberg, *JAH* 4 (1963) pp. 323ff.

[4] Comp. above, p. 202, and Fagnan, *REJ*, 28 (1894), p. 295.

concession made to the Jews by Yaʿqūb's son, Muḥammad al-Nāṣir, in permitting them, at their request, to wear yellow suits and turbans was, in fact, a kind of admission of the failure of the attempt made fifty years previously to Islamize African Jewry. At the same time, the remark made by an Arab historian in 1224 that there was not a single synagogue in the Maghreb may be correct.[1] In those days, the Jews were no doubt still wary of building synagogues, which would have provoked their enemies, preferring to hold their services unobtrusively in semi-private rooms.

Of Muḥammad al-Nāṣir's son, Yaḥyā, we are told that in 629/1231, in the reign of his father's brother, he came down from the hills, captured Marrakesh, destroyed the Christian church that had then been built, killed many Jews and Banū Farkhān and looted their property, and entered the *qaṣba* (fortress).[2] Just as there can be no doubt that the author of this report is referring to the church of the Christian garrison then stationed in the capital, it is clear that he means Jews openly adhering to their faith, and not forced converts.[3]

The Fez Community

Already at that time many Jews were living in Fez, in a neighbourhood still known as Funduq al-Yahūdī. This name suggests that there were buildings there used as *funduqs* (hostelries) for foreign Jewish traders who came to Fez on business.[4] We find such *funduqs* in the 13th century in Mediterranean coastal towns. At the beginning of the 14th century, we find in Fez a Castilian colony of representatives and agents of companies who cooperated with Jewish merchants from Majorca; the latter lived alternately in Majorca and Fez.[5]

The Sultan Yaʿqūb (1258-1286), the founder of the Merinid dynasty, transferred his capital to Fez and, finding the Old City too small, built outside its walls, in 1276, the *al-Madīna al-Bayḍā*, the White City, known to this day as Fās al-Jadīd (New Fez), as distinct from Fās al-Bālī (Old Fez). Here he erected his palace, the buildings of the *makhzan* (state

[1] Comp. Marrākeṣhi, *al-Muʿjib*, p. 223 (in Fagnan's translation, p. 265); also Munk, *Notice*, p. 45.

[2] *Rauḍ al-Ḳartas*, ed. Thornberg, p. 169 (Beaumier, p. 363); Cenival, *Hespéris* 7 (1927), p. 75.

[3] Comp. Dufourcq, *Espagne*, pp. 24 and 25 n. 9.

[4] Its exact place is given in Massignon, *Maroc*, p. 221, and Le Tourneau, *Fès*, fig. 10, p. 119; comp. also Guides Bleus, *Maroc*, p. 347.

[5] Comp. below, p. 380. For the Jewish *funduq* in Tunis see below, p. 372 n. 1, and Appendix ii.

administration) and houses for his soldiers and officials. It is reported that immediately before the founding of the New City the Muslims in the Old City rioted against the Jews. It is sometimes believed, therefore, that the Sultan transferred the Jews to one of the quarters of the New City, near his palace, so that it might be easier to protect them, but according to Leo Africanus the transfer took place in the early 15th century.[1] We shall later deal with the question when that quarter became a ghetto, separate from the city, and from when it bore the designation *mellāḥ*, which is the name for the Jewish quarter in Morocco to this day. The Sultan Yaʿqūb is also said to have used the poll-tax of the Jews for the benefit of needy sick persons and cripples. On another occasion, this revenue was used for the repair of a mosque.[2]

According to Arab sources, several Jews of the Ruqqāṣa family were courtiers of Yaʿqūb's son, the Sultan Yūsuf (1286-1307), who shared his amusements with them. One of them, the Khalīfa Ben Ḥayyūn, was his *ḥājib* (confidant). Ibn Khaldūn calls him *al-khalīfa al-kabīr*, *qahramān al-dār*, *i.e.* the great deputy, the majordomo; he belonged to the Jews who lived in the country as *muʿāhadūn*, *i.e.* by virtue of an *ʿahd* (protection) contract. The khalīfa's great influence upon his master aroused the envy of a Muslim courtier, who succeeded in inciting the latter against him, so that, by the Sultan's command, the khalīfa and his brother and brother-in-law were executed in 1302. Only the youngest member of the family escaped; he gained the confidence of the Sultan Sulaymān (1308-1310), and Jaime II, King of Aragon, on sending his ambassador, Castellnou, to conclude a pact with Morocco, recommended him to the Khalīfa b. Ruqqāṣa (1309). The latter was able to take revenge upon the courtier who had brought about the execution of his relatives, but his fate was no different from theirs. The sources of the history of the Ruqqāṣas intimate that the real cause of their persecution was intrigues and rivalries within the ruling family.[3]

This set of data, modest by itself, is important as testimony that from

---

[1] Comp. El-Jaznāi (14th and 15th centuries; comp. *GALS* II, p. 339), pp. 57 n. 3 and 34/83; Ibn al-Aḥmar (15th century; comp. *GALS* II, p. 340), *Histoire*, p. 14/63 (ed. Bouʿali, G. Marçais); ʿOmari (14th century; *GALS* II, p. 175), *Masālik al-Abṣār*, pp. 153f.; Beaumier, *Roudh*, p. 568; Leo Africanus, *Description*, pp. 233f.; *al-Ḥulal*, p. 137 (Dinur II/1, p. 368, no. 3 and note 72); Massignon, *Enquête*, p. 222; Terrasse, *Histoire* II, pp. 30f.; Le Tourneau, *Fès*, p. 66.

[2] Comp. Beaumier, *Roudh*, pp. 426 and 88.

[3] Ibn al-Aḥmar, *Histoire*, pp. 17/69 and 19/71; Ibn Khaldūn VII, pp. 232f. and 239; al-Nāṣirī, *k. al-Istiqṣa* III (Casablanca 1955), pp. 80 and 100 (the last two authors call this family Waqqāṣa); Dufourcq, *Espagne*, p. 395.

the early 14th century Morocco proper and its southern border region again offered conditions under which Jews could profess their faith openly.

From European Archives

The information culled from literary sources cannot fully close the gap in our knowledge, although it proves that the Jewish communities in North Africa did not disappear like their Christian counterparts (the latter ceased to exist although they could have found support in the units of Christian mercenaries formed in Morocco which enjoyed the same religious facilities as the Christian merchants in the ports of the Mediterranean coast).

Under these circumstances, the material in European archives acquires great importance. The Western European states and independent cities maintained commercial relations with North Africa. Political and economic motives played a significant part in the restoration of the Jewish communities in the seaports and capitals.

It will be remembered that precisely this region lapsed into chaos at the time of the Banū Hilāl and Banū Sulaym invasion, which led to the blocking of land communications and compelled traders to establish new commercial centres and use the sea routes. This trend continued as a result of the Crusades. Tunis, Bougie, Breshk, Tenes and Hūnayn became important commercial ports, but also centres of piracy, which developed along with commercial navigation. The pace of the development of those cities was increased by the flow of Muslim refugees from Andalusia, which began in the middle of the 13th century, and economic relations with Christian Europe grew closer. The representatives of the European countries that had established relations with the ports on the African Mediterranean coast were ordered, in their various capacities, to take care of their nationals, among whom we find also Jews. It was their duty to improve relations with the local rulers and to strengthen commercial ties. As far as we know, Venice was the first power that established a consulate in Tunis (in 1231). It was followed by Marseilles, Genoa, Pisa, Sicily and Aragon.[1] Christian traders took up residence in extra-territorial

---

[1] Comp. Brunschvig, *Berbérie* I, pp. 434-436, II, pp. 156-158 and 418; Julien, *Histoire* II, pp. 146 and 150f.; Dufourcq, *Espagne*, pp. 69f. Particular matters concerning the development of Tunis dealt with by A. Sayous, *Le Commerce des Européens à Tunis depuis la XII siècle* etc., Paris 1929, will be discussed in Appendix ii, Tunis.

funduqs that sprang up in Tunis and other ports. The earliest document in which the Catalan *funduq* and consulate in Tunis are mentioned is of 1253.[1] These developments eased the political situation of the Jews, in accordance with the rule that their position was much more favourable in countries where there were several religious minorities than where they were the only one. It was natural for Jewish merchants in European cities to establish business relations with their brethren in the countries with which they were trading. Those trends were not confined to the coastal towns. In the 13th and 14th centuries, Tlemcen enjoyed an economic position once held by Kairouan. The spreading influence of the Merinids, who during the siege of Tlemcen built their own city, Manṣūra—a kind of "New Tlemcen"—nearby, increased the economic importance of this centre, which was an intersection of trade routes from east to west: from "Africa" to Fez and the Atlantic coast, and from north to south: from the Mediterranean coast (Hūnayn, Oran) to Tāfilalet, Ghurāra and the Sudan. Hence the rise of the city's Jewish community, especially after the persecutions in Aragon and Majorca in 1391.[2]

A similar economic role was played by Fez, which, too, specialised in overseas trade, maintaining relations particularly with Granada. Ibn Khāldun regards it as the most important city in Africa, and Leo Africanus gives an enthusiastic description of its trade and material culture.[3]

This is the background against which Jewish life now unfolded. We possess clear evidence, derived from European archives, of the presence of Jews during that period in the Algerian-Tunisian region. A Geniza fragment of the twenties of the 13th century, supposed to make mention of Tunis and Qābes in connection with a Messianic movement, is not very revealing, but two letters of 1227 to the mayor of Pisa attest to a Jewish settlement at that time in Tunis and to its commercial relations with the Jews of Pisa. In one of the letters, two prominent Tunis Muslims recommend to the mayor a certain Jew who has come to Pisa to seek redress of some wrong. The other letter is a recommendation from another prominent Muslim for the same Jew, who has monetary claims against a Pisan Jew and his son-in-law, a convert to Christianity.[4]

---

[1] Comp. Dufourcq, *op. cit.*, p. 99.

[2] Dufourcq, *Espagne*, pp. 141-143, 149-153, 321-336 and 371-375.

[3] See Ibn Khaldūn's very instructive remarks in *Muqaddimah*, pp. 302/II 273, also 306f./II 282f.; see further Leo Africanus, *Description*, pp. 182-204; Marçais, *Berbérie*, p. 290; Julien, *Histoire* II, pp. 157 and 176f. (the conquest of Tūʾāt).

[4] The documents concerning the resettlement of the Jews in Tunis during the 13th-15th centuries will be discussed in Appendix ii.

In 1223, the Emperor Frederick II invaded the island of Jerba and transferred its inhabitants to Sicily. The Jews of Jerba formed a separate congregation in Palermo, and at their request the Emperor, in 1233, confirmed a special warden for them and permitted them to plant a date grove. They were ordered to plant henna and indigo, which had formerly been imported. The Jews of Jerba were thus familiar with the cultivation of date palms and industrial crops.[1]

About the middle of the 13th century, we find in Marseilles the trading establishment of the Jewish Ferrussol family, which did export and import business with the North African ports of Bougie, Algiers and Tenes. Some members of that ramified family seem to have resided in Bougie; at any rate, the papers state expressly in several cases that the African correspondents are Jews, and so they were no doubt in other cases as well. *E.g.*, most of the cargo of two ships sailing in 1248 from Marseilles to Bougie was consigned to Jews. The flourishing trade of the French Manduel family in Marseilles, which specialized in North African business in the years 1212-1240, was also, presumably, carried on with Jews. Documents of commercial relations between Bougie Jews and Majorca and Marseilles have also been preserved of the late 13th and early 14th centuries.[2]

Unlike Morocco, where the Jews enjoyed the special protection of the Merinid dynasty, and some even held influential positions—though with disastrous consequences to them and the Jews generally—the Jewish "denizens" in Tunisia and the kingdom of Tlemcen did not rise to the status of courtiers concerned with general political affairs. On the other hand, they were not exposed to the fury of riotous mobs. We find several interpreters, physicians and officials in the middle echelons. Our sources mention a few 1391 refugees who had access to the court of the ruler of Tlemcen, but a 15th. century Arab writer stresses that the chief physician in Tlemcen, despite his honoured position, refrained from meddling with affairs of state and thus kept out of trouble.[3]

In 1267, Moses of Tunis was Arabic interpreter to the Genoese traders resident in that city. The Jew Abraham, in 1421, translated a treaty between Florence and Tunis from Arabic into Italian, and in 1445,

---

[1] Schaube, *op. cit.*, p. 302; Baron, *SRH* IV, p. 160 and n. 11; Strauss, *The Jews in Egypt and Syria* II, pp. 24f., quotes a legendary story of how in 1388 the Jews of Jerba helped the Turks to occupy the island.

[2] See *HCM* I, pp. 292f., also pp. 171 and 175f.; Schaube, *op. cit.*, pp. 308f.; Julien, *Histoire* II, pp. 123f.

[3] Brunschvig, *Récits*, pp. 44f. and 107f.; comp. also below, pp. 393ff.

Abraham Fava drew up in Tunis the Latin text of a Tunisian-Genoese treaty. These translators probably hailed from Christian European countries, for persons knowing Latin and Italian were surely not to be found among the native Jews of Tunisia.[1]

However important were the ties of the North African countries with the North Italian and Southern French seaport republics, from the Jewish point of view, their ties with the Balearic Islands and the cities of Christian Spain, as first formed in the 13th century, were of greater significance. This was due to a long tradition of contacts between the Jews of North Africa and Muslim Spain and the Jewish population —steadily increasing from the second half of the 12th century—of the Christian Spanish kingdoms of Aragon and Castile. The Muslim successor states in North Africa were from the outset faced with the expansion and strengthening of Aragon. Jaime I (1213-1276), surnamed El Conquistador, and his successors Pedro III (1276-1285), Alfonso III (1285-1291) and Jaime II (1291-1327) conquered or gained control of the Balearic Islands (Majorca in 1230, other islands, progressively, by 1235, Minorca, finally, in 1286) and important regions on the south-eastern coast of the Pyrenean Peninsula (Valencia in 1238, Murcia in 1296). They also conquered Sicily (1282) and Sardinia (1297) and thereby became neighbours—enemies and allies by turns—of the three Maghreb states in the Eastern Mediterranean basin.

The areas thus coming under the sway of Aragon—in various forms: annexation, protectorate, rulers from the Aragonese royal house, etc.—had, as stated, Jewish inhabitants. Some had been settled in Majorca, the largest of the Balearic Islands, for centuries, at least since the Muslim conquest (903); they no doubt included many from North Africa, especially refugees from the Almohad persecutions, and others from European cities. The great majority concentrated in the capital, then known as Mudayna or simply Majorca (the name Palma was not used until the 17th century). Immediately after his conquest of Majorca, Jaime I's attitude towards the Jews took a favourable turn, and from then onwards, thoughout the 13th century, the policy of the Aragonese kings with regard to the Jews was marked by extreme tolerance both in Aragon itself and its dependencies. We find many Jews at their courts (and at those of the Castilian kings) in various capacities, especially as interpreters, agents, diplomats, and ambassadors to the North African Muslim countries and to Muslim Granada, ruled by the Naṣrids. Two

[1] Brunschvig, *Berbérie* I, p. 414.

Jews from Saragossa assisted Jaime I in diplomatic negotiations at the time of the conquest of the Balearics.

In 1286, Alfonso III ordered that the Jews Abraham and Samuel the sons of Jucef Abengelel be exempted from all taxes, except the poll-tax, in view of their many services to Pedro III and the fact that they were going on a mission to Morocco on Alfonso's behalf. We possess diplomatic instructions given to Abraham Abengelel in connection with that mission.[1] Jaime II, at the beginning of his reign (1291), sent Abraham to the King of Tlemcen, and Abraham took all his family with him.[2] Three years later, we find him (Abengelel) in the service of Sancho IV of Castile (1284-1295).[3] There can be little doubt that Abraham Abengelel is identical with Abrahim Avingalell, to whom Jaime I let a workshop at the entrance to the Jewish quarter of Valencia in 1276, upon the recommendation of the King of Tunisia and surely in view of his political services or business connections.[4] Political mediation in Tunis is alluded to in a document of Pedro III's last year (1285), ordering his representative in Tunis to make over to the Jew Salamon Abenzahit,[5] for two years, half the revenue due to the king from imposts on the hostelry in Tunis.[6]

In one of his poems, Todros b. Judah Abulafia praises Meir ben Musharif, of the Bene Shōshān, who had successfully carried out a mission to Marueccos (Marrakesh), following which "sighs (*anāḥōt*) had ceased and relief (*hanāḥōt*) had come." Meir was a courtier of Alfonso X of Castile (1252-1284), and his mission to Marrakesh probably took place in the early Merinid period.[7]

---

1 Abraham Abengalell went from Aragon to Granada in 1280 and 1283/4, Judas Abenhatens in 1287, Abraham Abenamies in 1290, Samuel Abengalell in 1293. Abraham and Samuel Abengalell went from Aragon to Morocco in 1287. See Dufourcq, *op. cit.*, pp. 200 n. 5; 205 n. 1; 210 nn. 1 and 2; 212f.; 217; 225; 325 n. 5; 327; comp. also Romano, *Homenaje á Millas Vallicrosa* II, p. 262 n. 103. On Joseph b. Galil, who stayed in Fez in 1307, comp. above, p. 368. He was probably a member of our Abengalell family, the name being uncommon. On Jewish agents in negotiations at the occupation of the Balearics comp. J. Amador de los Rios, *Historia social*, Madrid 1960, p. 215.

2 Régné, no. 1701; see also *ibid.*, nos. 810, 1514 and 2390.

3 Baer, *Spanien* II, p. 91; id., *Spain*, I, p. 410, n. 48.

4 Régné, no. 654; Dufourcq, *Espagne*, p. 127 and n. 2.

5 This as well as a number of other Arab surnames may be derived from a physical defect: *azwaṭ* means a person one of whose eyes is narrower than the other or has the pupil set lower (see Dozy *s.v.*). Zahūṭ, (similarly to Dahūd for Daʾūd) is the surname of the Baqrī family in the 18th and 19th centuries; see ch. Algeria in vol. II.

6 Régné, no. 1381; Baer, *Spain* I, p. 427 n. 23.

7 Comp. H. Brody, *Ẓiyunim* (Simhoni Memorial Volume), pp. 50-57; D. Yellin, *Gan Hammeshalim* (sic) etc. *Divan of Don Tadros* (*sic*) *Abu-l-ʿĀfiah*, Jerusalem 1932-1936, no. 569.

In the same year in which Samuel Abengalell proceeded on behalf of Jaime II, King of Aragon, to the court of the Naṣrids in Granada (1293), another Jew, the *al-faqui(m)* (*i.e.* court physician, rabbinic scholar, high official) Bondavi, left Aragon with his family on a important secret mission for the king to Tlemcen and Tunis.[1] He received very detailed instructions as to his task of concluding a peace treaty with Othman, the Sultan of Tlemcen. But his mission failed like earlier bids for the same objective.[2]

The Jewish interpreter Maimon b. Nono played an important part in the peace talks between Majorca and Tunis in 1329.[3]

In 1403 and 1405, the Jew Samuel Sala da Trapani travelled from Sicily to Tripoli on peace missions.[4] The choice of Jews for diplomatic missions appears to have been prompted not only by their personal qualifications but also by the presence of Jews at the courts of the North African rulers, which made it easier for the agents to establish contacts. We have seen above (p. 371) that in 1309 Jaime II asked high officials in Morocco, including the Jew Khalīfa b. Ruqqāṣa, to help his ambassador. A few years earlier (1294-5), Açach-Asac (= Isaac) carried out a mission to Jaime II King of Aragon on behalf of the Moroccan ruler Abū Ya'qūb Yūsuf.[5] By order of Abū Fāris, the Ḥafṣid ruler of Tunisia, the Jewish physician Bonjuha Bondavi went to Barcelona in the spring of 1400 to negotiate a peace pact with King Martin (1395-1410). Martin ordered the city authorities to exempt Bondavi and his two companions from wearing the prescribed Jewish badge.[6]

Jews from North Africa Settling in Spain

In keeping with his general policy of attracting Jews to his country, Jaime I, King of Aragon, Majorca, Valencia etc., gave orders to facilitate the migration of Jewish families from North Africa to his European possessions. A safe-conduct issued by him in Valencia, dated June 11th,

---

[1] Dufourcq, *Espagne*, pp. 225 and 329-335; Régné, *REJ*, 75 (1922), pp. 146f.; Brunschvig, *Berbérie* I, p. 107.

[2] Dufourcq, *op. cit.*, p. 331.

[3] Idem, *ibid.*, p. 506 n. 5.

[4] Milano, *Storia*, p. 172.

[5] Dufourcq, *op. cit.*, pp. 231 n. 1 and 346.

[6] Régné, *REJ*, 75 (1922), pp. 146f.; Brunschvig, *Berbérie* I, p. 224. Bonjuha Bondavi was probably a descendant of the Aragonese envoy Bondavin (see above, nn. 1 and 2). It is interesting to note that a Bondija ha-Kohen, who seems to have been an important person, is met with in Algiers at the same time; RIBaSH, *Resp.* no. 60.

1247, permits "all Jews and Jewesses" in Cigelmensa (Sijilmāsa) to move by sea or land and settle in Majorca, Barcelona, Valencia or in other places under his rule. Mentioned by name in the safe-conduct are Salomon Benammar, his wife Reana, his sons Jacob and Jucef, his daughters, Mona and Setaddar(!) [*Sitt Hadar*, *i.e.* Lady of Splendour?], and Juceff, Mona's husband; Isaach Ben Salomon, his wife Yamen, his sons Juceff and Jacob and his daughter Nini; Ammar (Salomon Benammar's brother) and his wife, sons and daughters; altogether, some twenty persons at least.[1]

We possess similar documents granted by the same King in 1270 to two brothers: Barchet (Barakat) and Mançer (Manṣūr) Avenmenage (Ibn Menashe), who lived in Alexandria, but may have been of Maghrebi origin.[2]

On February 17, 1278, Pedro III ordered his admiral, the commanders of the land forces and the crews of the royal navy to grant safe passage to some Jews from Tripoli, including one Hayon Benamar Albarach, who intended to settle in the kingdom.[3] This order may be a clue to the date of certain inscriptions discovered in the Tripolitanian-Libyan area.[4] Let us add that the safe-conduct granted to the Jews of Sijilmāsa in 1247 is an important link in the evidence of continuous Jewish settlement in that region. It fills the gap between Maimonides' letter and the information concerning the *payṭān* Judah b. Joseph Sijilmāsi in the early 15th century. Similar importance attaches to Pedro III's safe-conduct and the report of Samuel da Trapani's mission with regard to Tripoli.[5]

The Causes of the Renewal of Jewish Settlement

The policies of the rulers were undoubtedly an important factor in stabilizing the position of the Jews in North African countries. However, they do not by themselves account for the establishment or reestablish-

---

[1] Régné, no. 36. The full text of the safe-conduct was published in J. V. Villanueva, *Viaje literario á las iglesias de España* vol. 22 (Madrid 1852), p. 327, and reprinted in A. Pons, *Los judios del Reino de Mallorca* II, Madrid 1958, p. 203.

[2] Régné, no. 443; comp. also D. Romano, Los hermanos Abenmenasse, *Homenaje á Millas Vallicrosa* II, Barcelona 1955, p. 250 n. 25.

[3] Dufourcq, *op. cit.*, p. 243 and n. 8, p. 314 and n. 5; Régné, no. 691. The names of the others are also interesting: Isach Jucef Benbolfaratg al faquim, Ismael Honhazan Aliepdoni(!), Isach Abenjucef Annufusi, all Jews of Trebalos.

[4] See above, p. 134.

[5] See above pp. 354 n. 3; p. 377, and n. 4. Régné no. 1464 *REJ*, 67 (1914) (p. 70) the Jew Jacob the, sonof Issach Daray (i.e. from Darʿa) is mentioned.

ment of whole Jewish communities in many places along the coast and in the plain beyond, or for the prosperity of the settlements in the south, in the region bordering on the Sahara. Economic and demographic factors outside Africa played a considerable part in these developments. A most significant factor were the Jews of Majorca. Under Catalan-Aragonese rule, their number increased as a result of the policies of the Aragonese kings and the merchants of Barcelona, who sought the economic expansion of their country to Africa. The Jews of Majorca were in all respects efficient partners in this venture, both because of their familiarity with local conditions and the language and the possibility of using their ties with the indigenous and newly-settled Jews of North Africa. They developed trade by opening branches for brokering between the Christian traders in the *funduqs* and the Jewish retailers and pedlars in the oases of the southern steppe on the fringe of the Sahara.

Documents of many archives enable us to prepare an instructive list of Jewish traders and brokers and of transactions made in that extensive area. They contain names of people who lived in or originated from Majorca and Catalonia, and not of residents of Africa.

In 1276, Pedro III included Jewish traders in a diplomatic mission to the Maghreb, so that they might enjoy immunity during their stay in Africa and carry on their business without harassment.[1]

A Majorcan Jew, Çaadon Benada, complains under the date of July 1, 1289 to a Moroccan *baiulus* (royal official), in his own name and that of other Jews, about pirates from Valencia who had captured near Tenez (*sic*) a ship with goods belonging to him and others; they had also taken a Majorcan Jew named Jacob Bendallal and forced him to ransom himself with 150 gold doubloons.[2]

In September 1296, the ruler of Tlemcen complained to King Jaime II that a ship's captain from Valencia had confiscated at sea some goods being brought from Majorca by the Jew Maymon ben Atar, an inhabitant of Taount (modern Nemours), a seaport near Hūnayn. Under treaties signed between the rulers of Tlemcen and Jaime II's three predecessors, subjects of the Aragonese crown were forbidden to harm people from Tlemcen on land or at sea.[3]

In 1302, a treaty was signed between Bougie and Majorca which gave the Majorcan consul jurisdiction over all subjects of the king, including

---

[1] Dufourcq, *op. cit.*, p. 313 and n. 4.

[2] Baer, *Spanien* I/1, pp. 146f. Baer wrongly assumes that the piracy occurred near Tunis. The document itself has "Tenez."

[3] Dufourcq, *op. cit.*, pp. 347 nn. 4 and 5, 348 n. 2.

Jews. In fact, in 1303, the Consul Benet Blancas arrested in Bougie some Majorcan Jews charged with sodomy.[1]

In 1304 and 1305, ships arrived from Majorca in the ports of Taount, Cherchel and Tenes, and also in Algiers, despite a conflict between Aragon and that city. The Jew Solomon ben Zequi served as intermediary in trade talks with Breshk.[2]

Friendly relations between Majorcan Jewry and Bougie as a result of commercial ties were the reason why in 1304, when a conflict broke out between the two states, the Jews took no part in equipping a Majorcan fleet sent against Bougie.[3]

During hostilities between King Jaime II of Majorca and Tunis in 1308 and 1309, the Tunisian *makhzan* (treasury) confiscated, released and again confiscated goods of Majorcan Jews. Jaime II prohibited trading with Tunis and confiscated goods of five Tunisian subjects: three Jews, one Muslim and one Christian, and of six fidejussors: four Jews, one Muslim and one Christian.[4]

According to records of 1318 in the archives of the cathedral of Palma, property in Majorca and Fez was held by the Jews Isaac Levi, Samuel ben Shulal, Samuel, Hayyon and Mardokhay ben Harun Bacri, and Abraham and Yahya ben Natjar (= Najjār), who resided alternately in Majorca and Fez.[5]

Another record in the same archives (of 1330) mentions a power of attorney drawn up by the priest of the Catalans in Tenes for a Majorcan Jew living in that city.[6]

In 1319, a Jew in Ceuta acquired from King Jaime II of Aragon the right to trade in his country for four years.[7]

Abraham Malequi of Majorca traded with Morocco between 1302 and 1327; Solomon Malequi traded in Mostaganem in 1331.[8]

The volume of trade with Tlemcen is illustrated by figures for 1327: the value of goods imported from Barcelona, Valencia and Majorca was 15,000-20,000 dinars, and debts by Tlemcen merchants to Majorcan Jews exceeded 10,000 dinars. Catalan trade may be estimated at 80,000 dinars in Africa (Tunisia and Eastern Algeria) and 30,000 dinars in Morocco.

---

1 *Ibid.*, pp. 420-422 and esp. 422 n. 4; see Baer, *Spain* I, p. 407 n. 22.
2 *Ibid.*, p. 369 and n. 4.
3 *Ibid.*, pp. 446f.
4 *Ibid.*, p. 446 and nn. 3 and 4.
5 *Ibid.*, p. 465 and n. 4.
6 *Ibid.*, p. 141 n. 3.
7 *Ibid.*, p. 84 n. 6, p. 562 and n. 5.
8 *Ibid.*, p. 471 n. 5.

There can be no doubt that almost all the goods reached the customers through Jewish retailers and pedlars.[1]

We have given above (pp. 294-7) a list of goods exported from and imported to Africa from the 9th to the 12th century C.E. Records in European archives indicate that no change took place in the nature of goods exchanged between European Mediterranean countries and those of the south-western shore of the Mediterranean. Majorca and Catalonia bought grain in all the North African countries. Morocco exported grain to Seville *via* Safi, Anfa (near present-day Casablanca), Salé and Ceuta. Much in demand was sheep's wool, called *merini* (from the name of the Merinid dynasty). Paper from Fez, hides and furs of various domestic animals and variously processed were exported *via* Bougie and Tunis (Cordovan leather). White alum and feather alum were exported from Sijilmāsa. Other items were fish, corals, dates and cotton. We thus see that exports were mainly agricultural products and their derivatives, and raw materials.

Imports from Europe were clothing, textiles, jewelry, ironware, arms, lead, copper, tin and, rather surprisingly, salt and oil, of which a plentiful supply, of excellent quality, was available locally, as well as dried fruit; not surprising at all is the import of grain from Italy and Sicily to Jerba and Tunis, where years of severe drought were not infrequent.[2]

A great part of the goods exported from Africa were brought to the ports of exit from far away by Jewish pedlars, who sold them to purchasing agencies, receiving in return industrial products and "luxuries" that were thereupon marketed in the Berber-inhabited interior.[3]

The Treaty of 1360

The peace treaty concluded in 1360 between Abū Isḥāq Ibrāhīm, the Sultan of Tunis and Bougie, and Pedro IV of Aragon (1336-1387) repeatedly mentions both Catalan and Tunisian Jewry, who, like the other inhabitants of the two countries, are promised safety on the roads and protection against robbers. Tunisian citizens were not to pillage ships or cause damage to Pedro's subjects, whether Christians or non-Christians. Only the consul of the King of Aragon in Tunisia was to adjudge disputes between Christians and Jews originating from Catalonia. He was also to

[1] *Ibid.*, p. 553.
[2] *Ibid.*, pp. 544-548.
[3] *Ibid.*, p. 547, and comp. above, pp. 273f.

fix the amount of the imposts leviable from Catalan Christians and Jews. One article provides that no Tunisian Muslim or Jew shall be arrested in Pedro's country after the conclusion of the treaty, and if any such prisoners were found, they were to be released; the same applied to Pedro's subjects in Abū Isḥāq's country. Lastly, the Tunisian Sultan promised Pedro an annual payment of 2,000 gold dinars from the customs duties on goods imported and exported by his Christian and Jewish subjects.[1] In this treaty, Jews are thus expressly mentioned; in one of the earlier treaties between the two countries, concluded sixty years previously and which served as model for this one, they are not. The treaties between Pedro IV and the kings of Fez and Tlemcen (then a part of the Kingdom of Fez), and the correspondence between them of the years 1345-1362, which deal with the freedom of trade and security on the roads, also do not mention Jews. The treaty of 1360 is evidence of increasing Jewish participation in trade and permits the assumption of close relations between the Jews of Catalonia and Tunisia in the 14th century. This assumption finds further support in the post-1391 responsa literature. *E.g.*, Saul Astruq ha-Kohen, physician and rabbinical scholar, settled in Algiers and was close to the ruling circles already before the advent of the wave of refugees. Astruq Kohen in Hūnayn would receive deposits from the Maghreb while still resident in Valencia.[2]

A further indication of an increase of the Jewish population of Tunisia in the 14th century, is contained in a question addressed about 1460 to R. Ṣemaḥ Duran, the grandson of R. Simon b. Ṣemaḥ (RSHbaṢ) in Algiers. With the influx of new settlers into Tunis, the old synagogue in the *funduq*, built by the wearers of the "capos," *i.e.*, Jews wearing European dress, had become too small and had eventually been abandoned, also because of its great distance from the new Jewish quarter. The question indicates that nothing remained of it but the floor, which was really the roof of the *funduq*, and that the problem of its disposal had thus arisen. In Appendix ii, I have attempted to show that this synagogue was probably built between 1300 and 1360 and abandoned at the end of the 14th or the beginning of the 15th century. Fifty years later, nothing remained of the roof and walls of the synagogue.[3]

This set of data, modest in itself, is important as testimony that from

[1] Comp. Maximiliano A. Alarcón y Santón y Ramón García de Linares, *Los Documentos Árabes Diplomáticos del Archivo de la Corona de Aragón*, Madrid 1940, pp. 311-313; see also Brunschvig, *Berbérie* I, p. 408.

[2] RIBaSH, *Responsa* nos. 60 and 2.

[3] *Responsa Yakhin u-Boaz* I, no. 132.

the early 13th century North Africa proper and its southern border region again offered conditions under which Jews could profess their faith openly.

SUMMARY

The situation in the Maghreb, as described on the preceding pages, had a favourable effect on developments among the Jewish population. The rule that a country at enmity with its neighbours does not tend to subject its Jewish community to persistent unbearable oppression was again confirmed. We have observed a similar phenomenon in the first centuries of Arab rule in Africa, when the area was divided into several mutually hostile states, under whose aegis the Jews lived in comparative quiet. An analogous situation prevailed in the separate Christian kingdoms in Spain. This was correctly perceived by Eliyahu Kapsali, who says very clearly: "After the Edomites conquered Spain from the Ismaelites, the Jews who were in Spain came under Gentile rule . . . and they harassed the Jews, and repeatedly decreed conversion and expulsion upon them . . . and they killed . . . and the Jews suffered great tribulations . . . and they expelled the Jews . . . but for God's help . . . for there were not one or two kings in Spain but seven. And when one king expelled them, they would go to whichever king they thought most advisable and after a time the king who expelled them would absolve himself from his vow and take them back, and they would return to their cities. Thus did the Gentiles and the Jews all the time. And in this way there was never total expulsion from Spain, from the whole country, and the Jews were in Spain until this day."[1] On the other hand, the Jews were exposed to grave danger when a single, powerful realm emerged, as in the time of the Almoravids, the Almohad conquests and the union of the Catholic Kings of Castile and Aragon.

Political fragmentation is usually attended by ethnic and social fragmentation. Small states are unable to impose their general character on heterogeneous elements ruled by them and mould them into a uniform pattern; people of different origin, religious and social customs, and language, live side by side. This was particularly noticeable in the case of Tunisia and Tripolitania, which were open to waves of invaders from east and south reinforced by a stream of traders from Europe who

[1] *Debe Eliyahu* chap. 53; MS.B.M. Add. Or. 19971, fol. 44a (microfilm Ben-Zvi Institute, Jerusalem no. 5896).

settled very early (13th century) in the Tunisian port cities; the result was a medley of members of various peoples and classes who had to get along together if they were not to destroy each other. A social framework of this kind afforded room also for the Jews. In fact, we find them not only in the north, but in the south, in the border region between the desert and the settled country, as well.

Another factor making for a lessening of religious tension in the Maghreb was the Merinid dynasty, which did not belong to the aristocratic *shurafā*ʾ families of the house of the Prophet Muhammad and, owing to its opposition to the Almohads, showed no enthusiasm for the latters' religious reforms; this greatly reduced the heat of religious fanaticism.

The fact that in the second half of the 13th century—*i.e.*, in the early days of the Merinid regime—Jews from Spain went to Morocco on diplomatic missions on behalf of the kings of Aragon and Castile indicates that they knew of the presence of influential Jews at the court of the Moroccan rulers. Of course, upon the decline of the Merinids, their capital, Fez, became a centre of operations of the *shurafā*ʾ and afterwards of the cult of Idrīs, the founder of Fez, whose grave and whose body, miraculously preserved intact, were discovered in 1437. The population of Fez repeatedly responded to anti-Jewish incitement by the *shurafā*ʾ. There seems to be some truth in the notion that the rulers of Fez transferred the Jewish quarter near their own section of the city in order to protect the Jews under their patronage, although they did not always succeed in doing so.[1]

As we have seen, economic reasons contributed to the rehabilitation of the Jewish communities in the Ḥafṣid kingdom, which controlled the principal ports on the eastern part of the North African coast, where the maritime trade with Italy and other European countries developed from then on.

THE REFUGEES OF 1391

All this accounts for the fact that upon the onset of the 1391 catastrophe in the lands of the Aragonese crown in Catalonia and Majorca the refugees from those countries sought shelter in the cities of North Africa, in the area now known as Algeria. Many settled in the city of Algiers; this marked the beginning of its economic prosperity and development as

[1] Comp. Brunschvig, *Berbérie* II, pp. 416-420; Julien, *Histoire* II, p. 146; Le Tourneau, *Fès*, p. 599; *idem*, *Fez-Merinids*, pp. 16, 76. For the whole period see D. Corcos, The Jews in Morocco under the Merinides, *JQR*, 54-5 (1963-5).

an administrative centre, which elevated it to the status of capital in the 16th century. Others were absorbed into other cities of the Ziyanid and Ḥafṣid kingdoms, which then enjoyed a brief flowering season.[1]

After some time, the Merinid state sustained violent convulsions owing to the decline of the dynasty and attacks by Spain and latter Portugal, which saw an opportunity to supplant those who hindered the achievement of their political aims on the North African coast opposite their territories.[2]

The author of *Shebet Yehuda* gives a dismal picture of the reception of the refugees of 1391 in Africa: "But those who went to Arab countries endured untold suffering on the way, as they wrote to their relatives who had remained at home. Especially the villagers rose against them—saying that they were protecting their religion—and put them in chains, until the matter became known to the king. Part of them saved themselves by providing labour and money to their persecutors, and part were impelled by their tribulations to say: Let us make a captain, and let us return..." (cf. Num. 14:4).[3] As we shall see, this report refers to Morocco.

We know of R. Ephraim Enkawa (Ibn al-Nakawa) (1359-1442), who in 1393 spent some time in Marrakesh and had some trying experiences there, until he moved to Hūnayn and eventually found tranquillity in Agadir, a suburb of Tlemcen.[4] But apart from this and the preceding bit of information, we have no reports of suffering caused to refugees by the Muslim inhabitants. Of course, R. Isaac bar Sheshet mentions the grim days of the siege and capture of Algiers during one of the armed conflicts between the rival dynasties, but this was a calamity affecting the population as a whole.[5]

Abraham Zacuto likewise mentions only places in Algeria and Tunisia as refuges of Jews during the 1391 persecution.[6]

The afflux of the refugees of 1391 to certain regions and their virtual abstention from settling in others reflect the stability or instability of the general political situation in the areas concerned; they also point to the conditions of life of the Jews in the different zones. In this respect, a comparison with the refugees of 1492 is instructive: those of them who went to Africa settled in Morocco, which was bypassed by the great

---

[1] Comp. Julien, *op. cit.*, II, p. 160; Brunschvig, *op. cit.*, I, pp. 401f.

[2] Terrasse, *op. cit.*, II, pp. 93-116.

[3] Chap. 27.

[4] Comp. *Sha*ʿ*ar Kebod* etc., Tunis 1902, pp. 88b-89a. Gavison, *ʿOmer ha-Shikheḥa*, Livorno 1748, p. 137d, gives a description of his life in Tlemcen.

[5] RIBaSH, *Responsa*, no. 154; comp. Hershman, *Perfet*, p. 43.

[6] *Liber Juchassin*, ed. Filipowski, p. 225 a-b.

immigration wave of 1391. It seems that they shunned the coast of Algeria and Tunisia because of conditions in the interior and the danger of attacks from without.

One of the responsa of R. Isaac bar Sheshet indicates that the attitude of some earlier fugitives from forced conversion towards later arrivals was not always fair. The report reads as follows: "One day, a ship arrived here from Majorca with 45 forced conversos from Majorca, Valencia and Barcelona. The governor wanted to admit them into the city for reasons of self-interest, for he would collect from them one doubloon per head, an arrangement prompted by a certain person. They were originally admitted free of charge, and the *qāḍī* Ibn Meḥrez rebuked some Arabs who came and asked him not to let them land because of the rise in prices; he turned them out of the house angrily, saying: I thought you were true believers, but now I see that you are infidels. Is God unable to feed those along with the rest of mankind? Does man not live by every word that proceeds out of the mouth of the Lord? But that person called upon the people to urge the governor not to let them land, in order that they might return to Majorca and none of them come here."[1]

The Muslim governor thus originally allowed the refugees to land free of charge, and only at the instigation of a certain Jew did he prescribe an entry tax of one doubloon per person; this Jew was himself a refugee from Majorca, as R. Isaac remarks a few lines before. The qāḍī reprimanded the Muslims who alleged that the influx of many refugees caused a rise in prices, and the Jew sought to get the people to dissuade the governor from saving the refugees. It may not be superfluous to note that when Muslims expelled from Spain arrived in the Maghreb, they, too, met with a hostile attitude on the part of their coreligionists.[2]

In Tenes, the refugees were granted a reduction of the poll-tax and "king's tax" (*kharga de-malka*), which aroused the anger of the established residents.[3] Popular tradition has it that after the arrival of R. Ephraim Enkawa the king of Tlemcen permitted Jews to settle in his capital as a mark of appreciation for that miracle worker; up till then Jews lived in a suburb named Agadir.[4]

The refugees dispersed in the region, settled in the cities and began to organize themselves by the side of the veteran residents, sometimes as a separate community. As far as we know, a new community was established

---

1 RIBaSH, *Responsa*, no. 61 (f. 13b bottom).
2 For the attitude of the Muslims comp. Hamet, *Juifs*, p. 152 n. 2.
3 Simon Dūrān, *Responsa* III, no. 46.
4 Comp. Hershman, *Perfet*, p. 162.

only in Tlemcen, and it too, was not absolutely new, but a continuation of neighbouring Agạdir. We mainly find the refugees settling along the coast, from Hūnayn in the west via Oran, Mostaghanem, Tenes, Breshk, Algiers and Bougie to Tunis;[1] many settled in the capital, Tlemcen, and other cities of the plain, such as Miliana, Medea and Constantine. We shall yet discuss the absorption difficulties of the immigrants in the Jewish and non-Jewish environment and the many problems arising out of their having lived under conditions of forced conversion and religious coercion. We shall, moreover, give a comprehensive discussion of the importance of that immigration for the study of the geographical distribution, organizational and social structure and way of life of the veteran communities, the "residents," who had clung to their Judaism under conditions of external pressure and isolation from other diasporas. In this respect, only the collections of responsa of R. Isaac bar Sheshet and R. Simon ben Ṣemaḥ Dūrān, the most eminent of the refugees of 1391, who settled in Algiers, have so far been examined, while R. Simon's other writings, as well as later sources, have not found due attention.[2]

Some of the refugees achieved influential positions at the court of the Ziyanids and thereby gained control over their brethren. Simon b. Ṣemaḥ Dūrān says of Abraham Sasportas, of Majorca, that he was "powerful... through the medium of people of the court," and R. Isaac b. Sheshet sought his intervention to obtain freedom from customs duty for the books he had saved from Spain. Others who had connections with courtiers in Tlemcen were, *e.g.*, Abraham Mendīl and Yeshuʿah ben Moses.[3] Of Moses Gabbay, an important rabbinical scholar who settled in Hūnayn, we know that he retained his Aragonese passport and in 1394 went to Morocco on a mission on behalf of Juan I.[4] Wealthy and influential persons were to be found also among the second generation of refugees, such as R. Bonet, whom the king fined in the amount of one thousand gold dinars.[5] The Shulāl (Solal) family, of Majorca, likewise held an important position; we find members of it in Hūnayn, Tenes and Tlemcen. One of the Shulāls was the last nagid in Egypt prior to the Ottoman

---

[1] The existence of two separate communities in Bougie is confirmed by Solomon b. Simon Dūrān, *Responsa*, no. 568; comp. also Simon Dūrān, *Responsa* III, no. 45.

[2] The works referred to are I. Epstein, *Responsa*, and Hershman, *Perfet*. An essay on Simon b. Ṣemaḥ Dūrān of the seventies of the 19th century (Jaulus, *MGWJ*, 23-4 (1874-5) is now out of date.

[3] Comp. RIBaSH, *Responsa*, nos. 60 and 185, and Simon Duran, *Responsa* I, no. 62.

[4] Comp. Simon Dūrān, *Responsa* I, no. 33; Epstein, *Responsa*, pp. 98f.; Hershman, *Perfet*, pp. 114f.; Baer, *Spanien* I, pp. 720f.

[5] Comp. Solomon Dūrān, *Responsa*, no. 550, also no. 504.

conquest.[1] None of all these, however, played a really decisive role either within the Jewish community or at the court in Tlemcen. At any rate, we find no suggestion to the contrary in Jewish or Arab sources.

Tribulations and Persecutions in the 15th Century

In those days, an Ashkenazi scholar, R. Jacob ha-Kohen, came to Algiers, and R. Solomon, the son of R. Simon b. Ṣemaḥ, discussed halakhic questions with him. R. Jacob had one distinguished disciple, whom R. David Conforte, the author of *Kore ha-Dorot* mentions along with scholars then in Germany: "In the days of the said Ashkenazi rabbis (the author of *Terumat ha-Deshen*, R. Jacob ben Yehuda Weil, and R. Joseph Kolon) there lived R. Yeshaʿya (*sic*) ha-Levi b. Joseph ha-Levi, of the country of Tlemcen, a disciple of R. Jacob Askhenazi, who wrote *Halikhot ʿOlam*, a book on Talmudic precepts; expulsions and forced conversions caused him to flee from Tlemcen to Toledo in the year 5227/1467, as set out in the introduction to his book."[2]

Because of certain details, we will give some passages of R. Yeshuʿah ha-Levi's introduction *verbatim*: "... from the country of Tlemcen. All my days, I grew up among scholars, and my faith was salvatory strength (cf. Is. 36:6); I was born on the knees of scholars, and among their books I was nurtured. I listened to their words, and I inclined my ear unto their voice. I toiled much, and if I found little, I said: The Lord is my part (cf. Ps. 16:5). I sit in the house of the Lord all (my) days, and I attend at the doors of scholars, the keepers of my innermost archives. The table of the Gemara is laid before me. This is the table which is before the Lord (cf. Ez. 42:22)."

After this poetical portion, R. Yeshuʿah goes on to describe the event which caused him to leave Africa: "And it was in the year five thousand and 227 of the Creation (1467 C.E.) that the Lord's anger was kindled against his people, and he sent evil angels among them, wrath and indignation, and a blazing fire burnt them up or they were beaten in a mortar, and I departed out of the midst of the overthrow. And I left my house of study, the four cubits of the halakha. And I came to the land of Castile to keep my life from danger for a while. For that country had

---

[1] Comp. Simon Dūrān, *Responsa* II, nos. 53, 54, 136, 175, 238; III, nos. 207-213; Ṣemaḥ and Simon Dūrān, *Yakkin u-Boʿaz* I, nos. 65 and 136; Ben-Zvi, *Eretz-Israel we-Yishuba*, pp. 139 and 143f.

[2] David Conforte, *Kore ha-Dorot*, ed. D. Cassel, p. 27b.

become full of evil ... And when God caused me to wander from my father's house and from the land of my kindred, time tossed me to the city of Toledo, and lo, I met there a man greatly beloved ... the Nasi Don Vidal ben Labī ... he asked of me a difficult thing: to compose for him a treatise containing the methods of the Gemara, so that he might be able to cope, for the books which have been written here are inadequate even as regards the mere outline of the subject-matter..."[1]

In my opinion, the disturbances referred to by R. Yeshuʿah were due to incitement by the same circles which had a share in events that took place in Fez in 1438 and 1465, and that we shall discuss presently.

R. Abner ha-Ṣarfati (19th century) reports in *Yaḥas Fās* (Genealogy of Fez) that in the colophon of a handwritten Pentateuch he found a note on cruel pogroms that had occurred in Fez in 1438. Here is the account: In ancient times, Jews lived in the Old City of Fez, among the Arabs. They were expelled from there in 5198 (1438 C.E.) and went to settle in the *mellāḥ*, where several families built themselves houses. The reason for their expulsion were charges that they had poured wine into a vessel in a mosque. The *mellāḥ* was founded during the reign of the Emir Yaʿqūb, and the first deed of ownership of a house built there by a Jew bears the date of 1438.[2] A note in *Kissē Melākhīm* by Raphael Moses Albaz (a contemporary of Abner ha-Ṣarfati) is shorter: "Previously, in the year 854 (A. H. = 1449/50 C.E.), *i.e.* 5194/1438, (*sic*), the Jews were expelled from the Old City of Fez because of wine which had been found in a vessel in a house of prayer. It was a sudden, cruel expulsion. Some families went and built the *mellāḥ* of Fez, and many converted."[3]

These data are unclear and full of contradictions. The Emir Yaʿqūb referred to might be Abū Yūsuf Yaʿqūb (1258-1286), the founder of the Merinid regime in Fez. If so, we have to do here with an anachronism. But not impossibly he is an Emir Yaʿqūb who, together with an Emir Saʿīd, appears in Lane-Poole's list of emirs between the years 1416 and

---

[1] R. Yeshuʿah's *Halikhot ʿOlam* was printed in Sabionetta in 1567. It takes up the first 36 leaves of a slender pamphlet; fols. 37 and 38 contain Samuel ha-Nagid's Introduction to the Talmud. Solomon Dūrān's *Responsa* nos. 632-635 are addressed to "the great sage and Kabbalist R. Jacob ha-Kohen when he was staying here in Algiers"; the wording seems to indicate that he was not domiciled in Algiers.

[2] An abridged version of *Yaḥas Fās* in French translation was published by Y. D. Semah in *Hespéris* 19 (1934), pp. 79-94; comp. *ibid.*, pp. 91f.; also Eisenbeth, *Maroc*, p. 35.

[3] Ms. Sassoon 1007 (cf. D. Sassoon, *Ohel David*, p. 1064-1065) fol. 22b. For the discrepancies in the dates comp. also below, p. 431 n. 2. About the expulsion see below p. 400.

1424. However, from 1430 to 1465, the ruler of Fez was ʿAbd al-Ḥaqq, and his guardian during his minority was Abū Zakarīyā Yaḥyā al-Waṭṭāsī. Leo Africanus reports that the Jews were transferred to the New City of Fez in the days of Abū Saʿīd ʿOthmān (1398-1421). Previously, they lived in the Old City, but from time to time, upon the death of a king, the Moors plundered them. This is why Abū Saʿīd transferred them to the quarter formerly inhabited by the archers' guard, and on that occasion doubled their tax quota. Leo continues: "Here they live to this day, occupying a long and wide thoroughfare, where their stalls and synagogues are. The Jewish population has increased immeasurably, especially since the Jews were expelled by the kings of Spain."[1]

It seems that during the confusion which reigned in Fez in the early 15th century, the Jews suffered increasingly and that, for reasons of safety, those who had remained in the Old City also moved to the quarter near the palace. That quarter may from then on have been inhabited exclusively by Jews. Those troubles probably involved also loss of life. The date of 1438 does not seem accidental. That period was marked by intensified propaganda on the part of the *shurafāʾ*, descendants of Ḥasan, the Prophet Muhammad's grandson, who were laying claim to the kingship. They "discovered" the grave of Idrīs, the Prophet's great-grandson and founder of Fez, no doubt in order to inflame the Muslim masses. The same purpose was served by anti-Jewish and anti-Christian incitement, (it should be noted here that the influence of the *marabouts* was growing then in the whole of Africa).[2] It may have been given out that Jews could not be allowed to live near the tomb of a king descended from the Prophet. But we certainly cannot accept the view that general measures of forced conversion and expulsion took place at that time. Fez then had an important Jewish community, whose area included smaller communities, such as Tāza, on the caravan route Fez-Tlemcen. Algiers scholars in that period, R. Simon b. Ṣemaḥ Dūrān (d. 1444), his son, R. Solomon, and his grandson, R. Ṣemaḥ, were in touch with those communities and their learned leaders R. Isaac Nahmias, R. Solomon b. Falkon and R. Natan Busti, and their utterances would certainly have reflected any great calamity befalling Fez Jewry. A passage in a responsum of R. Solomon ben Simon to a learned Fezzi even suggests the contrary: "My heart is glad and I rejoice that you follow my words strictly. Al-

---

[1] Leo Africanus, *Description*, p. 234; comp. also Terrasse, *Histoire* II, pp. 93f.

[2] Comp. Terrasse, *op. cit.*, II, pp. 144ff.; Brunschvig, *Berbérie* I, p. 408; Massignon, *Maroc*, p. 125 sec. 99.

though you are badly off, you need not worry about your property."[1] This passage indicates that they were in straitened circumstances, but not in fear of attack.

One of the queries from Malaga addressed to R. Solomon ben Ṣemaḥ affords a glimpse of the relations then existing between the rabbis of Algiers, Spain, Jerusalem and Tunis. Moreover, incidentally and indirectly, it reveals the existence of a Jewish community in Marrakesh in those days.[2]

R. Isaac b. Alfara of Malaga, who settled and died in Palestine and to whom the query relates, wrote an account of his travels in Palestine which he sent to R. Simon ben Ṣemaḥ Dūrān. R. Abraham Zacuto saw the manuscript during his stay in the region (c. 1500) and inserted an epitome of it in one of his works.[3]

The presence of Jews in Fez in 1438/39 is known also indirectly from the story of the Infant Ferdinand of Portugal, who was held there as a hostage, with a Jew acting as liaison between him and his family in Portugal, while a merchant from Majorca—apparently also a Jew, a refugee from the island, for what would a Majorcan Christian be doing here?—supplied food to him and his retinue, which included a Jewish physician.[4]

However, matters in Fez became more difficult. *Shurafā'* propaganda in the country grew more intense, although the government was for the time being in the hands of regents of the Waṭṭāsid family, who ruled in the name of the orphaned minor, 'Abd al-Ḥaqq. When the latter grew up, he at first preferred the pleasures of the banquet hall and the harem to taking a firm stand towards his guardian, Abū Zakarīyā al-Waṭṭāsī. Eventually, however, he removed the Waṭṭāsids from the city, some by murder and some by banishment, leaving only one of them as a vizier without authority. In their stead, he appointed a Jew named Hārūn to be his all-powerful chamberlain. The appointment of that capable Jew was prompted also by the consideration that he would certainly not try to depose the Sultan in order to take his place.

[1] Comp. Simon Dūrān, *Responsa* II, nos. 169, 224; III, nos. 285-6; Solomon Dūrān, *Responsa* no. 406 (also no. 410); Ṣemaḥ and Simon Dūrān, *Yakhin u-Bo'az* I, nos. 65 and 109; II no. 3. Comp. Toledano, *Ner*, p. 47 and n. 21; Le Tourneau, *Fez-Merinids*, pp. 16, 30-31, 75.

[2] Solomon Dūrān, *Responsa*, no. 512; also published from a fragment MS in the Escorial by A. Neubauer in *Ha-Maggid*, 15 (1871), pp. 53a-b. On Jewish communities in Southern Morocco see above, p. 378 n. 1.

[3] *Juchassin*, ed. Filipowski, p. 228a-b.

[4] Comp. Lopes, *Historia* III, pp. 423-425; Kayserling, *Geschichte*, p. 46.

Tension between the three decisive factors in the state: the Sultan, the Waṭṭāsids and the *shurafā'* concentrated in Fez and the south of the country—which they controlled—now came to a head. A scapegoat was also ready. Venomous anti-Jewish incitement at once set in among the Muslim population. The chief inciter was the preacher (*khaṭīb*) at the great and famous *Jāmiʿ al-Qarawiyyin*. When the sultan and Hārūn were once absent from Fez, the preacher took advantage of the rumour of an attack by one of Hārūn's relatives upon a *sharīfa*, *i.e.* a woman of the family of the Prophet: by rousing the rabble, he frightened the clergy into outlawing the Jews. Almost the whole of the Jewish population of Fez is said to have been massacred then. Hārūn was killed before the eyes of his master by one of the Merinids. ʿAbd al-Ḥaqq himself, on returning to Fez, fell victim to the rabble, who butchered him like a sheep. With him ended the Merinid dynasty. The anti-Jewish riots later spread to other cities.

Evidence of the seriousness with which an attack on a descendant of Muḥammad was viewed is contained in a question addressed by R. ʿAmram ben Merwas of Oran to his eminent friend, R. Isaac b. Sheshet: "A Jew cursed a *kohen* and his ancestors violently in front of the people, and it was intended . . . to punish him because it was a *kohen* . . . and because in this country the Arabs are imitated in most matters; they say that a person who curses a relative of their Prophet must be severely punished, and the Jews say that a person who insults or curses a *kohen* must be dealt with similarly because a *kohen* is a descendant of Aaron."[1]

This question illuminates the background against which such extremely grave disturbances were apt to break out—especially if a *sharifa*, whose honour was particularly sacred, was reported to have been attacked and passions had been inflamed by malicious propaganda.[2]

The Vizier Hārūn

Direct and indirect references to the Jewish vizier, Hārūn, are to be found in a number of sources. A lively, almost firsthand account of the episode is preserved in the travel diary of ʿAbd al-Bāsiṭ, an Egyptian merchant and author, who was touring Spain and Africa at the time; he stopped over in Tlemcen when the tension prevailing in Fez made it impossible for him to get there. He used his stay in the capital of the

[1] RIBaSH, *Responsa*, no. 94.
[2] Comp. *EI s.v.* Sharīf.

Ziyanids to study medicine under a famous Jewish physician, who granted him an authorization (*ijāza*) to practise that profession. He is full of praise for his teacher, Moses ben Samuel al-Ashqar, a refugee from Malaga, declaring that he never saw a *dhimmī* of such excellent intellect and character (not surprisingly, he shows at the same time some prejudice, and even contempt, towards the Jews). ʿAbd al-Bāsiṭ expresses the opinion that Hārūn was a clever man and that, had his master listened to him, he would have saved both himself and his adviser. He does not conceal the fact that the influence of that rabble-rousing preacher in Fez was considerable, whereas a famous Muslim theologian in that city sanctioned the massacre only under duress. He also reveals the double-faced attitude of the superintendent of the *shurafā*ʾ, who wished to profit by the incitement without running any risk.[1]

Moroccan Jewry, Hārūn and ʿAbd al-Ḥaqq fell victims to the *shurafā*ʾs attempt to win the sympathy of the masses in their struggle for power, to which end they used the well-tried device of fanning religious fanaticism. Similar outbursts occurred during that period against Tūʾāt Jewry, whose settlement was liquidated.[2]

ʿAbd al-Bāsiṭ's Story

ʿAbd al-Bāsiṭ is one of the few Arab writers who pay attention to Jewish matters. Because of the importance of his account for the study of the period and the social background, some portions of his record may be quoted here:

"In that year (869), at the beginning of the month Rabīʿ I (November 1464), while I was still in Tlemcen, reports came from Fez of an enhancement of the power and affairs of the Jews through the Jewish vizier appointed by the lord of Fez, ʿAbd al-Ḥaqq al-Merīnī, after the latter had put to death several viziers of the Waṭṭās family, conceived a grudge against other members of it and expelled from Fez a group of Waṭṭasids who had revolted against him. The Jews of Fez gained control over the Muslims, wronged them and harmed them. Their affairs prospered and their influence increased, until the sultan, the vizier and the Jews underwent what we shall mention in the following.[3]

---

[1] R. Brunschvig published the MS. of ʿAbd al-Bāsiṭ, with a translation and introduction, in *Deux Récits de Voyage inédits en Afrique du Nord au XVe siècle*, Paris 1936; see there, pp. 8f. and 44/107, also pp. 12-14.

[2] Comp. below, p. 402.

[3] *Récits*, pp. 45f./109.

"On the eleventh thereof (of the month of Shawwāl, 869—June 7, 1465), a report reached Tlemcen from Fez that a large crowd of Fezzis had attacked the Jews in Fez and killed them to the last man. Only five men and six women, or fewer than these, survived; they escaped unnoticed. This was an important event and a great massacre, which ended with the murder (literally: slaughter) of ʿAbd al-Ḥaqq al-Merīnī, the ruler of Fez and lord of the Maghreb, notwithstanding his majesty and the splendour of his personality and kingship. And in his place arose one of the *shurafā'* of Fez, named Sherīf Muḥammad ibn ʿImrān. It is reported that ʿAbd al-Ḥaqq reigned over the kingdom of Fez for over thirty years and submitted to the viziers of the Waṭṭās family. Such was the custom in the countries of the Maghreb, in Fez. And it was the custom that decisions and the supreme command were with the viziers, and they were the masters of the people and the country, who issued orders and prohibitions in every matter; nothing was done in that kingdom without their sanction. The Merinid ruler was regarded by them as a tool, similarly to the caliphs in Egypt nowadays, in the era of the Turkish sultans (the Mamluks). Of course, they (the Merinids) were stronger than the caliphs there. ʿAbd al-Ḥaqq never ceased to use trickery against them (the Waṭṭasids) and to employ every device, until he eventually killed many of them and put to death the vizier Yaḥyā ibn Yaḥyā, who was mentioned earlier when some reference was made to ʿAbd al-Ḥaqq in the biographies of the year 99 (1459); with him, the son of the preceding vizier was killed . . . The B. Waṭṭās faction dispersed in consequence, and ʿAbd al-Ḥaqq took control of affairs. He appointed a vizier from among the B. Waṭṭās, conformable to his wishes and devoid of all decisive influence. His status as a vizier was similar to that of ʿAbd al-Ḥaqq as a king previously: without importance, without prestige, merely nominal. He (the ruler) appointed a Jew of Fez, named Hārūn ibn Baṭash, who was a moneychanger or dealt with the financial affairs of the viziers, and he made him a deputy vizier, restricting the powers of the vizier; he thereby wished to annoy the B. Waṭṭās, after he had killed many of them and imprisoned others in Meknes and had appointed from among them that insignificant vizier, whose name was likewise Abū al-Ḥasan ʿAli, and subdued him several times, until he had subdued him completely. ʿAbd al-Haqq put him (the vizier) aside in Fez as if he had been under his tutelage, and denied him any decisive influence in affairs of state. He did all this in order to annoy him and others, from among those who were in prison. Others, from among those who had escaped ʿAbd al-Ḥaqq, seized control of several districts of (the kingdom of) Fez. And that Jew remainded *de facto* vizier—there was no vizier but him, and he was the spokesman for the vizierate; and he remained faithful to his (Jewish) religion. This pleased ʿAbd al-Ḥaqq, for he annoyed and humiliated the B. Waṭṭās thereby.

"ʿAbd al-Ḥaqq kept him (the Jew) very close to him, and made him his confidant, until the whole kingdom was given into his hand. He trusted him because he thought it impossible that the Jew (as a non-Muslim) would exceed his authority, as ʿAbd al-Ḥaqq understood it. And the Jew had powers of command and prohibition in the kingdom of Fez, although he continued in the Jewish faith, and he was sometimes addressed by the title of vizier. In his days, the Jews of Fez and its districts became great; they were influential and important, and were obeyed and widely known. ʿAbd al-Ḥaqq was satisfied with this, and even pleased and delighted. And that Jew wore a sword on an iron belt engraved with the verse *al-kursī* (Sūra 2:256) and perhaps also with (the Muslim profession of faith) 'There is no God but Allah, and Muḥammad is Allah's messenger'. In the presence of his master he rode horses marked with the vizierial seal. And the ignorant mob would greet him with the title of vizier. On Friday, he would ride with the sultan to the Great Mosque, dismount and wait at the gate of the mosque until the sultan had gone inside, then sit down until the Friday service was over, and eventually get into the saddle again and return with the sultan. A great deal of objectionable things, corruption and transgressions manifested themselves in this accursed one, and the control of the Jews over the Muslims of Fez increased through him. The public could not bear them, hated ʿAbd al-Ḥaqq for this and sought his downfall, although the B. Waṭṭās, too, had sinned greatly against the citizens. But those had been Muslim viziers, unlike this accursed one, who was not of the (Muslim) faith.[1]

"Thereafter it happened that, in the same year, ʿAbd al-Ḥaqq left Fez on certain business, and the Jewish vizier with him. That Jew had appointed as his deputy in Fez a man—also a Jew, and a relative of his—named Saul ben Baṭash, an assistant at Government House in New Fez. It happened that this Jew summoned a woman of the *shurafāʾ* in a certain matter and spoke to her insultingly; some say that he struck her, or the like. The incident came to the knowledge of the preacher of Fez, Sayyidī Abū ʿAbdallah Muḥammad. He and the Muslims were greatly vexed because of the Jews, their influence and their control over the Muslims. In his sermon on Friday at the Great Jāmiʿ of Fez, named *Jāmiʿ al-*

---

[1] As to this description comp. Leo Africanus, pp. 235-241; also Terrasse, *Histoire* II, p. 70.

Qarawiyyin, he always preached about the Jews and also dared to incite and encourage the people: perhaps they would rise up because of this for Allah's sake and revolt. And the matter became known, and he became famous because of this. And when the insult to that *sharīfa* occurred, he dedicated his soul to Allah, left his house and loudly proclaimed in the streets and alleys of Fez: He who will not go forth for the sake of Allah has no *muruwwa* (Beduin chivalry) and no religion! And he went on to shout: Holy war, holy war! He also ordered others to issue this call in the streets of Fez, and the people heard it and presently revolted with him. They were joined by the great multitude from all 'the low places' (Sūra 22:28) in Fez; they took him and began to stream to the house of the *sherīf* Muḥammad ibn ʿImrān, who was *mazwār* (in charge) of the *shurafā*ʾ in Fez, similarly to the *naqīb* (supervisor) of the *ashrāf* in those countries. But he, in spite of his status, personal authority and great energy, when the preacher came in to him and tried to stir him up (against the Jews), did not respond, contending that it was improper for him to revolt while there were theologians in Fez who had not yet been asked for an opinion in the matter. They (the crowd) hastened to the theologians and assembled them, including the greatest of them at that time, the scholar and *muftī*, my lord the *sheikh* and *imām*, the greatest of sages, *sayyidī* Abū ʿAbd Allah Muḥammad al-Qaurī. He and the other assembled persons were brought to the house of the *sayyid* the *sherīf*. The preacher hastened to say to them: Go forth with us to the holy war; fight for the renewal of Islam! The crowd repeated his words and then said: If you will not fight together with us, you will be the first whom we shall fight; for you, *shurafā*ʾ and theologians, are content to be ruled by Jews. Then they shouted again: Holy war, holy war! meaning to incite them thereby. They demanded of al-Qaurī that he give a theological opinion, but he refused to do so, claiming that he was afraid of the authorities. They continued to prod him, after preparing a written question on the incident and on what that Jew and the Jews had done, saying that it constituted a violation of the Covenant,[1] and even more than that. They drew their swords and called out to al-Qaurī: We, too, have authority and power. We have risen up for Allah's sake and pledged our lives. This is the question which we ask you to answer according to the law of Allah, blessed be he. If you will not do so, we shall let the world do without you, for your are a theologian who does not act in conformity with his theology. They added other

[1] *I.e.*, the restrictions on non-Muslims in Muslim lands ascribed to the Caliph ʿOmar I (634-644) and known as the "Covenant of ʿOmar."

things in the same vein. And they gave him no rest until he wrote with his own hand a permit to kill the Jews, and another permit to revolt against them, and even against the sultan. When he had finished writing, they hastened to the *ḥāra* (the Jewish quarter) and wielded their swords against the Jews, killing as many of them as Allah wanted them to kill; they did not omit even one until they had killed the last, so as to clear the quarter of them. This was a glorious day in Fez and a great slaughter. A numerous Jewish community was killed on that day. Afterwards they turned to the palace of the government, devastated it and killed the Jew who was in it, namely the deputy of the vizier.

"Thereafter they set over them the aforementioned *sayyid sherīf* Muḥammad ibn ʿImrān, took him to the said palace and prepared themselves to do homage to him as their lawful ruler. It was then suggested to them by experienced and sensible persons from among the educated and intelligent that they must not proceed in this way before they had defeated the sultan ʿAbd al-Ḥaqq, lest ill befall them. Thereafter they decided that the notables of Fez and the sherif should write to ʿAbd al-Ḥaqq, who was absent from Fez, telling him of the incident and of the uprising and revolt of the people and informing him that the government palace would have been plundered if they had not calmed the people by bringing the *sayyid sherīf* into it, 'and he will take your place until Your Highness returns and the affairs of the Muslims and the people are settled, and nothing will be removed from your control.' They sent him (ʿAbd al-Ḥaqq) a letter containing all this and similar phrases. When the letter reached him, he at once made preparations for returning to Fez. But his Jewish vizier hastened to him and said: Your return will not be a happy one. What they have written is trickery. May it please my lord —Allah lend him victory—to go to Tāza or some other city until this flame has died down and the cause of my lord become strong again, and afterwards go to Fez—that will be well. The Jew's advice was sound, but, as the saying goes: When a person's fate is sealed, he becomes struck with blindness. ʿAbd al-Ḥaqq reprimanded the Jew, saying, You have been wrong from beginning to end, all this is because of you; there is no merit in you. There was one of the Merinids present; he witnessed the sultan's outburst against the Jew. That man promptly pierced the latter with his lance, in the presence of the sultan, so that he dropped dead right in front of ʿAbd al-Ḥaqq. He thereby hoped to win the goodwill of the people of Fez when they heard of his action.

"That murderer advised ʿAbd al-Ḥaqq to settle the matter quickly by returning to Fez, and others of ʿAbd al-Ḥaqq's entourage concurred in this advice. It was a fatal suggestion, which brought about the end of ʿAbd al-Ḥaqq's reign. The sultan travelled hurriedly, so that he arrived in Fez ahead of his soldiers, accompanied by only a few men. Most of his soldiers sensed that it was not safe to be with him, that disaster awaited him, and they therefore slowed down their progress. Afraid of being killed by the mob, they put as great a distance as possible between themselves and ʿAbd al-Ḥaqq. He entered Fez with only three members of his suite. When the people of Fez learnt of his arrival, they went to meet him, ostensibly in order to welcome him. With them went a group of people known as *al-wakkāra** (people of the lupanars) who are like the *zuʿar*** (procurers, underworld characters) in those countries. As soon as they saw ʿAbd al-Ḥaqq, they rebelled against him, shouting to one another: Holy war, holy war! When the soldiers who were with ʿAbd al-Ḥaqq heard this, they deserted him. He was seized by the arms and dragged from his horse. This happened near the abattoir of Fez. He was held at the abattoir, as is done to sheep, and slaughtered without resistance at his appointed time. This took place on the 22nd Ramaḍān of that year (14th May, 1465).

"The crowd returned to Fez and paid homage to the *sayyid sherīf* Muḥammad ibn ʿImrān as their lawful ruler, thanked him by the *bayʿa* (investiture) and made him king. When this became known to the B. Waṭṭās, they wanted to return to Fez and enter the city, but the people of Fez prevented them from doing so. The *sherīf* wished to remain king, and he convened members of the two factions, the royal B. Merīn and the vizierial B. Waṭṭās. And there was disagreement between the people of Fez and those outside the city.

"Thereafter the people of the cities distant from Fez learnt of these events. They rose against the Jews of the cities and did to them what the people of Fez had done to their Jews. The Jews were thus befallen by a calamity the like of which had never occurred before; as many of them as Allah—blessed be he—decreed were killed.

"Thereafter Fez and the districts were the scene of disasters, wars, rebellions, disturbances, corruption, devastation and loss of life. During this intermediate period, the Franks seized several cities in the coastal region, such as Tanja and Aṣīla (Arzila). Eventually, the B. Waṭṭās gained control of Fez: they ousted the *sayyid sherīf* Muḥammad from there after about four years. The *sherīf* had ruled only in Fez itself; he had had no control of the rest of the country; the districts had all been in the

* See Dozy, s.v. وكر ** *Idem*, s.v. زعر; also I.M. Lapidus, *Muslim Cities in the Later Middle Ages*, 1967, *s.v.*

hands of the B. Waṭṭās. The latter were themselves divided into two opposing factions: the Arabs of Khloṭ belonged to one faction, the Shāwiyya to the other."[1]

References to the Events in Other Sources

As stated, those events are referred to in a number of other sources, Hebrew, Arabic and Portuguese.

The Jewish Chronicles of Fez, written in the 19th century, probably on the basis of oral tradition, contain a rather vague account: in the year 5225 (1465), the Muslims in Fez, finding one of them slain, accused the Jews of his murder, attacked the Jewish quarter and did there as they pleased; men, women and children were killed on that occasion, and only a few families escaped.[2]

There is no reference here to the Jewish vizier, Hārūn, which shows that this Jewish tradition is unconnected with the story that was current among Arabs and Christians.[3] Whereas most of the sources fix the time of the Jewish vizier as indicated above, there is one version which dates the episode after the expulsion from Spain and introduces details of clothes regulations recalling what we know of the Almohad period.[4] The different versions of the events in Fez prompted the following obscure utterance in *Shebeṭ Yehuda*: "The Thirty-Third (Destruction). In the great city of Fez was a great massacre of Jews, but as I have not found it recorded in writing, I will not describe it here; I have come across numerous extensive oral reports that differ from one another and that are not worth noting since the story is not authenticated."[5] It must be admitted that if these doubts relate to a story of the destruction of the whole Jewish population of Fez in the days of ʿAbd al-Ḥaqq they are very justifiable, for, unlike the Arabs and the late Jewish Chronicles, the Jews of that generation say nothing about a wholesale massacre in Fez, and it

---

[1] *Récits*, pp. 49-55/113-121.

[2] Comp. Toledano, *Ner*, pp. 45f. (relies on *Yaḥas Fās*). The same description appears in *Kissē Melākhīm*, MS. Sassoon 1007, fol. 22b-23a.

[3] Until ʿAbd al-Bāsiṭ's account was published, the oldest available source was al-Zarkashi *Taʾrīkh al-Dawlatayn*, Tunis 1289 H., p. 141 (transl. Fagnan, *Chronique*, pp. 258-260); who calls Hārūn *raʾīs al-dawla*, head of the government. Comp. also al-Jannābī, Fagnan, *Extraits*, pp. 312f. Another version is quoted in Massignon, *Enquête*, p. 223, from MS. Rabāt 505, according to which three Jews then held the high positions of vizier, *ḥājib* (chamberlain) and *ṣāhib al-shurṭa* (chief of police), comp. Cour, *Etablissement*, pp. 36f.; Brunschvig, *Récits*, p. 113. For the Christian sources comp. Castries-Cenival, *ABP* III, p. 426, also Lopes, *Historia* III, pp. 441f.

[4] Comp. Kayserling, *REJ*, 39 (1899), pp. 315-317, also Toledano, *Ner*, p. 73.

[5] Ed. Shohet, p. 90.

is inconceivable that they should have formed a conspiracy of silence concerning such a shocking event. The occurrence of a massacre can certainly not be deduced from the following utterance of R. Ḥayyim Gagin: "And in the spring of my life, tribulations caused me to leave Fez for the kingdom of Castile, so that I might have peace for the study of the Tora, for drinking of the beautiful waters."[1]

The events in Fez during that century are referred to in a note at the beginning of a *pinqas* of the Fez community for the years 5639/1879–5685/1925. The note was copied from an original written in 5449/1689, based on an ancient source. Despite some obscure passages, certain traits lend it great credibility: the candour with which the unknown author describes the causes of the persecutions, the mention of Hārūn, the admission of the manhandling of a Muslim woman, the admission of the drinking of wine in a mosque, and the mention of clothing regulations. It therefore merits a full translation although, as stated, it is not clear in every particular.[2]

The persecution which took place in Fez which is called the Hārūn (!) Persecution was as follows. There were two brothers, one a king and one a rebel. Once (?) the Gentiles of the city rebelled and sent for the other [the rebel] and let him in and made him king, and the other [the deposed one] swore that if he was restored to the kingship he would not appoint a minister or commander other than a Jew. And because of our sins he was restored to the kingship and kept his oath and set a Jew named Hārūn over the city as deputy. And the Jews became proud, and they transgressed laws and contravened precepts and did deeds that ought not to be done, and some of them took a Gentile married woman and beat her cruelly; and she screamed and begged for mercy and they did not listen to her, and they went on beating her so that the Gentiles assembled and wreaked death and destruction upon the Jews until they had killed all the males except those who changed their religion—until in the general killing they killed a woman, and her two children came out (of her womb); and they took them in a vessel and brought them before the king; and they spared the women, and he [the king] issued a proclamation among the Gentiles that they should no longer smite the Jews. After ten days,

[1] Comp. Toledano, *Ner*, p. 46 n. 18.

[2] The MS., Ben-Zvi Institute no. 2651, is illegible in some places. The text published by J. Bennaïm in *Malkhey Rabbanan*, Jerusalem 1931, 96 c-d (*s.v.* Gavison), which he found in an ancient MS. written by Moses Gavison, is in part much better. The translation follows whichever is the better version in the place in question. For Moses Gavison and his father Jacob see *op. cit.*, 96b and 71a. I am indebted to Mr. A. David for drawing my attention to the Ben-Zvi Institute MS.

the king assembled all those who had changed their religion and said to them: I know and am certain that you have not changed your religion voluntarily; therefore anyone who wishes to revert to Judaism shall do so.[1] So everyone who took his life in his hands, cast himself upon the Holy One, blessed be he, and said: I am a Jew, remained alive; he survived, he, his children and his children's children; and it was said that the first who had said: I am a Jew was one of the Banū al-Lajām. And this persecution took place in the year of "the tender and delicate woman."[2] And twenty-five years before it, there was, also in Fez, the fierce persecution called the al-Khāḍa (!)[3] Persecution. It occurred because the Jews had become so arrogant and lawless that they went to the Great Mosque, stopped up the source of the water pouring forth there and filled the marble basin from which the water poured with wine and drank there all night, and at daybreak they went away, leaving one Jew there drunk and asleep. And the Gentiles came and found him there, and they killed all the male Jews who were there, and only those escaped who changed their religion. And they killed children and women and brought Jews from another place and settled them in their stead. And during the second persecution, it was decreed that the Jews might only wear a garment made of hair. All this I found written on some faded paper, and I copied it in order that it might be remembered. I, the poorest of my clan, the smallest on earth, the lowliest of all, Moses the son of the honourable teacher and rabbi, Rabbi Jacob Gavison, may the Lord protect him and keep him alive. Tuesday, the 17th of Tammuz (may God turn it to the good), 5449/1689.

A far echo of those events may be contained also in an elegy by an unknown poet, published by H. Schirmann and concerned mainly with the capture of Oran by the Spaniards in 1509, to be discussed below. As usual, the elegist begins by mentioning earlier tribulations; after a reference to the events of 1391 comes the following passage:

"And now, in my days, I am the man that hath seen affliction by the rod of wrath. / Enemies arose against my congregation, the seed of Edom and the sons of Qeṭūra. / At first the people of the West, the possessors of the axe and the hoe, / killed man and woman together and desecrated Tora

[1] This is in accordance with the Muslim principle *lā ikrāh fi-l-dīn* "there is no coercion in religion"; Sura 2:256; comp. Saʿid al-Antāki, *Taʾrīkh*, ed. Cheikho Beyrout, Paris 1909, p. 235. Cf. Hirschberg, *Bar-Ilan Annual* IV-V (1965), pp. 433f. and 470.

[2] *I.e.*, 5225/1665: The Hebrew letter-numerals for 5225 spell the word *harakkah* "the tender woman"; see Deut. 28, 56.

[3] So Bennaïm. This seems to be a variant of Arabic *al-ḥauḍ* "water basin for ritual ablutions at a mosque (usually designated by the Persian word *shadarrawān*)."

scrolls. / And they sought their hidden treasures and filled their bellies with dainties. / More recently against me arose a well-known enemy from Meghila,[1] / Killed the houses of Gorerīn and Ta'ūtī and desecrated the house of him who is terrible in his doing (comp. Ps. 66:5). / And after him arose an enemy in Dar'a and destroyed the whole house of prayer, / and they also imposed upon them laws wicked and hard without pity."[2]

These lines are followed by an account of the "destruction" in Spain and Portugal, and the elegy winds up with the story of the capture of Oran. Considering the apparently chronological order of presentation, we may suppose that by the deeds of the people of the West are meant the occurrences in Fez and other cities at the end of the Merinid regime.

The reference to the "well-known" enemy from Meghila and his misdeeds in Ghurāra and Tū'āt—for this is how we must correct the MS. readings "Gorerin" and "Ta'ūtī"—is fairly transparent. A Jewish population in Tu'āt, a large oasis on the edge of the Sahara, on the border between Algeria and Morocco, is known from the early 14th century onwards.[3] In the late 15th century, a marabout shaykh named Muḥammad al-Meghīlī, who had been expelled from Fez, arrived there and engaged in unbridled incitement against the Jews, who were very influential there and in Sijilmāsa and the neighbouring districts. He charged that they were practising sorcery and did not comply with the discriminatory regulations. According to Arab sources, he killed many wealthy Jews in Tū'āt and compelled the others to wear special clothing and conspicuous distinctive badges. According to Leo Africanus, this happened in the year of the expulsion of the Jews from Spain.[4]

In the Dar'a Valley, we find at that time the Banū Sa'd, *i.e. shurafā'* who derived their origin from Ḥasan, a grandson of the Prophet Muḥammad, and who later founded the Moroccan royal dynasty which ousted the B. Waṭṭās. Of the Sherīf Muhammad al-Shaykh al-Qā'im (1510-17), it is reported that he regarded himself as a religious and moral reformer and whipped and mulcted the Jews. He did so also in Tunis on his way to Mecca, thereby angering the Emir of Tunisia, who summoned him into his presence. He did the same in Cairo, where the Mamluk sultan Kansūh al-Ghaurī was then in power. In view of this latter fact, we may assign his

[1] See *G. B. Maroc*, p. 360 bottom.

[2] Schirmann, *Kīnōt*, p. 49 = p. 71.

[3] Comp. above, pp. 369.

[4] Comp. Corcos, *Jews* I-II, pp. 277 n. 11; III-IV, 73 and n. 96. It may be worth noting that Leo Africanus, *Description*, p. 431, mentions a caravan of Jews with which he traversed that region. The whole problem will be discussed in vol II.

actions to the early 16th century, and the poet not impossibly refers to him. Still, the author of the elegy may have heard of other similar happenings, prior to the time of Muhammad al-Qā'im.[1]

The active, vehement anti-Jewish policy of the *shurafā'* at that time, in the early days of their political struggle, may have been prompted by a desire to win the sympathies of the masses, and an additional reason may have been the wish to show that their religious zeal was greater than that of the sultans of the Waṭṭās dynasty, who were tolerant towards the Jews and admitted refugees from Spain and Portugal. Later, when the position of the *shurafā'* consolidated, Muḥammad al-Mahdī himself became tolerant towards the Jews, who thereupon supported him and his heir.[2]

The Settlement of the Refugees of 1492 and 1497

The eighty years of the rule of the Banū Waṭṭās dynasty in Morocco (1472-1554) were marked by a violent struggle with its Sherifian Banū Saʿd rivals, which led to a gradual shrinking of their territory in the interior and a Portuguese invasion of the Atlantic coast, closing most of the ports to the sultans. It was also a fateful period for the local Jewish community. The expulsions from Spain and Portugal and the events preceding and following them, and the political contest of the three forces in the area: the sultans, the *shurafā'* and the kings of Portugal, decisively affected Moroccan Jewry. Its spiritual physiognomy and socio-economic structure, as well as its status and place within the Moroccan state, were determined during that period.

At the end of 5252 (summer 1492), refugees from Spain affected by the "Christian kings'" expulsion edicts began to stream to Morocco. One of them, Abraham ben Solomon of Ardutiel, who settled in Fez and whose *Sefer ha-Qabbala* continues the work of Abraham ben Daud, describes the tribulations of the exiles on reaching Moroccan soil. Although the port of Salé (Ṣelā) was not in Christian-controlled territory, it was there that, according to Abraham ben Solomon, two Christian Gentiles ('uncircumcised'), Thomas and Julian, violated Jewish women; the reference is probably to Christian traders or sea-captains who took advantage of the refugees' plight. Count Vasco Coutinho de Borba, the

[1] Comp. the account of al-Jannābī—two generations after Muḥammad al-Qā'im—in Fagnan, *Extraits*, pp. 340 and 361. According to R. Haim Gagin, persecutions of Jews occurred in the Tāfilālet in 1526; Toledano, *Ner*, p. 61.

[2] Comp. H. Terrasse, *Histoire* II, p. 132. Unlike the Jews, the Muslims expellees spread hatred against Spain and Christian Europe.

Portuguese governor of Arzila (1490-1501, 1505-1514), prevented the refugees from proceeding to nearby Qṣar al-Kabīr, which was ruled by the King of Morocco.[1] Meanwhile, Beduin robbers learnt of their intended movement; they set upon the defenceless convoy leaving Arzila and despoiled it completely, thus stripping men, women and children of all their belongings; they did the same to those coming from al-ʿArāʾish (Larache). A better fate befell those who landed at the port of Bādis (Velez de la Gomera), the only outlet to the Mediterranean in the hands of the sultan of Fez and therefore of great political importance. The local ruler, Mulay Manṣūr, a member of the royal family, received them willingly and enabled them to proceed to Fez.[2] The *Sefer ha-Qabbala* pays special tribute to the great king, the benevolent Gentile, Mulay Shaykh (*i.e.* Muḥammad al-Shaykh, 1472-1505, the first King of Fez of the Waṭṭās dynasty), "who received the Jews in the whole of his kingdom and was kind to them."[3] *Shebet Yehuda* likewise notes the friendly attitude of the King of Fez, although it has much to say about cruelties and wrongs then inflicted upon the refugees in Morocco.[4]

The plight of the refugees who came to Fez and Oran is also mentioned by Abraham Zacuto. He praises the charity of the Jews of Algiers, who in 1499 redeemed fifty of their coreligionists for 700 gold ducats; they had been imprisoned for two years in Seville and then brought to Algiers. "It is a small community quantitatively, but great in quality," concludes R. Abraham.[5]

The statements in Jewish sources as to the favourable attitude of the first Waṭṭāsi ruler towards the Jews are confirmed by the ingenuous account of a contemporary non-Jewish writer, Leo Africanus. In his time, the Jews of Bādis lived in one street, and many of them dealt in wine, as befits the inhabitants of a port city frequented by sailors of different

---

[1] See about him Steinschneider, *Geschichtsliteratur* p. 98-9. The story about his cruelty is confirmed by Lattes, *Excerpta*, p. 76. For more details about de Borba see Castries-Cenival, *ABP* V, p. 161 (index). Incidentally, de Borba was among the attackers of Azemmour in 1513, and the Jews helped the Portuguese to capture the city; *ibid.*, I, pp. 403ff.

[2] Manṣūr is mentioned in Zambaur, *Manuel*, p. 80, and Massignon, *Maroc*, p. 266.

[3] *MJC* I, pp. 112f.; see also Lattes, *op. cit.*, pp. 75-6 and 90.

[4] Ed. Shohet, pp. 122f.; comp. also Marx, *Studies in Jewish History and Booklore*, p. 86; Usque, *Consolation*, transl. by Cohen, p. 200; Joseph ha-Kohen, *Emek ha-Bakha* (ed. Letteris), pp. 103f. Elbaz's account in *Kissē Melakhim* (MS. Sassoon 1007), fol. 23a and b is a combination of that of Abraham b. Solomon and that of *Shebet Yehuda*; it was published—from another MS.—by N. Ben-Menahem in *Areshet* II (1962), pp. 399f.

[5] *Juchassin* ed. Filipowski, p. 227a and b.

countries.[1] In Tadlā, an important commercial centre on the Fez-Marrakesh route, which was also a caravan junction between east and west, there were two hundred Jewish families, and one wealthy Jew there was a major taxpayer.[2] In Fez itself, which became a commercial metropolis, a centre of international trade, the number of Jews increased enormously, especially after the expulsion from Spain.[3] Marmol, who visited Morocco in the first half of the 16th century, speaks of 10,000, but this seems exaggerated.[4] In Tāza, Leo found five hundred Jewish families.[5] We have already mentioned his testimony concerning the small communities scattered in the mountains, which included also Karaites.[6] His reports concerning Asfī (Safi), Azemmour and Ṭīṭ will be cited below in connection with Portuguese affairs. The general picture emerging from these accounts is that of a Jewish population living under conditions of shocking degradation, but not exposed to attacks on their persons or property.[7]

Owing to their man-made and other troubles, many refugees were at first in so desperate a plight that part of them were unable to hold out and returned to Christian countries, including Spain. Judah Ḥayyāṭ, a refugee rabbi who made the painful journey from Spain to Morocco and thence to Italy, reports on it in the introduction to his *Minḥat Yehuda*. Some portions of his report may be given here.

After he had escaped to Morocco and settled in a place he does not name, but which is presumably in the northern part of the country, a Muslim refugee from the Spanish city where he had officiated as a rabbi falsely asserted that he had ordered his congregation to ridicule the Prophet Muhammad when the Jews joined the Christians in celebrating the capture of Granada from the Muslims. "And one Ismaelite from Spain, from the same locality as I, arrived there (for they, too, had been expelled) and told slanderous stories about me, and people believed him as if there had been three witnesses. They smote me, they wounded me, they took away my veil from me and threw me into a deep pit with snakes and scorpions in it. They presently sentenced me to be stoned to death, but promised that if I changed my religion they would make me captain

[1] *Description*, p. 275.
[2] *Ibid.*, pp. 142f. and 147.
[3] *Ibid.*, p. 234.
[4] Marmol, *Afrique*, pp. 170 and 300.
[5] *Description*, p. 303; comp. also above, 368.
[6] See above p. 270. and esp. *Description* p. 114.
[7] Massignon, *Maroc*, pp. 158f., gives a list of *mellāḥs* that existed at that period. Comp. also above pp. 367ff.

over them without dowry or gift. But Judah yet rules with God, and is faithful with the saints (Hos. 12:1). And the God in whom I put my trust frustrated their design. When I had been there for almost forty days in darkness and gloom, with scanty bread and water by measure, my belly cleaving to the ground, in hunger and in thirst and in nakedness and in want of all things, God stirred up the spirit of the Jews in Chechaouen, and they came thither to redeem me, and I rewarded them for my redemption by giving them nearly two hundred books which I had."[1]

The aid given to R. Judah Ḥayyaṭ by the Jews of Chechaouen suggests that he was imprisoned in one of the ports in the north of the country controlled by independent sheykhs, and the reference to the books indicates that it was possible after all to save part of one's valuable possessions.

R. Judah goes on: "After getting out of there, I went to the great city of Fez. There was a famine in the city, so that we ate the grass of the field. Every day I worked a mill at the house of some Arabs, with both my arms, for a small, extremely thin slice of bread, not fit even for dogs. At night, my belly cleaved to the ground and because of the great cold of autumn and because we had no covering against the cold nor houses to lodge in, we made ditches in the dung that was in the city and put our bodies therein, and thus came true the verse Lam. 4:5."

After some vicissitudes, Rabbi Ḥayyaṭ arrived in Naples. There he was taken prisoner by the king of France and again ill-treated. From there he went to Venice. He eventually settled in Mantua, where he wrote his work, a commentary on the Kabbalistic *Maʿareket ha-Elōhūt*.[2]

An account of the refugees' plight is contained in the introduction to an elegy on the expulsion from Spain by Abraham ben Solomon ha-Levi Buqarāṭ: "And out of their number we, 12.000 persons, came to the kingdom of Tlemçen. And about three thousand of the people fell dead at that time . . . And the rest of them walked in the markets and broad places naked, without clothes. Jews[3] wandered in the streets, embraced dunghills. And famine prevailed over them in that year; it held them tightly in its grip. And they were weary with bearing the burden, and numberless many of them returned to the kingdom of Castile and changed

[1] Comp. Marx, *Studies*, pp. 205-6.

[2] *Maʿarekhet ha-Elōhūt*, ed. Zolkva (Zólkiew), 1879, p. 3. On the author see Baer, *Spain* II, p. 426; G. Shalom, *Tarbiz*, 24 (1965), p. 169; Ben-Sasson, *Zion*, 26 (1961), p. 27 and n. 16. The rendering of the narrative in Steinschneider, *Polemische und apologetische Literatur*, Leipzig 1877, p. 375, is not accurate.

[3] A pun on *Ibrim*—Hebrews and *ivrim*—blind men; see Lam. 4:14.

their honour (religion). (cf. Ps. 106:20). This applies to such of them as came to the kingdom of Portugal and such as came to the kingdom of Fez. . ."[1]

A similar relation by an unknown contemporary author, who himself seems not to have been a refugee, was published from a MS.[2]

"Many of the exiled Spaniards went to Mohammedan countries, to Fez, Tlemçen and the Berber provinces, under the rule of the King of Tunis. On account of their large number, the Muslims did not allow them into their cities, and many of them died in the fields from hunger, thirst and lack of everything. . . A Jew in the Kingdom of Tlemcen, named Abraham the viceroy who ruled the Kingdom, made part of them come to his Kingdom and he spent a large amount of money to help them. The Jews of Northern Africa were very charitable toward them. As part of those who went to Northern Africa found no rest and no place that would receive them, they returned to Spain and became converts. . ."[3]

The latter accounts agree with that of Judah Ḥayyaṭ, and the authors are influenced by the phraseology of the Book of Lamentations. It should be noted that they complain mainly of difficult objective conditions, and not of the attitude of the authorities. Judah Ḥayyāṭ ascribes his imprisonment in Northern Morocco to a slanderous charge.

The figure given by Buqarāṭ seems exaggerated in the light of the evidence of Abraham ibn Abi Zimra, who reports that some 200 persons came to Tlemcen from Granada; it is unlikely that sixty times that number fled to the city from other places.[4] Buqarāṭ himself left Tlemçen, and in 5267/1507 we find him in Tunis, writing the introduction to his notes on Rashi's Bible commentary.

We may cite a passage from *Debey Eliyahu* by Eliyahu Kapsali of Candia, a contemporary of the events, though he lived far from the scene. He no doubt heard the story from eye witnesses, since it is confirmed by the sources quoted, except for the portion given only in resumé, for which we have found no corroboration. A certain vagueness of Kapsali's account may be due to its second-hand character.

"Some went to the land of Ismael, to Oran, Algiers and Bougie, which are far from the port of Cartagena.[5] Thousands and tens of thousands of

[1] Comp. Ben-Sasson, *Tarbiz*, 31 (1962), pp. 59-71.

[2] See Marx, *Studies*, pp. 77-105.

[3] *Ibid.*, p. 86; the English translation by Marx, pp. 94-5; comp. above, pp. 403-404.

[4] Gavison, *'Omer*, p. 138a.

[5] In Spain.

ships came to the port of Oran. The inhabitants of the country, the Canaanites, on seeing the great number of ships, complained and said: Lo, they are making the country narrow for us; and they are coming as enemies, to destroy us and take us as slaves and bondwomen, and to take away our money. Assemble yourselves and let us go to the fortified cities and fight for ourselves and our children. And so they did: they shot at the ships with cannon and other instruments of destruction and destroyed part of the Jews. But in the end, when they learnt of the expulsion, the king received them kindly, for an intercessor stood up for them at the palace in the person of the late R. Doriham.[1] After they had landed, they moved about, trying to find a place where their foot might rest. And the country could not sustain them because they were more numerous than locusts—they were countless. The king then built them houses of boards and planks outside the city walls, and they dwelt under oak trees and birch trees, the shade of which is beneficial... And they made sheds for their cattle, sheds with pens all round. And they built themselves solid huts. The sons gathered wood, and the father (handled) hammers, beams and thorns(!), and the Lord (!), saved them by all these activities; Joshua [2] made them hewers of wood."[3]

Kapsali then describes a fire which, starting in a bakehouse, destroyed part of the camp, watched by a shocked crowd of local Jewish inhabitants.

Three distinguished refugee scholars from Spain stayed for a time in Morocco. Jacob Beyrab relates: "From the day of the expulsion and persecution in Spain I was all the time a religious guide in Israel and a rabbi for five thousand Jewish houses in the city of Fez, well known among the public; I was then a beardless youth of eighteen, and there were great scholars there, and although I suffered hunger and thirst and want of everything etc. ..."[4] Abraham Zacuto, while attending R. Isaac Shulāl's academy in Jerusalem, engaged in preparing tables for coordinated calendars; he remarks that he did so also "in Salamanca in Castile and in Fez and Tlemcen and in Tunis."[5] R. David ibn Abi Zimra (RaDBaZ) is said to have gone to Fez at the time of the expulsion and from there to

---

[1] Marx, *Studies*, p. 94, n. 44, assumes that this is miswritten for Abraham, the name of a person mentioned previously (p. 407).

[2] According to Luzzatto, "Joshua" is a metaphor for God.

[3] Addenda by S. D. Luzzatto to M. M. Wiener, *Emek Habacha von R. Joseph ha Cohen*, Leipzig 1858, pp. 16-17 (Hebrew part).

[4] *Responsa*, ed. Venice, fol. 298b (Lemberg, fol. 68b). According to Gavison, *Omer ha-Shikheḥa* p. 68c he passed Tlemcen on his way to Palestine.

[5] Comp. D. Sassoon, *Ohel David* I, p. 510; Shohet, *Zion*, 13/14 (1948/49), pp. 43 and 46.

Egypt.[1] It is surely accidental that the aforementioned scholars are the only ones of whom we know that they sojourned in North Africa while seeking a place of refuge.

However, most of the Spanish and Portuguese exiles in Morocco settled down, establishing themselves in the seaports and the major cities of the interior. In fact, it seems that they did not establish themselves exclusively in the cities. The settlement of the ramified Pereṣ family in the Dades region in the Central Atlas Mountains is described by one of its members, who migrated to Europe, as follows:

"... And the members of my family lived in the kingdom of Old Castile ... and the nations were jealous of them ... saying, Let them be expelled from our country ... And the majority of the children of Pereṣ left, a great multitude, and they ran to and fro on the other side of the Ocean, in a part of Africa, and they dwelt beyond Migdal Eder (a pun, cf. Gen. 35:21), that is the kingdom of the king of Morocco, and they bought from him a city named Dades and set up gates, and they lay down safely, and no stranger, not of their father's house and bearing their name, passed in their midst; and they would marry no woman of another family even though they be made to fall down as corpses, but only of their own family from youth, and they were fruitful and multiplied from day to day and the land was not able to bear them that they might dwell together as brethren and associates, and they bought further from the king a neighbouring city, named Tilith, and that property cost them dear. And they live in those places to this day, and great rabbis and eminent sages are in their midst, who expound the Tora in seventy ways, and they observe the Tora and the precepts with exceeding strictness ..."[2]

Yehuda Pereṣ's above utterances must serve as indicative of the history not only of one family, but of many others, whose sons did not perpetuate their memory. Even such tombstones as have been preserved supply no additional information concerning those Jews. The Spanish refugees would set up stones in human shape without inscriptions, such as we find in the cemeteries of Tetuan and Tangiers.[3] Where it was usual

---

[1] Sambari, *MJC* I, p. 157; Azulai, *Shem ha-Gedolim s.v.*

[2] Comp. *Peraḥ ha-Lebanon*, Berlin 1712, Introduction. For the Pereṣ family in Spain see Baer, *Spanien* II, p. 424. Slouschz, *Travels*, p. 486, mentions that he brought some tombstones from Dades to the Museum of Rabat; he quotes an inscription of 1615.

[3] A survey of old anthropomorphic tombstones of Chechaouen, Tetouan, Al-Qṣar al-Kebir (Alcazarquivir) and Tangiers was published by Millas-Valicrosa and Laredo in *Sefarad*, 6 (1946), pp. 63-72; 9 (1949), pp. 421-432. For Muslim tombstones of the same type see Bourilly, *Éléments*, pp. 112f.

to engrave names and dates, the slab bearing the inscription was laid face downwards by order of the Muslim authorities, so that the carving became blurred and filled with earth in the course of time.

The presence of Jews in that area in those days (the first quarter of the 16th century) is incidentally confirmed by the wondrous tale of a Jewish tribe in the Sahara, told by two Muslim horsemen, members of a caravan that brought wine from the oasis of Skoura in the Dades region; clearly, only Jews carried on wine-making at that time.[1]

Further confirmation comes from a third source, independent of the two others. A pamphlet by Ḥayyim Gagin concerning a dispute between refugees and residents in the year 5268/1526 over the examination of ritually unfit meat invokes the practice of the veteran communities of "Darʿa and the district of Todgha and the district of Sūs and the district of Ghōzōla (Guezzoula)". These areas are on the southern edge of the Atlas, bordering on Dades and Skoura. According to Gagin, the dispute was referred to the court of the sultan Abū Ḥasan ʿAli (1524-1554), called (also in this source) Bū Ḥasūn, who had been installed shortly before and who was then in Meknes to make peace with one of his associates.[2]

Summing up, we may note that even in the Atlas region the refugees settled in the vicinity of veteran Jewish residents. However, in the absence of precise data, the numerical relation between the two strata cannot be estimated. Nor do we know what proportion of the Jews were descendants of those who had experienced the Almohad persecution and how many had come to the Maghreb subsequently, in the 200 years between the rise and the decline of the Merinids. Although our sources are more informative with regard to the period of the expulsions, we cannot say, either, how many refugees came direct from Spain and how many *via* Portugal, or how many came from the latter upon the 1497 expulsion and how many earlier. This problem merits a special discussion.

Diplomatic Agents

R. Elia Kapsali, the author of *Debey Eliyahu*, heard from a Portuguese refugee that about 1508 the King of Fez had sent a Jew as his "ambassa-

[1] Colin, *Juifs nomades*, pp. 55-65; also below, p. 434. The wine produced by the Jews of Tāza was famous, as noted by Leo Africanus, *Description*, p. 303, and Marmol, *Afrique*, p. 300.

[2] The relevant portions of this pamphlet were published by Toledano in *Ner*, pp. 58-68, from a copy made by him; comp. especially p. 62. For the Guezzoula tribe comp. Massignon, *Maroc*, p. 198 sec. 228, and map p. 70; *G. B. Maroc*, p. 437.

dor" to Portugal. The ambassador took ten Jews to accompany him. Among them was the refugee.[1]

At the court of the Waṭṭasid sultan in Fez, great influence was wielded by Jacob Rosales, "prominent among the Jews, popular with most of his brethren," and Moses Abuṭām (or Abuṭāt), who is described as overbearing towards the Jews, corrupt and an informer; these two represented the refugees with Bū Ḥasūn.[2] Both Jewish groups must have felt confident of the latter's favourable attitude towards them, for it would surely not have occurred to the parties in a religious controversy to appeal to a hostile ruler. Bū Ḥasūn was presently overthrown in Fez by his nephew Aḥmad (1524-1550) and had to content himself with the Bādis-Velez region; here, too, he employed Jews in diplomatic tasks. One of them, Abraham Cordovi—a refugee judging by his name—went on a mission to Portugal in 1532. A report of 1549 shows that Bū Ḥasūn had a Jewish secretary, who is once called Sananes. It is not unlikely that his first name was Menahem.[3]

Jacob Rosales was a respected merchant who maintained his connections with Portugal after settling in Fez; he figures in an account by David Reubeni, who was in Portugal in 1526. Reubeni sent signet rings to him and to an unnamed nagid.[4] After a time, we find Rosales in Portugal both on business and on a mission on behalf of Aḥmad, King of Fez, to whose diplomatic staff he belonged; he went repeatedly to the court of King João III (1521-1557), taking letters there and back. In 1533, he maintained close contact with a French officer who had come to Fez on a mission on behalf of his country. In the following year, he went to João on behalf of Aḥmad for peace talks, which were terminated by the 1538 treaty.[5] It seems quite certain that Rosales was a *converso* from Portugal, although his name as a Christian is nowhere mentioned.[6]

[1] Lattes, *Excerpta* p. 90.

[2] Comp. Toledano, *op. cit.*, pp. 64 and 72.

[3] Castries-Cenival, *ABP* II, pp. 562, 583f., (Cordovi); *ibid.*, IV, pp. 239, 246 and 248f.; *ABE* I, pp. 187-189. We know a Menahem Senanes who lived at the beginning of the 17th century and may have been a grandson of our Sananes. That Sananes was a *respetor* (= *repositarius*, an agent at the king's court), who conducted the affairs of the community; Vajda, *Recueil*, pp. 29, 39-40.

[4] Toledano, *op. cit.*, pp. 62f. and 72; Corcos, *Jews* IV, p. 79 n. 109; Reubeni's account, *MJC* II, p. 218.

[5] Castries-Cenival, *ABP* II, pp. 476-481, 518-520, 596f., 645f.; *ABF* I, Ser. I, pp. 16 and 28; *ABE* I, p. 78. See also Corcos, *Sefunot*, 10 (1966), pp. 104-106.

[6] A strange coincidence should be noted. In 1500, we find the captain Antonio Bocarro, a *converso*, in Safi. One of his descendants, Manuel Bocarro Frances, known as Jacob Rosales, lived in Hamburg in the middle of the 17th century; Kellenbenz, *Sephardim*, pp. 338-344.

In 1537, another Jew, Jacob Rute (Rōtī), who was the nagid of the Fez community about the middle of the century, undertook an official mission for the King of Fez. He had been appointed interpreter in Safi (Asfī) in 1523. The assumption that he was the son of Abraham ben Zamiro of Safi is based on an error that is easy to explain.[1] David Reubeni's story refers to an old Jew, Abraham Rut(e) of Asfi, who visited Reubeni in Tavira when on his way to the king of Portugal "to gain honour for himself . . . so that the king might set him over all the Jews." In Reubeni's opinion, Abraham Rut(e) was "the most modest Jew in that kingdom."[2] He was probably the ancestor of the well-known Fezzi family of Rute; he who traced that family to Abraham ben Zamiro must have confused the modest Abraham with the prominent one.[3]

We do not know when Jacob Rute and his brother Moses left Safi. Presumably their departure had something to do with arms deals with the king of Portugal. This would account for the fact that in the thirties we find Jacob at the court in Fez in the honoured position of a secretary-interpreter concerned with foreign affairs, especially relations with Portugal; as such he was greatly assisted by his brother Moses, now resident in Arzila and acting as his agent and representative in that region. Jacob himself visited Arzila, and he also travelled to Portugal to expedite the negotiations in person.[4] In a letter dated August 14th, 1537, the governor of Tangier reported to his king that Jacob had come to him with powers of attorney from the King of Fez and the *qā'id* of Chechaouen, Mulay Ibrāhīm. The Muslim courtiers in Fez did not easily agree that this mission should be entrusted to a Jew, although his good relations with the Portuguese court were known; some said it would be better to send a Muslim notable accompanied by Jacob as interpreter and adviser.[5] Jacob also served as a secretary-interpreter when the Portuguese ambassador de Tavora came to Fez in 1541. The ambassador told his king that

[1] R. Ricard's statement, *ABP* IV, p. 106, that Jacob Rute was the son of Abraham ben Zamiro, relies on an order appointing Jacob interpreter in Safi; comp. Sousa-Veterbo, *Noticia de alguns arabistas*, Coimbra, 1906, pp. 69f.; I have not been able to as much as see this very rare work, not available even at the Library of the British Museum.

[2] Comp. *MJC* II, pp. 212f. The name Rut (rather than Rute) occurs also in *ABA* II, pp. 11 and 48.

[3] The name Abraham was frequent in the Rute family; comp. Toledano, *Ner*, pp. 80, 93 and 96; Vajda, *Recueil*, p. 15. See also Corcos, *Sefunot*, 10 (1966), pp. 106-111.

[4] In Portuguese documents, Jacob is mentioned from 1536 as being in personal contact with de Redondo, the governor of Arzila, comp. *ABP* III, pp. 69f. and 72.

[5] Comp. *ibid.*, p. 184.

Jacob was a high dignitary at the court of Fez, that he had furthered the cause of Portugal and that the king should therefore be grateful to him.[1]

Similar appreciation is reflected in the letters of Vargas, a Portuguese agent who was in Fez in the years 1539-1544. According to him, the ruler of Fez insisted that only Jacob was authorized to speak in his name and that no account should be taken of what others purported to say on his behalf. Vargas stresses that Jacob was helpful to him and Tavora in the conduct of the talks. The Pope also recognized his usefulness and gave him a travel permit for all Christian countries.[2]

Jacob was in Portugal on a mission for his master in the years 1541-1543. Here, however, he was grievously wronged by João III, so that the king of Fez deemed it necessary to defend his secretary and to summon Vargas for a talk on the matter. The wrong was the outcome of personal intrigues against Jacob. The task assigned this time to the emissary of Fez was difficult in any case because of the precarious political situation. Each side suspected the other of planning to betray it by making peace with the Saʿdī *sherīf*. Portugal's then maturing decision to evacuate the important African ports was regarded by the ruler of Fez as indirect assistance to the latter. In this atmosphere of distrust, the Portuguese launched various accusations against Jacob and Moses. Moses was imprisoned at the instigation of the Inquisition, of which we shall have more to say below. (p. 438). The intention of the Portuguese to expel the Jews from Arzila deepened Jacob's disappointment at their ingratitude, especially as his brother was a resident of that city. From then onwards, so Vargas reports, relations between him and the Portuguese cooled. The king of Fez stoutly defended his subject, Moses Rute, and his intervention finally bore fruit. In 1544, we find Moses in Arzila, continuing his efforts to mediate between his brother and Vargas, who had moved thither.[3] Jacob himself proceeded to Arzila a year later for negotiations between the Kingdom of Fez and Portugal. When the Portuguese ambassador came to Velez (in 1547/48), he was carrying three letters of accreditation: to the king of Fez, to the ruler of Velez and to Jacob Rute.[4]

The Rute family was intimately involved in the life of the Jewish community, refugees and veterans alike. According to the Inquisition, Jacob Rute helped converso immigrants in Fez to settle down in their new surroundings and aided them in even more significant ways. One

[1] Comp. *ibid.*, p. 470.
[2] *Ibid.*, pp. 203f., 206 and 218; comp. Lopes, *Expansão*, p. 192.
[3] *ABP* III, pp. 554f.; IV, pp. 75, 80 and 83.
[4] Published in D. Lopes, *Anais de Arzila*, Lisbon 1919, II, pp. 403-405.

document mentions the *converso* Rui Mascarenhas, who planned to go to Portugal to revert to Christianity and then had second thoughts, went back to Fez and openly professed Judaism. Jacob Rute assisted him out of his own pocket and raised a sum of money for him from others. Another neo-Christian, of Lisbon, a cannoneer by trade, arrived in Fez, returned to Judaism under Jacob's guidance and offered his services to the king of Fez. Two youths who had acted in similar fashion declared that they had done so with the privity of Jacob Rute. Though statements to the Inquisition cannot be relied upon, the foregoing particulars do not seem impossible under the circumstances then prevailing in Portugal and its African ports.[1]

According to documents in our possession, Jacob Rute was the nagid of the Fez community in 1550. We know of other members of the Rute family, scholars, negidim and men of affairs, who were active in Fez and Marrakesh after Jacob.[2]

Spain and Portugal in the African Maghreb

The supplement to the *Sefer ha-Qabbala* by Abraham of Adrutiel winds up with a reference to the 1496/7 persecution, as a result of which several refugee scholars came from Portugal to Fez. Abraham describes the Portuguese king, Manuel (1495-1521), as an uncircumcised evildoer, the son by a concubine of Dom João II, who died of poison in 1495—in reality, he was his nephew—and he says that Manuel became king because João left no son worthy of the succession.[3] *Shebeṭ Yehuda*, on the other hand, calls Manuel "a good man" (*ḥāsīd*). These opposing views reflect Manuel's policy towards the Jews, which, let us add at once, was also that of his son and heir, João III, and of their predecessors in the 15th century. The dichotomy is particularly striking in the attitude of the kings towards the Jews of the Maghreb, both veterans and refugees.[4]

ʿAbd al-Bāsiṭ concludes his remarks on ʿAbd al-Ḥaqq al-Merīnī with

---

[1] According to *Shebeṭ Yehuda*, p. 126, the persecutions in Lisbon in 1506 broke out on account of Guano Rodrigo Mascarenhas, a Jewish customs official.

[2] Comp. *Kerem Ḥemer* II, nos. 23 and 25; Vajda, *Recueil*, pp. 15, 22, 38 and 47; Toledano, *Ner*, pp. 80, 93 and 96; *ABA* II, pp. 11 and 48; comp. also Benaïm, *Malkhey Rabanan*, pp. 76b (Isaac Rute) and 66a (Jacob Rute). The biography of Jacob is reviewed by Corcos, *Maroc*, pp. 106-111.

[3] *MJC* I, pp. 113f.; Joseph ha-Kohen, *Emek ha-Bakha*, pp. 107 and 105, holds the same opinion.

[4] Ed. Shohet, p. 126; but comp. Introduction, p. 10.

the statement that the Franks—which in this case means the Portuguese—took advantage of the confusion following his murder to seize several coastal cities. It is true that at this stage Portuguese penetration was the direct result of the situation then prevailing in the Maghreb, but the striving of the Christian states of the Iberian Peninsula for a foothold on the African coast was of long standing, manifesting itself from the late 14th century. Castile profited by the weakness of the Merinids to encourage their rivals for the throne. In retaliation, the Merinid ruler incited pirates to attack Spanish ships, whereupon the king of Castile, Enrique III, in 1399, captured and destroyed Tetouan, put half of the population to death and sold the remainder into slavery. The city's rehabilitation began only at the end of the 15th century, upon the arrival of the Jewish and Muslim refugees from Spain.

The Capture of Ceuta and Arzila

After João I of Portugal had concluded a peace treaty with Castile in 1411, ensuring the stability of his rule, he tried his luck in the African Maghreb. In 1415, the Portuguese captured Ceuta, the port opposite Gibraltar, as a bridgehead for further conquests, thereby ushering in a new era in the history of Morocco and Portugal. That era ended in the middle of the 16th century with the complete discomfiture of Portugal and the evacuation of all the cities held by her, except three: Ceuta and Tangier in the north, and Mazagan in the south.[1]

Present-day Portuguese scholars differ as to the significance of these conquests for their country: some approve and others disapprove of them. At the same time, they try to discover the motives of that bold endeavour of a small, poor nation, which at the beginning of the conquests numbered not more than a million and which presumed to impose its sway on a populous country with a culture not lower than its own and rich in natural resources. They regard the capture of Ceuta as inspired by the vision of a metropolis of trade with India. Some credit João I's son, Dom Henrique, who took up residence in the Maghreb, with the idea of sailing along the Atlantic coast to map out a trade route to the Far East not blocked

[1] In the 13th century, the European powers tried to penetrate into that region; comp. Beaumier, *Roudh*, pp. 566f.; Brunschvig, *Berbérie* I, p. 49. See also the interesting paper read by Louis Jadin, L'Afrique et Rome depuis l'époque des découvertes jusqu'au XVIIe siècle, at the XIIe Congrès International des Sciences Historiques in Vienna 1965, *Rapports* II, pp. 33-69; esp. pp. 33, 39-41.

by intervening Muslim territories. Those negating the importance of Portuguese Ceuta point out that it is vouchsafed only a few lines in Leo Africanus's account, while many pages are devoted to Fez.[1]

Ceuta was considered a penal colony. The Portuguese Royal Archives contain receipts for payments, in money and goods, of the special tax for the maintenance of ironsmiths in Ceuta, who presumably manufactured weapons, and for the maintenance of the fleet at Tangier. These documents itemize the imposts collected in the thirties of the 15th century from the Jews in the almuxarifado (collection district) of Guarda and from the people of Syntra (Cintra), Vallada, Muja, Lisbon, Setubal and Coimbra.[2] They permit the conclusion that the maintenance of the bridgehead on the Moroccan coast was a burden on Portugal, especially when the advance of the invading army was stopped and there were setbacks and failures (such as the expedition against Tangier in 1437).

The second stage of the invasion began at the end of the reign of Alfonso V, surnamed the African (1438-1481), after a long preparatory period, when circumstances were favourable thanks to the confusion following the fall of the Merinids. After the capture of Arzila (1471),[3] Alfonso changed the title "King of Portugal and the (European) Maghreb"[4] to "King of Portugal and of the Maghrebs, this side and the other of the sea in Africa."[5] In the same year, he occupied Tangier and began to move southward along the Atlantic coast, in which Portugal had long been interested. The local *qā'ids* (commanders) recognised Portuguese suzerainty over Azemmur (1486) and Safi (1488). In 1505, the conquerors established the fortress of Agadir.[6] Three years later, Safi was occupied and became an important base; Azemmur was seized in 1513. The Portuguese now established other fortresses along the coast—in Mazagan and (Old) Mogador—and made themselves masters of the important Moroc-

---

[1] The discussion of this point is summed up by Lopes in *Historia*, pp. 396-421, and *Expansão*, pp. 131-142. See also Terrasse, *Histoire* II, pp. 112ff.; Julien, *Histoire* II, pp. 195f.; Leo Africanus, *Description*, p. 267.

[2] Azevedo, *Documentos* I, doc. 13, pp. 26 and 28-33; doc. 17, p. 41 (Tangier); doc. 131, pp. 163-166; doc. 132, p. 169; doc. 94, pp. 556 and 558; Lopes, *Expansão*, p. 141.

[3] In Arabic: Azīlī (Ibn Ḥawqal, 79), later also Aṣīla.

[4] Rey de Portugall e de Algarve; comp. Azevedo, *Documentos* I, doc. 13, p. 18; *ibid.*, doc. 95, p. 560.

[5] Rei de Portugal e dos Algarves, daquém e dalém mar em África; comp. Lopes, *Historia* III, p. 450; *Expansão*, p.153. In Arabic his title is *sulṭān Burtkāl wa-l-Gharbayn*, i.e. ruler of Portugal and the two Maghrebs; comp. *ABP* I, p. 83. See also Fernandes, *Description*, p. 30.

[6] In Portuguese sources: Santa Cruz de Aguer (du Cap de Gué).

can ports. The Waṭṭásids retained only two outlets to the sea, Salé and Bādis-Velez.[1]

In the areas they began to penetrate, the Portuguese found Jewish communities. According to Abraham Zacuto, what led to the capture of Ceuta (1415) was that the townspeople had readily received fugitive *conversos* from Castile and thus aroused the anger of João I.[2] This motive for the invasion is quite unlikely and is not mentioned by any Christian source. However, we should not therefore doubt the very existence of a Jewish population in the city. In fact, part of it may have been descendants of forced converts to Islam of the generation of Joseph ben Yehuda ibn ʿAqnīn.[3]

Don Isaac Abarbanel, in a letter to Yeḥiel of Pisa, a wealthy Italian Jew, reports that about 250 Jews were taken prisoner after the capture of Arzila and transferred to Portugal. Most of them were redeemed through the efforts of Don Isaac and a committee set up for the purpose. Here are some extracts from that letter:

"Lo, our lord the King (Alfonso V)—may God prolong his reign, stood and measured the earth, a great many people; he set up the standard for the nations ... and he passed over to the land of Africa to inherit habitations not his, and he encamped there against the city of Arzila, a royal city, full of people ... and the people went up to the city ... and they took the city ... afterward he took him the city of Tangier. And whereas the unhappy Jewish people resident in Arzila were scattered and separated within the city, one here and one there ... and all the persons departing from the city in captivity, young and old, daughters of Zion and men of the children of Israel, were two hundred and fifty. And when we saw the dear children of Zion ... we, individual members of the community, agreed to proclaim liberty to the captives and the opening of the prison to them that were bound and to give the ransom of their lives from our silver and our gold, be it little or be it much.

And I, your servant, and the other leaders, juster and better men than I am, appointed from the congregation twelve officers, like the number of the tribes of Israel, to perform the charitable act of bringing out the prisoners from prison ... and for as much money as they were worth and

---

[1] The Portuguese conquests are described in *ABP* I, pp. VII-XVI, Lopes, *Expansão*, pp. 154-163, also *idem*, *Historia de Arzila*, Coimbra 1924.

[2] *Juchassin* ed. Filipowski, pp. 225b and 226a (the date is misprinted as (5)125/1365 for (5)175/1415). For the whole problem of Jewish participation in the Portuguese conquest see Corcos, *Sefunot*, 10 (1966), pp. 58-60.

[3] See above, pp. 356ff. About the Jewish population in later times see Corcos, *op. cit.*, p. 74 and n. 93.

within a few days, at most ten, we redeemed one hundred and fifty persons, and here in this city and in the other cities ... two hundred and twenty persons; and their redemption cost ten thousand doubloons.[1]

We do not know whether any Jews remained in Arzila after the conquest or whether those we find there in the days of Manuel and João III were new settlers. The capture of Arzila and Tangier was followed by a thirty years' lull in military operations, when the Portuguese increased their influence in the coastal region by political means. The local *qā'ids* accepted Portuguese patronage, but retained their independent status *vis-à-vis* the local population. Those were the days of the 1492 and 1497 expulsions, and many of the growing mass of refugees seem to have settled in the Atlantic coast region. In the early 16th century, military operations resumed with all their attendant features: the establishment of garrisons, the annexation of cities to the Kingdom of Portugal, the appointment of military and civil governors, the building of fortresses. We now find Jews fighting shoulder to shoulder with the Portuguese, and rushing to their aid when they were in distress. Most important of all, nearly the whole of the political negotiations between Portugal and the Maghreb devolved on them. A wealth of material on this subject is preserved in Portuguese archives and ancient writings. Its volume might give the impression of a potential field of research into the life of large groups, but in fact its importance consists in glimpses of the daily life of a few families residing in the seaports near the border and maintaining varied relations with the royal courts of Portugal and Morocco, the *shurafā'* and the *qā'ids*, and the Jewish, Muslim and Christian local populations. Those small communities were centres for the redemption of captives and two-way trading in various commodities, both material and spiritual, including the passing of political information and military intelligence, definitely smacking of espionage in which Jews engaged like other inhabitants of the country. Those documents also permit certain conclusions as to life in the interior of Morocco not revealed by other sources.[2]

The refugees who came to Africa were not prominent persons—court dignitaries, wealthy people and great religious scholars—but members of the middle classes: merchants, agents and craftsmen, especially iron-

---

[1] *Otzar Nehmad* 2 (1857), pp. 66f.

[2] For the redemption of Christian captives by Jews see *ABP* II, pp. 319, 323 and 328. For insinuations or direct accusations of espionage see, e.g. *ABP* I, pp. 466, 512 and 681; II, pp. 134, 344f. and 516f.; III, pp. 46-49, 282, 313-315 and 406-408; IV, pp. 253f.; V, p. 113 n. 2; *ABE* I, pp. 267-270; *ABA* II, p. 8.

workers and weaponsmiths. The latter were very badly needed by the Portuguese, which is why, when they fled from Spain to Portugal in 1492, they were charged only half the tax fixed for permission to enter.[1] Later, when tension between Portugal on the one hand and the king of Fez and the Saʿdite *ṣherīf* on the other increased, there were complaints of arms smuggling into the Maghreb and of *converso* armourers moving to Marrakesh.[2] These developments naturally displeased the Christians. During the period under review, many advantages awaited those who settled in the ports under Portuguese protectorate. For one thing, they found Jewish communities there, though not large ones. Moreover, their knowledge of the Spanish and Portuguese languages and national customs, as well as their connections with the authorities of their former countries of residence, helped them to become useful middlemen in the emergent relations between the conquerors and the local population. Obviously, the Portuguese did not at first examine who had been forcibly baptized and since returned to Judaism. It was only towards the end of their rule, when the Inquisition had been established in Portugal, that they remembered this point.[3]

In view of certain peculiar features of the history of the Jews in the cities of the region, it seems appropriate to deal specially with these and the prominent families living in them.

ASFĪ—SAFI

According to Leo Africanus, who visited the city in 1500, it had about 100 Jewish families. It was ruled by a Berber *qāʾid* under Portuguese suzerainty. Meanwhile, intrigue and dissension were rife among the local sheykhs, and there were signs of rebellion against the king of Portugal.[4] We know, moreover, of a plot hatched by the *qāʾid* with the Spaniards through the intermediary of a Jew. Reaction was swift: the *qāʾid* and his Jewish emissary were murdered, and the Portuguese navy and army moved against the city and occupied it (1508).[5]

---

[1] Kayserling, *Geschichte*, pp. 112f., also 59f.; Baer, *Spain* II, p. 511 n. 13. Reubeni has much to say about *conversos* skilled in the use of firearms; *MJC* II, pp. 181 and 199, also 178 and 208f.

[2] *Converso* armourers from Spain went to Morocco; *e.g.*, *ABP* III, pp. 220-222, and see below, pp. 396, 398 and nn. 243, 251. So did Muslim refugees, Terrasse, *Histoire* II, p. 132.

[3] See below, pp. 436ff.

[4] Leo Africanus, *Description*, pp. 117-121; and comp. *ABP* II, pp. 115ff.

[5] Fernandes, *Description*, p. 37. The whole Muslim population seems to have been

On that occasion, King Manuel promised the Jews of the city that he would never expel them or force them to become Christians. If a Jew should voluntarily agree to embrace Christianity, he would be allowed to live as a Jew until his baptism: and if the interests of the king should require the evacuation of the Jews, they would be given two years to prepare their departure and might take all their property with them. Such promises were probably also made in other places. We shall later see that they were not kept in the case of Safi, whereas the king and the local governor took care of the Jews and their property upon the evacuation from Azemmour and even upon the expulsion from Arzila.[1]

The archives reveal that relations between the Jews and the local Portuguese administration in Safi were at first satisfactory. The numerous documents include no complaint like that lodged in 1509 by the Safi Muslims against the Governor Diogo de Azambuja and his soldiers, concerning lawless conduct towards their womenfolk.[2] Worthy of note is a refugee family named Ben Zamiro, which played a dominant role in the life of the city. One of its members, Abraham, was appointed town rabbi by the king. At the end of 1510, Safi was under siege. According to a report sent to the king, one sector of the city wall was entrusted to the Jews under the command of the brothers Isaac and Ismael, of the Ben Zamiro family. Another source reports that the two brothers had been in Azemmour at the time and, on learning that the governor of Safi, Nuno Fernandes de Ataide, was hard pressed, decided to come to his aid; they equipped two frigates, enlisted a crew of two hundred Jews and entered Safi harbour one night, unnoticed by the besiegers. The Jews were joyfully received by the commander and the population. At daybreak, they attacked the enemy, inflicting heavy losses, and then returned to the city in high spirits and excellent order. The Moors, seeing the city so well defended, raised the siege.[3] It should be noted that a similar episode is reported to have occurred about half a century later. A Jew of Azemmour, Samuel Valenciano, organized assistance for Safi, then besieged by the Arabs. Without entering into a critical analysis of these sources, it cannot be doubted that they are reliable testimony of good relations between the Jews and the Portuguese authorities.[4]

---

rebelliously disposed towards the Portuguese; comp. *ABP* I, pp. 179-89 (177-8), also pp. 74-5 and 83-4. Corcos, *Sefunot* 10 (1966), pp. 63-69, discusses Portuguese-Jewish relations in Asfi and Azemmour.

[1] *ABP* I, pp. 174 and 271.

[2] *Ibid.*, pp. 177 (French)/189 (Arabic).

[3] Mendoca, *Iornada*, p. 90; Góis, *Crónica* III, p. 46 (= Ricard, *Portugais*, p. 62).

[4] Comp. *ABP* I, p. 273 n. 5.

Other records show that the Jewish community made a cash contribution to the cost of maintaining the city wall and that the amount was paid through Abraham ben Zamiro, the government-appointed rabbi of Safi. The Jews also supplied manpower for repairs and for cleaning the trench encircling the wall.[1]

Together with R. Abraham, the documents of 1512/13 mention Mūsa Dardeiro, interpreter to the governor. Ataide and another high official praise him in their letters to the king, representing him as a friend and servant of the throne. As usual, he engaged also in political mediation, conducting talks with the Arabs. He was assassinated in 1512, and Abraham Zamiro says in one of his letters that Dardeiro paid with his life for his loyalty to Portugal. An investigation revealed that Yaḥyā Taʿfūft, the *qāʾid* of Safi, and other Muslim notables had killed him because he reported their anti-Christian machinations to the governor.[2]

Relations with Yaḥyā Taʿfūft, the local Muslim leader, ostensibly a supporter of Portuguese rule, remained strained. Yaḥyā regarded the Jews as his rivals for the king's favour and repeatedly charged that they acted as interpreters for his enemies and that the latter met at the houses of the Jews. The governor suggested punishing the Jews to placate Yaḥyā.[3] Yaḥyā's spiteful reference to Jews who were of no benefit to the city seems to have prompted Manuel to order the expulsion of certain persons; that he gave such an order is apparent from a letter of the governor of Safi to the king of the beginning of 1519, reporting its execution. By the time the letter was written, thirty families had left in two caravans; others were due to follow soon, and thus the number of the Jews was to be reduced in accordance with the order.[4]

We have already noted (p. 412,) that Jacob Rute was appointed interpreter in Safi in 1523 and that Abraham Rut(e) of Asfi was in Portugal in 1527 and there strove to secure his appointment to high office. In 1538 and 1541, Joseph Levi was the interpreter in Safi, and the governor suggested allocating him a fixed salary in recognition of his faithful service and the devotion of his father, who had served the governor of Agadir and been put to death by the Saʿdi *sherif* in Sūs.[5]

---

[1] *ABP* I, pp. 271-273, 300 and n. 1; II, p. 47.

[2] Comp. *ABP*, index, *s.v.*

[3] *Ibid.*, II, pp. 100/103, 115f., 134 and 161-163.

[4] *Ibid.*, pp. 222-224.

[5] *Ibid.*, III, pp. 140 and 419f.; comp. also below, p. 429 n. 3. The events in Safi are reviewed in Lopez, *Historia* III, pp. 471-486. Massignon, *Maroc*, p. 266, gives a list of the independent *qāʿids* under the last Waṭṭāsids.

Azemmour

This city and its vicinity also had various strata of Jewish inhabitants: old settlers, refugees and "neo-Christians," before its capture by the Duke Dom Jaime Bragance on the 3rd September, 1513.[1] Azemmour fell to him without bloodshed through the help tendered to him by the Jews. Leo Africanus charges the Jews with treason for opening the gates to the duke after being promised that they would not be harmed.[2] But a Portuguese source, apparently trying to minimize the part of the Jews, merely says that Jacob ben Adibe reported the situation in Azemmour: the Moors were in confusion and intended to abandon the city.[3] On entering Azemmour, the duke, in accordance with his promise, instructed one of his high officials, the *corregedôr*,[4] to see to the safety of the Jews, and the latter immediately directed the Portuguese to the city's grain stores.[5] The king granted the Jews various privileges—*inter alia*, that they would have to pay no more than one oka [6] per house, *i.e.* family, in tax—and appointed Joseph Adibe chief rabbi of the community.[7] The Jews lived in a separate quarter, and the Muslim refugees who wished to return to the city stipulated that they should be housed next to the Jews, also in a separate quarter; this quarter was outside the *qaṣba*, and its inhabitants asked to be allotted room inside, so that they might seek shelter there in an emergency. Here, too, the Jews contributed to the financing of various defence items, such as the digging of a trench, and to the construction of a bridge.[8]

Later, King Manuel forbade the settlement of *conversos* in Azemmour, but the governor of the city remonstrated. The ban does not seem to have always been strictly enforced, for in 1537 a complaint was made against neo-Christians, both Jews and Muslims, who had married local girls and were practising their former religions.[9]

---

[1] Old settlers: *ABP* III, pp. 83f. Reubeni, *JMC* II, p. 199, tells of Jews from Hymyir who came to Portugal. He undoubtedly means Jews living among the Awlād ʿAmrān, who were encamped in the region; *ABP* II, p. 31. Abraham b. Zamiro conducted negotiations with them; *ibid.*, p. 325, also I, p. 85 n. 2, and Massignon, *Maroc*, p. 70. Neo-Christians: *ABP* I, pp. 453 and 462.

[2] *Description*, pp. 125-127.

[3] Góis, *Chronica* III, p. 167 (= Richard, *Portugais*, p. 109f.); *ABP* I, pp. 400-408.

[4] Mayor, municipal judge, tax commissioner.

[5] *ABP* I, pp. 411/428f.

[6] A silver coin of 3.05 gr. weight; comp. Massignon, *Maroc*, p. 103.

[7] *ABP* I, p. 175 n. 1.

[8] *Ibid.*, pp. 475f.; II, pp. 40, 248 and 344f.

[9] See below, p. 437.

During Manuel's reign, the Adibe family played a very important role in Azemmour. In Arabic documents, the name appears in the form al-Dhīb, but the family came from Spain and one of its members had been persecuted by the Inquisition.[1] As mentioned, Joseph Adibe was chief rabbi; he also carried out political assignments in the negotiations between the King of Portugal and the *qā'ids*.[2] Yaḥyā Adibe was the official translator in Azemmour, with a fixed annual salary, and when he was in Lisbon in 1514, the king ordered a robe of honour like that worn by the *qā'id* of Azemmour to be delivered to him. In 1530, he was in Fez, where he had contacts with the king's goldsmith, a Jewish *converso* judging by his name, who told him about the mood prevailing at court with regard to peace. About the same time, he conducted armistice talks with the *qā'id* of Salé.[3]

Other members of the family, Jacob and Moses, were engaged in commerce, the collection of customs duty on behalf of the authorities and various other activities. Their status aroused envy, and someone complained to King João III (1521-1557) that the governor of Azemmur listened only to the advice of the Adibes. The king seems to have heeded this complaint: the family's prestige waned, and only Yaḥyā retained his position.[4] In the second quarter of the century, members of the Ben Zamiro family, which until then was mainly active in Safi, are frequently heard of in Azemmour.

There may be a connection between the decline of the Adibe family and the serious complaints voiced to the king by the physician Rodrigo, a neo-Christian settled in Azemmour, in letters of the years 1527 and 1528. Jewish suppliers, whom he does not mention by name, are said by him to be exploiting their concession to flay the poorer residents. He points out the wrong done to clerks and hired labourers: they lose on the sale of goods given them in lieu of wages and have to pay heavily for the commodities they need. In his opinion, the suppliers should not be allowed a profit exceeding one third of the value of the goods. Matters had improved when Abraham ben Zamiro was awarded the supply contract, but when the former contractors won it again, the people were seized with despair. Rodrigo thought that the governor of the city was to blame for the situa-

---

1 *ABP* II, pp. 31 and 90. The family as a whole, without first names, is mentioned many times; comp. *ABP*, Index, *s.v.*; Baer, *Spain* II, p. 326: Ben Adube; the *converso* Moses *ABP* V, pp. 120 n. 3 and 520.

2 *ABP* II, pp. 90-92.

3 *ABP* I, pp. 609 and n. 1, and n. 1; II, pp. 59f., 490f. and 531-533.

4 Ibid., II, p. 321 n. 1, comp. also I, 508f., and II, pp. 313/317.

tion. The *qā'ids*, too, complained against the governor; he had insulted a Jew in their service, and they threatened that if he continued to treat their emissaries in this way they would allow no one to enter Azemmour.[1]

About that time, a neo-Christian, that is to say, a Jew, arrived in Azemmour whose wife and children were still in Beja in Portugal. He had originally wished to settle in Safi, but had not been permitted to do so because he was suspected of intending to move to the Muslim part of the country. When the governor of Azemmour imposed a fine on him which he was unable to pay, the local neo-Christians, including the physician Rodrigo, contributed to its payment.[2]

In the years 1528-1530, we find Abraham ben Zamiro and Francisco Gomes as agents responsible for the payment of the soldiers stationed in Azemmour. From a statement by the governor Mascarenhas, we gather that they at first carried out their obligations, but that the payments were discontinued following Abraham's arrest in Portugal; according to the terms of the contract, only he was authorized to make them. We shall later (p. 434) discuss the identity of this Abraham ben Zamiro.[3]

In the years 1536-1539, one Jaquo Daroque is mentioned repeatedly in orders to reimburse to him expenses incurred for the upkeep of certain Moors (including the *qā'id* of the *ṣherīf*) and cash payments made to them. He was probably a person trusted by the Portuguese with whom official visitors were quartered and who was supposed to keep an eye on their movements.[4]

In 1541, the Portuguese were faced with the necessity of evacuating Azemmour owing to pressure by the troops of the Sa'di *sherīf*, whose sphere of influence extended up to that city. King João III, wishing the local Jews to be removed to Arzila unscathed, ordered Leite and Mascarenhas, governors of the two cities, to make appropriate arrangements. The order was subsequently readdressed to the new governor of Azemmour, Fernando de Noronha, who was to take the Jews to al-'Arā'ish (Larache), Arzila, Tangier or Ceuta. If the evacuees were without means of subsistence, the governor was to provide for them. Moreover, he was to select two Jewish notables to assist him in evaluating immovable property, for

---

[1] *ABP* II, pp. 418-428. Our Rodrigo is probably identical with Mestre Rodrigo, the court physician of João II and Manuel I; but see *ibid.*, p. 420 n. 1.

[2] *Ibid.*, p. 423 and n. 2.

[3] *ABP* II, pp. 491-494 and 536-542; below, 434-5. Gomes also seems to have been a Jew or a *converso*; comp. about him *ibid.* II, p. 330 n. 1.

[4] *Ibid.* III, pp. 41, 133, 135 and 207.

which receipts were to be given. The Jews were to send a representative to the royal court in Lisbon to settle their debts, whereupon the receipts for their property would come into force and they would receive compensation for the latter. The evacuees all left for Tangier in four vessels.[1]

During the negotiations between the Portuguese and the Saʿdi *sherīf*, an important and dangerous mission was entrusted to some Azemmour Jews. They were to explore the situation, watch developments and movements in the *sherīf's* army and carry letters. One of them, Breguis, was extradited to the *sherīf* and paid with his life for his loyalty to the Portuguese.[2]

Ṭit-Mazagan

South of Azemmour, in the Duqāla region, were the twin port cities of Ṭiṭ and Mazagan. Near the latter, the Portuguese built a powerful fortress, which they held even after the evacuation of Safi and Azemmour. In 1502, the inhabitants of the area complained to the king of Portugal about his agent in Mazagan, who had made himself obnoxious to Muslims, Jews and Christians alike.[3] In view of the delicate position of Ṭiṭ, the king of Fez appointed a Jew his representative in the city, and a Christian his treasurer and tax-collector. It was one of the last points held by the Waṭṭāsids, who, when it fell to the Portuguese, evacuated the Muslim population and resettled it near Fez.[4] On that occasion, the Jews presumably moved to neighbouring Mazagan. In 1527, Abraham ben Zamiro was appointed official interpreter in the latter locality, but he preferred to reside in Azemmour.[5]

The Jews of Mazagan still appear in a document of 1541. In 1542, the Christian civil population of that city was evacuated to Portugal. At the same time, the king approved measures taken by the governor with regard to the Jewish merchants, but unfortunately the document in question does not permit us to tell what they were.[6]

---

[1] *Ibid.* III, pp. 352-355 and 516f.

[2] A vivid description of those dangerous activities is given *ibid.*, pp. 313-315 and 406-408. On Breguis see *ibid.*, pp. 240, 408-411, 440-442 and 448-450. For the general situation in Azemmour comp. Lopes, *Historia* IV, pp. 82-84 and 88; *idem*, *Expansão*, p. 194 and passim.

[3] *APB* I, pp. 74f. and 86. The site of Ṭiṭ: *G. B. Maroc*, p. 177.

[4] Leo Africanus, *Description*, p. 121.

[5] *ABP* IV, p. 106 n. 2. See also below, p. 435 n. 1.

[6] *Ibid.* III, p. 337; IV, pp. 94f.

Tetouan, Arzila and Other Northern Cities

Portuguese sources are scant of material concerning the Jews in that northern portion of Morocco which 400 years later (1912) came under Spanish protectorate. The affairs of Tetouan Jewry are not directly referred to at all, although that city undoubtedly had a Jewish community by 1530, when Ḥayyim Bibas was appointed rabbi there.[1] Something may indeed be gathered from the letters of priests and monks sent to the region to redeem Christian captives and who made propaganda among the Jews; they did so with the permission of the Muslim rulers, who were amused by the wrangles between Jews and Christians. One of the church emissaries reports in detail his disputations at the synagogue of Tetouan, where he saw little children learning to read. Other letters deal with missionary activities among the Jews of Ceuta.[2]

Certain parts of the region were inhabited by Castilians—veteran Christians—who engaged in pig-raising and robbery. Vargas, the representative of the king of Portugal in Fez, advised the king to forbid neo-Christians and Castilians to raise pigs, which was distasteful to the local population. Of the Castilians he says that they are robbers and murderers, responsible for the killing of a Jew and a Moor travelling from Arzila to Qṣar al-Kabīr and the recent killing of a wealthy Jew of Chechaouen, an agent of Mulay Muḥammad ben Rashīd, and his Moorish companion;[3] The Jews of Chechaouen at the end of the preceding century were mentioned above in connection with the story of Judah Ḥayyāṭ.[4]

Meanwhile, the position of the Portuguese in Africa weakened steadily. In 1541, it was still possible to consider the removal of the Jews of Azemmour to Arzila, while early in 1542 João III ordered the Jews of Arzila to be expelled directly to Fez. Mascarenhas, the governor of the city, asked permission to postpone the execution of the order on the grounds that the inhabitants owed much money to the Jews, as a result of the recent bad times, and that the expulsion of the Jews would force the latter to collect the debts at once, thus causing great damage to the debtors. If the king agreed to a two-year postponement, as the Jews had been promised, or if they might remain at least until the next harvest, the delay would enable the people to pay their debts without difficulty.

Vargas in Fez learnt of the proposed expulsion of the Jews and apprised

---

[1] Toledano, *Ner*, p. 89.
[2] *ABP* IV, pp. 282f. and 379f.
[3] *Ibid.* III, pp. 281f. and 291-293.
[4] See above, p. 406.

the king of a rumour circulating in this connection: the Portuguese were expelling the Jews because they intended to pull out of Arzila and Tangier; this news had a most depressing effect on Jacob Rute. At the end of the year, Mascarenhas used a different argument to persuade João to modify the decree for the expulsion, which apparently had been postponed until after the harvest in accordance with his request. Morocco was in a state of anarchy, and it was imperative for at least four or five wealthy Jewish families to remain in Arzila to report what was going on in the country. The Jews were thus necessary for Portuguese intelligence.[1]

The last reference to Jews in the region dates from 1547. As a result of war propaganda, the security situation had deteriorated and nomads had risen against the government. In the valley of the Verga (Ouergha) river, which descends from the Rif Mountains and flows into the Sebou, a caravan from Fez was attacked and robbed, and the Jewish travellers were killed.[2]

The Southern Sector of the Coast

In the three-cornered struggle for control of Morocco, particular importance attached to the southern sector of the coast and its hinterland because it was here that the Saʿdī rise to power began. The opposition of the *shurafāʾ* to Portuguese control of the coastal region increased steadily, and after broadening their base in the Darʿa Valley, they took hold of the Sūs Valley. Their purpose was twofold: to drive out the hated Portuguese and to destroy the remaining power of their Waṭṭāsid rivals. Their efficient tools were the marabouts, heads of fanatical religious orders, whose influence on the populace was growing. Their advance along the Sūs Valley to the approaches of the Atlantic coast (1511-1517), and the capture of Marrakesh (1523), brought them into direct contact with the Portuguese, who held all the ports from which short and convenient routes lay to *shurafāʾ*-occupied territory. The *shurafāʾ* were as yet too weak to attack the Portuguese army directly, and Aḥmad al-Aʿraj, a brother of the *sherīf* Muḥammad al-Shaykh al-Mahdī, recognised the suzerainty of João III when proclaiming himself ruler of Marrakesh (1525).

This sector of the coast likewise had an old-established Jewish popula-

---

[1] *ABP* III, pp. 352-355; IV, pp. 19, 25f. and 120.

[2] *Ibid.*, p. 196.

tion. Though non-Jewish sources usually mention only individual Jews, these obviously had not come there by chance. Leo Africanus reports a conversation he had with an old Jew in Massa, at the outlet of the Sūs into the Ocean, concerning the frequency of whale carcasses on the local beach. That man and the family he surely had can hardly have been the only Jews in the area.[1] In fact, in an Arabic memorandum dated 1510, the people of Massa complain to King Manuel, under whose protectorate they have been since 1496, that the servants of a Portuguese agent in Azemmour, J. Lopes, seized a Jewish notable proceeding with a Muslim on a business trip to one of the nomad tribes. They denounce a Jew named Ibn Zamīr—*i.e.*, a member of the Zamiro family—who has sworn that the Jew of Massa will not go free. In the end, the prisoner was ransomed with a cash payment and "a couple of large Jewish books". That merchant of Massa, again, may be presumed to have had business partners and relatives in the city. We have to do here with a clash between refugees (Ibn Zamīr) and veteran residents induced by business rivalry.[2]

North of Massa, on a towering cliff overlooking the mouth of the Sūs river, the Portuguese built the famous fortress of Agadir. We find some Jews here, such as a physician—described as ignorant—who was a "neo-Christian", *i.e.*, a *converso*; a certain incompetent interpreter was probably also a Jew.[3] Besides, documents mention Jews of unspecified social status. Jews sometimes engaged in the import of goods from overseas which according to papal bulls must not be brought into Moorish lands lest the latter's war potential be increased. In view of the importance of the region, it is not surprising that the Portuguese should have been interested in collecting information on current events. For that purpose, and for the maintenance of contact with the rival rulers, the Waṭṭāsids and the *shurafā'*, they conveniently used Jews. As early as 1514, Isaac ben Zamiro of Safi negotiated with the governor of Marrakesh for the establishment of a Portuguese protectorate.[4] On another occasion, the governor of Safi sent a Muslim to gather information among the Jews of Marrakesh, and a Jew who arrived in Azemmour from Marrakesh brought letters from various prisoners.[5]

A not inconsiderable number of refugees were living in Marrakesh at that time. Among them was a physician, who in 1512 was removed from

---

[1] Leo Africanus, *Description*, p. 88.
[2] *ABP* I, pp. 233-239; Lopes, *Historia* III, pp. 542 and 544.
[3] *ABP* I, pp. 471, 475 and 563.
[4] *Ibid.*, pp. 572f., 642-646 and 688.
[5] *Ibid.* III, p. 137.

some position he held.[1] *Converso* experts in the weapon and metal industry also flocked to Marrakesh, so that a Christian resident of Safi, worried about the safety of the Portuguese, complains that the Jews not only make weapons, but teach the Muslims to make them.[2]

Intelligence work was rather dangerous. A Jew named Meir Levi was an intelligence agent of the governor of Agadir. He was helped by relatives who lived in Marrakesh and occasionally went to Taroudant, then the residence of the *sherīf* Muhammad al-Shaykh. It is not to be assumed that he moved about the area without the help of local Jews. He was eventually captured and was executed in Sūs by order of the *sherīf*.[3]

Jews were not lacking among the supporters of the *shurafā'*. Joseph ha-Kohen, the author of *'Emeq ha-Bakha* (The Vale of Tears) and *Dibrey ha-Yāmīm* (Chronicles), has heard of the *shurafā'* Aḥmad al-A'raj and Muḥammad al-Mahdi; he notes that a Jew foretold the *sherīf* Muhammad the greatness of the dynasty founded by him, and that Muḥammad built Taroudant, *i.e.*, Sūs.[4]

When in 1541 Muhammad al-Mahdī reduced the fortress of Agadir by cannon fire from a very favourable strategic position, the Jews—according to Portuguese documents—caused the death of many Christians in Agadir by treason.[5] The *sherīf*'s victory marked a decisive turn of events, heralding the retreat of the Portuguese, just as the capture of Arzila seventy years earlier had opened up the Atlantic coast to them; King João resolved to evacuate all the southern ports, except well-fortified Mazagan. Other Portuguese documents indicate that these developments perturbed the Portuguese-Jewish traders in Marrakesh; they began to remove their property from the city and requested a pledge from the *sherīf* that they would be allowed to join the Christians should an emergency arise.[6]

The evacuation of the coastal cities enormously enhanced the prestige of the Sa'dīs, and Muhammad al-Mahdī was able to occupy Fez and expel the Waṭṭāsi king (1549). During the fighting, many Jews fled to Meknes, already in the hands of the *sherīf*, and the latter treated them well; he even lightened their tax burden. In 1554, Muhammad al-Mahdī

---

[1] *Ibid.* I, pp. 337 and 344; II, pp. 147f.

[2] *Ibid.* III, pp. 220-222.

[3] *Ibid.*, pp. 417-422. See also above, p. 421.

[4] *Dibrey ha-Yāmīm*, Amsterdam 5493/1733, p. 134b; cf. Gedalya b. Yahya, *Shalshelet* p. 96a.

[5] *ABP* III, p. 360; Cenival, *Chronique de Santa Cruz*, pp. 70 n. 2 and 156 n. 1. Lopes, *Historia* IV, p. 126; *idem, Expansão*, pp. 197f. and 207f.

[6] *ABP* III, pp. 406-409.

became ruler of all Morocco, but his rule lasted only three years; he was murdered by a Turkish officer who had infiltrated his bodyguard, which consisted of Turkish mercenaries, and had won his confidence.[1] According to an Arab source, Muhammad's son avenged his father with the help of a Jew. When the encirclement of the Turks in Taroudant, who were under the command of the *sherīf*'s assassin, brought no results, the Jewish supplier of that garrison advised Mulay ʿAbd Allah, the *sherīf*'s son and heir, to retreat into the mountains and spread the rumour that he and his troops were going to Fez. The Turks, on the other hand, were advised by the Jew to abandon Taroudant, where they were always in danger of encirclement, and to withdraw *via* Sijilmāsa to Tlemcen, where a large Turkish force was standing. The plan was adopted and the Turkish troops left. After a day, ʿAbd Allah attacked them and wiped them out, although they fought valiantly and inflicted heavy losses upon the *sherīf*'s army.[2]

This last stage of the war of the B. Waṭṭās and their Turkish auxiliaries against the Saʿdī *shurafāʾ* is the subject of a detailed account, different from that cited above, in the *Dibrey ha-Yāmīm* (Chronicle) of the Ibn Danān family, which is the principal Jewish source on the rule of the *shurafāʾ* of the Saʿdī and Filālī dynasties.[3] Here is the account, partly *verbatim* and partly summarized:[4]

In Kislev, 5214 (end of 1553), the *sherīf* Muhammad al-Shaykh learnt that Bū Ḥasūn had called the Turks from Algiers to his aid and was marching against Fez. In the first battle, the *sherīf* was defeated, but in the second, the Turks were routed by the fire of Muley ʿAbd Allah's guns. However, the Christian gunners and mercenaries, betraying their master, went over to the Turks. This forced the *sherīf* to abandon the fight, leaving guns, ammunition, equipment and a large quantity of food. He escaped to Marrakesh, and Bū Ḥasūn entered Fez in 5214 (1554) with his Turkish auxiliaries. Turks and local bandits penetrated from the Muslim *mellāḥ* into the Jewish, looting, killing eleven persons, and driving many from their houses. "And the Lord raised up a saviour for Israel, a Jew from al-Jazāʾir (Algiers) who was nagīd of al-Jazāʾir, and the Lord

---

[1] Gedalia b. Yahya, *Shalshelet ha-Qabbala*, p. 96a; *ABE* I, pp. 133-136, 150-164 and 267-270; Terrasse, *Histoire* II, pp. 165-172.

[2] Colin, *Chronique*, pp. 31-36; comp. Fagnan, *Extraits*, pp. 385-387.

[3] All the later Jewish chronicles rely on this one, which is based on contemporary accounts.

[4] I am indebted to Professor G. Vajda for a photocopy of a MS. of this chronicle, of which he has published a French translation under the title: *Un Recueil de textes historiques judéo-marocains*, Paris 1951.

rewarded his deeds by the grant of an *amān* (*i.e.* letter of safety) for the Jews of Fez from the Turkish sultan, whose name is Mulay Muhammad Sāliḥ. And when we saw the crowd enter the *mellāḥ*, the chronicler continues, we informed the said Algerian Jew; he was at the gate of the *mellāḥ*, which was closed. He informed the *qā'id* and the sultan, and they entered the *mellāḥ* and drove out all those who had penetrated into it, killing many of them, and thus saved the people from pillage and death. Israel's God rescued us by a saviour, whose name is Khalfūn al-Gharbi. Afterwards we paid the Turkish sultan 20,000 Sūsi dinars as an advance payment. The Turks left the city after thirty-nine days, and Bū Ḥasūn remained in the city. His son was the vizier in Meknes. And in the year 5214 (1554), Saul ben Shem Tob ibn Ramūkh was sheykh (of the Jews)." Eventually—during the same year—the *sherīf* Muhammad defeated his enemies and entered Fez. Bū Ḥasūn was killed and his body desecrated. The Jews paid Mulay Muhammad 20,000 dinars, after paying the same amount in that year to the Turks and 22,000 dinars to Bū Ḥasūn. They also gave Muhammad al-Shaykh 4,000 pieces of soap; in addition, all Jews paid individual amounts. May God have mercy upon those who remained! Furthermore, Mulay Muhammad demanded from the Jews 10,000 ṣaḥfa [1] of grain, and they compounded with him for 42,000 Sūs dinars. In 5218 (1558), in the month of Shebat, an epidemic broke out in Old Fez, and on the 1st of Adar, the scourge reached the *mellāḥ*. In the same year, Mulay Muhammad died on the way to Sūs. The Turks murdered him treacherously in his tent; although his whole army was with him, no one lifted a finger to save him. The Turks went to Sūs and remained there for a time. They robbed the Jews, raped many Jewish women and also abducted a number of Jews; then they left to return to their own country. ʿAbd Allah, Mulay Muhammad's son, and the *qā'id* Bū Kabīr, who was in charge of the defence of Marrakesh, went to war. To reduce the number of rivals for the rulership, ʿAbd Allah put to death eleven sons and grandsons of Muhammad. ʿAbd Allah, and his brothers annihilated the Turks. Although the Turks attempted to attack Fez again that year, they were defeated, and the *sherīf* ʿAbd Allah returned safely to the city.[2]

---

[1] A measure of capacity; see Dozy *s.v.*

[2] *Recueil*, pp. 11-13. This account is confirmed by Spanish sources; comp. *ABE* II, pp. 151f. See also Toledano, *Ner*, pp. 90-92; Toledano used MSS. of *Yaḥas Fes* and *Kissē Melakhim*, both of which, as stated above, draw on the Danān chronicle. *Kissē Melakhim*, MS. Sassoon, 24b, says that Mulay Muhammad was murdered "in the year (5)318 (of the Creation i.e. 1557/58 C.E.), which corresponds to the year 974 H.".

It should be noted that the Jewish source makes no mention of the story of the Jewish supplier and that it stresses the heavy taxes the Jews had to pay, in contrast to what other sources say of alleviations granted to them.

Distinguished Refugee Families

In our survey of the communities in coastal cities, we repeatedly came across the names of the Zamiro,[1] Adibe [2] and Levi families, who played important parts in their respective localities. In certain cases, the persons and the tasks undertaken and very successfully accomplished by them exceeded the narrow local framework and assumed general political significance. This was due to a variety of factors: personal ability, ramified family connections and the special social position of the Spanish and Portuguese refugees, which fitted them for liaison work between the Portuguese conquerors on the one hand and the disunited Muslim rulers on the other. Members of the same family often led in all fields: the political, economic and internal Jewish. This phenomenon was not confined to a single generation: we find it repeated, on a large scale, after approximately one hundred and two hundred years.

One of the outstanding figures of the period was Abraham b. Meir Zamiro, rabbi, physician and, in time, politician as well.

Abraham ben Zamiro originated from Spain. This is attested, *inter alia*, by three of his letters. One is in archaic but correct Castilian, with a Portuguese flavour, the two others in Portuguese betraying Castilian influence.[3] There is a tradition that the Ibn Zamiros had lived in Granada. Upon the expulsion, Abraham migrated to Malaga (1493), and in the same year we find him in Oran, where he wrote the *piyyut* "My soul, how long wilt thou be foolish?". On arrival in Morocco, the Ibn Zamiros at first settled in Fez, and from there they moved to Safi and Azemmour. According to a contemporary, Abraham Gavison, Abraham ben Zamiro

---

But 974 H. is 1566 C.E.! A similar discrepancy in synchronization was pointed out above (p. 389, n. 3). We have not to do here with errors, but with a different system of Hijra chronology, the principle of which I have not been able to discover.

[1] The most usual form of this name in both Hebrew and Arabic is Zamiro(u), but Zīmur and Zimrā (the latter influenced by the family name of David b. Zimrā) occur as well. In European sources the transliteration varies: Esmiro, Zemeron, Zimero, Zimra etc. The name may be derived from Zamora, the name of a town in Northern Spain. Comp. Baer, *Spanien* II, p. 423, also p. 304.

[2] Comp. above, pp. 422ff.

[3] *ABP* I, pp. 281-283, 357-361 and 619-629.

was surnamed *Goren Nakhon* (well-prepared threshing-floor), since he was familiar with the Bible, Maimonides' *The Guide of the Perplexed* and its commentaries and most of the Decisors, as well as with the treasures of language and poetry. He was outstanding in Arabic poetry as well.[1]

Abraham ben Zamiro was also remarkable for his courage: he did not leave Safi when it was under siege. By a decree of 1510, Manuel I appointed him chief rabbi of the city. The appointment had at first gone to his brother, Isaac, but when the king learnt that Abraham had always been the local rabbi and that the governor of Safi, Diogo de Azambuja, had confirmed him in his office, Isaac's appointment was cancelled. Abraham was restored to his position and given both civil and criminal jurisdiction over the Jews. The Jews of Safi had a prison of their own; appeals against the rabbi's judgments were heard before the governor.[2]

Abraham ben Zamiro's activities were not confined to the communal field. He took part in negotiations carried on by the Portuguese with the Maghrebi rulers and with Beduin tribes.[3] In Arabic documents he is sometimes called *ribbi* (rabbi) and sometimes *al-ḥazzān al-Yahūdī* (the Jewish community leader).[4]

His fame spread to Portugal, and David Reubeni pays high tribute to him. The relevant passage occurs in the account of David's relations with Maghreb Jewry:

When the ambassador of the king of Fez arrived in Portugal, he brought with him letters to Reubeni from the Jews of Fez and R. Abraham of Safi and asked that they be answered. About the same time, A Jew of Safi, named Joseph Cordiella[5] brought a letter from the *sherīf* whose territory lay beyond the kingdom of Fez and who had Jews among his subjects. They "dwell on a great mountain. The name of the mountain is al-Sūs and it is at the end of the world, and those Jews under his rule sow and reap, and most of them are poor, and they are strong, and there came before me one of them, a *kohen*, whose heart was like a lion's; he was not of the Jews who live under Ismaelite rule." At the request of that *sherīf*, R. Abraham Zamiro came to him, "and this R. Abraham is a great

[1] Gavison, *ʿOmer ha-Shikheḥa*, pp. 106a, 126d and 135c; Toledano, *Ner*, pp. 72 and 88f.; Voinot, *Pèlerinage*, p. 48; *ABP* IV, p. 106. Comp. also Ben-Naïm, *Malkhe Rabbanan*, p. 13a and b; D. Corcos, *Sefunot* 10 (1966), pp. 57 and 59-69.

[2] *ABP* I, pp. 175 n. 1 and 265-270.

[3] Goís, *Crónica* III, p. 160; *ABP* I, p. 231 n. 4; II, pp. 413, 415, 432 and 434. The redemption of captives: *ibid.* II, pp. 319 and 323-328. On Taʿfūft comp. also Lopes, *Historia* III, pp. 480 and 489-496.

[4] *ABP* II, 348f., 359, 413 and 434.

[5] A Yuçaf Cordiella is found in Spain in the 14th century; see Baer, *Spanien* II, pp. 169 and 189f.

man, greatly honoured by the Christians and their kings and by the Ismaelites and their kings." Abraham had returned from that mission before the last New Year (5287) and made a full report to Reubeni. The measure of Reubeni's esteem for Abraham is apparent from his statement that one of the five flags he made was intended for b. Zamiro of Safi. Reubeni notes incidentally that his servant Joseph Cordiella denounced R. Abraham to the king of Portugal for the alleged killing of a Christian girl. Reubeni persuaded him to desist from this accusation.[1]

Reubeni's account might seem purely fictional, but is confirmed by documents in the Royal Archives.

Abraham was engaged at that time in most lively negotiations with the king of Fez and several *qā'idṣ* and with the *sherīf* Aḥmad al-Aʿraj, a brother of Muhammad al-Shaykh al-Mahdī, concerning the conclusion of a peace treaty. Abraham visited the *sherīf,* who in one of his letters informs the governor of Safi that Abraham will transmit his conditions to him orally. Some of these letters are of September, 1526 *i.e.* before the New Year, 5297. In October of that year, Ben Zamiro was sent to the *sherīf* to deal with the redemption of prisoners.[2]

We have already mentioned (p. 410) a report by two Berber horsemen of the existence of a Jewish tribe in the Sahara. That report, written down in Arabic by Judah ben Zamiro, Abraham's nephew, somehow found its way into the Portuguese Royal Archives; it is datable to February, 1527.[3] It does not seem accidental that a report of Jews living on the Sūs Mountain reached Portugal about the same time as Reubeni wrote his account.[4]

We have found one Abraham ben Zamiro as an agent of the authorities in Azemmour in the years 1528-1530 (p. 424). We are inclined to identify him with our R. Abraham, who had until then been active in Safi, although we do not know the reasons for his leaving it. There may have been dissensions within the community, which counted among its members Abraham Rute, who aspired to an official position among the Jews and applied for it to the king of Portugal about that time; it will be remembered that Jacob Rute was appointed interpreter at Safi in 1523.[5] But the problem is further complicated by an Abraham ben Zamiro who

[1] *MJC* II, pp. 180ff., 192 and 212.

[2] *ABP* II, pp. 348f., 356, 364-367 and 371f.; also *ibid.*, pp. 413, 416, 432 and 434.

[3] Comp. G. S. Colin, Juifs nomades, p. 55.

[4] *MCI* II, p. 180. On Jewish desert dwellers comp. *Mann*, *REJ*, 74 (1922), pp. 150-152.

[5] Comp. above, p. 412.

was appointed interpreter in Mazagan in 1527 and whom it is difficult to identify with Abraham ben Zamiro of Safi and Azemmour.[1] Moreover, Ben Zamiro's imprisonment in Portugal is unexplained,[2] it may have been due to renewed accusations by Joseph Cordiella after he left Reubeni. In any case, some of the adventurism tinging all the activities of those involved in Portuguese-African politics attached to the Jewish participants as well.

The Zamiros were a ramified family, and several other of its members took an active part in communal life and national trade and maintained regular contact with the authorities.

Isaac, Abraham's brother, was one of the defenders of Safi, the commander of a sector of the wall, and later was concerned with wheat purchases for the Portuguese and negotiated with the king of Marrakesh for the recognition of Portuguese suzerainty. He undertook a mission to the king of Portugal, and the governor of Safi asked his master to listen to everything Isaac said. The various documents enable us to follow Isaac's political activities and trade in textile fabrics from Portugal until 1539.[3]

Maïl (Ismael) took part in the defence of Safi with Isaac and acted as interpreter on several occasions. In 1523, he dealt with the redemption of a Christian captive on the instructions of the king of Portugal.[4]

Popular legend invested the Zamiros with an aura of saintliness. In Safi, near the *Dār al-Makhzen* (government house), a small building is still shown in which, according to tradition, the seven Ben Zamiro brothers ("Beney Zamira") are buried. It became the object of mass pilgrimages throughout the year, in which even Muslims participated; it was especially resorted to on Lag be-'Omer.[5]

Members of the second generation are likewise mentioned in the sources. We already know Judah, who gives us the description of the Jewish tribe in the Sahara and who calls Abraham his father's brother.[6]

---

[1] *ABP* IV, p. 106 n. 2. Comp. Cenival, *ibid.* II, p. 352 n. 1. Richard, *ibid.*, pp. 477 and 481, maintains that Abraham b. Zamiro of Safi and Abraham of Azemmur are also different persons. Colin, *Juifs Nomades*, pp. 56f., pays no attention to this point.

[2] *ABP* I, pp. 477-481, and above, p. 424.

[3] *ABP* I, pp. 271, 273, 311, 443f., 572f. (negotiations with the "king" of Marrakesh), 642, 645f. and 688; II, pp. 165-167 and 453f.; III, pp. 139, 193-197 and 229; Bennaïm, *Malkhe Rabbanan*, p. 77a.

[4] *ABP* I, pp. 271, 273 and 667f.; II, pp. 324-328. For the defence of Safi see above, p. 420.

[5] Y. D. Semah, *Bulletin de l'Enseignement public du Maroc*, Juin 1938, p. 308; Voinot, *Pèlerinage*, pp. 47-49.

[6] Comp. above, pp. 410, 434.

Another nephew of Abraham was Solomon-Sulaymān, who also took a hand in politics; on returning from Marrakesh in 1541, he gave the governor of Safi a detailed report of the mood prevailing among the *shurafā*ʾ. In 1556, we find him in prison in Cadiz, and a message from João III to his ambassador in Spain notes that he has been arrested by the Spaniards for carrying letters from the court of Lisbon to the *sherīf* and that it is therefore fitting to regard him as a political prisoner and demand the release of his person and goods.[1] In prison, Solomon met with an acquaintance from the Maghreb, Belchior Vaz de Azevedo, a corsair and adventurer. The latter had formerly lived in Arzila and had spent twelve years at the court of the *sherīf* of Sūs. Azevedo seems to have imported arms for the Moroccan rulers and, at the same time, supplied sacred books to the Jews. The import of those goods was forbidden by the popes and persecuted by the secular authorities.[2] Still other members of the Zamiro family are mentioned in contemporary sources.[3]

The Church and the Inquisition

For a long time, the Portuguese authorities deliberately ignored the problem of the neo-Christians, both Jews and Muslims, who had settled in the African zone in the hope of being able to elude the watchfulness of the Church and revert to the religion of their fathers. Hunting them would have hindered the development of the cities and the strengthening of ties in which the Portuguese were greatly interested; the neo-Christians were closer to them in some respects than other strata of the population. Therefore, when instructions came from the royal court—no doubt following complaints by zealous priests and monks—that neo-Christians should be debarred from settling in the region, the local governors either ignored these instructions or challenged them with well-founded arguments. A letter from Azemmour to Manuel of 1514 explains that there are only ten neo-Christians in the city (the reference is no doubt to families) —craftsmen and merchants who benefit the population; they all took part in the capture of the city and then remained in it, so that the king has no reason to demand their removal.[4]

---

[1] *ABP* III, pp. 406-409, and V, pp. 50-54. Although unproved, the identity of the two Solomons seems very probable.

[2] *ABA* I, pp. 28f., 44-9; *ABP* IV, p. 56, also pp. 200-202; P. de Cenival, *Chronique de Santa Cruz*, Paris 1934, pp. 70 n. 2, 155-6; Willan, *Trade*, p. 127.

[3] Comp. e.g., Enkaoua, *Resp. Kerem Ḥemer* II, no. 31; *ABP* I, p. 655; II, pp. 438f.; also *EJ* (ed. 1972) *s.v.* Benzamero.

[4] *ABP* I, pp. 490 and 497.

In 1537, a Christian priest in Azemmour complains that Jewish and Muslim *conversos* marry local—*i.e.*, Jewish and Muslim—women and live according to their old religion. In his reply, the governor states that the king has ordered him to refrain from all action in this matter. At the same time, he expresses the hope that a local branch of the Inquisition will soon be opened.[1] The fear of that institution indeed casts its shadow upon the lives of the Portuguese conversos. Meanwhile, its establishment in Portugal was postponed again and again. In Rome and Lisbon, Jews were trying to avert the calamity by ransom payments, bribes to cardinals and personal influence, and their efforts were successful for many years, until the eventual setting-up of the Inquisition in 1547.[2] The *conversos* in Portugal foresaw this development; many tried to escape to the African region, and thence to Morocco, while there was still time. The stream of *converso* refugees swelled in the thirties of the century, but it had certainly set in upon the beginning of forced conversions, and exit bans had been issued every now and then.[3]

Assiduous priests anticipated the official establishment of Inquisition tribunals: when the stream of Marranos increased, they began, as early as 1537, to prepare prosecution files against them. Those mentioned as reverting to Judaism in Azemmour include Manuel Rodrigues, who observes the Sabbath according to Jewish custom, Moses Adibe (of Tavira), Juão Nunes Velho, Isaac Cabeca and others. A Christian knight resident in Azemmour who visited Fez in 1541 hastens to report that he found some neo-Christian grain merchants, whom he mentions by name, living in the Jewish quarter there; when he debated the meaning of a biblical passage with a Jew, one of them promptly came to the latter's aid.[4]

The Old Christian Vargas, who resided in Fez from 1539 as a grain broker and political emissary and had a close-up view of events, said immediately upon arrival that the Jewish *conversos* who migrated from Portugal to Africa should be watched. In time, his utterances became more aggressive. He suggested prohibiting *conversos* travelling from one

---

[1] *Ibid.* III, pp. 83f. Similar accusations against Muslim *conversos* *ibid.* II, pp. 476 and 479.

[2] Joseph ha-Kohen, *Emek ha-Bakha*, p. 107, says that the sanguinary Inquisition activities began in 1539; but see Kayserling, *Geschichte*, pp. 154, 186ff., 213, 226ff. and 256.

[3] Kayserling, *ibid.*, pp. 143 and 156; see also *ABE* I, p. 51, for a similar ban on an inhabitant of Seville.

[4] *ABP* V, pp. 119-123. The question arises whether this Isaac Cabeca is identical with the person of that name mentioned in Willan, *Trade*, p. 127.

city to another by land, since they would escape to Tetouan *en route* and there revert to Judaism; he intimated that the Rutes in Arzila helped such people and should therefore be expelled.[1]

It is easy to realize that a delicate situation had arisen for the Portuguese governors and agents. Military pressure by the *shurafāʾ* was increasing, and Portuguese ruling circles were aware that it would not be possible to withstand it and that insufficiently fortified cities would have to be evacuated. The emigration of *conversos*, who included experts in the manufacture of arms and in international trade, especially in war materials, undoubtedly strengthened the enemies of Portugal.[2] We know, *e.g.*, that the Saʿdī *shurafāʾ* had cannon and ammunition not of Moroccan manufacture. It was inadvisable, therefore, to annoy the Jews in the region and neighbouring areas by oppressive measures and thus cause them to join the anti-Portuguese front. This accounts for the double-facedness of Portuguese policy in this respect, as reflected in contemporary correspondence.

That policy is palpably demonstrated by the story of Moses Rute, which involves a variety of aspects. The 1538 treaty between Portugal and the Kingdom of Fez contained a clause permitting Jews to visit and do business in Portuguese-controlled cities. However, the Jews were unable to benefit by this clause owing to the incitement carried on by a Franciscan monk of Spanish origin. The latter bore an especial grudge to Moses Rute, who was then living in Arzila, but was a subject of the King of Fez. The intervention of Vargas, the Portuguese agent in Fez, in favour of Rute—under pressure from the king—was unavailing. When Moses went to Tangier, the Inquisition caught hold of him, and he was jailed for offences against the regulations of the "Holy Office". This happened in 1542. A consequent severance of relations with Portugal, as demanded by the sons of King Aḥmad, was avoided only by the efforts of Jacob Rute, who knew that such a step would do no good. Vargas did everything to obtain Moses' release, warning of possible retaliatory action by the King of Fez against the Christians, which would affect him, too. He unsuccessfully urged the Spanish monk to reveal what was behind the affair. Ostensibly, Moses was charged with ill-treating a Christian captive, but that was certainly not the real reason for his arrest. It seems more likely that the

[1] *ABP* III, p. 201; IV, pp. 55-58.

[2] Comp. above, p. 419 and n. 2; also *ABEs* I, pp. 44-52; Lopes, *Historia* IV, p. 97; *ABF* I, Ser. I, pp. 28f. and 44-49 (the complaint by the Portuguese ambassador in Paris in 1562).

clergy wished to punish him for aiding *conversos*. He was eventually released, went back to Arzila and continued his political activity.[1]

The Church used gentle methods as well. Increasing demands for the introduction of the Inquisition were paralleled by intensified missionary activity among the refugees in Morocco. In 1531, a Franciscan was permitted by the king of Fez to preach in the synagogues of the Jewish quarter; he found no response.[2] In 1548/49, a Jesuit, João Nunes Barreto, charged with the care and redemption of Portuguese prisoners in Tetouan, debated with the elders and rabbis in the local synagogue while the congregation was assembling for prayers. His interpreter was an Islamized Christian, who thus wished to demonstrate his attachment to the religion and country he had betrayed. The Jesuit claims that a great rabbi afterwards came to his house to tell him that he had been convinced by his arguments and was prepared to leave his wife and go with his two sons to Ceuta and be baptised there. In the following year, the same monk claims to have persuaded other Jews to go to Ceuta and embrace Christianity. We also find Jesuits debating with Jews in Ceuta itself.[3]

There is no reason to believe all the stories of the conversion of Jews, but there were certainly persons who returned to Spain or Portugal and the bosom of the Church. Incidents of this kind are reported by Jewish sources as well.[4]

Spanish Conquests

The activity of priests of Spanish origin was in part the result of Spain's growing interest, from the end of the 15th century, in events in the western sector of North Africa. During that century, the internal affairs of Castile had prevented Spaniards from taking an active part in African conquests. When the Catholic Kings, Ferdinand of Aragon and Isabel of Castile, had overcome dynastic difficulties and established themselves on the throne of the united kingdom, they applied their energies to improving the situation in the interior and on the borders, and especially wiping out

---

1 See Ricard's review of the 'Rute Affair," *APB* IV, pp. 108-111; also Corcos, *Maroc*, p. 108 n. 282; Moses' stay in Arzila is confirmed by letters from Vargas to João III, *ibid.*, pp. 140 and 145-148.

2 *ABEs* I, pp. 7-37. Comp. also the story of a Christian's Jewish wife in Fez who in 1540 testified before the king and the rabbis that she had been a Christian for eleven years; *ABP* III, pp. 272f.

3 *ABP* IV, pp. 282f., 303f., 308f. and 379f.; Gomes dos Santos, *Mélanges Lopes-Cenival*, p. 238.

4 Comp. the story of Moses Benzamero of Fez who was baptized at the Escorial in 1589, changed his name to Pablo de Santa-Maria and became a "councillor of the king"; Ricard, *Hespéris* 24 (1937), p. 136, and 32 (1945), pp. 85f.

the Muslim Kingdom of Granada, the last remnant of the Arab conquest on the Iberian Peninsula. Only when this had been accomplished did they join in the struggle for the African coastland. Until then, they had kept aloof, benefiting by the efforts of the Portuguese, their unconscious allies, who diverted the attention of the Moroccan rulers from Granada. Of course, after the liquidation of Granada, Columbus's sensational discoveries turned the minds of the Spaniards to wider horizons than the Kingdom of Fez. It was easy, therefore, for the Catholic Kings to be generous towards their smaller neighbour, to agree to a division of areas of influence and conquest and, in 1494, to sign a treaty with the king of Portugal, João II, recognising his right to conquer the Kingdom of Fez. The Spaniards indeed did not abide by the terms of that treaty, for they seized control of Velez (1508), but they contended that this was a separate state, independent of Fez. The main features of that agreement were reaffirmed by the Treaty of Cintra of 1509, except that Melilla and Qasasa (Qaçaça) were now to remain Spanish.[1]

In 1545, Contreras, a Franciscan monk in Tetouan, suggested to Carlos I, King of Spain and (as Charles V) Holy Roman Emperor (see p. 443), to have Morocco conquered by the crown prince Philip.[2] In the last decade of Portuguese and Waṭṭāsid rule, Spain became more and more interested in Moroccan affairs.[3]

During the 15th century, the Jewish communities in the region had lived in comparative quiet. The refugees of 1391 were absorbed, and the tension between the two strata wore off. As ʿAbd al-Bāsiṭ notes apropos of a refugee doctor, the Jews had no high-flown ambitions: they did not aspire to politically influential positions at the courts of the rulers, an aspiration which would in the end have been visited upon themselves and their coreligionists.[4] The few references in Jewish literature to the kings and viziers show that their attitude towards the Jewish subjects was not unfavourable. The court was accessible to bribery, which was practised through special go-betweens.[5] According to a Flemish traveller, Anselme

[1] These relations and developments are reviewed by Cenival, *ABP* I, pp. 203-212; Lopes, *Expansão*, pp. 161f.; Bauer-Landauer, *Relaciones* III, pp. I-XIX.

[2] *ABEs* I, pp. 101-116.

[3] Lopes, *Historia* IV, pp. 121-124; *ABEs* I, pp. 361f.; 642-645; Richard, *Hespéris* 24 (1937) pp. 300ff.

[4] Brunschvig, *Deux Récits*, p. 45/108.

[5] Comp. Simon b. Zemaḥ Dūrān, *Resp.* II, no. 61. The reference seems to be to the Ḥafṣid ruler Abū Fāris (1394-1434); on his grandson Othman (1435-1485), mentioned by Solomon b. Simon Dūrān, *Resp.* no. 479, see Brunschvig, *Berbérie* I, p. 241, and especially p. 261ff. Cases of bribery are mentioned, *e.g.*, by Simon b. Semaḥ Dūrān, *Resp.* I, no. 62; III, no. 59.

Adorne, the Jews in Tunis, which he visited in 1470, lived in degrading conditions, but nothing is known of threats to their physical safety; Adorne himself mentions that Jews travelled by ship to Alexandria together with Muslims and Christians.[1] In Constantine, the Jews lived among the general population, not in a special quarter.[2]

The division of areas of influence and conquest between Spain and Portugal at the end of the 15th century was no secret to the Jews, who discerned the political trends even before they had consolidated into treaties. This accounts for the fact that the refugees of 1492 and 1497 did not go to the cities coveted by the Spaniards: they did not wish their persecutors to catch up with them. Of the more important refugees, only a few stayed in those cities, and only for a short time. Abraham Zacuto and his son and Abraham ha-Levi Buqarāt spent several years in Tunis (1500-1507), and so did Moses Alashqar. Here Zacuto completed his *Sefer ha-Yuḥasin* and Buqarāt his *Sefer ha-Zikkaron*, a commentary on Rashi to the Pentateuch.[3]

In 1509, Spain launched a campaign of conquest along the Mediterranean coast. This time, the pact with Portugal was kept; the attack began at Oran, east of the Moroccan ports. Cardinal Ximenes took advantage of the religious fanaticism of the Spaniards and the disunity of the Muslim states to proclaim a crusade. The Spanish navy set out on a "holy war," while its real assignment was a secular one: to seize the maritime bases of trade with Africa and to eliminate Muslim piracy.[4]

Upon the capture of Oran (1509), about 4,000 persons were killed by order of Cardinal Ximenez, about 5,000 were led into captivity, and two mosques were converted into churches. The sufferings of the Jewish community are described in an elegy by a contemporary *payṭān*, which will be dealt with in a special section on Oran (vol. ii).

After Oran, it was Bougie's and Tripoli's turn to come under the Spanish yoke, and the same fate befell Tenes and Mostaganem. Chronicles report that the Jews of Bougie and Tripoli were led into captivity and exile. We find some of them as refugees in Italy.[5] Others found their way

---

[1] Brunschvig, *Deux Récits*, pp. 185ff. and 220.

[2] Idem, *Berbérie* I, p. 388.

[3] Comp. Filipowski, *Juchassin*, Introd., p. VI, and p. 223a. In the introduction to his commentary (Livorno 1645), Buqarāt gives the date when he wrote it as (5)267 = 1507 C.E. For Buqarāt see also above, pp. 406-7.

[4] A short account of the campaign: Fisher, *Barbary Legend*, pp. 33-35.

[5] Joseph ha-Kohen, *Emek ha-Bakha*, p. 110; Gedalya, *Shalshelet*, p. 95b; Vogelstein-Rieger, *Geschichte der Juden in Rom* II, p. 31. Appendices 12 and 13 contain many names attesting to the North African origin of their bearers, e.g., Bahlūl (not Kahlūl or Kutlūl).

to Egypt.[1] According to a late tradition, 800 families moved from Tripoli eastward to Tājūra.[2] Dapper, not generally a very reliable source, says that the number of Jews in Tlemcen decreased after Abū ʿAbd Allah's death (1517).[3]

The city of Algiers was forced to surrender one of the islands at the harbour entrance to the Spaniards; they built fortifications and installed guns on it, and the city was now within range of their fire. The small Jewish community which existed here before the expulsions of 1492 and 1497 and which, according to Abraham Zacuto, was noted for ransoming captives brought over from Spain, probably held its own even under the difficult conditions now arising. Some of the former captives may have settled in Algiers.[4]

The Spanish army did not try to penetrate into the interior of the country, and it is doubtful whether Ximenez ever intended it to do so. The situation of the Spanish garrisons, therefore, was not auspicious; they received no regular supplies, since they were under siege both on the landside, owing to the hostility of the Muslim population, and on the seaside, owing to interference by Turkish pirates. However, the kingdoms of the Ziyanids and Ḥafṣids, in the territories of which the Spaniards had established themselves, were so exhausted that they could not avail themselves of the existing favourable circumstances to force the European invaders to evacute the ports, as the *sherīf* Muhammad al-Mahdī had done in Morocco.

It was the Turkish corsairs who dislodged the Spaniards from the coastal cities. They were at first under the command of al-ʿArūj and later under that of his famous brother Khayr al-Dīn, known in European literature as Barbarossa, the red-bearded one. It was an act of great political wisdom for Khayr al-Dīn to recognise the overlordship of the powerful Ottoman sultans, Selim I Yāwūz, who conquered Egypt in 1517, and his son Sulayman, surnamed al-Qānūnī, the Legislator, in Turkey

---

[1] The refugees from Tripoli in Egypt came into notice by the dispute between R. Levi b. Ḥabib and R. Jacob Beyrab concerning a girl who had been married in Tripoli against her will; Beyrab, *Responsa*, no. 56; Levi b. Ḥabib, Quntres ha-Semikha, *Responsa*, ed. Venice, p. 318b (ed. Lemberg, p. 77a); Abraham Adādī, *Wayiqra Abraham*, *Resp.* Yore Deʿah, p. 4 (16c); comp. Dimitrowsky, *Sefunot* 7, (1963), pp. 97-100.

[2] More about that town in vol. II.

[3] There is some truth in what Dapper says in *Description*, p. 161, but the main cause of the decline of the community was the struggle between the Spanish and the Turks for possession of the town; comp. below, p. 444.

[4] *Juchassin*, ed. Filipowski, p. 227b.

and the Magnificent, in Europe. Ferdinand of Aragon had died in 1516, and the Spanish throne had devolved upon his grandson, King Charles I, a Habsburg on his father's side, known in German history as the Emperor Charles V. As heir to two crowns, he was the ruler of an empire in Europe, Asia and America "over which the sun never set." By accepting Ottoman suzerainty, the corsairs assured themselves of military and political assistance from a power that was a match for Charles V. The struggle between the invaders and the Spaniards was nevertheless hard; it lasted over sixty years and was marked by many vicissitudes. The command of the Turkish forces was finally entrusted to generals directly subordinate to the Sublime Porte in Constantinople. Further particulars of the events of those days will be given in the chapter dealing with the situation in Algeria during the 16th century.

We know very little of the fate of the Jews in those parts during that period. In view of Charles V's cruelty at the conquest of Tunis in 1535—the figures of 70,000 killed and 40,000 captives are given—the account of the sufferings of the Jews by Joseph ha-Kohen does not seem exaggerated: the Jews, too, of whom there were many, in part fled into the desert, in part were slain, and in part were taken captive and sold as slaves; about a hundred and fifty were redeemed by the communities in Naples and Genoa.[1]

During the siege of Algiers by Charles (1541), the Jews lived in great fear, and they exulted when the Spaniards were defeated without having set foot in the city. In memory of their miraculous rescue, they appointed days of fasting and rejoicing on the 3rd and 4th of the month of Ḥeshvan, when *piyyūṭīm* composed by the rabbis of Algiers were to be recited.[2] In the same year, Bougie was captured by foreign invaders. A question addressed to Rabbi Abraham ibn Ṭawāh indicates that the Jews in the city were plundered; most of them were taken captive, and only a minority escaped.[3] The Jews also had their share of suffering upon the capture of Mahdiyya by Andrea Doria's fleet in a fierce battle between him and the *ra'īs* Dragut, the Turkish commander in the area.[4]

---

[1] *Emek ha-Bakha*, pp. 117f.; *Dibrey ha-Yamim*, p. 102a. Comp. also Gedalya, *Shalshelet*, p. 95b; Assaf, *KS*, 14 (1937/38), pp. 548f.; Fisher, *Barbary Legend*, pp. 78 and 313f.; Julien, *Histoire* II, p. 258; Montmorency, *Barbary States*, p. 89.

[2] To be dealt with vol. II. chap. Algeria.

[3] Simon b. Zemaḥ Dūrān, IV/3 (*Responsa* of Abraham ibn Ṭawāh), no. 24.

[4] Joseph ha-Kohen, *Dibrey ha-Yamim*, p. 135b, calls Mahdiya "Afrika", as was the use in contemporary Arabic literature. According to Cazès, *Essai*, p. 120, the refugees from Mahdiya went to Moknine, a small place half-way between Mahdiya and Sousse.

At the end of the reign of Charles V, who in 1555 renounced his crowns and retired to a monastery, the Turks took Tripoli and later expelled the troops of the *sherīf* Muhammad al-Mahdī from Tlemcen. The latter city changed hands several times between the Spaniards, the Turks and the *sherīf*'s Berber soldiers. The Jews suffered from these changes more than the rest of the population. Joseph ha-Kohen reports: "It was in the year 5203, *i.e.* 1543, that Manṣūr plotted against his master, the king of Tlemcen in Barbary. He called the Spaniards who were in Oran, and they came to the city in force and pillaged it, and the Jews, too, of whom there were many there, were led captive by the enemy, and they were sold as slaves in the month of Adar. Some were redeemed in Oran and some in Fez, and some were led to Spain and estranged from the Lord, the God of Israel."[1] Armed intervention did not end here. About a year later, Khayr al-Dīn's son, Ḥasan Pasha, set out to take revenge upon Manṣūr and the Spaniards, and then it was the other way again—and each retaliatory action brought trouble for the Jews. The sons of the nagid and some Jews who were with them, who were fleeing for their lives, were seized on the road to Debdou, thrown into prison and forced to redeem themselves with a heavy ransom.[2]

Gavison's *ʿOmer ha-Shikheḥa* relates: "Tlemcen was captured by the idolators in the year 5202 (1542) . . . and about 1,500 Jews were killed or taken prisoner. Some Jews went to Fez to ask the local community to ransom the captives, but they could not redeem all of them because of their great number and of prices that were higher than they were worth. Some of the people had fled prior to being taken, hoping to get away, and were subsequently caught because the inhabitants of the place to which they had fled betrayed them to the idolaters . . . Some had not fled, but indolently stayed where they were until they were captured. When they arrived, Rabbi Judah ʿUziel ruled that those who had fled and thus done what they could—young folk, children and old people—should be redeemed first."[3]

Spanish sources report that the Jews in Tlemcen, where Ottoman rule was firmly established, and those in Oran, which remained Spanish

---

[1] *Emek ha-Bakha*, p. 120.

[2] *Dibrey ha-Yamim*, p. 127b.

[3] Gavison, *ʿOmer ha-Shikheḥa*, p. 29b. A reference to one of the invasions of Tlemçen occurs in a responsum of Solomon Dūrān: "the enemy invaded Tlemcen and all the kethuboth (marriage contracts) were lost, and when those of the community who remained had settled down again ......" (Simon b. Zemaḥ Dūrān, *Responsa* IV/1, n. 16(7b). Comp. also Julien, *Histoire* II, pp. 262 and 267.

until 1792 (with an interval from 1708 to 1732), took an active part in the political schemes hatched in both places.[1]

Tunisia was the last country of the region to be annexed to the Ottoman Empire. After a brilliant victory over the Spaniards, Sīnān Pasha, in 1574, erased the last symbolic remnants of the rule of the Ḥafṣids and turned their state into a Turkish pashalik. Thus vanished Spain's dream of holding a continuous chain of port cities along the entire North African coast. She retained only Mellila, Mers al-Kabīr and Oran.

Four years after the establishment of the Pashalik of Tunisia, King Sebastian of Portugal (1557-1578), who, with the help of a deposed *sherīf*, tried to revive Portuguese aspirations in North Africa, was killed in the Battle of the Three Kings (see vol. II) at Qṣar al-Kabīr in Northern Morocco. Upon his death (and that of the two Saʿdī *shurafāʾ* who took part in the battle), his design lapsed. Of the three ports still in Portuguese hands, two, Ceuta and Tangier, fell to Spain, leaving only Mazagan. The attempt by European states to establish continous areas of control beyond the Mediterranean was shelved for approximately three hundred years.

Summing up, we should note the different attitudes adopted by the Spaniards and the Portuguese towards the local inhabitants, and especially the Jews, in the areas under their control. It is doubtful whether the tolerant approach of the Portuguese stemmed from feelings of human kindness. The kings of powerful Spain thought that they might treat Jews and Muslims cruelly, and their propaganda knew how to whitewash their crimes. The rulers of little Portugal, on the other hand, who also had plans for large-scale conquests, were compelled to pursue an opportunist course both at home and in North Africa. João II was prepared to admit the Jews expelled from Spain and promised them temporary refuge in his country because he needed their money to finance his war in Africa. The same policy is even more apparent in the attitude of Manuel, variously surnamed "the Wicked" and "the Virtuous," and of his son, João III.[2]

The middle of the 16th century marked the beginning of a new era for North Africa. Simultaneously with the rise of the independent Sherifian kingdom, two territories took shape to the east of it: Algeria and Tunisia, from which latter Tripolitania was to split off subsequently. There was a kind of historical justice in the forms of organization and degree of

---

[1] About the activities of the Cansinos and Sasportas' see vol. II.

[2] One of the objects of Fisher's *Barbary Legend* was to show up the biased attitude of European sources as to that period of North African history; comp. the Introduction and, *e.g.*, p. 48 n. 5.

independence of these countries. The Outer Maghreb, which had fought the Portuguese and Turks by its own efforts, achieved a sovereign state under *shurafā'* of the Sa'dī dynasty. The people of Algeria, Tunisia and Tripolitania, who had not been able to defend themselves against the Spaniards unaided, came under the protectorate of the Ottoman Empire and were subject to forms of administration which differed from territory to territory.

From now on, we have to do with four territories, each with a definite physiognomy of its own and its own particular destiny. The new political frameworks had considerable influence on the history of Maghreb Jewry, which began to develop along three or four different lines.

APPENDIX I

R. ZACHARIAH AGHMĀṬI AND TWO OF HIS CONTEMPORARIES

The end of the Almoravid and the beginning of the Almohad era are, in every respect, one of the least known periods of the history of the Jews in the Maghreb (including Spain). Religious and social persecution, migration within the area and emigration to neighbouring Christian states and the Muslim East—Egypt and Asia—are the causes of wide gaps in the source material, so plentiful for earlier times.

In those days there lived, or at any rate were born and brought up, in the Maghreb three rabbinic scholars whose life stories are completely unknown to us.

According to their writings, they must be regarded as disciples, or disciples' disciples, in spirit of the great North African scholars Rabbenu Ḥananel, R. Nissim ben Jacob of Kairouan and R. Isaac Alfasi. They cannot be assigned to the circle whose centre was the *beyt midrash* of Lucena, since none of them is mentioned by R. Abraham ibn Daud, the authoritative contemporary historian, who was well informed about the main centres of rabbinic learning in his day, and especially about the Lucena scholars. But the existence of other seats of learning not within the purview of Ibn Daud, is attested by two well-known rabbis, Joseph ben Judah ibn ʿAqnīn ha-Sefaradi and Joseph ben Judah ibn Simon, a disciple of Maimonides.[1] The abovementioned scarcity of information compels us to cull every detail wherever we can find it.

One of the scholars to be discussed here is R. Zachariah ben Judah Aghmāṭi.[2] For reasons to be set out hereunder he may perhaps be assigned, approximately, to the years 1120-1195, though his very existence, and his identity, were not known until the past generation. He hailed from Morocco, as attested by his cognomen (*nisba*): Aghmāṭ was a large urban centre some 40 kms. south-east of Marrākesh, with many Jewish inhabitants.[3] No biographical details concerning R. Zachariah are known

[1] For them see above, pp. 356ff.

[2] Mentioned briefly p. 349.

[3] Idrīsi (1099-1166) describes Aghmāṭ as a pleasant locality with a Jewish population; R. Dozy and M. J. Goeje, *Description*, pp. 69 and 79f. For the destruction of the Jewish community see above, pp. 124ff, p. 142 n. 17. For Aghmāṭ generally in those

from external sources; even his name is nowhere mentioned. But from 1928 onwards, both short and more extensive fragments of a commentary on several Talmud tractates by an anonymous author were published —from Geniza documents kept in Leningrad and Cambridge and at the British Museum—chiefly on account of utterances of a rabbi frequently quoted therein, whose initials, RBS, were not at first correctly interpreted.[1]

The name and date of the author of the commentary, R. Zachariah ben Judah, were established by a MS the acquisition of which by the British Museum was announced in 1933.[2] From it, a commentary on the Tractate Berakhot was published in 1938; the title-page bears the author's full name and indicates that he wrote a *ner* (lamp)[3] to all the Halakhot Rabbati—*i.e.* the *Halakhot* of Alfasi—and that he composed his commentary in the years 1189-1191. Clearly, he did not in a mere two years

---

days see *EI*² *s.v.* (Lévi-Provençal). Murābiṭi dinars were minted in Aghmāṭ; H. W. Hazard, *The Numismatic History of Late Medieval North Africa*, New York 1952, p. 11, and Goitein, *Society* I, pp. 235f. For the two townlets now on the site see *Les Guides bleus*, Maroc, p. 160.

[1] Here is a list of these publications, in the order of their appearance: B. M. Lewin, *Otzar ha-Geonim*, Thesaurus of the Gaonic Responsa and Commentaries, Haifa-Jerusalem, 1928-1941. L. Ginzberg, *Geniza Studies in Memory of Doctor Solomon Schechter*, II, New York 1929. J. N. Epstein, Rabbenu Baruch mi-Ḥaleb, *Tarbiẓ* 1/4 (1930), pp. 27-62. J. Leveen, A Digest of Commentaries on the Babylonian Talmud, *The British Museum Quarterly* VII (1932/33), pp. 76f. S. Assaf, Ḥeleq mi-Perush Qadmon etc., *Abhandlungen zur Erinnerung an Hirsch Perez Chajes*, Wien 1933. M. D. Ben-Shem (ed.), *Hanner* by R. Zekharya son of R. Yehuda Agamati (*sic*) in the year 4949 (1189), Jerusalem 1948. J. Leveen (ed.), *A Digest of Commentaries on the Tractates Bābhā Ḳammā, Bābhā Mᵉṣiᶜā and Bābhā Bhāthᵉrā of the Babylonian Talmud, compiled by Zachariah Ben Judah Aghmāti*, London 1961. S. Abramson, *Be-Merkazim ubi-Tefuzot bi-Tekufat ha-Geonim*, Jerusalem 1965. In the following notes, these publications are referred to only by author and page, except J. Leveen's second publication, which is referred to as *Commentaries*.

[2] B.M.Or. 11361. See J. Leveen, *l.c.* Epstein (p. 31), who could not have known of the existence of the MS, calls him Anonymous.

[3] This is what the commentary is called on the title-page of the MS fol. 1b. At the end of the Tractate Berakhot we read: This lamp (*būṣīnā*) is the first of all the lamps . . . (Ben-Shem p. 122). From R. Zachariah's words at the end of his commentaries on Baba Kama (J. Leveen, *Commentaries*, 59b) and Baba Meẓiᶜa (*ibid.*, 162a), it appears that he called his commentary on each tractate lamp (*būṣīnā*): . . . this is the first of all the lamps . . ., this is the second of all the lamps (the end of the commentary on Baba Batra is missing in the MS). *Ner* or *būṣīnā* as the name of a commentary is a borrowing from Arabic, where the word *sirāj* is often used in this way; see Brockelmann, *GALS* III, Index of Titles. Famous in Jewish literature are Maimonides' *Sirāj*, an Arabic commentary on the Mishna, and the *Sirāj* of R. Isaac ibn Ghiyāt, which has variously been translated as *Sefer ha-Ner* and *Sefer ha-Maor*; see Assaf, *Tarbiẓ* 3, Jerusalem (1932), pp. 213f. and 339. It may be noted that the critical commentaries on Alfasi's *Halakhot* by R. Zerahya ha-Levi of Lunel are called *Sefer ha-Maor ha-Gadol* and *Sefer ha-Maor ha-Qatan*.

collect all his material and work it up into a continuous commentary. The date no doubt relates to the final editing of notes accumulated in the course of many years' study of Alfasi's *Halakhot*.[1]

The fragments of the commentary that have come down to us deal with the Tractates Berakhot, Shabbat, Erubin, Baba Kama, Baba Meẓiʿa and Baba Batra. R. Zachariah's work is really, in the main, a selection from the teachings of the Geonim and the First (post-Gaonic) Generations (of rabbis) and herein lies its great importance.[2] The fragments do not originate from the same sçribe and even the extant editing is not uniform. Some are early, others late, as a comparison of parellel passages will show.[3]

R. Zachariah makes ample use of Arabic, both in presenting his own ideas and those of others. He uses that language in three kinds of material: short comments on single Hebrew and Aramaic words which were not sufficiently understood by students;[4] short substantive comments;[5] quotations from ancient or contemporary Arabic sources, sometimes running into many lines, as the occasion required.[6] His frequent resort to

[1] The expression "Halakhot" *tout court* refers to Alfasi's work, which contains summaries of talmudic discussions and the decisions of the issues involved. R. Zachariah calls Alfasi *ha-Rab* without the addition of a name; see, *e.g.*, his commentary on Baba Meẓiʿa, MS Cambridge, *Geniza Studies in Memory of Doctor Solomon Schechter* II, pp. 386 and 390, also 386, and J. Leveen, *Commentaries*, p. 62b: and so wrote my teacher, ha-Rab, of blessed memory.

[2] See, *e.g.*, Abramson, who compares portions of R. Zachariah's commentaries with corresponding passages of R. Hay's responsa contained in Gaonic responsa collections.

[3] Ben-Shem, note 12 and p. 13, note 24*, already observed that the portion of the commentary on Berakhot published by S. Assaf from the Leningrad MS was older than the British Museum MS published by himself. But he failed to keep his promise of a systematic discussion of the variations between the two MSS, and especially of the omission of the Arabic quotations contained in the British Museum MS. These omissions indicate that the Leningrad MS was written in a country where Arabic was not very well known, which is why long passages were left out. There are also many textual variations between the portions of the commentary on Baba Meẓiʿa published by Ginzberg from the Cambridge MS, and B.M.Or. 10013, the commentaries published by J. Leveen, *op. cit.*, in facsimile. As to the portions of the commentary on Baba Meẓiʿa published from the Oxford MS by J. N. Epstein, *op. cit.*, Appendix I, pp. 46-51, see below, p. 456 and p. 453 n. 1.

[4] See *e.g.*: Ginzberg, p. 389; Assaf, p. 38 (comp. Epstein, p. 28); Ben-Shem, p. 21 (in the name of R. Nissim); *ibid.*, pp. 74, 75 and 95; J. Leveen, *Commentaries*, pp. 1a-b, 2a, 3a, 4a, 5a and 52b.

[5] Assaf, pp. 34 (= Ben-Shem, p. 17) and 37; Ben-Shem, pp. 84f. (in the name of R. Baruch) and 114; J. Leveen, *Commentaries*, pp. 1a, 52a and 62.

[6] Ginzberg, pp. 383f., 387, 391f., and 393; Assaf, pp. 33f. (Rab Hay); Ben-Shem, p. 77; J. Leveen, *Commentaries*, p. 5a (comp. Z. P. Chajes (ed.) Solomon Benhaytom, *Commentary on the Tractate Mashqin*, p. 77) and 167a-b (Maimonides' Mishna commentary and explanations).

Arabic indicates that he was writing for people thoroughly familiar with it. Below we shall deal with a fragment of an anonymous contemporary commentary which shows none of the features we have found in R. Zachariah.[1]

In view of the sources used by him, it seems safe to assume that in order to pursue his studies he left his native Aghmāṭ for Muslim Spain, which in those days was one of the two main centres of rabbinic learning.

So did other Moroccan Jews, known to us by their names and activities, They are R. Moses Darʿi and R. Joseph ben Mellāl, which latter, as his name indicates, originated from the same region as Aghmāṭi; both Darʿi and Ben Mellāl were disciples of R. Joseph ibn Megāsh, himself the most distinguished disciple of Alfasi when the latter had settled in Spain in his old age. R. Joseph ibn Megāsh succeeded Alfasi in Lucena and, as shown by questions addressed to him from Morocco, was famous in the whole of that country. The place of destination of one of his responsa, given as "the mountain", may be Aghmāṭ.[2]

It is not improbable that R. Zachariah, too, in his youth, studied under R. Joseph ibn Megāsh (d. 1141), whom he frequently quotes in his commentary. R. Zachariah was familiar with the teachings and commentaries of the Geonim, from the early ones down to Rab Hay and R. Samuel bar Ḥofni, and with those of the famous African scholars, Rabbenu Ḥananel and R. Nissim ben Jacob; he recorded their utterances, especially those of R. Ḥananel. He was also conversant with the utterances of the Spanish-Jewish scholars preceding him, R. Isaac ibn Ghiyāt and, as stated, R. Joseph ibn Megāsh. He knew the Mishna commentary of Maimonides, his contemporary, and quoted it in his own commentary.[3]

In addition to Eastern, North African and Spanish rabbis, R. Zachariah mentions Western European scholars who preceded him by about two

---

[1] See p. 453 and n. 1; p. 456 and nn. 2-5.

[2] R. Moses Darʿi was widely known in his time as a harbinger of the Messiah; see Maimonides, *Epistle to Yemen*, ed. A. S. Halkin, New York 5712, pp. 99-103. R. Joseph ibn Mellāl is referred to in the letter of a Cairo merchant published by Hirschberg, *Y. F. Baer Jubilee Volume*, Jerusalem 1960, p. 151, l. 19, and note *ibid.* Comp. S. Baron, *SRH* V, pp. 201f., 384 n. 66; VI, p. 361 note 50; also above, pp. 120-122, and 352. The responsa of R. Joseph ibn Megāsh, Warsaw 1870, articles 93, 101, 137 and 152, where the Moroccan communities are mentioned, are discussed by me above pp. 349, 352, 354. Comp. also I. Ta-Shmah, *Kiryath Sepher* 46 (1971), p. 551. Mellāl is a small locality in the Darʿa Valley; see *Les Guides bleus*, Maroc, p. 442. It has given its name to a textile fabric; see above p. 278 n. 4.

[3] See the Index of Authors in J. Leveen, *Commentaries*, pp. 17f. R. Zachariah adds to Maimonides' name the blessing for the living ("may the Almighty protect him and keep him alive"); see, *e.g.*, J. Leveen, *Commentaries*, pp. 5a and 12a.

generations, viz. R. Gershom and Rashi.[1] This and his knowledge of Maimonides' Mishna commentary suggest that if, like Moses Darʿi and Joseph ibn Mellāl, he returned to Morocco after his first period of study, he must have left it again during one of the waves of Almohad persecutions and gone to Christian Europe, viz. to Spain, where the process of liberation from Muslim rule was in full swing, or to Provence—apparently to settle there for good.

A peculiar feature of R. Zachariah's work is the frequency of references to R. Baruch ha-Sefaradi, which are proportionately more numerous than those to the Geonim and their early successors. But for certain difficulties, to be discussed presently, one might regard this as an indication that R. Baruch was the teacher under whose guidance he studied. But here the question arises where and when R. Zachariah studied under R. Baruch. And if he was not taught by him personally but through his writings, there is still the question where he became acquainted with R. Baruch's work (or works?), of which nothing has so far been discovered in the original version, all his teachings being incorporated in the utterances of other scholars.[2]

R. Baruch was known from references in the writings of R. Isaiah (ben Mali) di Trani (c. 1180-1250), who sometimes calls him R. Baruch of Aleppo, but mostly just R. Baruch. R. Isaac (ben Moses), called *Or Zaruaʿ* after his *magnum opus* (c. 1180-1260), refers to him as R. Baruch bar Samuel *me-Erez Yawan* ("of the land of Greece", but see below), or simply as R. Baruch.[3] According to J. N. Epstein, R. Baruch bar Samuel was "one of the most famous Talmud commentators . . . his commentaries are frequently mentioned by German, Italian, Southern French and

[1] Epstein, pp. 42 and 61, says that he found only one reference to Rabbenu Gershom; see now the index mentioned in the preceding note.

[2] Even assuming that R. Zachariah studied under R. Baruch, he evidently had his comments before him in writing, and incorporated them into his own commentary, years after R. Baruch's death. R. Zachariah generally indicates the beginning and end of R. Baruch's words and always adds to his name the blessing for the dead; see, *e.g.*, J. Leveen, *Commentaries*, pp. 7b, 15a, 16a, 20a-b and 67b. He mentions Rabbenu Ḥananel in the same way; see *ibid.*, pp. 11b, 12a, 14a-b, 19b and 21b.

[3] See Epstein, pp. 27f. Scholars were indeed named after their countries of origin: "Sefaradi" (*e.g.*, Maimonides, Leveen, *Commentaries*, p. 5a) or "Maghrebi", "Maʿarabi" (*e.g.*, Joseph the son of Judah ibn Simon Maʿarabi, see Al-Harīzī, *Taḥkemoni*, ed. Kaminka, 1899, p. 362; Nahum ha-Maʿarabi, one of the translators of the Epistle to Yemen; Rab Solomon Ner ha-Maʿarab in a poem by Abraham ibn Ezra, see Z. P. Chajes (ed.), *The Commentary on the Tractate Mashqin* by Rabbenu Solomon ben Hayatom, Berlin 5670/1910, p. XIV; see also above, p. 87; but it was derogatory for a Jew to be surnamed *Yewāni*, ('a pagan Greek'), which is why the expression *me-Ereẓ Yāwān* was chosen.

Spanish rabbis...".[1] The Gaon Samuel ben ʿAli, in an epistle addressed to Aleppo, mentions incidentally that his father, the Gaon ʿAli, would receive epistles and questions from there, *inter alia* from R. Baruch.[2] When the fragments of the Berakhot commentary with the frequent mention of "RBS" were discovered in the Leningrad library, Epstein interpreted these initials as "R. Baruch Sefaradi" and decided that the R. Baruch referred to in the Gaon's epistle, in the fragments of the Berakhot commentary (which were available to him even before Assaf published them).[3] by R. Isaiah di Trani and by R. Isaac Or Zaruaʿ was one and the same person. Epstein endorsed the long-standing view that the expression *me-Ereẓ Yāwān* in *Or Zaruʿa* refers to Southern Italy and maintained that R. Baruch had grown up and been educated there.[4]

But this thesis is disproved by R. Baruch's use of the phrase "as we do in Spain",[5] which indicates that the surname Sefaradi does not denote the origin of his family, but that he himself was born and bred in that country. The many Arabic passages in quotations of his utterances confirm the view that he lived in an Arabic-speaking area. If he once explains a word by reference to the "language of Edom," this may well be Spanish, and not Italian.[6]

The Gaon Samuel ben ʿAli's statement that R. Baruch corresponded with his father permits us to conjecture that R. Baruch lived approximately from the late 11th to the middle of the 12th century.[7] He thus belonged

[1] Epstein, p. 27; see also the list of scholars *ibid.*, pp. 32-39.

[2] Assaf, *Tarbiẓ* 1/2, (1930), p. 61.

[3] Epstein's solution (p. 29) was confirmed by a passage in the British Museum MS: "These *pisqey ḥalīfīn* (decisions concerning substitution) are by R. Baruch the son of R. Samuel Sefaradi, may their memories be blessed"; J. Leveen, *Commentaries*, p. 97b. B. M. Lewin had taken those initials to mean "R. Saadia (?)"; L. Ginzberg and J. Leveen (in 1933) had suggested "R. Baruch (the son of Isaac Albalia)".

[4] Epstein, pp. 28 and 32. As to *Or Zaruʿa*, see, *e.g.*, Part IV, article 51 (Jerusalem 5647), fol. 9, col. 2, twice.

[5] Ben-Shem, p. 32.

[6] The reference is to the word *askala*, which is absent in Babli, Baba Batra 73[a], but appears in Yerushalmi, Baba Batra V,1 (15a) and in the Tosefta, *ibid.*, IV, 1. R. Isaac Or Zaruʿa (in the place indicated in note 4) reports in the name of R. Baruch that "there are those who say (that an *askala* is) a small ladder by which one boards a ship ... and so it is called in the language of Edom". This explanation surprised R. Isaac: how comes it that a scholar *me-Ereṣ Yāwān* does not interpret *askala* by the corresponding Greek word σχαλίς? See also *ʿArukh s.v.*, where we are told at the end that "the corresponding foreign word is *asqala*" (Nathan b. Jechiel, *Aruch Completum*², Vienna 1926).

[7] The basis for this estimate is as follows. R. Baruch exchanged letters with the Gaon ʿAli, the father of the Gaon Samuel (see above, n. 1). We do not know how long ʿAli held office, but on the strength of Assaf's reasoning (*Tarbiẓ* 1/1 (1929),

to the generation preceding that of R. Zachariah, but of course their lifetimes overlapped for some thirty to forty years; from this point of view there is no difficulty in assuming that R. Zachariah studied under R. Baruch.

It seems very difficult to give a definite or even a reasonable, well-founded tentative answer to the question when R. Baruch left the Maghreb, how he got to Aleppo, how it was that his teachings came to be widely known in Christian Europe or where they came to the notice of an anonymous commentator who refers to him as "the great rabbi, may God protect him" and "our rabbi Baruch, may his glory be enhanced", which indicates that the author was R. Baruch's contemporary and had seen his commentary with his own eyes.[1]

May I, with all due reserve, make a suggestion in the matter, supported by the facts already stated and those set out in the following.

R. Baruch left Muslim Spain at a mature age, possessed of comprehensive learning and fully-developed intellectual powers. He went to the Christian-controlled part, probably even before the Almohads ruled the Maghreb. Possibly intending to reach Palestine, like Judah Halevi, or one of the Eastern centres of rabbinic studies, Baghdad or Aleppo, he stopped on the way, teaching and writing his book, which circulated among the rabbis of Christian Europe. He probably passed through Southern Italy whence, perhaps, his surname *me-Ereẓ Yāwān*. In his old age, by then a famous scholar, he reached Aleppo, where he presently began to correspond with the Gaon ʿAli in Baghdad. Aleppo was then an important centre of rabbinic learning, as we know from the epistles of the Gaon Samuel ben ʿAli.[2] It also became a haven for refugees from Almohad persecution: R. Joseph ben Judah Hamaʿarabi of Ceuta, a disciple of Maimonides, and the poet R. Judah ben ʿAbbās, a friend of Judah Halevi.[3] Relations between the Babylonian academy, especially R. Samuel ben ʿAli, and the scholars who remained in the Maghreb for the time being continued during the persecutions.[4]

---

pp. 105f.) Epstein (p. 31) assumes that he died before 1150, and R. Baruch died about 1160. Therefore, and in view of other information, we are surprised at Epstein's conclusion (p. 31, last line) that "all this places R. Baruch before 1140". The identification of R. Baruch with the son of R. Isaac Albalia is untenable also in view of the fact that Abraham ben Daud, *SHQ*, pp. 61 and 63, does not say that R. Baruch ben Isaac ever left Spain.

[1] See Epstein, pp. 53 and 56f., also p. 45.

[2] See Assaf, *Tarbiẓ* 1/1, p. 126, and 1/2, p. 61; also Epstein, p. 31.

[3] Above, pp. 350, 359.

[4] Above, p. 360.

Epstein tried to strengthen his thesis of R. Baruch's South Italian origin by referring to R. Solomon ben Hayatom, author of a commentary on the Tractate Mashqin (Mo'ed Qatan), who is likewise frequently mentioned by contemporary scholars.[1] R. Solomon's stock of Italian words and method of teaching have given rise to the assumption that he grew up and was educated in Southern Italy. But precisely from this angle there is reason to doubt or at least qualify that assumption. As against the twenty-five words counted in it by H. P. Chajes, R. Solomon's commentary contains thirty Arabic words. As to the Greek words, Chajes is doubtful whether the author knew that language at all.[2]

The use of Italian is indeed *prima facie* evidence that the author lived for quite a long time in Italy, but equal evidential value attaches to the use of Arabic words, which suggests the influence of Arab culture.[3] On the other hand, we can hardly draw far-reaching conclusions from references to Jewish, and perhaps also non-Jewish, customs in Arab-Muslim countries: "a custom prevails among laundrymen in the land of Ismael"; "it is the custom of the sons of Kedar (= Arabs) to pour vinegar on a *gabshushit* that comes from Spain and wash their heads with it";[4] "such as Spaniards, of Granada and Cordoba and all their surroundings, people with bare heads."[5] All that appears with certainty from these references is that the author wished to interpret the Tractate Mashqin by means of the realities of his own day and age.

At the same time, it is surprising that R. Solomon speaks of contemporary Palestinian customs: "and they take him (a dead person) to Hebron or to whatever place they wish etc."; "as *all the people in the surroundings of Hebron still* do *today* (to the dead) (underscoring mine)—they send their dead to Hebron"; "and thus they are wont to do (to stamp with the foot (comp. Ezek. 6, 11)) in Palestine *to this day*."[6]

According to the sources identified by Chajes in R. Solomon's commentary: Rashi; Alfasi; R. Isaac ben Ghiyāt; R. Tobias, the author of *Leqaḥ*

---

[1] See Epstein, pp. 29 and 32, also pp. 27f.

[2] *Op. cit.*, (p. 451 n. 3.), pp. XXXI-XXXIV.

[3] We should be careful to distinguish between Southern Italy and Sicily. In Italy, Arab rule ceased during the first half of the 10th century, while in Sicily it lasted about a century longer. The Arab cultural centre which continued to exist in Sicily under the Normans in the 11th and 12th centuries, did not notably affect Southern Italy.

[4] P. 90, l. 7-8 from the bottom. R. Solomon means the mud at the sea shore, which dries into *gabshushit*, piles; comp. R. Ḥananel, Erub. 8a. Clearly those Arabs dwelt in Spain or in its vicinity.

[5] *Op. cit.*, p. XIII, where there are further quotations and also the references to the pages of the main part of the book.

[6] *Ibid., ibid.*

Tob; and R. Nathan, the author of the *ʿArukh*, he surmises that the "Rabbi Solomon, light of the West" in one of the poems of Abraham ibn Ezra is our R. Solomon. He assigns him to the first half of the 12th century.[1] During that period, Palestine was under Crusader rule, and it is inconceivable that Jews should have been living in and near Hebron in appreciable numbers without being mentioned by the Jewish travellers then visiting the country: Benjamin of Tudela and Petaḥya of Regensburg.[2] As we cannot advance R. Solomon's lifetime to the second half of the 11th century, we must assume that he relies on a tradition that had come to his knowledge. In fact, Benjamin of Tudela reports: "And there (in the Cave of Machpelah) are many barrels full of bones of Jews, because the Jews used to bring their dead there, each the bones of his fathers, and deposit them there to this day."[3]

Incidentally, the custom of burial in Hebron is also mentioned in a letter of Nachmanides of 1267: "I am bound for Hebron, the city of the tombs of our forefathers, to prostrate myself on them and, with God's help, to hew out a tomb there for myself."[4] Thus, the restorer of Jewish settlement in Jerusalem wished to be buried in Hebron.

In sum: even if we disregard the references to customs in Eastern countries, there can be no doubt that, in addition to the use of the Arabic language, we must pay attention to the surname Sefaradi which R. Isaiah di Trani gives his countryman, R. Solomon, surely on the basis of reliable traditions.[5] It seems likely that R. Solomon hailed from Spain, and that he also received his rabbinic education in that country. The uncertainty prevailing on this point is due to the great mobility of rabbinic scholars in those days, a phenomenon which will be dealt with at the end of this discussion.

Comparing the sources used by the three, R. Baruch ben Samuel, R. Zachariah ben Judah and R. Solomon ben Hayatom, and their exegetic methods, we may conclude that they were all born and educated in a rabbinic environment in a country under Muslim rule—the first two in

[1] See *ibid.*, pp. XIVf. and XXVf.

[2] See *Masʿot Rabbi Benjamin*, ed. Adler, London 1907, p. 27; R. Petaḥya, *Sibbub*, ed. Grünhut, pp. 33-4. R. Benjamin saw two Jewish dyers in Bethlehem; *ibid.*, p. 26.

[3] Note the expression "still . . . today" and "to this day" used by R. Benjamin and R. Solomon (see above, p. 454 n. 6).

[4] A. Yaʿari, *Iggerot Ereṣ-Yisrael*, Tel Aviv 1943, p. 85; B. Z. Kedar, *Tarbiẓ* 41 (1971), pp. 93-4.

[5] Chajes, *op. cit.*, p. XII and note 2, relies also on Abraham Epstein. The initials RaSHY may have to be read "Rabbi Shelomo Yatom (or Yishaqi)" and there may be a copyist's error for "Ben Hayatom"; see also J. N. Epstein, p. 29.

the Maghreb (in the wider sense) and R. Solomon presumably so. Perhaps we may also assume that all three were decisively influenced by one *beyt midrash*, whose methods of study were based on those of R. Ḥananel, R. Nissim ben Jacob and Alfasi; the latter's writings were well known to them. For the time being, we cannot locate that *beyt midrash*, but it was certainly not in Lucena.[1] Our thesis would account for the similarity of the methods of the three scholars. The special character of the three is brought out very clearly by a comparison with an anonymous author, a fragment of whose commentary on Baba Meẓi'a was published by Epstein from an Oxford MS as Appendix I to his paper on R. Baruch.[2]

A collation of that author's commentary on Baba Meẓi'a 7a-15a with the corresponding passage in R. Zachariah [3]—which indeed comprises only a few pages—reveals a series of formal and substantive differences.

The anonymous author's commentary is on the Gemara, that of R. Zachariah on Alfasi's Halakhot. At the former's time of writing, R. Baruch was still alive,[4] while R. Zachariah always adds to his name the blessing for the dead. The two utterances of R. Baruch quoted in the anonymous commentary are not quoted, or referred to in any way, by R. Zachariah. Their language and style indicate that they were not written in this form by R. Baruch, whose style is well known to us from R. Zachariah's many quotations. They are translations into Hebrew and have been adapted to the mode of expression of R. Ḥananel, whose influence is recognisable throughout the anonymous commentary.[5] The latter contains no reference to the Geonim or the "First (post-Gaonic) Generations" and no explanations of individual words by means of equivalents in foreign languages, as we find in Rashi and as are frequent also in the commentaries of R. Baruch, R. Solomon and R. Zachariah; and especially, there is not a single word of Arabic, the language familiar to the Spanish scholars, We may thus conclude that the anonymous commentary originates from Christian Europe, perhaps from Italy, the presumed country of origin of R. Ḥananel.

We still have to discuss the mobility of the three scholars, a quality they share with other rabbis in the Maghreb in the days of Muslim rule, with

---

[1] See above, p. 447.
[2] Epstein, pp. 45-59.
[3] Leveen, *Commentaries*, pp. 64b-68b.
[4] See Epstein, p. 53 and nn. 1 and 4, and pp. 56f.
[5] At the same time, Epstein, p. 45, denies that we may have to do here with a commentary by R. Ḥananel rather than a "commentary which makes much use of, abridges and adds to R. Ḥananel's commentary".

many of their Muslim colleagues, and also with many European Jewish scholars.

From the middle of the 10th century, African Maghrebi scholars show a tendency to migrate to the Spanish Maghreb, which tendency increases in the 11th and early 12th centuries owing to the economic and spiritual attraction of that centre. But the growing political disarray of Muslim Spain after the onset of the Reconquest led, even before the Almohad persecution, to the emigration of Jews to Christian Spain, Provence, Italy and Oriental countries. The three scholars are representative of the exodus from North Africa and Spain. R. Zachariah presumably went to Northern Spain or Provence, R. Baruch spent the latter part of his life in Aleppo, and R. Solomon ben Hayatom settled in Italy.

Let us sum up. This Appendix deals with three unknown 12-th century Maghrebi rabbinic scholars, viz. R. Zachariah ben Judah, of whom we spoke first, his great teacher, R. Baruch, and R. Solomon Benhayatom, who belonged to the same circle, at any rate as far as his method is concerned. Our purpose has been twofold: to show how they migrated to different parts of the Mediterranean world and to clarify a few points of their biographies and exegetic procedures. There is still much room for research into their work in all respects: language, methodological dependence, sources etc.[1] Such research will no doubt greatly enlarge our knowledge of Maghreb Jewry.

---

[1] We have already (on p. 449 n.1) referred to S. Abramson's study, which demonstrates he need for more such comparative research.

APPENDIX II

TUNIS

(The Rehabilitation of a Community after the Almohad Persecutions)

The main purpose of this Appendix is to show how by coordinating widely scattered details the gap of our knowledge of the history of Maghrebi Jewry, beginning with the time of the Almohad persecutions, may ultimately be closed.

A community on which information would seem to be particularly scarce is that of Tunis. Still, we shall find that the assembled references fuse into an important segment of the history of Tunis Jewry, covering a period of approximately 300 years (1160-1470). Moreover we may assume that developments in other places on the Mediterranean coast during that period were more or less on the same lines.

Among the responsa in *Yākhīn u-Boʿaz* I, whose author is R. Ṣemaḥ Dūrān (a son of R. Solomon (RaSHBaSH) and grandson of R. Simon ben Ṣemaḥ (RaSHBaṢ), who was active in Algiers in the second half of the 15th century, there is one (no. 132) that deals with the permissibility of the sale of a dilapidated and abandoned synagogue at the Jewish merchants' inn in Tunis and the construction of a new synagogue with the proceeds. It is addressed to R. Joseph Zimron "while he was still living in Tunis", as it says in the heading—probably before he moved to Constantine. R. Ṣemaḥ sent other responsa to R. Joseph Zimron when the latter was living in Constantine.[1] In the opening of one of these (no. 126) we read "after I arrived from Majorca" and the date 5228/1468. R. Ṣemaḥ was in Majorca for a cure in 5225/1465 (no. 124), and I assume that the two responsa addressed to R. Joseph Zimron in Tunis (nos. 132 and 133) were written several years previously.[2] If so, they are not later than the end

[1] Nos. 78-80, 126 and 149-150.

[2] R. Joseph ben R. Abraham Zimron was a pupil of the RaSHBaSH, and the latter's responsa include some addressed to "our oldest pupil" in Bougie (nos. 12-18, 225 and 288-294) or in Constantine, which name is spelt in different ways (nos. 19-46, 235-246, 327-331, 482-496, 596-602 and 613). Incidentally, we find the name of Joseph ben Abraham Zimron mentioned in some MS fragments in the Escorial written during the life of his teacher RaSHBaSH; Neubauer, *Ha-Maggid* 15 (1871), p. 53 b. Nos. 12 and 225 indicate that after completing his studies with the RaSHBaSH, R. Joseph

of the fifties of the 15th century. This date is of some importance because of the historical content of no. 132.

The halakhic discussion concerning the permissibility of selling the communal synagogue embodies some information about its founders and earliest congregants, as well as about its shape. Our sources being poor in details of this kind, that information is of particular importance, especially as it is based on reliable traditions and on evidence taken by R. Ṣemaḥ as to conditions prevailing in his time.

The portions of the responsum that are of historical interest may be given here textually, because they allow us a glimpse into the life of the Jewish community in Tunis.

"To Our Beloved and Dear R. Joseph Zimron (may God protect him and keep him alive) when he was still in Tunis . . . Thought must be given to the synagogue in Tunis concerning which it has been asked whether it may be sold or not . . .

Even if you say that it was not financed and built by Jews from all over the world or by the wearers of the round cape (*capos*), but by the local inhabitants, there can be no doubt that it was dedicated to Jews from all over the world, so that every Jew wearing the round cape who came to

---

lived with his family in Bougie, where he engaged in commerce—at any rate he was not one of the local *dayyanim* (see no. 229). While in Constantine, R. Joseph corresponded with the RaSHBaSH and his son R. Ṣemaḥ, as well as with his son R. Aaron (see *Yakhin u-Boʿaz* I, at the beginning of no. 126: "You find it difficult to accept what my lord brother, the wise R. Aaron, may God preserve him, wrote in reply to questions from Constantine while I was on the island of Majorca"). R. Aaron apparently replied to those questions after the death of the RaSHBaSH; his answers did not commend themselves to R. Joseph, who therefore submitted the same questions to R. Ṣemaḥ after the latter's return from Majorca. It is true that the RaSHBaSH would answer questions in his own name during his father's, the RaSHBaṢ's, lifetime (see nos. 287 and 294), but we cannot attribute such a practice to RaSHBaSH's son R. Aaron, who was quite undistinguished and would not be known to us as a responsa writer but for the testimony of R. Ṣemaḥ. It thus seems likely that the RaSHBaSH died during R. Ṣemaḥ's stay in Majorca, at the age of sixty-one or sixty-two (he was born in 1404). The probable chronological order of the responsa to R. Joseph Zimron is therefore as follows: 1. From the RaSHBaSH, to Bougie and later to Constantine; 2. from R. Aaron, immediately after his father's death, to Constantine; 3. from R. Ṣemaḥ, after his return from Majorca, to Constantine. Two responsa of R. Ṣemaḥ to "our beloved, dear" R. Joseph in Tunis do not fit into this scheme. They seem early; their tone is friendly, as appropriate between men who had studied together under the RaSHBaSH. I therefore believe that we have to do here with a kind of comradely advice sought by R. Joseph, who had recently been in Tunis, before he arrived in Constantine or even Bougie. If so, they were written during the RaSHBaSH's lifetime, and the addition of "deceased" after his name at the end of no. 133 belongs to the scribe. However, the matter requires further consideration. For R. Ṣemaḥ's stay in Majorca see Baer's very interesting remarks, *Spain* II, p. 496, n. 30.

Tunis from the four corners of the earth, by sea or by land, might come to it and pray in it; you cannot say that if it was built on behalf of some particular individuals, only they and their descendants, and not wearers of the round cape, may pray there. In fact, every wearer of the round cape who came to Tunis by sea or land has resorted to that house to pray there without hindrance since the day of its establishment until the present day. It is thus dedicated to all Jews by common consent... In my view, this synagogue, which has become a permanent ruin, should be abandoned and not built up again because it is very far from the Jewish quarter. Efforts should be made to build another synagogue within the Jewish quarter, so that people may attend services early in the morning and late in the evening, which they are not able to do at the ruined synagogue because of its remoteness. They should leave the latter in its desolation and build a new synagogue in the Jewish quarter in order to pray there, pour out their hearts to the Lord and fast and call solemn assemblies, thus fulfilling the duty of congregational prayer morning, evening and noon ... When that synagogue was first built, the people were few, and all the Jews who were there were able to pray in it even when other sojourners came and joined them; the place would hold them all. Now, however, that house cannot hold all the Jews who are there and who wish to pray in it, because they are now a large community and the house is too small for them, which was not the case before. Nor was the place out of the way before, because the people who built it were staying at the *pūndāq* (inn) where the synagogue was built and were able to pray there always without inconvenience or special effort, every day —evening, morning and noon. But now things are different because the Jews are not now living at the *pūndāq* or in its vicinity; they live in a quarter very far from the inn where the synagogue was, so that they are not able to go and pray at that house three times a day but only in the morning, and not all the people but only a few—the remnants whom the Lord calls those who are anxious for His word—because of the great distance. For the two reasons I have mentioned, viz. the smallness of the house in relation to the number of worshippers, whom it cannot accommodate all, and the great distance from the Jewish quarter, which prevents people from worshipping there regularly..., they are obliged to build another synagogue, which will have room for the whole congregation so that they will go and say their prayers there every day...

From what you have written, it appears that that synagogue was a small penthouse on a building not itself sacred and that the ceiling and walls of that penthouse have now collapsed, so that nothing sacred remains but the floor, *i.e.* a roof." (*Yākhīn u-Boʿaz* I, no. 132, *fol.* 41a-42a).

Probably the *funduq* itself has also been abandoned at that time because some of in RaSHBaSH's responsa deal with a privately owned *funduq* in Tunis (see below, para. 33).

Let us now point out the relevant facts emerging from our responsum:

1. The place of the synagogue makes it most plausible that she was established by "wearers of the round cape"[1] on the roof of the inn[2] at which they used to stay, and also by Jews "from all over the world".[3]

2. Though very small, the synagogue was at first sufficient for both the local wearers of the round cape and the visiting traders wearing that garment who came to Tunis by sea or land.

3. After a time, the synagogue could no longer hold all intending worshippers. Moreover, the Jewish quarter moved far away from the inn, and Jews no longer resided at the inn or anywhere else in the neighbourhood.

4. The desolate, abandoned synagogue fell into utter ruin. Its walls collapsed, and only its floor, *i.e.* the roof, or part thereof, on which the synagogue had been built, remained.

5. In R. Ṣemaḥ Dūrān's time, the question of selling the remnants of the synagogue arose, and he was consulted about it.

All these facts are vague, of unknown date, except for the estimated date of R. Ṣemaḥ's reply. Our task is to discover particulars likely to dispel this vagueness and fill in the blanks.

Let us begin with some general matters.

Christian traders from European cities who in the Middle Ages maintained relations with ports on the southern shore of the Mediterranean constructed residential buildings and warehouses for themselves

[1] More about this word below, p. 462.

[2] Chapels were usually attached to the inns of Christian merchants trading in Muslim lands under special treaties or capitulations, the service being held by a priest of the denomination (see below p. 462 n. 1). Since the Antiquity and till recent times there existed in some places on the side of the synagogue a room (or more) to accomodate travellers, who could not afford to pay for lodging; S. Klein, *MGWJ* 76 (1932), pp. 545-55; *ibid.* 77 (1933), pp. 81-4; comp. also below nn. p. 474 n. 1 and 2.

[3] In the original: *baʾey ʿolām.* As to this expression, contrasted with *beney ʿir* "the townspeople" at the beginning of R. Ṣemaḥ's responsum, *cp.* e.g. RaDBaZ, *Responsa* II, no. 248 (ed. Sudzilkow, Part I, 31, 4): כל באי עולם הבאים דרך ים פרנקייא או מתורכייא ... "from all the world who come by sea, from countries of the Franks or from Turkey ..." A. Sayous, *Le Commerce des Européens à Tunis depuis le XII siècle jusqu'à la fin du XVI*, Paris 1929, traces back the existence of a Jewish *funduq* in the city of Tunis to the 12th century. They dwelled also in a faubourg outside the city, called *bled el-Yahoud.* Sayous does not indicate the source of his information.

that were known as *funduqs* (Hebrew pronunciation: pūndāq). Commercial treaties between European trading cities and Muslim states ensured immunity for the *funduqs* and safety of life and property and freedom of religious worship, including the right to build churches, for their inhabitants. As a rule, the *funduqs* were situated near the harbour and formed a distinct administrative unit, with autonomous jurisdiction, separate from the Muslim town.[1] One of the first cities to trade with Tunis and Tunisia seems to have been Pisa, whose ships are mentioned in Geniza documents of the 12th century.[2] As far as we know, the earliest commercial treaty between Pisa and Tunis was signed in 1157.[3] The Catalan *funduq* and consulate in Tunis were established in 1253.[4] Altogether, trade relations between Tunis and European ports expanded after the accession of the Ḥafṣid dynasty in Tunisia. According to Adorne, a Flemish-born Christian traveller and contemporary of R. Ṣemaḥ Dūrān, there were Genoese, Venetian, Pisan and Florentine *funduqs* in Tunis. All these buildings were near the Sea Gate, *i.e.* the France Gate of the period of the French protectorate over Tunisia.[5] The Jewish *funduq* which had been established by the wearers of the round cape in accordance with the rights they enjoyed as foreign traders—and which suited their needs and those of their neighbours, was undoubtedly situated in the same area. To be sure, in R. Ṣemaḥ ben Dūrān's time, Jews had already ceased to live in it. More on this below.

"Wearers of the round cape" is a frequent appellation in contemporary literature for Jews of Spanish origin. By royal decree, the Jews of Aragon were forced already in the 13th century to wear distinctive cloaks known as *cape ronde*, whence the appellation "wearers of the *capos* or *caperon*[*de*].[6]

[1] L. de Mas Latrie, *Traités de Paix et de Commerce et documents divers concernant les relations des chrétiens avec les Arabes de l'Afrique septentrionale au Moyen Age*, Paris 1866, I, Introduction, pp. 89-92; gives an exhaustive description of the *funduqs*, their legal status, the rights of their inhabitants, etc. See also Ch. E. Dufourcq, *L'Espagne Catalane et le Maghreb aux XIIe et XIVe siècles*, Paris 1965, pp. 69-70.

[2] See Hirschberg, *Yitzhak F. Baer Jubilee Volume* (Hebrew), Jerusalem 1960, p. 142 (margin, l. 31); a document from Goitein, *Sefer Hodu* (still in MS), No. 97, is mentioned on p. 148 in the note to l. 30/1 (see also *infra* p. 464 n. 4).

[3] See Mas Latrie, *op. cit.*, *II Documents*, pp. 23-26.

[4] See Dufourcq, *op. cit.*, pp. 95 and 415.

[5] R. Brunschwig, *Deux Récits de Voyage inédits en Afrique du Nord au XVe siècle*, 1936, pp. 186-7; Dufourcq, *op. cit.*, pp. 69-70.

[6] See RaSHBaSH, no. 413. RDBaZ, no. 910, mentions a quarrel in Cairo between the *coposiyin* on the one hand and the Maghrebis and Tunisians on the other, resulting in separate worship. He notes that the *coposiyin* are Catalan expellees; he clearly means those of them who originally settled in Tunis and Algeria and quarrelled with the established residents of North Africa over prayer customs. On the *capos* edict in

Generations later, the *capos*, originally marks of shame, became robes of honour of Spanish expellee rabbis in Turkey, who refused to discard them on the Sabbath in spite of the ban pronounced by their Eastern colleagues.[1]

Another important fact attesting to the legal status of the inhabitants of the Jewish *funduq*: the synagogue was erected on the roof of the building, which is surprising in several respect. It is not in accordance with Jewish tradition ("Out of the depths have I cried unto thee, O Lord", Ps. 130:1). It contradicts everything known to us of the location of synagogues in Muslim and Christian towns. Both in the Islamic domain and in countries under Christian rule, the Jews were not allowed by either custom or law to build synagogues in raised and conspicuous positions; they therefore built them in low places, concealed from view by surrounding structures, or behind façades simulating residential buildings. On the other hand, the establishment of a synagogue in a penthouse seems perfectly plausible under the special conditions enjoyed by the round-caped traders. The area of the inns was outside the jurisdiction of Muslim Tunis, and the Christians, too, were free to build places of worship in conspicuous positions.[2] The Christian neighbours, themselves foreign traders, could hardly object to the action of the Jews for two reasons: 1. by doing so, they would have compromised their own right of public worship; 2. the European consuls, under whose patronage all these traders were living and who were their supreme judicial authorities, were certainly not anxious to become involved in religious disputes.[3]

The construction of the synagogue on the roof of the inn suggests that it was a small, makeshift penthouse, though perfectly sufficient for the needs of the permanent residents of the inn and of the visiting traders who put up there from time to time when passing through Tunis. This is the conclusion reached by R. Ṣemaḥ Dūrān at the end of his responsum.

The findings so far arrived at, on the basis of R. Ṣemaḥ's responsum, with regard to the probable origin, legal status, and number of the inn's residents do not answer the questions as to the circumstances of the

Aragon see Régné, Catalogue des actes de Jaime Ier etc. (1213-1291), REJ, 60 (1910)—70 (1920), no. 1117 (dated 1284; the alfaqui Samuel is exempted from wearing a *capo*). R. Solomon ben Adret, Responsa V, no. 183, mentions the great expense incurred by the Jews to obtain a mitigation of the decree requiring them to wear large badges "until the prescribed size was reduced by half and wearers of the (Jewish) cape (*gelima*) were no longer obliged to wear the badge." For particulars see A. Neuman, *The Jews in Spain*, Philadelphia 1942, II, pp. 201-2; 205-6; 327, n. 135; and 345 (*capa rotunda*).

[1] See Hirschberg in *Religion in the Middle East*, Cambridge 1969, I, p. 186.

[2] See Brunschvig, *Deux Récits*, p. 187.

[3] Dufourcq, *op. cit.*, p. 69; and see, e.g., *ibid.*, p. 422, on the powers vested in the Consul Blancas.

establishment of the wearers of the round cape at the inn and the founding of the synagogue, the period of time that passed until the number of residents at the inn had become too great, and the reasons why they deemed it necessary to move to another quarter, far away from their original abode. To solve these questions, we must first of all marshal the different testimonies in our possession as to the presence of Jews in Tunis from the days of the Almohads to the time of R. Ṣemaḥ Dūrān.

1. Upon the conquest of Tunis by al-Mu'min (1160), Jews and Christians were given the choice between conversion and death.[1] This cruel measure, leaving no option of emigration, was designed to cow the inhabitants of the other, as yet unconquered parts of the country into submitting to Almohad rule.

2. A responsum of Maimonides (1135-1205) relates to an incident connected with Tunis. A merchant, probably from Sicily, "travelled to Tunis, where he sold and bought goods and dispatched a letter to L. . . . He then left Tunis and presently went down with his goods in a shipwreck."[2]

3. A letter from Maimonides to his son contains the following passages: "And you should always be extremely cautious of the people who live [in the coastal area] between Tunis and Alexandria and also of those who live in the mountains of Barbary. . ."[3]

4. A Tunisian chronicler, Zarkashi (wrote about 1523) reports:

"In the year 595/1199, al-Manṣūr (1184-1199) ordered the Jews to wear the *shikla*: shirts (*qumuṣ*) of material an ell (*dhirāʿ*) square and cloaks (*barānis*) with blue hoods (*qalānis*)."[4]

Al-Marrākeshi (1185-after 1223) dwells at length on the order issued by al-Manṣūr to the Jews of the Outer Maghreb, but the garments mentioned by him are quite different.[5] Zarkashi obviously had another source before him, which recorded events in the form they took in Tunisia.

The sources quoted in paragraphs 2-4 show clearly that the Jews returned to Tunis, and to Tunisia generally, not long after their persecution by al-Ma'mūn. Their position in time became so secure that a foreign Jew could stay and trade in Tunis. Maimonides' warning to his son against the Jews living between Tunis and Tripolitanis indicates that

---

[1] Ibn al-Athir, XI, pp. 134-135 and 159-160.

[2] *Responsa*, ed. Blau, I, no. 87, pp. 135f.

[3] See above, p. 165.

[4] *Ta'rīkh al-Dawlatayn al-Muwaḥḥadiyya wa-l Ḥafsiyya*, Tunis 1889, p. 11 (French translation: E. Fagnan, *Chronique des Almohades*, Constantine 1895, pp. 19f.).

[5] R. Dozy (ed.), *The History of the Almohades etc.*, Leyden 1881 (second ed.), p. 223; comp. above p. 201.

he knew not only that there were Jews in that area but that they were not persecuted. Upon al-Manṣūr's accession, the region knew serious troubles when the Almoravid ruler of Majorca, ʿĀli ibn Ghāniya captured Bougie and gained control of the whole area east of it. Al-Manṣūr marched against him two years later and reconquered Tunis, Qābes, Tozeur and Qafṣa after severe fighting. Zarkashi notes that the battle for Qafṣa was particularly fierce.[1] The Jews no doubt took advantage of these unsettled conditions in order to get rid of oppressive restrictions.[2]

5. From a Geniza fragment of the twenties of the 13th century which mentions Tunis and Qābes in connection with a Messianic movement it can be surmised, at least, that both towns had a Jewish population.[3]

6. A letter of recommendation of the 20th Shawwāl, 624 (3rd October, 1227) from Tunis to Pisa.[4] Omar ibn Abū Bekr al-Ṣābūni, of Tunis, a courtier of the local ruler, recommends the bearer of the letter, Omar ibn Abī Jayyid the Israelite, also of Tunis, to the Podestà Ubaldo Visconti, the lord of Bish (= Pisa).[5] Omar ibn Abū Jayyid has a claim in Pisa against Abdhin the Jew, his son-in-law Bitura [6] (the Jew), who has become a Christian, and others. The Muslim courtier asks the podestà to help the claimant obtain what is due to him. Although in possession of valid documents, the latter is unable to collect the debt since the debtors are on friendly terms with Pisan notables. The writer asks for a study of the documents and concludes by reiterating his request, stressing that the claimant is his protégé (*jār*). He promises sympathetic attention in the event of a similar request on the part of the podestà of Pisa.

7. A letter of 1237 from two Muslims, subjects of the king of Tunisia, to Ubaldo Visconti, the podestà of Pisa. *Inter alia* they request the podestà to help Bonaut the Jew, of Tunis, who has come to Pisa to seek redress

---

[1] See Zarkashi, *l.c.*; Léo l'Africain gives a different sequence of events; comp. *Description*, pp. 379f. and notes.

[2] At any rate, their position in that part of the Maghreb was not so precarious as in Morocco; comp. above, ch. II at the end.

[3] Assaf, *Zion*, 5 (1939/40), p. 122, l. 8, and p. 123, l. 36 (*Sources and Studies* (Hebrew), p. 147).

[4] Published in M. Amari, *I Diplomi arabi del real archivio fiorentino*, Firenze 1863, pp. 83-85.

[5] In Jewish Geniza documents we have found two forms: פישאוין and פישוין (Pisans); see p. 462 n. 2. *Yosifon*, cap. I, ed. Huminer, p. 45, writes נהר פישאה.

[6] Both names seem strange; Amari transliterates them as Abidsin and Beitura. Does the second name stand for Bitas or for a similar sounding name, *e.g.* Ventura? Comp. below, para. 33.

in a legal matter. By acting upon their recommendation he will earn the gratitude of the king and all the people of Tunis.[1]

8. For the year 648/1250, Zarkashi reports that the *shikla* was enforced in Tunis.

It is interesting to note that this measure, too, was taken after a revolt —in this case against the Ḥafṣid ruler al-Mustanṣir the First (1249-1277)— had been put down. It might seem that the rebels had found it to their advantage to ease the restrictions imposed on the Jews. But then the *shikla* may have fallen into disuse in the course of time.[2]

9. In 1267, Moses of Tunis was the Arabic clerk or secretary of the Genoese traders resident in Tunis.[3]

10. In 1276, King Jaime I of Aragon let to Abraham Avin Galell a workshop at the entrance to the Jewish quarter of Valencia; he did so on the recommendation of the king of Tunis, no doubt in view of Abraham's political services or business connections.[4]

11. King Pedro III of Aragon, in a document of 1285, the last year of his reign,[5] orders his representative in Tunis to make over to the Jew Solomon ibn Zahut[6] half of the revenues falling due to the king from imposts on the local *funduq* (of the Aragons) during a period of two years.

12. In 1293, the Jew Bondavi, surnamed *al-Faqīh*[7] travelled with his family to Tlemcen and Tunis on a secret mission on behalf of King Jaime II of Aragon. The fact that he took his family with him points to a rather extended stay in Africa and to the existence of organized Jewish communities in the places where he was sent.[8]

---

[1] The latter was published in Latin translation in Amari, *Diplomi arabi*, p. 291, and Mas Latrie, *Traités*, II Documents, pp. 30-31. Bonaut seems to be a variant of Bonet.

[2] *Ta'rikh*, p. 25/45.

[3] Brunschvig, *La Berbérie orientale*, I, p. 414; Mas Latrie, *op. cit.*, *II Documents*, p. 122, n. 1.

[4] Régné, No. 654; see also Dufourcq, *op. cit.*, p. 127 and n. 2. Abraham Avin Galell, in the service of the kings of Aragon (and Castile), is mentioned several times more in Aragonese documents; see Régné nos. 810, 1514, 1701 and 2390; above p. 376 and notes; Baer, *Die Juden im christlichen Spanien*, II, Berlin 1936, p. 91; *ibid.*, p. 491, n. 49.

[5] Régné, No. 1381; Baer, *op. cit.*, p. 502, n. 23.

[6] In the document: Abenzahit. We may have to do here with an appellation denoting a physical defect, as usual in Arabic. *Za'ūṭ* means a man with a drooping eyelid or the pupil of one of whose eyes is lower. Zahut (like Dahud for Da'ūd) is the cognomen of the Bacri family, famous in Algeria in the 18th and 19th centuries.

[7] In Arabic: scholar of religious law, but in Spanish court parlance *al-faqui* is the learned physician, the trustworthy official.

[8] Régné, nos. 2481-2483; see above p. 377 and Dufourcq, *op. cit.*, pp. 329-331. As for the name Bondavi, see the end of n. 3 to p. 470.

13. Some important information of a kind very rare in Muslim sources is preserved in Zarkashi's Chronicle:[1]

Abū ʿAli Omar, the *qāḍī al-ankiḥa* (marriages), died in the year 731/1330.[2] There had been tension between him and ʿAbd al-Rafīʿ, the *qāḍī al-jamāʿa*[3] (of the community, *i.e.* the chief qadi), both for personal reasons and over matters of principle. Abū ʿAli was once asked whether marriage contracts (*ʿuqdat nikāḥ*) made between protected persons (*dhimmī*) and witnessed by Muslims were valid. He answered in the affirmative. Ibn ʿAbd al-Rafīʿ rejected Abū ʿAli's view, but the latter instructed the notaries (*ʿudūl*)[4] of Tunis to confirm such contracts. He wrote a book maintaining the permissibility of hearing suits between protected persons and of confirming their legal documents and marriage contracts; he called it *Idrāk al-Ṣawāb fi Ankiḥa Ahl al-Kitāb* (Reaching the Right Conclusions as to Matrimonial Matters of the People of the Book). The chief qadi thereupon wrote a book propounding the opposite view.

Zarkashi adds that two other Muslim jurists likewise disagreed in these matters. The argument against confirmation was in this case that protected persons do not adhere to Islamic law in their contracts, which was countered with the remark that "we do not ask them about what is allowed according to our law (*sharʿ*) and it does not trouble us if they transgress it."

Without going into the historico-legal implications of the marriage contracts—the so-called *ṣadāq*—made between Jews before Muslim authorities, the validity of which was a subject of controversy among Tunis clerics, we gather from Zarkashi's words that some such contracts were made not later than the first third of the 14th century, *i.e.* about three generations before the arrival in North Africa of expellee scholars from Spain and Majorca (1391). Contracts of this kind are mentioned as a matter of course in the responsa of R. Isaac b. Sheshet and R. Simon b. Ẓemaḥ Dūrān.[5]

[1] *Taʾrikh*, p. 56.

[2] In the Maghreb countries (including Spain), the special post existed of qāḍī for the drawing up and confirmation of marriage contracts; see E. Tyan, *Histoire de l'organisation judiciaire en pays d'Islam*, Paris 1938, I, p. 156. This post seems to have been particularly important in Tunis, since its local incumbent is frequently mentioned by Zarkashi; see, e.g., *op. cit.*, pp. 29 and 135f.

[3] See Tyan, *op. cit.*, p. 185.

[4] See Tyan, *op. cit.*, pp. 349ff., esp. p. 345 n. 1; comp. also index, *s.v.* shuhūd. For the attitude of the Jewish authorities towards the Muslim notaries see above, pp. 240ff.

[5] See, *e.g.*, RIBaSH, *Responsa*, nos. 102 and 148; RaSHBaṢ, *Responsa* II, no. 200; RaSHBaSH, no. 477.

The very existence of the *ṣadāq* contracts reflects a socio-religious reality of a special kind. This reality and the legal significance of the marriage deeds will be discussed elsewhere.

14. During the war between King Jaime II of Majorca (1291-1327) and Tunisia in 1308, the Ḥafṣid government confiscated the goods of Majorcan Jews in Tunis. The goods were subsequently released, but later confiscated again (1309). The documents mention goods of three Jewish, one Muslim and one Christian, traders as well as of four Jewish, one Muslim and one Christian, agents. The agents no doubt lived in Tunis.[1]

15. At the negotiations for a commercial and political treaty, conducted in the year 1329 by the Consul Blacas on behalf of the young King Jaime III of Majorca, Blacas was assisted by a Jewish interpreter, Maymon ben Nono.[2]

16. In 1330 the Jew Joseph Asusi (*i.e.* of Sousse in Tunisia), a customs farmer of the Ḥafṣid kingdom of Tunis, tried to levy customs and imposts from Catalan traders—both Christians and Jews—in excess of the agreed rates, in violation of the peace treaty signed between the two countries in 1329.[3]

17. The peace treaty concluded in 1360 (for a period of ten years) between Abu Isḥāq Ibrāhīm, Sultan of Tunis and Bougie, and King Pedro IV of Aragon (1336-1387) contains the earliest express references to Jewish inhabitants both of Catalonia and of Tunisia. The nationals of both states are assured of safety on the highways and protection against robbers. Tunisian citizens are forbidden to rob ships and cause damage to Pedro's subjects, both Christians and others. The consuls of the King of Aragon in Tunisia are to have exclusive jurisdiction in matters between Christians and Jews hailing from Catalonia. They are to collect the usual fees from their Christian and Jewish nationals. One article provides that no Muslim or Jewish Tunisian shall be taken captive in Pedro's domains and that, if such captives be found, they shall be set free; the same is to apply to Pedro's subjects in the lands of Abu Isḥāq. Lastly, the Tunisian sultan promised Pedro a share of 2,000 great gold dinars annually in the customs duty on goods imported and exported by his Christian and Jewish subjects.[4]

---

[1] Dufourcq, *op. cit.*, p. 446. About the influx of Majorcan Jews to North Africa before 1391, see Baer, *Spain* II, p. 46.

[2] *Ibid.*, p. 506, no. 5.

[3] *Ibid.*, p. 507, n. 3.

[4] The Arabic original and a Castilian translation were published in Maximiliano A. Alarcón y Santón y Ramón García de Linares, *Los documentos árabes diplomáticos*

Here is a translation of the summarizing passage of the Arabic text of the treaty:[1]

"Whosoever travels by land or by sea from the said exalted seat of His Honour [2] or from his other lands to the lands of the said magnificient King Pedro [3] shall be entitled to protection (*aman*) of his person and property; no imposts shall be levied from him in respect of his commerce except the old customary imposts, whether he be in transit or a resident. The same shall apply to people from the lands of the said magnificent Pedro who come to the said exalted seat of His Honour—may Allah the Most High guide him—or to his other lands. And this shall be so throughout the duration of the said peace.

If they (the subjects of Pedro) build inns for themselves as their dwelling-places at the said exalted seat of His Honour, and erect houses and storageplaces for themselves, no one but members of their company [4] shall live there with them, except with their consent.

If they have consuls at the said exalted seat of His Honour or in the other lands under his (the Tunisian ruler's) control, these shall decide disputes between Catalan Christians and Jews from their lands, either in their favour or against them;[5] only their consuls, appointed in that behalf, shall judge between them.

The consul shall receive his (the ruler's) letter at the said seat of His Honour or in his other lands, wherever he (the consul) has jurisdiction over their communities.[6]

After the conclusion of this peace, no Muslim or Jew from the said seat of His Honour or from his (the ruler's) other lands shall be taken captive or become a slave in the lands of the magnificent King Pedro. And if such should be found to have happened, he (the person in question) shall be set free. Nor shall one of the people (who come)

---

del Archivo de la Corona de Aragón, Madrid 1940, No. 140 bis, 25 Ṣafar 761 = 15 January 1360, pp. 311-320; see also next note.

[1] Isidro de Las Cagigas, in *Hespéris* 19 (1934), pp. 65-77, published a contemporary Latin translation of the treaty that differs from the original in certain particulars: there are several enlargements; the Jews are mentioned expressly only once; typical Arabic expressions are translated freely, etc.

[2] In the original: *ḥaḍra* "presence", a typically Arabic epithet for a ruler or notable. The Latin translation has *Nobilis Ciuitas Tunis*, the Castilian *excelsa Majestad*.

[3] In the original: *Enbir*. *En* is a Castilian honorific always tacked on to the bearer's name; Bir—Pier, Pedro.

[4] In the original: *ṣanf*, i.e. merchants' or artisans' guild.

[5] I.e. whether they are plaintiffs or defendants.

[6] The original uses the term *ṭā'ifa*—community; the reference is to Christians and Jews.

from the lands of the magnificent King Pedro to the lands of the said seat of His Honour, Christian or Jew, be taken captive or become a slave after the conclusion of this peace. And if such should be found to have happened, he (the person in question) shall be set free."

18. "And then (in 1391) they came to Algiers, Oran, Bougie and Tunis [1] because of those persecutions (the anti-Jewish measures taken in that year), and R. Maymūn bar Saadia came to Constantine."[2]

19. In 1400, King Abū Fāris of Tunisia (1394-1434) sent the physician Bonjuha Bondavi to King Martin of Aragon (1395-1410) in Barcelona to negotiate a peace treaty. Martin ordered the Barcelona city authorities to exempt Bondavi and his two companions from having to wear the distinctive Jewish badge.[3]

20. A rather peculiar affair is reported in a responsum of R. Isaac bar Sheshet to R. Samuel Ḥalayo in Breshk, which is mainly concerned with Sabbath laws (no. 93). It incidentally answers a question concerning a man who had become converted to Judaism at Maṭmaṭa.[4] The fact that he is said to have subsequently reverted to Islam would indicate that he was a Muslim prior to his conversion. He would tell about things he was able to do by means of incantations. "But his eventual behaviour shows that he is a swindler and a liar, for we have heard that he backslid in Tunis because the traders there enticed him. He allowed himself to be enticed and submitted himself for pieces of silver and was baptized there. Afterwards he wished to return, but the community did not accept him. He thereupon reverted to Islam and is now a Muslim."

The (Christian) traders mentioned in the responsum undoubtedly lived in one of the *funduqs* of the traders' colony. The Jews in Tunis were obviously not prepared to accept the apostate partly for fear lest the Muslim authorities accuse them of causing a Muslim to abandon his

---

[1] This does not seem to be an instance of the very frequent miswriting "Tunis" for "Tenes". If Abraham Zacuto had meant Tenes, he would have mentioned at least one of the rabbis who were there at the time and who were in contact with Algiers.

[2] Abraham Zacuto, *Sefer Yuhasin*, ed. Filipowski, p. 225a.

[3] Brunschvig, *La Berbérie orientale*, I, p. 224 (also p. 414). The source referred to by Brunschvig: Llagostera, *Itinerari del rei Marti*, I (Institut Estudis catalans 1911-12), II (*ibid.*, 1912-13) is not available in Jerusalem. The name Bondavi, already met with under para. 12 above, was not used in this form in Spain, where it occurs as Bondia; see also RIBaSH, *Responsa*, no. 60, where Bondia ha-Kohen, an Algiers notable, is mentioned; in no. 171 the RIBaSH addresses himself to מאישטרי בונגידיש בונדוי in Calir (Cagliari), Sardinia. On the other hand, the name Bonjuha is very frequent; see Baer, *Die Juden im christlichen Spanien*, Berlin, 1929, I Index.

[4] The Maṭmaṭa region extends southward to Qābes. In a settlement known as Maṭmaṭa, Jews dwelt in caves.

religion. In Maṭmaṭa, far from the centre of government, the Jews had not been apprehensive of official reaction—perhaps also because the conversion had taken place in private. The fact that a rabbi in Algiers was queried from Breshk (west of Algiers) concerning something that had happened in Tunis shows that the incident had become widely known.

21. A Tunis scholar, R. Ḥayyim Melīli, lived in the days of R. Isaac bar Sheshet and R. Simon ben Ṣemaḥ Dūrān and addressed questions to them. Their subjects suggest that he may have been familiar with commercial matters.[1]

22. R. Benjamin ʿAmmār of Bougie, in a question to R. Simon ben Ṣemaḥ (*Tashbeṣ* II, no. 61), says that the king has assigned living quarters to a Jewish courtier ("one of his servants") who came with him from Tunis and that the latter may have infringed a *haskama* (agreement) concerning rights of possession. The reference is probably to the ruler of Tunis, Abū Fāris, and the courtier may be the physician Bondavi, mentioned in para. 19 above, or the interpreter Abraham (paras. 26 and 27).

23. Tunis is mentioned some more times in the RaSHBaṢ's responsa. From questions addressed to him by a resident of that city, R. Isaac ben R. Saadia ha-Kohen, and the style of his answers we may conclude that the questioner was an educated man, interested in both exoteric and occult learning.[2] One responsum begins: "... Your words were few in quantity but great in quality. Your waters issue from the sanctuary. They attest that you are proficient in the Talmud and the Aggadot and in occult learning and also in the art of poetry, that your eye has seen everything precious, that you delight in the law of the Lord, that you are eager to study and study again every single book and story." (*Tashbeṣ* II, no. 236).

R. Ḥayyim Melīli and R. Isaac ben R. Saadia ha-Kohen are evidence that Tunis in the late 14th and the first third of the 15th century had men

[1] See RIBaSH, no. 70, as well as *Tashbeṣ* II, no. 196, concerning the guardianship over the property of his nephew; in *Tashbeṣ* we are told that he was "well versed in accounts". *Tashbeṣ* I, no. 14, deals with the sale of wine to non-Jews; no. 93, with the lifting of the prohibition of a woman. R. Ḥayyim's surname suggests that he came from the Mediterranean port of Melilla in Morocco.

[2] *Tashbeṣ* II, nos. 236-237; III, nos. 50-57. The address preceding III, nos. 50-57; "Tunis, to the learned Rabbi Saadia" is incomplete; we should read "R. Isaac ben R. Saadia (ha-Kohen)". In nos. 56 and 57, the RaSHBaṢ reacts to criticism of his responsa II, 236 and 237, which had been found inadequate. He addresses his critic in the second person, which means that R. Isaac ben R. Saadia (and not R. Saadia) is the addressee of these responsa. His concern with the Kabbala is strikingly apparent in nos. 54 and 56.

who pursued the study of the Law not just because they were *dayyānim*.

24. Other responsa mention Tunis only incidentally, as in the story of a minor girl, a captive from Tū'āt, whom her captors have sold to a Jew in Tunis.[1]

25. More important is a responsum to Constantine, in which RaSHBaṢ says that Tunis has a *beyt din* of its own and a *dayyān* to whom he refers as "His Honour" although he has detected a flaw in his reasoning.[2]

"Tunis" Miswritten for "Tenes" [3]

The graphic and phonetic similarity between Tunis and Tenes (the name of an Algerian seaport half-way between Algiers and Mostaganem) caused mistakes in the headings of some of the RaSHBaṢ's responsa. According to its heading, *Tashbeṣ* I, no. 125, was sent to "Tunis, to the faithful who are there," while the text itself says that the matter under reference began to be reconsidered upon the arrival of the *dayyān* R. Samuel Ḥakīm; the latter, according to all available testimony, lived in Tenes, so that Tunis must be a miswriting.[4]

According to the heading of *Tashbeṣ* II, nos. 5-14, these responsa were sent to Tunis. The questioner is R. Joseph (ben Nathanel) Sasportas, who has *Tashbeṣ* II, no. 245, addressed to him in Tenes. Thus, as regards the printed headings, the matter is undecided;[5] but it is accepted that R. Joseph Sasportas lived in Tenes, then a centre of Jewish learning.[6] It is interesting to note that the reading "Tunis" for "Tenes" occurs also in one of the semi-legendary stories of R. Joseph Sambari. In his biography of the RIBaSH he says: "And they smuggled him (the RIBaSH) from there (from Majorca) to the lands of Ismael, to Tunis. And Edom (*i.e.* the Christian authorities in Majorca) sent the governor of Tunis five talents, that he might deliver him up and let them do with him as they pleased.

[1] *Tashbeṣ* III, no. 178; see also no. 263.

[2] *Ibid.*, no. 217.

[3] A letter to the Gaon Hay mentions one Salīm ibn al-Ṭansāwī, who had left Kairouan. In this case, the references may be to a man from Tunis, and not from Tenes; see Mann, *Texts and Studies I*, p. 144, l. 18. In a letter addressed to Nahrāy b. Nissim we read about a *wakīl* (representative of merchants) in Tunis; most probably this city is meant and not Tenes; T.-S. 8. 18; Ashtor, *Zion*, 30 (1965), p. 64, n. 22.

[4] See *Tashbeṣ* II, nos. 59 and 249 (cp. also I, no. 103). The RIBaSH, too, wrote to R. Samuel in Tenes: nos. 41, 42 and 98-100.

[5] The heading of *Tashbeṣ* II, nos. 239, 254 and 255 do not indicate R. Joseph Sasportas's place of residence, but the heading of no. 264 mentions Tenes.

[6] The RIBaSH wrote to the *dayyānim* and leaders of the community of תנסש (no. 15) and to a scholar of that locality, R. Isaac (no. 162). The RaSHBaṢ sent responsa to R. Mordekhai Najjār (II, no. 60), R. David ha-Kohen Shulāl (II, no. 136, 175 and 238), and R. Joseph ben Abba (III, no. 133-134).

But the Jews smuggled him out from there to the city of Algiers and he was saved."[1]

26. In December, 1423, the Jew Abraham in Tunis translated into Latin the peace and commercial treaty concluded in 1421 by the Tunisian ruler Abū Fāris (mentioned under Paras. 19 and 22 above) with Florence and Pisa.[2]

27. In 1445 in Tunis, Abraham Fava the Interpreter translated the Arabic text of the Tunis-Genoese treaty of 1433 into Latin.[3] We may assume that he is identical with the Abraham mentioned in the preceding paragraph.

28. A Jew in Tunis held a promissory note from one of the dignitaries of the Tunisian ruler 'Uthmān (1435-1488), who in time transferred the dignitary to Algiers as governor. The Jew, wishing to collect the debt, sent an appropriate authorization to Algiers. In the meantime, a complication occurred in that the dignitary was recalled to Tunis; but while still in Algiers, being an honest man, he paid the debt, in cash and in hides, against a receipt. The Algerian Jew who had collected the debt sent the hides to Majorca by another Jew, who was forced there to change his religion. The legal problems arising in this connection were submitted to the RaSHBaSH (no. 479).

From the point of view of our subject, it is interesting to note that a Jewish merchant in Tunis had connections with a Muslim courtier in Tunis who likewise engaged in commerce. We incidentally learn that Jews exported hides from Algiers to Majorca. The question is not later than the early sixties of the 15th century, the time of the RaSHBaSH's death.

The collection of the RaSHBaSH's responsa includes also questions addressed to him directly from Tunis.

29. A resident of Tunis married a woman also resident in that city, and they subsequently moved to Mostaganem. Years later the husband returned to Tunis and again took up residence there, whereas the wife had meanwhile settled in Oran. The husband demanded that his wife join him in Tunis, where there were "merchants among whom he can live, while

---

[1] *Dibrey Yosef*, Art. 55, MS. AIU No. 130, p. 49; Ms. Bodl. No. 2410, p. 40. The matter is not referred to in the excerpts published by Neubauer in *MJC* I.

[2] M. Amari, *Diplomi arabi*, pp. LXXI, 151-64; 326-30, 430; L. Mas-Latrie, *Traités*, I, pp. 256-7, II, pp. 344-54. For the date of the translation, 1423 or 1424, see Mas-Latrie, *op. cit.*, p. 344.

[3] *Ibid.*, pp. 142-143.

he is afraid of travel because of Arab creditors who make false claims against him, but who can do nothing to him in Tunis." (no. 337).

Living conditions and security were satisfactory in those days in the capital of the Ḥafṣid kingdom, but not in the domain of the Banu Ziyyān, where Mostaganem and Oran were situated. The term "merchants" refers to wholesalers engaged in overseas trade, and perhaps more particularly, to the Christian traders then in Tunis.[1]

30. In a Tunis synagogue, a transient rabbi perceived a custom which seemed most peculiar to him. On the Sabbath, when the heads of the community assembled to read the portions of the Law, water was served to congregants that were thirsty (no. 274). This custom originated in the fact that—as we already know from a responsum of R. Ṣemaḥ, the son of the RaSHBaSH—there was as yet no permanent synagogue in Tunis.

31. The referral to the RaSHBaSH of a question as to what was then a very common occurrence (no. 275: mourning for an infant who died after thirty days) indicates that there was not at that time in Tunis a rabbinic authority who might have decided it; see para. 34 below.

32. On the other hand, a question concerning the engagement of a prayer leader (no. 241) shows that communal life in Tunis was comparatively well organized.

33. Out of a group of responsa, nos. 347-352, sent to a well-educated man in Tunis, R. Ḥayyim ben Joseph Barbut, some (347 and 349-351) deal with a *funduq* left by his father-in-law.

There is clear evidence here that at least one private *funduq* existed in the Jewish quarter of Tunis in the middle of the 15th century (see above p. 461). At the beginning of that century, we find a *hospitium Venture hebrei* in Bologna, in which foreign Jews were given accommodation. The Jewish communities under Venetian rule were the first to establish *fondachi* (inns) for foreign merchants, where they were provided with food and lodgings. Some of these inns were leased to private persons.[2]

In 1495, the anonymous pupil of Obadya Bertinoro complains that he found no proper inn—with rooms, tables and beds—on his journey from Beirut to Jerusalem via Damascus. At the end of the day he sometimes came to a dilapidated house without a roof, called "alḥan" (= *khān*),

---

[1] The Christian traders included also Marranos who had not reverted to Judaism; see *Yakhin u-Boʿaz* I, no. 75. R. Uziel al-Haʾik, *Mishkenot ha-Roʿim*, fol. 103, col. 1, calls the traders from Christian European cities *taggarey mata*, no doubt to indicate the special status always accorded to traders from Europe.

[2] I. Sonne, *HUCA* 16 (1941) Hebrew part pp. 51-2; Baron, *The Jewish Community* II, pp. 11-12.

where bread, fruit and eggs were sold but no shelter was available; people stayed in the courtyard with their donkeys.[1]

34. Another group of responsa, nos. 247-258, are likewise addressed to R. Ḥayyim Barbut. No. 247 suggests that the questioner lived in a place where there were no *dayyānim*, so that he was compelled to turn to the RaSHBaSH; cp. para. 31 above. Nos. 250-256 contain theoretical discussions of customs, *leshonot* (utterances of early Talmud commentators) and the like, which were frequent subjects of responsa correspondence between old-established communities and the Algerian rabbis.

35. Two questions from R. Moses Orgali (nos. 258 and 259) are further evidence that Tunis had not in those days a competent rabbi or *dayyān*, so that after a brawl at synagogue the disputants were compelled to apply to the RaSHBaSH, through the intermediary of R. Moses, for the correct interpretation of a certain rule in the Tractate Ketubot, as well as concerning a matter of ritually unfit food. The fact that a brawl occurred at synagogue confirms our assumption that a well-ordered synagogue did not then exist in Tunis.

36. Some of the questions addressed to the RaSHBaSH by a well-educated man, R. Ḥasdāy Najjār (nos. 93-111; 627-628), reflect the way of life of a community whose well-to-do and educated members engage in overseas trade: Reuben deposits some books with Simon and goes overseas (no. 98); Simon, who holds a promissory note for 300 pounds, goes overseas (no. 99); ox and goat hides are an important item of overseas trade (nos. 104 and 105); Reuben pledges some books for 300 dinars (no. 106); a Christian trader, that is, a foreigner, buys some hides wholesale from Jews (no. 107).[2]

37. The responsum from R. Ṣemah to R. Joseph Zimron (*Yākhīn u-Boʿaz* I, 132) has been dealt with above, pp. 458 ff., but its chronological place is here.

38. A Flemish nobleman, Anselm Adorne, visited Mediterranean countries in 1471-1472. A considerable portion of his account of that trip is devoted to Tunis (1470). At first he speaks of the inns of Christian traders from Europe and the honoured position of the local Christians of the royal guard. Then comes the following passage:

---

[1] A. Neubauer, *Jahrbuch für die Geschichte der Juden und des Judentums*, 3 (1863) p. 276. In the following this traveller complains a second time that even in the towns no inns exist as it is usual in Italy, and the stranger is obliged to find private lodgings.

[2] RaSHBaSH, no. 478, deals with the affairs of Shushān Zurāfa, a veteran resident (judging by his name), who went overseas as an agent (*mitʿasseq*) on behalf of a Christian trader doing business with a Jew in Bougie.

"The Jews, on the other hand, have no freedom. They must all pay a heavy (poll-) tax. They wear special clothes, different from those of the Moors. If they did not do so, they would be stoned, and they therefore put a yellow cloth on their heads or necks; their women dare not even wear shoes. They are much despised and hated, more than even the Latin Christians, who are called Frangi here."[1]

Adorne does not mention the wearers of the round cape—the Jewish traders from Europe—and he may not have been aware of their existence. At any rate, their status does not seem to have been better than that of the local Jews; this may be inferred from his remark that the Frangi—the European Christians—were not well treated, in contrast to the respected position of the native Christians as the king's soldiers. Adorne's account indicates the existence of a sizable Jewish community in Tunis, thus confirming our conclusion from the responsa of contemporary Algerian rabbis. His remark concerning the despised condition of the Jews may explain the fact that they had as yet no synagogue worthy of the name: the authorities may not have permitted its construction, in accordance with the well-known "Omar's Regulations", which, *inter alia*, forbid the building of synagogues and churches in Muslim countries.

The data on Jews in Tunis from the Almohad persecutions (1160) to Adorne's visit (1470), which we have been able to collect and arrange in the foregoing paragraphs, are milestones in the development of the Tunis community over a period of approximately 300 years (of course, not all of them contribute in equal measure to our historical knowledge). The increase in the volume and frequency of the responsa within a short time indicates that the community grew and its contact with the religious-legal centre in Algiers became regular. As for the material in European archives, there can hardly be a doubt that its systematic, minute examination will disclose much fresh information as to the role of Tunis Jewry in the relations between Tunisia and the states of Southern Europe. Meanwhile, the documents already known attest to the rehabilitation and development of the community, which because of its numerical growth and perhaps for other reasons as well—left the *funduq* for a different neighbourhood.

The salient feature of the early material is that most of it concerns commerce and political-historical relations with the cities and states of Christian Europe; though direct and indirect references to these subjects

[1] Brunschvig, *Deux Récits*, Adorne (p. 29b/158), p. 192. In note 3, Brunschvig says: "En tunisien actuel, 'Européen' se dit encore Franji, pl. Franj." See above, p. 96 n. 2 and p. 91. Comp. E.J.[2] VII, 51-2 s.v. Franco.

occur throughout, from the letter of recommendation to the Podestà of Pisa (para. 6) to R. Ṣemaḥ Dūrān's responsum. Tunis Jewry thus appears to have played an important part in this sphere. Of course, this conclusion may be affected by the fact that much of the material comes from the archives of Christian Europe. However, the testimony of the rabbinic sources concerning the Tunis community, and especially its educated members, also tends to indicate that its strength did not lie in learning or social activities. The nature of the questions addressed to the RIBaSH and the RaSHBaṢ by R. Ḥayyim Melīli (para. 21), suggests that he was particularly conversant with commercial matters. The RaSHBaSH's responsa contain numerous references to overseas trade.

It seems that the passage in R. Ṣemaḥ Dūrān's responsum that require the Tunis community "to build another synagogue, which will have room for the whole congregation, so that they will go and say their prayers there every day" contains a hidden reproach. It appears surprising that many years after the synagogue at the *funduq* was abandoned the growing community still had no synagogue for daily congregational prayers. Of course, Adorne (para. 38) reports that the Jews lived under conditions of degradation, but so they did throughout the Maghreb, and he stresses that the position of European Christians was similar; in any case, he seems to exaggerate somewhat, for elsewhere he indicates that relations between passengers of the three faiths on a Genoese ship appeared to be normal; the Christians observed Sunday, the Jews Saturday and the Muslims Friday as their day of rest.[1]

The data assembled help to clarify the picture emerging from R. Ṣemaḥ's responsum. Its vague and uncertain contours, lacking support by names or dates, become sharp and definite. It is a picture of wearers of the round cape, *i.e.* Jewish traders from Christian Europe, especially from Majorca and Aragon, who have come to a Maghrebi seaport where there is a district of European *funduqs*, whose residents enjoy immunity of both their persons and property. These traders have likewise built a *funduq*, taken up permanent residence in it and installed a little synagogue in a penthouse on the roof. This *funduq* is also used by wearers of the round cape who spend only a short time in the city in connection with their business.[2] They of course share in the use of the synagogue, as is stressed in R. Ṣemaḥ's responsum: "In fact, every wearer of the round cape who came to Tunis by sea or land has resorted to that house to pray there."

---

[1] See *Deux Récits*, p. 220.

[2] Transient traders are mentioned, *e.g.*, by the RaDBaZ; see p. 461 n. 3 above.

As to international law, the 1360 peace treaty (para. 17) grants them the same rights as are enjoyed by the permanent residents of the *funduqs*.

The little synagogue was probably established in the late 13th or early 14th century. Records of that time (paras. 11-12, 14-17) attest to expanding international relations. The Jews are not expressly mentioned in the treaty concluded at the end of 1301 between Jaime II of Aragon and ʿAbd Allah, the ruler of Tunis, although they are implicitly referred to where the treaty speaks of Muslims and non-Muslims.[1] But in a document of 1330 we read that the Jewish customs agent in Tunis is trying to extort sums in excess of the legal rate from Catalan-Jewish traders (para. 16).

The 1360 peace treaty (para. 17) reflects a radically different situation. It repeatedly mentions Jewish traders, which points to an increase in the number of wearers of the round cape in Tunis; a further increase no doubt occurred, especially, in and after 1391 (persecutions in Majorca and Aragon). They seem to have included only a very small proportion of religious scholars. Judging by his name, R. Ḥayyim Melīli, *i.e.*, the man from Melilla, already mentioned above (p. 477) and repeatedly referred to in the responsa of the RIBaSH and the RaSHBaṢ (para. 21) was not a 1391 refugee. It is uncertain whether the well-educated R. Isaac ben R. Saadia ha-Kohen (para. 23) was a veteran resident or an expellee. On the other hand it seems that the book-owning traders referred to above (Para. 36) were expellees.

In the 15th century we find several Jews in positions of honour at the Ḥafṣid court. One of them was a member of the king's retinue in Bougie, another was sent on a diplomatic mission (paras. 19 and 22). A significant change seems to have occurred at that time in the Tunis community as regards both its size and nature. The numerical increase was the cause that there was no longer room for all of them at the *funduq* and the synagogue, so that they moved to a fairly distant neighbourhood. This is expressly stated in R. Ṣemaḥ Dūrān's exposé. Adorne's remarks concerning the special yellow headgear of the Jews indicate that he is referring to native-born residents and not to foreign traders, who wore the round cape, the distinctive mark of Jews from Christian countries. The contempt shown to the wearers of the yellow headgear, and their fear of transgressing the discriminatory regulations, likewise indicate that the reference is to people not enjoying the protection of a European state.

The results of our inquiry may be summed up as follows: Jewish settlement in Tunis (or Tunisia) did not cease with the Almohad per-

---

[1] See Alarcón, *op. cit.* (p. 468 n. 4), no. 116, pp. 247-253.

secutions. The sources testify to commercial relations with Jews outside Tunisia, esp. Italy. The influx of Jewish merchants from Christian countries began at a very early period, possibly in the first half of the 13th century. The rehabilitation of the Tunis community was slow at the beginning but gathered momentum in the 14th and 15th cent.

For the sake of completeness let us very briefly review the history of the Tunis community until the end of Ḥafṣid rule (1574).

In the late 15th and early 16th centuries references to the Tunis community become fewer. The apportionment of spheres of influence and potential conquest between Spain and Portugal, with the eastern part of the North African Mediterranean coast allotted to Spain, was no secret to the Jews, who noticed political trends before they had crystallized in treaties. This is why the waves of expellees of the years 1491-1496 avoided the cities coveted by the Spaniards. But an anonymous source remarks that some of them went to the Berber provinces under the king of Tunis.[1] We know indeed that the famous astronomer R. Abraham Zacuto and his son Samuel spent some time in Tunis after their expulsion from Spain, and it was here that Abraham Zacuto completed his *Sefer ha-Yuhasin*.[2] R. Abraham ha-Levi Buqarāt wrote his commentary on Rashi to the Pentateuch in Tunis.[3] A third scholar who spent some time there was R. Moses Alashqar.[4] They all left Tunis before Spain launched its campaign of conquest along the Mediterranean coast (1509).

A few years later, Tunis Jewry suffered as a result of hostile propaganda by the fanatically religious Muhammad al-Qā'im, founder of the Saadi dynasty in Morocco (1510-1517). An Arab chronicler, al-Jannābī, reports that while passing through Tunis on a pilgrimage to Mecca (c. 1515), al-Qā'im made inflammatory speeches against the Jews and levied contributions from them. The king of Tunis (Muḥammad V?) thereupon summoned him to appear before his council, where he defended himself impertinently.[5]

In view of the cruelty known to have been shown by the soldiers of the

---

[1] Marx, *Studies*, p. 86/94.

[2] See ed. Filipowski, London 1857, pp. 22a and 223a.

[3] In the introduction to *Sefer ha-Zikkārōn*, Leghorn 5605 (1844/45), he says: "And this began to be written while I was in exile, caught in the thicket of wandering, as a wayfaring man that turneth aside to tarry for a night, here in the city of Tunis, may the Lord found it well, in the year two hundred and sixty-seven of the sixth millennium of the Creation (1507)".

[4] R. Simon, the son of the RaSHBaSH, sent a responsum to him in Tunis; *Yakhin u-Boʿaz*, II, no. 23. R. David Conforte, *Kore ha-Dorot*, 31 b, does not record the fact of his stay in Tunis, nor is he fully aware that he was an expellee.

[5] Fagnan, *Extraits*, p. 340. About al-Qā'im cf. above, pp. 402-3.

Emperor Charles V upon the capture of Tunis from the "Algerian pirate" Khayr al-Dīn (1535)—we are told of 70,000 killed and 40,000 captives[1]—R. Yosef ha-Kohen's account of the sufferings of the Jews does not seem exaggerated:

"And the Emperor Charles made war upon Tunis in Barbary, and he took it on the twenty-first of the month of July in the year five thousand two hundred and ninety-five (1535), and Tunis lost all its glory at that time, and the Jews, of whom there were many, in part fled into the desert, hungry, thirsty and completely destitute, and the Arabs plundered everything they brought with them; and many died at that time, some were smitten with the edge of the sword when the uncircumcised came to the city, and some went into captivity before the enemy, and they had no saviour on the day of the Lord's wrath... and they sold them as men-servants and maidservants at the four corners of the earth, in Naples and in Genoa; the Italian communities redeemed many at that time, may God remember it in their favour."[2]

No records seem to have been preserved of what happened to the Tunis community during the century following this catastrophe. The few hints in responsa of Algiers rabbis, and the reports of the settlement of Livornese traders, are outside the scope of this Appendix.

---

[1] Christian sources confirm that Charles's troops did not spare peaceful citizens. Those who were not killed were sold into slavery; libraries, mosques and buildings of artistic value were ravaged or destroyed. See G. Fisher, *Barbary Legend*, Oxford 1957, pp. 78 and 313-4.

[2] *ʿEmeq ha-Bakha*, Cracow 1895, pp. 117-118; *idem, Dibrey ha-Yamim le-Malkhey Ṣarfat u-le-Malkhey Ottoman*, Amsterdam 1733 p. 102a; Gedalya ben Yahya, *Sefer Shalshelet ha-Qabbāla*, Amsterdam 1697, p. 95b; on the redemption of Tunisian captives in Italy see also S. Assaf, *KS*, 14 (1936-8), pp. 548-9.

SELECT BIBLIOGRAPHY

The elements "Abī", "Abū", "b", "B" and "Ibn", the Arabic article "al-", the Hebrew article "ha-" and the diacritic signs have been disregarded in establishing the alphabetical order of items. At the beginning of a line, the Arabic article is indicated by a dash.

ʿAbd al-Ḥakam, Ibn, *Futūḥ*—Ibn ʿAbd al-Ḥakam, *Conquête de l'Afrique du Nord et de l'Espagne*[2], texte et traduction par A. Gateau, Alger, 1948.

Abraham b. Nathan of Lunel, *Sefer ha-Manhig*, 1855. —
אברהם בן נתן הירחי המנהיג, ברלין תרט״ו.

Abramson, S., *Ba-Merkazim*, 1965. —
ש. אברמסון, במרכזים ובתפוצות בתקופת הגאונים, ירושלים 1965.

——, ed., *R. Nissim Gaon*, libelli quinque, 1965, —
רב נסים גאון, ירושלים, תשכ״ה.

Acta Sanctorum ... collegit ... I. Bollandus, Antverpiae, 1643.

Aelius Spartianus, 'De vita Hadriani,' *Scriptores Historiae Augustae*, vol. I.

—Aḥmar, Ibn, *Histoire des Benī Merīn, rois de Fās, intitulée Rawdat en-Nisrīn*, ed. et trad. C. Bouáli et G. Marçais, Paris, 1917.

Alarcon y Santon, M.A., y Garcia de Linares, R., *Los Documentos Arabes Diplomáticos del Archivo de la Corona de Aragón*, Madrid-Granada, 1940.

Albeck, Sh., ed., *Sefer ha-Eschkol*, 1910 (1935). —
שלום בן יחזקאל אלבק, האשכול, ברלין, תר״ע [מהדורת חנוך אלבק, ירושלים, תרצ״ה].

Albertini, E., *L'Afrique Romaine*, Alger, 1950.

Albertini, E., Marçais, G., Yver, G., *L'Afrique du Nord française dans l'Histoire*, Paris, 1937.

Alḥārizi, Y., *Taḥkemōni*, ed. Kaminka, 1899. —
אלחריזי ר׳ יהודה, תחכמוני, הוצאת א. קמינקא, ווארשא תרנ״ט.

Altmann, A., Stern S.M., *Isaac Israeli*, London, 1958.

Applebaum, Sh., *Greeks and Jews*, 1969. —
ש. אפלבאום, יהודים ויוונים בקיריני הקדומה, ירושלים, 1969.

Applebaum, S., *Teucheira*—S. Applebaum, 'The Jewish Community of Hellenistic and Roman Teucheira in Cyrenaica', *Scripta Hierosolymitana VII*, 1961, pp. 27-52.

Aptowitzer, V., R. Chuschiel und R. Chananel, *Jahresbericht der Isr.-Theol. Lehranstalt in Wien 1933*.

ʿAqnīn, Ibn, *Divulgatio*, ed. A. Halkin, 1964. —
הלקין א. ש., הוציא את המקור הערבי ותרגם. ר׳ וסף בן יהודה בן יעקב אבן עקנין, התגלות הסודות והופעת המאורות; פירוש שיר השירים, ירושלים תשכ״ד.

Arukh Completum, ed. A. Kohut, 1926. —
נתן בן יחיאל, ערוך השלם, וינה תרפ״ו, הוציא חנוך יהודה קאהוט.

Ashtor formerly: Strauss, E., *Egypt* [or] *Toledot ha-Yehudim*, 2 vol. 1944-51. —
שטראוס א., תולדות היהודים במצרים וסוריה תחת שלטון הממלוכים, שני כרכים, ירושלים תש״ד–תשי״א.

——, *The Jews in Spain*, 2 vol., 1960-6. —
אשתור א., קורות היהודים בספרד המוסלמית, ירושלים 1960—1966.

Assaf, S., *Batey ha-Din we-Sidreyhem*, 1924. —
ש. אסף, בתי הדין וסדריהם אחרי חתימת התלמוד, ירושלים 1924.

——, *Gaonica*, 1933. —
ש. אסף, מספרות הגאונים, ירושלים, 1933.

——, *Responsa I* (1927). —
ש. אסף, תשובות הגאונים ולקוטי ספר הדין להרב ר׳ יהודה ברצלוני ז״ל, ירושלים תרפ״ז.
——, *Responsa II* (1929). —
ש. אסף, תשובות הגאונים מתוך ׳הגניזה׳, ירושלים תרפ״ט.
——, *Responsa III* (1942). —
ש. אסף, תשובות הגאונים מכתבי־יד שבגנזי קמברידז׳, ירו־שלים תש״ב.
——, *Sefer ha-Shetaroth le-Rav Hāi*, 1930. —
ש. אסף, ספר השטרות לרב האי, ירושלים, תר״צ.
——, Sources, 1946.
ש. אסף, מקורות ומחקרים בתולדות ישראל, ירושלים תש״ו.

—Athīr, Ibn—Abū Ḥasan ʿAlī . . . Muḥ . . . Ibn al-Athīr, *al-Kāmil fi 't-taʾrīkh*, 7 vols, Cairo, 1348-53 H.

Avigad, N., 'A Depository of Inscribed Ossuaries in the Kidron Valley,' *IEJ* 12 (1962), pp. 1-12.

Avi-Yona, M., *In the Days of Rome and Byzantium*, 1946. —
מ. אבי־יונה, בימי רומא וביזאנטיון, ירושלים, 1946.

Azevedo, P. De, *Documentos das chancelarias reais anteriores a 1531 relativos a Marrocos*, I-II, Lisboa, 1915-1934.

Bacher, W., *Anfünge der hebräischen Grammatik*, Leipzig, 1895.

Baer Fritz, *Spanien* Fritz Baer, *Die Juden im christlichen Spanien* I, 1-2, Berlin, 1929-1936.

——, *Spain*, Fritz Baer, *A History of the Jews in Christian Spain*, 2 vol., Philidelphia, 1961-6.

—Balādhurī—Al-Beladsori, *Liber expugnationis regionum*, ed. de Goeje, Leiden, 1866, reprinted 1968.

Baneth, D. H., *Iggerot ha-Rambam, Epistulae*, 1946. —
ד. צ. בנעט, אגרות הרמב״ם, חוברת ראשונה, חליפת המכתבים עם ר׳ יוסף בן יהודה, ירושלים תש״ו.

Baney, M. M., 'Some Reflections of Life in North-Africa in the Writings of Tertullian,' Patristie Studies, LXXX, 1958.

-Barceloni, Yehuda b. Barsilai, *Sefer ha-ʿIttim*, 1903. —
יהודה בר ברזילי אל ברצלוני, ספר העתים, הוציאו יעקב שור, קראקא, ה׳ תרס״ג.

——, —Yehuda b. Barsilai aus Barcelona, *Sepher Haschetaroth, Dokumentenbuch*, ed. S.Z. Halberstam, Berlin, 1898. —
ספר השטרות להרב הנשיא רבינו יהודה בר׳ ברזילי הברצלוני, הר״ל שלמה זלמן חיים האלברשטאם, ברלין תרנ״ח.

Baron, S.W., *A Social and Religious History of the Jews*², New York, 1952 ff.

Bartarelli, L.V., *Guida d'Italia, Possedimenti e Colonie*, Milano, 1929.

Bartoccini, R., 'Scavi e rinvenimenti in Tripolitania', *Africa Italiana*, 2 (1928/9), pp. 187-200.

Bauer-Landauer, I., *Relaciones de Africa*, 5 vol., Madrid, 1922-3.

-Bekrī—Al-Bakrī, *al-Masālik wa-l-Mamālik*, ed. de Slane, Algiers, 1857 (ed.² ibid., 1910); and *Description de l'Afrique Septentrionale*², ed. de Slane Algiers, 1911-13.

Beaumier, A., *Roudh el Kartas, Histoire des Souverains du Maghreb*, Paris, 1860. (for the Arabic text see Zarʿ, Ibn Abī).

Beinart, H., *Sefunot* VIII (1964), pp. 319-334. —
ביינארט, ח., פאס: מרכז לגיור · · · במאה הט״ז, ספונות ח, תשכ״ד, עמ׳ שיט שלד׳.

Benbenishti, Ḥ., *Keneset ha-Gedola*, 1658. —
חיים בן ישראל בנבנשתי, כנסת הגדולה, ליוורנו ת״ח.

Ben-Naim, *Malkhe Rabbānān*, 1931. —
יוסף בן נאים, מלכי רבנן, ירושלים, תרצ״א

Benjamin b. Moses Nahāwendī, *Mas'at Binyamin*, 1834. —
בנימין (בן משה) הנהאונדי, משאת בנימין, גוזלוו־אבפטוריה, 1834

Bergmann, J., *Jüdische Apologetik im neutestamentlichen Zeitalter*, Berlin, 1908.

Bergstraesser, G. *Grundzüge des islamischen Rechts*, hgg. von Joseph Schacht, Berlin & Leipzig, 1935.

Beyrab, J., *Responsa*, 1958. —
יעקב בירב, שאלות ותשובות, ירושלים, תשי״ח.

Bialik-Ravnitzki, *Shirey Shelomo ibn Gabirol*, 1924-1932. —
ח״נ ביאליק וי״ח רבניצקי, שירי שלמה בן יהודה אבן גבירול, שבעה ספרים, ברלין, תרפ״ד תל־אביב, תרצ״ב

Bikkurey ha-ʿIttīm, 12 fasc., 1828-31. —
בכורי העתים י״ב קונטרסים, ווינן, תקפ״ח־תקצ״ב.

Blau, L., *Das altjüdische Zauberwesen*², Berlin, 1914.

Bontwetsch, N. [G], *Doctrina Iacobi nuper Baptizati*, Göttingen, 1910.

Bourilly, J., *Ethnogr.*— J. Bourilly, *Éléments d'ethnographie marocaine*, Paris, 1932.

Brauer, E., *Ethnologie der jemenitischen Juden*, Heidelberg, 1934.

Brockelmann, C., *Geschichte der arabischen Literatur*, 2 vol., Leiden, 1943-49; Supplementbände, 3 vol., Leiden, 1937-42.

Brunschvig, R., *Deux récits de voyage inédits en Afrique du Nord*, Paris, 1936.

——, *La Berbérie orientale sous les Ḥafṣides*, 2 vol., Paris, 1940-1947.

Buber, S., 'Einleitung und Ergänzungen zum Aruch,' *Jubelschrift Graetz*, Breslau, 1887. [in Hebrew part: pp. 1-47].

Cagnat, R., et Merlin, A., *Inscriptions latins d'Afrique*. Paris, 1923.

Carcopino, J., *Le Maroc antique*, Paris, 1948.

Cassel, D., ed., *Rechtsgutachten der Geonim*, Berlin, 1848. —
תשובות גאונים קדמונים, מאת דוד קאססעל, ברלין, תר״ח.

Castries, H. De, et Cenival, P. De, *Les sources inédites de l'histoire du Maroc*, Paris, 1905.

Cazès, D., *Essai sur l'histoire des Israélites de Tunisie depuis les temps les plus reculés*, Paris, 1888.

Colin, G. S., 'Des Juifs nomades retrouvés dans le Sahara marocain au XVIe siècle,' *Mélanges Lopes-Cenival*, Lisboa, 1945.

Conforte, D., *Kore ha-Dorot*, ed. D. Cassel, 1866. —
קונפורטי דוד, קורא הדורות, הוצ׳ דוד קאססעל, ברלין תר״ו.

Corcos, D., 'The Attitude of the Almohadic Rulers towards the Jews,' *Zion* 32 (1967), pp. 137-60.

——, 'The Jews of Morocco under the Marinides,' five parts: *JQR* 54 (1963/4), pp. 271-87; 55 (1964/5), pp. 55-81, 137-50.

——, 'Maroc,' *Sefunot X*. —
יהודי מארוקו מגירוש ספרד ועד אמצע המאה הט״ז, ספונות י, עמ׳ נג קיא.

Coronel, N., ed., *Gaonäische Gutachten*, 1871. —
תשובות הגאונים, נ. נ. קורונל, ויען תרל״א.

Cour, A., *L'établissement des dynasties des Chérifs au Maroc . . . 1509-1830*, Paris, 1904.

Danān, Saadia Ibn, *Seder ha Dorot*, in Edelman, *Ḥemda Genūza* (*q.v.*).

Dapper, O., *Description de l'Afrique*, Amsterdam, 1686.

Davidson, I., *Thesaurus of Medieval Hebrew Poetry*, vol. I, 1925.

Diehl, E., *Inscriptiones Latinae Christianae Veteres*, 3 vol., Berlin, 1925-1931.

Diesner, H. J., *Geschichte des Vandalenreichs, Aufstieg und Untergang*, Stuttgart, 1966.

Delattre, A. L., *Gamart ou la Nécropole Juive de Carthage*, Lyon, 1895.

Desparmet, J., *Algérie - Coutumes, Institutions, Croyances des Musulmans de l'Algérie*, Tome I², Alger, 1948.

Dinur, B., Tōledōt Yisrāēl, 1958-63. —
דינור, בן ציון, תולדות ישראל, סדרה שניה–ישראל בגולה, ספרים א–ד, תל־אביב, תשי״ח־תשכ״ג.

Diringer, D., *Le Iscrizioni antico-ebraiche*, Firenze, 1934.

Doutte, E., *Magie et religion dans l'Afrique du Nord*, Alger, 1909.

Dozy, R., ed., *The History of the Almohades* by . . . al-Marrakoshi, Leyden, 1881.

Dufourcq, C. E., *L'Espagne catalane et le Maghreb aux XIIIe et XIVe siècles*, Paris, 1965.

Dūrān Simon b. Zemaḥ, *Responsa*, see *Teshūbōth, etc.*

Edelman, Z. H., *Ḥemda Genūza*, 1856. —
צבי הירש עדעלמאן, חמדה גנוזה, קאניגסבערג תרט״ז.

——, *Iggeret ha-Shemad*, printed in Edelman, *Ḥemda Genūza*.

Enkawa, E., *Shaᶜar Kebod*, 1902. —
אפרים אלנקאוה, שער כבוד ה׳ תונס תרס״ב.

Eppenstein, S., *Beiträge zur Geschichte und Literatur im gaonäischen Zeitalter*, Berlin, 1913.

——, Joseph [Wa]ᶜAqnin, *Ṭibb al-Nufūs*; translation of chap. 27 in *Sokolow Jubilee Volume*, Warsaw 1904. —
ספר היובל, הובל שי לכבוד נחום סאקאלאוו, ווארשא, תרס״ד, עמ׳ 371–388.

Epstein, A., *Eldad ha-Dani*, 1891. —
א. עפשטיין, אלדד הדני, פרעשבורג תרנ״א.

Epstein, I., *The Responsa of Rabbi Simon B. Ẓemaḥ Duran*, London, 1930.

Ezra, M. Ibn, *Shīrat Israel*, 1924. —
משה אבן עזרא, שירת ישראל, תרגום בן־ציון הלפר, ליספיה, 1924.

Faḍl Allāh al-ᶜOmari, *Masālik el-Abṣār*, trad. Gaudefroy-Demombynes, Paris, 1927.

Fagnan, E., *Extraits inédits relatifs au Maghreb*, trad. et annot., Alger, 1924.

——, 'Le signe distinctif des Juifs au Maghreb,' *REJ* XXVIII, 1894.

Fernandes, V., *Description de la Côte d'Afrique de Ceuta au Sénégal*, ed. P. de Cenival et Th. Monod, Paris 1938.

Ferrère, F., *La Situation religieuse de l'Afrique romaine* (Thesis), Paris, 1897.

——, *De Victoris Vitensis libro qui inscribitur Historia Persecutionis* (Thesis), Paris, 1898.

Fischel, W., *Jews in the Economic and Political Life of Mediaeval Islam*, London, 1939.

Fischer, Marcus, *Geschichte der Juden unter der Regierung Mohadi's und Imam Edris*, Prag, 1817. —
מאיר פישר, תולדות ישורון תחת ממשלת מאהאדי ואימאם עדריס, מלכי מוריי־טאניא, פראג 1817.

Fisher, G., *Barbary Legend*, Oxford, 1957.

Frend, W. H. C., *The Donatist Church*, Oxford, 1952.

Friedmann, K., *Miscellanea*— K. Friedmann, 'Le fonti per la storia degli Ebrei di Cirenaica, nell' antichità', *Miscellanea di studi ebraici in memoria di H. P. Chajes*, Firenze, 1930, pp. 39-55.

——, 'La grande ribellione giudaica sotto Traiano,' *GSAI*, n.s., II, 1931, pp. 108-124.

——, 'Condizioni e cultura degli Ebrei di Cirenaica,' *GSAI*, n.s. II, 1934, pp. 323-334.

——, *Atene*—K. Friedmann, 'Gli Ebrei in Cirenaica prima della conquesta araba', *Atene e Roma*, X, 1929, pp. 199-210.

Futūḥ, see ᶜAbd al-Ḥakam.

Garcia Figueras, T., et Sancho Mayi, H. *Documentos para el studio del Abastecimiento de las plazas Portuguesas*, Tanger, 1939.

Gattefosse, J., *Drac*—J. Gattefosse, 'Juifs et Chretiens du Dra[c] avant l'Islam,' *Bulletin de la Société de Préhistoire du Maroc*, 9e année, 1935, pp. 39-66.
Gautier, E.F., *La Conquête du Sahara*, Paris, 1925.
——, *Le Passé de l'Afrique du Nord*, Paris, 1952.
Gavison, A., *ʿOmer ha-Shihkeḥa*, 1748. —
ר׳ אברהם ב״ר יעקב גבישון, עומר השכחה, ליוורנו, 1748 (בהקדמה אשרה״ו–1752).
Gedalya b. Yahya, *Shalshelet*, 1697. —
גדליה בן יחיא, ספר שלשלת הקבלה, אמשטרדם תנ״ז.
Ghirelli, A., *El Páis Bereber*, Madrid, 1942.
Ginzberg, L., *Die Haggada* —L. Ginzberg, *Die Haggada bei den Kirchenvätern etc.*, Berlin 1900.
——, *Geonica*, I-II, New York 1909.
——, *The Legends of the Jews*, 7 vol., Philadelphia, 1909-38.
Ginze Kedem I-VI, 1922-1940. —
גנזי קדם, מאסף מדעי לתקופת הגאונים, ערוך בידי ב״מ לוין חיפה־ירושלים תרפ״ב־ת״ש.
Ginzey Schechter, ed. L. Ginsberg, 1928-9. —
גינצבורג, ל., גנזי שכטר, א–ג, ניו־יורק תרפ״ח–תרפ״ט.
Ginzey Yerushalem, 1901. —
גנזי ירושלם, חוברת שניה, ש״אווערטהיימער, ירושלים תרס״א.
Gois, Damiao de, *Crónica do felicissimo Rei D. Manuel*, 4 vol., Coimbra, 1949-1955.
Goitein, S. D., *Jewish Education* [or] *Sidrey Hinūkh*. —
גויטיין ש. ד. סדרי חינוך בימי הגאונים ובית הרמב״ם, מקורות חדשים מהגניזה, ירושלים, תשכ״ב.
——, *Society* — S. D. Goitein, *A Mediterranean Society*, I-II, 1967-1971.
——, *Studies in Islamic History and Institutions*, Leiden, 1966.
——, 'La Tunisie du XIe siecle,' *Études d'Orientalisme dédiées à la mémoire de Lévi-Provençal*, t. II, Paris, 1962, pp. 559-578.
Golvin, L., *Le Maghreb Central à l'Époque des Zirides*, Paris, 1957.
Gottheil, G. and Worrell, W. H. *Fragments from the Cairo Genizah in the Freer Collection*, New York, 1927.
Gramaye, J. B., *Africae illustratae*, Libri X, Tournay, 1623.
Gravière, J. de la, *Les Corsaires Barbaresques et la Marine de Soliman le Grand*, Paris, 1887.
Gray, J., *The Jewish Inscriptions in Greek and Hebrew at Tocra, Cyrene and Barce*, Cyrenaican Expedition of the University of Manchester, Manchester, 1956.
Gsell, St., *Histoire ancienne de l'Afrique du Nord*, 8 vol., Paris, 1913-1928.
——, *De Tipasa Mauretaniae Caesariensis Urbe*, Thesis, Algerii, 1894.
Güdemann, M., *Geschichte des Unterrichtswesens und der Kultur der abendländischen Juden*, etc., 3 vol., Wien, 1880-1888.
Guernier, E., *L'apport de l'Afrique à la pensee humaine*, Paris, 1952.

Halkin, A.S., ed., *Iggeret* —
הלקין, אברהם שלמה, אגרת תימן לרבנו משה בן מימון, המקור הערבי ושלשת התרגומים העבריים ונוסף עליהם תרגום אנגלי מאת בועז כהן, ניו־יורק, האקדמיה האמריקנית למדעי היהדות, תש״ב.
Hameiri, *Beyt-Abōt*, 1821. —
מנחם בן שלמה המאירי, בית אבות, שאלוניקי, 1821
-Harawi, Abu l-Hasan ʿAli, *Guide des Lieux de Pèlerinage*, ed. Janine Sourdel-Thomine, Damas, 1953.
Harkavy, A., 'Responsa der Geonim,' in his *Studien und Mitteilungen* IV, Berlin, 1887. —

זכרון לראשונים וגם לאחרונים, חלק ראשון, זכרון לראשונים, מחברת רביעית, א. א. הרכבי, ברלין, תרמ״ז.

——, 'Zikhron', *Studien und Mitteilungen* V, Peterburg 1891. —
הרכבי, א. א., ספר הגלוי—זכרון לראשונים ה, חוברת ראשונה: השריד והפליט מספר האגרון וספר הגלוי, פטרבורג, תרנ״ב.

Hawqal, Ibn, *Opus geographicum*, ed. J. H. Kramers, Leiden, 1937-1939, *BGA* II².

Hershman, A., *Perfet*, Jerusalem 1956. —
הרשמן אברהם, רבי יצחק בר ששת (הריב״ש), דרך חייו ותקופתו, ירושלים תשט״ז.

Hirschberg, J. W., [H.Z.] *Der Diwān des as-Samauʾal ibn ʿAdijā*', Kraków, 1931.

——, *Elath*, The Eighteenth Archaeological Convention (1962), Jerusalem, 1963. —
ח״ז הירשברג, היישובים היהודיים באיזור של מפרץ אילת בימי הביניים, אילת הכינוס הארצי השמונה־עשר לידיעת הארץ, ירושלים תשכ״ג, עמ׳ 182—193.

——, *Israel in Arabia*, 1946. —
ישראל בערב. קורות היהודים בחמיר וחג׳אז מחורבן בית שני ועד מסעי־הצלב, תל־אביב תש״ו.

——, *Inside Maghreb* [or] *Me-Erez*, 1957. —
מארץ מבוא השמש, עם יהודי אפריקה הצפונית בארצותיהם, ירושלים תשי״ז.

——, *Nissim*. —
רבינו נסים ב״ר יעקב מקירואן, חיבור יפה מהישועה, תירגם מהמקור הערבי והקדים מבוא ירושלים תשי״ד.

Hitti, Ph. K., *History of the Arabs*³, London, 1943.

Hopkins, J. F. P., *Government*—J. F. P. Hopkins, *Medieval Muslim Government in Barbary*, London, 1958.

Horeb—*Horeb, Devoted to Research in Jewish History and Literature*, New York —
חורב מאסף מוקדש לתולדות ישראל וספרותו ניו־יורק.

Horowitz, Ch. H., ed. *Toratan shel Rishonim, Halachische Schriften der Geonim*, 1881.—
תורתן של ראשונים, שני חלקים, חיים מאיר הלוי הורוויץ, פראנקפורט ע״נ מיין תרמ״ב.

ʿIdhārī al-Marrākushi Ibn: R. Dozy, *Histoire de l'Afrique du Nord*², 2 vol., ed. G. S. Colin & E. Lévi-Provençal, Leiden, 1948-51.

Idris, H. R., *La Berberie orientale sous les Zirides*, Paris, 1962, 2 vols.

—Idrīsī—R. Dozy et M. J. de Goeje, *Description de l'Afrique et de l'Espagne par Edrisi*, Leyde, 1866.

Iggeret R. Scherira Gaon, cd. B. Lewin, 1921. —
אגרת רב שרירא גאון, [הוצאת] ב״מ לוין, חיפה, 1921.

Initiation à l'Algérie, Paris, 1957.

Initiation au Maroc, Paris, 1945.

Initiation à la Tunisie, Paris, 1950.

Isaac Bar Sheshet, *Responsa*, 1546-7. —
תשובות הרב רבינו יצחק בר ששת, קושטנטינה, ש״ו–ש״ז.

——, *New Responsa*, Munkatsh, 1901. —
שו״ת הריב״ש החדשות לרבינו יצחק בר ששת, מו״ל דוד פרענקיל, מונקאטש, תרס״א.

—Jaznaī, *Zahrat al-Ās*, ed. et trad. A. Bel, Alger, 1923.

Julien, Ch.-André, *Histoire de l'Afrique du Nord*², t. I-II, Paris, 1951-1952.

——, *History of North Africa from the Arab Conquest to 1830*. Edited and revised by R. Le Tourneau; translated by John Petrie, New York, 1970.

Juster, J., *Les Juifs dans l'Empire Romain*, t. I-II, Paris, 1914.

——, 'La condition légale des Juifs sous les rois visigots,' *Études d'Histoire Juridique offertes a P. F. Girard*, pp. 275-335.

Kahana, D. *Abraham ibn Ezra*. 1894. —
כהנא דוד: רבי אברהם אבן עזרא, קובץ חכמת הראב״ע, ורשה, תרנ״ד.

Kahrstedt, U., *Kulturgeschichte der römischen Kaiserzeit*,[2] Bern, 1958.
Katz, M., *Iggeret*, 1950. — כ״ץ משה, אגרת ר׳ יהודה אבן קוריש, תל־אביב, ׳דביר׳ תש״ב/1950.
Kayserling, M., *Geschichte der Juden in Portugal*, Leipzig, 1876.
Kellenbenz, H., *Sephardim an der unteren Elbe*, Wiesbaden, 1958.
Khaldūn, Ibn, *Kitāb al-ʿIbar*, Būlq, 1284 H. — ʿAbdurraḥmān Ibn Khaldūn, *Kitāb al-ʿIbar*, Būlāq, 1284 H., 7 vols.
——, *Muqaddima*, Būlāq, 1284 H. — ʿAbdurraḥmān Ibn Khaldūn, *Muqaddimat* [*Kitāb al-ʿIbar*], Part one, Būlāq, 1284 H.
Kirstein, E., Nordafrikanische Stadtbilder; Antike und Mittelalter Libyen und Tunesien[2]. Heidelberg, 1966.
Kisse Melakhim, by R. M. Albaz, MS. Sassoon 1007.
Kitāb al-Fiqh, Cairo, 1354-58 H. — ʿAbdurraḥmān al-Jazīrī, *Kitāb al-Fiqh ʿalā 'l-madhāhib al-arbaʿa*. 4 vols. Cairo, 1354-58 H. Reprinted 1950.
Klar, B., *Aḥimaʿaṣ*, 1944. — מגילת אחימעץ, והיא מגילת יוחסין לרבי אחימעץ בירבי פלטיאל, מהדורת ב. קלאר, ירושלים, תש״ד.
——, *Erez Kinnaroth*, 1950. — ב. קלאר, טבריה בתקופת הגאונים, ארץ־כנרות, 1950.
——, Meḥqārīm we-ʿIyūnīm, — ב. קלאר, מחקרים ועיונים בלשון, בשירה ובספרות, תל־אביב, 1954.
Kolmansperger, F., *Von Afrika nach Afrika, Unsichtbare Revolution im schwarzen Erdteil*, Mainz, 1965.
Kornemann, E., *Weltgeschichte des Mittelmeerraumes*, Zweiter Band, München, 1948.
Krauss, S., *Synagogale Altertümer*, Berlin—Wien, 1922.
Kubbel, L. E., and Matveev, V. V., 'Drevniye i sredniye vekoviye istočniki po etnografii i istorii narodov Afriki,' *Arabskiye istočniki VII-X vekov*, Moscow-Leningrad, 1960.

La Chapelle, F. de, 'Esquisse d'une Histoire du Sahara Occidental,' *Hespéris XI*, 1930, pp. 35-96.
Lane-Poole, S., *The Mohammedan Dynasties*, Paris, 1928.
Laredo, A.I., *Bereberes y Hebreos en Marruecos*, Madrid, 1954.
La Ronciere, Ch. de *La Découverte de l'Afrique au Moyen Age*, 3 vol., Caire, 1925-1927.
Lattes, M., *Excerpta—De Vita et Scriptis . . . Eliae Kapsali excerpta . . .* Patavii, 1869. — מ. לאטיש, לקוטים שונים מס׳ דברי אליהו לר׳ אליהו קפשאלי, פאדובה, 1869.
Leiter W. ed., *Shaare Teshubah*, Responsa of G., Pittsburg, 1946. — תשובות הגאונים, שערי תשובה, זאב וואלף לייטער, פיטסבורג תש״ו.
Leon l'Africain, *Description de l'Afrique*, Nouvelle édition traduite par A. Épaulard, Paris, 1956.
Leschi, L., *Études d'Épigraphie, d'Archéologie et d'Histoire Africaines*, Paris, 1957.
Le Tourneau R., *Fès avant le Protectorat*, Casablanca, 1949.
——, *Fez—Merinids*—R. Le Tourneau, *Fez in the Age of the Marinids*, University of Oklahoma Press, Norman, Oklahoma, 1961.
——, *The Almohad Movement in North Africa in the twelfth and thirteenth centuries*, Princeton, 1969.
Levi b. Ḥabib, *Quntrues ha-Semikha*, 1865. — ר׳ לוי בן חביב, שאלות ותשובות, למברג 1865, דפים נא, א–פא, ח.
Levi Della Vida, G., 'Due iscrizioni imperiali neo puniche', *Africa Italiana* VI, 1935, pp. 1-29.
——, 'Le iscrizioni neopuniche della Tripolitania,' *Libya, Rivista della Tripolitania* III, 1927, pp. 91-116.

——, 'Iscrizioni neopuniche di Tripolitania,' *Rendiconti della Classe di Scienze morali, storiche e filologiche*, Accademia Nazionale dei Lincei, ser. VIII, vol. IV, 401-412.

——, 'Il teatro augusteo di Leptis Magna, etc.' *ibid.* VI (1938!), pp. 104-109.

Lévi-Provençal, E. *Documents inédits d'histoire almohade*, Paris, 1928.

——, *Extraits des Historiens Arabes du Maroc*², Paris, 1929.

——, *Islam d'Occident*, Paris, 1948.

——, *Traités*—E. Lévi-Provençal, *Documents arabes inédits sur la vie sociale et économique*, Paris, 1955.

Levy, R., *The Social Structure of Islam*, Cambridge, 1957.

Lewicki, T., *Źródła arabskie do dziejów Słowiańszczyzny*, Wrocław, 1956.

Lewin, B. M., *Iggeret Sherira* G., see *Iggeret*.

Lewis, A. R., *Naval Power and Trade in the Mediterranean A.D. 500—1100*. Princeton, 1951.

Lopes, D., *Historia da expansão Portuguesa no mundo*, Vol. I, Lisboa, 1937.

——, *Historia de Portugal, Direccão literaria de Damião Peres*, vol. I-IV, 1928-1932.

Maʿarekhet ha-Elōhūt, 1879. —
מערכת האלהות מהגאון רבינו פרץ בעל התוספת · · · ועם פירוש הגאון רבינו יהודה חייט קראו מנחת יהודה, זאלקווא תקל״ט.

Maimonides, *Iggarot*, 1712. —
רבינו משה המיימוני, אגרות ושאלות תשובות, אמשטרדם תע״ב.

——, *Responsa*, 1859. —
קובץ תשובות הרמב״ם ואגרותיו, לפסיא תרי״ט.

——, *Responsa*, ed. A. Freimann, Jerusalem 1934. —
אברהם חיים פריימן, תשובות הרמב״ם, ירושלים תרצ״ד.

——, *Responsa*, ed. J. Blau, 3 v l., Jerusalem 1957-61. —
יהושע בלאו, תשובות הרמב״ם א–ג, ירושלים ה׳ תשי״ח–תשכ״א.

—Maqarrī, *Nafḥ al-ṭīb*.—Aḥmad b. Muḥ. at-Tilimsānī al-Maqarrī, *Nafḥ aṭ-ṭīb min ğuṣn al-Andalus ar-raṭīb*, Cairo 1358-61.

Marx, A., *Studies*—A. Marx, *Studies in Jewish History and Booklore*, New York, 1944.

Mayer, L. A., *Mamluk Costume*, Geneva, 1952.

Mann, J., *J.* —J. Mann, *The Jews in Egypt and in Palestine under the Fāṭimid Caliphs*, 2 vol., Oxford 1920-1922.

——, *Texts and Studies*, I, Cincinnati, 1931.

—Maqdisī—Al-Moqaddasi, *Descriptio imperii moslemici*, ed. de Goeje, BGA III.

Marçais, G., *L'Architecture musulmane d'Occident*, Paris, 1954.

——, *La Berbérie Musulmane*, 1946.

Marcy, G., *Les inscriptions libyques bilingues de l'Afrique du Nord*, Paris, 1936.

Margaliouth, M., *Ha-Ḥillūqim*, 1938 —
מרגליות מ., החילוקים שבין אנשי המזרח ובני ארץ ישראל, ירושלים תרצ״ח.

de Marmol, L. *Descripción general de Affrica*, Granada, 1573.

Massignon, L., *Enquête sur les corporations Musulmanes d'artisans et de commerçants au Maroc*, Paris, 1925.

——, *Le Maroc*, Alger, 1906.

Mazahéri, A., *La vie quotidienne des Musulmans au Moyen Age*, Paris, 1951.

Megāsh, Joseph Ibn, *Responsa*, 1870. —
אבן מיגאש, יוסף הלוי, שאלות ותשובות, ורשה 1870.

Mercier, E., 'Une page de l'histoire de l'invasion arabe: La Kahena,' *REC* XII, 1868, pp. 241-254.

Masālik, see Bakrī.

—Masʿudī, *Murūj al-Dhahab*.— Abu 'l-Ḥasan ʿAlī b. al-Ḥusayn, *Murūj adh-dhahab*, Baghdad, 4 parts.

Meir b. Baruch, see Rothenburg.
de Mendoca H., *Iornada de Africa*, Lisboa, 1607.
Merlin, Alfred, *Inscriptions latines de la Tunisie*, Paris, 1944.
Mesnage, P., 'Le Christianisme en Afrique,' *Revue Africaine* 1913, pp. 361-700.
Mez, A., *Die Renaissance des Islams*, Heidelberg, 1922.
Mieses, M., 'Les Juifs et les Etablissements puniques en Afrique du Nord,' *REJ* XCII-XCIV, 1932-1933.
Mirski, A., *Ibn Khalfūn*, Jerusalem, 1961. —
מירסקי, אהרן, שירי ר׳ יעחק אבן־כ׳לפן, ירושלים תשכ״א.
Monceau, P., 'Les colonies juives dans l'Afrique Romaine,' *REJ* XLIV, 1902, pp. 1-28.
——, *Histoire littèraire de l'Afrique Chrétienne*, I, Paris, 1901.
de Montmorency, J. E. B. 'The Barbary States in the Law of Nations,' *Transactions of the Grotius Society*, IV, 1919, pp. 87-94.
Motylinski A., 'Chanson Berbère de Djerba,' *Bulletin de Correspondance Africaine* III, 1885, pp. 461-464.
Müller J., ed., *Responsen*, 1888. —
תשובות גאוני מזרח ומערב, העתיק יואל הכהן מיללער, ברלין.
Munk, S., 'Notice sur Joseph ben Iehouda . . . disciple de Maimonide,' *JA* 1842, pp. 5-72.
Musafya, Y., ed., *G. Responsa*, 1864. —
תשובות הגאונים, מאת י׳ מוסאפיה, מקיצי נרדמים, ליק תרכ״ד.

—Nāṣirī, *al-Istiqṣā'*, Cairo, 1312 H. — Abu 'l-'Abbās Aḥmad b. Khālid an-Nāṣirī, *Kitāb al-istiqṣā' li-akhbār duwal al-maghrib al-aqṣā*, Cairo, 1312 H.
Neubauer, A., *Aus der Petersburger Bibliothek*, Leipzig, 1866.
——, *Mediaeval Jewish Chronicles*, I-II, Oxford, 1887-1895.
Neumann, A. A., *The Jews in Spain*, I-II, Philadelphia, 1942.
Nissim, R., *Ha-Mafteaḥ*, ed. J. Goldenthal, 1847. —
ספר המפתח של מנעולי התלמוד שחברו מורנו ורבנו ניסים בן כבוד מורנו ורבנו יעקב ז״ל, השתדלתי בהדפסתו יעקב גאלדענטהאל, וין 1847.
Nuzha—Nozhet el hadi, Histoire de la dynastie saadienne au Maroc (*1511-1870*) *par Mohammed . . . Eloufrāni*, publ. et trad. O. Houdas, Paris, 1888-1889.

Obermann, J., *Studies in Islam and Judaism, The Arabic Original of Ibn Shahin's Book of Comfort*, New Haven, 1933.
Ortega, M. L., *Los Hebreos en Marruecos*[4], Madrid, 1934.
Ontiveros y Herrera, E. G., *La Politica Norte-africana de Carlos I*, Madrid, 1950.
Ozar ha-Geonim, ed. B. M. Lewin, 1928-1941. —
לוין, ב. מ., אוצר הגאונים, תשובות גאוני בבל ופירושיהם, ירושלים, תרפ״ח–תש״א.
Ostrogorsky, G., *Geschichte des byzantinischen Staates*, München, 1952.
Ozar Tob (Hebrew annex to *MWJ*)—
אוצר טוב, כולל דברים עתיקים מתוך כ״י מועתקים.

Pelissier, E., et Remusat, J. P. A. *Histoire de l'Afrique de . . . el-Kaīrouāni*, Paris, 1845.
Perfet, *Responsa*, see Isaac bar Sheshet.
Petaḥya, *Sibūb* ed. Grünhut, 1904-5. —
ר׳ פתחיה, סיבוב מהדורת גרינהוט, ירושלים, 1904–1905.
Petschenig, M., *Historia persecutionis Africae Provinciae*, Vindobonae, 1881.
Picard, G. Ch., *La civilisation de l'Afrique romaine*, Paris, 1959.
——, *Les religions de l'Afrique Antique*, Paris, 1954.
Pinsker, S., *Liqqutey Qadmoniyoth*, 1870. —
ש. פינסקער, לקוטי קדמוניות לקורות דת בני מקרא, וויען, 1870.

Pirenne, H., *Economic and Social History of Medieval Europe*, New York, n.d.

——, *Medieval Cities*, New York, 1956.

——, *Mohammed and Charlemagne*, New York, 1957.

Poznanski, S., *Harkavy-Festschrift*, 1909. —
פוזנאנסקי ש. א. אנשי קירואן, ספר היובל לא. א. הרכבי, זכרון לאברהם אליהו, פטרבורג, תרס״ט, 175–220.

Power, E., *Medieval People*, London, 1954.

Preisendanz, K., *Papyri Graecae Magicae*, *Die griechischen Zauberpapyri*, hgg. und übersetzt, I-II, Berlin, 1928-1931.

-Qalqashandī, *Ṣubḥ al-Aʿshā*, Cairo, 1331-8 H. — Abu 'l-ʿAbbās Aḥmad al-Qalqashandi, *Ṣubḥ al-aʿshā*, Cairo, 1331-1338 H.

Qebūzat Ḥakhāmim, see Warnheim W.

Qohelet Shelomo, see Wertheimer, S. A.

Quraysh, Ibn, *Y. Risāla*, ed. J. J. L. Barges et D. B. Goldberg, *Epistola de studii targum utilitate*, Paris 1857.

Rabinowitz, L., *Adventurers* — L. Rabinowitz, *Jewish Merchant Adventurers*, London, 1948.

Rachmuth, M., 'Die Juden in Nordafrika bis zur Invasion der Araber,' *MGWJ* 50, 1906, 22-58.

Rang, S., et Denis, F. *Fondation de la Régence d'Alger*. *Histoire de Barberousse*, Paris, 1837.

S. J. L. Rapoport, *Bikkurey ha-ʿIttim* —
שי״ר, תולדות רבינו חננאל בן רבינו חושיאל, בכורי העתים, לתקצ״ב ווין 1831.

Rauḍ al-Qirṭās, see Zarʿ, Ibn Abī.

Régné, J., 'Catalogue des actes de Jaime Ier, Pedro III et Alfonso III, rois d'Aragon, concernant les Juifs (1213-1291),' *REJ* LX, 1910—LXX, 1920.

Reynolds, J. M., and Ward-Perkins, J. B. *The Inscriptions of Roman Tripolitania*, Rome-London, 1952.

Ricard, R., *Les Portugais au Maroc de 1495 à 1521*, Rabat, 1937.

Romanelli, P., *Storia delle provincie romane dell' Africa*, Roma, 1959.

Rosanes, S., *Histoire des Israélites de Turquie*, 1930-8. —
רוזאניס שלמה, דברי ימי ישראל בתוגרמה, א–ה, תל־אביב, תר״צ–סופיא, תרצ״ז–תרצ״ח.

Rosenthal, F., *Ibn Khaldūn*, *The Muqaddimah*, transl. from the Arabic, I-III London, 1958.

Rothenburg, Meir [b. Baruch de], *Shaʿarey Teshūbōth*, 1891. —
שערי תשובות מהר״ם רוטנבורג, הוצאת מקיצי נרדמים, ברלין, 1891.

Rubin, B., *Das Zeitalter Iustinians*, Berlin, 1960.

Salama, P., *Les Voies Romaines de l'Afrique Du Nord*, Alger, 1951.

Salzman M., *Ahimaaz b. Paltiel*—The Chronicle of Ahimaaz, 1924.

Sassoon, D. S., ed., *Diwan of Shemuel Hannaghid*, 1934. —
דיואן שמואל הנגיד, נערך, ע״י דוד ששון אוקספורד 1934.

Sauvaget, J., *La poste aux chevaux dans l'empire des Mamelouks*, Paris, 1941.

Sayous, A., *Le Commerce des Européens à Tunis depuis le XIIe siecle* . . ., Paris, 1929.

Sbornik — Palestinskiy sbornik. Moscow-Leningrad, 1954 ff.

Schaube, A., *Handelsgeschichte der romanischen Völker des Mittelmeergebietes*, München und Berlin, 1906.

Schechter, S., *Saadyana*, Cambridge, 1903.

Schiffers, H., *Die Sahara und die Syrtenländer*, Stuttgart, 1950.

Schirmann J., *Qinōt*, 1939. —

שירמן ח., קינות על הגזרות בארץ־ישראל, אפריקה, ספרד, אשכנז וצרפת, הדפסה מיוחדת מ׳קבץ על יד׳ ספר ג (יג), ירושלים, תרצ״ט.

Schürer, E., *Geschichte des jüdischen Volkes im Zeitalter Jesu Christi*[3-4], I-III, Leipzig, 1901-1909.

Sefer Ḥasīdīm, ed. Wistinetzki, 1924. —
ספר חסידים עפ״י נוסח כ״י, ערך והו״ל י. ויסטינצקי, פרנקפורט ע״ב מיין, 1924.

Sefer Ha-Qabbalah—The Book of Tradition by Abraham Ibn Daud, ed. by Gerson D. Cohen, Philadelphia 1967.

Sefer ha-Yishub II, ed. by Assaf, S.-Mayer, L. A., 1944. —
ספר הישוב. כרך שני: מימי כיבוש ארץ־ישראל על־ידי הערבים עד מסעי הצלב; בעריכת ש. אסף ול. א. מאיר, ירושלים תש״ד.

Shaʿarey Ẓedeq, G. Responsa, 1792. —
שערי צדק. . . תשובות הגאונים, שאלוניקי, תקנ״ב.

Shebeṭ Yehuda, ed. *Shoḥet*, 1947. —
שבט יהודה לר׳ שלמה ן׳ ורגה, הגיה וביאר עזריאל שוחט, ערך והקדים מבוא יצחק בער, ירושלים, תש״ז.

Simon, M., 'Le Judaïsme berbère dans l'Afrique ancienne,' *RHPhR* XXVI, 1946.

Skoss, L., *Dictionary*—L. Skoss, *The Hebrew-Arabic Dictionary of the Bible known as Kitāb Jāmiʿ al-Alfāẓ*, I-II, New Haven, 1936-1945.

Slane, William Mc Guckin de, *Les prolegomènes d'Ibn Khaldoun*, 3 vol., Paris, 1863-68.

Slouschz, N., *Azkara* [IV] —
נ׳ סלושץ, השמדות בדורו של הרמב״ם, אזכרה, קובץ תורני מדעי ערוך בידי י״ל הכהן פישמן, כרך ד, ירושלים תרצ״ז/ח.

——, 'Etude sur l'Histoire des Juifs et du Judaisme au Maroc,' *Archives Marocaines* 1905-6, Paris.

——, N., *Les Hebréo-Phéniciens*, Paris, 1909.

——, *Judéo-Hellènes et Judeo-Berbères*, 1909.

——, *Thesaurus of Phoenician Inscriptions*, 1942. —
אוצר הכתובות הפיניקיות, תל־אביב תש״ב, עמ׳ 155–206.

——, *Travels in North Africa*, Philadelphia, 1927.

——, 'Un voyage d'études juives en Afrique,' *Mémoires de l'Académie des Inscriptions*, t. XII, 2e partie, 1913.

Solomon b. Simon [Dūrān], R., *Responsa*, 1742. —
ספר הרשב״ש, שו״ת ר׳ שלמה בן שמעון בן צמח (דוראן), ליוורנו תק״ב.

Soualah Mohammed, *La Société Indigène de l'Afrique du Nord*, I-II[3], III, Alger, 1946.

Squarciapino, M. Fl., *Leptis Magna*, Basel, 1966.

The Joshua Starr Memorial Voume, New York, 1953.

Steinschneider, M., *Die arabische Literatur der Juden*, Frankfurt, 1902.

Strauss, see Ashtor.

Ṭaʿam Zeqénīm, ed., E. Ashkenazy, 1865. —
טעם זקנים, קבוץ (!) חבורים וכתובים ושירים בענייני החכמה והאמונה והמדע, אספתים ולקטתים אליעזר אשכנזי, תושב תוניס, תרט״ו פפד״מ.

Tarbiẕ—Tarbiẕ a Quarterly for Jewish Studies, Jerusalem, 1930 — תכבוץ למדעי הרוח, ירושלים, תר״ץ

TaShBeZ—Teshūbōth Shimeon b. Zemaḥ, four parts, Amsterdam, 1738.
Part 4: *Ḥūṭ ha-Meshulash*, three sections:
IV/1—Responsa R. Solomon Dūrān.
IV/2—Responsa R. Solomon Ẓeror.
IV/3—Responsa R. Abraham ibn Tawāh. —
תשובות ר׳ שמעון בן צמח דוראן, אמשטרדם, תצ״ח. בספר אר בעה חלקים. שלושת החלקים הראשונים הם תשובותיו של רשב״ץ. בחלק הרביעי הנקרא ׳חוט המשולש׳ שלושה טורים: הטור הראשון: תשובות ר׳ שלמה דוראן; הטור השני:

תשובות ר׳ שלמה צרור: הטור השלישי: תשובות ר׳ אברהם אבן טוואה.

Tcherikover, V., *Hellenistic Civilization and the Jews*, Philadelphia 1959.

——, *The Jews in Egypt*, 1945. —

צ׳ריקובר א., היהודים במצרים בתקופה ההלניסטית־הרומית לאור הפאפירולוגיה, ירושלים תש״ה.

Tchernowitz, H., *Toledot ha-Poseqim*, 1945-6. —

חיים טשרנוביץ, תולדות הפוסקים, ג חלקים, ניו–יורק, תש״ה–תשו.

Terrasse, H., *Histoire du Maroc*, I-II, Casablanca, 1949-50.

Thomassy, R., *Le Maroc et ses caravanes*[2], Paris, 1845.

Tissot, Ch., *Geographie comparée de la Province Romaine d'Afrique*, I-II, avec notes par Salomon Reinach, Paris, 1884-8.

Toledano, J. M., *Lumière* [or] *Ner*, 1911. —

טולידאנו י. מ., נר המערב, ירושלים, תרע״א.

——, *Sārid u-Pālit*, n.d. —

שריד ופליט, אוסף לדברי תורה ולמדע היהדות וכו׳, חמ״ד, חש״ד.

Toutain, J., *De Saturni dei in Africa cultu*, (Thesis), Paris, 1894.

Tritton, A. S., *Materials on Muslim Education in the Middle Ages*, London, 1957.

Tyan, E., *Histoire de l'Organisation Judiciare en pays d'Islam*, t. I-II, Paris-Harissa (Liban), 1938-1943.

Tykocinski, H., *The Gaonic Ordinances*, 1959. —

טיקוצינסקי ח., תקנות הגאונים, תל־אביב–ירושלים, תש״כ.

Uṣaybiʿa, Ibn Abi, *ʿUyūn al-Anbāʾ*. — Aḥmad b. Abī Uṣaybiʿa, *ʿUyūn al-ambāʾ fī ṭabaqāt al-aṭibbāʾ*, Cairo, 1299 H.

Vajda, G., *Un recueil de textes historiques judeo-marocains*, Paris, 1951.

Voinot L., *Pèlerinages Judéo-Musulmans du Maroc*, Paris, 1948.

Warmington, B. H., *The North African Provinces from Diocletian to the Vandal Conquest*, Cambridge, 1954.

Warnheim, W., *Qebuṣat Ḥakhāmīm, Wissenschaftliche Aufsätze gesammelt*, Wien 1861. —

קבוצת חכמים, כולל דברי מדע פרי עשתנות חכמים שונים

Weiss, A. H., *Dōr, dōr we-dorshāv*, 1924. —

א. ה. וויס, דור דור ודורשיו, ה חלקים, (נדפס מחדש) נויורק/ברלין, 1924.

Wensinck, A. J., *Miftāḥ*, 1934.—A. Y. Fansink, *Miftāḥ kunūz as-sunan*, Cairo, 1353 H.

Wertheimer, S. A., *Ginzey Yerushalayim*, 1901. —

גנזי ירושלים, חוברת שניה, ש״א ווערטהיימער, ירושלים, תרס״א.

——, *Qohelet Shelomo*, 1899. —

קהלת שלמה, שאלות ותשובות הגאונים הקדמונים, ש״א ווערטהיימער, ירושלים, תרנ״ט.

Wieder, N., *Islamic Influences on the Jewish Worship*, Oxford, 1947.

Williams, J. J., *Hebrewisms of West Africa*, New York, 1930.

Willan, T. S., *Trade, Studies in Elisabethan Foreign Trade*, Manchester 1959.

Wilde, R., 'The Treatment of the Jews in the Greek Christian Writers of the First Three Centuries,' *Patristic Studies*, LXXXI, Washington D.C., 1949.

Wolfensohn, Z. W., and Schneursohn, Sh. Z., ed., *Ḥemda Genūza* (G. Responsa), 1867. —

חמדה גנוזה והוא תשובות הגאונים, ז׳ וו׳ וואלפינזאהן ושניאור זלמן שניאורזאהן, ירושלים, תרכ״ז.

Yaʿari, A., *Iggerot*, 1943.

יערי אברהם, אגרות ארץ־ישראל, תל־אביב, תש״ג.

Yakhin u-Bōaz, *Responsa*, 1782. —

יכין ובועז, (שו״ת) ר׳ צמח ור׳ שמעון בני רשב״ש, ליוורנו, תקמ״ב.

Yāqūt, *Muʿjam.* — Shihāb ud-dīn Abī ʿAbdallāh Yāqūt, *Kitāb muʿjam al-buldān*, 10 vols, Cairo, 1323-35 H.

[A. M. Lunz], *Yerushalayim*, 13 vol., Jerusalem, 1882-1919. —
[א״מ לונץ], ירושלים, מאסף ספרותי לחקירת ארץ ישראל.

Yeshuʿah ha-Levi, *Halīkhōt ʿOlām*, 1567. —
ישועה הלוי, ספר הליכות עולם, סביוניטה, 1567.

Yosef ha-Kohen, *Dibrey ha-Yāmīm*, 1739. —
יוסף בן יהושע בן מאיר הכהן הספרדי, ספר דברי הימים למלכי צרפת ומלכי בית אוטומאן התוגר, אמשטרדם, תצ״ג/1739.

——, *Emeq ha-Bakha*, 1895. —
יוסף הכהן [הרופא], עמק הבכא, מהדורת מ. לטריס, קראקוב, 1895.

Yeivin, S., *Milḥemet Bar-Kochba*², Jerusalem, 1952. —
ש. ייבין, מלחמת בר־כוכבא, ירושלים, תשי״ב.

Zacuto, A., *Liber Juchassin*, ed. Filipowski, 1857. —
זכות אברהם, ס׳ יוחסין השלם, לונדון, 1857.

Zambaur, E. de, *Manuel de Généalogie et de Chronologie*, Hanovre, 1927.

Zarʿ, Ibn Abī, Rauḍ al-Qirṭās, 1935/6.—Ibn Abi Zarʿ, *Kitāb al-anīs al-muṭrib bi-rawḍ(at) al-qirṭās fī akhbār mulūk al-maghrib wa-taʾrīkh madīnat Fās*, Rabat, 1355 H.

—Zarkashī, *Taʾrīkh al-Dawlatayn*, 1289 H.—Abu ʿAbdallāh Muḥ. al-Luʾluʾī az-Zarkashī, *Taʾrīkh ad-dawlatayn al-Muwaḥḥiddiyya wa-l-Ḥafṣiyya*, Tunis, 1289 H.

Zion— Zion. A Quarterly for Research in Jewish History, Jersualem, 1936. —
ציון, רבעון לחקר תולדות ישראל.

ha-Zofeh me-Erez Hagar [later . . . *le-Ḥokhmat Israel*], vol. I-XV, Budapest 1911-1931.
הצופה מארץ הגר [· · לחכמת ישראל].

Zucker M., *Saadia*, 1959. —
צוקר מ. על תרגום רס״ג לתורה, ניו יורק תשי״ט.

ARABIC INDEX

GREEK INDEX

HEBREW INDEX

GENERAL INDEX

A

Abarbanel Isaac: letter to Yehiel of Pisa, 417

a. ᶜAmrān, policeman, 235

a. Ayyūb Solomon abū al-Muᶜallim, physician, 351

Ab beyt-dīn [*ha-gādol*] (head of the [Grand] court), 226; see also *beyt-dīn*

Abba Qartaginea R., 49

ᶜAbd al-Bāsiṭ, Egyptian merchant and author, 392-3, 414

ᶜAbd al-Ḥaqq, al-Merīnī, 390-2, 394, 397-8, 414

ᶜAbd al-Malik, caliph: 89, 90-2; transfers J. or Copts from Egypt to Kairouan, 144

ᶜAbd al-Masīḥ *al-Shammās* (deacon), 287

ᶜAbd al-Muʾmīn, Almohad ruler: 5, 118, 123, 126-8, 132, 138; death in 1163, 119, drive into Africa, 132; last years, 136-9; conquest of Tunis, 464; sents army to Spain, 119

ᶜAbdallah b. Muhammad al-Mahdī, *sherif:* avenges father's death, 430

a. ᶜAbdallah Muhammad al-Qaurī: *khaṭīb* (preacher) in Fez, 395-6

Abdhin: J. from Tunis in Pisa, 465

Abenamies Abraham: went to Morocco, 376 n.

Abengelel, family: 368; Abraham [Avingallel], 376, 466; Abraham and Samuel: exempted from taxes, 376; went to Morocco 376 n.; Samuel proceeds to Granada, 377; see also Galil

Abenhatens Judas: went to Morocco, 376 n.

Abenjucef Isach Annafusi, 378 n.

Abenzahit: receives revenues in Tunis, 367

Abī wa-ummī, see Ibn Quraysh, *Risala*

Abraham b. ᶜAlī, physician, 307

Abraham b. ᶜAṭā (=Nathan) nagid; 112-3, 211-3; 307, 311, 320; released from *ghiyār*, 198-9

Abraham b. Daud, historian, 111, 126, 160, 447; see also Story of four Sages

Abraham b. Ḥiyya ("Savasorda"), 235 n.

Abraham b. Jacob: sents questions to Bab., 108, 346

Abraham b. Jacob, J. traveller, 296

Abraham b. Jacob Darᶜī, in Fusṭāṭ: 355

Abraham b. Peraḥya Yajū of Mahdiya, 285

Abraham b. Solomon of Ardutiel, historian, 403, 404 n.

Abraham Malequi, merchant, 380

Abraham al-Qābesī, Bab. G., 97, 341

Abraham al-Qalᶜī R., 344

Abūdāni: brings Saadia's commentary to Fez, 108, 306

Abulafia Todros b. Judah, poet, 376

Abuṭām (Abuṭāt) Moses, 411

Asach [Asac = Isaac]: on mission to Jaime II of Aragon, 377

Academy, Academies: Bab. and Pal., 298, 312, 327; of Baghdad: later ties with Maghrebi scholars, 360; called *Ḥabūra* (Society), 214; donations for, 312; heads in Pal., 206; Pal.: early ties with Maghreb 298; of Kairouan, 321, 327; of Pumbeditha, 221; rivalry between Bab. academies 325; see also Gaon, Geonim

Account-books, 257

Aden, 132, *peqidim* (wardens) of merchants in, 293

Addison, L., on marriage customs in Morocco, 171

Adibe, family: 423; Jacob, 422-3; Joseph, 422; Moses, 423, 437; Yaḥya, official translator, 423

Adorne Anselm, Chr. merchant, 441

Adret Ibn, Solomon [RaShBA], 368

Africa, African(s): 44; J. Diaspora undervalued, 9-10; J. in Central A., 143, *kohanim*, 163-5; litigate before Alexander the Great, 41; relations with Spanish J., 13-15; Tal. distincts between Africans and Carthaginians, 45: "Afrika" = Mahdiya, 443 n.

Agadir: 1, 428; conquered by Portugal, 416; fortress reduced in 1541, 429

Agadir (suburb of Tlemcen): R. Ephraim Enkawa in, 385

B

I

J

K

L

N

O

P

T

Y

Z